COURTS, JUDGES, AND POLITICS

An Introduction to the Judicial Process

COURTS,

JUDGES,

AND POLITICS:

An Introduction to the Judicial Process

WALTER F. MURPHY
Princeton University

C. HERMAN PRITCHETT
University of Chicago

 Random House

NEW YORK

MANUFACTURED IN THE
UNITED STATES OF AMERICA

to Jerome G. Kerwin

PREFACE

This book is a collection of cases and essays which analyze and illustrate the functioning of the judiciary in the context of the American political process. It endeavors to make materials which are now scattered through the law reviews, court reports, and political science journals readily available for students of government, law, and public affairs. The goal is to organize these materials in a framework which will foster a clearer understanding of the role which American judges and courts, as they perform their historic function of settling disputes and dispensing justice, play in the process of democratic policy formation.

It is no longer a novel idea to suggest that law is not an exact science, or that judges are influenced by policy considerations in arriving at decisions where public policy issues are present. The U.S. Supreme Court has often been the subject of controversy because of the opinions it has rendered on constitutional or legal questions of wide public importance. Its members have often been attacked as reactionaries or radicals because of the policy consequences of their decisions.

Since the interpretation and application of the American Constitution are pre-eminently political tasks, the subject of constitutional law has been studied with due recognition of the policy positions taken by the justices. The decisions handed down by the Court have been carefully examined to determine what influences were at work, and the relationship of the social or economic philosophies of the justices to the opinions written has been the subject of endless speculation. However, these concerns have generally been incidental to a study of the legal doctrines themselves. The attention of most lawyers and scholars of the law has been primarily on the law produced, not on the process by which it was produced.

The authors and compilers of this volume are not lawyers but political scientists. Courts and judicial administration have of course always been of interest to political scientists, but until relatively recently there was little that was distinctively political in their approach. They examined the constitutional decisions of the Supreme Court just as lawyers would, though often handicapped by lack of legal training. They wrote biographies of justices, but the significance of these was more likely due to the literary skill of the author than to his political science training.

But political scientists have sought more and more to develop an approach to the judicial process which would give activities of the courts new meaning by placing them within the main stream of political relationships. This volume is a part of that effort. It endeavors to examine the policy significance and consequences of what judges do and how they do it. It is a behavioristic kind of analysis, and as such is comparable to the concern with process which has been increasingly prevalent in recent studies of government and social action. We have heard much talk of the governmental process, the administrative process, the legislative process. The process type of analysis contrasts generally with the institutional approach, in which attention is centered on governmental structures and their legal status, functions, and powers. Process analysis professes to go beyond the appearance to the reality, beyond the legal façade to the actual operating mechanisms.

With this general goal, the materials presented here undertake, in Part I, to indicate how the present-day conception of the judge developed, and to suggest the basic organization of our dual system of courts and the relations between lower and higher courts. In Part II there is a discussion of the two groups of specialists who operate the court system—the judges and the members of the bar. The third part traces out the various sources of power exercised by judges, and then more specifically examines the instruments through which judicial power is brought to bear in specific controversies.

Part IV concentrates upon the special characteristics which a controversy must possess to make it eligible for judicial treatment, and demonstrates how such controversies are often purposely formulated by interests which seek to use the power of the courts to support their own policy positions. Part V analyzes the reasoning processes which courts employ in deciding cases. The judicial method of establishing facts, perhaps the most distinctive characteristic of court procedure, is examined. After the facts are settled, the law applicable to those facts must be determined, and the process of judicial reasoning employed is followed in the various contexts of case law, statute law, and constitutional law.

Part VI follows the reasoning process into the labyrinth of the decisional stage. The speculative but always fascinating prospect of getting behind the face of the written opinions to discover the hidden sources of judicial preferences has stimulated many suggestive efforts toward establishing judicial motivations, and some of these efforts are presented here.

Part VII shifts the focus from the exercise of judicial power to restraints upon the courts. Both the executive and the legislature are incomparably stronger than the judiciary in the control of physical power, and the methods available to them to curb judges who have incurred their wrath or lost their confidence are pointed out. Less understood are the checks within the judicial system itself; while everyone knows that higher courts can review and reverse the decisions of lower courts, not so many are aware of the powers of resistance available to lower courts which disagree with the rulings of their superiors. There are in addition the restraints which judges, honoring the responsibilities of the judicial role and understanding the fragile underpinnings of their tremendous power, impose upon themselves.

Finally, Part VIII seeks to re-examine, in the light of the preceding intensive analysis of the judicial operation, the justification for judicial participation in democratic policy formation—an issue which has stirred controversy ever since Marshall forcefully and successfully stated the case for judicial supremacy.

The question of what materials to include and exclude in a book such as this presents a difficult problem, one influenced by high printing costs as well as by more scholarly considerations. Other political scientists trying to achieve the same goals would have made different choices. However, use of these cases and readings in teaching at Princeton and Chicago leads us to believe that we have brought together material that can be made the core of a rewarding and stimulating one-semester course.

We would have preferred presenting these cases and articles in their complete, original forms with their full plumage of documentation intact. But the size of such a book would have made its cost prohibitive. We have therefore had to edit most of the materials and in so doing to eliminate much bibliographical data. We hope that reading these selections will entice students to go to the original sources and also to use the selected references at the end of each introduction for investigating on their own the rich literature of the judicial process.

Acknowledgment is gratefully made to the individuals and publishers who gave their permission to reprint materials appearing in this volume. The authors also wish to acknowledge the aid received from Princeton University and from the Social Science Research Committee of the University of Chicago in meeting certain expenditures involved in preparation of this volume; and we wish to thank Louis Werner of the Princeton Class of 1961 for research assistance.

WALTER F. MURPHY
C. HERMAN PRITCHETT

CONTENTS

PART ONE

The Judiciary

1 / PERCEPTIONS OF THE
JUDICIAL ROLE

There are many ways of looking at law and at the function of judges. Three main schools of jurisprudence have influenced the development of the American legal system. The first is the *natural-law school,* which views law as justice or morality. Dating back to pre-Socratic Greece and receiving its earliest systematic statement from the Stoics and Cicero, it took roots in Roman law and also became a part of Christian theology. The natural-law theory is predicated on the existence of a universal and immutable set of principles imbedded in human nature. These principles are discernible, in the phrase of Thomas Aquinas, by "right reason," and thus can be known by all men. Man-made regulations become true law only insofar as they square with the standards of justice as defined by "right reason."

The natural-law concept of the judicial function blended with the role that the Germanic tribes ascribed to their king-judge. The law of these tribes was based on custom; and when elected ruler, the king swore to administer the justice to his people which his ancestors had administered to their ancestors. His function thus called for discovery of old rules rather than creation of new ones. The king-judge "found" the law which his predecessors had followed. So too under the natural-law theory, the judge

3

was ideally to apply deductive reasoning to general moral principles in order to discover what was just in a given situation.

Natural-law thinking permeated every Western legal system, including that of the common law. While English judges developed an extremely complex set of technical rules to govern both the substance and procedure of their decision-making, they also made continual efforts to justify their decisions in terms of principles of morality and abstract reason as well as by the existing legal rules. To cover the gaps where the common-law rules could not provide justice, a separate procedure called equity grew up along-side the more technically oriented law courts.

Analytical Jurisprudence

By the end of the eighteenth century, however, natural-law theory had experienced a period of intellectual decay. While its outward forms were preserved intact, it was often used by writers like Blackstone as a façade to protect the political and economic *status quo*. Natural-law theory was also subject to corruption in its precepts concerning the judicial function. Many judges began to equate the ideals of natural law with their own decision-making processes, and to use the verbiage of natural-law theory as a substitute for critical self-examination. Judges were thus able to conceive of their own personal value choices as ineluctable commands of justice, without even being aware that they were making subjective choices. Jeremy Bentham's efforts to expose and to reform the logical absurdities of the English legal system were in great part aimed at natural law, which he saw as lying at the root of contemporary judicial thinking.

It was John Austin, a disciple of Bentham, who laid the groundwork for the second important school of jurisprudence which influenced American law. Recognizing with Bentham that judges were actually "creating" law as often as they were "finding" it, and offended by the confusion that had resulted, Austin tried to make jurisprudence a truly ordered and consistent body of knowledge. Law, according to Austin, consisted only in "positive law," the commands of the sovereign, and was law "without regard to goodness or badness." The judge's task was to deduce from the more general commands of the sovereign the way a specific case should be decided. The syllogism was to be the instrument of the judge: the major premise would be the general command of the sovereign; the minor premise the instant case. The conclusions would follow by the rules of logic.

Austin did not deny the existence of natural justice; he simply denied its relevance to the operation of a legal system. To carry out its purpose of bringing about a logical order in the law, Austin's *school of analytical jurisprudence*, as it came to be called, devoted itself almost exclusively to defining various legal concepts and methodically arranging them in regularized and, where possible, hierarchical organization.

Ironically, in the United States at least, analytical jurisprudence was used to becloud even further the fact that judges exercised a considerable amount of personal choice in arriving at their decisions. The declaratory theory of the judicial function had been endorsed by John Marshall in 1824 in the case of *Osborn* v. *Bank of the United States:*

> Judicial power, as contradistinguished from the power of the laws, has no existence. Courts are the mere instruments of the law, and can will nothing. When they are said to exercise a discretion, it is a mere legal discretion, a discretion to be exercised in discerning the course prescribed by law. . . . Judicial power is never exercised for the purpose of giving effect to the will of the Judge; always for the purpose of giving effect to the will of the Legislature; or, in other words, to the will of the law.

American judges generally supported Marshall's rationalization of their decision-making process; but in the second half of the nineteenth century they also accepted analytical jurisprudence and simply added another string to their bow. A judge could justify his decision in terms of natural law or by logical deduction from the command of the sovereign as embodied in the Constitution. Most judges through the nineteenth century and even well into the twentieth continued to assert that their one and only job was to discover law. In 1936 Justice Roberts gave the classical statement of the declaratory theory in explaining how the Supreme Court had concluded that Congress had exceeded its authority in trying to set farm production quotas:

> It is sometimes said that the court assumes a power to overrule or control the action of the people's representatives. This is a misconception. . . . When an act of Congress is appropriately challenged in the courts as not conforming to the constitutional mandate the judicial branch of the Government has only one duty,—to lay the article of the Constitution which is invoked beside the statute which is challenged and to decide whether the latter squares with the former.[1]

As Thomas Reed Powell remarked, judges were claiming "that it is not they who speak but the Constitution that speaketh in them."

[1] *United States* v. *Butler.*

Sociological Jurisprudence

The declaratory theory of the judicial function was less than candid, and its decline was due to a number of factors, among which was the growth of *sociological jurisprudence*, the third school of legal thought which has shaped American law. Although some of its principles were borrowed from the ideas of German jurists, Roscoe Pound is generally recognized as the main figure in the establishment of the sociological school. To Pound and his followers, law was neither a matter of eternal justice nor of logical deduction from jural postulates. Rather, law was a part of the culture of a society, a set of fallible, man-made rules designed to resolve conflict among the competing interests in a society. While using logic as an instrument and recognizing concepts of justice as part of the societal milieu, sociological jurisprudence attempted to use economics, political science, psychology, and sociology to show how law could fulfill its basic conflict-resolving purpose. Pound denounced the declaratory concept of the judicial function as "a slot machine theory," and frankly accepted the fact that judicial discretion played a major role in "social engineering."

Sociological jurisprudence, of course, was not the only force operating to throw light on law and the business of judging. In philosophy, prag-matism with its conception of truth as a relation between things rather than as a separate entity was gaining popularity and undercutting much of the basis of the older legal theories. In psychology, Freud was expound-ing the notion of the unconscious and showing that the reasons men give for their behavior and the real reasons for their actions are often quite different. At about the same time, the Marxian economic interpretation of history made an impact even on nonsocialists like Charles Beard, and raised further doubts as to whether the announced motivation of public officials was a true explanation or merely a rationalization. Political scien-tists like A. F. Bentley began to investigate government and law not as the expression of philosophical theories but as the product of the struggle of group interests. "Law," Bentley wrote, "is activity, just as government is. It is a group process, just as government is. It is a forming, a systematization, a struggle, an adaptation, of group interests, just as government is."

In the legal profession there were similar intellectual upheavals. Oliver Wendell Holmes, lecturing at Harvard in 1880, heaped scorn on those who saw the common law as "a brooding omnipresence in the sky." "The life of the law," Holmes said, "has not been logic: it has been experience.

The felt necessities of the time, the prevalent moral and political theories, intuitions of public policy, avowed or unconscious, even the prejudices which judges share with their fellow-men, have had a good deal more to do than the syllogism in determining the rules by which men should be governed."[2] Then, attacking the mechanical declaratory theory, Holmes stated: "The very considerations which judges most rarely mention, and always with an apology, are the secret root from which the law draws all the juices of life. I mean, of course, considerations of what is expedient for the community concerned."[3]

Holmes continued his efforts "to wash the law in cynical acid" after his appointment to the Massachusetts Supreme Judicial Court and later to the United States Supreme Court. In 1908, Louis D. Brandeis, another Boston lawyer, began a new trend in legal advocacy, that of assembling a mass of factual data to prove to judges that a given piece of social legislation was reasonable. In 1916, Brandeis joined Holmes on the Supreme Court. A third judge, Benjamin N. Cardozo, also exerted a significant influence on the development of American juridical thinking. Where Holmes had been mainly a skeptical critic and Brandeis more of a social than a legal reformer, Cardozo openly accepted the principles of sociological jurisprudence and applied them in his own decisions on the New York Court of Appeals and later on the U.S. Supreme Court.

During the 1920's an offshoot group from the sociological school, calling themselves realists, mounted a fresh assault on the still highly orthodox declaratory theory. Led by such men as Jerome Frank, they often made fuller use of psychological knowledge than had their older colleagues. The realist critique of existing legal rules as myths to hide judicial policy-making was devastating; but, perhaps because of the general disillusionment of the 1920's, they made little positive contribution of their own to legal theory, other than to point out some of the problems which a viable theory of law and judging would have to face.

Policy and Judicial Practice

Nor were these intellectual currents the only forces undermining the accepted theory of judging. Supreme Court justices themselves often exposed the fact that there was a great deal of personal discretion in their work. For example, there were occasional flashes of candor, as when Justice Harlan told a group of law students that "if we don't like an act

[2] *The Common Law* (Boston: Little, Brown, 1881), p. 1.
[3] *Ibid.*, p. 35.

of Congress, we don't have much trouble to find grounds for declaring it unconstitutional."

Again, specific decisions were revealing. Although John Marshall had preached the declaratory theory while formulating a great deal of public policy, he skillfully avoided backing his Court into an untenable political position. His successors, however, were not always so adroit. The Taney Court, for instance, stepped clumsily beyond its sphere of competence when in 1857, in the Dred Scott case, it held that Negroes were not citizens of the United States, that Congress could not prohibit slavery in the territories, and that therefore the Missouri Compromise had been unconstitutional. In 1870, the Court by a 4-3 vote declared the Legal Tender Acts unconstitutional; little more than a year later it reversed itself and held by a 5-4 vote that the paper-money statutes were valid. In 1895, the Court divided 4-4 on the question whether Congress could legitimately levy an income tax. Then on rehearing one justice changed his mind, and the slim majority reversed "a century of error" to void the tax.

Charles Evans Hughes called these three cases "self-inflicted wounds." They laid bare the lawmaking and policy-shaping function of the judges. Moreover, these dramatic decisions were not rare exceptions: the social, economic, and political predilections of judges were often clearly visible beneath the onionskin of official opinions. From the last decade of the nineteenth century until 1937, judges seemed to "find" the law of the land in Herbert Spencer's sociology and in Manchester economics as frequently as in the Constitution.

The showdown came in 1937. In the preceding four years the Supreme Court had handed down twelve decisions voiding federal statutes and over thirty decisions striking down state laws. Most of the laws declared unconstitutional were efforts by state or federal authorities to regulate economic affairs. In one case a majority of the justices held that the federal government could not regulate wages and hours because the matter was local. In another case, five justices held that states could not regulate such matters even though they were local. "We seem," Justice Stone wrote, "to have tied Uncle Sam up in a hard knot."

The knot, however, did not stay tied. Fresh from his thundering triumph in the 1936 election, President Roosevelt announced his "Court-packing" plan by which he would be allowed to appoint one additional justice for every member of the Supreme Court over seventy years of age who did not retire, with the stipulation that the Court's membership never exceed fifteen. The bill was beaten in the Senate, but not before some of the justices modified their economic if not their constitutional thinking. The first break came when Justice Roberts switched his vote on state regulation of wages and hours, and then a few weeks later joined the former dissenters in forming a new majority to reverse the implications of earlier decisions and so to validate most of the New Deal.

For a time, at least, the wide range of personal discretion in the judging business stood as naked to public view as did the creative role of the judges in molding public policy. According to Max Lerner, Americans learned then that "judicial decisions are not babies brought by constitutional storks." Since that time the Supreme Court has had to perform its functions in the clear, hard light of public knowledge that judicial interpretation is policy formation, not merely legal exegesis. When the Supreme Court in 1954 unanimously reversed a sixty-year-old precedent and held that racial segregation in the public schools was unconstitutional, the decision was widely regarded as a policy decision in which the Court was registering the growth of national and world revulsion against racial discrimination. The current recognition of the courts as part of the political process no longer shocks or even surprises anyone in these sophisticated times.

This new emphasis upon the policy functions of the courts has been fatal to the conceptualism of an earlier day. The classic doctrine of the separation of powers had resulted in an utterly false idea of what officials actually do, not only in the courts but in the executive and legislative branches as well. The behavioristic type of analysis which has been characteristic of modern political science reveals that in all three branches, in somewhat varying degrees, policymaking, administrative, and adjudicative activities are going on.

This book offers an approach to the judicial process which places judging within the main stream of political relationships. Judicial policymaking is seen as a major and proper function, not as incidental or as the work of the wrong kind of judges. Judicial decisions are frankly recognized as influenced by the same sorts of pressures and motivations that bear on legislators and administrators.

At the same time the book endeavors to avoid a danger in discarding the separation-of-powers conceptualism, and that is the risk of going to the opposite extreme and refusing to concede any distinctive characteristics to the judicial process. It is just as false to argue that judges freely make policy decisions as to contend that they have no policy functions at all. There *is* a difference between legislative and judicial lawmaking. Judges *do* operate within a situational context different from that of policymakers elsewhere in government. The basic conditions of litigation mean that policy issues come before the courts in a more structured, less hectic form than legislators usually encounter. Any accurate analysis of judicial behavior must have as a major purpose to make fully clear the unique conditions under which judicial policymaking proceeds.

This study is concerned, then, with promoting a clearer, more realistic understanding of the way the American judicial system actually operates in the political process. Any such effort must take fully into account the fact that judges are men who are influenced in their judging by personal predilections, by their commitments to ethical norms, and by their understanding of the realities of political life. But at the same time it must never be forgotten that the freedom of the judge is limited by the institutional ethos and by the traditions of his calling. A judicial decision is an amalgam of personal judgment and institutional control.

SELECTED REFERENCES

Bentley, A. F., *The Process of Government* (Chicago: University of Chicago Press, 1908).

Cahill, Fred, *Judicial Legislation* (New York: Ronald Press, 1952).

Cairns, Huntington, *Legal Philosophy from Plato to Hegel* (Baltimore: Johns Hopkins University Press, 1949).

Cohen, Morris, "The Place of Logic in the Law," 29 *Harvard Law Review* 622 (1916).

Frank, Jerome, *Law and the Modern Mind* (New York: Brentano's, 1930).

Frank, John P., *Marble Palace* (New York: A. A. Knopf, 1958).

Frankfurter, Felix, "The Supreme Court," 3 *Parliamentary Affairs* 68 (1949).

Holmes, Oliver Wendell, *The Common Law* (Boston: Little, Brown, 1881).

Lerner, Max, "The Court and the Constitution as Symbols," 46 *Yale Law Journal* 1290 (1937).

Mason, Alpheus T., *Harlan Fiske Stone: Pillar of the Law* (New York: Viking, 1956).

———, *The Supreme Court from Taft to Warren* (Baton Rouge: Louisiana State University Press, 1958).

Patterson, Edwin S., *Jurisprudence* (Brooklyn: The Foundation Press, 1953).

Powell, Thomas Reed, *Vagaries and Varieties in Constitutional Interpretation* (New York: Columbia University Press, 1956).

Pound, Roscoe, "The Need for a Sociological Jurisprudence," 19 *Green Bag* 107 (1907).

———, "Scope and Purpose of Sociological Jurisprudence," 24 *Harvard Law Review* 591 (1911); 25 *ibid.* 140, 489 (1912).

———, *Social Control through Law* (New Haven: Yale University Press, 1942).

———, "A Survey of Social Interests," 57 *Harvard Law Review* 1 (1943).

Rommen, H., *The Natural Law* (trans. T. R. Handley; St. Louis: Herder, 1955).

Stone, Julius, *The Province and Function of Law* (Cambridge: Harvard University Press, 1950).

Wright, Benjamin F., *The Growth of American Constitutional Law* (Boston: Houghton Mifflin, 1942).

1.
"*[Judges] are the depositaries of the laws; the living oracles . . .*"

COMMENTARIES ON THE LAWS OF ENGLAND   *Sir William Blackstone**

. . . BUT HERE a very natural, and very material, question arises: how are these customs and maxims to be known, and by whom is their validity to be determined? The answer is, by the judges in the several courts of justice. They are the depositaries of the laws; the living oracles, who must decide in all cases of doubt, and who are bound by an oath to decide according to the law of the land. Their knowledge of that law is derived from experience and study . . . and from being long personally accustomed to the judicial decisions of their predecessors. And indeed these judicial decisions are the principal and the most authoritative evidence, that can be given, of the existence of such a custom as shall form a part of the common law. The judgment itself, and all the proceedings previous thereto, are carefully registered and preserved, under the name of *records,* in public repositories set apart for that particular purpose; and to them frequent recourse is had, when any critical question arises, in the determination of which former precedents may give light or assistance. . . . For it is an established rule to abide by former precedents, where the same points come again in litigation: as well to keep the scale of justice even and steady, and not liable to waver with every new judge's opinion; as also because the law in that case being solemnly declared and determined, what before was uncertain, and perhaps indifferent, is now become a permanent rule which it is not in the breast of any subsequent judge to alter or vary from according to his private sentiments: he being sworn to determine, not according to his own private judgment, but according to the known laws and customs of the land; not delegated to pronounce a new law but to maintain and expound the old one. Yet this rule admits of exception, where the former determination

American ed.; Chicago: Callaghan & Cockcroft: 1871, I, 69–70.

* Eighteenth-century English jurist whose *Commentaries* (1765–68) became one of the most influential writings in Anglo-American legal theory.

is most evidently contrary to the divine law. But even in such cases the subsequent judges do not pretend to make a new law, but to vindicate the old one from misrepresentation. For if it be found that the former decision is manifestly absurd or unjust, it is declared, not that such a sentence was *bad law,* but that it was *not law;* that is, that it is not the established custom of the realm, as has been erroneously determined. . . .

2.   *"[Courts] may truly be said to have neither FORCE nor WILL, but merely judgment . . ."*

THE FEDERALIST, NO. 78   *Alexander Hamilton*

. . . WHOEVER ATTENTIVELY considers the different departments of power must perceive that, in a government in which they are separated from each other, the judiciary, from the nature of its functions, will always be the least dangerous to the political rights of the Constitution; because it will be least in capacity to annoy or injure them. The Executive not only dispenses honors, but holds the sword of the community. The legislature not only commands the purse, but prescribes the rules by which the duties and rights of every citizen are to be regulated. The judiciary, on the contrary, has no influence over either the sword or the purse; no direction either of the strength or of the wealth of the society; and can take no active resolution whatever. It may truly be said to have neither FORCE nor WILL, but merely judgment; and must ultimately depend upon the aid of the executive arm even for the efficacy of its judgment. . . .

Some perplexity respecting the rights of the courts to pronounce legislative acts void, because contrary to the constitution, has arisen from an imagination that the doctrine would imply a superiority of the judiciary to the legislative power. It is urged that the authority which can declare the acts of another void, must necessarily be superior to the one whose acts may be declared void. As this doctrine is of great importance in all the American constitutions, a brief discussion on the ground on which it rests cannot be unacceptable.

There is no position which depends on clearer principles, than that

every act of a delegated authority, contrary to the tenor of the commission under which it is exercised, is void. No legislative act, therefore, contrary to the Constitution, can be valid. To deny this, would be
to affirm that the deputy is greater than his principal; that the servant
is above his master; that the representatives of the people are superior
to the people themselves; that men acting by virtue of powers may do
not only what their powers do not authorize, but what they forbid.

If it be said that the legislative body are themselves the constitutional
judges of their own powers, and that the construction put on them is
conclusive upon the other departments, it may be answered, that this
cannot be the natural presumption, where it is not to be collected from
any particular provisions in the Constitution. It is not otherwise to be
supposed, that the Constitution could intend to enable the representatives of the people to substitute their *will* to that of their constituents.
It is far more rational to suppose, that the courts were designed to be
an intermediate body between the people and the legislature, in order,
among other things, to keep the latter within the limits assigned to
their authority. The interpretation of the laws is the proper and peculiar province of the courts. A constitution is, in fact, and must be regarded by the judges, as a fundamental law. It therefore belongs to
them to ascertain its meaning, as well as the meaning of any particular act proceeding from the legislative body. If there should happen to
be an irreconcilable variance between the two, that which has the
superior obligation and validity ought, of course, to be preferred; or,
in other words, the Constitution ought to be preferred to the statute,
the intention of the people to the intention of their agents.

Nor does this conclusion by any means suppose a superiority of the
judicial to the legislative power. It only supposes that the power of
the people is superior to both; and that where the will of the legislature, declared in its statutes, stands in opposition to that of the people,
declared in the Constitution, the judges ought to be governed by
the latter rather than the former. They ought to regulate their decisions by the fundamental laws, rather than by those which are not
fundamental. . . .

3.   *"He only judges the law because he is obliged to judge a case."*

JUDICIAL POWER IN THE UNITED STATES   *Alexis de Tocqueville**

. . . I AM NOT aware that any nation of the globe has hitherto organized a judicial power on the principle adopted by the Americans. The judicial organization of the United States is the institution which the stranger has the greatest difficulty in understanding. He hears the authority of the judge invoked in the political occurrences of every day, and he naturally concludes that in the United States judges are important political functionaries; nevertheless, when he examines the nature of the tribunals, they offer nothing which is contrary to the usual habits and privileges of those bodies; and the magistrates seem to him to interfere in public affairs by chance, but by a chance which recurs every day. . . .

The first characteristic of judicial power in all nations is the duty of arbitration. But rights must be contested in order to warrant the interference of a tribunal; and an action must be brought to obtain the decision of a judge. As long, therefore, as a law is uncontested, the judicial authority is not called upon to discuss it. . . . When a judge in a given case attacks a law relating to that case, he extends the circle of his customary duties, without however stepping beyond it; since he is in some measure obliged to decide upon the law, in order to decide the case. But if he pronounces upon a law without resting upon a case, he clearly steps beyond his sphere, and invades that of the legislative authority.

The second characteristic of judicial power is that it pronounces on special cases and not upon general principles. If a judge, in deciding a particular point, destroys a general principle by passing a judgment which tends to reject all the inferences from that principle and consequently to annul it, he remains within the ordinary limits of his functions. But if he directly attacks a general principle without hav-

Democracy in America (1835), Ch. 6.

* French political analyst whose observations of nineteenth-century American society have become classic.

ing a particular case in view, he leaves the circle in which all nations
have agreed to confine his authority; he assumes a more important,
and perhaps a more useful, influence than that of the magistrate, but
he ceases to represent the judicial power.

The third characteristic of the judicial power is its inability to act
unless it is appealed to, or until it has taken cognizance of an affair.
This characteristic is less general than the other two; but notwithstanding the exceptions, I think it may be regarded as essential. The
judicial power is by its nature devoid of action; it must be put in
motion in order to produce a result. When it is called upon to repress
a crime, it punishes the criminal; when a wrong is to be redressed, it
is ready to redress it; when an act requires interpretation, it is prepared to interpret it; but it does not pursue criminals, hunt out wrongs,
or examine into evidence of its own accord. . . .

The Americans have retained these three distinguishing characteristics of the judicial power; an American judge can only pronounce a
decision when litigation has arisen, he is only conversant with special
cases, and he cannot act until the case has been duly brought before
the court. His position is therefore perfectly similar to that of the
magistrate of other nations; and he is nevertheless invested with immense political power. . . . The cause of this difference lies in the
simple fact that the Americans have acknowledged the right of the
judges to found their decisions on the Constitution, rather than on
the laws. In other words, they have left judges at liberty not to apply
such laws as may appear to them to be unconstitutional.

I am aware that a similar right has been claimed—but claimed in
vain—by courts of justice in other countries; but in America it is recognized by all the authorities; and not a party, nor so much as an individual, is found to contest it. This fact can only be explained by the
principles of the American constitutions. . . . In the United States, the
Constitution governs the legislator as much as the private citizen: as it
is the first of laws, it cannot be modified by a law; and it is therefore
just that the tribunals should obey the Constitution in preference to
any law. This condition is essential to the power of the judicature; for
to select that legal obligation by which he is strictly bound is the
natural right of every magistrate.

In France the Constitution is also the first of laws, and the judges

have the same right to take it as the ground of their decisions; but
were they to exercise this right, they must perforce encroach on rights
more sacred than their own, namely, on those of society, in whose
name they are acting. In this case the State-motive clearly prevails
over the motives of an individual. In America, where the nation can
always reduce its magistrates to obedience by changing its Constitution, no danger of this kind is to be feared. Upon this point therefore
political and logical reason agree, and the people as well as the judges
preserve their privileges.

Whenever a law which the judge holds to be unconstitutional is
argued in a tribunal of the United States, he may refuse to admit it
as a rule; this power is the only one which is peculiar to the American
magistrate, but it gives him immense political influence. Few laws
can escape his searching analysis; for there are few which are not
prejudicial to some private interest or other, and none which may not
be brought before a court of justice by the choice of the parties, or by
the necessity of the case. But from that time a judge has refused to apply any given law in a case, that law loses a portion of its moral sanction. The persons to whose interests it is prejudicial learn that means
exist of evading its authority; and similar suits are multiplied, until it
becomes powerless. One of two alternatives must then be resorted to:
the people must alter the Constitution, or the legislature must repeal
the law.

The political power which the Americans have entrusted to their
courts of justice is therefore immense; but the evils of this power are
considerably diminished by the obligation which has been imposed
of attacking the laws through the courts of justice alone. If the judge
had been empowered to contest the laws on the ground of theoretical
generalities; if he had been enabled to open an attack or to pass a
censure on the legislator, he would have played a prominent part in
the political sphere; and as the champion or the antagonist of a party,
he would have arrayed the hostile passions of the nation in the conflict.
But when a judge contests a law, applied to some particular case in an
obscure proceeding, the importance of his attack is concealed from the
public gaze; his decision bears upon the interest of an individual, and
if the law is slighted it is only collaterally. Moreover, although it be
censured, it is not abolished; its moral force may be diminished, but

its cogency is by no means suspended; and its final destruction can only be accomplished by the reiterated attacks of judicial functionaries. It will readily be understood that by connecting the censureship of the laws with the private interests of members of the community, and by intimately uniting the prosecution of the law with the prosecution of an individual, the legislation is protected from wanton assailants and from the daily aggressions of party-spirit. The errors of the legislator are exposed whenever their evil consequences are most felt; and it is always a positive and appreciable fact which serves as the basis of a prosecution.

I am inclined to believe this practice of the American courts to be at once the most favorable to liberty as well as to public order. If the judge could only attack the legislator openly and directly, he would sometimes be afraid to oppose any resistance to his will; and at other moments party-spirit might encourage him to brave it every day. The laws would consequently be attacked when the power from which they emanate is weak, and obeyed when it is strong. That is to say, when it would be useful to respect them, they would be contested; and when it would be easy to convert them into an instrument of oppression, they would be respected. But the American judge is brought into the political arena independently of his own will. He only judges the law because he is obliged to judge a case. The political question which he is called upon to resolve is connected with the interest of the parties, and he cannot refuse to decide it without abdicating the duties of his post. He performs his functions as a citizen by fulfilling the strict duties which belong to his profession as a magistrate. It is true that upon this system the judicial censureship which is exercised by the courts of justice over legislation cannot extend equally to all laws, in as much as some of them can never give rise to that precise species of contestation which is termed a lawsuit; and even when such a contestation is possible, it may happen that no one cares to bring it before a court of justice. The Americans have often felt this disadvantage, but they have left the remedy incomplete, lest they should give it efficacy which might in some cases prove dangerous. Within these limits, the power vested in the American courts of justice of pronouncing a statute to be unconstitutional forms one of the most powerful barriers which has ever been devised against the tyranny of political assemblies.

4.
"The decisions of the courts on economic and social questions depend upon their economic and social philosophy ..."

ANNUAL MESSAGE TO CONGRESS (1908)   *Theodore Roosevelt*

THE CHIEF lawmakers in our country may be, and often are, the judges, because they are the final seat of authority. Every time they interpret contract, property, vested rights, due process of law, liberty, they necessarily enact into law parts of a system of social philosophy; and as such interpretation is fundamental, they give direc- tion to all law-making. The decisions of the courts on economic and social questions depend upon their economic and social philosophy; and for the peaceful progress of our people during the twentieth century we shall owe most to those judges who hold to a twentieth century economic and social philosophy and not to a long outgrown philosophy. . . . Of course a judge's views on progressive social philosophy are entirely second in importance to his possession of a high and fine character. . . . But it is also true that judges, like executives and legislators, should hold sound views on the questions of public policy which are of vital interest to the people.

The legislators and executives are chosen to represent the people in enacting and administering the laws. The judges are not chosen to represent the people in this sense. Their function is to interpret the laws. The legislators are responsible for the laws; the judges for the spirit in which they interpret and enforce the laws. We stand aloof from the reckless agitators who would make the judges mere pliant tools of popular prejudice and passion; and we stand aloof from those equally unwise partisans of reaction and privilege who deny the proposition that, inasmuch as judges are chosen to serve the interests of the whole people, they should strive to find out what those inter- ests are, and, so far as they conscientiously can, should strive to give effect to popular conviction when deliberately and duly expressed by the lawmaking body. The courts are to be highly commended and staunchly upheld when they set their faces against wrongdoing or tyranny by a majority; but they are to be blamed when they fail to recognize under a government like ours the deliberate judgment of the majority as to a matter of legitimate policy, when duly expressed by the legislature. Such lawfully expressed and deliberate judgment should be given effect by the courts, save in the extreme and exceptional cases where there has been a clear violation of a constitutional provision. . . . To protest against tyranny, to protect minorities from oppression, to nullify an act committed in a spasm of popular fury, is to render a service to the Republic. But for the courts to arrogate to themselves functions which properly belong to the legislative bodies is all wrong, and in the end works mischief. The people should not be permitted to pardon evil and slipshod legislation on the theory that the court will set it right; they should be taught that the right way to get rid of a bad law is to have the legislature repeal it, and not to have the courts by ingenious hair-splitting nullify it. A law may be unwise and improper; but it should not for these reasons be declared unconstitutional by a strained interpretation, for the result of such action is to take away from the people at large their sense of responsibility and ultimately to destroy their capacity for orderly self restraint and self government. Under such a popular government as ours, founded on the theory that in the long run the will of the people is supreme, the ultimate safety of the Nation can only rest in training and guiding the people so that what they will shall be right, and not in devising means to defeat their will by the technicalities of strained construction.

5.
"The prophecies of what the courts will do in fact . . .
are what I mean by the law."

THE PATH OF THE LAW   *Oliver Wendell Holmes**

WHEN WE study law we are not studying a mystery but a well known profession. We are studying what we shall want in order to appear before judges, or to advise people in such a way as to keep

10 *Harvard Law Review* 39 (1897). Copyright 1897 Oliver Wendell Holmes.

* Justice, Massachusetts Supreme Judicial Court, 1882–99; Chief Justice, Massachusetts Supreme Judicial Court, 1899–1902; Associate Justice, U.S. Supreme Court, 1902–32.

them out of court. The reason why it is a profession, why people will pay lawyers to argue for them or to advise them, is that in societies like ours the command of the public force is intrusted to the judges in certain cases, and the whole power of the state will be put forth, if necessary, to carry out their judgments and decrees. People want to know under what circumstances and how far they will run the risk of coming against what is so much stronger than themselves, and hence it becomes a business to find out when this danger is to be feared. The object of our study, then, is prediction, the prediction of the incidence of the public force through the instrumentality of the courts.

The means of the study are a body of reports, of treatises, and of statutes, in this country and in England, extending back for six hundred years, and now increasing annually by hundreds. In these sibylline leaves are gathered the scattered prophecies of the past upon the cases in which the axe will fall. These are what properly have been called the oracles of the law. Far the most important and pretty nearly the whole meaning of every new effort of legal thought is to make these prophecies more precise, and to generalize them into a thoroughly connected system. . . . The primary rights and duties with which jurisprudence busies itself again are nothing but prophecies. One of the many evil effects of the confusion between legal and moral ideas, about which I shall have something to say in a moment, is that theory is apt to get the cart before the horse, and to consider the right or the duty as something existing apart from and independent of the consequences of its breach, to which certain sanctions are added afterward. But, as I shall try to show, a legal duty so called is nothing but a prediction that if a man does or omits certain things he will be made to suffer in this or that way by judgment of the court;—and so of a legal right. . . .

The first thing for a business-like understanding of the matter is to understand its limits, and therefore I think it desirable at once to point out and dispel a confusion between morality and law, which sometimes rises to the height of conscious theory, and more often and indeed constantly is making trouble in detail without reaching the point of consciousness. You can see very plainly that a bad man has as much reason as a good one for wishing to avoid an encounter with the public force, and therefore you can see the practical importance of the distinction between morality and law. A man who cares nothing for an ethical rule which is believed and practised by his neighbors is likely nevertheless to care a good deal to avoid being made to pay money, and will want to keep out of jail if he can.

I take it for granted that no hearer of mine will misinterpret what I have to say as the language of cynicism. The law is the witness and external deposit of our moral life. Its history is the history of the moral development of the race. The practice of it, in spite of popular jests, tends to make good citizens and good men. When I emphasize the difference between law and morals I do so with reference to a single end, that of learning and understanding the law. For that purpose you must definitely master its specific marks, and it is for that that I ask you for the moment to imagine yourselves indifferent to other and greater things.

I do not say that there is not a wider point of view from which the distinction between law and morals becomes of secondary or no importance, as all mathematical distinctions vanish in presence of the infinite. But I do say that that distinction is of the first importance for the object which we are here to consider,—a right study and mastery of the law as a business with well understood limits, a body of dogma enclosed within definite lines. I have just shown the practical reason for saying so. If you want to know the law and nothing else, you must look at it as a bad man, who cares only for the material consequences which such knowledge enables him to predict, not as a good one, who finds his reasons for conduct, whether inside the law or outside of it, in the vaguer sanctions of conscience. . . . The prophecies of what the courts will do in fact, and nothing more pretentious, are what I mean by the law. . . .

. . . You may assume, with Hobbes and Bentham and Austin, that all law emanates from the sovereign, even when the first human beings to enunciate it are the judges, or you may think that law is the voice of the Zeitgeist, or what you like. It is all one to my present purpose. . . . In every system there are such explanations and principles to be found. It is with regard to them that a second fallacy comes in, which I think it important to expose.

The fallacy to which I refer is the notion that the only force at work in the development of the law is logic. In the broadest sense, indeed, that notion would be true. . . . The danger of which I speak is not the admission that the principles governing other phenomena also govern the law, but the notion that a given system, ours, for instance, can be worked out like mathematics from some general axioms of conduct. This is the natural error of the schools, but it is not confined to them. I once heard a very eminent judge say that he never let a decision go until he was absolutely sure that it was right. . . .

This mode of thinking is entirely natural. The training of lawyers is a training in logic. The processes of analogy, discrimination, and deduction are those in which they are most at home. The language of judicial decision is mainly the language of logic. And the logical method and form flatter that longing for certainty and for repose which is in every human mind. But certainty generally is illusion, and repose is not the destiny of man. Behind the logical form lies a judgment as to the relative worth and importance of competing legislative grounds, often an inarticulate and unconscious judgment, it is true, and yet the very root and nerve of the whole proceeding. You can give any conclusion a logical form. You always can imply a condition in a contract. But why do you imply it? It is because of some belief as to the practice of the community or of a class, or because of some opinion as to policy, or, in short, because of some attitude of yours upon a matter not capable of exact quantitative measurement, and therefore not capable of founding exact logical conclusions. Such matters really are battle grounds where the means do not exist for determinations that shall be good for all time, and where the decision can do no more than embody the preference of a given body in a given time and place. We do not realize how large a part of our law is open to reconsideration upon a slight change in the habit of the public mind. No concrete proposition is self-evident, no matter how ready we may be to accept it, not even Mr. Herbert Spencer's Every man has a right to do what he wills, provided he interferes not with a like right on the part of his neighbors. . . .

I think that the judges themselves have failed adequately to recognize their duty of weighing considerations of social advantage. The duty is inevitable, and the result of the often proclaimed judicial aversion to deal with such considerations is simply to leave the very

ground and foundation of judgments inarticulate, and often unconscious, as I have said. When socialism first began to be talked about,
the comfortable classes of the community were a good deal frightened. I suspect that this fear has influenced judicial action both here
and in England, yet it is certain that it is not a conscious factor in the
decisions to which I refer. . . . I cannot but believe that if the training
of lawyers led them habitually to consider more definitely and explicitly the social advantage on which the rule they lay down must be
justified, they sometimes would hesitate where now they are confident, and see that really they were taking sides upon debatable and
often burning questions.

So much for the fallacy of logical form. Now let us consider the
present condition of the law as a subject for study, and the ideal
toward which it tends. . . . The development of our law has gone on
for nearly a thousand years, like the development of a plant, each
generation taking the inevitable next step, mind, like matter, simply
obeying a law of spontaneous growth. It is perfectly natural and right
that it should have been so. Imitation is a necessity of human nature.
. . . Most of the things we do, we do for no better reason than that our
fathers have done them or that our neighbors do them, and the same
is true of a larger part than we suspect of what we think. The reason
is a good one, because our short life gives us no time for a better, but
it is not the best. It does not follow, because we all are compelled to
take on faith at second hand most of the rules on which we base our
action and our thought, that each of us may not try to set some corner
of his world in the order of reason, or that all of us collectively should
not aspire to carry reason as far as it will go throughout the whole
domain. In regard to the law, it is true, no doubt, that an evolutionist
will hesitate to affirm universal validity for his social ideals, or for the
principles which he thinks should be embodied in legislation. He is
content if he can prove them best for here and now. He may be ready to
admit that he knows nothing about an absolute best in the cosmos, and
even that he knows next to nothing about a permanent best for men.
Still it is true that a body of law is more rational and more civilized
when every rule it contains is referred articulately and definitely to an
end which it subserves, and when the grounds for desiring that end
are stated or are ready to be stated in words.

At present, in very many cases, if we want to know why a rule of law has taken its particular shape, and more or less if we want to know why it exists at all, we go to tradition. We follow it into the Year Books, and perhaps beyond them to the customs of the Salian Franks, and somewhere in the past, in the German forests, in the needs of Norman kings, in the assumptions of a dominant class, in the absence of generalized ideas, we find out the practical motive for what now best is justified by the mere fact of its acceptance and that men are accustomed to it. The rational study of law is still to a large extent the study of history. . . . It is a part of the rational study, because it is the first step toward an enlightened scepticism, that is, toward a deliberate reconsideration of the worth of those rules. When you get the dragon out of his cave on to the plain and in the daylight, you can count his teeth and claws, and see just what is his strength. But to get him out is only the first step. The next is either to kill him, or to tame him and make him a useful animal. For the rational study of the law the black-letter man may be the man of the present, but the man of the future is the man of statistics and the master of economics. It is revolting to have no better reason for a rule of law than that so it was laid down in the time of Henry IV. It is still more revolting if the grounds upon which it was laid down have vanished long since, and the rule simply persists from blind imitation of the past. . . .

. . . I look forward to a time when the part played by history in the explanation of dogma shall be very small, and instead of ingenious research we shall spend our energy on a study of the ends sought to be attained and the reasons for desiring them. As a step toward that ideal it seems to me that every lawyer ought to seek an understanding of economics. The present divorce between the schools of political economy and law seem to me an evidence of how much progress in philosophical study still remains to be made. In the present state of political economy, indeed, we come again upon history on a larger scale, but there we are called on to consider and weigh the ends of legislation, the means of attaining them, and the cost. We learn that for everything we have to give up something else, and we are taught to set the advantage we gain against the other advantage we lose, and to know what we are doing when we elect.

There is another study which sometimes is undervalued by the practical minded, for which I wish to say a good word, although I think a good deal of pretty poor stuff goes under that name. I mean the study of what is called jurisprudence. Jurisprudence, as I look at it, is simply law in its most generalized part. Every effort to reduce a case to a rule is an effort of jurisprudence, although the name as used in English is confined to the broadest rules and most fundamental conceptions. One mark of a great lawyer is that he sees the application of the broadest rules. . . . Theory is the most important part of the dogma of the law, as the architect is the most important man who takes part in the building of a house. . . .

6.   *"We cannot transcend the limitations of the* ego *. . ."*

THE NATURE OF THE JUDICIAL PROCESS   *Benjamin N. Cardozo**

THE WORK of deciding cases goes on every day in hundreds of courts throughout the land. Any judge, one might suppose, would find it easy to describe the process which he had followed a thousand times and more. Nothing could be farther from the truth. Let some intelligent layman ask him to explain: he will not go very far before taking refuge in the excuse that the language of craftsmen is unintelligible to those untutored in the craft. Such an excuse may cover with a semblance of respectability an otherwise ignominious retreat. It will hardly serve to still the pricks of curiosity and conscience. In moments of introspection . . . the troublesome problem will recur, and press for a solution. What is it that I do when I decide a case? To what sources of information do I appeal for guidance? In what proportions do I permit them to contribute to the result? In what proportions ought they to contribute? If a precedent is applicable, when do I refuse to follow it? If no precedent is applicable, how do I reach the rule that will make a precedent for the future? . . . At what

New Haven: Yale University Press, 1921, pp. 9–13, 18–21, 43, 66–67, 105–106, 113–114, 141, 161–162. Copyright 1921 Yale University Press. Reprinted with permission.

* Judge, New York Court of Appeals, 1913–26; Chief Judge, New York Court of Appeals, 1926–32; and Associate Justice, U.S. Supreme Court, 1932–39.

point shall the quest be halted by some discrepant custom, by some consideration of the social welfare, by my own or the common standards of justice and morals? Into that strange compound which is brewed daily in the cauldron of the courts, all these ingredients enter in varying proportions. I am not concerned to inquire whether judges ought to be allowed to brew such a compound at all. I take judge-made law as one of the existing realities of life. There before us is the brew. Not a judge on the bench but has had a hand in the making. The elements have not come together by chance. *Some* principle, however unavowed and inarticulate and subconscious, has regulated the infusion. It may not have been the same principle for all judges at any time, nor the same principle for any judge at all times. But a choice there has been, not a submission to the decrees of Fate; and the considerations and motives determining the choice, even if often obscure, do not utterly resist analysis. . . . [T]here will be need to distinguish between the conscious and the subconscious. . . . More subtle are the forces so far beneath the surface that they cannot reasonably be classified as other than subconscious. It is often through these subconscious forces that judges are kept consistent with themselves, and inconsistent with one another. . . . There is in each of us a stream of tendency, whether you choose to call it philosophy or not, which gives coherence and direction to thought and action. Judges cannot escape that current any more than other mortals. All their lives, forces which they do not recognize and cannot name, have been tugging at them—inherited instincts, traditional beliefs, acquired convictions; and the resultant is an outlook on life, a conception of social needs, a sense in James's phrase of "the total push and pressure of the cosmos," which, when reasons are nicely balanced, must determine where choices shall fall. In this mental background every problem finds its setting. We may try to see things as objectively as we please. None the less, we can never see them with any eyes except our own. . . .

We reach the land of mystery when constitution and statute are silent, and the judge must look to the common law for the rule that fits the case. He is the "living oracle of the law" in Blackstone's vivid phrase. Looking at Sir Oracle in action, viewing his work in the dry light of realism, how does he set about his task?

The first thing he does is to compare the case before him with the precedents, whether stored in his mind or hidden in books. I do not mean that precedents are ultimate sources of the law, supplying the sole equipment that is needed for the legal armory, the sole tools . . . "in the legal smithy." Back of precedents are basic jural conceptions which are postulates of judicial reasoning, and farther back are the habits of life, the institutions of society, in which those conceptions have had their origin, and which, by a process of interaction, they have modified in turn. None the less, in a system so highly developed as our own, precedents have so covered the ground that they fix the point of departure from which the labor of the judge begins. Almost invariably, his first step is to examine and compare them. If they are plain and to the point, there may be need of nothing more. *Stare decisis* is at least the everyday working rule of our law. . . . It is a process of search, comparison, and little more. Some judges seldom get beyond that process in any case. Their notion of their duty is to match the colors of the case at hand against the colors of many sample cases spread out upon their desk. The sample nearest in shade supplies the applicable rule. But, of course, no system of living law can be evolved by such a process, and no judge of a high court worthy of his office views the function of his place so narrowly. If that were all there were to our calling, there would be little of intellectual interest about it. The man who had the best card index of the cases would also be the wisest judge. It is when the colors do not match, when the references of the index fail, when there is no decisive precedent, that the serious business of the judge begins. He must then fashion Law for the litigants before him. In fashioning it for them, he will be fashioning it for others. . . . Every judgment has a generative power. It begets its own image. . . .

. . . We go forward with our logic, with our analogies, with our philosophies, till we reach a certain point. At first, we have no trouble with the paths; they follow the same lines. Then they begin to diverge, and we must make a choice between them. History or custom or social utility or some compelling sentiment of justice or sometimes perhaps a semi-intuitive apprehension of the pervading spirit of our law must come to the rescue of the anxious judge, and tell him where to go. . . .

The final cause of law is the welfare of society. The rule that misses its aim cannot permanently justify its existence. "Ethical considerations can no more be excluded from the administration of justice . . . than one can exclude the vital air from his room and live." Logic and history and custom have their place. We will shape the law to conform to them when we may; but only within bounds. The end which the law serves will dominate them all. . . . I do not mean, of course, that judges are commissioned to set aside existing rules at pleasure in favor of any other set of rules which they may hold to be expedient or wise. I mean that when they are called upon to say how far existing rules are to be extended or restricted, they must let the welfare of society fix the path, its direction and distance. . . .

There has been much debate among foreign jurists whether the norms of right and useful conduct, the patterns of social welfare, are to be found by the judge in conformity with an objective or a subjective standard. . . . So far as the distinction has practical significance, the traditions of our jurisprudence commit us to the objective standard. I do not mean, of course, that this ideal of objective vision is ever perfectly attained. We cannot transcend the limitations of the *ego* and see anything as it really is. None the less, the ideal is one to be striven for within the limits of our capacity. This truth, when clearly perceived, tends to unify the judge's function. His duty to declare the law in accordance with reason and justice is seen to be a phase of his duty to declare it in accordance with custom. It is the customary morality of right-minded men and women which he is to enforce by his decree. . . .

My analysis of the judicial process comes then to this, and little more: logic, and history, and custom, and utility, and the accepted standards of right conduct, are the forces which singly or in combination shape the progress of the law. Which of these forces shall dominate in any case must depend largely upon the comparative importance or value of the social interests that will be thereby promoted or impaired. . . .

If you ask how [the judge] is to know when one interest outweighs another, I can only answer that he must get his knowledge just as the legislator gets it; from experience and study and reflection; in brief, from life itself. Here, indeed, is the point of contact between the legislator's work and his. The choice of methods, the appraisement of values, must in the end be guided by like considerations for the one as for the other. Each indeed is legislating within the limits of his competence. No doubt the limits for the judge are narrower. He legislates only between gaps. He fills the open spaces in the law. How far he may go without traveling beyond the walls of the interstices cannot be staked out for him upon a chart. He must learn it for himself as he gains the sense of fitness and proportion that comes with years of habitude in the practice of an art.

. . . [Yet] the judge, even when he is free, is still not wholly free. He is not to innovate at pleasure. He is not a knight-errant roaming at will in pursuit of his own ideal of beauty or of goodness. He is to draw his inspiration from consecrated principles. He is not to yield to spasmodic sentiment, to vague and unregulated benevolence. He is to exercise a discretion informed by tradition, methodized by analogy, disciplined by system, and subordinated to "the primordial necessity of order in the social life." Wide enough in all conscience is the field of discretion that remains. . . .

Our survey of judicial methods teaches us, I think, the lesson that the whole subject matter of jurisprudence is more plastic, more malleable, the moulds less definitively cast, the bounds of right and wrong less preordained and constant, than most of us . . . have been accustomed to believe. . . . So also the duty of a judge becomes itself a question of degree, and he is a useful judge or a poor one as he estimates the measure accurately or loosely. He must balance all his ingredients, his philosophy, his logic, his analogies, his history, his customs, his sense of right, and all the rest, and adding a little here and taking out a little there, must determine, as wisely as he can, which weight shall tip the scales. . . .

7.   *". . . does a man cease to be himself when he becomes a Justice?"*

THE JUDICIAL PROCESS AND THE SUPREME COURT   *Felix Frankfurter**

JUDGES ARE men, not disembodied spirits. Of course a judge is not free from preferences or, if you will, biases. But he may deprive a bias of its meretricious authority by stripping it of the un-

98 *Proceedings of the American Philosophic Society* 233 (1954). Copyright 1954 American Philosophic Society. Reprinted with permission.
* Associate Justice, U.S. Supreme Court, 1939–.

critical assumption that it is founded on compelling reason or the coercive power of a syllogism. He will be alert to detect that though a
conclusion has logical form it in fact represents a choice of competing
considerations of policy, one of which for the time has won the day.

An acute historian recently concluded that those "who have any
share of political power . . . usually obtain it because they are excep-
tionally able to emancipate their purposes from the control of their
formulated wishes and impressions." For judges, it is not merely a desirable capacity "to emancipate their purposes" from their private
desires; it is their duty. It is a cynical belief in too many quarters . . .
that it is at best a self-delusion for judges to profess to pursue disinterestedness. It is asked with sophomoric brightness, does a man cease to
be himself when he becomes a Justice? Does he change his character
by putting on a gown? No, he does not change his character. He
brings his whole experience, his training, his outlook, his social, intellectual, and moral environment with him when he takes a seat on the
supreme bench. But a judge worth his salt is in the grip of his function. The intellectual habits of self-discipline which govern his mind
are as much a part of him as the influence of the interest he may have
represented at the bar, often more so. . . .

To assume that a lawyer who becomes a judge takes on the bench
merely his views on social or economic questions leaves out of account
his rooted notions regarding the scope and limits of a judge's authority.
The outlook of a lawyer fit to be a Justice regarding the role of a
judge cuts across all his personal preferences for this or that social
arrangement. . . .

Need it be stated that true humility and its offspring, disinterestedness, are more indispensable for the work of the Supreme Court than
for a judge's function on any other bench? These qualities alone will
not assure another indispensable requisite. This is the capacity for
self-searching. What Jacques Maritain said in another connection applies peculiarly to members of the Supreme Court. A Justice of that
Court cannot adequately discharge his function "without passing
through the door of the knowing, obscure as it may be, of his own
subjective."

This is not to say that the application of this view of the judge's
function—that he is there not to impose his private views on society,
that he is not to enforce personalized justice—assures unanimity of

judgments. Inevitably there are bound to be differences of opinion. And it would be pretense to deny that in the self-righteous exercise of this role obscurantist and even unjustifiable decisions are sometimes rendered. . . . The answers that the Supreme Court is required to give are based on questions and on data that preclude automatic or even undoubting answers. If the materials on which judicial judgments must be based could be fed into a machine so as to produce ineluctable answers, if such were the nature of the problems that come before the Supreme Court, and such were the answers expected, we would have IBM machines doing the work instead of judges. . . .

The core of the difficulty is that there is hardly a question of any real difficulty before the Court that does not entail more than one so-called principle. Anybody can decide a question if only a single principle is in controversy. Partisans and advocates often cast a question in that form, but the form is deceptive. In a famous passage Mr. Justice Holmes has exposed this misconception:

> All rights tend to declare themselves absolute to their logical extreme. Yet all in fact are limited by the neighborhood of principles of policy which are other than those on which the particular right is founded, and which become strong enough to hold their own when a certain point is reached. . . . The boundary at which the conflicting interests balance cannot be determined by any general formula in advance, but points in the line, or helping to establish it, are fixed by decisions that this or that concrete case falls on the nearer or farther side.

This contest between conflicting principles is not limited to law. In a recent discussion of two books on the conflict between the claims of literary individualism and dogma, I came across this profound observation: "But when, in any field of human observation, two truths appear in conflict it is wiser to assume that neither is exclusive, and that their contradiction, though it may be hard to bear, is part of the mystery of things." But judges cannot leave such contradiction between two conflicting "truths" as "part of the mystery of things." They have to adjudicate. If the conflict cannot be resolved, the task of the Court is to arrive at an accommodation of the contending claims. This is the core of the difficulties and misunderstandings about the judicial process. This, for any conscientious judge, is the agony of his duty.

2 / JUDICIAL ORGANIZATION AND JURISDICTION

The task of judging in the United States is performed under organizational arrangements more complex and confusing than those encountered in almost any other country. There are, first of all, two complete systems of courts, federal and state, with all the attendant problems of defining their respective jurisdictions. Then there are fifty separate state systems, which with few exceptions are set up on models and assumptions dating from the eighteenth century, if not earlier. While the concern of this book is primarily with the judicial function in the federal courts, a quick view of the characteristics of the state judicial system is appropriate.

The Judicial System in the States

The American approach to court organization has been strongly localistic. The pattern was established when the country was sparsely settled and methods of communication and transportation were primitive. Courts needed to be close to be convenient, and the result was the widespread adoption of the justice-of-the-peace system to provide courts on a neighborhood basis. At the next higher level, courts tended to be established with relation to the distance a man could travel in a day on horseback.

These local courts and judicial districts, once set up, have proved very difficult to modify.

Another dominant characteristic of the state court system has been the layers of courts, often with overlapping jurisdiction. Justices of the peace or other part-time magistrates, where they still exist, constitute the lowest level of trial courts. They typically are authorized to grant money judgments up to a certain amount (often about $300), and as criminal courts they can try only minor offenses. They are not courts of record, and, if their decisions are appealed, an entirely new trial must be held in the next highest court. Municipal or county courts are the courts of first instance for most civil, criminal, and probate proceedings. Circuit or district courts are also trial courts, typically covering several counties and handling the more important civil and criminal business.

At the appellate level, the states typically provide a set of inferior appellate courts in addition to the state supreme court. The easy availability of appellate consideration and the tremendous volume of appeals carried to the higher courts are characteristics in which the American legal system differs markedly from English and continental systems of justice. This practice grew first of all from the widespread assumption that litigants were entitled to carry disputes through all the levels of the appellate courts. Perhaps more important, however, was the view which the appellate judges themselves took of their function. Their role was primarily, as Hurst says, "to declare the law, rather than merely to decide the case." So the appellate courts did not see cases as a whole. They saw rather a succession of legal issues, which it was their job to settle. If legal error was found in the trial, the case would go back to the trial court for further proceedings, which in turn might be appealed on other legal issues.

American appellate procedure was further complicated by choice of the writ of error as the main instrument for securing review. This was one of the most technical of the writs developed by the English law courts, and it limited the reviewing court to a consideration of the formal record of the case. An appeal took on the status almost of a new and more expensive lawsuit, as assignments of error were prepared, records printed, and the evidence transcribed. Many appeals were decided simply on the basis of error in appellate procedure.

The channels which connect courts in a hierarchy permit cases to be appealed upward and orders pertaining to cases to be sent downward. Traditionally there has been little use of these hierarchical relationships for purposes of administrative supervision of lower state courts by higher courts. The American state judicial system has been a decentralized operation. There has been no central authority with responsibility for the state of the judicial business, or with power to shift judicial manpower from areas with few cases to those with congested calendars. The notion of judicial independence, it has been assumed, requires judicial autonomy. Judges have had to answer to no one for the efficiency of their courts or the volume of work they perform.

However, some movement toward centralization of judicial power, and even in some limited way toward judicial unification, has taken place in a few states. Starting with Chicago in 1906, a number of the larger cities set up unified municipal courts to replace the haphazard collection of justices of the peace and other local courts which had been created over the years. These unified courts were administered by a chief judge with authority to assign judges according to the needs of judicial business. But this control was, of course, limited to a single level of courts, and did not achieve any rationalization of the contacts between levels in the judicial hierarchy. In any case, the impetus of the municipal court movement had largely been lost by 1930.

The current battleground of judicial reform in the states is over unification of state court systems, and the goal is the establishment of administrative control from the center to use judicial manpower most effectively and to reduce appeals. By 1955 some thirteen states and the District of Columbia had set up an office of judicial administration or administrative chief judge. But it was not until New Jersey acted in 1948 that any state set up a completely integrated judicial system, with all judges except those on the supreme court subject to interchange and to assignment by the chief justice. Much remains to be done to bring effective administrative direction and unification to state judicial hierarchies, but the trends are definitely in that direction.

Law and Equity

The American legal system has made great strides in at least one important area of judicial administration. Historic English practice created a dichotomy between cases in law and cases in equity. In its early development the common law had gone through periods of extreme rigidity during which persons were simply turned away if their suits could not be settled by the issuance of certain specific technical writs or orders. These litigants began appealing to the king for his personal justice. By the fourteenth century such petitions for grace were being referred for settlement to the king's chancellor. Out of this practice, courts of chancery or equity grew up alongside the courts of law. In the United States, the functions of these two types of tribunals have now largely been merged, though the two different kinds of procedure have been retained. In 1955, only four states still had separate chancery courts.

This administrative reform has been carried out without serious damage to the flexibility of equity, though centuries of operation have limited the kinds of disputes which equity will handle and the types of orders which will be issued. Today, litigants who have suffered, or are about to suffer, a real injury and who have no redress from common or statutory law can still have their cases heard by a judge, sitting without a jury, who will attempt to do justice by giving a decision shaped to fit the special circumstances of each individual situation.

The Federal Court System

The federal courts are organized in a simple and logical arrangement, but this was achieved only after a long period of legislative adjustment. The district courts, one or more of which is located in every state, are the trial courts of the federal system. Initially there were also federal circuit courts which were trial courts for some classes of cases, but they were finally abolished by statute in 1911. Appeals from the decisions of the district courts go to the courts of appeals, created by Congress in 1891, and known until 1948 as circuit courts of appeals. For judicial purposes the country is divided into ten numbered circuits; an eleventh court of appeals sits in the District of Columbia. There are from three to nine circuit judges in each circuit, and a panel of three normally sits in deciding a case.

There are also a few specialized courts in the federal system. The Customs Court, for example, is a trial court for disputes on customs duties, and there is a Court of Customs and Patent Appeals which reviews decisions of the Customs Court and Patent Office determinations. The Court of Claims adjudicates claims against the United States. The Tax Court is technically not in the judicial branch, but is rather an executive agency for reviewing decisions of the Internal Revenue Service.

At the apex of the federal hierarchy is the United States Supreme Court. Created directly by the Constitution, the Supreme Court is primarily an appellate court, but the Constitution does define two categories of cases which can be heard in the Court's original jurisdiction, i.e., without prior consideration by any other court. These are cases in which a state is a party, and those affecting ambassadors, public ministers, and consuls.

However, the Court generally does not have to accept a suit invoking its original jurisdiction unless it feels there is a compelling reason of public policy.

All the remaining business of the Supreme Court comes to it in its appellate jurisdiction, which it exercises, as the Constitution says, "with such Exceptions, and under such Regulations as the Congress shall make." In the post-Civil War period Congress used this authority over the Court's appellate jurisdiction to withdraw from its consideration a politically embarrassing case in which the Court had already heard argument. The Supreme Court in *Ex parte McCardle* (1869) agreed that such action was within congressional power. In 1957 Senator Jenner of Indiana sought reprisal against the Court's decisions in certain national security cases by a bill withdrawing the Court's appellate jurisdiction in five specific kinds of cases. The defeat of this proposal has made it less likely that such a limitation on the Court's jurisdiction will ever again be seriously proposed.

Except in the limited classes of cases where there is an appeal to the Supreme Court as of right, review is sought by filing with the Court a petition for writ of certiorari to a state supreme court or federal court of appeals. This writ, if granted, directs the lower court to send up the record in the case for review. The Court now receives over 1,500 petitions for certiorari each year. The petitions are reviewed by all members of the Court, and are granted on the affirmative vote of four justices. Usually no reason is given when petitions are denied, but in general the Court accepts only cases which present substantial issues of law or policy. However, the Court has on many occasions refused to review decisions involving issues of major importance.

The federal judiciary has been affected by the same trends toward centralization and administrative control noted in the state courts. The federal developments were largely due to the interest of Chief Justice Taft in improved judicial administration. Congress in 1922 passed a statute authorizing the Chief Justice to assign district judges to temporary service anywhere in the country, provided their senior circuit judge certified that they could be released. The same statute created the Conference of Senior Circuit Judges, which was to meet annually in Washington on call of the Chief Justice to discuss the functioning of the federal courts.

This annual meeting proved useful, though the Conference had little in the way of formal authority. It was soon apparent that any active program of administrative improvement would have to be based on statistical data about the federal courts and their work loads and practices which were not then available. With the support of the Conference and the Attorney

General, Congress passed the Administrative Office Act in 1939, creating the Administrative Office of the United States Courts. The director of this office was to gather statistics on the work of the federal courts, and also to prepare the judiciary budget for approval by the conference of senior circuit judges. The 1939 act also created a judicial council in each circuit, with general supervisory responsibilities for the district courts in the circuit. Finally, the act called for an annual conference in each circuit, attended by all the circuit and district judges along with representatives of the bar, to discuss the improvement of judicial administration.

The name of the Conference of Senior Circuit Judges was subsequently changed to the Judicial Conference of the United States, and by a 1957 statute the district judges in each circuit were directed to elect one of their number to attend the annual conference. All of this machinery has done a great deal toward tightening up the administration of the federal courts, providing the data on which remedial action can be based, and developing legislative proposals affecting the judiciary for submission to Congress.

Federal Jurisdiction

The jurisdiction of the federal courts is defined by Article III of the Constitution on two different bases: subject matter and nature of the parties involved. The subject matter classifications are (1) all cases in law and equity arising under the Constitution; (2) all cases in law and equity arising under the laws of the United States; (3) all cases in law and equity arising under treaties made under the authority of the United States; and (4) all cases of admiralty and maritime jurisdiction. Any case falling in these four fields can be brought into the federal courts, regardless of who the parties to the controversy may be.

Issues arising under the first three of these headings—Constitution, laws, and treaties—are referred to generally as "federal questions." A plaintiff seeking to bring a case into the federal courts on one of these grounds must set forth on the face of his complaint a substantial claim as to the federal question involved. Cases appealed from state supreme courts are often refused review by the Supreme Court on the ground that no substantial federal question is involved.

The second basis for federal court jurisdiction is in terms of the parties involved. Article III of the Constitution extends federal jurisdiction to controversies (1) to which the United States is a party; (2) between two or more states; (3) between a state and citizens of another state; (4) between citizens of different states; (5) between a state, or the citizens thereof, and foreign states, citizens, or subjects; and (6) to all cases affecting ambassadors, other public ministers, and consuls. Matters involving these classes of parties can be brought in the federal courts, no matter what the subject matter.

Of these classes, the first and the fourth are by far the most important in the generation of litigation. The United States enters federal courts as a party plaintiff in a great number of civil and criminal suits every year, and it can also be haled into court as a defendant in situations where it has waived its sovereign immunity and given its consent to be sued. When no consent to sue the government has been given, it may be possible to sue officials acting for the government, particularly if they are alleged to be acting beyond their statutory authority or under an unconstitutional statute.

Suits between citizens of different states are commonly referred to as arising under the "diversity of citizenship" jurisdiction of the federal courts. The purpose of opening the federal courts to such cases was originally to provide a neutral forum for the determination of such disputes, since the state courts might be biased in favor of their own citizens and against "strangers" from other states. Today there is less likelihood of such bias, and many persons—including Supreme Court justices—have urged the abolition of this class of federal jurisdiction. In 1958 Congress undertook to reduce the number of such cases in the federal courts by limiting them to disputes involving more than $10,000.

Suits falling under federal jurisdiction can also be brought in state courts, except in those areas—such as federal criminal, admiralty, patent, and bankruptcy cases—where Congress has given the federal courts exclusive jurisdiction. In all other areas the state and federal courts have concurrent jurisdiction over Article III cases. A suit meeting the tests of federal jurisdiction which is filed in a state court can by appropriate action be transferred to a federal court for trial. States have occasionally sought to place restrictions on the right of removal of civil suits from state to federal courts, particularly where out-of-state corporations are concerned, but such laws have usually been declared unconstitutional. Where state courts do exercise federal jurisdiction, they are of course bound by the "supremacy clause" of the Constitution. Article VI, after making the Constitution, laws, and treaties of the United States "the supreme Law of the Land," continues: "and the Judges in every State shall be bound thereby, any Thing in the Constitution or Laws of any State to the Contrary notwithstanding."

The complication of a dual system of courts is one which other leading federal governments, such as Australia, Canada, and India, have avoided. In these countries there is only one federal court, superimposed on a complete system of state courts. By contrast the American system may often seem to be cumbersome and productive of confusion and delays in the administration of justice. However, processes of co-operation and adjustment have largely solved the many potential conflicts in the dual system of courts.

SELECTED REFERENCES

Abraham, Henry J., *Courts and Judges* (New York: Oxford University Press, 1959).

Bunn, Charles W., *A Brief Survey of the Jurisdiction and Practice of the Courts of the United States* (5th ed.; St. Paul: West Publishing Co., 1949).

Douglas, William O., *We the Judges* (New York: Doubleday, 1956), Ch. 3.

Frankfurter, Felix and James M. Landis, *The Business of the Supreme Court* (New York: Macmillan, 1928).

Hart, Henry M., Jr. and Herbert Wechsler, *The Federal Courts and the Federal System* (Brooklyn: The Foundation Press, 1953).

Hurst, James Willard, *The Growth of American Law* (Boston: Little, Brown, 1950), Chs. 5, 6, 8, 9.

Mayers, Lewis, *The American Legal System* (New York: Harper, 1956), Chs. 1–3.

Parker, John J., "The Integration of the Federal Judiciary," 56 *Harvard Law Review* 563 (1943).

Stern, Robert L. and Eugene Gressman, *Supreme Court Practice* (2d ed.; Washington, D.C.: BNA, Inc., 1954).

Vanderbilt, Arthur, *Men and Measures in the Law* (New York: A. A. Knopf, 1949).

Willoughby, W. F., *Principles of Judicial Administration* (Washington, D.C.: The Brookings Institution, 1929).

1.   *". . . our system of courts is archaic . . ."*

THE CAUSES OF POPULAR DISSATISFACTION WITH THE ADMINISTRATION
OF JUSTICE   *Roscoe Pound**

. . . CAUSES LYING in our judicial organization and procedure [are] the most efficient causes of dissatisfaction with the present administration of justice in America. For I venture to say that our system of courts is archaic and our procedure behind the times. Uncertainty, delay and expense, and above all, the injustice of deciding cases upon points of practice, which are the mere etiquette of justice, direct results of the organization of our courts and the backwardness of our procedure, have created a deep-seated desire to keep out of court, right or wrong, on the part of every sensible business man in the community.

Our system of courts is archaic in three respects: (1) in its multiplicity of courts, (2) in preserving concurrent jurisdictions, (3) in the waste of judicial power which it involves. The judicial organizations of the several states exhibit many differences of detail. But they agree in these three respects.

THE MULTIPLICITY OF COURTS

(1) Multiplicity of courts is characteristic of archaic law. In Anglo-Saxon law, one might apply to the Hundred, the Shire, the Witan, or the king in person. Until Edward I broke up private jurisdictions, there were the king's superior courts of law, the itinerant justices, the county courts, the local or communal courts and the private courts of lordships; besides which one might always apply to the king or to the Great Council for extraordinary relief. When later the royal courts had superseded all others, there were the concurrent jurisdictions of King's Bench, Common Pleas and Exchequer, all doing the same work, while appellate jurisdiction was divided by King's Bench, Exchequer

Address before the American Bar Association, 1906. Reprinted with permission of the author.

* Dean Emeritus, Harvard Law School.

Chamber and Parliament. In the Fourth Institute, Coke enumerates seventy-four courts. Of these, seventeen did the work that is now done by three, the County Courts, the Supreme Court of Judicature and the House of Lords. At the time of the reorganization by the Judicature Act of 1873, five appellate courts and eight courts of first instance were consolidated into the one Supreme Court of Judicature. It was the intention of those who devised the plan of the Judicature Act to extend the principle of unity of jurisdiction by cutting off the appellate jurisdiction of the House of Lords and by incorporating the County Courts in the newly formed Supreme Court as branches thereof. The recommendation as to the County Courts was not adopted, and the appellate jurisdiction of the House of Lords was restored in 1875. In this way the unity and simplicity of the original design were impaired. But the plan, although adopted in part only, deserves the careful study of American lawyers as a model modern judicial organization. Its chief features were (1) to set up a single court, complete in itself, embracing all superior courts and jurisdictions, (2) to include in this one court, as a branch thereof, a single court of final appeal. In the one branch, the court of first instance, all original jurisdiction at law, in equity, in admiralty, in bankruptcy, in probate and in divorce was to be consolidated; in the other branch, the court of appeal, the whole reviewing jurisdiction was to be established. This idea of unification, although not carried out completely, has proved most effective. Indeed, its advantages are self-evident. Where the appellate tribunal and the court of first instance are branches of one court, all expense of transfer of record, of transcripts, bills of exceptions, writs of error and citations is wiped out. The records are the records of the court, of which each tribunal is but a branch. The court and each branch thereof knows its own records, and no duplication and certification is required. Again, all appellate practice, with its attendant pitfalls, and all waste of judicial time in ascertaining how or whether a case has been brought into the court of review is done away with. One may search the recent English reports in vain for a case where an appeal has miscarried on a point of practice. Cases on appellate procedure are wanting. In effect there is no such thing. The whole attention of the court and of counsel is concentrated upon the cause. On the other hand, our American reports bristle with fine points of appellate procedure. More than four percent of the digest paragraphs of the last ten volumes of the American Digest have to do with Appeal and Error. In ten volumes of the Federal Reporter, namely volumes 129 to 139, covering decisions of the Circuit Courts of Appeals from 1903 till the present, there is an average of ten decisions upon points of appellate practice to the volume. Two cases to the volume, on the average, turn wholly upon appellate procedure. In the ten volumes there are six civil cases turning upon the question whether error or appeal was the proper mode of review, and in two civil cases the question was whether the Circuit Court of Appeals was the proper tribunal. I have referred to these reports because they represent courts in which only causes of importance may be brought. The state reports exhibit the same condition. . . . All of this is sheer waste, which a modern judicial organization would obviate.

EXISTING CONCURRENT JURISDICTIONS

(2) Even more archaic is our system of concurrent jurisdiction of state and federal courts in causes involving diversity of citizenship; a system by virtue of which causes continually hang in the air between two courts, or, if they do stick in one court or the other, are liable to an ultimate overturning because they stuck in the wrong court. A few statistics on this point may be worth while. In the ten volumes of the Federal Reporter referred to, the decisions of the Circuit Courts of Appeals in civil cases average seventy-six to the volume. Of these, on the average, between four and five in a volume are decided on points of federal jurisdiction. In a little more than one to each volume, judgments of Circuit Courts are reversed on points of jurisdiction. The same volumes contain on the average seventy-three decisions of Circuit Courts in civil cases to each volume. Of these, six, on the average, are upon motions to remand to the state courts, and between eight and nine are upon other points of federal jurisdiction. Moreover, twelve cases in the ten volumes were remanded on the *form* of the petition for removal. In other words, in nineteen and three-tenths percent of the reported decisions of the Circuit Courts the question was whether those courts had jurisdiction at all; and in seven percent of these that question depended on the form of the pleadings. A system that permits this and reverses four judgments a year because the cause was

brought in or removed to the wrong tribunal is out of place in a modern business community. All original jurisdiction should be concentrated. It ought to be impossible for a cause to fail because brought in the wrong place. A simple order of transfer from one docket to another in the same court ought to be enough. There should be no need of new papers, no transcripts, no bandying of cases from one court to another on orders of removal and of remand, no beginnings again with new process.

THE WASTE OF JUDICIAL POWER
(3) Judicial power may be wasted in three ways: (1) By rigid districts or courts or jurisdictions, so that business may be congested in one court while judges in another are idle, (2) by consuming the time of courts with points of pure practice, when they ought to be investigating substantial controversies, and (3) by nullifying the results of judicial action by unnecessary retrials. American judicial systems are defective in all three respects. The Federal Circuit Courts and Circuit Courts of Appeals are conspicuous exceptions in the first respect, affording a model of flexible judicial organization. But in nearly all of the states, rigid districts and hard and fast lines between courts operate to delay business in one court while judges in another have ample leisure. In the second respect, waste of judicial time upon points of practice, the intricacies of federal jurisdiction and the survival of the obsolete Chinese Wall between law and equity in procedure, make our federal courts no less conspicuous sinners. . . .

Each state has to a great extent its own procedure. But it is not too much to say that all of them are behind the times. We struck one great stroke in 1848 and have rested complacently or contented ourselves with patchwork amendment ever since. The leading ideas of the New York Code of Civil Procedure marked a long step forward. But the work was done too hurriedly and the plan of a rigid code, going into minute detail, was clearly wrong. A modern practice act lays down the general principles of practice and leaves details to rules of court. The New York Code Commission was appointed in 1847 and reported in 1848. If we except the Connecticut Practice Act of 1878, which shows English influence, American reform in procedure has stopped substantially where that commission left it. In England, beginning with 1826 and ending with 1874, *five* commissioners have put forth *nine* reports upon this subject. As a consequence we have nothing in America to compare with the radical treatment of pleading in the English Judicature Act and the orders based thereon. We still try the *record*, not the *case*. We are still reversing judgments for nonjoinder and misjoinder. The English practice of joinder of parties against whom relief is claimed in the alternative, rendering judgment against any that the proof shows to be liable and dismissing the rest, makes an American lawyer rub his eyes. We are still reversing judgments for variance. We still reverse them because the recovery is in excess of the prayer, though sustained by the evidence.

But the worst feature of American procedure is the lavish granting of new trials. In the ten volumes of the Federal Reporter referred to, there are, on the average, twenty-five writs of error in civil cases to the volume. New trials are awarded on the average in eight cases a volume, or nearly twenty-nine percent. In the state courts the proportion of new trials to causes reviewed, as ascertained from investigation of the last five volumes of each series of the National Reporter system, runs over forty percent. . . . In one case in my own state an action for personal injuries was tried six times, and one for breach of contract was tried three times and was four times in the Supreme Court. When with this we compare the statistics of the English Court of Appeal, which does not grant to exceed twelve new trials a year, or new trials in about three percent of the cases reviewed, it is evident that our methods of trial and review are out of date.

A comparison of the volume of business disposed of by English and by American courts will illustrate the waste and delay caused by archaic judicial organization and obsolete procedure. In England there are twenty-three judges of the High Court who dispose on the average of fifty-six hundred *contested* cases, and have before them, in one form or another, some eighty thousand cases each year. In Nebraska there are twenty-eight district judges who have no original probate jurisdiction and no jurisdiction in bankruptcy or admiralty, and they had upon their dockets last year forty-three hundred and twenty cases, of which they disposed of about seventy percent. England and Wales, with a population in 1900 of 32,000,000, employ for their whole civil litigation ninety-five judges, that is, thirty-seven in the Supreme Court and

House of Lords and fifty-eight county judges. Nebraska, with a population in 1900 of 1,066,000, employs for the same purpose one hundred and twenty-nine. But these one hundred and twenty-nine are organized on an antiquated system and their time is frittered away on mere points of legal etiquette. . . .

2.   *". . . each court is a kingdom unto itself."*

MODERN COURTS FOR ILLINOIS   *Louis A. Kohn**

. . . OUR OUTMODED judicial system . . . today is substantially as provided in our 1848 Constitution when Illinois was a rural state of 800,000 compared with a highly industrialized state of today of more than 9,000,000 people. . . .

At the top of our court structure is a Supreme Court made up of seven judges elected from seven districts. Cook County alone represents 55 percent of the state's population and generates almost 60 percent of the Supreme Court business, but is included in the Seventh Supreme Court District with four adjacent counties. The present member from that District is a resident of Lake County.

The Supreme Court is ham-strung with the requirement that it must take a wide variety of cases of little legal significance. This burden impairs its ability to consider cases involving important questions and to exercise properly the rule-making and administrative powers which it claims to have. There is no chief justice elected as such and this office is rotated annually. There is no administrative director and no statistics of the business of our state courts are compiled.

Except for the designation of appellate court judges, no power of assignment of judges is exercised. Outside Cook County, appellate court judges, who are actually elected as circuit judges, also serve as trial judges, and in many cases have great difficulty in doing justice to both jobs.

On the trial court level we have a multiplicity of courts, completely

42 *Journal of the American Judicature Society* 42 (1958). Copyright 1958 American Judicature Society. Reprinted with permission.

* Member Illinois Bar; General counsel, Committee for Modern Courts.

free of outside administrative supervision, and each court is a kingdom unto itself. The overlapping jurisdiction of various courts has, in too many cases resulted in fruitless and protracted litigation, delaying ultimate determination of the controversy on the merits and in costly duplication of court facilities and waste of judicial manpower.

Throughout the state (except in Chicago) justices of the peace and police magistrates, compensated by fees assessed against defendants, preside over the courts not of record, and all appeals from their decisions involve trials *de novo*. In every county there is a county court of limited jurisdiction and the judge need not be a lawyer—and if he is a lawyer he often engages in the practice of law. Downstate the circuits often cover a number of counties and between terms of court there is no tribunal available to grant equitable relief and to try felonies and other important matters. In many areas, there are unreasonable delays in the trial of cases; the worst congestion is in Cook County where in common law jury cases it is in excess of four years. . . .

Judges, justices of the peace and police magistrates are all elected. In the case of Supreme Court judges, judges of the Circuit Court and the Superior Court of Cook County, candidates are nominated at party conventions and elected at a special judicial election. Predominance of purely political considerations in the selection of candidates, the inability of voters, particularly in metropolitan centers, properly to pass on their qualifications, and the lack of voter interest in these special elections, have led to widespread criticism of the elective system. Other judicial officers are nominated in primaries and then elected in a general election. Judicial candidates are often required to make substantial campaign contributions to the party and mend their political fences, and too often personal and professional qualifications are given secondary consideration. Finally, judges cannot be made to retire because of disability, and removal for cause is solely by impeachment and legislative address, which procedures are so clumsy that I believe impeachment has only been tried once.

Our committee sought to cure these many defects and submitted to the 1953 session of the legislature a most comprehensive proposal, which was approved by the organized bar and won the support of a great majority of the newspapers in the state and many civic groups spearheaded by a state-wide citizens committee. Likewise the legislative committee in its final report approved the plan but with several dissents. Leading authorities stated that it if were adopted the proposal would set the pattern for the rest of the country.

The major provisions of the 1953 plan were as follows: There would be a *single trial court*—the circuit court—made up of appropriate branches with jurisdiction to try all justiciable matters. There would be at least one division in each county with a full-time judge resident in the county. All existing courts would be consolidated under the circuit court so that the troublesome questions arising out of overlapping jurisdictions could no longer arise and there would be more efficient utilization of judicial manpower. There would be three grades of judges: circuit judges, associate judges and magistrates, and all incumbent judges, J.P.'s and police magistrates would be assimilated into the appropriate category. All judicial officers would be required to be lawyers, to devote full-time to their judicial duties and would be prohibited from political activity and from making political contributions. Recognizing that in some areas full-time lawyers would not be available, there was a provision for special magistrates who would not be subject to the restrictions referred to. The master in chancery and the fee system of compensation would be abolished.

On the *upper court level* there would be an appellate court made up of three districts, one for Cook County and two downstate. It would in most cases be the court of last resort as generally there would be only one appeal. Direct appeal to the Supreme Court would exist only in few instances as where a constitutional question of a capital case resulting in imposition of a sentence were in order and in a few other cases of direct appeal. That court would also have original jurisdiction in a very limited number of specified cases. The Supreme Court would review decisions of the appellate court when that court certified that its decision was of such importance and that it ought to be reviewed by the Supreme Court. In all other decisions of the appellate court, the Supreme Court would have discretionary jurisdiction. The Supreme Court would have full rule-making powers subject to substantive law. General administrative authority would be exercised through the chief justice, who would serve a three-year term, over all courts with power of assignment over all judges. There would be an administrative director and staff as in the federal system and an annual judicial conference.

The legislature was given power to provide for voluntary or involuntary retirement of judges at such an age as may be fixed by law. Provision was also made for a judicial commission to remove judges for disability or for other cause.

With respect to judicial selection, the proposal would have substituted for the present elective method the non-partisan commission method, following closely the Missouri plan with what we thought might be some improvements. There would be one nominating commission for the upper courts and one for each circuit, made up of an equal number of lawyers and non-lawyers. The lawyers would be elected by the lawyers in the appropriate district or circuit, and the method of selecting the lay members would be left up to the legislature. The commission would submit not less than 2 nor more than 5 names to the governor and he would have to make his appointment to fill the vacancy within 90 days or it would devolve upon the Supreme Court. The appointees would serve for a full year and thereafter until the general election. If approved, an appointee would then serve a full term. All judges would be allowed to stand for reelection without opposition and party designation. Magistrates would be appointed by the circuit court without definite term. The legislature was further empowered to change the method of selection, provided the proposal were approved by a majority of the voters voting on the issue.

. . . This far reaching reform, in spite of the opposition of justices of the peace and strenuous objection to the selection provisions, received the required two-thirds vote in the Senate with one vote to spare and in the House failed by about 25 votes. . . .

3.   *"The business of the courts is very big business indeed."*

IMPROVING JUDICIAL ADMINISTRATION   *William J. Brennan, Jr.**

          . . . THE BUSINESS of the courts is very big business indeed. The stuff of that business is of course litigation. The volume of litigation is increasing enormously and, at least in the larger states, the

28 *Pennsylvania Bar Association Quarterly* 238 (1957). Copyright 1957 Pennsylvania Bar Association. Reprinted with permission.
* Associate Justice, U.S. Supreme Court, 1956–.

courts, state and federal, are bogging down under the strain. Calendar congestion is a problem of such gravity at some places as to threaten an actual breakdown in the administration of justice itself. . . .

. . . In New Jersey there is no problem of calendar congestion in any court of the state. An automobile accident suit and every other kind of suit can be tried not more than nine months after it is brought, and in most counties within six months. Better still, only one out of five actions ever goes to trial at all, because four of them are voluntarily settled without trial.

How was it done? . . . Simply by abandoning an archaic system of 17 virtually autonomous courts and substituting an integrated court system operated much as a business corporation under rules of practice, procedure and administration devised by the Supreme Court as the Board of Directors, and supervised by the Chief Justice as Executive Head, assisted by a presiding judge in each county functioning much like the branch head of any far-flung business. To this was added an Administrative Director of the Courts, to gather and interpret statistics as to pending cases, and an assignment power in the Chief Justice to assign judges anywhere in the state as court work required. Calendar control in the several counties is made the responsibility of the presiding judge of the county, called significantly, the Assignment Judge, and is operated under uniform calendar control rules with the help of the Administrative Director and under the direction of the Chief Justice. Judges are empowered to grant all relief, legal or equitable, as justice requires. Pleadings are simplified and after issue joined, litigants are allowed broad discovery of one another's claims and defenses, through deposition, interrogatory and inspection practices. Before trial, a pretrial conference of lawyers and judge is mandatory in civil causes in the upper courts, to settle factual and legal issues, stipulate facts to save trial time, mark exhibits and explore the possibilities of settlement.

That system became effective late in 1948 when, like today's problem in almost every other jurisdiction of the country, certainly in all other populous states, trial lists were two or more years in arrears, and some cases actually were pending up to eight years. Within three years, by 1951, all arrears were cleared up and current cases were being tried, when tried at all, within six to nine months. New Jersey has probably experienced the impact of increased litigation, particularly from automobile accidents, to as great or a greater degree than most other states. Yet since the calendars became current in 1951, they have remained current and no one fears the future, such is the flexibility of the system and the strength of the business practices and organization which account for the result. . . .

It is inconceivable that the citizens of other states will continue much longer to put up with systems of autonomous courts free from any sort of control within or without, the judges concerned with their own court only and brooking no interference from judges of other courts, or indeed even from other members of their own court. The exorbitant waste from overlapping jurisdictions, duplication of personnel and organization is itself enough to stimulate demands for modernization; that demand is now becoming insistent with the bite of calendar congestion and its attendant unconscionable delays and multiplication of technicalities. Separate courts for law issues, separate courts for equitable issues, for criminal causes, for matrimonial causes, for domestic relations cases, for any other kind of specialty of the law are definitely on the way out. A judge worthy of the name is fully qualified to dispense any relief that justice requires and most states now follow the practice of combining these powers in the judges of a court of general jurisdiction. Another court for the trial of petty criminal causes and civil matters where small amounts are involved, plus a Supreme Court to hear appeals, and perhaps an intermediate appellate court if appeal volume is large, suffice for a court system. The vast federal court business is handled by a system of but three courts, the District Courts, the Courts of Appeal and the Supreme Court; a state court system should not require more. New Jersey's system is essentially a three tier system: the first tier, the Supreme Court; the second tier, a Superior Court of three Divisions (one of the Divisions an intermediate appellate court) and a county court, both with general jurisdiction of all cases, civil and criminal; and the third tier, the criminal and civil courts of limited jurisdiction. The judges of the Superior and County Courts are interchanged between the Courts, and in the case of the Superior Court Judges, within the law, chancery and appellate divisions of that court, as the business of the court requires. All Superior Court Judges and Judges of the County Court are subject to assignment and are assigned by the Chief Justice to handle the work of both courts indiscriminately as required by the business of the several counties, disclosed by the statistics gathered by the Administrative Director, for the most efficient and prompt dispatch of court business throughout the state.

It is obviously essential to efficient business administration that the rule making body (in New Jersey it is the Supreme Court) have power to formulate the rules of practice, procedure and administration to govern the conduct and dispatch of court business. . . . Rules are prepared for most [courts] by the legislatures. That was also the case in New Jersey under the former court system but the inflexibility of that method, in a field where flexibility is of paramount importance, persuaded the framers of the new constitution to vest that power in the Supreme Court.

The new [New Jersey] constitution also established the Office of the Administrative Director of the Courts. That office performs the task without which efficient administration of any business would be impossible. That office keeps a perpetual inventory of the caseload in all the courts and collects and interprets other pertinent statistical data to be able to detect threatened trouble spots to enable the Chief Justice to deal with them before they grow to the size of a problem. That office is also charged with the responsibility continuously to study operations and develop procedures the better and more efficiently to process court business.

There is another conduit of information which features the New Jersey system and is worthy of mention. Every judge of the state files a weekly report of his week's activities with the Administrative Director. That report shows his hours on the bench each day, the names of the cases handled during the day and the time given to each. Some judges are more effective in their work than others, some give more satisfaction to the bar and the public than others, some are more diligent, more conscientious, more devoted to their work than others. These individual differences cannot be changed administratively; but there should and can be equality in the number of hours each judge of the same court spends in the courtroom. This weekly report operates to assure that there will be no inequalities in the burden of judicial work among the judges and that the public will have the full services of the entire corps of judges during working hours.

That report also includes other information helpful to the prompt disposition of judicial business. If the judge reserves decision in any matter, he notes the fact on his weekly report and on each subsequent weekly report until the matter is decided. If the office of the Administrative Director notes that the decision is reserved an undue length of time, an inquiry of the judge for a reason usually results in its prompt disposition. This device has made a valuable contribution toward the goal of minimizing unnecessary delays in the handing down of decisions made by the judge rather than by the jury.

You may ask whether this centralized administration and supervision of the daily work of the judges poses any threat to the independence of decision which is the absolute essential of the judicial function. I think every judge in the New Jersey courts will be quick to say that rather than impair their independence of decision, such administration and procedure enhances their independence to do right and justice as they see right and justice in every case. Relieved of the worry every good judge feels when he is grappling with a new problem while old ones are not yet decided, he brings the full vigor of his talents to bear on the new. New Jersey has historically espoused the system of strong judges under which judges are free to direct the judicial process to the end of right and justice upon the merits. It is as true in New Jersey today as it has ever been that the trial judge is not a mere umpire of the dispute of contending lawyers and litigants but the active agent of justice so to guide the trial and the protagonists that right and justice on the merits shall result. . . .

Now, obviously judges should be independent in rendering decisions. The error crept in when this independence was carried over to administration. In any large institution, whether it be court, government agency, or business firm, someone must run the show on the administrative side. Some one must be boss. When a modern court system is established there should be an administrator at the head of the entire organization, as there is in the executive branch. This should be the permanent chief justice of the supreme court. He should be given specific powers of administration—studying docket conditions, shifting judges as needed, appointing administrative judges below, requiring statistical information, and so on. In addition, he should have general administrative control over the entire structure, as well as superior authority to the administrative judges in the trial court. . . .

> *". . . the Supreme Court must . . . decide only those cases which present questions whose resolution will have immediate importance far beyond the particular facts and parties involved."*

4.

WORK OF THE FEDERAL COURTS   *Fred M. Vinson**

. . . ONCE AGAIN this year the Supreme Court ended its term [in June, 1949] with all business, in readiness for disposition, having been disposed of. That statement has much less meaning today than formerly, for a similar order has been entered in each of the 20 preceding years. The days before passage of the 1925 Act . . . when it took eighteen to twenty-four months for the Court to reach a case on its docket, are forgotten, and it is assumed by everyone, as it should be, that the Supreme Court is current in its work. The Court will soon have been operating under its basic jurisdictional statute for a quarter of a century, and experience has eloquently proved the wisdom of its architects. As you well know, the obligatory jurisdiction of the Court, other than its original jurisdiction as set out in the Constitution, is restricted to cases in which the validity of a treaty or statute of the United States is drawn in question and the decision is against its validity, to cases in which the validity of a state statute is drawn in question on the ground of its being repugnant to the Constitution, treaties or laws of the United States and the decision is in favor of its validity, and to review of certain district court decisions which, by statute, are appealable directly to the Supreme Court. All other cases come within the Court's discretionary jurisdiction, and, as has been the custom for some years past, the Court takes such cases only when at least

Address before the American Bar Association, September 7, 1949, 69 S. Ct. v. Reprinted with the permission of the West Publishing Company.
* Chief Justice of the United States, 1946–53.

four justices feel that the public importance of the question presented requires its consideration by the Supreme Court.

This selective process is one that consumes much of the Court's time, and its importance is often overlooked because of the more general public interest in the Court's published opinions. Throughout the year, in term time and vacation alike, each justice considers carefully every appeal and petition for certiorari or other relief filed with the Clerk, together with responses and records in each case. Since the number of such applications has reached approximately fifteen hundred in each of the past several years, you can well understand the magnitude of the task.

During the past term of Court, only about 15% of the petitions for certiorari were granted, and this figure itself is considerably higher than the average in recent years. While a great many of the 85% that were denied were far from frivolous, far too many reveal a serious misconception on the part of counsel concerning the role of the Supreme Court in our federal system. I should like, therefore, to turn to that subject very briefly.

The Supreme Court is not, and never has been, primarily concerned with the correction of errors in lower court decisions. In almost all cases within the Court's appellate jurisdiction, the petitioner has already received one appellate review of his case. The debates in the Constitutional Convention make clear that the purpose of the establishment of one supreme national tribunal was, in the words of John Rutledge of South Carolina, "to secure the national rights & uniformity of Judgmts." The function of the Supreme Court is, therefore, to resolve conflicts of opinion on federal questions that have arisen among lower courts, to pass upon questions of wide import under the Constitution, laws, and treaties of the United States, and to exercise supervisory power over lower federal courts. If we took every case in which an interesting legal question is raised, or our *prima facie* impression is that the decision below is erroneous, we could not fulfill the Constitutional and statutory responsibilities placed upon the Court. To remain effective, the Supreme Court must continue to decide only those cases which present questions whose resolution will have immediate importance far beyond the particular facts and parties involved. Those of you whose petitions for certiorari are granted by the Supreme Court will know, therefore, that you are, in a sense, prosecuting or defending class actions; that you represent not only your clients, but tremendously important principles, upon which are based the plans, hopes, and aspirations of a great many people throughout the country. Lawyers might be well-advised, in preparing petitions for certiorari, to spend a little less time discussing the merits of their cases and a little more time demonstrating why it is important that Court should hear them. . . . What the Court is interested in is the actual, practical effect of the disputed decision—its consequences for other litigants and in other situations. A petition for certiorari should explain why it is vital that the question involved be decided finally by the Supreme Court. If it only succeeds in demonstrating that the decision below may be erroneous, it has not fulfilled its purpose.

Our 1948 Term was a busy one. The number of cases disposed of during the term amounted to 1,434—a total surpassed only in the 1946 Term, my first on the Court, when 1,520 appeals, petitions, and applications were disposed of. These figures take on added significance when compared with the statistics for the pre-war years, 1929–1940, when the Supreme Court handled an average of only 937 cases a year. Thus the post-war years have shown an increase of over 50% in the volume of applications directed to the Supreme Court. This fact calls for some explanation.

In 1930, the Supreme Court received twenty-two petitions for certiorari filed under the *in forma pauperis* statute . . . which provides that the Supreme Court and other federal courts may grant leave to poor persons to proceed without payment of filing fees upon the filing of an oath of poverty. Each year thereafter, the number of *in forma pauperis* petitions for certiorari grew larger until, in 1946, a total of 528 were received. Most of these petitions came from prisioners, state and federal, who challenged the legality of their convictions or detention in post-trial proceedings. 455 such petitions were filed last term. In addition, requests for other kinds of relief, such as original writs of habeas corpus, mandamus, prohibition, and the so-called common law writ of certiorari, have mounted each year until they reached a peak of 247 last term. Most of these applications were also filed by prisoners under the *in forma pauperis* section of the Judicial Code. The total of these petitions for certiorari and other relief thus reached 702 last term, of which 686 had matured and were acted upon. . . .

The tremendous increase in the number of *in forma pauperis* applications has not brought about a corresponding increase in the total number of cases granted review. Last term only 18 such cases—approximately 4% of the petitions—were granted, as compared with 22% of the Appellate Docket petitions. This is not hard to account for, since most of the petitions are prepared by prisoners without legal assistance and are without legal merit. The burden involved in filing, recording, and examining six or seven hundred such petitions a year is, however, very considerable, especially since they follow no particular form, are sometimes handwritten, and usually contain so much that is superfluous that the real issues are difficult to uncover. . . .

The right of a prisoner who claims the denial of a federally protected right to petition the Supreme Court is an extremely important one. Many, if not most, of the cases in which the Court has spelled out the requirements of a fair trial under the Due Process Clause of the Fourteenth Amendment have come up as *in forma pauperis* petitions. However, the fact that the volume of such petitions has reached the six-hundred mark in each of the past three or four years and that ninety-six out of every one hundred have little or no legal merit suggests that something should be done to try to stem the flow. I firmly believe, despite the burden, that the right to petition the Supreme Court should remain and should not be made any more difficult. . . .

5.   *"A review on writ of certiorari is not a matter of right . . ."*

U.S. SUPREME COURT RULES, RULE 19: CONSIDERATIONS GOVERNING REVIEW ON CERTIORARI

1. A REVIEW on writ of certiorari is not a matter of right, but of sound judicial discretion, and will be granted only where there are special and important reasons therefor. The following, while

neither controlling nor fully measuring the court's discretion, indicate the character of reasons which will be considered:

(a) Where a state court has decided a federal question of substance not theretofore determined by this court, or has decided it in a way probably not in accord with applicable decisions of this court.

(b) Where a court of appeals has rendered a decision in conflict with the decision of another court of appeals on the same matter; or has decided an important state or territorial question in a way in conflict with applicable state or territorial law; or has decided an important question of federal law which has not been, but should be, settled by this court; or has decided a federal question in a way in conflict with applicable decisions of this court; or has so far departed from the accepted and usual course of judicial proceedings, or so far sanctioned such a departure by a lower court, as to call for an exercise of this court's power of supervision.

2. The same general considerations outlined above will control in respect of petitions for writs of certiorari to review judgments of the Court of Claims, of the Court of Customs and Patent Appeals, or of any other court whose determinations are by law reviewable on writ of certiorari.

6.   *"Wise adjudication has its own time for ripening."*

STATE V. BALTIMORE RADIO SHOW

A MAN WAS *arrested by Baltimore police on suspicion of the brutal murder of a small girl. While he was in custody, and before he came to trial, a local radio station made a "devastating" broadcast giving details of the suspect's previous criminal record and his re-enactment of the crime. The radio station was found guilty of contempt of court for this broadcast, but the Maryland Court of Appeals reversed the conviction, relying upon three Supreme Court decisions in which the right of the press to comment on matters pending in court*

338 U.S. 912, 70 S. Ct. 252, 94 L. Ed. 562 (1950).

*had been upheld. A petition for writ of certiorari to review the deci-
sion of the Maryland appellate court was denied by the Supreme
Court. Normally no explanation is given by the justices for denial of
certiorari, but in this instance Justice Frankfurter, who had been opposed to the doctrine of the three Supreme Court cases cited by the
state court, wrote an opinion explaining the consequences of denial of
the writ.*

OPINION OF MR. JUSTICE FRANKFURTER respecting the
denial of the petition for writ of certiorari. . . .

This Court now declines to review the decision of the Maryland
Court of Appeals. The sole significance of such denial of a petition for writ of certiorari need not be elucidated to those versed
in the Court's procedures. It simply means that fewer than four members of the Court deemed it desirable to review a decision of the
lower court as a matter "of sound judicial discretion." . . . A variety of
considerations underlie denials of the writ, and as to the same petition
different reasons may lead different justices to the same result. This is
especially true of petitions for review on writ of certiorari to a State
court. Narrowly technical reasons may lead to denials. Review may be
sought too late; the judgment of the lower court may not be final; it
may not be the judgment of a State court of last resort; the decision
may be supportable as a matter of State law, not subject to review by
this Court, even though the State court also passed on issues of federal
law. A decision may satisfy all these technical requirements and yet
may commend itself for review to fewer than four members of the
Court. Pertinent considerations of judicial policy here come into play.
A case may raise an important question but the record may be cloudy.
It may be desirable to have different aspects of an issue further illu-
mined by the lower courts. Wise adjudication has its own time for
ripening.

Since there are these conflicting and, to the uninformed, even confusing reasons for denying petitions for certiorari, it has been suggested from time to time that the Court indicate its reasons for denial.
Practical considerations preclude. In order that the Court may be enabled to discharge its indispensable duties, Congress has placed the

control of the Court's business, in effect, within the Court's discretion. During the last three terms the Court disposed of 260, 217, 224 cases, respectively, on their merits. For the same three terms the Court denied, respectively, 1,260, 1,105, 1,189 petitions calling for discretionary review. If the Court is to do its work it would not be feasible to give reasons, however brief, for refusing to take these cases. The time that would be required is prohibitive, apart from the fact as already indicated that different reasons not infrequently move different members of the Court in concluding that a particular case at a particular time makes review undesirable. It becomes relevant here to note that failure to record a dissent from a denial of a petition for writ of certiorari in nowise implies that only the member of the Court who notes his dissent thought the petition should be granted.

Inasmuch, therefore, as all that a denial of a petition for a writ of certiorari means is that fewer than four members of the Court thought it should be granted, this Court has rigorously insisted that such a denial carries with it no implication whatever regarding the Court's views on the merits of a case which it has declined to review. The Court has said this again and again; again and again the admonition has to be repeated.

The one thing that can be said with certainty about the Court's denial of Maryland's petition in this case is that it does not remotely imply approval or disapproval of what was said by the Court of Appeals of Maryland. The issues canvassed in the opinions of that court, and which the State of Maryland has asked us to review, are of a nature which very readily lend themselves to misconstruction of the denial of this petition. The present instance is peculiarly one where the redundant becomes the necessary.

It becomes necessary to say that denial of this petition carries no support whatever for concluding that either the majority or the dissent in the court below correctly interpreted the scope of our decisions in *Bridges* v. *California* . . . *Pennekamp* v. *Florida* . . . and *Craig* v. *Harney.* . . . It does not carry any implication that either, or neither, opinion below correctly applied those decisions to the facts in the case at bar.

The issues considered by the Court of Appeals bear on some of the basic problems of a democratic society. Freedom of the press, properly conceived, is basic to our constitutional system. Safeguards for the fair administration of criminal justice are enshrined in our Bill of Rights. Respect for both of these indispensable elements of our constitutional system presents some of the most difficult and delicate problems for adjudication when they are before the Court for adjudication. It has taken centuries of struggle to evolve our system for bringing the guilty to book, protecting the innocent, and maintaining the interests of society consonant with our democratic professions. One of the demands of a democratic society is that the public should know what goes on in courts by being told by the press what happens there, to the end that the public may judge whether our system of criminal justice is fair and right. On the other hand our society has set apart court and jury as the tribunal for determining guilt or innocence on the basis of evidence adduced in court, so far as it is humanly possible. . . .

These are issues that this Court has not yet adjudicated. It is not to be supposed that by implication it means to adjudicate them by refusing to adjudicate. . . .

7.   *"The real meaning of a denial of certiorari is not what the justices say it is."*

WHAT THE SUPREME COURT DID NOT DO DURING THE 1951 TERM

Fowler V. Harper* and George C. Pratt†

. . . THE COURT has succeeded in cloaking its certiorari behavior in such a shroud of mystery that any explanation of what happens is the sheerest guesswork. Justice Frankfurter is the most vocal member of the Court in connection with its discretionary jurisdiction, but what he says from time to time is not very helpful. In

101 *University of Pennsylvania Law Review* 439 (1953). Copyright 1953, the University of Pennsylvania. Reprinted with permission. This was the third in a series of articles Professor Harper did on denials of certiorari.

* Professor of Law, Yale Law School.

† Practicing attorney, member of the New York bar.

1950 he purported to throw some light on the subject. His comments did little more than suggest that the Court sometimes has denied certiorari because the record was "cloudy" or because the time was not "ripe" for decision. He apparently believes that it is impractical or unnecessary to inform the bar of the nation as to what makes the certiorari machinery tick. . . .

Now, the old question, what is the meaning of a denial? To quote Justice Frankfurter again:

> Inasmuch, therefore, as all that a denial of a petition for a writ of certiorari means is that fewer than four members of the Court thought it should be granted, this Court has rigorously insisted that such a denial carries with it no implication whatever regarding the Court's views on the merits of a case which it has declined to review. The Court has said this again and again; again and again the admonition has to be repeated.
>
> The one thing that can be said with certainty about the Court's denial of [the petition in this case] is that it does not remotely imply approval or disapproval of what was said by [the lower court].

Once in the 1950 term and twice during the past term these views were reasserted. Justice Frankfurter's most recent effort to explain the lack of significance of a denial of certiorari was his memorandum of November 17, 1952, on the denial of a rehearing on the petition in the *Rosenberg* case to which Justice Black noted his dissent. Again Justice Frankfurter sought to clear up the "misconception" concerning a denial of the writ. "It means," he said, "and all that it means is, that there were not four members of the Court to whom the grounds on which the decision of the Court of Appeals was challenged seemed sufficiently important when judged by the standards governing the issue of the discretionary writ of certiorari." Reduced to simple language, the result of Justice Frankfurter's position seems to be as follows: For the first time in American history, two persons have been condemned to death for espionage in what is legally regarded as "peace" time—an offense comparable to that for which Klaus Fuchs got fifteen years. Even though all nine members of the Supreme Court may regard this conviction and sentence as contrary to law, it may be that this case was not reviewed on the merits for reasons which it is not "practical" to reveal to the bar and the public.

Perhaps denials *do not* imply the way the Court feels about the decision or the opinion below. But, the opinion below stands as law. And whether the justices like it or not, lawyers and judges *do* attach significance to such denials. During the past year a man was executed because the Court of Criminal Appeals of Texas regarded a denial of certiorari as *approval* by the Supreme Court of a local practice of doubtful constitutionality. In Galveston County, Texas, Negroes are effectively barred from sitting on juries in capital trials of other Negroes by the action of the local prosecutor in peremptorily challenging the Negro members of the jury panel. On appeal to the Court of Criminal Appeals, one Ross, convicted of murder, challenged the constitutionality of this practice. In answer, the Texas court said:

> The identical question was decided adversely to the appellant in McMurrin v. State, Tex. Cr. App. . . . This was also a case from Galveston county. . . . The Supreme Court of the United States refused a writ of certiorari. . . . *In our view their holding is conclusive against the contention in the instant case.*

After this decision, Ross petitioned for Supreme Court review of the constitutionality of this technique for excluding Negroes from juries. In the face of the statement by the Texas court that the Supreme Court had *held* this practice to be constitutional, the petition was denied, Justice Douglas alone recording his dissent as he had also done in the *McMurrin* case.

It is bad when the public views a denial of certiorari as a decision on the merits; is is worse when the bar does the same. But when the judiciary also takes the same view, an observer is entitled to question where the trouble lies and whether the Court is properly discharging its obligations by an occasional admonition from one justice that such denials mean only that a bare minority of the Court did not want to review the case. The real meaning of a denial of certiorari is not what the justices *say* it is. It is to be found in the reactions of the public, the bar and especially the judiciary. Law is not what is said in memoranda essays; it is the behavior of judges, lawyers, and of prosecuting attorneys in Galveston County, Texas.

The following table is presented for whatever it may be worth on this problem:

DECISIONS OF THE COURT AFTER GRANTING CERTIORARI

	1949	*1950*	*1951*	*3 year total*	*3 year percentage*
Cases from Federal Courts:					
Affirmed	32	28	45	105	38%
Reversed	52	61	55	168	62%
Total	84	89	100	273	
Cases from State Courts:					
Affirmed	10	3	5	18	32%
Reversed	7	17	15	39	68%
Total	17	20	20	57	
Cases from both Federal and State Courts:					
Affirmed	42	31	50	123	37%
Reversed	59	78	70	207	63%
Total	101	109	120	330	

These figures present the other side of the certiorari process, *i.e.*, how the Court disposes of the cases in which it grants review. In theory, the Court grants certiorari in those cases which present issues of general importance. Neither the merits of a case nor the actual decision in the court below is in itself supposed to affect the Court's decision to grant or deny certiorari except, perhaps, when the decision below is in conflict with past decisions of the Supreme Court. Yet, during the last three years the Court *reversed* the decision below in 207 of its certiorari cases, while it *affirmed* in only 123 cases—69% more reversals than affirmances. As to certiorari cases coming up from the state courts, there was an even greater difference, the Court having reversed 39 cases and affirmed only 18—more than twice as many reversals as affirmances.

In view of these facts, one wonders about Mr. Justice Frankfurter's repeated admonitions that denials of certiorari carry no indication of the Court's opinion on the merits of the cases. In any particular case that may be true. But if the cases are viewed as a whole, it would seem that, since the grants of certiorari came most often in cases where the Court disapproved of the decisions below, the denial of certiorari may imply at least some degree of approval of the decision below. . . .

PART TWO

Judge and Company

3 / STAFFING THE COURTS

In every Western nation judges form an elite group. They are usually set aside from the rest of society by a unique uniform and by a specialized form of education, as well as by the degree of power which they exercise over the lives of their fellow citizens. Because of the scope of judicial power, staffing this policymaking elite is one of the principal problems of government. Three means—or some combination of these—are generally used today to select judicial personnel: (1) establishing the judiciary as a separate profession, entrance to which is regulated much the same as in medicine or law; (2) allowing political officials to appoint men to the bench; or (3) permitting the people as a whole to elect their judges.

Continental nations using the civil-law system have tended to make the judiciary a distinct professional career, one separate even from the practice of law. In France, for example, to become a judge a man must be at least twenty-five years old, have graduated from a recognized law school, and have passed a special set of examinations. Once in the judicial profession he becomes a career civil servant whose position and promotion largely depend on the Ministry of Justice.

In Britain, on the other hand, judges from the time of the Norman conquest have been appointed by the king. Indeed, through much of the

Middle Ages judges were regarded merely as assisting the sovereign's personal administration of justice. Early English judges were usually clergymen attending the royal household. But, by the beginning of the fifteenth century, kings were also staffing their courts from among the serjeants of the law trained in the Inns of the Court, a practice which slowly grew over the centuries until judicial office became a virtual monopoly of the legal profession.

British judges held their positions only at the pleasure of the king, and their terms of office expired on the death of the sovereign who had appointed them. This dependence on royal favor frequently made for judicial subservience. Their long struggle for free government convinced the English that an independent judiciary was vital to the type of constitutional rule they desired, but not until 1701 did the Act of Settlement provide that judges should serve during good behavior, with removal contingent upon Parliamentary approval. And it was not until 1760 that a judge's commission did not expire on the death of the king who had appointed him.

The British belief in the value of an independent judiciary was transplanted to America, and royal abuse of this principle was one of the grievances which gave a moral tinge to the cause of the Revolution. The Declaration of Independence accused George III of having "made Judges dependent on his Will alone, for the Tenure of their Offices, and the Amount and Payment of their Salaries."

After the Revolution, American states generally provided that judges should be appointed by one or both houses of the legislature or by the governor with the consent either of a special legislative council or of the legislature itself. Only one state allowed the governor full appointing power. At the constitutional convention in 1787, the Framers were presented with several plans for choosing federal judges. Those delegates, like Franklin, Mason, Gerry, and Ellsworth, who opposed a strong executive, wanted to adhere to the dominant state practice and vest the appointing authority in Congress. Others, like Hamilton, Madison, and Morris, wanted the executive to appoint judges. It was Hamilton who first suggested that the President nominate and the Senate confirm, but this obvious compromise was twice rejected by the convention before it was finally approved. Following British practice, the new Constitution provided that federal judges should serve during good behavior.

The third method of judicial selection, that of popular election, has been almost exclusively a development of American state government.

Vermont provided for election of some judges in 1777, followed by Georgia in 1802 and Indiana in 1816, but by 1832 only Michigan elected all of its judges. The tides of Jacksonian democracy, however, reached even the courts; and each of the states admitted to the Union from 1846 until 1959 provided for election of all or most judges. In 1960, two-thirds of the states still used election as one of the chief means of judicial selection. As a corollary of popular election, there has been a trend to limit judges to definite terms of office.

The Federal System in Operation

In the actual operation of the federal system, the real—as opposed to the legal—power of the President to make judicial appointments varies with the court involved. At the Supreme Court level the President has wide discretion. He is influenced, of course, by many considerations, such as matters of geographic and ethnic representation, and the anticipated reaction of the bar and the public, as well as the climate of opinion in the Senate. But, by and large, the President may take as his principal concern the general position of the nominee and the way he can be expected to vote once on the Court.

Presidents have also been mindful of past political services in selecting nominees, both as a reward for these services and as an indication of future behavior. As Lincoln explained, "We cannot ask a man what he will do [if appointed], and if we should, and he should answer us, we should despise him for it. Therefore we must take a man whose opinions are known." John Marshall had been a Federalist stalwart as a state politician, as a member of the House of Representatives, as a diplomat, and as Secretary of State before becoming Chief Justice. Roger Brooke Taney had faithfully fought by Jackson's side during the struggle over the Bank of the United States. David Davis had managed Lincoln's campaign for the 1860 nomination. John Marshall Harlan the elder had been one of the leaders in the 1876 Republican convention's nomination of Rutherford B. Hayes, and George Sutherland had served as one of Harding's top advisers during the 1920 presidential race.

In nominating judges for the courts of appeals, whose jurisdiction covers several states, the President has much less freedom of choice; but it is at the district court level that presidential power is most circumscribed. Where neither Senator from the state involved is from the President's party, the Justice Department will normally mediate among state and local party leaders and interest groups to secure agreement on a nominee. But where the state has a Senator from the President's party, that Senator ordinarily plays a decisive part in the final choice among candidates. If there are two Senators from the party, the process of securing agreement on the same candidate is often difficult.

The rule of Senatorial courtesy—that a Senator from the President's party must approve appointments within his state—has been expanded so that, as President Taft expressed it, the Chief Executive has only a veto power over the selection of district judges, not full nominating authority. According to Dean Wigmore, consistent practice has amended the Constitution so that it reads: "The individual Senator from the State where an appointment is to be made shall nominate." It has become commonplace for the nomination of a district judge to be announced by the sponsoring Senator, and in 1930 Senator David Reed of Pennsylvania candidly explained to the Senate how a particular judge came to be nominated:

> I thought for a while that I had found a good man in Luzerne County, which is where Wilkes-Barre is, and then I thought I had found a man in Tunkhannock. . . . All of these men I considered. I wanted to get the best one. . . . So far as this being somebody else's choice, it is not. It is my choice. It is my free choice, uninfluenced by General Atterbury [of the Pennsylvania Railroad] or anyone else.

Senator Reed may have been describing an unusual situation. As an elected official often dependent on local political leaders and interest groups, a Senator must make his choice with reference to considerations similar to those the President would weigh, though his scale is calibrated to state rather than national politics.

The President and the Senate

The Senate thus acts as a real brake on executive discretion in the selection of judges. Washington saw one of his Supreme Court nominees rejected by the Senate, and in the nineteenth century the Senate refused to confirm twenty-two Supreme Court choices, over 25 per cent of those nominated. In apparent contrast, during the present century Judge John J. Parker has been the sole nominee to the Supreme Court rejected by the Senate—a defeat due partly to the opposition of labor and Negro organizations and partly to the perennial friction between executive and legislative power. Although there has been serious opposition to several other nominees, only Louis D. Brandeis in 1916 was in real danger of failing to receive confirmation.

This record perhaps indicates that Presidents have been choosing judicial personnel with a careful regard to Senatorial moods as much as it shows any lapse of Senatorial power. In 1937, for example, after his defeat on the Court-packing bill, President Roosevelt decided to nominate Senator Hugo L. Black to fill the vacancy left by the retirement of Willis Van Devanter. Roosevelt chose Black for a number of reasons. First, the President wanted a man who would understand the economic reality of the times, and Black's staunch liberal record, which antedated the New Deal, indicated he would be sympathetic to government regulation of the economy. Second, Black's pugnacity and scathing sarcasm had made him *persona non grata* to many of the conservatives who had just beaten the President. Third, Roosevelt's revenge would be complete since these conservatives would not be able to block Black's confirmation because of the Senate's custom of approving without question the appointment of members of their own "club."

In an entirely different political context, President Eisenhower resorted to the use of recess appointments. When the Senate is not in session, the President may appoint a man to serve until the end of the next session of Congress. Since Congress now usually adjourns sometime in the summer until early January, and the Supreme Court begins its term in October, a recess appointment may present the Senate with a *fait accompli.* Although Eisenhower successfully used this method with three of his first four nominations, George Washington was less fortunate. Washington had given a recess appointment to Rutledge as Chief Justice; but when the President sent Rutledge's name to the Senate, confirmation was refused.

Delay in confirmation can be used as a means of Senatorial coercion of the executive. In 1959, for instance, the Judiciary Committee held up action on thirteen of Eisenhower's lower-court nominations for most of the first session of the Eighty-sixth Congress. Blame for this extended delay was generally placed on the committee chairman, James O. Eastland of Mississippi, whose racist views had caused him to become disaffected with the federal judiciary. A few days before the end of the session, however, the real story became known. Eisenhower had nominated a man for a Texas district judgeship, a post to which Senate Majority Leader Lyndon Johnson wanted to send his own choice. Since Johnson was a Democrat, the rule of Senatorial courtesy did not apply; but Johnson was able to use his influence to bottle up all thirteen nominations. Faced with this situation, the Justice Department arranged a capitulation. Eisenhower's nominee withdrew and Johnson's man was named in his place. Within three days of this new nomination, the Judiciary Committee had approved all the nominees and the Senate had confirmed them.

The Mechanics of the Appointing Process

The mechanics of the appointing process are relatively simple. The President usually depends heavily on the Attorney General's staff to screen candidates and to maintain liaison with Congress and interested pressure groups. When the list of candidates has been narrowed, the FBI runs a full loyalty-security check, and the Justice Department seeks the approval of the American Bar Association's Committee on the Federal Judiciary. This committee then conducts its own inquiry, seeking the views of the legal profession. The practice in both the Truman and Eisenhower administrations was to nominate no one on whom the bar report was negative.

When the nomination is sent to the Senate, the matter is referred to the Committee on the Judiciary. The committee chairman is allowed to read the FBI report, but the other Senators are not. At the same time the committee clerk sends out a "blue slip" to the Senators from the nominee's state, asking their views. If a Senator does not answer within a week, the committee rules assume that he has no objection. The clerk, however, customarily inquires as to the cause of the delay; and if the Senator is investigating the nominee, the committee will postpone further action until the Senator has completed his inquiry.

Next, the committee chairman appoints a subcommittee which sets a date for hearings. In the case of lower-court judges, these hearings are usually perfunctory, if the Justice Department has maintained proper liaison with Senators. The Senators from the nominee's state and a few other character witnesses testify in glowing terms. Only occasionally is there more than token opposition from Senators, though not infrequently a few cranks ask to be heard.

It sometimes happens, however, that Senators use these hearings to exert legislative pressure on either the executive or the judiciary. In 1958, for example, the Supreme Court was under heavy attack from both conservative Republicans and southern Democrats who charged the Court with usurping legislative authority. The Judiciary Committee had before it a number of bills to curb the Court, including one measure which would have removed the Court's appellate jurisdiction in five significant areas of constitutional interpretation. As a compromise, Senator O'Mahoney of Wyoming suggested that future judicial nominees be asked to affirm belief in the limited nature of judicial power. At hearings in March, 1958, Senator Eastland asked George H. Casswell, nominated for a district judgeship in Florida, to stand and give a sworn answer to the following question:

> Do you, in contemplation of the necessity of taking an oath to support and defend the Constitution of the United States, understand that such oath will demand that you support and defend the provisions of Article 1, Section 1 of the Constitution, that "all legislative power herein granted shall be vested in a Congress of the United States . . ." and that therefore you will be bound by such oath not to participate knowingly in any decision to alter the meaning of the Constitution itself or any law as passed by the Congress and adopted under the Constitution?

Taken by surprise, Casswell meekly complied, but the Attorney General at his next press conference branded the oath as "silly." Persuaded more by the opposition of liberal Senators than by the anger of the Attorney General, the committee later toned down the oath to a simple question about belief in the separation-of-powers doctrine.

In contrast to the usual bland character of hearings on lower-court nominees, the proceedings an appointment to the Supreme Court involves are often elaborate and explosive. Interest groups can use these hearings as a forum to voice their views on the course of constitutional law and Senators can utilize the publicity of the occasion to express opposition to the candidate, the President, or the Court. Thus in 1958 southern Senators tried to turn the hearings on Justice Potter Stewart into a debate on the merits of school desegregation.

Before the second administration of Franklin D. Roosevelt, a Supreme Court nominee usually did not attend the hearings. Beginning, however, with the nomination of Felix Frankfurter, it has become normal practice for the nominee to appear as a witness and be subjected to committee interrogation—though in 1949 Sherman Minton, then a court of appeals judge, declined to testify in his own behalf lest he be asked about "highly controversial and litigious issues affecting the Court."

After the hearings, the subcommittee reports to the full Judiciary Committee, and the question of confirmation is discussed and voted upon. In executive session, the Senate debates and decides the issue.

Since 1929 these debates have been public; before that time it was the custom for the Senate to hold secret sessions on confirmation proceedings.

The Judicial Role

The judiciary plays no official role in the selection of judges. Frequently, however, judges take an important part in choosing their colleagues, either in consulting with executive officials, Senators, spokesmen for bar associations or other interest groups, or directly with party leaders. Justice Samuel Miller, for instance, constantly dabbled in appointment politicking and made strenuous efforts to get his brother-in-law appointed to the Supreme Court. Chief Justice William Howard Taft was instrumental in the selection of Pierce Butler and Edward Sanford. According to Harold L. Ickes, Justice Harlan F. Stone's advice was influential in Roosevelt's decision to nominate Felix Frankfurter; and Roosevelt, when considering a successor to Charles Evans Hughes, accepted the outgoing Chief Justice's recommendation and promoted Stone to the center chair. After Stone's death, President Truman discussed the matter of a new Chief Justice with Hughes, and, so Justice Robert H. Jackson thought, with several of the associate justices.

The Judicial Elite: A Collective Portrait

Judges, we have said, form an elite group in Western nations. This is particularly true in the United States. What is the character of this elite? On the federal level, at least, all are lawyers—an expected but nevertheless important fact in light of the specialized training and generally conservative spirit of the American bar. Most have been very successful lawyers either in private practice or in politics. Most judges have played, at some time in their lives, an active part in politics, and the overwhelming majority have been affiliated with the party of the President who nominated them. Available statistics show that each President from Grover Cleveland to Dwight Eisenhower has chosen from 82.2 to 98.6 per cent of federal judges from the ranks of his own party; the over-all average is close to 95 per cent.

John Schmidhauser[1] has sketched a collective portrait of the ninety-one

[1] "The Justices of the Supreme Court: A Collective Portrait," 3 *Midwest Journal of Political Science* 1 (1959). Detroit: Wayne State University Press. Reprinted with permission.

men who sat on the Supreme Court from 1789 to 1957. Schmidhauser found that "throughout the entire history of the Supreme Court, only a handful of its members were of essentially humble origin. Nine individuals selected in widely scattered historical periods comprise the total. The remaining eighty-two (90%) were not only from families in comfortable economic circumstances, but were chosen overwhelmingly from the socially-prestigeful and politically-influential gentry class in the late eighteenth and nineteenth century or the professionalized upper middle-class thereafter." Equally meaningful for social origin was the fact that nearly two-thirds of the justices "were drawn from politically active families, and of perhaps greater significance, a third of this group were chosen from a relatively narrow circle of families—families which have been distinctive in their possession of traditions of judicial service."

The justices themselves have generally been politically active people. In fact, George Shiras was the only justice out of the ninety-one who had not participated in practical politics before going to the Court. Twenty-six out of thirty-four pre-Civil War appointees had been primarily politicians, and the over-all percentage for the 168 years covered by Schmidhauser's study was 53.9 per cent. This figure would be considerably larger if some or all of the twenty-four men who had pursued lower-court judicial careers were included in the "politician" category. Only four Supreme Court justices have been primarily law-school professors, and all were appointed by Franklin Roosevelt. Of the fourteen justices who were neither "politicians," lower-court judges, nor professors, eleven were chiefly corporation lawyers and three noncorporation lawyers.

Religiously, most Supreme Court justices have been members of high-status Protestant sects (Episcopalian, Presbyterian, French Calvinist, Congregationalist, or Unitarian), though in the twentieth century there has been a marked tendency for each President to keep a Catholic on the Court, and since 1916 to have a Jew on the bench. Ethnically, Schmidhauser found that only five justices were not natural-born American citizens, and three of these five were appointed by George Washington. Most of the justices—94.6 per cent—came from predominantly western European stock—English, Welsh, Scotch-Irish, Irish, French, Dutch, or Scandinavian—and some 57.2 per cent from British or Welsh backgrounds. Of the justices born in the United States, the majority have come from small towns or urban areas, with the percentage of rural-born justices steadily declining.

Noting the high educational level of Supreme Court appointees, Schmidhauser concluded that "the recruitment process has generally rewarded those whose educational backgrounds, both legal and non-legal, have comprised the rare combination of intellectual, social and political opportunities which have generally been available only to the economically comfortable and socially prominent segment of the American population."

Improving the Selection System

Both popular election and political appointment have come under sharp criticism as poor methods of staffing the courts. Election, it is often said, can turn a judge's eyes from the law to popular opinion of the moment, or at least divert his attention from administering justice to running a re-election campaign. It is charged that many men who would make excellent judges will not expose themselves to the sort of campaign expected of politicians, and that many other candidates cannot bear the heavy expenses of campaigning. This last defect can lead to dependence on the money and skills of a political machine and to an unhealthy influence in the courtroom. In fact, the assertion has been made that popular election merely transfers the appointing power from elected officials to party bosses.

The appointment method, in turn, has been severely attacked as a form of patronage, a potential—and sometimes actual—corrupter not only of judges but of public faith in decent government. The American Judicature Society and the American Bar Association have been conducting campaigns to have the selection of judges taken "out of politics," and more authority put in the hands of bar groups. Through its Committee on the Federal Judiciary the A.B.A. already exercises what comes close to a veto over federal appointments; but some of its officers have been urging that they be given the names of all candidates under consideration and that the Bar Association be allowed to rank these candidates. This is only one short step away from permitting the bar to name those who should be considered in the first place. Benjamin Franklin once suggested that allowing lawyers to select judges would be wise, since lawyers would invariably choose the best men of their profession in order to divide their practices among themselves. While Franklin was indulging his sense of humor, his suggestion does emphasize that attorneys have special interests of their own which do not always coincide with those of the community at large. The question raised by the plans to increase bar association control is whether taking judicial appointments "out of politics" really means taking them out of a form of politics in which the decision-makers must face frequent popular re-election, only to throw appointments into bar association politics where there is no popular control.

As a compromise between appointing and electing judges, Albert Kales proposed in 1914 that judges be initially appointed for a specific term and then be subject to popular re-election. In 1934 California substantially adopted Kales' idea; and in 1940 Missouri enacted a variation which has received wide endorsement as a practical answer to improving judicial selection. Under the Missouri Plan, several commissions are established to nominate judges at different court levels. The appellate commission consists of seven members: the chief justice of the state, three lawyers elected by the state bar association, and three men appointed by the governor, none of whom can be a public officeholder or an official of a political party. With the exception of the chief justice, these members serve for six years, with their terms staggered so that two retire every other year. The commission nominates three men for each judicial vacancy. The governor must appoint one of the three. At the next election after the new judge has served for twelve months, his name is put on the ballot with the question whether he should be retained in office. If elected, he serves a definite term, twelve years for an appellate judge, six years for a trial judge. At the end of this term he is eligible for re-election.

The Ideal Judge

Any particular method of judicial recruitment is only a means to an end, and no method can be rationally evaluated unless the end is understood. In short, the basic question is: What do we ask from our judges? The answer is a paradoxical one. Senator Harper of South Carolina said in 1826 that judges "ought to possess, in a high degree, talent, firmness, and integrity; and more than these, the individuals discharging duties on the Bench should . . . all be statesmen. . . . They should be without the manner, party, or passions, and views of politicians; they should be perfectly acquainted with men, with the workings of human passions without being subject to the influence of passions."

Senator Harper was asking for rare men, but he was also reflecting the American image of the ideal judge. We want a man of integrity, but also a man of learning and experience. Law and society are not separate entities; therefore we want a man who is a statesman as well as a legal craftsman. We want a judge who is detached in his outlook, yet familiar with the economic, social, and political problems of the times; a man who has a sense of underlying popular sentiment as well as an ability to distinguish transitory moods from basic attitudes. We want a man who understands politics in the broadest sense of the word, but a man who is above narrow partisanship.

It is doubtful whether any system of selection could consistently recruit such paragons; but, with all its shortcomings, the federal appointing process has over the years provided personnel whose integrity, skill, and sense of statecraft have been well above the state average. This has been due in part to the high prestige of the judicial office. The fact that there are few lawyers who would not be willing, even anxious, to exchange a lucrative private practice for the psychic income of the judicial robe creates a vast reservoir from which officials of both parties may draw men of great talent.

In part, the success of the federal system has been due to the power of the judiciary. Rarely has a President or a Senator knowingly put a weak or incompetent man in a position from which he could sabotage crucial public policies. In part, too, the federal record has been due to the ballot box. A President's right to choose judges from within the ranks of his own political party is one of the accepted rules of the American political game—as long as the men nominated are honest and capable. Evidence of corruption in the nominating process, or of ineptitude in selection, would be a deadly campaign weapon in the hands of the opposition.

Federal success can also be attributed to the fact that once appointed the judge is independent, removable only for criminal action and largely responsible only to his own conscience. More than one President has been sorely disappointed because a party man became his own man when promoted to the bench. Unpredictability, John P. Frank has written, "is almost the clearest feature of the appointment process. . . . [T]he number of surprises is great and no President can be sure of what he is getting." This has been true from the early years of the nineteenth century when anti-Federalist Presidents sent justice after justice to the Court to curb John Marshall's influence, only to see their votes captured by the Chief Justice. As one judge put the matter, whatever the politics involved in the nominating process, "the judicial appointee to a life position has the last say—if only he will say it."

SELECTED REFERENCES

Cooley, Rita W., "Judicial Appointments in the Eisenhower Administration," 34 *Social Science* 10 (1959).

Evans, Evan A., "Political Influence in the Selection of Federal Judges," 1948 *Wisconsin Law Review* 330.

Ewing, Cortez A. M., *The Judges of the Supreme Court, 1789–1937* (Minneapolis: University of Minnesota Press, 1938).

Fairman, Charles, "Mr. Justice Bradley's Appointment to the Supreme Court and the Legal Tender Cases," 54 *Harvard Law Review* 977 (1941).

Fox, Edward J., Jr., "The Selection of Federal Judges: The Work of the Federal Judiciary Committee," 43 *American Bar Association Journal* 685 (1957).

Frank, John P., "The Appointment of Supreme Court Justices," 1941 *Wisconsin Law Review* 172–210, 343–379, 461–512.

Harris, Joseph P., *The Advice and Consent of the Senate* (Berkeley: University of California Press, 1953).

Haynes, Evan, *The Selection and Tenure of Judges* (Newark: National Conference of Judicial Councils, 1944).

Hurst, James Willard, *The Growth of American Law* (Boston: Little, Brown, 1950), Ch. 7.

Hyde, Laurance M., "The Missouri Method of Choosing Judges," 41 *Journal of the American Judicature Society* 74 (1957).

Laski, Harold J., "The Technique of Judicial Appointment," 24 *Michigan Law Review* 529 (1926).

Martin, E. M., *The Role of the Bar in Electing the Bench in Chicago* (Chicago: University of Chicago Press, 1936).

Mason, Alpheus T., *Brandeis: A Free Man's Life* (New York: Viking Press, 1946), Chs. 30–31.

Mayers, Lewis, *The American Legal System* (New York: Harper, 1955), Ch. 12.

Miller, Ben R., "Politics and the Courts," 42 *American Bar Association Journal* 939 (1956).

Peltason, Jack W., *Federal Courts in the Political Process* (New York: Random House, 1955), Ch. 4.

Ratner, Sidney, "Was the Supreme Court Packed by President Grant?" 50 *Political Science Quarterly* 343 (1935).

Rogers, William P., "Judicial Appointments in the Eisenhower Administration," 41 *Journal of the American Judicature Society* 38 (1957).

Schmidhauser, John R., "The Justices of the Supreme Court: A Collective Portrait," 3 *Midwest Journal of Political Science* 1 (1959).

Schubert, Glendon A., Jr., *Constitutional Politics* (New York: Holt, Rinehart & Winston, 1960), Ch. 2.

Sears, Kenneth C., "The Appointment of Federal District Judges," 25 *Illinois Law Review* 54 (1930).

Vanderbilt, Arthur T., *Judges and Jurors* (Boston: Boston University Press, 1956).

Wigmore, John H., "The President Shall Nominate," 25 *Illinois Law Review* 929 (1931).

1.
> *"[A judge] is not . . . fitted for the position unless he is a party man, a constructive statesman . . ."*

THEODORE ROOSEVELT TO HENRY CABOT LODGE

July 10, 1902

Personal

Dear Cabot:

 . . . . NOW AS TO Holmes. . . . First of all, I wish to go over the reasons why I am in his favor. He possesses the high character and the high reputation both of which should if possible attach to any man who is to go upon the highest court of the entire civilized world. His father's name entitles the son to honor; and if the father had been an utterly unknown man the son would nevertheless now have won the highest honor. The position of Chief Justice of Massachusetts is in itself a guarantee of the highest professional standing. Moreover, Judge Holmes has behind him the kind of career and possesses the kind of personality which make a good American proud of him as a representative of our country. He has been a most gallant soldier, a most able and upright public servant, and in public and private life alike a citizen whom we like to think of as typical of the American character at its best. The labor decisions which have been criticized by some of the big railroad men and other members of large corporations constitute to my mind a strong point in Judge Holmes' favor. The ablest lawyers and greatest judges are men whose past has naturally brought them into close relationship with the wealthiest and most powerful clients, and I am glad when I can find a judge who has been able to preserve his aloofness of mind so as to keep his broad humanity of feeling and his sympathy for the class from which he has not drawn his clients. I think it eminently desirable that our Supreme Court should show in unmistakable fashion their entire sympathy with all

Henry Cabot Lodge, *Selections from the Correspondence of Theodore Roosevelt and Henry Cabot Lodge, 1894–1918* (New York: Scribner's, 1925), I, 517–519. Reprinted with permission.

proper effort to secure the most favorable possible consideration for the men who most need that consideration.

Finally, Judge Holmes' whole mental attitude, as shown for instance by his great Phi Beta Kappa speech at Harvard, is such that I should naturally expect him to be in favor of those principles in which I so earnestly believe.

. . . In the ordinary and low sense which we attach to the words "partisan" and "politician," a judge of the Supreme Court should be neither. But in the higher sense, in the proper sense, he is not in my judgment fitted for the position unless he is a party man, a constructive statesman, constantly keeping in mind his adherence to the principles and policies under which this nation has been built up and in accordance with which it must go on; and keeping in mind also his relations with his fellow statesmen who in other branches of the government are striving in cooperation with him to advance the ends of government. Marshall rendered such invaluable service because he was a statesman of the national type, like Adams who appointed him, like Washington whose mantle fell upon him. Taney was a curse to our national life because he belonged to the wrong party and faithfully carried out the criminal and foolish views of the party which stood for such a construction of the Constitution as would have rendered it impossible to preserve the national life. The Supreme Court of the sixties was good exactly in so far as its members represented the spirit of Lincoln.

This is true at the present day. The majority of the present Court who have, although without satisfactory unanimity, upheld the policies of President McKinley and the Republican party in Congress, have rendered a great service to mankind and to this nation. The minority —a minority so large as to lack but one vote of being a majority—have stood for such reactionary folly as would have hampered well-nigh helplessly this people in doing efficient and honorable work for the national welfare, and for the welfare of the islands themselves, in Porto Rico and the Philippines. No doubt they have possessed excellent motives and without a doubt they are men of excellent personal character; but this no more excuses them than the same conditions excused the various upright and honest men who took part in the wicked folly of secession in 1860 and 1861.

Now I should like to know that Judge Holmes was in entire sympathy with our views, that is with your views and mine and Judge Gray's, for instance, just as we know that ex-Attorney General Knowlton is, before I would feel justified in appointing him. Judge Gray has been one of the most valuable members of the Court. I should hold myself as guilty of an irreparable wrong to the nation if I should put in his place any man who was not absolutely sane and sound on the great national policies for which we stand in public life.

Faithfully yours,
Theodore Roosevelt

2.   *". . . 'if any of you die, I'll disown you.'"*

PRESIDENT TAFT'S APPOINTMENTS TO THE SUPREME COURT

*Daniel S. McHargue**

. . . TAFT DEPLORED the practice of using the Supreme Court as the last refuge of senility; he wanted, or said he wanted, a younger Court. Yet the President's first appointment was one which definitely over-rode this consideration. The death of Justice Peckham on October 24, 1909, opened the way for the first of Taft's six Supreme Court nominations. . . .

President Taft had long admired Horace H. Lurton, with whom he had sat as United States Circuit Judge. Lurton had served in the Confederate Army, had advised on Democratic Party politics, had been a justice of the Supreme Court of Tennessee for seven years, and chief justice of the same court for a short time before he was appointed United States Circuit Court Judge in 1893. Lurton had also served as professor of law at Vanderbilt University from 1898 to 1910, and was Dean of the Law School during the last five years of the period mentioned, while acting as Circuit Judge.

Taft had unsuccessfully urged President Roosevelt to give Lurton the place Justice Shiras vacated and the place Justice Brown vacated,

12 *Journal of Politics* 478 (1950). Copyright 1950 Southern Political Science Association. Reprinted with permission.
* Associate Professor of Political Science, University of Michigan.

and now that Taft was President, he earnestly desired to put his old friend and colleague on the Supreme Court bench. But Lurton was sixty-five years of age, older than the President thought a man should be at the time he ascended the highest bench, so Taft had to subject himself to considerable soul-searching before he arrived at a decision. . . . Some three weeks after Peckham's death, Taft wrote to Circuit Judge John W. Warrington of Cincinnati, Ohio, saying in part:

> I say this to you most confidentially . . . that you can be very sure that my first impulse and my strong and continuing impulse is to appoint Lurton to the Supreme Bench. I have a good deal of opposition to him in the pressure from New York to have a candidate, and also to Lurton's age. But I feel strongly, as you express it, that the consideration of age ought to weigh much less heavily in a case where a man has reached his ripest judicial power and is able by reason thereof to take his place on the bench and begin writing opinions there as if he had always been there, than in the case where you take a man from the bar, or indeed from the state bench, with his lack of familiarity with the nice distinctions in reference to the jurisdiction and the Federal practice.

Taft added a postscript suggesting that friends of Lurton seek to line up the support of the Senate Judiciary Committee. One week later Taft wrote to William B. Sanders of Cleveland, Ohio, saying:

> . . . Nothing I could do in my Presidential term would give me more pleasure than that appointment. Whether I can make it or not is dependent on the issue of an investigation I am making just at present. Have you any means of reaching the Judiciary Committee of the Senate, and especially Knute Nelson of Minnesota, in respect to the matter? . . .

The President had received a great many letters since the time when a vacancy was left by Peckham, either recommending Lurton or arguing against his nomination. Lurton himself was keeping up an active correspondence with Secretary of War Dickinson with respect to the strategy and progress of his candidacy, and most of Lurton's letters to Dickinson were sent on by the latter to Taft.

In one of his letters to Dickinson, Lurton claimed commitments of support from some eighteen senators of whom two were working actively in his behalf; described the efforts of four governors, one judge, and others prominent in politics who were pressing for his nomination; expressed some concern over the position which the New England senators might take; and told how he had assigned the task of approaching them to the president of the New York Life Insurance Company. . . .

Many persons had written to Taft asking that Lurton not be named because they felt Lurton to be anti-labor. Among them were A. B. Garretson, president of the Order of Railway Conductors; Edward A. Moseley, secretary of the Interstate Commerce Commission; D. L. Cease, editor and manager of *The Railroad Trainman;* Samuel Gompers of the American Federation of Labor; and W. G. Lee, president of the Brotherhood of Railroad Trainmen. President Taft was undisturbed by such protests. . . .

Finally, on December 13, 1909, Taft sent Lurton's name to the Senate. Three days later Taft wrote to Justice Harlan, "I have yours of December 13th and thank you for speaking to Senator Nelson. I have no doubt he will help in the appointment." The Senate confirmed Lurton's nomination one week after it was received. . . .

Justice Brewer died on March 28, 1910, and President Taft had to name a second Supreme Court justice. Many candidates were recommended as Brewer's successor, but the President knew whom he wanted. The previous year he had met and been tremendously impressed with the talents of Charles Evans Hughes, the Governor of New York. The President had remarked a few months after he met Hughes that if ever he had the chance he would offer Hughes the Chief Justiceship. Archie Butt noted that Taft had said some four months prior to Brewer's death:

> If I am defeated for the next nomination, I think it will be by Hughes. And I don't think he will allow his name to be used unless he really feels that I have no chance to win. . . . I will have a chance to offer him a seat on the Supreme Bench. He will be inclined to accept, and he will waver and he will then consult his wife, and she, I think, will be the final influence which will cause him to decline it. But if he doesn't accept the Judiciary, I expect to see him President some day. . . .

Less than one month after the vacancy on the bench occurred, Taft wrote to Hughes offering him the place and intimating that he might later be made Chief Justice. Taft indicated some reasons why Hughes might decline including his excellent prospects of becoming President, his desire to continue as Governor, and the alternative certainty of a large income should he turn to private practice. However, Taft argued that if Hughes preferred a judicial career to a political one, he might as well make the switch at this time, explained that Hughes need not leave the Governorship until October when only a few months would remain of his term, and said, "The Chief Justiceship is soon likely to be vacant and I should never regard the practice of never promoting associate justices as one to be followed." But in a postscript Taft added:

> P.S. Don't misunderstand me as to the Chief Justiceship. I mean that if that office were now open, I should offer it to you and it is probable that if it were to become vacant during my term, I should promote you to it; but, of course, conditions change so that it would not be right for me to say by way of promise what I would do in the future. Nor, on the other hand, would I have you think that your declination would prevent my offering you the higher place, should conditions remain as they are.

Two days later Hughes accepted the offer. . . . The concluding paragraph read as follows:

> Your expressions regarding the Chief-Justiceship are understood and most warmly appreciated. You properly reserve entire freedom with respect to this and I accept the offer you now make without wishing you to feel committed in the slightest degree. Should the vacancy occur during your term, I, in common with all citizens would desire you to act freely and without embarrassment in accordance with your best judgment at that time.

The President nominated Hughes on April 25, 1910, and the Senate confirmed the nomination on May 2, 1910. . . .

Hughes was without judicial experience and was to be the only one of Taft's nominees to the highest Court who had never before sat as a judge. . . . Whether Taft was motivated by a desire to shelve the man he considered his chief competitor for the next Republican presidential nomination is not certain. . . .

On December 12, 1910, President Taft, a Republican, a Northerner, and a Unitarian, nominated Justice White, a Democrat, a Southerner, and a Catholic, to the Chief Justiceship. . . . The center chair on the bench had been left vacant by the death of Chief Justice Fuller on

July 4, 1910, but Taft delayed his nomination until Congress met in December, 1910; meanwhile another vacancy occurred through the resignation of Justice Moody on November 20, 1910. The President was be-
sieged with recommendations and the Attorney General had several
lists of candidates prepared. . . .

Justice Holmes wrote to Sir Frederick Pollock saying:

> The President said he meant to send for me and talk about the new
> appointments. . . . As to the Chief Justiceship I am rather at a loss.
> I should bet he will appoint Hughes, who has given up a chance of
> being Republican nominee for the Presidency, but I know nothing. I
> think White who is next in Seniority to Harlan (too old, etc.) the
> ablest man likely to be thought of. I don't know whether his being a
> Catholic would interfere. I always have assumed absolutely that I
> should not be regarded as possible—they don't appoint side Judges as a
> rule, it would be embarrassing to skip my Seniors, and I am too old.
> I think I should be a better administrator than White, but he would
> be more politic. . . .

President Taft wrote to Chauncey Depew in October, 1910, saying,
". . . if Mr. Root were five years younger I should not hesitate a moment about whom to make chief justice. . . ." That the President was
seeking some one whose age and energy and disposition would promise
years of hard work was indicated in a statement he made to a part of
his cabinet in July, shortly after Fuller's death. Taft had heard that
Justice Harlan, the Senior Associate Justice, whom Taft regarded as extremely indolent, thought he should be promoted to the center chair.
Taft was furious and said, "I'll do no such damned thing . . . I won't
make the position of chief justice a blue ribbon for the final years of
any member of the court. I want someone who will coordinate the
activities of the court and who has a reasonable expectation of serving
ten or twenty years on the bench."

Taft asked Attorney General Wickersham to sound out the justices
and ascertain whom they desired as their leader. Wickersham reported
back that the Court preferred Justice White. White was a Democrat, a
Confederate veteran, and a Roman Catholic. Wickersham and Taft
both realized that some criticism would be bound to result if such a
man were named, but neither felt that any of White's allegiances should
be held against him. . . .

In early December, Taft made his decision and told Assistant Secretary of the Treasury Charles D. Hilles, "I have decided whom I will appoint chief justice . . . and in doing so I have driven another nail in my political coffin." . . .

Various motives have been attributed to Taft in naming White. One author believes the two main factors were Taft's feeling that White had been right in the Insular Case decision and his conviction that White was the best man to direct his trust-busting campaign. . . . Most authorities agree that Taft appointed White because he knew and approved his constitutional views. One author claimed that, "Taft was probably influenced by his desire to break the 'Solid South' politically." . . .

In selecting White, Taft ignored the precedent of not promoting an Associate Justice and the precedent of choosing as Chief Justice only men of the same political party as the President. . . . The Senate confirmed White's nomination the same day it was received. . . .

It is interesting to note that Taft had said Senator Elihu Root was too old to be Fuller's successor as he was sixty-five years of age. Edward D. White was sixty-five years of age when he was named to take Fuller's place. The President had claimed he wanted a man who promised many years of usefulness on the bench, but he told Archie Butt that, ". . . Hughes is young enough to wait, and if he makes good on the bench I may yet be able to appoint him." . . .

It had been known for some time prior to Justice Moody's retirement on November 20, 1910, that President Taft would soon have to name someone to take his place. Candidates were advanced from all sections of the country. . . .

On December 12, 1910, President Taft named Willis Van Devanter to take Moody's place. Van Devanter had been Commissioner to revise the Wyoming statutes, City Attorney of Cheyenne, Wyoming, member of the Territorial Legislature of Wyoming, Chief Justice of the Supreme Court of Wyoming, Chairman of the Republican State Committee of Wyoming, delegate to the Republican National Convention of 1896, member of the Republican National Committee, Assistant Attorney General of the United States assigned to the Department of the Interior, and had been United States Circuit Judge for the eighth circuit since 1903. . . .

Many of Van Devanter's political, railroad, and judicial friends sent letters of recommendation in his behalf. There were several letters asking that Van Devanter not be named, including one from A. A. Johnson, ex-president of the University of Wyoming, who claimed Van Devanter owed too much to great corporations, particularly the Union Pacific.

Van Devanter's most earnest supporter was Senator Warren of Wyoming. President Taft wrote Warren acknowledging clippings sent in Van Devanter's behalf and in another letter took cognizance of Warren's recommendation of Judge Van Devanter. About the same time Judge Van Devanter wrote to Secretary of Commerce and Labor Charles Nagel, "I am not a candidate for the court in the sense in which the term generally is used." He asked that his name be withdrawn if it would spare the President any embarrassment and took up some four pages defending himself against the charge that he had not written his fair share of opinions in the territorial court. Apparently Warren's campaign for Van Devanter did not go too smoothly at one stage late in the game, for only one week prior to the nomination, Warren wrote to Taft:

> I fear I was unfortunate enough to vex or annoy you in our interview on last Saturday. I am sorry, for it was farthest from my intention to do so.
> Please discontinue consideration of the name of Judge Van Devanter in connection with immediate appointments to the Supreme Bench.

Two days before Van Devanter was nominated, Senator J. C. Burrows wrote President Taft that he had wired United States Circuit Judge Henry Severens, "Do you think Van Devanter better than Hook?" and that Severens wired back, "Yes." On December 12, 1910, the day Taft nominated Van Devanter, Senator Warren wrote to Taft thanking him and enclosing telegrams from Van Devanter and C. W. Burdick, Chairman of the Republican State Central Committee of Wyoming, expressing gratitude to Senator Warren for what he had done to bring about the nomination. . . . The Senate confirmed on December 15, 1910.

Just why President Taft chose Van Devanter is uncertain. He was probably influenced by the fact that of the Westerners whom he considered geographically available, Van Devanter had fewer enemies who protested his proposed nomination than did his chief competitors.

On the surface, at least, Taft's fourth appointment in 1910, that of Joseph R. Lamar, appeared to result from something less than a careful search. One author claims Taft ". . . was hard pressed to find another man. He had run out of first-rate ideas, and in the absence of a grab bag from which he could choose at random, it was necessary to assign to Attorney General Wickersham the task of hunting up someone to take the job." . . .

On December 11, 1910, Archie Butt noted, "Not only does White get the Chief Justiceship, but Lamar gets one of the other places. I am delighted, of course, that the South seems to be reaping the benefit of her conservatism . . ." Taft wrote his brother, Charles P. Taft, "I shall make my judicial appointments tomorrow, and I shall be greatly relieved when they go in. I am not sure that I shall suit everybody, but I shall at least suit myself."

Lamar had practiced law in Augusta, served two terms in the Georgia legislature, had written extensively on jurisprudence in Georgia, had been one of three commissioners who recodified Georgia's laws, had served two years on the Supreme Court of Georgia, and had again practiced in Augusta since 1906. Among those who had recommended his appointment were former Associate Justice Brown, Joseph Brown, Governor of Georgia, J. F. Hanson, president of the Central of Georgia Railroad System, Congressman William Adamson of Georgia, Congressman Hardwick, William Lamar, former Congressman from Florida, the Supreme Court judges of Georgia. . . .

We know that Taft had met Lamar some months before when in Augusta and had been attracted to him. But Lamar was greatly surprised when he was nominated for the bench and feared he would not be confirmed as he was a Southerner, a Democrat, and had represented railroads and other corporations. However, his nomination was confirmed by a unanimous vote. . . .

President Taft's last opportunity to name a justice came with the death of Justice Harlan on October 14, 1911. The Department of Justice appointment clerks established a list that mentioned fifty-one candidates including William Borah of Idaho, William Jennings Bryan of Nebraska, William Hook of Kansas, Frank Kellogg of Minnesota, Mahlon Pitney of New Jersey. . . . President Taft offered Harlan's place to Secretary of State Philander Knox, who had previously served as Attorney General under President Benjamin Harrison, but Knox declined.

Finally, on February 19, 1912, Taft nominated Mahlon Pitney of New Jersey as Harlan's successor. Pitney had served two terms in Congress, was temporary chairman of the Republican state convention of New Jersey in 1895, a member of the New Jersey Senate where he became Republican floor leader and then president, a judge of the Supreme Court of New Jersey from 1901 to 1908, and had been Chancellor of New Jersey since 1908.

A New York newspaper, the *Evening Post,* claimed Pitney's nomination was announced after a delegation of New Jersey lawyers headed by former Attorney General John Griggs called on Taft. . . .

The day he sent Pitney's name to the Senate, President Taft wrote letters to the leading backers of disappointed candidates. To Congressman D. R. Anthony, who had been Judge Hook's chief proponent, Taft wrote as follows:

> I am very sorry to disappoint you; but after giving the matter the fullest consideration, I have concluded that I must go to New Jersey for a Justice. This relieves the situation so far as Hook is concerned, in that it leaves him open to promotion when vacancies occur for the consideration of my successor. There are reasons that I explained to you why I prefer to pass the Eighth Circuit and go to the Third, which has not had a justice for eight or ten years. . . .

The President also wrote to Senators Penrose and Oliver of Pennsylvania detailing his reasons for selecting Pitney and trying to convince them that the selection of a New Jersey man would not prejudice Pennsylvania's chances of having one of its men named to the bench should a vacancy occur while Taft was still President.

Pitney's nomination was greeted with mixed reactions. The New Jersey Senate complimented Taft on making a wise choice as did several individuals, but the President also received some protests. One account of Pitney's nomination said, "Because of his drastic rulings against peaceful picketing, his appointment was bitterly opposed by labor organizations, but the Senate, after three days' discussion, confirmed it by a vote of fifty to twenty-six." Pitney was confirmed on March 13, 1912, and two days later John Kirley, President of the National Association of Manufacturers, wrote to Taft congratulating him on the nomination and confirmation. He observed that it was pitiful that there were some Senators who would not endorse Pitney because of the protests of labor agitators.

It is reported that on the last day of his term as President, Taft told the newspaper correspondents that, "Above all other things . . . he was proudest of the fact that six of the nine members of the Supreme Court, including the Chief Justice, bore his commission. 'And I have said to them,' Taft chuckled, 'Damn you, if any of you die, I'll disown you.' "

It is true that in naming as many Democrats as Republicans to the highest bench, Taft paid less attention than any other President to the principle of appointing only members of the President's own party. It is also true that while Taft was concerned with maintaining a geographical balance, he seldom appointed a resident of the circuit which had just lost its representation on the bench. . . .

It has already been mentioned that Taft was extremely anxious to be appointed to the Supreme Court. In the light of that fact it might be argued that he was seeking by his appointment of Democrats to create a sentiment in favor of his own appointment by a Democratic President at a later date. It is not known that Taft was influenced by any such ulterior motive, but it should be noted that many Democrats urged President Wilson to ignore partisan considerations in his judicial appointments, as Taft had done, and nominate former President Taft to the nation's highest bench.

Certainly the election of November, 1910, gave Taft reason to feel that it might be wise to placate Southern Democrats. The Republicans not only lost the House of Representatives to the Democrats, an indication that the Democrats might win the next presidential election, but also had their majority in the Senate cut from seventeen to seven. One month later Taft elevated Justice White, a Democrat from Louisiana, to the Chief Justiceship and filled one of the vacancies on the bench with Joseph R. Lamar, a Democrat from Georgia. . . .

It might also be argued that Taft chose White instead of Hughes for the Chief Justiceship because of his desire to occupy that place himself at some future time. Hughes was only forty-eight years of age and could be expected to outlive Taft. White was sixty-five, while Taft was only fifty-three and could hope to succeed White. It is not known that any such consideration affected Taft's decision not to elevate Hughes even though he had practically promised the place to Hughes. However, it is interesting to note that Taft succeeded White as Chief Justice, and Hughes later took Taft's place in the center chair.

Like other Presidents, Taft sought to control the Supreme Court's construction of the constitution by appointing men to that bench whose constitutional views he felt coincided with his own. Hence, he chose men whose views he knew and approved. All six of Taft's appointees in large measure shared his "real politics," though only half of them shared his "nominal politics" in the sense of partisan affiliation. They would probably not have been considered for appointment had not their fundamental political and economic views been closely akin to those of the President.

Taft's selections were likely influenced in varying degrees by personal, political, and party considerations. He seemed to feel that the Democratic Party's hold on the "Solid South" could be broken. . . . Possibly Taft hoped only for the more limited objective of a favorable reaction on the part of the border states in the next election.

It has already been suggested that Taft may have appointed Hughes in order to remove him as a contender for the next Republican presidential nomination. Both Van Devanter and Pitney had strong supporters within the Republican Party who would be pleased by their appointments and Taft could hope for support from Wyoming and New Jersey in the forthcoming election as a result of selecting their residents to the bench. However, it is not certain that Taft was in any way affected by such considerations. . . .

3.   *"It turned out that was pretty good strategy . . ."*

HOW I GOT TO BE A FEDERAL JUDGE   *Joseph Samuel Perry**

I THOUGHT that instead of giving a lecture on some philosophical question I would relate how I became a federal judge. Some of the younger lawyers might be interested in hearing about the

Speech before the Chicago Bar Association, November 20, 1951.
* U.S. District Judge, Northern District of Illinois.

avenue I travelled to that appointment. There are, of course, many avenues . . . but I will tell you how I got there.

To begin with, if you want to be appointed to that office in Illinois, you almost have to be a Democrat. There are some States where one could be a Republican, but not in Illinois. In Minnesota, for example, you could be appointed if you were a Republican—that is, if you were a dangerous Republican who might defeat some Democrat who wanted to be elected to a particular office.

I started out by being born a Republican. Now I know that doesn't sound very good for a fellow who was born in Alabama, but there is one county down there—Winston County—which was known as the Free State of Winston during the Civil War. They had no slaves and so they did not fight on the Confederate side in the Civil War. They either hid out in the bluffs or they ran across the border at night and fought in the Union Army. They still vote Republican and they have never elected a Democrat in the history of the county. Not even Roosevelt carried Winston County.

I was born right near the edge of that county and my grandfather, John Brown—no relation to the famous John Brown—was an old Republican, and my mother was a Republican, and so, as I say, I was born a Republican.

After my mother's death, which occurred when I was four, my father moved down into a Democratic county where I "got educated." Of course, I became a Democrat. It was not until I was about 17 years old and went back to the vicinity of Winston County to teach school that I learned that my mother's people had been Republicans and that I had been born of a Republican mother.

After I enlisted in World War I and had served overseas, I returned and went to work in the coal mines. By that time, of course, the unions had gotten there and I joined the union, as my friend here said, and I was getting along fine. Then John Lewis came down and called a strike in the summertime when we had very little work anyway and when it couldn't hurt the coal company. That made me mad. I got so mad that I quit coal mining and went to college and got an education.

So that was another step forward. I came up here, went to the University of Chicago and got a master's degree. Then I got a doctor's degree and felt highly educated.

Then I moved out to DuPage County and, because of the college education I had acquired, I almost became a Republican. However, before I could completely backslide, my friend Elmer Schaefer, over here—Walter Schaefer's brother—who had gone to law school with me, began to work on me. He saw I was getting a little weak and he induced me to rejoin and affiliate myself with the Democratic party. And so, because I had a good evangelist working on me, I stuck with the Democratic party.

Of course, I became active in DuPage County. I will be frank about it. At first I talked around amongst the Republicans about doing some work—there was no Democratic party out there—but the Republicans didn't need me. Well, after I became converted to the Democratic party again, or was saved again, so to speak, I proceeded to organize the Democratic party out there and to make it tough for the Republicans. The result was that we finally had the framework of a party. Later, with the aid of the late Governor Henry Horner and a few other good Democrats, I landed in the legislature and kept working along and served my term there. Then I got out of politics and came back and practiced law.

And then I gambled. I saw a man—Paul Douglas—who looked as though he might be elected to the United States Senate. I backed him and as a result I had his support. My political friendship with my good friend Scott Lucas, in the meantime, had grown bit by bit and Scott was not mad at me.

Since we are talking confidentially I will be perfectly frank with you folks in admitting that I tried to obtain this appointment seven years ago and learned then that it requires not one but two senators. At that time I was out of politics and they did not need me. Therefore, I decided that this time if I wanted that appointment I had better get back into politics—which I did. When I learned, as I soon did, that everyone shoots at the top man—that he is everyone's target—I went to each of the senators and said "Listen here, if you are going to back me, for heaven's sake don't make me number one. Be sure to back me and get me on the list but don't make me number one."

As it turned out that proved to be pretty good strategy because everybody else was shot off and, no use lying about it, I helped to shoot them off. The result of it was I landed on top. (Laughter.) I have the job now and I am going to stick.

4.   *"I believe that the Senators are entitled to know how you feel . . ."*

THE BRENNAN HEARINGS

SENATOR JOSEPH MC CARTHY of Wisconsin. . . . On the basis of that part of his record that I am familiar with, I believe that Justice Brennan has demonstrated an underlying hostility to congressional attempts to expose the Communist conspiracy.

I can only conclude that his decisions on the Supreme Court are likely to harm our efforts to fight communism.

I shall, therefore, vote against his confirmation unless he is able to persuade me today that I am not in possession of the true facts with respect to his views.

I shall want to know if it is true that Justice Brennan, in his public speeches, has referred to congressional investigations of communism, for example, as "Salem witch hunts," and "inquisitions," and has accused congressional investigating committees of "barbarism."

I have evidence that he has done so. . . .

I would like to ask Mr. Brennan a few questions if I may. . . . Do you approve of congressional investigations and exposure of the Communist conspiracy set up?

Mr. BRENNAN. Not only do I approve, Senator, but personally I cannot think of a more vital function of the Congress than the investigatory function of its committees, and I can't think of a more important or vital objective of any committee investigation than that of rooting out subversives in Government.

Senator McCARTHY. You, of course, I assume, will agree with me—

Hearings before the Committee on the Judiciary, U.S. Senate, on the Nomination of William J. Brennan to be an Associate Justice of the U.S. Supreme Court, 85th Congress, 1st Session, pp. 5, 17–22, 34.

and a number of the members of the committee—that communism is not merely a political way of life, it is a conspiracy designed to overthrow the United States Government.

Mr. BRENNAN. Will you forgive me an embarrassment, Senator. You appreciate that I am a sitting Justice of the Court. There are presently pending before the Court some cases in which I believe will have to be decided the question what is communism, at least in the frame of reference in which those particular cases have come before the Court.

I know, too, that you appreciate that having taken an oath of office it is my obligation not to discuss any of those pending matters. With that qualification, whether under the label communism or any other label, any conspiracy to overthrow the Government of the United States is a conspiracy that I not only would do anything appropriate to aid suppressing, but a conspiracy which, of course, like every American, I abhor.

Senator McCARTHY. Mr. Brennan, I don't want to press you unnecessarily, but the question was simple. You have not been confirmed yet as a member of the Supreme Court. There will come before that Court a number of questions involving the all-important issue of whether or not communism is merely a political party or whether it represents a conspiracy to overthrow this Government.

I believe that the Senators are entitled to know how you feel about that and you won't be prejudicing then any cases by answering that question.

Mr. BRENNAN. Well, let me answer it, try to answer it, this way, Senator. Of course, my nomination is now before the Senate for consideration, nevertheless since October 16 I have in fact been sitting as a member of the Court. The oath I took, I took as unreservedly as I know you took your own, and as I know every Senator took his. And I know, too, that your oath imposes upon you the obligation to ask just such questions as these.

But I am in the position of having an oath of my own by which I have to guide my conduct and that oath obligates me not to discuss any matter presently pending before the Court. . . .

Senator McCARTHY. Mr. Brennan, we are asked to either vote to confirm or reject you. One of the things I have maintained is that you have adopted the gobbledegook that communism is merely a political party, is not a conspiracy.

The Supreme Court has held that it is a conspiracy to overthrow the Government of this country. I am merely asking you a very simple question.

It doesn't relate to any lawsuit pending before the Supreme Court. Let me repeat it.

Do you consider communism merely as a political party or do you consider it as a conspiracy to overthrow this country?

Mr. BRENNAN. I can only answer, Senator, that believe me there are cases now pending in which the contention is made, at least in the frame of reference in which the case comes to the Court, that the definitions which have been given by the Congress to communism do not fit the particular circumstances. . . .

Senator McCARTHY. You know that the Congress has defined communism as a conspiracy. You are aware of that, aren't you?

Mr. BRENNAN. I know the Congress has enacted a definition, yes, sir.

Senator McCARTHY. And I think it is important before we vote on your confirmation that we know whether you agree with that?

Mr. BRENNAN. You see, Senator, that is my difficulty, that I can't very well say more to you than that there are contending positions taken in given cases before us. . . .

Senator McCARTHY. . . . This is all important, I would like to know whether or not the young man who is proposed for the Supreme Court feels that communism is a conspiracy or merely a political party. Now just so you won't be in the dark about my reason for asking that, the Daily Worker, all of the Communist-lip papers, and the Communist witnesses who have appeared before my committee, I assume the same is true of Senator Eastland's committee, have taken the position that it is merely a political party. I want to know whether you agree with that. That will affect your decision. It will affect my decision on how to vote on your confirmation. I hope it will affect the decision of other Senators.

Mr. BRENNAN. Senator, believe me I appreciate that what to one man is the path of duty may to another man be the path of folly, but

I simply cannot venture any comment whatever that touches upon any matter pending before the Court.

Senator McCarthy. Mr. Brennan, I am not asking you to touch upon anything pending before the Court. I am asking you the general question:

Do you consider communism merely as a political party or do you consider it as a conspiracy to overthrow this country? . . .

Mr. Brennan. Senator, I cannot answer, I am sorry to say, beyond what I have. . . .

Senator O'Mahoney. Just let me clarify this. The Senator from Wisconsin has made it perfectly clear, as I understand it, that he is not asking the Justice to make any statement with respect to a pending case. Therefore, the oath of office that the Justice may have taken is not involved.

Senator McCarthy. Right.

Senator O'Mahoney. There is now pending before the Senate a resolution, sent here by the executive branch of the Government, by the President of the United States, who appeared before us in a joint session of Congress in which he asked Congress to pass a resolution authorizing him to employ the Armed Forces of the United States in the defense of any nation in the Middle East, undescribed though the Middle East was in the resolution, at the request of any nation there, which was being attacked by international communism.

Now the question I think that is in the mind of the Senator from Wisconsin is the question which I think has already been settled and on which you must have clear views. Do you believe that international communism is a conspiracy against the United States as well as against all other free nations?

Mr. Brennan. Yes, that question I answer definitely and affirmatively. I did not understand that was the question the Senator was asking me. . . .

Senator Jenner. May I interrupt right there? Does the Senator from Wyoming and does the Senator from Wisconsin draw a distinction between international communism and communism?

Senator O'Mahoney. I don't.

Senator McCarthy. I don't draw a distinction.

Senator JENNER. I would like to know Mr. Justice Brennan's answer to that. Do you draw a distinction between international communism and communism?

Mr. BRENNAN. Let me put it this way, Senator. This is the difficulty. There are cases where, as I recall it, the particular issue is whether membership, what is membership, and whether if there is membership, does that come within the purview of the congressional statutes aimed at the conspiracy? I can't necessarily comment on those aspects because they are actual issues before the Court under the congressional legislation.

Senator JENNER. That is why it raises a question in my mind. In other words, if we have a Communist Party in the United States and the congressional committee has ascertained that it is hooked up with international communism, yet the domestic party might contend they are just national Communists, would that influence your thinking?

Mr. BRENNAN. Nothing would influence my thinking. All I am trying to get across is that I do have an obligation not to discuss any issues that are touched upon in cases before the Court.

Senator JENNER. I think in the question that Senator O'Mahoney placed—read the question, will you, please, Mr. Reporter, and the answer?

(Question and answer read.)

Senator JENNER. Delete the word "international" and just leave in the word "communism," what would be your answer?

Mr. BRENNAN. Of course, I accept the findings as they have been made by the Congress. The only thing I am trying to do, Senator, is to make certain that nothing I say touches upon the actual issues before us growing out of that legislation as applied in particular cases. . . .

Senator JENNER. My question, Mr. Chairman, was not based on cases pending. My question was in a similar vein.

In view of that would you answer the question?

Mr. BRENNAN. The answer is "Yes." I'm sorry to have confused the gentlemen.

The CHAIRMAN. Senator McCarthy, you may proceed.

Senator MCCARTHY. Let's see if we finally have the answer to this, Mr. Justice. You do agree that communism, striking the word "international" from it, communism does constitute a conspiracy against the United States—I am not talking about any case pending.

Mr. BRENNAN. Yes.

Senator McCARTHY. Thank you. . . .

Senator O'MAHONEY. Mr. Chairman, let me address the question to the nominee, Associate Justice Brennan. I read it again from the statement filed with this committee under date of February 26, 1957, by Mr. Charles Smith.

> You are bound by your religion to follow the pronouncements of the Pope on all matters of faith and morals. There may be some controversies which involve matters of faith and morals and also matters of law and justice. But in matters of law and justice, you are bound by your oath to follow not papal decrees and doctrines, but the laws and precedents of this Nation. If you should be faced with such a mixed issue, would you be able to follow the requirements of your oath or would you be bound by your religious obligations?

Mr. BRENNAN. Senator, I think the oath that I took is the same one that you and all of the Congress, every member of the executive department up and down all levels of government take to support the Constitution and laws of the United States. I took that oath just as unreservedly as I know you did, and every member and everyone else of our faith in whatever office elected or appointive he may hold. And I say not that I recognize that there is any obligation superior to that, rather that there isn't any obligation of our faith superior to that. And my answer to the question is categorically that in everything I have ever done, in every office I have held in my life or that I shall ever do in the future, what shall control me is the oath that I took to support the Constitution and laws of the United States and so act upon the cases that come before me for decision that it is that oath and that alone which governs. . . .

5.   *". . . the sense of the Senate . . ."*

THE PROBLEM OF RECESS APPOINTMENTS

MR. HART. . . . Mr. President, I believe that the practice of making interim appointments to the High Bench and the appointee taking his place on the Court is one which should cease. . . . I felt a great handicap in properly interrogating the nominee when the nominee is a Justice of the Court and has been sitting for some 6 months. I am reasonably sure that it is embarrassing and difficult for a nominee under such circumstances to have to come before the Senate committee and be subjected to questions which may in some manner bear on cases before the Court.

It is my considered opinion that the Senate might well inform the President that it is the sense of this body that the practice of making such interim appointments—a practice which had not been followed for more than 52 years before the interim appointment of Chief Justice Warren—is seriously hampering the Senate in fully performing its constitutional duties. I suggest further that it is not in the best interest of the Supreme Court, the nominee who may be involved and, conceivably, litigants before the Court during such interim period.

It should be remembered that it is for the benefit of litigants, not for the comfort of the Senate or of the appointee, that appointments to the Federal Court are for a lifetime. It is done to assure the judge's complete independence of mind. I would suggest that something less than that is the case when the judge is sitting in the Court and must come before a Senate committee where hearings are held.

. . . I desire to make it clear that I do not feel . . . that the Senate should withhold its advice and consent from this nominee. Actually I believe a better case might be made that the Senate—faced with an interim appointee—should have moved with more speed to bring the matter to an early decision, while at the same time taking some positive action to indicate its views to the President that extreme restraint be practiced in making further interim appointments.

Fifteen Justices of the Supreme Court have been given recess ap-

105 *Congressional Record* 7467 (1959).

pointments and were subsequently confirmed by the Senate. But for more than 100 years before the appointment in 1953 of Chief Justice Warren, no recess appointee to the Supreme Court took his seat in advance of Senate confirmation. The only instances previous to 1953 where an interim appointee took his seat in advance of confirmation were Justice Rutledge in 1795, and Justice Curtis, in 1851. In this administration we have seen interim appointees taking seats on the bench and participating in decisions prior to Senate confirmation in the instances of Chief Justice Warren, Justice Brennan, in 1956, and now Justice Stewart, appointed October 14, 1958, taking his seat the same day, and now awaiting confirmation. . . .

I for one advise the present administration that I feel interim appointments to the Court are most unfortunate and should be avoided except in the most extreme cases. Certainly the participation of such an appointee in Court work prior to Senate confirmation is unwise. I realize that this may cause difficulties during the interim months when the Court is under strength, particularly at a time when the Court may be evenly divided on many crucial cases. However, it is my feeling that in such situations the Senate of the United States would understand the need for all due speed, and would be far better able to perform its constitutional responsibilities in giving its advice and consent.

For myself, I believe Justice Potter Stewart will make an outstanding Justice. I believe he answered many difficult questions put to him during the hearings with honesty and with a show of most substantial ability. His record as a judge of the Sixth Circuit Court of Appeals, which circuit includes Michigan, was outstanding. I expect to vote for the confirmation of his nomination, and welcome the opportunity to do so.

Mr. DIRKSEN. I wish to make one comment on the observations of the distinguished Senator from Michigan. The Constitution does not make it mandatory on the President to make interim or recess appointments. It says that the President has the power to do so. Consequently, he may do so or not, as he may delay the matter or not, as he chooses. Many nominations have become practical considerations.

One other matter comes sharply to mind. I believe it was at the end of the first session of the 85th Congress that the name of a judge was pending before the Committee on the Judiciary when a circumstance came to the attention of one member of the committee who felt that we ought to bring the nominee before us for further testimony. It was the last week of the session. Having concluded the testimony—and it was a little on the dramatic side—the Senator in question suggested that the nomination go over for a week. But by going over for a week, the Senate adjourned, and that was the end of the matter. So the nomination automatically had to be a recess appointment, if it was to be effective at all.

But there are problems of judicial congestion today. If the Senate is not in session, and there is a hiatus period, I doubt very much whether it is wise to incur a long delay and thus burden the other members of the court, whether it be a court of district judges or appellate judges, or members of the Supreme Court. . . .

Mr. HART. I was not unmindful of those considerations. Still, for more than 100 years the Nation and its judicial establishment survived and avoided a situation which I think we all agree should be avoided if it is at all possible to do so.

In the absence of a showing of urgency, I think it is very desirable that an appointee not sit until after the Senate, through its committee, has had an opportunity to review his qualifications to sit on the Supreme Court.

SENATE RESOLUTION 334
86th Congress, 2d Session

Introduced by Mr. Hart, June 16, 1960, and referred to the Committee on the Judiciary; Reported August 22, 1960; Considered, Amended, and Passed, August 29, 1960. . . .

Whereas one of the solemn constitutional tasks enjoined upon the Senate is to give or withhold its advice and consent with respect to nominations made to the Supreme Court of the United States, doing so, if possible, in an atmosphere free from pressures inimical to due deliberations; and

Whereas the nomination of a person to the office of Justice of the Supreme Court should be considered only in the light of the qualifications the person brings to the threshold of the office; and

Whereas Presidents of the United States have from time to time made
    recess appointments to the Supreme Court, which actions were
    unquestionably taken in good faith and with a desire to promote
    the public interest, but without a full appreciation of the dif-
    ficulties thereby caused the Members of this body; and
Whereas there is inevitably public speculation on the independence of
    a Justice serving by recess appointment who sits in judgment
    upon cases prior to his confirmation by this body, which specula-
    tions, however ill founded, is distressing to the Court, to the
    Justice, to the litigants, and to the Senate of the United States:
    Now, therefore, be it

Resolved, That it is the sense of the Senate that the making of recess appointments to the Supreme Court of the United States may not
be wholly consistent with the best interests of the Supreme Court, the
nominee who may be involved, the litigants before the Court, nor indeed the people of the United States, and that such appointments,
therefore, should not be made except under unusual circumstances and
for the purpose of preventing or ending a demonstrable breakdown
in the administration of the Court's business.

6.
*"There is no means of insuring that judges will carry
out the policies of the people except partisan choice of
judges . . ."*

POLITICS, THE BAR, AND THE SELECTION OF JUDGES

*Francis D. Wormuth and S. Grover Rich, Jr.**

    . . . TWO PROPOSALS for the selection of judges have at-
tracted attention in Utah recently: the so-called Missouri plan, which
was defeated by a gubernatorial veto in 1949, and nonpartisan election, which was enacted by the legislature in 1951. Both plans are

3 *Utah Law Review* 459 (1953). Copyright 1953, University of Utah. Reprinted
with permission.
* Professors of Political Science, University of Utah.

based on the assumption that the judicial function is nonpolitical, and that the selection of judges should also be nonpolitical; they therefore undertake to remove the influence of parties and political considerations in the choice of judges. The political scientist's criticism of both plans rests on his conviction that the judicial function is necessarily political, and that parties are essential to democratic government. If this is true, judges should be chosen in a partisan manner. The traditional methods of executive appointment and partisan election meet this test; the issue between these two is not canvassed here.

The belief that the selection of judges should be nonpolitical is comparatively recent. Of course the framers of the federal Constitution expected all federal offices to be filled on a nonpartisan basis; but as soon as factions and parties developed, partisan appointment to the judiciary became the rule. Presidents Washington and Adams appointed only Federalists to the Supreme Court; Presidents Jefferson, Madison, and Monroe appointed only Democratic-Republicans. Of all the judges who have adorned the Supreme Court, only eight did not belong to the same party as the President who appointed them. It is notorious that gubernatorial appointments have likewise been partisan. . . .

. . . Under the attacks of the "muckrakers," political parties came into disrepute in the early nineteen hundreds. Together with the initiative, the referendum, and the direct primary, nonpartisanship was intended to break the grip of corrupt political machines. In addition, nonpartisan election derived support from the high prestige enjoyed by business as compared with politics. There was a demand that government be taken out of the hands of partisan politicians and placed "on a sound business basis." This kind of argument seemed especially applicable to the judiciary. On the theory that judges were neutral referees rather than political officers, several states adopted nonpartisan election for judgeships. The movement has now lost much of its earlier fascination, and nonpartisan balloting has been abandoned in several areas. Nevertheless, now and again it is adopted in a new community, and nearly half of the nation's voters are still called upon to make some of their electoral choices from nonpartisan ballots. . . .

If the judiciary administers a supernal code to which it has infallible access, its work is in no way partisan, and the judges should not be chosen through partisan channels. Divine appointment would then be the proper method of recruitment. But if constitutions and statutes are subject to alternative constructions, if the political and social views of the judges determine their decisions—if judges, after all, are human—they are policy-forming officers.

If it is necessary to call a witness on this question, let him be a man of the conservative temper of William Howard Taft: "Some one has said, 'Let me make the ballads of the country, and I care not who makes the laws.' One might also say, paraphrasing this, 'Let any one make the laws of the country, if I can construe them.'" Learned Hand made the same point when he said that "[T]he words a judge must construe are empty vessels into which he can pour nearly anything he will."

Inescapably, then, judges are vested with political powers. In Holmes' words, "Judges do, and must, legislate." And in so doing, it may be added, they inevitably are influenced by their personal views. Mr. Justice Brandeis, in the words of his biographer, was "like his conservative colleagues . . . inclined to translate his economic and social views into the constitution." But can any judge do otherwise? No amount of mumbo-jumbo about "objectivity" can conceal the facts. . . .

Inevitably judges formulate public policy. It is a commonplace of political science that policy-forming officers should be in sympathy with the official formulators of policy. Judges should be lions, said Francis Bacon, but lions under the throne. In a democracy they should execute the policies of the people. This is a simple condition of orderly and efficient government. There is no practical means by which the people can formulate policy in a democracy except through the machinery of partisan politics. There is no means of insuring that judges will carry out the policies of the people except partisan choice of judges—whether by executive appointment or by popular election.

So little are these matters understood that the very word "partisan" has a bad odor. It connotes jobbery and corruption, while the word "nonpartisan" is equated with "virtue." But jobbery and corruption are by no means synonymous with a party system. They can occur under any governmental form. On the other hand, practical experience has shown that democracy and a party system are synonymous.

Only through a party system can issues be formulated and presented to the voters; only through a party system can the majority of the voters choose policy-forming officers committed to executing the program they have indorsed. It is late in the day to insist that judges stand above politics, that their decisions are dictated by abstract rules, that their views on public issues play no part. Their views on public issues are bound to play a part.

The significant question, then, is whether the judges are to implement the views indorsed by a majority of the voters. If a court is able to frustrate the popular desire for long, "The people will," as Abraham Lincoln said, "have ceased to be their own rulers, having . . . resigned their government into the hands of that eminent tribunal." One suspects that this is a covert purpose of at least some of those who desire nonpartisan selection of judges.

From what has been said it should be clear that the political choice of judges should not be confused with the sale of public office; that the political qualities of the good judge are not partisan qualities of the ward boss; that judges should be chosen not merely because their views on policy agree with those of the majority of the voters but for their competence, their training, and their judicial temperament. The political qualifications of a judge are no substitute for the nonpolitical qualifications. But the political qualifications equally with the others must be met; they are indispensable in a democracy. Neither is it intended to suggest that the popular will should prevail over constitutional prohibitions by any other means than the orderly process of constitutional amendment. This is an entirely distinct issue. Distortions of constitutions can be carried out as effectively by "nonpartisan" judges—judges who represent minority views—as by partisan judges who represent majority views. The history of judicial interpretation of the Fourteenth Amendment is too well known to require rehearsal here. Nor is it intended to suggest that the constitutional ideals of the separation of powers and the independence of the judiciary should be ignored. Certainly judges should no more improvise rules to promote than to thwart the popular will. All that is intended is to argue that judges should reflect settled public opinion; that is, they should have enough sympathy with popular programs to prevent them from sabotaging such programs. Anyone who is familiar with the tortuous course of interpretation of constitutional provisions and social legislation in the period 1890–1937 will agree that sabotage is not too strong a word to describe what judges entertaining minority views have done in the past.

The sponsors of the Missouri plan are at least dimly aware of these objections. They argue that democracy is retained and even strengthened under the Missouri plan because the voters pass on the judges' records at periodic intervals. This, of course, is an empty pretense. Conceivably a voter might make a choice between two candidates for a judgeship on some other basis than party or caprice. It is not conceivable, however, that he can discharge the duty which the Missouri plan places on him. He cannot canvass the judge's decisions—at the trial level, these are not even reported—over a period of 6 or 12 years and determine whether the cases were rightly decided. If he could, judicial ability would be so widely distributed that there would be no need for a Missouri plan. The plebiscite in which the voters are given a choice between a definite proposal ("Should X be retained as judge?"), and an unnamed alternative they cannot control, is the most familiar window-dressing of despotism. "Shall Napoleon be First Consul of the French?" "Shall Louis Napoleon be Emperor of the French?" All such questions cannot but receive huge affirmative votes. . . . Under the Missouri plan the participation of the voters in the strictest sense is meaningless. The choice of the governor in appointment is limited to the three names proposed to him by the commission. Complete power over the judiciary rests in the hands of this anonymous and politically irresponsible group of seven men, three of whom—and surely the most influential three—are directly chosen by the state bar association. The hand is the hand of Esau, but the voice is the voice of Jacob. . . .

It cannot be said that nonpartisan elections in which two or more candidates are named fulfill the purposes of democracy much more satisfactorily than the Missouri plan. The voter is deprived of the guidance—often pitifully inadequate, to be sure—as to the views of the candidate which a party designation affords. He votes on the basis of vague recollections of names he has seen in the newspapers, unless the incumbent has the advantage of being so designated, or of appearing first on the ballot, in which case the incumbent is practically assured of re-election.

Popular election of judges has weaknesses that have been expounded so often that they need no repetition here. Certainly making elections nonpartisan has not done away with these weaknesses. . . . The average voter—vaguely aware of the role money plays in elections —naively believes that while political parties are under obligation to those who foot their bills, the nonpartisan candidate is somehow "independent." Actually, nonpartisanship only insures that the public remain unaware of the candidate's supporters and the commitments he makes. Unable to obtain financial support from the established parties, the nonpartisan judicial candidate is compelled to solicit funds from among fellow members of the bar, thereby incurring obligations to the very persons who will appear before his court if he is elected. . . .

Many of these evils were apparent at the first institution of nonpartisan election of judges. In 1914, William Howard Taft found nonpartisan election to be decidedly inferior to partisan election. Later experience confirmed his judgment. Raymond Moley, in his report of the Seabury investigation of the New York City magistrates' courts in 1930–31, summarized the effect of nonpartisan election:

> . . . More recent attempts to keep out party politics by a nonpartisan ballot have aroused the dogs of another kind of politics. Appeal to the people by a judge of anything except a very high court means appeal to race, religion, and other political irrelevancies. It means cheap stunts for gaining publicity and slavery to the newsgathering exigencies of the city desk. This may be called the politics of nonpartisanship. With every judge his own political leader, his ear must be to the ground constantly, instead of, as under the old system, at those fortunately infrequent moments when the oracular voice of the boss rumbled a veiled request or an outspoken order. . . .

Parties are indispensable to democracy. But nonpartisan elections enfeeble the party system. (This is, of course, precisely what its originators intended.) Removing party labels from the ballots has weakened the incentive to engage in party activities, making it more difficult for party organizations to recruit funds and new members. Particularly at the local level, which is a vital level, party organization is likely to disappear. Further, nonpartisan election interferes with the recruitment of candidates for partisan positions. . . . It has likewise proved to be true that a man who has identified himself as a partisan is unlikely to become a candidate for nonpartisan office. The amount of talent available for both classes of offices has been drastically reduced.

Certainly discretionary executive appointment and partisan election of judges have their weaknesses. But they are not fatal weaknesses; nor do the newer methods overcome these weaknesses. The evils of election are not removed by making elections nonpartisan; the evils of appointment are hardly avoided by entrusting the power of appointment to an irresponsible committee. It is not even true that these methods accomplish their announced objective of taking "politics" out of the choice of judges. The determination of policy *is* politics. Whenever men are to be selected for positions which involve the determination of public policy, there will always be persons and groups interested in the selection of certain candidates and the defeat of others. Nonpartisan choice does not mean that a policy-forming position has suddenly become politically neutral. It merely means that the people are deprived of the only instrument—admittedly a weak and erratic instrument—for insuring that policy determination responds to majority sentiment. This instrument is political parties.

. . . The traditional methods of judicial selection no doubt have their faults, but these remedies are worse than the disease.

7.   *"[A Supreme Court Justice must have] five years of judicial service."*

S. 1184, 85TH CONGRESS, 1ST SESSION

FEBRUARY 14, 1957: Mr. Talmadge introduced the following bill; which was read twice and referred to the Committee on the Judiciary.*

Be it enacted by the Senate and House of Representatives of the United States of America in Congress assembled, That section 1 of title 28, United States Code, is amended by adding at the end thereof the following new paragraph:

* This bill, and more than a dozen similar measures introduced in the Eighty-Fifth Congress, died in committee. [Eds.]

"No person shall be appointed after the date of enactment of this paragraph to the office of Chief Justice of the United States or to the office of Associate Justice of the Supreme Court unless, at the time of his appointment, he has had at least five years of judicial service. As used in this paragraph 'judicial service' means service as an Associate Justice of the Supreme Court, a judge of a court of appeals or district court of the United States, or judge of the highest court of a State." . . .

8.   *"Greatness in the law is not a standardized quality . . ."*

THE SUPREME COURT IN THE MIRROR OF JUSTICES   *Felix Frankfurter*

. . . DURING THE one hundred and sixty-seven years since the day appointed for its first session, ninety Justices have sat on the Supreme Court. The number of men over so long a period would seem to be sufficient to afford some light on the kind of experience or qualifications that may be deemed appropriate for service on the Court. Indeed, the actualities about the men who were appointed to the Court may well be wiser guides than abstract notions about the kind of men who should be named. Of the ninety Justices I shall consider seventy-five, omitting contemporary and relatively recent occupants of the Court. . . . I refer to the suggestion, indeed the assumption that, since the Supreme Court is the highest judicial tribunal, prior "judicial service" is not only a desirable, but an indispensable, qualification.

What is the teaching of history on this? Of the seventy-five Justices, twenty-eight had not a day's prior judicial service. Seven more had sat on some bench from a few months to not more than two years. Nine sat six years or less. Measures have been proposed that would require "judicial service" of not less than five years in a lower federal court or as a member of the highest court of a State; some bills demand ten years of such service. A five-year requirement would have ruled out at least thirty-five of the seventy-five judges (in fact more, because several of the Justices who had had judicial experience did

105 *University of Pennsylvania Law Review* 781 (1957). Copyright 1957 University of Pennsylvania. Reprinted with permission.

not sit on a federal bench or on the highest court of a State), and the ten-year requirement would have barred certainly forty-five of our seventy-five Justices.

Who were these Justices who came on the Supreme Court without any "judicial service," without even the judicial experience of an Iredell, who at the age of twenty-six sat on the Superior Court of his State, North Carolina, only long enough—six months—to resign. They begin with . . . James Wilson and include Bushrod Washington, Marshall, Story, Taney, Curtis, Campbell, Miller, Chase, Bradley, Waite, Fuller, Moody, Hughes, Brandeis, Stone and Roberts. Of the twelve Chief Justices within our period, five had not had any judicial experience at the time of their appointment as Chief Justice and two more had had none when they first came on the Court.

Apart from the significance of a Chief Justice as the administrative head of the Court what of the quality of judicial service of the men who came on the Court totally devoid of judicial experience? Assessment of distinction in the realm of the mind and spirit cannot exclude subjective factors. Yet it is as true of judges as of poets or philosophers that whatever may be the fluctuations in what is called the verdict of history, varying and conflicting views finally come to rest and there arises a consensus of informed judgment. It would indeed be a surprising judgment that would exclude Marshall, William Johnson, Story, Taney, Miller, Field, Bradley, White (despite his question-begging verbosities), Holmes, Hughes, Brandeis and Cardozo in the roster of distinction among our seventy-five. I myself would add Curtis, Campbell, Matthews and Moody. (Some might prefer the first Harlan or Brewer or Brown.) Of the first twelve, five had had judicial experience and seven none before coming on the Court; of the others only Matthews can be counted a judge, for a brief period, before he came to Washington. Of the sixteen Justices whom I deem pre-eminent, only six came to the Court with previous judicial experience, however limited. It would require discernment more than daring, it would demand complete indifference to the elusive and intractable factors in tracking down causes, in short, it would be capricious, to attribute acknowledged greatness in the Court's history either to the fact that a Justice had had judicial experience or that he had been without it.

Greatness in the law is not a standardized quality, nor are the elements that combine to attain it. To speak only of Justices near enough to one's own time, greatness may manifest itself through the power of penetrating analysis exerted by a trenchant mind, as in the case of Bradley; it may be due to persistence in a point of view forcefully expressed over a long judicial stretch, as shown by Field; it may derive from a coherent judicial philosophy, expressed with pungency and brilliance, reinforced by the *Zeitgeist*, which in good part was itself a reflection of that philosophy, as was true of Holmes; it may be achieved by the resourceful deployment of vast experience and an originating mind, as illustrated by Brandeis; it may result from the influence of a singularly endearing personality in the service of sweet reason, as Cardozo proves; it may come through the kind of vigor that exerts moral authority over others, as embodied in Hughes.

The roll-call of pre-eminent members of the Supreme Court who had had no judicial experience in itself establishes, one would suppose, that judicial experience is not a prerequisite for that Court. It would be hard to gainsay that this galaxy outshines even the distinguished group that came to the Court with prior experience on state courts, though these judges included the great names of Holmes and Cardozo. It has been suggested that the appearance on the Court of Marshall, Story, Taney, Curtis, Campbell, Miller, Bradley, Hughes and Brandeis, all without prior judicial experience, is "a curious accident." But this accident has been thrown up by history over a period of one hundred and fifty years. . . .

. . . Apart from meaning that a man had sat on some court for some time, "judicial service" tells nothing that is relevant about the qualifications for the functions exercised by the Supreme Court. While it seems to carry meaning, it misleads. . . . The Supreme Court is a very special kind of court. "Judicial service" as such has no significant relation to the kinds of litigation that come before the Supreme Court, to the types of issues they raise, to qualities that these actualities require for wise decision.

To begin with, one must consider the differences in the staple business of different courts and the different experiences to which different judicial business gives rise, and the bearing of different experiences so generated on the demands of the business of the Supreme

Court. Thus, there is a vital difference, so far as substantive training is afforded, between the experience gained on state courts and on the lower federal courts. There are the so-called federal specialties whose importance for the Supreme Court has copiously receded since the Evarts Act of 1891, but is still relevant to its work. One would suppose that if prior judicial experience would especially commend itself for Supreme Court appointments, the federal courts would furnish most materials for promotion. History falsifies such expectation. Of the forty-seven Justices who had had some kind of prior judicial experience, no matter how short, fifteen came from the federal courts—Trimble, Barbour, Daniel, Woods, Blatchford, Brewer, Brown, Howell E. Jackson, McKenna, Day, Lurton, Taft, Sanford, Van Devanter and John H. Clarke—whereas thirty-two had only experience on state courts.

How meagerly the experience on a state court, even if of long duration, prepares one for work on the Supreme Court is strikingly borne out by the testimony of the two Justices who are indubitably the two most outstanding of those who came to the Supreme Court from state courts. After having spent twenty years on the Supreme Judicial Court of Massachusetts, part of it as Chief Justice, in the course of which he wrote more than a thousand opinions on every conceivable subject, Mr. Justice Holmes found himself not at all at home on coming to the Supreme Court. Listen to what he wrote to his friend Pollock after a month in his new judicial habitat:

> Yes—here I am—and more absorbed, interested and impressed than ever I had dreamed I might be. The work of the past seems a finished book—locked up far away, and a new and solemn volume opens. The variety and novelty to me of the questions, the remote spaces from which they come, the amount of work they require, all help the effect. . . .

Nor did Cardozo, after eighteen years on the New York Court of Appeals, five of them as Chief Judge, in the course of which he gained the acclaim of the whole common-law world, find that his transplantation from Albany to Washington was a natural step in judicial progression. On more than one occasion he complained to friends (sometimes as bitterly as that gentle soul could) that he should not have been taken from judicial labors with which he was familiar and which were congenial to him, to types of controversies to which his past experience bore little relation and to which, though these were the main concern of the Supreme Court, he was not especially drawn. . . .

But, it may be suggested, if experience on a state court does not adequately prepare even the greatest of judges for the problems that are the main and certainly the most important business of the Supreme Court, judicial experience intrinsically fosters certain habits of mind and attitudes, serves to train the faculties of detachment, begets habits of aloofness from daily influences, in short, educates and reinforces those moral qualities—disinterestedness and deep humility—which are indeed preconditions for the wise exercise of the judicial function on the Supreme Bench. Unhappily, history again disappoints such expectation. What is more inimical for good work on the Court than for a Justice to cherish political, and more particularly Presidential, ambition? . . . Sad and strange as it may be, the most numerous and in many ways the worst offenders in this regard have been men who came to the Court from state courts, in some instances with long service on such courts. Their temperamental partisanship and ambition were stronger than the disciplining sway supposedly exercised by the judiciary. To be sure, there have been instances of such political ambition by those who came on the Court without judicial experience. Salmon P. Chase, of course, is a conspicuous example. But I think it is fair to say that fewer Justices who had had no prior judicial experience dallied with political ambition while on the Court than those who came there with it. And it deserves to be noted that the most vigorous, indeed aggressive hostility to availability of a member of the Court for a Presidential nomination came from one who had no prior judicial experience, Chief Justice Waite. . . .

. . . What of the lower courts as a training ground for the Supreme Bench? The fact is that not one so trained emerges over a century and a half among the few towering figures of the Court. Oblivion has overtaken almost all of them. Probably the most intellectually powerful of the lot, Mr. Justice Brewer, does not owe the weight of the strength that he exerted on the Court to his five years on the circuit court after his long service on Kansas courts. Surely it is safe to attribute it to the native endowment that the famous Field strain gave him. Mr. Justice Van Devanter was undoubtedly a very influential member of the so-called Taft Court. But he was that essentially on the procedural aspect of the Court's business and by virtue of the extent to which Chief Justice Taft leaned on him. . . .

One is not unappreciative of Chief Justice Taft by saying that his significance in the Court's history is not that of an intellectual leader but as the effective force in modernizing the federal judiciary and in promoting jurisdictional changes to enable the Court to be capable of discharging its role in our federal scheme. Moreover, it was not Taft's eight years of service on the Sixth Circuit, highly esteemed as it was, that led President Harding to make him Chief Justice White's successor after Taft's twenty years of separation from active concern with law. . . .

Not only is the framework within which the judicial process of the Supreme Court operates drastically different from the jurisdictional and procedural concern of other courts but the cases that now come before the Court, and will increasingly in the future, present issues that make irrelevant considerations in the choice of Justices that at former periods had pertinence. Mastery of the federal specialties by some members of the Court was an obvious need of the Court in days when a substantial part of the Court's business related to such specialties. Thus, when maritime and patent cases appeared frequently enough on the Court's docket, it was highly desirable to have a judge so experienced in these fields as was Judge Blatchford when he was named to the Court. . . . And since the business that came to the Court in times past reflected to no small degree sectionally different economic interests, geographic considerations had their relevance. . . . All this has changed. Not only in the course of a hundred years but in the course of fifty years. Today there is a totally different flow of business to the Court from what it was a hundred years ago; it is predominantly different from what it was fifty years ago. . . .

. . . Whereas a hundred years ago, private common-law litigation represented the major part of the Court's business, and fifty years ago, constitutional cases apart, public and private law business was equally divided, today private litigation has become virtually negligible. Constitutional law and cases with constitutional undertones are of course still very important, with almost one-fourth of the cases in which written opinions were filed involving such questions. Review of administrative action, mainly reflecting enforcement of federal regulatory statutes, constitutes the largest category of the Court's work, comprising one-third of the total cases decided on the merits. The remaining significant categories of litigation—federal criminal law, federal jurisdiction, immigration and nationality law, federal taxation—all involve largely public law questions.

The Court was of course from the beginning the interpreter of the Constitution and thereby, for all practical purposes, the adjuster of governmental powers in our complicated federal system. But the summary of the contemporaneous business before the Court that is reflected in written opinions statistically establishes these constitutional adjudications and kindred public law issues as constituting almost the whole of Supreme Court litigation. It is essentially accurate to say that the Court's preoccupation today is with the application of rather fundamental aspirations and what Judge Learned Hand calls "moods," embodied in provisions like the due process clauses, which were designed not to be precise and positive directions for rules of action. The judicial process of applying them involves a judgment on the process of government. The Court sits in judgment, that is, on the views of the direct representatives of the people in meeting the needs of society, on the views of Presidents and Governors, and by their construction of the will of legislatures the Court breathes life, feeble or strong, into the inert pages of the Constitution and the statute books.

Such functions surely call for capacious minds and reliable powers for disinterested and fair-minded judgment. It demands the habit of curbing any tendency to reach results agreeable to desire or to embrace the solution of a problem before exhausting its comprehensive analysis. One in whose keeping may be the decision of the Court must have a disposition to be detached and withdrawn. To be sure, these moral qualities, for such they are, are desirable in all judges, but they are indispensable for the Supreme Court. Its task is to seize the permanent, more or less, from the feelings and fluctuations of the transient. Therefore it demands the kind of equipment that Doctor Johnson rather grandiloquently called "genius," namely, "a mind of large general powers accidentally determined to some particular direction as against a particular designation of mind and propensity for some essential employment." . . .

If these commonplaces regarding the reach of the powers of the Supreme Court and the majesty of the functions entrusted to nine mere mortals give anyone the impression that a Justice of the Court is left at large to exercise his private wisdom, let me hasten to say as quickly and as emphatically as I can that no one could possibly be more hostile to such a notion than I am. These men are judges, bound by the restrictions of the judicial function, and all the more so bound because the nature of the controversies that they adjudicate inevitably leaves more scope for insight, imagination, and prophetic responsibility than the types of litigation that come before other courts. It was the least mentally musclebound and the most creative mind among Justices, Mr. Justice Holmes, who, with characteristic pithiness, described his task as "that of solving a problem according to the rules by which one is bound.". . .

The search should be made among those men, inevitably very few at any time, who give the best promise of satisfying the intrinsic needs of the Court, no matter where they may be found, no matter in what professional way they have manifested the needed qualities. Of course these needs do not exclude prior judicial experience, but, no less surely, they do not call for judicial experience. One is entitled to say without qualification that the correlation between prior judicial experience and fitness for the functions of the Supreme Court is zero. The significance of the greatest among the Justices who had had such experience, Holmes and Cardozo, derived not from that judicial experience but from the fact that they were Holmes and Cardozo. They were thinkers, and more particularly legal philosophers. . . .

4 / THE BAR

Law, Bentham observed, is not made by the judge alone but by "judge and company." And by far the most numerous members of this judicial company are the lawyers. The function of the legal profession is twofold: to explain the intricacies of the rules of law to potential litigants and also to advocate the interests of clients before judges and jurors so as to convince them that those interests deserve the protection of the legal system.

Popular attitude toward the bar has been curiously ambivalent. On the one hand, the lawyer has been rewarded with social status. His profession ranks with those of physicians and scientists on the prestige ladder. He is constantly given the trust and confidence of his clients. His advice is deemed so important that the federal Constitution, like most state constitutions, specifically guarantees the right to counsel in court proceedings. In addition, the lawyer is time and again elected to public office. From one-half to two-thirds of Senators and Congressmen and a considerable number of Presidents have been lawyers.

On the other hand, the lawyer has characteristically been the object of deep distrust and resentment, and the butt of sharp satire. Plato was wary of the divisive force of lawyers in a society. The churchmen in the

Middle Ages feuded with the "civilians," the Roman lawyers. In the Puritan Revolution, the Levellers—a group far more moderate than their title implied—referred to lawyers as "vermin and caterpillars." The satire of Dean Swift in the next century was devastating. Often frustrated in his efforts at legal reform, Bentham claimed attorneys were "obsequious to the whisper of interests and to the beck of power." In 1939 Fred Rodell of the Yale Law School castigated the legal profession as "a high class racket." "In tribal times," Rodell wrote, "there were the medicine men. In the Middle Ages, there were the priests. Today there are the lawyers. For every age, a group of bright boys, learned in their trade and jealous of their learning, who blend technical competence with plain and fancy hocuspocus to make themselves masters of their fellow men."

This ambivalence toward the bar is understandable and perhaps inevitable since the practicing part of the legal profession—unlike its upper strata, the judges—has seldom been successful in cloaking its activities with the protection of a myth of self-denying impartiality. Lawyers have a technical competence which is not only scarce but in great demand in a society which regulates itself by complicated legal rules. This need brings relatively high income and social prestige to the profession. But, while money, prestige, and expertise are marks of power, power can also breed resentment.

Character of the Bar

In England, the legal profession is divided into two groups: a small, rather select number of barristers, who alone can argue cases before the courts; and solicitors, who meet with clients, draw up legal documents, and, where a client must go to court, contact and "brief" the barrister who will argue the case. While there is no such formal distinction between lawyers in the United States, an even higher degree of specialization has grown up.

Until the end of the Civil War, a lawyer typically had a face-to-face relationship with his clients and might handle all sorts of problems, serving as an arbiter and counselor among his neighbors. The Civil War and the growth of large corporate enterprises did much to change these relationships. The new business system needed the lawyer's skills both to expand its potentialities and to defend it against attacks from labor and farm groups. The lawyer became, as Adolph A. Berle has said, "an intellectual jobber and contractor in business matters." Lawyers assumed the task of remolding the legal framework of a predominantly agrarian society to fit, as well as to protect and foster, the interests of a burgeoning industrial system.

But the attorney has become more than the servant of the huge corporation. Lawyers have infiltrated the top levels of business management. There is a well-worn path from the legal staff to the board of directors of banks, railroads, and industrial plants. Sullivan and Cromwell, one of the nation's largest law firms, has held sixty-five directorships at one time. Nor is this progression from adviser to director restricted to business. While no solid statistics are available, much the same phenomenon can be seen in university administration and in the high ranks of labor organizations.

The country and small-town lawyer can still enjoy the personal relationships of the early nineteenth century, but to meet the demands of industrialization the bulk of the legal profession has had to change its mode of operation. The large urban law office is organized much like a small but efficient factory. At the top are the firm's partners. Often these men are well-known public figures; some have been of the stature of Elihu Root, Charles Evans Hughes, John W. Davis, or Thomas E. Dewey. At the next level are the salaried associate lawyers, usually not known outside of the profession but still highly competent craftsmen who have been selected because of their proficiency. Below them are the lawyer-clerks, young men just out of law school; below these are accountants, investigators, and stenographers. The firm will be divided into departments, and sometimes subdepartments, each one handling only a single type of legal problem.

Of necessity, much of this work is impersonal. The partner—who often makes his practice a stepping stone to business or political positions —utilizes his contacts to attract the large numbers of wealthy clients who are needed to pay for the high overhead costs of maintaining the firm and its staff. The young lawyer does most of the grinding research, waiting for the time when his own contacts, professional reputation, and capital will enable him to reach the level of partner or to branch out into business or politics, perhaps to return in a few years as a partner in another large firm.

Specialization within the profession has also created a shadowy, but nonetheless real, social stratification among lawyers. The upper class, of course, is made up of the partners of the large firms, counsel for big corporations, and government lawyers at the Attorney General, Solicitor General, and Assistant Attorney General rank. The upper middle class might be viewed as composed of professors at Ivy League and other prestige law schools, government counsel just below the Assistant Attorney General rank, and partners in the established and prosperous but not necessarily large urban firms. Country lawyers and professors at lesser-known law schools make up the lower middle class together with the highly mobile associates in the bigger offices. In the lowest class in the profession are those attorneys who specialize in criminal law, divorce cases, and personal injury suits. Members of this last group—men like Clarence Darrow, Melvin Belli, and Gerry Geisler—are frequently in the public spotlight. There is, however, a distinct tendency within the legal profession to look down on these lawyers, and the statistics in the last chapter on the background of Supreme Court justices indicate that the bar has made its notions of social status felt.

Legal Education

In England during the Middle Ages, lawyers were trained at Inns of the Court by practitioners rather than by university faculty. This tradition of practical training rather than the formal university education of the continental lawyer carried over to America; and up through the middle of the nineteenth century the typical attorney had received his preparation for the bar by working as an apprentice to a lawyer or by reading law on his own. In the late eighteenth century, however, several professorships of law were established at American colleges. Among the more important were those held by George Wythe at William and Mary, Chancellor Kent at Columbia, and James Wilson at the College of Philadelphia. Wythe's students included John Marshall as well as one of Marshall's great antagonists, Spencer Roane, Jeffersonian Chief Justice of Virginia.

At about the same time that colleges were beginning to add law to their curricula, attorneys set up a number of private schools to give a more systematic version of the practical apprenticeship training. The most influential of these was run by Judge Tapping Reeve at Litchfield, Connecticut, from 1784 to 1823 and was carried on after Reeve's death until 1833. Reeve's school, conducted most of the time by himself and one assistant, trained over one thousand young men in the law. Two of his students (Aaron Burr and John C. Calhoun) became Vice-Presidents; three others became Supreme Court justices; thirty-four, state supreme court judges; six, cabinet members; fourteen, governors; twenty-eight, Senators; and a hundred and one, members of the House of Representatives. But, as brilliant as some of this private instruction was, most of these schools had closed by the end of the first third of the nineteenth century. Competition from the colleges, from less expensive apprenticeship training, and from the publication of several comprehensive treatises which covered almost all of the then existing fields of law was too intense.

The coming of age of the university law school can be dated from 1870 when Christopher Columbus Langdell was appointed dean of the Harvard Law School. Langdell brought about a revolution in the study and teaching of law. Convinced that law could be reduced to a relatively small number of principles which could be found in appellate court opinions, he abandoned lectures in favor of the casebook method. In addition, he recruited a full-time faculty, and helped make the teaching of law a recognized career within the legal profession.

Although some of his teaching ideas were seriously modified, Langdell's influence spread to other universities and the law school gradually became the main source of legal education. In 1953 some 93 per cent of American lawyers had attended law school and about 80 per cent had graduated. Progress was not immediate, however, nor is it yet complete. It was not until the last decade of the nineteenth century that law schools began to require that their students have had some college training; and it was not until 1921 that the American Bar Association went officially on record as demanding two years of college work as a prerequisite for admission to law school. In 1952 the American Association of Law Schools adopted three years of college work as an admission standard, but not as a requirement. It is difficult, if not impossible, however, for a student to be admitted to the better law schools without having graduated in the upper section of his college class and without having done quite well in a special "Law Aptitude" examination. Still, the American Bar Association's survey of the legal profession, completed in 1953,[1] showed that while some 80 per cent of American lawyers had attended college, less than half were college graduates.

Admission to the Bar

"Membership in the bar," Cardozo said for the New York Court of Appeals in 1917, "is a privilege burdened with conditions." Each state sets up standards for admission to the bar and for the conduct of practicing attorneys. While these rules vary greatly from state to state, they all draw essentially on the English statute of 1402, promulgated during

[1] Albert P. Blaustein and Charles O. Porter, *The American Lawyer* (Chicago: University of Chicago Press, 1954).

the reign of Henry VI: "All attorneys should be examined by the justices, and in their discretion, only those found to be good and virtuous, and of good fame, learned and sworn to do their duty, be allowed to put upon the roll and all others put out." "Good moral character" and technical competence have remained the two basic requirements for bar admission. The definition of these terms, however, differs from state to state. The A.B.A. study reported that although in 1953 every state conducted some sort of inquiry into the background of candidates, only thirty-nine states required all fledgling lawyers to take a written bar examination. Only twenty states demanded a law degree; three required merely a high-school education; and two set no minimal educational standards whatever.

Admission to the bar means no more than that the candidate is allowed to practice in the courts of the admitting state. To be admitted to the courts of another state requires an entirely new procedure, though most states, while demanding that a migrant lawyer become a bona fide local resident, do not ask an established attorney to take the student bar examination.

Standards for admission to practice before federal courts are even less fixed. To become a member of the Supreme Court bar, a lawyer must only: (1) have been admitted for three years to practice before the highest court of his state; (2) be in good standing before that court (i.e., not under suspension or disbarment); (3) be sponsored by two members of the Supreme Court bar; (4) pay a $25 fee. Lower federal courts have only minimal consistency in their admission standards; sometimes two district judges in the same state will prescribe different rules. In general, however, if an attorney is a resident of the area covered by the court's jurisdiction, has been admitted to practice before state courts, and is in good standing, he will be allowed to argue before federal courts.

The standards of professional conduct for practicing lawyers are high, almost idealistic; policing the bar, however, is a difficult task. Each state provides a method of disciplining attorneys for unethical, or illegal, conduct. Some states leave the matter largely up to bar associations; others put discipline in the hands of the courts. Increasingly, states are requiring both judges and the bar to share this onerous work. In Illinois, for example, the two major bar groups, the Chicago Bar Association and the Illinois Bar Association, have grievance committees which receive and investigate complaints against lawyers, and hold hearings which are conducted much like a trial, though usually not in public unless the lawyer under investigation so requests. At the completion of the hearing the committee files findings of fact and of law which are reviewed by the bar association's board of governors. If there is a recommendation that the lawyer be suspended or disbarred, the record is sent to the state supreme court, which holds final hearings and imposes the discipline.

The difficulties in policing the legal profession are increased by the fact that, by and large, being a member of the bar does not entail actually joining a bar organization. In 1953 only twenty-five states had "integrated bars," that is, bar associations which all lawyers in the state were compelled by law to join and to which they were amenable for their conduct. All other bar associations, however influential, were strictly voluntary. The American Bar Association, for instance, had in 1956 a membership of only 82,000 out of well over 200,000 practicing attorneys.

Indeed, the first bar organization in this country dates back only to 1869 when the Columbus, Ohio, Bar Association was founded. The Association of the Bar of the City of New York was organized in 1870, and eight years later the A.B.A. was formed. The National Bar Association was organized by Negro lawyers in 1925, since the A.B.A. excluded them from membership because of their race. In protest against the "laissez faire" ideology of the A.B.A., a group of liberal lawyers seceded in 1936 and established the National Lawyers Guild. In 1953, Attorney General Herbert Brownell put the Guild on the Attorney General's list of subversive organizations. The legal stigma, but not the public image, was later removed when the Guild took Brownell to court and he was unable to substantiate his charges.

Conservatism and the Bar

Although the views of individual lawyers and lawyers' groups represent every possible shade of political thinking, and even the Communist party has a fair share of attorneys, the character of the American bar as a whole is generally conservative. There are a number of reasons behind this conservatism, such as the possible effect of social background and present income. Perhaps it is a combination of three psychological pulls which is chiefly responsible for the bar's conservatism. The first is the nature of Anglo-American law itself. The common law has historically attempted to use old rules to cope with new situations, only changing those rules after their failure has become clear. Where change has resulted, the process has customarily been one of slow, step-by-step modification rather than of swift or fundamental revision.

The second factor responsible for the bar's conservatism is that lawyers as a profession have a heavy investment in preserving established legal rules. Law school, expensive and time-consuming, trained them in these rules; and their practice has made these rules familiar working tools. When basic legal principles become unsettled, a lawyer's advice loses some of its expertise, and he has to go through a painful period of relearning. Although the total amount of litigation may be directly proportional to the degree of uncertainty in the law, such uncertainty makes an attorney's work far more difficult and can cause the loss of important clients. This danger is one of the reasons why successful counsel usually develop extra-legal skills in predicting the behavior of judges, jurors, and clients.

The third factor is that of association with large corporations. Depending on specific circumstances, such association could be a conservative or a liberal influence. But, since in this century the interests of most business groups have been largely in protecting the changes in the legal system made after the Civil War, this third factor has reinforced other conservative tendencies. As we saw earlier in this chapter, the highest social status—and the highest income—goes to those firms which specialize in corporate affairs. A lawyer must have the confidence of the business community to become a trusted and informed adviser on legal policy; and continually advocating his clients' interests cannot help but have a deep influence on a lawyer's thinking and—if he wishes to retain those clients—on his actions as well. Moreover, members of this upper stratum of the profession do not remain as hired defenders of business interests, but are often co-opted into top management circles where they share those same business interests.

SELECTED REFERENCES

Arnold, Thurman, *The Symbols of Government* (New Haven: Yale University Press, 1935).

———, *The Folklore of Capitalism* (New Haven: Yale University Press, 1937).

Berle, Adolph A., Jr., "Modern Legal Profession," 9 *Encyclopedia of the Social Sciences* 340.

Blaustein, Albert P. and Charles O. Porter, *The American Lawyer* (Chicago: University of Chicago Press, 1954).

Cheatham, Elliott E., *Cases and Materials on the Legal Profession* (2d ed.; Brooklyn: The Foundation Press, 1955).

Drinker, Henry S., *Legal Ethics* (New York: Columbia University Press, 1953).

Hurst, Willard, *The Growth of American Law* (Boston: Little, Brown, 1950), Chs. 12, 13.

Mills, C. Wright, *White Collar* (New York: Oxford University Press, Galaxy ed., 1956), pp. 121–129.

Pirsig, Maynard E., *Cases on the Legal Profession* (Minneapolis: West Publishing Co., 1957).

Pound, Roscoe, *The Lawyer from Antiquity to Modern Times* (Minneapolis: West Publishing Co., 1953).

Robinson, Edward S., *Law and the Lawyers* (New York: Macmillan, 1935).

Rodell, Fred, *Woe unto You, Lawyers!* (New York: Reynal and Hitchcock, 1939).

Symposium, "The Lawyer's Role in Modern Society," 4 *Journal of Public Law* 1 (1955).

Twiss, Benjamin, *Lawyers and the Constitution* (Princeton: Princeton University Press, 1942).

1.   *". . . there was a society of men among us . . ."*

GULLIVER'S TRAVELS   *Jonathan Swift**

      I ASSURED his honor, "that law was a science in which I
had not much conversed, farther than by employing advocates, in vain,
upon some injustices that had been done me: however, I would give
him all the satisfaction I was able."

     I said, "there was a society of men among us, bred up from their
youth in the art of proving by words multiplied for the purpose, that
white is black, and black is white, according as they are paid. To this
society all the rest of the people are slaves. For example, if my neighbor
has a mind to my cow, he has a lawyer to prove that he ought to have
my cow from me. I must then hire another to defend my right, it being
against all rules of law that any man should be allowed to speak for
himself. Now, in this case, I, who am the right owner, lie under two
great disadvantages: first, my lawyer, being practised almost from his
cradle in defending falsehood, is quite out of his element when he
would be an advocate for justice, which is an unnatural office he
always attempts with great awkwardness, if not with ill will. The second disadvantage is, that my lawyer must proceed with great caution,
or else he will be reprimanded by the judges, and abhorred by his
brethren, as one that would lessen the practice of law. And therefore
I have but two methods to preserve my cow. The first is, to gain over
my adversary's lawyer with a double fee, who will then betray his
client, by insinuating that he has justice on his side. The second way is,
for my lawyer to make my cause appear as unjust as he can, by allowing the cow to belong to my adversary: and this, if it be skillfully
done, will certainly bespeak the favor of the bench. Now your honour
is to know, that these judges are persons appointed to decide all controversies of property, as well as for the trial of criminals, and picked
out from the most dexterous lawyers, who are grown old or lazy; and

The Works of Jonathan Swift (Edinburgh: Constable & Co., 1814), XII, 319–322.
* Swift (1667–1745) was probably the greatest satirist in English literature.

having been biased all their lives against truth and equity, lie under such a fatal necessity of favouring fraud, perjury, and oppression, that I have known some of them refuse a large bribe from the side where justice lay, rather than injure the faculty, by doing any thing unbecoming their nature or their office.

"It is a maxim among these lawyers, that whatever has been done before may legally be done again; and therefore they take special care to record all the decisions formerly made against common justice and the general reason of mankind. These, under the name of precedents, they produce as authorities to justify the most iniquitous opinions; and the judges never fail of directing accordingly.

"In pleading, they studiously avoid entering into the merits of the cause, but are loud, violent, and tedious in dwelling upon all circumstances which are not to the purpose. For instance, in the case already mentioned, they never desire to know what claim or title my adversary has to my cow; but whether the said cow were red or black; her horns long or short; whether the field I graze her in be round or square; whether she was milked at home or abroad; what diseases she is subject to, and the like; after which they consult precedents, adjourn the cause from time to time, and in ten, twenty, or thirty years come to an issue.

"It is likewise to be observed, that this society has a peculiar cant and jargon of their own, that no other mortal can understand, and wherein all their laws are written, which they take special care to multiply; whereby they have wholly confounded the very essence of truth and falsehood, of right and wrong; so that it will take thirty years to decide whether the field left me by my ancestors for six generations belongs to me, or to a stranger three hundred miles off.

"In the trial of persons accused for crimes against the state, the method is much more short and commendable: the judge first sends to sound the disposition of those in power, after which, he can easily hang or save a criminal, strictly preserving all due forms of law."

Here my master interposing, said, "it was a pity that creatures endowed with such prodigious abilities of mind, as these lawyers, by the description I gave of them, must certainly be, were not rather encouraged to be instructors of others in wisdom and knowledge." In answer to which I assured his honour, "that in all points out of their own trade they were usually the most ignorant and stupid generation among us, the most despicable in common conversation, avowed enemies to all knowledge and learning, and equally disposed to pervert the general reason of mankind in every other subject of discourse as in that of their profession."

2. *"The government of democracy is favorable to the political power of lawyers . . ."*

THE TEMPER OF THE LEGAL PROFESSION *Alexis de Tocqueville*

IN VISITING the Americans and in studying their laws, we perceive that the authority they have entrusted to members of the legal profession, and the influence which these individuals exercise in the government, is the most powerful existing security against the excesses of democracy.

This effect seems to me to result from a general cause, which it is useful to investigate, as it may be reproduced elsewhere. . . .

Men who have more especially devoted themselves to legal pursuits derive from occupation certain habits of order, a taste for formalities, and a kind of instinctive regard for the regular connection of ideas, which naturally render them very hostile to the revolutionary spirit and the unreflecting passions of the multitude.

The special information that lawyers derive from their studies ensures them a separate station in society, and they constitute a sort of privileged body in the scale of intelligence. This notion of their superiority perpetually recurs to them in the practice of their profession: they are the masters of a science which is necessary, but which is not very generally known; they serve as arbiters between the citizens; and the habit of directing the blind passions of parties in litigation to their purpose inspires them with a certain contempt for the judgment of the multitude. To this it may be added, that they naturally constitute *a body;* not by any previous understanding, or by an agreement which directs them to a common end; but the analogy of their studies and the uniformity of their proceedings connect their

Democracy in America (1835), Ch. 16.

minds together, as much as a common interest would combine their endeavors.

A portion of the tastes and of the habits of the aristocracy may consequently be discovered in the characters of lawyers. They participate in the same instinctive love of order and formalities; and they entertain the same repugnance to the actions of the multitude, and the same secret contempt of the government of the people. I do not mean to say that the natural propensities of lawyers are sufficiently strong to sway them irresistibly; for they, like most other men, are governed by their private interests, and the advantages of the moment.

In a state of society in which the members of the legal profession cannot hold that rank in the political world which they enjoy in private life, we may rest assured that they will be the foremost agents of revolution. But it must then be inquired whether the cause which induces them to innovate and destroy is accidental, or whether it belongs to some lasting purpose which they entertain. It is true that lawyers mainly contributed to the overthrow of the French Monarchy in 1789; but it remains to be seen whether they acted thus because they had studied the laws or because they were prohibited from cooperating in the work of legislation. . . .

I do not, then, assert that *all* the members of the legal profession are at *all* times the friends of order and the opponents of innovation, but merely that most of them usually are so. In a community in which lawyers are allowed to occupy without opposition that high station which naturally belongs to them, their general spirit will be eminently conservative and anti-democratic. . . .

The government of democracy is favorable to the political power of lawyers; for when the wealthy, the noble, and the prince are excluded from the government, lawyers are sure to occupy the highest stations in their own right, as it were, since they are the only men of information and sagacity, beyond the sphere of the people, who can be the object of the popular choice. If, then, they are led by their tastes to combine with the aristocracy and to support the crown, they are brought in contact with the people by their interests. They like the government of democracy without participating in its propensities and without imitating its weaknesses; whence they derive a twofold authority from and over it. The people in democratic states do not mistrust the members of the legal profession, because it is known that they are interested in serving the popular cause; and the people listen to them without irritation, because they do not attribute to them any sinister designs. The object of lawyers is not, indeed, to overthrow the institutions of democracy, but they constantly endeavor to give it an impulse which diverts it from its real tendency by means which are foreign to its nature. Lawyers belong to the people by birth and interest, and to the aristocracy by habit and taste; they may be looked upon as the connecting link between the two great classes of society. . . .

This aristocratic character, which I hold to be common to the legal profession, is much more distinctly marked in the United States and in England than in any other country. This proceeds not only from the legal studies of the English and American lawyers, but from the nature of the law and the position which these interpreters of it occupy in the two countries. The English and the Americans have retained the law of precedents; that is to say, they continue to found their legal opinions and the decisions of their courts upon the opinions and decisions of their forefathers. In the mind of an English or American lawyer a taste and a reverence for what is old is almost always united with a love of regular and lawful proceedings. . . .

In America there are no nobles or literary men, and the people are apt to mistrust the wealthy; lawyers consequently form the highest political class and the most cultivated portion of society. They have therefore nothing to gain by innovation, which adds a conservative interest to their natural taste for public order. If I were asked where I place the American aristocracy, I should reply without hesitation that it is not composed of the rich, who are united by no common tie, but that it occupies the judicial bench and the bar.

The more we reflect upon all that occurs in the United States, the more we shall be persuaded that the lawyers, as a body, form the most powerful, if not the only, counterpoise to the democratic element. In that country we easily perceive how the legal profession is qualified by its powers, and even by its defects, to neutralize the vices which are inherent in popular government. When the American people are intoxicated by passion or carried away by the impetuosity of their ideas, they are checked and stopped by the almost invisible influence of their legal counselors, who secretly oppose their aristocratic propensities to the nation's democratic instincts, their superstitious attachment to what is old to its love of novelty, their narrow views to its immense designs, and their habitual procrastination to its ardent impatience.

The courts of justice are the most visible organs by which the legal profession is enabled to control the democracy. The judge is a lawyer who, independently of the taste for regularity and order that he has contracted in the study of law, derives an additional love of stability from his own inalienable functions. His legal attainments have already raised him to a distinguished rank among his fellow citizens; his political power completes the distinction of his station and gives him the inclinations natural to privileged classes. . . .

> *". . . departures from the fiduciary principle do not usually occur without the active assistance of some member of our profession . . ."*

3.

THE PUBLIC INFLUENCE OF THE BAR *Harlan F. Stone**

NO TRADITION of our profession is more cherished by lawyers than that of its leadership in public affairs. We dwell upon the part of lawyers in the creation of the Federal Constitution and in the organization of the national government and of our federal and state judicial systems. The rôle they played in politics and government in the first half of the last century is a familiar part of our history. . . . In a very real sense they were guardians of the law, cherishing the legitimate influence of their guild as that of a profession charged with public duties and responsibilities. . . .

All this is justly the subject of pride to lawyers. The records of almost any Bar Association meeting reveal our readiness to turn back to these pages of a glorious past, because they portray those ideals of

48 *Harvard Law Review* 1 (1934). Copyright 1934 Harvard Law Review Association. Reprinted with permission.

* Associate Justice, U.S. Supreme Court 1925–41; Chief Justice of the United States, 1941–46.

our profession to which we would most willingly pay tribute. Yet candor would compel even those of us who have the most abiding faith in our profession, and the firmest belief in its capacity for future usefulness, to admit that in our own time the Bar has not maintained its traditional position of public influence and leadership. Although it tends to prove the point, it is not of the first importance that there are fewer lawyers of standing serving in the halls of legislatures or in executive or administrative posts than in earlier days. Public office is not the only avenue to public influence. . . . But it is not without its lesson for us that most laymen, at least, would deny that there is today a comparable leadership on the part of lawyers, or a disposition of the public to place reliance upon their leadership where the problems of government touch the law.

We cannot brush aside this lay dissatisfaction with lawyers with the comforting assurance that it is nothing more than the chronic distrust of the lawyer class which the literature of every age has portrayed. It is, I fear, the expression of a belief too general and too firmly held for us to shut our eyes to it. . . .

The coercive power of the state no doubt has its part to play in any civilization. We cannot do without the policeman, yet we cannot count his night stick as our most potent civilizing agency. . . . We know that unless the urge of individual advantage has other curbs, unless we may have recourse to other forces of social betterment, and unless the more influential elements in society conduct themselves with a disposition to promote the common good, society cannot function. . . .

Throughout the history of Anglo-American civilization, the professional groups have been among the most significant of those non-governmental agencies which promote the public welfare. Although in smaller measure, during the rapid growth of our industrial system their function has been not unlike that of the medieval guilds. They have exerted direct control over their members by training, by selection, by punishment, by reward. Among these groups the position of the Bar has been one of peculiar importance and significance. While it has not inherited the completely independent status of the English bar, to no other group in this country has the state granted comparable privileges or permitted so much autonomy. No other is so closely related to the state, and no other has traditionally exerted so powerful an influence on public opinion and on public policy. That influence in the past has been wielded chiefly in the courts, in the forum of local communities, in legislative halls, in the councils of government. . . .

In appraising the present-day relationship of the lawyer to his community, we cannot leave out of account either the altered character of public questions or the change in the function which the lawyers, as a class, are called upon to perform. It was in 1809 when Jefferson wrote: "We are a rural farming people; we have little business and few manufactures among us, and I pray God it will be a long time before we have much of either." Profound changes have come into American life since that sentence was penned. The first half of the nineteenth century saw the beginnings of a shift from that idyllic scene, and in the second half the transformation was complete from a young nation made up of isolated groups of agricultural pioneer communities, scattered through the vast territory east of the Mississippi River, to an industrial state, in which, in our own day, we have witnessed the domination of law and politics by inexorable economic forces. Public problems are no longer exclusively questions of individual right. They involve an understanding of the new and complex economic forces we have created, their relationship to the lives of individuals in widely separated communities engaged in widely differing activities, and the adaptation to those forces of old conceptions of law developed in a different environment to meet different needs.

The American Bar, like most other elements in the life of the nation, was ill prepared for a change so swift and sweeping. From the beginning of the commercial expansion in England almost to our own day, the problems of the law were those of an intensely individualistic society. An adequate technique, and skill in using it, engaged the attention of its practitioners. Its historical background and moral content, and more or less abortive attempts to reform its procedure, were the chief considerations of its philosophers. . . .

The changed character of the lawyer's work has made it difficult for him to contemplate his function in its new setting, to see himself and his occupation in proper perspective. No longer does his list of clients represent a cross section of society; no longer do his contacts make him the typical representative and interpreter of his community. The demands of practice are more continuous and exacting. He has less time for reflection upon other than immediate professional undertakings.

He is more the man of action, less the philosopher and less the student of history, economics, and government.

The rise of big business has produced an inevitable specialization of the Bar. The successful lawyer of our day more often than not is the proprietor or general manager of a new type of factory, whose legal product is increasingly the result of mass production methods. More and more the amount of his income is the measure of professional success. More and more he must look for his rewards to the material satisfactions derived from profits as from a successfully conducted business, rather than to the intangible and indubitably more durable satisfactions which are to be found in a professional service more consciously directed toward the advancement of the public interest. Steadily the best skill and capacity of the profession has been drawn into the exacting and highly specialized service of business and finance. At its best the changed system has brought to the command of the business world loyalty and a superb proficiency and technical skill. At its worst it has made the learned profession of an earlier day the obsequious servant of business, and tainted it with the morals and manners of the market place in its most anti-social manifestations. In any case we must concede that it has given us a Bar whose leaders, like its rank and file, are on the whole less likely to be well rounded professional men than their predecessors, whose energy and talent for public service and for bringing the law into harmony with changed conditions have been largely absorbed in the advancement of the interests of clients. . . .

I mention these changes now, not to condemn, but to describe them. . . . When we know the significant facts in the professional life of the lawyers of the present generation and appraise them in the light of the altered world in which we live, we shall better understand how it is that a Bar which has done so much to develop and refine the technique of business organization, to provide skillfully devised methods for financing industry, which has guided a world wide commercial expansion, has done relatively so little to remedy the evils of the investment market; so little to adapt the fiduciary principle of nineteenth century equity to twentieth century business practices; so little to improve the functioning of the administrative mechanisms which modern government sets up to prevent abuses; so little to make law more readily available as an instrument of justice to the common man.

Notwithstanding all the pressures of modern economic life upon the lawyer, and his absorption with the demands of client-caretaking, we could make no greater mistake than to assume that ours has become a profession without ideals. Even the lawyer's devotion to the interests of his clients is a manifestation of a selfless loyalty to an ideal, though it may not always be seen in true perspective in relation to the public interest which it is also his duty to serve. No one familiar with the history of the Bar, knowing its life and personnel, can doubt that it has the idealism, the will to sacrifice, the capacity for leadership, which will continue to enable it to play well its part. No professional class has greater pride in its traditions or higher aspirations for its future. None will respond more willingly, with generous expenditure of time and effort, to the intelligent call for action. But none so much needs to know the facts which reveal, in clear relief, its altered position in the social structure and the manner in which under new conditions it is meeting its public responsibilities. None, unless it be the scientists, can be more profoundly moved by facts.

But like most other elements of the community, we are in a sense the victim of changes, of whose nature and effect we are still not wholly aware. Hence it is that the Bar needs to know and to focus its attention upon the facts, not in the form of assumptions or generalizations, nor yet on the details of petty misconduct in its disreputable outer fringes, but upon data patiently assembled and organized so as to show with the powerful impact of revealed truth the extent to which devotion to private interests has obscured our vision of the public welfare. . . .

I venture to assert that when the history of the financial era which has just drawn to a close comes to be written, most of its mistakes and its major faults will be ascribed to the failure to observe the fiduciary principle, the precept as old as holy writ, that "a man cannot serve two masters". . . . There is little to suggest that the Bar has yet recognized that it must bear some burden of responsibility for these evils. But when we know and face the facts we shall have to acknowledge that such departures from the fiduciary principle do not usually occur without the active assistance of some member of our profession, and that their increasing recurrence would have been impossible but for the complaisance of a Bar, too absorbed in the workaday care of private interests to take account of these events of profound import or to sound the warning that the profession looks askance upon these, as things that "are not done".

We must remember, nevertheless, that the very conditions which have caused specialization, which have drawn so heavily upon the technical proficiency of the Bar, have likewise placed it in a position where the possibilities of its influence are almost beyond calculation. . . . Without the constant advice and guidance of lawyers business would come to an abrupt halt. And whatever standards of conduct in the performance of its function the Bar consciously adopts must at once be reflected in the character of the world of business and finance. Given a measure of self-conscious and cohesive professional unity, the Bar may exert a power more beneficent and far reaching than it or any other non-governmental group has wielded in the past. . . .

Apart from the procedure of formulating new methods of discipline and new specifications of condemned practices, we must give more thoughtful consideration to squaring our own ethical conceptions with the traditional ethics and ideals of the community at large. The problems to which the machine and the corporation give rise have outstripped the ideology and values of an earlier day. The future demands that we undergo a corresponding moral readjustment. Just as the lawyers of 1790 to 1840 took a leading part in fashioning the country's ideals to suit political change, so we must now shoulder the task of relating them to business and economic change.

All this cannot be done in those occasional and brief intervals when the busy lawyer secures some respite from the pressing demands of clients to participate in the festivities of bar association meetings. It requires study and investigation, the painstaking gathering of data and their portrayal in such fashion that we may know the facts and, knowing them, develop a consciousness of their implications for our profession.

With so much to be done we must look to those elements in the profession best qualified for doing it. A generation ago that search must have begun and ended with practicing lawyers. But paralleling the development of the practicing bar has come, in the past fifty years, the steady growth in public esteem and influence of a new force in American legal life, that of the rapidly increasing group of university law teachers, devoting their lives to the task of advancing the cause of legal science for which they have been specially selected and trained. Members of the Bar, they nevertheless make up a distinct professional group within the Bar. . . . It is they who have taken the initiative in the most important reforms undertaken by the Bar in the past twenty years. They originated and have chiefly guided the movements espoused by the Bar for the enactment of uniform laws, the restatement of the law, the improvement in standards of admission to the Bar, and the reform of civil and criminal procedure. It is they who today represent the most cohesive, disinterested and potent single force operating within the profession to establish its public relationships on a higher plane. . . .

. . . Their detachment, their scholarly resources, their growing influence with the Bar, all indicate plainly enough that it is they who must take the more active part in solving the problems which weigh upon our profession perhaps as never before. They, as can no others, may assemble and portray the facts which reveal, so that all may see, the manner in which the Bar is performing its functions and, portraying them, stir the latent idealism of lawyers to carry on.

It is equally true that the Bar cannot sit by and leave the burden entirely upon the law schools. In the light of information which they may make available the Bar must assume the responsibility of consciously bringing its conduct to conform to new standards fitting the times in which we live. And unless history reverses itself the coöperation and support of leaders of the Bar will not be wanting. . . .

4.   *"The Lawyer's Duty in Its Last Analysis."*

CANONS OF PROFESSIONAL ETHICS

15. HOW FAR A LAWYER MAY GO IN SUPPORTING A CLIENT'S CAUSE.

NOTHING OPERATES more certainly to create or to foster popular prejudice against lawyers as a class, and to deprive the profession of that full measure of public esteem and confidence which

Canons of Professional Ethics of the American Bar Association, Canons 15, 22, 32.

belongs to the proper discharge of its duties than does the false claim, often set up by the unscrupulous in defense of questionable transactions, that it is the duty of the lawyer to do whatever may enable him to succeed in winning his client's cause.

It is improper for a lawyer to assert in argument his personal belief in his client's innocence or in the justice of his cause.

The lawyer owes "entire devotion to the interest of the client, warm zeal in the maintenance and defense of his rights and the exertion of his utmost learning and ability," to the end that nothing be taken or withheld from him, save by the rules of law, legally applied. No fear of judicial disfavor or public unpopularity should restrain him from the full discharge of his duty. In the judicial forum the client is entitled to the benefit of any and every remedy and defense that is authorized by the law of the land, and he may expect his lawyer to assert every such remedy or defense. But it is steadfastly to be borne in mind that the great trust of the lawyer is to be performed within and not without the bounds of the law. The office of attorney does not permit, much less does it demand of him for any client, violation of law or any manner of fraud or chicane. He must obey his own conscience and not that of his client.

22. CANDOR AND FAIRNESS.

The conduct of the lawyer before the Court and with other lawyers should be characterized by candor and fairness.

It is not candid or fair for the lawyer knowingly to misquote the contents of a paper, the testimony of a witness, the language or argument of opposing counsel, or the language of a decision or a textbook; or with knowledge of its invalidity, to cite as authority a decision that has been overruled, or a statute that has been repealed; or in argument to assert as a fact that which has not been proved, or in those jurisdictions where a side has the opening and closing arguments to mislead his opponent by concealing or withholding positions in his opening argument upon which his side then intends to rely.

It is unprofessional and dishonorable to deal other than candidly with the facts in taking the statement of witnesses, in drawing affidavits and other documents, and in the presentation of causes.

A lawyer should not offer evidence which he knows the Court

should reject, in order to get the same before the jury by argument for its admissibility, nor should he address to the Judge arguments upon any point not properly calling for determination by him. Neither should he introduce into an argument, addressed to the court, remarks or statements intended to influence the jury or bystanders.

These and all kindred practices are unprofessional and unworthy of an officer of the law charged, as is the lawyer, with the duty of aiding in the administration of justice.

32. THE LAWYER'S DUTY IN ITS LAST ANALYSIS.

No client, corporate or individual, however powerful, nor any cause, civil or political, however important, is entitled to receive nor should any lawyer render any service or advice involving disloyalty to the law whose ministers we are, or disrespect of the judicial office, which we are bound to uphold, or corruption of any person or persons exercising a public office or private trust, or deception or betrayal of the public. When rendering any such improper service or advice, the lawyer invites and merits stern and just condemnation. Correspondingly, he advances the honor of his profession and the best interests of his client when he renders service or gives advice tending to impress upon the client and his undertaking exact compliance with the strictest principles of moral law. He must also observe and advise his client to observe the statute law, though until a statute shall have been construed and interpreted by competent adjudication, he is free and is entitled to advise as to its validity and as to what he conscientiously believes to be its just meaning and extent. But above all a lawyer will find his highest honor in a deserved reputation for fidelity to private trust and to public duty, as an honest man and as a patriotic and loyal citizen.

> *"I don't see why we should not come out roundly and say that one of the functions of a lawyer is to lie for*
5. *his client . . ."*

THE ETHICS OF ADVOCACY   *Charles P. Curtis**

I

I WANT FIRST of all to put advocacy in its proper setting. It is a special case of vicarious conduct. A lawyer devotes his life and career to acting for other people. . . . His loyalty runs to his client. He has no other master. Not the court? you ask. . . . No, in a paradoxical way. The lawyer's official duty, required of him indeed by the court, is to devote himself to the client. The court comes second by the court's, that is the law's, own command.

Lord Brougham, in his defense of Queen Caroline, in her divorce case, told the House of Lords: "I once before took occasion to remind your Lordships, which was unnecessary, but there are many whom it may be needful to remind, that an advocate, by the sacred duty which he owes his client, knows in the discharge of that office but one person in the world—that client and no other. . . . Nay, separating even the duties of a patriot from those of an advocate, and casting them if need be to the wind, he must go on reckless of the consequences, if his fate it should unhappily be to involve his country in confusion for his client's protection."

Lord Brougham was a great advocate, and when he made this statement he was arguing a great case, the divorce of Queen Caroline from George IV before the House of Lords. Plainly he was exerting more than his learning and more than his legal ability. Years later he explained to William Forsythe, the author of a book on lawyers called *Hortensius*, who had asked him what he meant. Before you read Brougham's reply, let me remind you that the king, George IV, was the one who was pressing the divorce, which Brougham was defending, and that George had contracted a secret marriage, while he was heir

4 *Stanford Law Review* 3 (1951). Copyright 1951 Stanford University. Reprinted with permission.
* Author and practicing attorney; died 1959.

apparent, with Mrs. Fitzherbert, a Roman Catholic. Brougham knew
this, and knew too that it was enough to deprive the king of his
crown under the Act of Settlement. Brougham wrote:

> The real truth is, that the statement . . . was a menace, and it was
> addressed chiefly to George IV, but also to wiser men, such as Castle-
> reagh and Wellington. I was prepared, in *case of necessity,* that is, in
> case the Bill passed the Lords, to do two things—first, to resist it in
> the Commons *with the country at my back;* but next, if need be, to
> dispute the King's title, to show he had forfeited the crown by marry-
> ing a Catholic, in the words of the Act, "as if he were naturally dead."
> What I said was fully understood. . . .

Lord Brougham's menace has become the classic statement of the
loyalty which a lawyer owes to his client, perhaps because being a
menace it is so extreme. And yet the Canons of Ethics is scarcely
more moderate, ". . . entire devotion to the interest of the client,
warm zeal in the maintenance and defense of his rights and the exertion of his utmost learning and ability. . . ."

The person for whom you are acting very reasonably expects you to
treat him better than you do other people, which is just another way
of saying that you owe him a higher standard of conduct than you
owe to others. . . . A lawyer, or a trustee, or anyone acting for another,
has lower standards of conduct toward outsiders than he has toward
his clients or his beneficiaries or his patrons against the outsiders. He
is required to treat outsiders as if they were barbarians and enemies.
The more good faith and devotion the lawyer owes to his client, the
less he owes to others when he is acting for his client. It is as if a man
had only so much virtue, and the more he gives to one, the less he has
available for anyone else. . . .

You devote yourself to the interests of another at the peril of yourself. Vicarious action tempts a man too far from himself. Men will do
for others what they are not willing to do for themselves—nobler as
well as ignoble things. . . .

II

. . . I tried to find a situation in which a lawyer may be in duty
bound to lie for his client. I asked an eminent and very practical judge.
He told me he hoped I was joking. I went to two leaders of the bar,

both ex-presidents of bar associations. One said, "No, I don't believe there is such a situation." The other said, "Why, of course, there are." But he has not yet given me one.

Finally I thought I had one. It was the case of a lawyer who, I felt very sure, had lied to me when he told me that he did not represent a certain man. I was secretary of the Grievance Committee of the Bar Association at the time, and I was trying to find out whether this man had been blackmailed by some other lawyers. I went to this lawyer and asked him. If he had even admitted to me that he had represented this man, I should have been pretty sure that the man had indeed been blackmailed, for I knew that he had not gone to his regular counsel, but to a different lawyer, in order to keep the whole affair secret. The lawyer told me he did not even know the man.

I recall thinking then that this lawyer was doing just right by lying to me, but I don't know who else agreed with me. My lawyer had gone on to make the same denial to the Grievance Committee, and later, when the Bar Association brought proceedings for his disbarment, in the course of those proceedings, persisted in his denial before the court itself. He was not disbarred, but he was subsequently reprimanded and suspended.

I take it that it is inadmissible to lie to the court. A lawyer's duty to his client cannot rise higher than its source, which is the court. Perhaps my lawyer did wrong to lie to the Grievance Committee, but I am not so sure. I know he did right to lie to me, and I am inclined to hope that in his place I should have lied to the Grievance Committee as well.

It may be that it all depends on whether you are asked the question by someone who has a right to ask it. If he has no right to ask and if simple silence would, or even might, lead him to the truth, then, I believe your lawyer is in duty bound to lie. For the truth is not his, but yours. It belongs to you and he is bound to keep it for you, even more vigorously than if it were only his own. He must lie, then, beyond the point where he could permissibly lie for himself. But this only illuminates the problem from a different angle, the right to ask instead of the duty to answer. Let me give you a situation in which a lawyer must lie to someone who does have the right to ask him the question.

A lawyer is called on the telephone by a former client who is unfortunately at the time a fugitive from justice. The police want him and he wants advice. The lawyer goes to where his client is, hears the whole story, and advises him to surrender. Finally he succeeds in persuading him that this is the best thing to do and they make an appointment to go to police headquarters. Meanwhile the client is to have two days to wind up his affairs and make his farewells. When the lawyer gets back to his office, a police inspector is waiting for him, and asks him whether his client is in town and where he is. Here are questions which the police have every right to ask of anybody, and even a little hesitation in this unfortunate lawyer's denials will reveal enough to betray his client. Of course he lies.

And why not? The relation between a lawyer and his client is one of the intimate relations. You would lie for your wife. You would lie for your child. There are others with whom you are intimate enough, close enough, to lie for them when you would not lie for yourself. At what point do you stop lying for them? I don't know and you are not sure.

To every one of us come occasions when we don't want to tell the truth, not all of it, certainly not all of it at once, when we want to be something less than candid, a little disingenuous. Indeed, to be candid with ourselves, there are times when we deliberately and more or less justifiably undertake to tell something less or something different. Complete candor to anyone but ourselves is a virtue that belongs to the saints, to the secure, and to the very courageous. . . .

I don't see why we should not come out roundly and say that one of the functions of a lawyer is to lie for his client; and on rare occasions, as I think I have shown, I believe it is. Happily they are few and far between, only when his duty gets him into a corner or puts him on the spot. Day in, day out, a lawyer can be as truthful as anyone. But not ingenuous. . . .

I have said that a lawyer may not lie to the court. But it may be a lawyer's duty not to speak. Let me give you a case from the autobiography of one of the most distinguished and most conscientious lawyers I or any other man has ever known, Samuel Williston. In his autobiography, *Life and Law,* he tells of one of his early cases. His client was sued in some financial matter. . . . Williston, of course, at once got his client's letter file and went through it painstakingly, sorting, arranging, and collating it. The letters . . . told the whole story.

. . . Trial approached, but the plaintiff's lawyers did not either demand to see the correspondence, nor ask for their production. "They did not demand their production and we did not feel bound to disclose them." At the close of the trial, "In the course of his remarks the Chief Justice stated as one reason for his decision a supposed fact which I knew to be unfounded. I had in front of me a letter that showed his error. Though I have no doubt of the propriety of my behavior in keeping silent, I was somewhat uncomfortable at the time."

This was a letter, a piece of evidence, a fact. Suppose it had been a rule of law. Suppose the Chief Justice had equally mistakenly given as a reason for his decision some statute or regulation which Williston knew had been repealed or amended, and it was not a letter but a copy of the new statute which he had in front of him. Williston would have interrupted the Chief Justice and drawn his attention to it. This is sometimes debated, but it is beyond dispute that this would have been Williston's duty, and there is no doubt at all that he would have performed it as scrupulously as he respected his duty to his client. . . .

III

The classical solution to a lawyer taking a case he knows is bad is Dr. Johnson's. It is perfectly simple and quite specious. Boswell asked Johnson whether as a moralist Johnson did not think that the practice of law, in some degree, hurt the nice feeling of honesty.

"What do you think," said Boswell, "of supporting a cause which you know to be bad?"

Johnson answered, "Sir, you do not know it to be good or bad till the Judge determines it. I have said that you are to state facts fairly; so that your thinking, or what you call knowing, a cause to be bad, must be from reasoning, must be from your supposing your arguments to be weak and inconclusive. But, Sir, that is not enough. An argument which does not convince yourself, may convince the Judge to whom you urge it: and if it does convince him, why, then, Sir, you are wrong, and he is right." . . .

No, there is nothing unethical in taking a bad case or defending the guilty or advocating what you don't believe in. It is ethically neutral. It's a free choice. There is a Daumier drawing of a lawyer arguing, a very demure young woman sitting near him, and a small boy beside her sucking a lollypop. The caption says, "He defends the widow and the orphan, unless he is attacking the orphan and the widow." And for every lawyer whose conscience may be pricked, there is another whose virtue is tickled. Every case has two sides, and for every lawyer on the wrong side, there's another on the right side.

I am not being cynical. We are not dealing with the morals which govern a man acting for himself, but with the ethics of advocacy. We are talking about the special moral code which governs a man who is acting for another. . . .

IV

The fact is, the "entire devotion" is not entire. The full discharge of a lawyer's duty to his client requires him to withhold something. If a lawyer is entirely devoted to his client, his client receives something less than he has a right to expect. For, if a man devotes the whole of himself to another, he mutilates or diminishes himself, and the other receives the devotion of so much the less. This is no paradox, but a simple calculus of the spirit. . . .

A lawyer should treat his cases like a vivid novel, and identify himself with his client as he does with the hero or the heroine in the plot. Then he will work with "the zest that most people feel under their concern when they assist at existing emergencies, not actually their own; or join in facing crises that are grave, but for somebody else." . . . I can only add that this zest may deepen into a peculiar and almost spiritual satisfaction, as wide as it is deep. . . .

How is a lawyer to secure this detachment? There are two ways of doing it, two devices. . . . One way is to treat the whole thing as a game. I am not talking about the sporting theory of justice. I am talking about a lawyer's personal relations with his client and the necessity of detaching himself from his client. Never blame a lawyer for treating litigation as a game, however much you may blame the judge. The lawyer is detaching himself. A man who has devoted his life to taking on other people's troubles, would be swamped by them if he were to adopt them as his own. . . .

The other way is a sense of craftsmanship. Perhaps it comes to the same thing, but I think not quite. There is a satisfaction in playing a game the best you can, as there is in doing anything else as well as you can, which is quite distinct from making a good score. . . . A lawyer may have to treat the practice of law as if it were a game, but if he can rely on craftsmanship, it may become an art. . . .

6.
"I only hope that this insidious essay will not mislead some gullible young lawyer . . ."

SOME REMARKS ON MR. CURTIS' "THE ETHICS OF ADVOCACY"
*Henry S. Drinker**

. . . MR. CURTIS to the contrary notwithstanding, no man can be either too honest, too truthful, or too upright to be a thoroughly good lawyer, and an eminently successful one. A lawyer does not acquire valuable clients by getting a reputation for being willing to practice any kind of chicanery in their behalf. It is too apt to occur to the good client that the lawyer who, when "in a corner" or "on the spot," will lie for him, may, in a similar corner, lie *to* him for the lawyer's own advantage.

A lawyer need never lie for his client. Mr. Curtis cites no instances in his thirty-three years of practice where he himself has been called on or even tempted to do so. The only case he gives of a lie by another lawyer was that to the grievance committee, for which the liar, despite Mr. Curtis' apparent approval, was ultimately suspended by the court.

Mr. Curtis' primary thesis is apparently that the lawyer's duty of "entire devotion to the interest of the client" is so unqualified that one of the functions of a lawyer is even to lie for him. . . .

Of course no one could say that an occasion might not possibly

4 *Stanford Law Review* 349 (1952). Copyright 1952 Stanford University. Reprinted with permission.

* Author and attorney. Chairman, Committee on Professional Ethics of the American Bar Association.

arise when there was no alternative except the truth or a lie and when the consequences of the truth were such that the lawyer might be tempted to lie. This, however, would not make it right for him to do so. When Mr. Curtis intimates that in his opinion a lawyer's duty to his client is higher than that to the court, he ignores the established principle of privileged communications. At the very beginning of the development of the common law, it was agreed by lawyers, judges, and legislators and embodied in decisions, in statutes, and in canons of ethics that in order to encourage the client to tell his whole story to the lawyer, facts which the client disclosed to his lawyer are "privileged" and may not be disclosed by the lawyer without the client's permission.

It was for this reason that Mr. Williston could not disclose the injurious letter from the files which the client had turned over to him for examination. It was for this reason that the lawyer could not tell the police officers where his client had telephoned him that he was hiding. When the police officers asked the lawyer, there was no necessity for him to lie. He should have said: "If I knew, my duty as a lawyer would forbid my telling you." . . .

Mr. Curtis quotes from a characterization of New York financiers, politicians, lawyers, and judges during the corrupt period following the civil war, as if such corruption were a normal feature of the lawyers of today. This attitude pervades his whole article. When he says: "The more good faith and devotion the lawyer owes to his client, the less he owes to others when he is acting for his client. . . ." he is as wrong as are those who intimate that a businessman who makes a dollar steals it from someone else. . . .

He also makes much of the principle that a lawyer is justified in representing a client whom he believes to be guilty, or in taking a case which he believes is unsound. The reason for this is that our legal system is based on the principle that justice is best attained by each side having a lawyer whose duty is to present it as well as it can be presented, with a judge and jury to decide the issue. It has been found, and the experience of every lawyer will corroborate this, that a case which at first sight appeared unsound or hopeless sometimes turns out later to be sound. No matter how flagrant a crime, nevertheless under our system the criminal has a right to have his guilt established in accordance with due procedure and with the rules of evidence, and the Constitution guarantees him the right to representation by a lawyer who will give him all the protection which the law affords, and no more. . . .

I only hope that this insidious essay will not mislead some gullible young lawyer into believing that the law as practiced by the hundreds of fine lawyers throughout this country is actually what Mr. Curtis makes it out to be, instead of the noble profession that it is, represented by "men who could not for any fee or reward of any sort or kind be induced for a single instant to yield to temptation or to lower themselves to win the bread of shame by the arts of chicanery."

7. *"I will not counsel or maintain any suit which shall appear to me to be unjust . . ."*

OATH OF ADMISSION

I DO SOLEMNLY SWEAR:

I will support the Constitution of the United States and the Constitution of the State of ——;

I will maintain the respect due to Courts of Justice and judicial officers;

I will not counsel or maintain any suit or proceeding which shall appear to me to be unjust, nor any defense except such as I believe to be honestly debatable under the law of the land;

I will employ for the purpose of maintaining the causes confided to me such means only as are consistent with truth and honor, and will never seek to mislead the Judge or jury by any artifice or false statement of fact or law;

I will maintain the confidence and preserve inviolate the secrets of my client, and will accept no compensation in connection with his business except from him or with his knowledge and approval;

Oath of Admission recommended by the American Bar Association.

I will abstain from all offensive personality, and advance no fact prejudicial to the honor or reputation of a party or witness, unless required by the justice of the cause with which I am charged;

I will never reject, from any consideration personal to myself, the case of the defenseless or oppressed, or delay any man's cause for lucre or malice.

SO HELP ME GOD.

Judicial Power

PART THREE

Judicial Power

5 / SOURCES OF JUDICIAL POWER

The roots of judicial power can be found in the nature of human society itself. Since men's wants, if not their needs, are virtually without limit and the resources to satisfy those wants are scarce, competition and conflict are almost inevitable in a community based on an individualist ethic. A third party for peaceful settlement of disputes is thus a prerequisite to large-scale group organization, a necessity which even primitive peoples have recognized and tried to meet.

In a nation whose political organization is as complex as that of the United States, disputes between individuals form only one part—and a relatively simple part, however large—of the business of courts. Clashes between organized interest groups, between individuals or groups and the established rules of society, between executive and legislative officials, or between officers of different levels of government, constitute the more difficult grist for the judicial mill. "Hardly any question," Alexis de Tocqueville noted in 1835, "arises in the United States that is not resolved sooner or later into a judicial question."

Courts, Statutes, and the Constitution

It might seem at first glance that judicial discretion is at its maximum when operating strictly under judge-made rules of law, and consequently that statutes and written constitutions restrict the power of the bench. This, of course, can be the case; but statutes and constitutions can also be turned into fecund sources of judicial power. All legislation has to be applied to specific situations, and such application requires interpretation. As Bishop Hoadley warned King George I, "Whosoever hath an absolute authority to interpret any written or spoken laws, it is he who is truly the Law-giver to all intents and purposes, and not the person who first wrote or spoke them."

To function with any degree of success, the American political system needed an umpire to interpret—if not to create—its fundamental principles. First, there was the basic fact of a written constitution. Traditionally, common-law courts had interpreted laws passed by Parliament; and by the terms of Article VI the Constitution was "law," the "supreme Law of the Land." Although the Constitution did not expressly confer upon judges authority to decide what governmental activity did or did not conform to its provisions, Supreme Court justices assumed in *Yale Todd's Case* (1794), *Hylton* v. *United States* (1796), and *Calder* v. *Bull* (1798) that they did possess such power.

Whether the Framers actually intended to confer this right on the courts has been the subject of much speculation by lawyers, politicians, and historians. The protest of Justice Gibson of the Pennsylvania Supreme Court that "the grant of a power so extraordinary ought to appear so plain, that he who should run might read" hit the argument for judicial review at its weakest point. The issue, however, was settled for all practical purposes by John Marshall's opinion in *Marbury* v. *Madison* (1803). Marshall's reasoning was syllogistic. Major premise: The Constitution is the supreme law of the land and judges take an oath to support that Constitution. Minor premise: It is the province of the judiciary to interpret the law. Conclusion: Judges must not enforce a statute which they believe to be in violation of a provision of the Constitution.

If judges could declare acts of Congress invalid, it followed that they could also refuse to apply Executive Orders. The year after *Marbury* v. *Madison*, Marshall accepted this conclusion in his opinion for the Court in *Little* v. *Barreme*, a dispute growing out of the quasi-war with France in the 1790's. An act of Congress had authorized the navy to seize American ships bound *to* any port under French control. Acting under an Executive Order from President Adams directing capture of American vessels bound *to* or *from* French ports, Captain Little of the frigate *Boston* seized *The Flying Fish*, which had just left a French port in Haiti. Marshall held that, in the absence of any stated congressional policy, the President might have legally ordered capture of American ships trading with the French, but that once Congress had specifically legislated on the matter valid presidential policy had to conform to that of Congress.

Like a system of separated powers, a federal system of government stands in need of an umpire. The Supreme Court was quick to take on this function, though here the justices acted with the explicit approval of Congress, which had provided in the Judiciary Act of 1789 that the Supreme Court might review and reverse court decisions upholding the constitutionality of state statutes. In 1797, *Ware* v. *Hylton* ruled that a Virginia statute was inconsistent with the terms of the treaty of peace with Great Britain and therefore invalid under the national supremacy clause of the Constitution. In 1810, the Court in *Fletcher* v. *Peck* held a Georgia statute to be in violation of the constitutional clause forbidding states to impair the obligation of contracts.

These early decisions could be used to support three different types of claims for judicial power. The first, and narrowest, claim was that of judges to supremacy over judicial procedures as outlined in Article III and elsewhere in the Constitution. For instance, judges would have authority to refuse to enforce a statute which allowed a treason conviction on the testimony of one witness rather than the two required by the Constitution. Secondly, and less narrowly, judges could claim they were supreme within their own department to the extent of being able to deny other public officials the use of judicial machinery to enforce policies which judges considered unconstitutional. Nothing in these two claims challenged the equal authority of the President or Congressmen to run their own departments free of judicial authority or to follow their own constitutional views when not resorting to the courts.

The third, and broadest, claim—one foreshadowed rather than articulated in these decisions—was one of supremacy not only over judicial proceedings, but also over the other political processes insofar as constitutional questions were involved. Once more the argument for such supremacy would be structured along syllogistic lines: Government officials take an oath to support the Constitution; the Supreme Court is the authoritative interpreter of the Constitution; therefore, Government officials are oath-bound to obey Supreme Court interpretations of the Constitution *whenever* they make policy decisions.

Acceptance of this last claim would establish the Supreme Court as the balance wheel in the national government's system of separated powers and as the arbiter between federal and local officials. Such acceptance would obviously give the justices far more than brokers' fees.

As participants as well as umpires in the political struggle, they would be able to define not only their own power but also that of the other participants. This broadest claim of judicial supremacy has often been rejected, especially by "strong" presidents like Jackson or Lincoln, who have pointed out that they took an oath to support the Constitution itself, not the judicial gloss on that document. But in general this assertion of ultimate judicial power has been accepted, and it was the fruition of this development which Charles Evans Hughes described in 1908 when he said, "We are under a Constitution, but the Constitution is what the judges say it is."

The Cult of the Robe

While claiming for the Supreme Court the role of guardian of the chastity of the Constitution, John Marshall had delicately avoided the hard fact that the Constitution seldom yields a scientifically objective meaning, even to skilled investigation. As Justice Robert Jackson was to observe in 1952, the materials of constitutional interpretation are often "as enigmatic as the dreams Joseph was called upon to interpret for Pharaoh." The declaratory theory of the judicial function obscures the fact that constitutional interpretation necessarily involves a highly personalized choice among conflicting public policies; and, as was pointed out in Chapter 1, Marshall did not hesitate to embrace this concept of the judge as devoid of will, operating only as a competent and disinterested technical expert in matters constitutional.

The natural law's declaratory theory of how judges ought to decide cases was subtly transformed into a myth explaining how judges *did* decide. Every society has its myths; indeed, because of the limits of human reason it is probable that every society must have myths to justify—and perhaps conceal—the gaps between its announced norms and its actual practices. Just as the myth that judges in private law disputes only "find" law was a price that had to be paid to keep individuals from resorting to violence, so the myth of the judge as the neutral expert who decides policy disputes by reference to a transcendent— and inscrutable—body of law was necessary to hold together the intricate patterns of government organization which had been woven into the tapestry of the American Constitution.

Anthropologists have found that in primitive societies myths and magic help to ease tensions by means of wish fulfillment. They allow man to exercise, at least in his own mind, control over a hostile and mysterious universe. Applying this lesson to the American legal system, it might be concluded that because our political organization needed an impartial umpire, one was created by a wish-fulfilling myth. The analogy can be stretched too far, however. It is simply not true that acceptance of the Court in this role was automatic or immediate. And, when it has been out of tune with the dominant interests in society, either within the nation as a whole or as represented in the other branches of government, the Court has been subjected to more than its share of criticism. John Marshall, Roger Brooke Taney, Charles Evans Hughes, and Earl Warren have all seen the very foundations of the Court's power gravely threatened by legislative or executive attack.

When, on the other hand, judicial decisions have been in harmony with the dominant interests of society, the justices have been the object of lavish praise, bordering on adulation. "We have made idols of [judges]," Senator Norris once complained. "They have black gowns over their persons. Then they become something more than human beings."

The modern revival of the judicial myth can be dated from the last two decades of the nineteenth century. This was the time of the founding of the American Bar Association, which operated in its early days, in Edward S. Corwin's phrase, as "a juristic sewing circle for laissez-faire." As the justices bestowed on the new corporations a special status as wards of the Court, the supposed distinction between will and judgment became a divinely revealed truth, one confirmed by decision after decision upholding principles of Spencerian sociology and classical economics against populist efforts at reform.

The judicial robe played an obvious and important role in this process, cloaking judges with religious symbolism. As William Howard Taft observed in 1908: "It is well that judges should be clothed in robes, not only, that those who witness the administration of justice should be properly advised that the function performed is one different from, and higher, than that which a man discharges as a citizen in the ordinary walks of life; but also, in order to impress the judge himself with the constant consciousness that he is a high priest in the temple of justice and is surrounded with obligations of a sacred character that he cannot escape. . . ."[1]

When, in 1937, Roosevelt's attack on the Court precipitated a judicial reversal on crucial questions of government regulation of the economy, the Court lost its special constituency, and its non-policy-making myth

[1] *Present Day Problems* (New York: Dodd, Mead, 1908), pp. 63–64. Reprinted with permission of Dodd, Mead.

was somewhat tarnished. But old myths, like old soldiers, fade away rather slowly. Once created, the judicial myth gave to judges a source of power which had an existence separate from that of the interest groups which had nourished it. In 1954, the myth still possessed sufficient vitality to be invoked by some of the defenders of the school segregation decisions. Many liberals of the 1950's blandly repeated the conservative creed of the period from 1890 to 1937 that the Supreme Court, in striking down repressions of freedom, was only following the explicit commands of the Constitution.

Legitimization

Groups whose interests are being protected by constitutional or statutory law as currently interpreted by judges have solid cause to foster the judicial myth. The matter, however, goes far deeper. In a pluralistic society many important public policies will adversely affect the aims and interests of a number of powerful individuals and groups. This antagonism will not only create opposition to the wisdom of the policies involved but will also stir up controversy as to the very authority of government to pursue such policies. To meet this situation there must be some means of legitimizing political decisions.

According to Max Weber, governmental action is justified by one or more of three basic means. The first is by appeal to tradition, to the fact that a particular policy is in harmony with historic practice. The second means consists of an appeal to legality, to a rational set of rules which have been given the force of law in a community. The third method Weber called "charismatic." Some leaders are "touched with grace." They govern by the force or sanctity of their personalities rather than by applying traditional or legal rules.

Just as any stable political system must, American government provides many means of legitimizing political action. The campaign speech and the ballot box are among those most frequently used. But the judiciary, especially the Supreme Court, in its role as impartial arbiter plays a significant part here. A Supreme Court decision upholding the constitutionality of a contested statute usually utilizes all three of Weber's modes of legitimation. First, the justices will customarily integrate the law into historical practice, a feat which sometimes requires a good deal of ingenuity. Next the justices will explain how the statute conforms to the Constitution, that vague but fundamental set of rules underlying

American society. Last, the justices bring to bear all the political magic with which the cult of the robe endows them to stamp their history and law with the seal of near-infallibility.

This part in the process of legitimizing policy decisions means that judges have a more positive role to play in the American political system than that of merely declaring statutes unconstitutional. Their share in the legitimizing function also acts as a source of judicial power. Since many of their policy decisions will inevitably engender challenges of a fundamental nature, elected officials will often need the judicial blessing or at least have good cause to fear the malediction of judges. This need may inhibit use of the various counter-weapons which legislators and administrators have at their disposal to check judicial power.

New Myths for Old

The widespread adverse reaction to Roosevelt's Court-packing plan showed that the charisma of the Court rested on a far more complex basis than the immediate popularity of its decisions. The old judicial myth had taken hold even among those liberals who openly deplored the laissez-faire uses to which court power was being put. Much of the strength of that myth was due to the fact that the concept of the impartial, impersonal judge who interpreted the Constitution as mechanically as if it were a private contract had become an ideal of American society. As such an ideal it had been as important in shaping judicial behavior as in influencing public attitudes toward the bench. Judges seldom cynically exploited the myth. However willingly, they were usually its captives as much as were lay believers. And, as captives, judges generally did try to behave as neutral technicians. They were rarely guilty of deliberate deception of others. Their failure was one of self-deception, of not being able to differentiate between the provisions of a constitution "designed to endure for ages to come" and their own social and economic predilections. Only in this century, and especially since 1937, have judges come both to recognize and openly confess their deep personal involvement in policy-making.

This new candor has not been an unmixed blessing. Since 1937 the Justices of the Supreme Court have often seemed in great doubt about their proper function in the political system. The judiciary stands in need of a fresh justification for its policy-making role, but candor makes the creation of mythology difficult. If judges are unwilling—or unable—to become the subject of a new myth, their prestige, and consequently much of their power, will hang on their ability to persuade the losers in litigation, other government officials, and the public at large of judicial competence, integrity, and disinterestedness. The old myth can be criticized on many counts, but it did recognize that those who hold political power are unwilling to allow those considered to be rivals for power to sit in judgment on their policy-making prerogatives; and it was based on an understanding of the harsh social fact that unimpeachable logic is often an inadequate answer to the demands of self-interest.

SELECTED REFERENCES

Arnold, Thurman W., *The Symbols of Government* (New Haven: Yale University Press, 1935).

Beard, Charles A., *The Supreme Court and the Constitution* (New York: Macmillan, 1912).

Black, Charles L., Jr., *The People and the Court* (New York: Macmillan, 1960).

Cardozo, Benjamin N., *The Nature of the Judicial Process* (New Haven: Yale University Press, 1921).

——, *Law and Literature* (New York: Harcourt, Brace, 1931).

Crosskey, William W., *Politics and the Constitution* (Chicago: University of Chicago Press, 1953), 2 vols.

Frank, Jerome, *Law and the Modern Mind* (New York: Brentano's, 1930).

——, "The Cult of the Robe," 28 *Saturday Review of Literature* 12 (Oct. 13, 1945).

——, *Courts on Trial* (Princeton: Princeton University Press, 1949), Chs. 4, 5.

Frank, John P., *Marble Palace* (New York: A. A. Knopf, 1958).

Frankfurter, Felix, "The Supreme Court and the Public," 83 *The Forum* 329 (1930).

Gerth, H. H. and C. Wright Mills (eds.), *From Max Weber: Essays in Sociology* (New York: Oxford University Press, 1946), Ch. 4.

Gray, John C., *The Nature and Sources of the Law* (New York: Columbia University Press, 1909).

Hand, Learned, *The Bill of Rights* (Cambridge: Harvard University Press, 1958).

Hughes, Charles Evans, *The Supreme Court of the United States* (New York: Columbia University Press, 1928).

Mason, Alpheus T., *The Supreme Court from Taft to Warren* (Baton Rouge: Louisiana State University Press, 1958).

———, "The Supreme Court: Temple and Forum," 48 *Yale Review* 524 (1959).

Rodell, Fred, *Nine Men* (New York: Random House, 1955).

Twiss, Benjamin, *Lawyers and the Constitution* (Princeton: Princeton University Press, 1942).

1. *"It is, emphatically, the province and duty of the judicial department, to say what the law is."*

MARBURY V. MADISON

BEFORE GOING *out of office after their crushing defeat in 1800, the Federalists enacted the Judiciary Act of 1801. While this law made several needed reforms its creation of many new judicial posts —to which Adams nominated and the lame-duck Senate confirmed deserving Federalists—made it vulnerable to a charge of court-packing. In signing and delivering the commissions the night before Jefferson's inauguration, Adams' Secretary of State, John Marshall, neglected to deliver a number of appointments to justice-of-the-peace courts in the District of Columbia. The new Secretary of State, James Madison, refused to deliver some of these commissions. William Marbury, one of the disappointed appointees, brought suit in the Supreme Court under a provision of the Judiciary Act of 1789 which Marbury claimed gave the Court original jurisdiction in such cases.*

It was expected that Marshall and the other Federalist justices would order the commission delivered and that Jefferson would defy the Court's authority. Marshall opened his opinion with a nine-thousand-word indictment of Jefferson's ethics, asserting that Marbury was morally entitled to his commission. Next the Chief Justice held that the laws of the United States afforded Marbury a remedy. The third point was whether Marbury had sought the proper remedy. Marshall stated that that portion of the Act of 1789 on which Marbury relied enlarged the original jurisdiction of the Supreme Court as defined in Article III of the Constitution. This apparent conflict raised the issue of whether the justices should follow a statute when it ran counter to their interpretation of the Constitution.

MR. CHIEF JUSTICE MARSHALL delivered the opinion of the Court. . . .

1 Cranch 137, 2 L. Ed. 60 (1803).

The question whether an act, repugnant to the constitution, can become the law of the land, is a question deeply interesting to the United States: but, happily, not of an intricacy proportioned to its interest. It seems only necessary to recognize certain principles, supposed to have been long and well established, to decide it. That the people have an original right to establish for their future government, such principles as, in their opinion, shall most conduce to their own happiness, is the basis on which the whole American fabric has been erected. The exercise of this original right is a very great exertion; nor can it, nor ought it, to be frequently repeated. The principles, therefore, so established, are deemed fundamental: and as the authority from which they proceed is supreme, and can seldom act, they are designed to be permanent.

This original and supreme will organizes the government, and assigns to different departments their respective powers. It may either stop here, or establish certain limits not to be transcended by those departments. The government of the United States is of the latter description. The powers of the legislature are defined and limited; and that those limits may not be mistaken, or forgotten, the constitution is written. To what purpose are powers limited, and to what purpose is that limitation committed to writing, if these limits may, at any time, be passed by those intended to be restrained? The distinction between a government with limited and unlimited powers is abolished, if those limits do not confine the persons on whom they are imposed, and if acts prohibited and acts allowed, are of equal obligation. It is a proposition too plain to be contested, that the constitution controls any legislative act repugnant to it; or that the legislature may alter the constitution by an ordinary act.

Between these alternatives, there is no middle ground. The constitution is either a superior paramount law, unchangeable by ordinary means, or it is on a level with ordinary legislative acts, and, like other acts, is alterable when the legislature shall please to alter it. If the former part of the alternative be true, then a legislative act, contrary to the constitution, is not law; if the latter part be true, then written constitutions are absurd attempts, on the part of the people, to limit a power, in its own nature, illimitable.

Certainly, all those who have framed written constitutions contemplate them as forming the fundamental and paramount law of the nation, and consequently, the theory of every such government must be, that an act of the legislature repugnant to the constitution is void. This theory is essentially attached to a written constitution, and is, consequently, to be considered, by this court, as one of the fundamental principles of our society. It is not, therefore, to be lost sight of, in the further consideration of this subject.

If an act of the legislature, repugnant to the constitution, is void, does it, notwithstanding its invalidity, bind the courts, and oblige them to give it effect? Or, in other words, though it not be law, does it constitute a rule as operative as if it was a law? This would be to overthrow, in fact, what was established in theory; and would seem, at first view, an absurdity too gross to be insisted on. It shall, however, receive a more attentive consideration.

It is, emphatically, the province and duty of the judicial department, to say what the law is. Those who apply the rule to particular cases, must of necessity expound and interpret that rule. If two laws conflict with each other, the courts must decide on the operation of each. So, if a law be in opposition to the constitution; if both the law and the constitution apply to a particular case, so that the court must either decide that case, conformably to the law, disregarding the constitution; or conformably to the constitution, disregarding the law; the court must determine which of these conflicting rules governs the case: this is of the very essence of judicial duty. If then, the courts are to regard the constitution, and the constitution is superior to any ordinary act of the legislature, the constitution, and not such ordinary act, must govern the case to which they both apply.

Those, then, who controvert the principle, that the constitution is to be considered, in court, as a paramount law, are reduced to the necessity of maintaining that courts must close their eyes on the constitution, and see only the law. This doctrine would subvert the very foundation of all written constitutions. . . . It would declare, that if the legislature shall do that which is expressly forbidden, such act, notwithstanding the express prohibition, is in reality effectual. It would be giving to the legislature a practical and real omnipotence, with the same breath which professes to restrict their powers within narrow limits. . . .

The judicial power of the United States is extended to all cases arising under the constitution. Could it be the intention of those who gave this power, to say, that in using it, the constitution should not be looked into? That a case arising under the constitution should be decided, without examining the instrument under which it arises? This is too extravagent to be maintained. In some cases, then, the constitution must be looked into by the judges. And if they can open it at all, what part of it are they forbidden to read or to obey?

There are many other parts of the constitution which serve to illustrate this subject. It is declared that "no tax or duty shall be laid on articles exported from any state." Suppose, a duty on the export of cotton, of tobacco, or of flour; and a suit intended to recover it. Ought judgment to be rendered in such a case? ought the judges to close their eyes on the constitution, and only see the law?

The constitution declares "that no bill of attainder or *ex post facto* law shall be passed." If, however, such a bill should be passed, and a person should be prosecuted under it; must the court condemn to death those victims whom the constitution endeavors to preserve?

"No person," says the constitution, "shall be convicted of treason, unless on the testimony of two witnesses to the same overt act, or on confession in open court." Here, the language of the constitution is addressed especially to the courts. It prescribes, directly for them a rule of evidence not to be departed from. If the legislature should change that rule, and declare one witness, or a confession out of court, sufficient for conviction, must the constitutional principle yield to the legislative act?

From these, and many other selections which might be made, it is apparent that the framers of the constitution contemplated that instrument as a rule for the government of courts, as well as of the legislature. Why otherwise does it direct the judges to take an oath to support it? This oath certainly applies, in an especial manner, to their conduct in their official character. How immoral to impose it on them, if they were to be used as the instruments, and the knowing instruments, for violating what they swear to support! . . . Why does a judge swear to discharge his duties agreeably to the constitution of the United States, if that constitution forms no rule for his government? if it is closed upon him, and cannot be inspected by him? If such be

the real state of things, this is worse than solemn mockery. To prescribe, or to take the oath, becomes equally a crime.

It is also not entirely unworthy of observation, that in declaring
what shall be the supreme law of the land, the constitution itself is
first mentioned; and not the laws of the United States, generally, but
those only which shall be made in pursuance of the constitution, have
that rank.

Thus, the particular phraseology of the constitution of the United
States confirms and strengthens the principle, supposed to be essential
to all written constitutions, that a law repugnant to the constitution is
void; and that courts, as well as other departments, are bound by that
instrument.

The rule must be discharged.

2.   *"The grant of a power so extraordinary ought to appear
so plain, that he who should run might read."*

EAKIN V. RAUB

PERHAPS THE *most effective answer to John Marshall's
reasoning in* Marbury v. Madison *was given by Justice Gibson of the
Pennsylvania Supreme Court in a dissenting opinion in an otherwise
unimportant case. Note that Gibson's statement that the Pennsylvania
Constitution does not specifically mention judicial review is equally
true of the federal Constitution.*

GIBSON, J. . . .

. . . I begin, then, by observing that in this country, the powers of
the judiciary are divisible into those that are POLITICAL and those that
are purely CIVIL. Every power by which one organ of the government
is enabled to control another, or to exert an influence over its acts, is
a political power. . . . [The judiciary's] civil, are its *ordinary* and *appropriate* powers; being part of its essence, and existing independently
of any supposed grant in the constitution. But where the government

12 Sergeant & Rawle 330 (1825).

exists by virtue of a *written* constitution, the judiciary does not necessarily derive from that circumstance, any other than its ordinary and
appropriate powers. Our judiciary is constructed on the principles of
the common law, which enters so essentially into the composition of
our social institutions as to be inseparable from them, and to be, in
fact, the basis of the whole scheme of our civil and political liberty.
In adopting any organ or instrument of the common law, we take it
with just such powers and capacities as were incident to it at the common law, except where these are expressly, or by necessary implication, abridged or enlarged in the act of adoption; and, that such act is
a written instrument, cannot vary its consequences or construction.
. . . Now, what are the powers of the judiciary at the common law?
They are those that necessarily arise out of its immediate business;
and they are therefore commensurate only with the judicial execution
of the municipal law, or, in other words, with the administration of
distributive justice, without extending to anything of a political cast
whatever. . . . With us, although the legislature be the depository of
only so much of the sovereignty as the people have thought fit to impart, it is nevertheless sovereign within the limit of its powers, and
may relatively claim the same pre-eminence here that it may claim
elsewhere. It will be conceded, then, that the ordinary and essential
powers of the judiciary do not extend to the annulling of an act of the
legislature. . . .

The constitution of *Pennsylvania* contains no express grant of political powers to the judiciary. But, to establish a grant by implication,
the constitution is said to be a law of superior obligation; and, consequently, that if it were to come into collision with an act of the legislature, the latter would have to give way. This is conceded. But it is
a fallacy, to suppose that they can come into collision *before the
judiciary*. . . .

The constitution and the right of the legislature to pass the act, may
be in collision. But is that a legitimate subject for judicial determination? If it be, the judiciary must be a peculiar organ, to revise the proceedings of the legislature, and to correct its mistakes; and in what
part of the constitution are we to look for this proud pre-eminence?
Viewing the matter in the opposite direction, what would be thought
of an act of assembly in which it should be declared that the Supreme

Court had, in a particular case, put a wrong construction on the constitution of the United States, and that the judgment should therefore be reversed? It would doubtless be thought a usurpation of judicial power. But it is by no means clear, that to declare a law void which has been enacted according to the forms prescribed in the constitution, is not a usurpation of legislative power. . . .

But it has been said to be emphatically the business of the judiciary, to ascertain and pronounce what the law is; and that this necessarily involves a consideration of the constitution. It does so: but how far? If the judiciary will inquire into anything besides the form of enactment, where shall it stop? There must be some point of limitation to such an inquiry; for no one will pretend that a judge would be justifiable in calling for the election returns, or scrutinizing the qualifications of those who composed the legislature. . . .

. . . In theory, all the organs of the government are of equal capacity; or, if not equal, each must be supposed to have superior capacity only for those things which peculiarly belong to it; and, as legislation peculiarly involves the consideration of those limitations which are put on the law-making power, and the interpretation of the laws when made, involves only the construction of the laws themselves, it follows that the construction of the constitution in this particular belongs to the legislature, which ought therefore to be taken to have superior capacity to judge of the constitutionality of its own acts. But suppose all to be of equal capacity in every respect, why should one exercise a controlling power over the rest? That the judiciary is of superior rank, has never been pretended, although it has been said to be co-ordinate. It is not easy, however, to comprehend how the power which gives law to all the rest, can be of no more than equal rank with one which receives it, and is answerable to the former for the observance of its statutes. Legislation is essentially an act of sovereign power; but the execution of the laws by instruments that are governed by prescribed rules and exercise no power of volition, is essentially otherwise. . . . It may be said, the power of the legislature, also, is limited by prescribed rules. It is so. But it is, nevertheless, the power of the people, and sovereign as far as it extends. It cannot be said, that the judiciary is co-ordinate merely because it is established by the constitution. If that were sufficient, sheriffs, registers of wills, and recorders of deeds, would be so too. Within the pale of their authority, the acts of these officers will have the power of the people for their support; but no one will pretend, they are of equal dignity with the acts of the legislature. Inequality of rank arises not from the manner in which the organ has been constituted, but from its essence and the nature of its functions; and the legislative organ is superior to every other, inasmuch as the power to will and to command, is essentially superior to the power to act and to obey. . . .

. . . had it been intended to interpose the judiciary as an additional barrier, the matter would surely not have been left in doubt. The judges would not have been left to stand on the insecure and ever shifting ground of public opinion as to constructive powers; they would have been placed on the impregnable ground of an express grant. They would not have been compelled to resort to the debates in the convention, or the opinion that was generally entertained at the time. . . . The grant of a power so extraordinary ought to appear so plain, that he who should run might read. . . .

What I have in view in this inquiry, is the supposed right of the judiciary to interfere, in cases where the constitution is to be carried into effect through the instrumentality of the legislature, and where that organ must necessarily first decide on the constitutionality of its own act. The oath to support the constitution is not peculiar to the judges, but is taken indiscriminately by every officer of the government, and is designed rather as a test of the political principles of the man, than to bind the officer in the discharge of his duty: otherwise it is difficult to determine what operation it is to have in the case of a recorder of deeds, for instance, who, in the execution of his office, has nothing to do with the constitution. But granting it to relate to the official conduct of the judge, as well as every other officer, and not to his political principles, still it must be understood in reference to supporting the constitution, *only as far as that may be involved in his official duty;* and, consequently, if his official duty does not comprehend an inquiry into the authority of the legislature, neither does his oath. . . .

But do not the judges do a positive act in violation of the constitution, when they give effect to an unconstitutional law? Not if the law has been passed according to the forms established in the constitution.

The fallacy of the question is, in supposing that the judiciary adopts
the acts of the legislature as its own; whereas the enactment of a law
and the interpretation of it are not concurrent acts, and as the judiciary is not required to concur in the enactment, neither is it in the
breach of the constitution which may be the consequence of the
enactment. The fault is imputable to the legislature, and on it the
responsibility exclusively rests. . . .

But it has been said, that this construction would deprive the citizen
of the advantages which are peculiar to a written constitution, by at
once declaring the power of the legislature in practice to be illimitable. . . . But there is no magic or inherent power in parchment and
ink, to command respect and protect principles from violation. In the
business of government a recurrence to first principles answers the
end of an observation at sea with a view to correct the dead reckon-
ing; and for this purpose, a written constitution is an instrument of
inestimable value. It is of inestimable value, also, in rendering its first
principles familiar to the mass of people; for, after all, there is no
effectual guard against legislative usurpation but public opinion, the
force of which, in this country is inconceivably great. . . . Once let
public opinion be so corrupt as to sanction every misconstruction of
the constitution and abuse of power which the temptation of the moment may dictate, and the party which may happen to be predomi-
nant, will laugh at the puny efforts of a dependent power to arrest it
in its course.

For these reasons, I am of opinion that it rests with the people, in
whom full and absolute sovereign power resides, to correct abuses
in legislation, by instructing their representatives to repeal the ob-
noxious act. . . . On the other hand, the judiciary is not infallible; and
an error by it would admit of no remedy but a more distinct expression of the public will, through the extraordinary medium of a convention; whereas, an error by the legislature admits of a remedy by
an exertion of the same will, in the ordinary exercise of the right of
suffrage,—a mode better calculated to attain the end, without popular
excitement. . . .

But in regard to an act of [a state] assembly, which is found to be
in collision with the constitution, laws, or treaties of the *United States,*

I take the duty of the judiciary to be exactly the reverse. By becoming parties to the federal constitution, the states have agreed to several limitations of their individual sovereignty, to enforce which, it was thought to be absolutely necessary to prevent them from giving effect to laws in violation of those limitations, through the instrumentality of their own judges. Accordingly, it is declared in the sixth article and second section of the federal constitution, that "This constitution, and the laws of the *United States* which shall be made in pursuance thereof, and all treaties made, or which shall be made under the authority of the *United States,* shall be the *supreme* law of the land; and the *judges* in every *state* shall be BOUND thereby: anything in the *laws* or *constitution* of any *state* to the contrary notwithstanding."

This is an express grant of a political power, and it is conclusive to show that no law of inferior obligation, as every state law must necessarily be, can be executed at the expense of the constitution, laws, or treaties of the *United States.* . . .

3.   *"I have an oath . . ."*

DWIGHT D. EISENHOWER, PRESS CONFERENCE, AUGUST 20, 1958

QUESTION. J. Anthony Lewis, *New York Times*: Sir . . . I just wondered whether you would talk to us at all about your personal feeling on the principle involved, basically the principle of school integration, and whether you believe there should—you personally favor the beginning of an end to segregated schools?

THE PRESIDENT. I have always declined to do that for the simple reason that here was something that the Supreme Court says, "This is the direction of the Constitution, this is the instruction of the Constitution"; that is, they say, "This is the meaning of the Constitution."

Now, I am sworn to one thing, to defend the Constitution of the United States, and execute its laws. Therefore, for me to weaken public opinion by discussion of separate cases, where I might agree

Public Papers of the Presidents: Dwight D. Eisenhower, 1958 (Washington: Government Printing Office, 1959), p. 625.

or might disagree, seems to me to be completely unwise and not a good thing to do.

I have an oath; I expect to carry it out. And the mere fact that I could disagree very violently with a decision, and would so express myself, then my own duty would be much more difficult to carry out I think.

So I think it is just not good business for me to do so.

4.   *". . . co-ordinate branches should be checks on each other."*

THOMAS JEFFERSON TO ABIGAIL ADAMS

AFTER HE *became President, Jefferson pardoned a number of prisoners who had been convicted under the Sedition Act. In 1804 he explained to the wife of the former President why he had taken such action.*

. . . YOU SEEM to think it devolved on the judges to decide on the validity of the sedition law. But nothing in the Constitution has given them a right to decide for the Executive, more than the Executive to decide for them. Both magistrates are equally independent in the sphere of action assigned to them. The judges, believing the law constitutional, had a right to pass a sentence of fine and imprisonment; because that power was placed in their hands by the Constitution. But the executive, believing the law to be unconstitutional, were bound to remit the execution of it because that power had been confided to them by the Constitution. That instrument meant that its co-ordinate branches should be checks on each other. But the opinion which gives to the judges the right to decide what laws are constitutional, and what are not, not only for themselves in their own sphere of action, but for the legislature and executive also in their spheres, would make the judiciary a despotic branch.

Andrew A. Lipscomb (ed.), *Writings of Thomas Jefferson* (Washington: Thomas Jefferson Memorial Association, 1903), XI, 50–51.

5.
> *"[A state decision] may be re-examined and reversed or affirmed in the Supreme Court of the United States."*

JUDICIARY ACT OF 1789, SECTION 25

THAT A final judgment or decree in any suit, in the highest court of law or equity of a State in which a decision in the suit could be had, where is drawn in question the validity of a treaty or statute of, or an authority exercised under the United States, and the decision is against their validity; or where is drawn in question the validity of a statute of, or an authority exercised under any State, on the ground of their being repugnant to the constitution, treaties or laws of the United States, and the decision is in favour of their validity, or where is drawn in question the construction of any clause of the constitution, or of a treaty, or statute of, or commission held under the United States, and the decision is against the title, right, privilege or exemption specifically set up or claimed by either party, under such clause of the said constitution, treaty, statute or commission, may be re-examined and reversed or affirmed in the Supreme Court of the United States . . . .

1 *U.S. Statutes at Large* 85-86.

6.
> *"The constitution . . . was . . . established, not by the states . . . but . . . by 'the People of the United States.'"*

MARTIN V. HUNTER'S LESSEE

IN 1813 *the Supreme Court had reversed a decision of the Virginia Court of Appeals regarding the protection afforded land rights of British citizens by the Jay Treaty. The Virginia high court, however, refused to obey this decision or to acknowledge the authority of the Supreme Court, claiming that while state judges were obliged to obey the Constitution, laws, and treaties of the United States, they*

1 Wheaton 304, 4 L. Ed. 97 (1816).

*were not bound to obey the Supreme Court's interpretations of these
acts. State and federal judges were officers of two different sovereignties and neither had an obligation to obey the decisions of the other.
With this refusal, the case was again brought before the Supreme
Court.*

STORY, J., delivered the opinion of the court. . . .

The constitution of the United States was ordained and established,
not by the states in their sovereign capacities, but emphatically, as
the preamble of the constitution declares, by "the People of the
United States." There can be no doubt, that it was competent to the
people to invest the general government with all the powers which
they might deem proper and necessary; to extend or restrain these
powers according to their own good pleasure, and to give them
a paramount and supreme authority. As little doubt can there be,
that the people had a right to prohibit to the states the exercise of
any powers which were, in their judgment, incompatible with the
objects of the general compact; to make the powers of the state governments, in given cases, subordinate to those of the nation, or to
reserve to themselves those sovereign authorities which they might
not choose to delegate to either. The constitution was not, therefore,
necessarily carved out of existing state sovereignties, nor a surrender
of powers already existing in state institutions, for the powers of the
states depend upon their own constitutions; and the people of every
state had the right to modify and restrain them, according to their
own views of policy or principle. . . .

This leads us to the consideration of the great question, as to the
nature and extent of the appellate jurisdiction of the United States.
We have already seen, that appellate jurisdiction is given by the
constitution to the supreme court, in all cases where it has not original
jurisdiction; subject, however, to such exceptions and regulations as
congress may prescribe. It is, therefore, capable of embracing every
case enumerated in the constitution, which is not exclusively to be
decided by way of original jurisdiction. . . . The appellate power is
not limited by the terms of the third article to any particular courts.
The words are, "the judicial power (which includes appellate power)
shall extend to all cases," &c., and "in all other cases before mentioned

the supreme court shall have appellate jurisdiction." It is the case, then, and not the court, that gives the jurisdiction. If the judicial power extends to the case, it will be in vain to search in the letter of the constitution for any qualification as to the tribunal where it depends. It is incumbent, then, upon those who assert such a qualification, to show its existence, by necessary implication. If the text be clear and distinct, no restriction upon its plain and obvious import ought to be admitted, unless the inference be irresistible.

If the constitution meant to limit the appellate jurisdiction to cases pending in the courts of the United States, it would necessarily follow, that the jurisdiction of these courts would, in all the cases enumerated in the constitution, be exclusive of state tribunals. . . .

But it is plain, that the framers of the constitution did contemplate that cases within the judicial cognisance of the United States, not only might, but would, arise in the state courts, in the exercise of their ordinary jurisdiction. With this view, the sixth article declares, that "this constitution, and the laws of the United States which shall be made in pursuance thereof, and all treaties made, or which shall be made, under the authority of the United States, shall be the supreme law of the land, and the judges in every state shall be bound thereby, anything in the constitution or laws of any state to the contrary notwithstanding." It is obvious, that this obligation is imperative upon the state judges, in their official, and not merely in their private, capacities. . . .

It must, therefore, be conceded, that the constitution not only contemplated, but meant to provide for cases within the scope of the judicial power of the United States, which might yet depend before state tribunals. It was foreseen, that in the exercise of their ordinary jurisdiction, state courts would incidentally take cognisance of cases arising under the constitution, the laws and treaties of the United States. Yet, to all these cases, the judicial power, by the very terms of the constitution, is to extend. . . .

It has been argued, that such an appellate jurisdiction over state courts is inconsistent with the genius of our governments, and the spirit of the constitution. That the latter was never designed to act upon state sovereignties, but only upon the people, and that if the power exists, it will materially impair the sovereignty of the states,

and the independence of their courts. We cannot yield to the force
of this reasoning; it assumes principles which we cannot admit, and
draws conclusions to which we do not yield our assent.

It is a mistake, that the constitution was not designed to operate
upon states, in their corporate capacities. It is crowded with provisions which restrain or annul the sovereignty of the states, in some
of the highest branches of their prerogatives. The tenth section of the
first article contains a long list of disabilities and prohibitions imposed
upon the states. Surely, when such essential portions of state sovereignty are taken away, or prohibited to be exercised, it cannot be
correctly asserted, that the constitution does not act upon the states.
The language of the constitution is also imperative upon the states,
as to the performance of many duties. . . . The courts of the United
States can, without question, revise the proceedings of the executive
and legislative authorities of the states, and if they are found to be
contrary to the constitution, may declare them to be of no legal validity. Surely, the exercise of the same right over judicial tribunals
is not a higher or more dangerous act of sovereign power.

Nor can such a right be deemed to impair the independence of
state judges. It is assuming the very ground in controversy, to assert
that they possess an absolute independence of the United States. In
respect to the powers granted to the United States, they are not
independent; they are expressly bound to obedience, by the letter of
the constitution; and if they should unintentionally transcend their
authority, or misconstrue the constitution, there is no more reason for
giving their judgments an absolute and irresistible force, than for
giving it to the acts of the other co-ordinate departments of state
sovereignty.

The argument urged from the possibility of the abuse of the revising power, is equally unsatisfactory. It is always a doubtful course,
to argue against the use or existence of a power, from the possibility
of its abuse. It is still more difficult, by such an argument, to ingraft
upon a general power, a restriction which is not to be found in the
terms in which it is given. From the very nature of things, the absolute right of decision, in the last resort, must rest somewhere—
wherever it may be vested, it is susceptible of abuse. In all questions
of jurisdiction, the inferior, or appellate court, must pronounce the

final judgment; and common sense, as well as legal reasoning, has conferred it upon the latter. . . .

It is further argued, that no great public mischief can result from a construction which shall limit the appellate power of the United States to cases in their own courts: first, because state judges are bound by an oath to support the constitution of the United States, and must be presumed to be men of learning and integrity; and secondly, because congress must have an unquestionable right to remove all cases within the scope of the judicial power from the state courts to the courts of the United States, at any time before final judgment, though not after final judgment. As to the first reason—admitting that the judges of the state courts are, and always will be, of as much learning, integrity and wisdom, as those of the courts of the United States (which we very cheerfully admit), it does not aid the argument. It is manifest that the constitution has proceeded upon a theory of its own, and given or withheld powers according to the judgment of the American people, by whom it was adopted. We can only construe its powers, and cannot inquire into the policy or principles which induced the grant of them. The constitution has presumed (whether rightly or wrongly, we do not inquire), that state attachments, state prejudices, state jealousies, and state interests, might sometimes obstruct, or control, or be supposed to obstruct or control, the regular administration of justice. . . .

This is not all. A motive of another kind, perfectly compatible with the most sincere respect for state tribunals, might induce the grant of appellate power over their decisions. That motive is the importance, and even necessity of uniformity of decisions throughout the whole United States, upon all subjects within the purview of the constitution. Judges of equal learning and integrity, in different states, might differently interpret the statute, or a treaty of the Unied States, or even the constitution itself: if there were no revising authority to control these jarring and discordant judgments, and harmonize them into uniformity, the laws, the treaties and the constitution of the United States would be different, in different states, and might, perhaps, never have precisely the same construction, obligation or efficiency, in any two states. The public mischiefs that would attend such a state of things would be truly deplorable; and it cannot be believed, that they could have escaped the enlightened convention which formed the constitution. What, indeed, might then have been only prophecy, has now become fact; and the appellate jurisdiction must continue to be the only adequate remedy for such evils.

There is an additional consideration, which is entitled to great weight. The constitution of the United States was designed for the common and equal benefit of all the people of the United States. The judicial power was granted for the same benign and salutary purposes. It was not to be exercised exclusively for the benefit of parties who might be plaintiffs, and would elect the national *forum*, but also for the protection of defendants who might be entitled to try their rights, or assert their privileges, before the same *forum*. Yet, if the construction contended for be correct, it will follow, that as the plaintiff may always elect the state court, the defendant may be deprived of all the security which the constitution intended in aid of his rights. Such a state of things can, in no respect, be considered as giving equal rights. . . .

It is the opinion of the whole court, that the judgment of the court of appeals of Virginia, rendered on the mandate in this cause, be reversed, and the judgment of the district court, held at Winchester, be, and the same is hereby affirmed.

JOHNSON, J.—It will be observed, in this case, that the court disavows all intention to decide on the right to issue compulsory process to the state courts; thus leaving us, in my opinion, where the constitution and laws place us—supreme over persons and cases, so far as our judicial powers extend, but not asserting any compulsory control over the state tribunals. In this view, I acquiesce in their opinion, but not altogether in the reasoning or opinion of my brother who delivered it. . . .

7.
> *"No state . . . officer can war against the Constitution without violating his undertaking to support it."*

COOPER V. AARON

IN 1955, *after the Supreme Court's decision in* Brown v. Topeka *declaring public school segregation unconstitutional, the Little Rock school board voluntarily drew up a plan for gradual integration. The NAACP attacked this plan as too slow, but it was approved by the lower federal courts. In 1956 the Arkansas legislature "nullified"* Brown v. Topeka *and passed a number of statutes to avoid desegregation. The Little Rock school board, however, persisted in its plan; and when the first Negro children showed up at Central High School in September, 1958, the Governor used the National Guard to bar their entry. After much legal maneuvering, mob violence, and federal military intervention, the colored children were admitted to the school. (Some of these documents are reprinted in Ch. 6.)*

At the end of the year the school board asserted that Central High School had become so disrupted by tension and turmoil that education had become impossible. The board therefore asked the district court that it be allowed to suspend desegregation for two and a half years, until popular feeling had calmed down. The district judge granted the request, but the Court of Appeals reversed the district judge. The board sought and obtained certiorari from the Supreme Court.

OPINION OF the Court by the CHIEF JUSTICE, MR. JUSTICE BLACK, MR. JUSTICE FRANKFURTER, MR. JUSTICE DOUGLAS, MR. JUSTICE BURTON, MR. JUSTICE CLARK, MR. JUSTICE HARLAN, MR. JUSTICE BRENNAN, and MR. JUSTICE WHITTAKER. . . .

The constitutional rights of respondents are not to be sacrificed or yielded to the violence and disorder which have followed upon the actions of the Governor and Legislature. . . . Thus law and order are not here to be preserved by depriving the Negro children of their constitutional rights. The record before us clearly establishes that

358 U.S. 1, 78 S. Ct. 1401, 3 L. Ed. 2d 5 (1958).

the growth of the Board's difficulties to a magnitude beyond its unaided power to control is the product of state action. Those difficulties, as counsel for the Board forthrightly conceded on the oral argument in this Court, can also be brought under control by state action.

The controlling legal principles are plain. The command of the Fourteenth Amendment is that no "State" shall deny to any person within its jurisdiction the equal protection of the law . . . the prohibitions of the Fourteenth Amendment extend to all action of the State denying equal protection of the laws; whatever the agency of the State taking the action . . . or whatever the guise in which it is taken. . . . In short, the constitutional rights of children not to be discriminated against in school admission on grounds of race or color declared by this Court in the Brown case can neither be nullified openly and directly by state legislators or state executive or judicial officers, nor nullified indirectly by them through evasive schemes for segregation whether attempted "ingeniously or ingenuously." . . .

What has been said, in the light of the facts developed, is enough to dispose of the case. However, we should answer the premise of the actions of the Governor and Legislature that they are not bound by our holding in the Brown case. It is necessary only to recall some basic constitutional propositions which are settled doctrine.

Article 6 of the Constitution makes the Constitution the "supreme Law of the Land." In 1803, Chief Justice Marshall, speaking for a unanimous Court, referring to the Constitution as "the fundamental and paramount law of the nation," declared in the notable case of Marbury v. Madison . . . that "It is emphatically the province and duty of the judicial department to say what the law is." This decision declared the basic principle that the federal judiciary is supreme in the exposition of the law of the Constitution, and that principle has ever since been respected by this Court and the Country as a permanent and indispensable feature of our constitutional system. It follows that the interpretation of the Fourteenth Amendment enunciated by this Court in the Brown Case is the supreme law of the land, and Art. 6 of the Constitution makes it of binding effect on the States "any Thing in the Constitution or Laws of any State to the Contrary notwithstanding." Every state legislator and executive and judicial officer is solemnly committed by oath taken pursuant to Art. 6, cl. 3 "to support this Constitution." Chief Justice Taney, speaking for a unanimous Court in 1859, said that this requirement reflected the framers' "anxiety to preserve it [the Constitution] in full force, in all its powers, and to guard against resistance to or evasion of its authority, on the part of a State. . . ." Ableman v. Booth. . . .

No state legislator or executive or judicial officer can war against the Constitution without violating his undertaking to support it. Chief Justice Marshall spoke for a unanimous Court in saying that: "If the legislatures of the several states may, at will, annul the judgments of the courts of the United States, and destroy the rights acquired under those judgments, the constitution itself becomes a solemn mockery. . . ." United States v. Peters. . . . A Governor who asserts a power to nullify a federal court order is similarly restrained. If he had such power, said Chief Justice Hughes, in 1932, also for a unanimous Court, "it is manifest that the fiat of a state Governor, and not the Constitution of the United States, would be the supreme law of the land; that the restrictions of the Federal Constitution upon the exercise of state power would be but impotent phrases. . . ." Sterling v. Constantin. . . .

It is, of course, quite true that the responsibility for public education is primarily the concern of the States, but it is equally true that such responsibilities, like all other state activity, must be exercised consistently with federal constitutional requirements as they apply to state action. The Constitution created a government dedicated to equal justice under law. The Fourteenth Amendment embodied and emphasized that ideal. State support of segregated schools through any arrangement, management, funds, or property cannot be squared with the Amendment's command that no State shall deny to any person within its jurisdiction the equal protection of the laws. The right of a student not to be segregated on racial grounds in schools so maintained is indeed so fundamental and pervasive that it is embraced in the concept of due process of law. . . . The basic decision in Brown was unanimously reached by this Court only after the case had been briefed and twice argued and the issues had been given the most serious consideration. Since the first Brown opinion three new Justices have come to the Court. They are at one with the Justices still on the Court who participated in that basic decision as to its correctness, and that decision is now unanimously reaffirmed. The principles announced in that decision and the obedience of the States to them, according to the command of the Constitution, are indispensable for the protection of the freedoms guaranteed by our fundamental charter for all of us. Our constitutional ideal of equal justice under law is thus made a living truth.

8.   *" 'We live by symbols' . . ."*

CONSTITUTION AND COURT AS SYMBOLS   *Max Lerner**

I. SYMBOLS IN POLITICS

Like children and neurotics, man as a political animal lives in a world riddled with bugbears and taboos—a dream world of symbols in which the shadows loom far larger than the realities they represent. Political thinkers as diverse as the English idealists and the classical Marxians have incurred a common fallacy: they have taken their own sense of the logical relation of things and read it into the way men behave. Actually men behave in their political lives with a disheartening illogicality. They live in a jungle of fear, filled with phantoms of what they have heard and imagined and been told. . . .

That is why men always find themselves forced to seek some symbol of divine right. Talk to the men on the street, the men in the mines and factories and steel mills and real-estate offices and filling-stations, dig into their minds and even below the threshold of their consciousness, and you will in the main find that Constitution and Supreme Court are symbols of an ancient sureness and a comforting stability. If you watch the black-robed justices as they come filing in, if you

46 *Yale Law Journal* 1290 (1937). Copyright 1937 Yale Law Journal Company. Reprinted with permission. Also reprinted in Max Lerner, *Ideas for the Ice Age* (New York: Viking, 1941), pp. 232–264.

* Professor of American Civilization, Brandeis University; formerly editor of *The Nation*.

listen to them read their opinions, you will be strong not to succumb to a sense of the Court's timelessness. Americans have been told that they are a people without a tradition, without a culture. And it does in truth seem surprising that the restless, unstable energies of the American people should have created anything that seems as deep-rooted and as timeless as the Supreme Court. Even today, in its new and imposing building, the Court still wears the ancient garments of divine right. . . . It has, to be sure, walked along the evolutionary path, but only as Orpheus once walked along the pathway out of Hell—with head turned backward.

What accounts for the extraordinary toughness and viability of the Court? . . . Most clearly and simply I should put it as follows: the nature and extent of the Supreme Court's power are best understood by seeing it as our basic instrument of sovereignty—an integral part of the American capitalist economic order. But the support of the judicial power lies largely in the psychological realm; its roots are in the minds of the people. Historically the judicial power must be seen as the instrument of the few; psychologically it is the symbol of the many. "We live by symbols," wrote Mr. Justice Holmes. It is to the Supreme Court and the Constitution as symbols that we must first turn. . . .

The Supreme Court as symbol goes hand in hand with the Constitution as symbol. Since the Supreme Court is popularly considered as exercising a guardianship over the Constitution, the result has been to invest the judges of the Court with all the panoply of sanctity with which the Constitution has itself been invested. This has had for American history an importance that can scarcely be overestimated. Constitutions, like all creations of the human mind and the human will, have an existence in men's imagination and men's emotions quite apart from their actual use in ordering men's affairs. This function has been called "constitutionalism," which Walton Hamilton has defined as "the name given to the trust which men repose in the power of words engrossed on parchment to keep a government in order." Edward S. Corwin . . . has pointed out that the Constitution has two aspects: it is an *instrument* and a *symbol*. As an instrument it must be viewed hard-headedly and used flexibly to promote the people's welfare in the present and future. As a symbol it is part of the mass mind, capable of arousing intense popular hysteria, loaded with a terrible inertia, its face turned toward the past.

II. CONSTITUTION INTO FETISH

To understand the fetishism of the Constitution one would require the detachment of an anthropologist. Every tribe needs its totem and its fetish, and the Constitution is ours. Every tribe clings to something which it believes to possess supernatural powers, as an instrument for controlling unknown forces in a hostile universe. This is true of civilized nations as well. Men need always something on which to fix their emotions, whether positively in the form of adoration or deification, or negatively in the form of a taboo. Like every people, the American people have wanted some anchorage, some link with the invariant.

> Change and decay in all around I see,
> Oh, Thou who changest not, abide with me.

And the Rock of Ages has been as essential in the politics of America as in its religion. In fact the very habits of mind begotten by an authoritarian Bible and a religion of submission to a higher power have been carried over to an authoritarian Constitution and a philosophy of submission to a "higher law"; and a country like America, in which its early tradition had prohibited a state church, ends by getting a state church after all, although in a secular form. . . .

What eased the path of Constitution-worship further was the fact that the new government was ratified on the ascending arc of a period of prosperity. It was thus possible to attribute to the government not only those effects which genuinely flowed from the stopping of the trade wars and the increased sense of confidence among the mercantile groups, but those also which, because of a war-locked Europe, were for a quarter-century to play economically into the hands of America. On the crest of this wave of prosperity the exultation over the new America was converted into the tradition of a perfect Constitution. Undoubtedly the sponsors of the new government were happy to have the decision about their work transferred from the plane of debate over principles to the plane of emotion and faith.

There were some, like James Madison in his famous tenth essay of the *Federalist*, who saw that faction founded upon disparate property interests lay at the core of all government; but that meant merely that they and others were grateful for the emergence of a rhetoric of the national interest to push class interests into the background. How Constitution-worship could be used thus was illustrated in the early jockeyings of the Federalists and anti-Federalists for positions of advantage. At first the anti-Federalists opposed ratification. But when it became clear that the new government was popular, the Jeffersonian party accepted its defeat and sought even to train the enemies' guns back on them. In doing this the Jeffersonians had the precedent of a skillful maneuver by which, in 1787 and 1788, the nationalists under the leadership of Hamilton had appropriated the name "Federalists" with all the emotional associations of decentralization and states' rights that went with it. It was a daring stroke, "this clearly conscious philological ambuscade into which the American masses fell." But Jefferson was no less daring and in the long run more effective when he and his party abandoned their opposition to the Constitution and became the eager rivals of the Federalists in worshiping it. Both parties showed an amazing unanimity in pointing out the perfections of the Constitution; they delighted in honoring it, and they measured their distance from each other by reciprocal charges of violating it and departing from its spirit. Their divergences were those of interpretation. . . .

But when we have allowed for the rhetoric of national unity, the persuasion of prosperity, the advantages of having a safety valve to let off the steam of party conflict; when we have added the propaganda of clergymen, lawyers, editors, teachers, we have not completed our analysis. Deeper than any of these were forces operating on the less conscious levels of the popular mind. One was the belief that ordinary people, as well as lawyers, have in word-magic. The American was the first written national Constitution. What matter that it was a broad pathway of government rather than a fixed and narrow code of law? The very definiteness with which the design for a government was set down in words on parchment was enough to command admiration and then reverence. What was wanted was a visible symbol of the things men hold dear. The American people had conquered a domain from its natives, wrested the sovereignty over it from the greatest power in Europe, fought their way to liberty. They wanted a visible mark of their accomplishment: *ecce signum.* And they wanted it all the more strongly as they began to suspect that in the process of consolidating their regime they had lost sight of their original impulsions and the goals they had dreamt of. . . . They found their peace in the safe haven of the Constitution. Here was the document into which the Founding Fathers had poured their wisdom as into a vessel; the Fathers themselves grew ever larger in stature as they receded from view; the era in which they lived and fought became a Golden Age; in that age there had been a fresh dawn for the world, and its men were giants against the sky; what they had fought for was abstracted from its living context and became a set of "principles," eternally true and universally applicable. . . . The Golden Age had become a political instrument. . . .

But the hunger for a national symbolism was not enough to solve the problems of sectional and class interests. . . . The politicians of the 1830's, like all politicians, finally fell under the sway of their own rhetoric. They actually believed in the efficacy of their legalistic arguments. They trusted in the sanctity of the Union within the symbolism of the Constitution to preserve the Union. The tragedy of Webster's "Reply to Hayne" was that symbolism did not prove enough.

While the war itself was a tragic defeat for the efficacy of the constitutional symbolism, the Northern victory only served to confirm that symbolism. As we shall see in the next section, however, the Constitution itself was no longer asked to bear unaided the burden of solving the problems which threatened the national unity. To the rhetoric of the Constitution was added the divine right of judges and the yeoman's work that the judicial power had to do. The heyday of constitutional symbolism was over with the Civil War. I do not say there was a slackening of constitutional fetishism. By no means. If anything, that fetishism grew in passion and intensity. But it no longer had to bear the heavy freightage of keeping party disputes in bounds and hemming economic conflicts within the ambit of peaceful political brawls. It is not too much to say that after the Civil War the *function* of constitutional symbolism became auxiliary to the cult of the judicial power. . . .

III. DIVINE RIGHT: AMERICAN PLAN

In a democracy in the twentieth century it may seem irreverent or whimsical or even merely literary to talk of divine right. Yet very little is clearer in the American scheme than the fact that the cult of the Supreme Court is the characteristic emotional cement by which American capitalism and American democracy are held together. The celebration of the Supreme Court in the capitalist America of the nineteenth and twentieth centuries performs the same social function as the celebration of kingship in the mercantilist Europe of the sixteenth to eighteenth centuries. On the main highways of the development of the Western world, what used to be the divine right of kings has been replaced by the divine right of judges. . . .

. . . America, which has carried capitalism to its highest peak of perfection, needed also a divine sanction of unusual potency with which to invest it. Because our parliamentary institutions—our Congresses and Presidents—are potentially too responsive to democratic impulses, the "higher law" was extended to hem in the acts of the people's representatives themselves. That "higher law" was located in the Constitution, but being divine it could not be contained even in that. So it overflowed and became a "brooding omnipresence in the sky" which could be brought to earth only when it was finally located in the minds of the men who took over the exclusive function of interpreting the Constitution. As Brooks Adams wrote in 1913, in his masterly *Theory of Social Revolutions,* by the "rule of reason" . . . the Court was taking over the authority of the church to "grant indulgences for reasonable causes." From the medieval church to American finance capitalism the wheel has come a full turn.

There are three principal elements in the pattern of divine right as it may be found in the popular mind. One is the fetishism of the Constitution, the second is the claim of the Court to the exclusive guardianship of the Constitution, and the third is the tradition of judicial neutrality. . . . What enabled the propertied groups, in the last analysis, to make use of the judicial power was the strength and evocative force of the constitutional tradition. . . . [But t]he fetishism of the Constitution, as a flexible instrument open to various construction, was in itself inadequate. In short, a *faith* was not enough. It had to be a faith deposited in a *power*. That power was the judicial power. The function of interpreting the Constitution had to be specialized in a single tribunal.

Thus arose the second element in the pattern of divine right: the exclusive claim of the Supreme Court to a guardianship of the Constitution. John Marshall and Joseph Story urged it very early in our history, primarily from the viewpoint of safeguarding the Federalist interests. Webster's "Reply to Hayne" is principally important as a defense, not so much of the Constitution, as of the judicial power. . . .

From Marshall through Taney, and increasingly after the Civil War, the Supreme Court offered to guard exclusively the charter of fundamental liberties. They offered to play the role of the Platonic guardians that watched over the mythical Greek republic; they were ready to furnish at once wisdom and militancy. Part of John Marshall's genius lay in his skill in pushing into the background the power that the Court was gaining over economic policy, and thrusting into the foreground its role of guardianship. This the later judges have encouraged by their continued utterances, and it has become the official theory of the Court's power. To be sure, the fact that the *role of guarding* the Constitution involved also the *power of deciding* what the Constitution was did not by a whit diminish the ardor of the Court in offering its services. Like a jealous Cyclops, it was willing to rule the domain that it guarded.

By the stress laid on this guardianship, the judges have been associated in our minds with the function of protection rather than with the struggle for power. This has been of enormous importance. It has conscripted to the service of the judicial symbol all the accumulated Anglo-Saxon tradition of the "rule of law." . . .

This brings us to the third element in the pattern of divine right: the tradition of judicial neutrality. The judges could not be proper guardians of the Constitution unless they approached it with detachment. We have somehow managed in our minds to place the judges above the battle. Despite every proof to the contrary, we have persisted in attributing to them the objectivity and infallibility that are ultimately attributes only of godhead. The tradition persists that they belong to no economic group or class; that they are not touched by economic interests; that their decisions proceed through some inspired way of arriving at the truth; that they sit in their robes like the haughty gods of Lucretius, high above the plains on which human beings swarm, unaffected by the preferences and prejudices that move common men. . . .

It is partly explained by our association of judges with the "rule of law." But even more it springs from a deep need in us for some final authority. We are, in a sense, a barbaric people, only several generations removed from the wilderness psychology. . . . We live in fear of . . . violence, and our exaggerated lip service to "law and order" and our cult of judges are functions of that fear. Most of us feel economically helpless in the midst of a ruthless exploitative capitalism; we feel alone in a vast impersonal urban civilization. We turn to "the law" as our final protection, and we read into the judges our hopes for someone who will be above the battle.

Most of us associate judges with the settlement of ordinary litigation, where political bias seems to us irrelevant; or with criminal trials, where the judge seems to sit as an avenging and impersonal deity, expressing through his function the sense and conscience of the community. What easier than to transfer this conception to the Supreme Court? Especially since there are four elements that seem to magnify the objectivity of the Supreme Court judges as compared with those of lower courts.

One is that they are in a "supreme" court, and presumably of some higher stature than ordinary mortals. The second is that they are appointed and not elected, and escape thus the grueling experience of a political campaign. The third is the greatness of the judicial tradition of the Supreme Court; some of our judges have actually been men of enormous ability; the fact that their ability has not been conspicuously in the direction of detachment is not generally known; what comes down to us is the almost Periclean devotion to their public trust shown by men like Marshall, Taney, and Holmes. The fourth factor, and perhaps the most important, is that we transfer our sense of the definitive and timeless character of the Constitution to the judges who expound it. . . . The judges become, thus, not ordinary men, subject to ordinary passions, but "discoverers" of final truth, priests in the service of a godhead. . . .

6 / INSTRUMENTS OF JUDICIAL POWER

Chapter 5 put particular emphasis on public esteem as a source of judicial power. The instrument which this esteem has helped shape is that of prestige, and prestige can become a bludgeon, especially when wielded by black-robed old gentlemen from whom the blood of political ambition has apparently drained. To criticize and oppose the judiciary when it operates at the peak of its prestige is often unwise and even occasionally illegal. Such acts can take on overtones of sacrilege and blasphemy, overtones which those who have benefited from a judicial decision frequently do their best to play up.

Decision and Opinion

There are, of course, many legal instruments which judges can use, the most obvious of which is their authority to hand down decisions in cases brought before them. A judge's authority varies, depending on the particular level of his court and on whether the case is heard with or without a jury. But even where the final decision is left to a jury, the judge's instructions to the jurors and his rulings as to what evidence they may or may not consider have great influence in determining the outcome of litigation.

Only slightly less important than the actual decisions are the opinions, especially those of appellate courts, which judges write to justify their rulings. Jurists from time immemorial have realized that carefully drafted statements of "the law" can have a strategic impact on public policy. John Marshall fully recognized the potential of a court pronouncement as an instrument with which to flay his opponents. His opinions in *McCulloch* v. *Maryland* and *Gibbons* v. *Ogden*, marking the constitutional expanse of the powers of the federal government, are among the most significant American political writings. Later justices have followed Marshall's practice, though not always with equal success.

The Injunction

Among the instruments shaped for the more specific exercise of judicial power, perhaps the most effective is the injunction. An injunction—a writ secured through an equity proceeding—is a command from a court directed to named defendants forbidding them to perform certain specified acts. The purpose of an injunction is not to punish or secure damages, but to prevent future injury or the continuation of a present injury. To obtain an injunction, a litigant must show that he has a real right at stake, that he is suffering or is about to suffer irreparable injury, that there is no action at law which offers him an adequate remedy, and that when "the equities are balanced," righting this wrong will outweigh any inconveniences or damage suffered by the defendant or by the public at large.

Normally only trial courts can issue an injunction, but an appellate court can instruct a trial judge to grant a restraining order in a given case. Under the Federal Rules of Civil Procedure, a judge may issue a temporary injunction without a hearing, but such a writ is to be granted only where it is necessary to preserve the *status quo* while the suit is being litigated, and the temporary writ can run no more than twenty days. A full trial must precede the issuance of a permanent injunction.

While an injunction is addressed only to named defendants, it binds those defendants, their servants, agents, attorneys, and employees, as well as all other persons who, knowing the injunction is in effect, conspire with the defendants. If the defendant is a public official, the injunction will run against the office rather than the man; that is, the defendant's successors in office are also bound. Judges have held that any private person or public official subject to the jurisdiction of a court can be bound by a federal court injunction. This broad category excludes only the

President of the United States. However, as a practical matter a federal court could not forbid legislators, state or federal, to vote for or against a bill, since no person could show immediate danger of injury to his legal rights until there was some move toward enforcement of the statute. Federal judges, however, claim authority to enjoin all state executive officials as well as federal executive officials below the level of the President from enforcing unconstitutional statutes or performing other acts which judges consider illegal.

The injunction thus gives judges a means not only of voicing disapproval of legislative or executive policy, but also of forbidding the carrying out of such policy. This power, however, may be extended too far. In the battle between the New Deal and the federal courts during the 1930's, some 1,600 injunctions were issued by district judges against the execution of various federal statutes. This tidal wave of restraining orders raised the cry of "government by injunction," and in 1937 Congress passed a statute denying a single federal judge authority to enjoin enforcement of an act of Congress. If such a suit is filed, the trial judge refers the matter to the chief judge of the circuit, who names a special three-judge tribunal to hear the case and, if necessary, issue an injunction. This is essentially the same procedure which, since 1911, has been followed in regard to injunction suits against state officials.

An interest group can also utilize the injunction as a weapon against competing groups as well as against governmental action. For several decades business groups used various statutes, particularly the Sherman Act, to secure injunctions against strikes, boycotts, and other union activity. In spite of a provision in the Clayton Act of 1914 which stated that the Sherman Act was not meant to apply to legal labor activities, federal courts continued to apply the anti-monopoly statute to unions. Finally, in 1932, Congress passed the Norris-La Guardia Act, sharply limiting the power of federal courts to issue injunctions in labor disputes. The Taft-Hartley Act authorized the issuance of labor injunctions for certain purposes, but the injunction can only be sought by the Attorney General, not by private individuals or interest groups.

The Great Writ

Called by Blackstone "the great writ of liberty," habeas corpus is an order from a judge directing a jailer or other official who has custody of a prisoner to bring that prisoner to court so that the judge may determine the legality of his detention. Originally the purpose of habeas corpus was to protect the jurisdiction of the English common-law courts against encroachments by courts of chancery or by the Crown. Gradually, however, the purpose of the writ shifted to become the classic means of protecting individuals against unlawful imprisonment. The Habeas Corpus Act of 1679 established the writ as one of the fundamental rights of English government, and American colonial practice generally accorded the writ the same high standing. Article I of the Constitution provides that the privilege of the writ of habeas corpus may not be suspended "unless when in Cases of Rebellion or Invasion the public Safety may require it."

Modern practice, while retaining the writ as protection against executive authority, has also made habeas corpus a means of tighter federal judicial control over state court proceedings. Until 1867, a person convicted of a crime could not apply for habeas corpus, but in that year Congress extended federal habeas corpus jurisdiction to "all cases" where a person is held in custody "in violation of the Constitution or laws or treaties of the United States."

Many state prisoners—about 750 a year during the last decade—have been using this statute as a means of challenging the validity of their convictions. Although the Supreme Court has said that a hearing on a habeas corpus petition is not a substitute for a retrial or an appeal, the distinction among these procedures is quite fine, making, as Justice Frankfurter once remarked, "an untidy area" in American law. While asserting that federal judges do not sit in habeas corpus cases to review the merits of the original trial, the justices have held that if there was a basic constitutional flaw in that trial—e.g., if the prisoner was coerced into confessing, if he was denied right to counsel, if his jury was illegally impaneled, or if the prosecutor knowingly used perjured testimony—the petitioner must be released, usually subject, however, to a new and legal trial.

As a potential judicial weapon against executive power, habeas corpus poses a threat of intra-governmental conflict, and on occasion the conflict has become a reality. In 1861, for instance, Chief Justice Taney ruled in *Ex parte Merryman* that only Congress, and not the President, could suspend the writ. Lincoln met this challenge to his war power by ignoring the order of the Chief Justice. Shortly thereafter the President averted another judicial rebuke by putting a District of Columbia judge under virtual house arrest to prevent him hearing a habeas corpus petition. After the war, the full Supreme Court sustained Taney's doctrine in *Ex parte Milligan;* but this decision could undo little of the military rule which Lincoln had imposed on the border states.

A similar conflict was carried on at a lower level in Hawaii during World War II between U.S. District Judge Delbert E. Metzger and Lieutenant General R. C. Richardson. Immediately after the attack on Pearl Harbor, the Governor of the territory, acting pursuant to his interpretation of the Hawaiian Organic Act of 1900, suspended the writ of habeas corpus, declared martial law, and requested the military commander in the area to exercise all the executive and judicial authority normally wielded by civil government. The commanding general proclaimed himself military governor and established military tribunals to try civilians for almost all offenses.

Judge Metzger, however, issued a writ of habeas corpus directing the release of two civilians held by the Army. General Richardson answered with an order prohibiting any judge in Hawaii from issuing such a writ. Metzger thereupon declared the general in contempt of court and fined him $5,000. At this point, the Justice Department sent out a peace emissary who worked out a compromise under which the judge remitted the fine and the general withdrew his anti-habeas corpus order, with the understanding that no prisoners would be released unless the trial court's decision was upheld on appeal.

In 1946, the Supreme Court sustained Judge Metzger's position, ruling in *Duncan* v. *Kahanamoku* that the Governor had exceeded the authority granted him by the Act of 1900. In spite of these and other judicial decisions sustaining the privilege of habeas corpus, it would appear, as Clinton Rossiter has observed, that in times of emergency executive officials will continue to impose military rule, by force if not by law.

The Contempt Power

Reinforcing the authority to issue writs is the contempt power. This is one of the oldest of judicial procedures and involves the power of a judge to protect the dignity of his court or to punish disobedience to his orders. If the act of contempt is committed in the presence of a federal judge, he simply slams down his gavel, and accuses, convicts, and sentences the contemnor. Such justice is swift, and the defendant has almost no procedural rights other than an appeal to a higher court. "Indirect contempts," those which occur outside the courtroom, commonly involve disobedience to a judicial order. In those situations, the judge must serve the accused with notice of the charge, allow him to be represented by counsel, and give him a hearing at which he may cross-examine witnesses and offer evidence on his own behalf.

There is a distinction between criminal and civil contempt, a distinction which, though often difficult to discern, is nonetheless important. The major identifying difference is one of purpose. The aim of a criminal contempt charge is to vindicate the dignity of the court, while a civil contempt action is intended to protect the rights of one of the litigants. The two types of action also differ as to procedure. In criminal cases, the prosecution is generally initiated by the judge or some other government official; the usual presumption of innocence present in a criminal trial applies, and the defendant must be found guilty beyond a reasonable doubt. Civil contempt proceedings are commonly initiated by one of the parties to a suit, and judgment can be made on the preponderance of the evidence. While the President may pardon for a criminal contempt conviction, it is doubtful that he can do so in civil contempt cases where the offended party is a private citizen.

Perhaps the most important difference between the two types of contempt action lies in the punishment meted out. A federal judge may impose a fine or prison sentence for criminal contempt. He has the same option in civil cases, but there his power is far more extensive. Since the object of a civil contempt action is to secure the rights of one of the parties, the sentence is normally conditional. For example, the judge may sentence the recalcitrant party to be imprisoned until he agrees to comply with the court's order. This, of course, could theoretically mean life imprisonment, a possibility which judges have recognized. The usual judicial explanation is that the prisoner carries the keys to his cell in his own pocket. He will be released as soon as he consents to obey the judge. Such an indeterminate sentence is obviously a far more powerful sanction than a specific fine or jail term.

Except in rare instances, a federal judge sits without a jury to hear contempt cases, a practice followed in almost all state judicial systems. Although in recent years several Supreme Court justices have tried to overturn this practice, judges have generally been jealous in guarding their contempt power. As the U.S. Supreme Court said in *In re Debs* in 1895: "In order that a court may compel obedience to its orders it must have the right to inquire whether there has been any disobedience thereof. To submit the question of disobedience to another tribunal, be it a jury or another court, would operate to deprive the proceeding of half its efficiency." Four years later, in declaring unconstitutional a state statute which extended the right to jury trial in contempt cases, the Virginia Supreme Court of Appeals announced: "The power to punish for contempts is inherent in the courts, and is conferred upon them by the constitution by the very act of their creation. It is a trust confided and a duty imposed upon us by the sovereign people, which we cannot surrender or suffer to be impaired without being recreant to our duty."

During the congressional debate on the 1957 Civil Rights Act, the absence of a right to a jury trial in most contempt proceedings became a key issue, and a compromise was worked out between northern liberals and southern Democrats. The 1957 Act, which allows the Attorney General to seek an injunction to protect Negroes against voting discrimination, maintains the traditional judicial authority to punish civil contempts without a jury, but somewhat restricts this authority in criminal cases. If, in a suit brought by the Attorney General under this statute, the judge imposes a sentence for criminal contempt which exceeds $300 or 45 days, the accused may demand, as a right, a new trial, this one by jury.

The most significant limitation on the contempt power, however, has been imposed by the Supreme Court. Historically, both state and federal judges have punished as contemptuous newspaper editorials which, while a trial was still in progress, criticized the judge's conduct. In 1941, the Supreme Court, by a 5-4 vote, held in *Bridges* v. *California* that the right to criticize judicial proceedings was protected by the First and Fourteenth Amendments and that only a "clear and present danger" to orderly administration of justice could justify contempt proceedings in such instances.

Executive Aid

Actually federal judges have little physical force of their own. Federal judges can only issue orders; it is up to the executive department to enforce judicial decrees. Even the marshals of the court are appointed by the President. The Constitution, of course, commands that the President "shall take Care that the Laws be faithfully executed," and specific congressional statutes direct executive assistance in carrying out court decisions. Without orders to the contrary, a marshal will enforce court decrees, and the Justice Department will co-operate in protecting the integrity of the judicial process. Occasionally, as in the case of *United States* v. *Peters* in 1809, when the Governor of Pennsylvania used militia to defy a Supreme Court judgment, or as in the mob violence in Little

Rock in 1957, additional force may be necessary to secure obedience to a court order. The marshal may summon a posse, as was done in the *Peters* case, or the President, as in the Little Rock affair, may send in federal troops.

On such occasions, when backed by the armed might of the Commander in Chief, judicial power may seem to be at its maximum. Yet the main function of the judicial process, at least from society's viewpoint, is to settle disputes peacefully. Cases raising questions concerning the very basis of economic and social relationships within a community cannot help but create deep cleavages of opinion. Since public esteem is among the chief sources of judicial power, community or class violence—unless drastically at odds with the sentiment of the overwhelming majority of the nation—against enforcement of a Supreme Court decision may be a sign that judicial power is approaching a dangerously low level.

SELECTED REFERENCES

Corwin, Edward S., "The Steel Seizure Case," 53 *Columbia Law Review* 53 (1953).

Fairman, Charles, *The Law of Martial Rule* (2d ed.; Chicago: Callaghan and Co., 1942).

Frankfurter, Felix and Nathan Greene, *The Labor Injunction* (New York: Macmillan, 1930).

"Injunctions," 43 *Corpus Juris Secundum* 397.

Jackson, Robert H., *The Supreme Court in the American System of Government* (Cambridge: Harvard University Press, 1955).

Mayers, Lewis, *The American Legal System* (New York: Harper, 1955), Chs. 4–8.

Murphy, Walter F., "Some Strange New Converts to the Cause of Civil Rights," *The Reporter,* June 27, 1957, pp. 13f.

———, "The Contempt Power of the Federal Courts," 18 *Federal Bar Journal* 34 (1958).

Note, "Civil and Criminal Contempt in the Federal Courts," 57 *Yale Law Journal* 83 (1947).

Note, "Contempt by Publication," 59 *Yale Law Journal* 534 (1950).

Note, "Enforcement of Court Orders," 2 *Race Relations Law Reporter* 1051 (1957).

Rossiter, Clinton, *The Supreme Court and the Commander in Chief* (Ithaca: Cornell University Press, 1951).

Schubert, Glendon A., Jr., "The Steel Case: Presidential Responsibility and Judicial Irresponsibility," 6 *Western Political Quarterly* 61 (1953).

Westin, Alan, *The Anatomy of a Constitutional Law Case* (New York: Macmillan, 1958).

Wright, Gordon K., *et al.*, "Civil and Criminal Contempts in the Federal Courts," 17 *Federal Rules Decisions* 167 (1955).

"... the seizure ... is illegal and without authority of
1.   law ..."

THE 1952 STEEL SEIZURE DISPUTE

IN APRIL, 1952, *during the middle of the Korean War,
the United Steel Workers, after long months of three-sided bargaining
among labor, government, and industry, called a strike which would
have shut down almost the entire steel production. On April 8, just
a few hours before the strike was to begin, President Truman issued
Executive Order 10340, directing Secretary of Commerce Charles
Sawyer to seize and operate the mills in the name of the United States
until the labor dispute had been settled. Government "seizure and
operation" consisted in sending telegrams to the eighty-five companies
concerned appointing each firm's president as manager for the government. All assets and liabilities were to remain with the owners,
though the fact that Sawyer was going to try to negotiate a wage
settlement with the workers might have affected the industry's profits.
The steel companies claimed that they would suffer irreparable injury from the government's action, and immediately brought suit in
the federal District Court for the District of Columbia, asking that
Sawyer be enjoined from operating their plants. Judge Walter Bastian
refused to issue a temporary injunction without a hearing; and on
April 9, a hearing was held before Judge Alexander Holtzoff. After
the proceedings, Holtzoff denied the companies' request, stating that
the injunction would, in fact, run against the President and also that
the steel companies had an adequate remedy at law in that they could
sue the government for any monetary loss due to the seizure.
On April 24 and 25, a hearing for a preliminary injunction was held
before Judge David A. Pine, and on April 29 Judge Pine decided for
the steel companies. The injunction was issued the following day.*

YOUNGSTOWN SHEET & TUBE COMPANY *v.* SAWYER

UNITED STATES DISTRICT COURT FOR THE DISTRICT OF COLUMBIA

Preliminary Injunction—Filed April 30, 1952

This cause came to be heard at this term upon motion of the plaintiffs for a preliminary injunction, and upon consideration thereof, the affidavits and briefs filed by the respective parties, and the arguments of counsel, and the Court having determined by its opinion filed herein on April 29, 1952, in which the Court's findings of fact and conclusions of law appear, that the seizure and taking possession on or about April 8, 1952 of the plaintiffs' plants, facilities and properties by the defendant was, and his continued possession thereof is illegal and without authority of law, and that irreparable damage will result to the plaintiffs unless the defendant is enjoined and restrained as hereinafter provided, it is by the Court this 30th day of April, 1952,

Adjudged and ordered, that, pending the final hearing and determination of this cause, the defendant, his officers, agents, servants, employees, and attorneys, and those persons in active concert or participation with them who receive actual notice of this order by personal service or otherwise, be, and hereby are, enjoined and restrained from continuing the seizure and possession of the plants, facilities and properties of the plaintiffs and from acting under the purported authority of Executive Order No. 10340. . . .

David A. Pine, Judge.

The Government secured a stay of this injunction from the Court of Appeals and petitioned the Supreme Court for certiorari. Certiorari was granted.

YOUNGSTOWN SHEET & TUBE COMPANY *v.* SAWYER

MR. JUSTICE BLACK delivered the opinion of the Court. . . .

It is urged that there were non-constitutional grounds upon which the District Court could have denied the preliminary injunction and

343 U.S. 579, 72 S. Ct. 863, 96 L. Ed. 1153 (1952).

thus have followed the customary judicial practice of declining to reach and decide constitutional questions until compelled to do so. On this basis it is argued that equity's extraordinary injunctive relief should have been denied because (a) seizure of the companies' properties did not inflict irreparable damages, and (b) there were available legal remedies adequate to afford compensation for any possible damages which they might suffer. . . . Arguments as to both rest in large part on the Government's claim that should the seizure ultimately be held unlawful, the companies could recover full compensation in the Court of Claims for the unlawful taking. Prior cases in this Court have cast doubt on the right to recover in the Court of Claims on account of properties unlawfully taken by government officials for public use as these properties were alleged to have been.

Moreover, seizure and governmental operation of these going businesses were bound to result in many present and future damages of such nature as to be difficult, if not incapable, of measurement. Viewing the case this way . . . we agree with the District Court and can see no reason why that [constitutional] question was not ripe for determination. . . .

The President's power, if any, to issue the order must stem either from an act of Congress or from the Constitution itself. There is no statute that expressly authorizes the President to take possession of property as he did here. Nor is there any act of Congress to which our attention has been directed from which such a power can fairly be implied. Indeed, we do not understand the Government to rely on statutory authorization for this seizure. There are two statutes which do authorize the President to take both personal and real property under certain conditions. However, the Government admits that these conditions were not met and that the President's order was not rooted in either of the statutes. . . .

Moreover, the use of the seizure technique to solve labor disputes in order to prevent work stoppages was not only unauthorized by any congressional enactment; prior to this controversy, Congress had refused to adopt that method of settling labor disputes. When the Taft-Hartley Act was under consideration in 1947, Congress rejected an amendment which would have authorized such governmental seizures in cases of emergency. . . .

It is clear that if the President had authority to issue the order he did, it must be found in some provision of the Constitution. And it is not claimed that express constitutional language grants this power to the President. The contention is that presidential power should be implied from the aggregate of his powers under the Constitution. Particular reliance is placed on provisions in Article II which say that "The executive Power shall be vested in a President . . ."; that "he shall take Care that the Laws be faithfully executed"; and that he "shall be Commander in Chief of the Army and Navy of the United States."

The order cannot properly be sustained as an exercise of the President's military power as Commander in Chief of the Armed Forces. The Government attempts to do so by citing a number of cases upholding broad powers in military commanders engaged in day-to-day fighting in a theater of war. Such cases need not concern us here. Even though "theater of war" be an expanding concept, we cannot with faithfulness to our constitutional system hold that the Commander in Chief of the Armed Forces has the ultimate power as such to take possession of private property in order to keep labor disputes from stopping production. This is a job for the Nation's lawmakers, not for its military authorities.

Nor can the seizure order be sustained because of the several constitutional provisions that grant executive power to the President. In the framework of our Constitution, the President's power to see that the laws are faithfully executed refutes the idea that he is to be a lawmaker. The Constitution limits his functions in the lawmaking process to the recommending of laws he thinks wise and the vetoing of laws he thinks bad. And the Constitution is neither silent nor equivocal about who shall make laws which the President is to execute. The first section of the first article says that "All legislative Powers herein granted shall be vested in a Congress of the United States . . . ." After granting many powers to the Congress, Article I goes on to provide that Congress may "make all Laws which shall be necessary and proper for carrying into Execution the foregoing Powers, and all other powers vested by this Constitution in the Government of the United States, or in any Department or Officer thereof."

The President's order does not direct that a congressional policy be executed in a manner prescribed by Congress—it directs that a presidential policy be executed in a manner prescribed by the President. . . .

The power of Congress to adopt such public policies as those proclaimed by the order is beyond question. It can authorize the taking of private property for public use. It can make laws regulating the relationships between employers and employees, prescribing rules designed to settle labor disputes, and fixing wages and working conditions in certain fields of our economy. . . .

It is said that other Presidents without congressional authority have taken possession of private business enterprises in order to settle labor disputes. But even if this be true, Congress has not thereby lost its exclusive constitutional authority to make laws necessary and proper to carry out the powers vested by the Constitution "in the Government of the United States, or any Department or Officer thereof."

The Founders of this Nation entrusted the lawmaking power to the Congress alone in both good and bad times. It would do no good to recall the historical events, the fears of power and the hopes for freedom that lay behind their choice. Such a review would but confirm our holding that this seizure order cannot stand.

The judgment of the District Court is

Affirmed.

MR. JUSTICE FRANKFURTER, DOUGLAS, JACKSON, BURTON, and CLARK each filed a separate concurring opinion. MR. CHIEF JUSTICE VINSON wrote a dissenting opinion for himself, JUSTICES REED and MINTON.

> *"If the federal court is to be merely an automaton stamping the papers an Attorney General presents, the judicial function rises to no higher level than an IBM machine."*

2.

UNITED STEELWORKERS V. UNITED STATES

IN 1959, *after another long series of wage negotiations, the United Steelworkers again called a strike. The Attorney General filed suit in the U.S. District Court for the Western District of Penn-*

361 U.S. 39, 80 S. Ct. 1, 4 L. Ed. 2d 12 (1959).

sylvania, asking for an eighty-day injunction under Section 208 of the Taft-Hartley Act. In support of his petition the Attorney General produced affidavits from the Secretary of Defense and other high government officials stating that a steel strike would not only disrupt the national economy but would also imperil national defense, particularly NATO commitments and various missile and atomic energy programs. The district judge granted the injunction, and the Court of Appeals affirmed. The steelworkers petitioned the Supreme Court for certiorari, asserting, among other points, that the conditions the Taft-Hartley law had laid down for the issuance of an injunction had not been met; and that even if such conditions had been met the injunction provisions of the statute were unconstitutional because they imposed duties on federal courts which were essentially legislative or executive in nature.

PER CURIAM. . . .

. . . In pertinent part, §208 provides that if the District Court—
"finds that . . . [a] threatened or actual strike or lock-out—

"(i) affects an entire industry or a substantial part thereof engaged in trade, commerce, transportation, transmission, or communication among the several States or with foreign nations, or engaged in the production of goods for commerce; and

"(ii) if permitted to occur or to continue, will imperil the national health or safety, it shall have jurisdiction to enjoin any such strike or lock-out, or the continuing thereof, and to make such other orders as may be appropriate. . . ."

The arguments of the parties here and in the lower courts have addressed themselves in considerable part to the propriety of the District Court's exercising its equitable jurisdiction to enjoin the strike in question once the findings set forth above had been made. These arguments have ranged widely into broad issues of national labor policy, the availability of other remedies to the executive, the effect of a labor injunction on the collective bargaining process, consideration of the conduct of the parties to the labor dispute in their negotiations, and conjecture as to the course of those negotiations in the future. We do not believe that Congress in passing the statute intended that the issuance of injunctions should depend upon judicial inquiries of this nature. Congress was not concerned with the merits of the parties' positions or the conduct of their negotiations. Its basic purpose seems to have been to see that vital production should be resumed or continued for a time while further efforts were made to settle the dispute. To carry out its purposes, Congress carefully surrounded the injunction proceedings with detailed procedural devices and limitations. The public report of a board of inquiry, the exercise of political and executive responsibility personally by the President in directing the commencement of injunction proceedings, the statutory provisions looking toward an adjustment of the dispute during the injunction's pendency, and the limited duration of the injunction, represent a congressional determination of policy factors involved in the difficult problem of national emergency strikes. This congressional determination of the policy factors is of course binding on the courts.

The statute imposes upon the courts the duty of finding, upon the evidence adduced, whether a strike or lock-out meets the statutory conditions of breadth of involvement and peril to the national health or safety. We have accordingly reviewed the concurrent findings of the two lower courts. Petitioner here contests the findings that the continuation of the strike would imperil the national health and safety. The parties dispute the meaning of the statutory term "national health"; the Government insists that the term comprehends the country's general well-being, its economic health; petitioner urges that simply the physical health of the citizenry is meant. We need not resolve this question, for we think the judgment below is amply supported on the ground that the strike imperils the national safety. Here we rely upon the evidence of the strike's effect on specific defense projects; we need not pass on the Government's contention that "national safety" in this context should be given a broader construction and application.

The petitioner suggests that a selective reopening of some of the steel mills would suffice to fulfill specific defense needs. The statute was designed to provide a public remedy in times of emergency; we cannot construe it to require that the United States either formulate a reorganization of the affected industry to satisfy its defense needs without the complete reopening of closed facilities, or demonstrate in court the unfeasibility of such a reorganization. There is no room in the statute for this requirement which the petitioner seeks to impose on the Government.

We are of opinion that the provision in question as applied here is not violative of the constitutional limitation prohibiting courts from exercising powers of a legislative or executive nature, powers not capable of being conferred upon a court exercising solely "the judicial power of the United States." . . . Petitioner contends that the statute is constitutionally invalid because it does not set up any standard of lawful or unlawful conduct on the part of labor or management. But the statute does recognize certain rights in the public to have unimpeded for a time production in industries vital to the national health or safety. It makes the United States the guardian of these rights in litigation. . . . The availability of relief, in the common judicial form of an injunction, depends on findings of fact, to be judicially made. Of the matters decided judicially, there is no review by other agencies of the Government. . . . We conclude that the statute entrusts the courts only with the determination of a "case or controversy," on which the judicial power can operate, not containing any element capable of only legislative or executive determination. We do not find that the termination of the injunction after a specified time, or the machinery established in an attempt to obtain a peaceful settlement of the underlying dispute during the injunction's pendency, detracts from this conclusion. . . .

Affirmed.

Concurring opinion of MR. JUSTICE FRANKFURTER and MR. JUSTICE HARLAN. . . .

. . . In view of such demonstrated unavailability of defense materials it is irrelevant that, as petitioner contended and the United States conceded, somewhat in excess of 15% of the steel industry remained unaffected by the stoppage, and that only about 1% of the gross steel product is ordinarily allocated to defense production.

However, petitioner also contested the sufficiency of the affidavits on the ground that they did not present the facts giving rise to the asserted emergencies with sufficient particularity to justify the findings made. This objection raises an issue which was essentially for the trier of fact, and the two lower courts found the affidavits sufficient. It is not for the judiciary to canvass the competence of officers of cabinet rank, with responsibility only below that of the President for the matters to which they speak under oath, to express the opinions set forth in these affidavits. Findings based directly upon them surely cannot be said to be "clearly erroneous." . . .

Moreover, under §208 the trier of these facts was called upon to make a judgment already twice made by the President of the United States: once when he convened the Board of Inquiry; and once when he directed the Attorney General to commence this action. His reasoned judgment was based upon the affidavits we have summarized, and it is not for us to set aside findings consistent with them. The President's judgment is not controlling; §208 makes it the court's duty to "find" the requisite jurisdictional fact for itself. But in the discharge of its duty a District Court would disregard reason not to give due weight to determinations previously made by the President, who is, after all, the ultimate constitutional executive repository for assuring the safety of the Nation, and upon whose judgment the invocation of the emergency provisions depends. . . .

The legislative history confirms what the provisions themselves amply reveal, that this portion of the Taft-Hartley Act contains a dual purpose, on the one hand to alleviate, at least temporarily, a threat to the national health or safety; and on the other to promote settlement of the underlying dispute of industry-wide effect. The former purpose is to be accomplished by the injunction, and by whatever additional remedies the President may seek and the Congress grant. . . . The latter purpose is to be accomplished by the command of §209 that the parties to the dispute "make every effort to adjust their differences"; by the secret ballot of employees provided by §209 with reference to the last offer of the companies; and finally by further action by the President and Congress pursuant to §210. To hold, as petitioner alternatively urged, that a District Court may enjoin only that part of the total stoppage which is shown to be the cause in fact of the peril, would at best serve only the purpose of alleviating the peril, while stultifying the provisions designed to effect settlement of the underlying dispute. . . .

Because the District Court's finding of peril to the national safety resulting from impediments to the programs for national defense was itself sufficient to satisfy the requirement of §208(a) (ii), it is not necessary to determine whether perils to defense exhaust the scope of "safety" as used in this statute, or to consider its findings with regard to peril to the national health.

Having decided that the strike was one which created a national emergency within the terms of the statute, the next question is whether, upon that finding alone, the "eighty-day" injunction for which the Government prayed should have issued, or whether the District Court was to exercise the conventional discretionary function of equity in balancing conveniences as a preliminary to issuing an injunction. The petitioner argued that under the Act a District Court has "discretion" whether to issue an "eighty-day" injunction, even though a national emergency be found. It argued that the district judge in this case did not consider that he had such "discretion." Alternatively, it argued that if the district judge did exercise "discretion" he abused it, for the broad injunctive relief he granted was not justifiable in this case. . . . We conclude that under the national emergency provisions of the Labor Management Relations Act it is not for the judiciary to exercise conventional "discretion" to withhold an "eighty-day" injunction upon a balancing of conveniences.

"Discretionary" jurisdiction is exercised when a given injunctive remedy is not commanded as a matter of policy by Congress, but is, as a presupposition of judge-made law, left to judicial discretion. Such is not the case under this statute. The purpose of Congress expressed by the scheme of this statute precludes ordinary equitable discretion. . . .

In the national emergency provisions of the Labor Management Relations Act Congress has with particularity described the duration of the injunction to be granted and the nature of specific collateral administrative procedures which are to be set in motion upon its issuance. We think the conclusion compelling that Congress has thereby manifested that a District Court is not to indulge its own judgment regarding the wisdom of the relief Congress has designed. Congress expressed its own judgment and did not leave it to a District Court. . . .

We come finally to the petitioner's contention that the grant to the District Courts by §208(a) of the Labor Management Relations

Act of jurisdiction to enjoin strikes such as this one is not a grant of
"judicial Power" within the meaning of Art 3, §2, of the Constitution,
and was therefore beyond the power of Congress to confer on the
District Courts. What proceedings are "Cases" and "Controversies"
and thus within the "judicial Power" is to be determined, at the least,
by what proceedings were recognized at the time of the Constitution
to be traditionally within the power of the judiciary in the English
and American judicial systems. Both by what they said and by what
they implied, the framers of the Judiciary Article gave merely the
outlines of what were to them the familiar operations of the English
judicial system and its manifestations on this side of the ocean before
the Union. Judicial power could come into play only in matters such
as were the traditional concern of the courts at Westminster and only
if they arose in ways that to the expert feel of lawyers constituted
"Cases" or "Controversies."

Beginning at least as early as the sixteenth century the English
courts have issued injunctions to abate public nuisances. . . . this
Court has impressively enforced the judicial power to abate public
nuisances at the suit of the Government. . . .

The jurisdiction given the District Courts by §208(a) of the Labor
Management Relations Act to enjoin strikes creating a national emergency is a jurisdiction of a kind that has been traditionally exercised
over public nuisances. The criteria for judicial action—peril to health
or safety—are much like those upon which courts ordinarily have
acted. Injunctive relief is traditionally given by equity upon a showing of such peril, and the court, as was traditional, acts at the request
of the Executive. There can therefore be no doubt that, being thus
akin to jurisdiction long historically exercised, the function to be performed by the District Courts under §208(a) is within the "judicial
Power" as contemplated by Art 3, §2, and is one which Congress may
thus confer upon the courts. It surely does not touch the criteria for
determining what is "judicial Power" that the injunction to be issued
is not a permanent one, and may last no longer than eighty days. . . .

MR. JUSTICE DOUGLAS, dissenting.

Great cases, like this one, are so charged with importance and
feeling that, as Mr. Justice Holmes once remarked . . . they are apt

to generate bad law. We need, therefore, to stick closely to the letter of the law we enforce to keep this controversy from being shaped by the intense interest which the public rightfully has in it. . . .

It is plain that the President construed the word "health" to include the material well-being or public welfare of the nation. When the Attorney General moved under §208 for an injunction in the District Court based on the opinion of the President and the conclusions of the board of inquiry, the union challenged the conclusion that "the national health or safety" was imperiled, as those words are used in the Act. The District Court found otherwise, stating five ways in which a continuance of the strike would, if permitted to continue, imperil "the national health and safety." . . .

. . . It is obvious that "national health" was construed to include the economic well-being or general welfare of the country. The Court of Appeals, in sustaining the injunction, was apparently of the same view. This seems to me to be an assumption that is unwarranted. I think that Congress when it used the words "national health" was safeguarding the heating of homes, the delivery of milk, the protection of hospitals, and the like. The coal industry, closely identified with physical health of people, was the industry paramount in the debates on this measure. The coal industry is indeed cited on the Senate side in illustration of the need for the measure. . . . There were those in the Senate who wanted to go so far as to outlaw strikes "in utilities and key nation-wide industries" in order to protect the "public welfare." . . . Reference was, indeed, made to strikes in industries "like coal or steel" among those to be barred in "the public interest." . . . But the Senate did not go that far. The Senate bill reached only situations where there was peril to the "national health or safety." The House bill went further and included cases where there was peril to "the public health, safety, or interest." The Senate view prevailed, that version being adopted by the Conference. . . .

To read "welfare" into "health" gives that word such a vast reach that we should do it only under the most compelling necessity. We must be mindful of the history behind this legislation. Re Debs . . . stands as ominous precedent for the easy use of the injunction in labor disputes. Free-wheeling Attorneys General used compelling public demands to obtain the help of courts in stilling the protests of labor. The revulsion against that practice was deep; and it led ultimately to the enactment of the Norris-LaGuardia Act. . . . We deal of course with a later Congress and an Act that sets aside by §208(b) pro tanto the earlier Act. What Congress has created Congress can refashion. But we should hesitate to conclude that Congress meant to restore the use of the injunction in labor disputes whenever that broad and all-inclusive concept of the public welfare is impaired. The words used—"national health or safety"—are much narrower. . . .

Nor can this broad injunction be sustained when it is rested solely on "national safety." The heart of the District Court's finding on this phase of the case is in its statement, "Certain items of steel required in top priority military missile programs are not made by any mill now operating, nor available from any inventory or from imports." Its other findings, already quoted, are also generalized. One cannot find in the record the type or quantity of the steel needed for defense, the name of the plants at which those products are produced, or the number or the names of the plants that will have to be reopened to fill the military need. We do know that for one and a half years ending in mid-1959 the shipments of steel for defense purposes accounted for less than 1% of all the shipments from all the steel mills. If 1,000 men, or 5,000 men, or 10,000 men can produce the critical amount the defense departments need, what authority is there to send 500,000 men back to work?

. . . Will a selective reopening of a few mills be adequate to meet defense needs? Which mills are these? Would it be practical to reopen them solely for defense purposes or would they have to be reopened for all civilian purposes as well? This seems to me to be the type of inquiry that is necessary before a decree can be entered that will safeguard the rights of all the parties. Section 208(a) gives the District Court "jurisdiction to enjoin" the strike. There is no command that it *shall* enjoin 100% of the strikers when only 1% or 5% or 10% of them are engaged in acts that imperil the national "safety." We are dealing here with equity practice which has several hundred years of history behind it. We cannot lightly assume that Congress intended to make the federal judiciary a rubber stamp for the President. His findings are entitled to great weight; and I along with my Brethren accept them insofar as national "safety" is concerned. But it is the

Court, not the President, that is entrusted by Article III of the Constitution to shape and fashion the decree. . . . If the federal court is to be merely an automaton stamping the papers an Attorney General presents, the judicial function rises to no higher level than an IBM machine. . . .

An appeal to the equity jurisdiction of the Federal District Court is an appeal to its sound discretion. One historic feature of equity is the molding of decrees to fit the requirements of particular cases. Equity decrees are not like the packaged goods this machine age produces. They are uniform only in that they seek to do equity in a given case. We should hesitate long before we conclude that Congress intended an injunction to issue against 500,000 workers when the inactivity of only 5,000 or 10,000 of the total imperils the national "safety." That would be too sharp a break with traditional equity practice for us to accept, unless the statutory mandate were clear and unambiguous. . . .

. . . It may be that it would be found impractical to send only part of the steelworkers back to work. The record in this case, however, is completely devoid of evidence to sustain that position. Furthermore, there is no indication that the District Court ever even considered such a possibility. I am unwilling to take judicial notice that it requires 100% of the workers to produce the steel needed for national defense when 99% of the output is devoted to purposes entirely unconnected with defense projects. . . .

3.   *" 'Don't argue with me.' "*

FISHER V. PACE, SHERIFF OF JASPER COUNTY, TEXAS

MR. JUSTICE REED delivered the opinion of the Court. While participating as counsel in the trial of a cause the petitioner, Joe J. Fisher, was adjudged guilty of contempt committed in the presence of the court by the District Court of Jasper County, Texas. The petitioner's client was the plaintiff in an action under the state

336 U.S. 155, 69 S. Ct. 425, 93 L. Ed. 569 (1949).

workmen's compensation law. The case was being tried before a jury and the parties had stipulated as to the average weekly wage of the claimant and the rate of compensation per week. The only remaining questions to be determined were as to the extent and duration of the incapacity resulting from an injury to the claimant's foot. . . .

OPENING ARGUMENT TO JURY OF PLAINTIFF'S ATTORNEY, JOE J. FISHER

"Now, bear in mind, gentlemen, that this is what we call a specific injury. . . . and the law states the amount of maximum compensation which a person can receive for such an injury, that is, one hundred and twenty-five weeks. . . . That is all we are asking. Now, that means one hundred and twenty-five weeks times the average weekly compensation rate.

"By Mr. Cox: Your Honor please—

"By the Court: Wait a minute.

"By Mr. Cox: The jury is not concerned with the computation; it has only one series of issues. That is not before the jury.

"By the Court: That has all been agreed upon.

"By Mr. Fisher: I think it is material, Your Honor, to tell the jury what the average weekly compensation is of this claimant so they can tell where he is.

"By the Court: They are not interested in dollars and cents.

"By Mr. Fisher: They are interested to this extent—

"By the Court: Don't argue with me. Go ahead. I will give you your exception to it.

"By Mr. Fisher: Note our exception.

"By the Court: All right.

"[By Mr. Fisher:] This negro, as I stated, can only recover one hundred and twenty-five weeks compensation, at whatever compensation the rate will figure under the law.

"By Mr. Cox: I am objecting to that discussion, Your Honor, as to what the plaintiff can recover.

"By the Court: Gentlemen! Mr. Fisher, you know the rule, and I have sustained his objection.

"By Mr. Fisher: I am asking—

"By the Court: Don't argue with me. Gentlemen, don't give any consideration to the statement of Mr. Fisher.

"By Mr. Fisher: Note our exception. I think I have a right to explain whether it is a specific injury or general injury.

"By the Court: I will declare a mistrial if you mess with me two minutes and a half, and fine you besides.

"By Mr. Fisher: That is all right. We take exception to the conduct of the Court.

"By the Court: That is all right; I will fine you $25.00.

"By Mr. Fisher: If that will give you any satisfaction.

"By the Court: That is $50.00; that is $25.00 more. Mr. Sheriff come get it. Pay the clerk $50.00.

"By Mr. Fisher: You mean for trying to represent my client?

"By the Court: No, sir; for contempt of Court. Don't argue with me.

"By Mr. Fisher: I am making no effort to commit contempt, but merely trying to represent the plaintiff and stating in the argument—

"By the Court: Don't tell me. Mr. Sheriff, take him out of the courtroom. Go on out of the courtroom. I fine you three days in jail.

"By Mr. Fisher: If that will give you any satisfaction; you know you have all the advantage by you being on the bench.

"By the Court: That will be a hundred dollar fine and three days in jail. Take him out.

"By Mr. Fisher: I demand a right to state my position before the audience.

"By the Court: Don't let him stand there. Take him out." . . .

Historically and rationally the inherent power of courts to punish contempts in the face of the court without further proof of facts and without aid of jury is not open to question. This attribute of courts is essential to preserve their authority and to prevent the administration of justice from falling into disrepute. Such summary conviction and punishment accords due process of law.

There must be adequate facts to support an order for contempt in the face of the court. Contrary to the contention of the petitioner the state Supreme Court evaluated the facts to decide whether there was sufficient evidence to support the judgment of the trial court and held that there was. . . . After a careful analysis of the facts as disclosed by the judgment of the trial court, the conclusion was reached that the conduct of the petitioner was clearly sufficient to support the power of the court to punish summarily the contempt committed in its presence.

The judgment of the Supreme Court of Texas must be affirmed. In a case of this type the transcript of the record cannot convey to us the complete picture of the courtroom scene. It does not depict such elements of misbehavior as expression, manner of speaking, bearing, and attitude of the petitioner. Reliance must be placed upon the fairness and objectivity of the presiding judge. The occurrence must be viewed as a unit in order to appraise properly the misconduct, and the relationship of the petitioner as an officer of the court must not be lost sight of. . . .

. . . On objection of the opposing counsel petitioner was stopped by the trial judge, but in the face of the court's decision he persisted in trying to tell the jury the effect of their answers. . . . In addition to this stubborn effort to bring excluded matter to the knowledge of the jury, the petitioner twice refused to heed the court's admonition not to argue the point. . . .

We see nothing in [the Supreme Court of Texas'] opinion or conclusion that indicates any disregard of petitioner's rights. The conduct of a judge should be such as to command respect for himself as well as for his office. We cannot say, however, that mildly provocative language from the bench puts a constitutional protection around an attorney so as to allow him to show the contempt for judge and court manifested by this record, particularly the last few sentences of the altercation.

The judgment of the Supreme Court of Texas accordingly is

Affirmed.

MR. JUSTICE DOUGLAS, with whom MR. JUSTICE BLACK concurs, dissenting.

The power to punish for contempt committed in open court was recognized long ago as a means of vindicating the dignity and authority of the court. . . . But its exercise must be narrowly confined lest it become an instrument of tyranny. Chief Justice Taft in *Cooke* v. *United States* . . . warned that its exercise by a federal court is "a delicate one and care is needed to avoid arbitrary or oppressive conclusions." The same restraint is necessary under our constitutional scheme when state courts are claiming the right to take a person by the heels and fine or imprison him for contempt without a trial or an opportunity to defend. . . .

It is said that the statement was improper under Texas practice.

But it took a ruling of the Texas Supreme Court to make it so, and even then Justice Sharp dissented. If Texas law on the point is so uncertain that the highest judges of the State disagree as to what is the permissible practice, is a lawyer to be laid by the heels for pressing the point? Yet it was for pressing the point of law on which the Supreme Court of Texas divided that Fisher was held in contempt. . . .

This lawyer was the victim of the pique and hotheadedness of a judicial officer who is supposed to have a serenity that keeps him above the battle and the crowd. That is as much a perversion of the judicial function as if the judge who sat had a pecuniary interest in the outcome of the litigation. . . .

MR. JUSTICE MURPHY, dissenting. . . .

A trial judge must be given wide latitude in punishing interference with the orderly administration of justice. . . . But the summary nature of contempt proceedings, the risk of imprisonment without jury, trial, or full hearing, make this the most drastic weapon entrusted to the trial judge. To sanction the procedure when it is patent that there has been no substantial interference with the trial, when a judge has used his position and power to successively increase the penalty for simple objections, is, I believe, a denial of due process of law. . . .

MR. JUSTICE RUTLEDGE, dissenting. . . .

Lawyers owe a large, but not an obsequious, duty of respect to the court in its presence. But their breach of this obligation in no case justifies correction by an act or acts from the bench intemperate in character, overriding judgment. Since the case comes here upon the sequence of events taken as an entirety, I do not undertake to separate one portion of the judgment from another. Accordingly, as the case stands here, I must take the entire sentence as infected with the fault I have noted. It follows, in my view, that the judgment should be reversed. Whatever the provocation, there can be no due process in trial in the absence of calm judgment and action, untinged with anger, from the bench.

4.
"Danger that calls for the presence of the State Patrol and the National Guard . . . cries aloud for such court action as was here taken."

INTEGRATION AND VIOLENCE AT CLINTON, TENNESSEE

IN 1956 *a federal district court ordered the school board of Anderson County, Tennessee, to begin desegregation the following fall. This order meant that about a dozen colored children would have to be enrolled along with eight hundred white students in Clinton High School. Late in August, John Kasper of Washington, D.C., head of the Seaboard White Citizens Council, came to Clinton to organize resistance to the desegregation order. He began a house-to-house campaign, telling his listeners, among other things, that permitting Negroes to enter the high school was the idea of the principal, D. J. Brittain, and that the Supreme Court was in favor of segregation. Kasper's success threatened to prevent the school from complying with the court's decree to end segregation; and school officials petitioned U.S. District Judge Robert Taylor to enjoin such interference.*

On August 29, 1956, Judge Taylor issued an injunction without giving notice to Kasper or the other defendants.

TAYLOR, DISTRICT JUDGE

TEMPORARY RESTRAINING ORDER

In this cause it appearing from sworn petition of D. J. Brittain, Jr., J. M. Burkhart, W. B. Lewallen, Sidney Davis and Walter E. Fisher that John Kasper, Tom Carter, Max Stiles, Ted Hankins, Leo Bolton and Mabel Currier and others whose names are not known by the petitioners at this time, are hindering, obstructing, and interfering with the carrying out of a memorandum order issued by this Court on January 1, 1956, in that, among other things, they have requested and urged the principal of the Clinton High School and the members of the County School Board of Anderson County to refuse to carry

Many of the following documents can be found at 1 *Race Relations Law Reporter* 872-879 (1956). Reprinted with permission.

out the aforesaid integration order of the Court; that they have formed and caused to be formed picket lines in front of Clinton High School of Anderson County and on August 28 and 29, 1956, caused a large crowd to form near the entrance to Clinton High School, and threatened and caused to be threatened several of the Negro students attending said high school, causing them in at least one instance to become afraid to attend school, and causing the parents of the students to become frightened and alarmed, one of whom caused a child to be removed from school; that anonymous letters have been written to parents of the students threatening them for permitting their children to attend school; that John Kasper has been one of the leaders in what appears to be a concerted movement to intimidate the parents, or some of them, who are sending their children to school, in an effort to prevent a continuation of school attendance; that on August 29, 1956, a crowd of people agitated by John Kasper attacked one of the Negro children of the school; that Kasper stated on various occasions that the Court had no authority to issue the aforesaid order of desegregation in the Clinton High School, and that it should not be obeyed.

It further appearing to the Court that the unlawful conduct of Kasper and the other named parties herein will continue unless a restraining order is issued prohibiting such acts, words, and conduct, and that if continued complainants will suffer immediate and irreparable injury, in that the Clinton High School will not continue to operate in an orderly manner and some of its students may suffer physical harm;

It is ordered and decreed by the Court that the aforementioned persons, their agents, servants, representatives, attorneys, and all other persons who are acting or may act in concert with them be and they hereby are enjoined and prohibited from further hindering, obstructing, or any wise interfering with the carrying out of the aforesaid order of this Court, or from picketing Clinton High School, either by words or acts or otherwise. . . .

This temporary restraining order is granted without notice to Kasper, Carter, Stiles, Hankins, Bolton, and Mabel Currier because of the matters hereinbefore set out and other matters of like tenor set forth in the complaint, and because it has been made to appear to the

Court that immediate action is necessary to prevent possible harm
to the students of Clinton High School.

A copy of the injunction was served on Kasper as he stood on the
steps of the county courthouse at Clinton, preparing to address a
crowd of almost a thousand people. Defying Judge Taylor's order,
Kasper immediately urged the crowd to resist school integration. The
next day, school officials petitioned Judge Taylor to hold Kasper in
contempt.

PETITION FOR CONTEMPT

I

That pursuant to the restraining order issued by Your Honor on
the 29th day of August, 1956, at 6:07 P.M. at Your Honor's offices
and chambers in the Federal Court House Building in Knoxville,
Tennessee, the defendant, John Kasper, one of the defendants named
in said restraining order, was duly served with said restraining order
by the United States Marshal while the defendant was on the Court
House steps or within the Court House building within the Town of
Clinton, Tennessee, at approximately 7:45 P.M. on the 29th day of
August, 1956.

II

Immediately upon receiving the aforesaid restraining order from
the Marshal of the United States District Court, the said defendant,
John Kasper, immediately stepped outside of the Court House door
in the Town of Clinton, Tennessee, where a large crowd of approximately eight hundred to one thousand people had gathered as per
prearrangements made by the defendant, John Kasper, and announcement by him during the preceding hours of the day, and the said
John Kasper began to address the crowd. The defendant looked at
the restraining order in front of the crowd while standing on the
Court House steps and said, "I have just been served with an injunction from the Federal Court." "We will now find out who our enemies
are." He then proceeded to read the names of the petitioners. He

called out the name of the petitioner, D. J. Brittain, Jr. He then called out to the crowd assembled, "He is our enemy." "We must get him." "I will not allow your children to be deprived of an education because a weak-kneed man like Brittain refuses to push those niggers out of school." While addressing the crowd, the defendant, John Kasper, further stated, "I will stay here until those niggers are out of Clinton High School." The petitioners further allege and show to the Court that the defendant Kasper then proceeded to tell his audience that those persons not specifically named in the restraining order could go ahead with their activities over at the Clinton High School. He further stated that the Federal Courts could serve all sorts of restraining orders on them, but that they did not have to obey said restraining orders unless they wanted to.

III

Petitioners further show to the Court that the defendant Kasper, on the morning of August 30th at approximately eight o'clock A.M., appeared in front of the high school grounds in the Town of Clinton, Tennessee, remaining some two hundred feet away from the main entrance door of said high school and standing apart from the large gathering or group of persons gathered there, proceeded to stop individuals walking up and down the street and converse with them in the general locality where large groups were gathered. The petitioners allege and show to the Court that the defendant Kasper's presence was designed, on this occasion, to further violate the orders of this Honorable Court. The petitioners aver that all of the above acts and conduct on the part of the defendant Kasper were in direct violation of the orders of this Honorable Court; and that his conduct was in wilful disregard of the order of this Court; and that the said defendant, John Kasper, is guilty of a criminal contempt of Your Honor's Court, under Title 18, Section 401, Subsection 3, of the United States Code Annotated.

The petitioners therefore pray that Your Honor issue an order of arrest for the person of John Kasper for criminal contempt of the orders of this Honorable Court, and that he be brought before Your Honor instanter to answer for his aforesaid contempt in accordance with law. . . .

Acting on this petition, Judge Taylor issued an order for Kasper's attachment (arrest).

TAYLOR, DISTRICT JUDGE

ORDER FOR ATTACHMENT

. . . It is ordered that a writ of attachment be forthwith issued commanding the Marshal of this Court and his deputies to attach said John Kasper and have his body before this Court in the United States Courthouse at Knoxville, Tennessee, forthwith, to stand trial upon the charge of criminal contempt set out in this order and to show cause why he should not be punished therefor and that a copy of this order be served upon the said John Kasper at the time he is apprehended.

That the Clerk of this Court will transmit to the Marshal an original and attested copy of said attachment and two attested copies of this order dated August 30, 1956.

On August 31, 1956 Judge Taylor held a hearing on the contempt petition.

TAYLOR, DISTRICT JUDGE

On this 31st day of August, 1956, came the attorney for the petitioners, D. J. Brittain, Jr., J. M. Burkhart, Sidney Davis, W. Buford Lewallen, and Walter E. Fisher, and the defendant, John Kasper, appeared in proper person and by attorney.

IT IS ADJUDGED that the defendant has been convicted upon his plea of not guilty and a finding of guilty, of the offense of wilfully violating the provisions of the temporary restraining order issued by this Court at 6:07 P.M. on August 29, 1956 as charged in the writ of attachment, and the Court having asked the defendant whether he has anything to say why judgment should not be pronounced, and no sufficient cause to the contrary being shown or appearing to the Court,

IT IS ADJUDGED that the defendant is guilty as charged of criminal contempt of this Court.

IT IS ADJUDGED that the defendant is hereby committed to the custody of the Attorney General or his authorized representative for imprisonment for a period of ONE (1) YEAR from and after this date.

IT IS ORDERED that the Clerk deliver a certified copy of this judgment and commitment to the United States Marshal or other qualified officer and that the copy serve as the commitment of the defendant.

Kasper appealed and was released on $10,000 bond pending the decision of the Court of Appeals. In the first few days of September, 1956, the picketing, threats, and minor outbursts of violence exploded into riots, and Clinton was in danger of mob rule. Governor Clement sent in state police and later called out the National Guard. Order was restored after several days, and state officials arrested and tried Kasper on a charge of sedition. Acquitted, Kasper returned to Clinton in November and took up his agitation again. He was arrested on a second charge of contempt and was awaiting trial on this new charge when the Court of Appeals for the 6th Circuit decided his appeal on June 1, 1957.

KASPER *v.* BRITTAIN

Before SIMONS, CHIEF JUDGE, and McALLISTER and MILLER, CIRCUIT JUDGES.

SIMONS, CHIEF JUDGE. . . .

The question whether the district court had jurisdiction of the controversy and the power to enforce its order by the injunctive process need give us little trouble. In Brown v. The Board of Education [1954] the Supreme Court concluded that in the field of public education segregation is a denial of equal protection of the laws. The constitutional principle there decided was implemented by the mandate for decree in [1955], wherein the cases there considered were remanded to the district courts to take such proceedings and enter such orders and decrees consistent with the opinion, as are necessary and proper to admit the parties to the cases to the public schools on a racially nondiscriminatory basis, with all deliberate speed. By the holdings there announced . . . the district court was bound to issue its injunctional order, requiring the School Board to desegregate the High Schools of Anderson County. Moreover, in di-

245 F. 2d 92, 2 *Race Relations Law Reporter* 792 (1957).

recting this to be done, the district judge acted with all deliberate speed, in conformity with our decision and the decision of the Supreme Court, when he commanded the School Board to desegregate by the fall term of 1956. . . .

The right to speak is not absolute and may be regulated to accomplish other legitimate objectives of government. The First Amendment does not confer the right to persuade others to violate the law. . . . Appellant had urged the crowd to disregard the orders of the court and to continue pressure upon the school officials until Negroes were eliminated from the Clinton High School. This, clearly, was not a mere exposition of ideas. It was advocacy of immediate action to accomplish an illegal result, sought to be avoided by the restraining order. The clear and present danger test, as applied by Judge Learned Hand, and adopted by the Supreme Court in the Dennis case, is here met by the mob violence that followed the urgings of the appellant. Danger that calls for the presence of the State Patrol and the National Guard, with the use of bayonets and tear gas, is, we think, within the narrowest limits of the concept and cries aloud for such court action as was here taken.

The contention that the procedure followed by the trial court constituted a denial of procedural due process because the temporary restraining order was not served upon the appellant, wherefore, he could not be guilty of violating it, is simply not applicable to the facts of record. The restraining order was served upon the appellant by the Marshal, who, with his deputy, gave clear and persuasive evidence of its service upon the appellant, the reading to him of the injunctional order, and the delivery to him of the citation, after which the appellant held up the paper and said to the crowd: "The Marshal served a temporary injunction on me and I have to appear over at Knoxville at the Federal Court Building tomorrow at 1 o'clock for a hearing. . . . You are all cordially invited to come over and we will demonstrate. . . . I will be with you folks until every Nigger is run out of the Clinton School." The Marshal's evidence was corroborated by his deputies and other witnesses. The suggestion of the appellant that the court's observation that it was of the *opinion* that the appellant knew about the restraining order is not a finding of fact, is but a captious play upon words.

The insistence of the appellant that the case was closed when the original defendants had complied with the court's order, so that he could not be guilty of criminal contempt for speaking against it must be rejected as clearly without merit. The Federal Court is always empowered to enforce its decrees by orderly process. . . . So, with the contention that the procedure followed constituted an improper use of Federal Police power, since the State Police power had not been exhausted, is equally untenable. The Federal Courts are empowered to protect Constitutional federal rights even though State power may equally be so exercised.

The contention that the sentence imposed upon the appellant was excessive is, likewise, rejected. Punishment is not "cruel and unusual," unless it is so greatly disproportionate to the offense committed as to be completely arbitrary and shocking to the sense of justice. . . . That is not the case here.

Finally, an injunctional order issued by a court must be obeyed, however, it may seemingly be challenged as invalid. This principle has long been accepted and is crystallized in the classic comment of Mr. Chief Justice Taft in Howat v. Kansas . . . wherein, speaking for a unanimous court, he said: "It is for the court of first instance to determine the question of the validity of the law and until its decision is reversed for error by orderly review, either by itself or by a higher court, its orders, based on its decision, are to be respected." . . . So only, may the dignity of courts be maintained and Constitutional rights be ab initio preserved.

Judgment affirmed.

Following this failure, Kasper petitioned the U.S. Supreme Court for certiorari.

KASPER *v.* BRITTAIN

Petition for Writ of Certiorari to the United States Court of Appeals for the Sixth Circuit, denied.

Meanwhile, in July, 1957, Kasper had been convicted on the second contempt charge. Again released on bond pending determination of

355 U.S. 834, 78 S. Ct. 54, 2 L. Ed. 2d 46 (October 14, 1957).

a petition for a new trial, he ran afoul of state officials and was jailed on vagrancy and school-dynamiting charges. In November, 1957, Judge Taylor denied Kasper's motion for a retrial and imposed a sentence of six months. Taken to the Federal penitentiary at Tallahassee, Florida, Kasper was placed in an integrated cell block.

5.   *The President "shall take Care that the Laws be faithfully executed."—U.S. Constitution, Art. II, Sec. 3.*

UNITED STATES CODE, TITLE 10 (1958)

Sec. 332. *Use of militia and armed forces to enforce Federal authority.*

WHENEVER THE President considers that unlawful obstructions, combinations, or assemblages, or rebellion against the authority of the United States, make it impractical to enforce the laws of the United States in any State or Territory by the ordinary course of judicial proceedings, he may call into Federal service such of the militia of any State, and use such of the armed forces, as he considers necessary to enforce those laws or to suppress the rebellion.

Sec. 333. *Interference with State and Federal Law.*

The President, by using the militia or the armed forces, or both, or by any other means, shall take such measures as he considers necessary to suppress in a State, any insurrection, domestic violence, unlawful combination, or conspiracy, if it—

(1) so hinders the execution of the laws of that State, and of the United States within the State, that any part or class of its people is deprived of a right, privilege, immunity, or protection named in the Constitution and secured by law, and the constituted authorities of that State are unable, fail, or refuse to protect that right, privilege, or immunity, or to give that protection; or

(2) opposes or obstructs the execution of the laws of the United States or impedes the course of justice under those laws.

In any situation covered by clause (1), the State shall be considered to have denied the equal protection of the laws secured by the Constitution.

Sec. 334. *Proclamation to disperse.*

Whenever the President considers it necessary to use the militia or the armed forces under this chapter, he shall, by proclamation, immediately order the insurgents to disperse and retire peaceably to their abodes within a limited time.

6.
> *"I . . . do command all persons engaged in such obstruction of justice to cease and desist therefrom . . ."*

THE LITTLE ROCK INCIDENT

PURSUANT TO *a plan which had been voluntarily adopted by the School Board and later approved by the federal courts, Little Rock's Central High School was ready to admit ten Negroes on opening day, September 3, 1957, when Governor Faubus intervened.*

STATE OF ARKANSAS
EXECUTIVE DEPARTMENT

PROCLAMATION

To all to whom these presents shall come—Greetings:

WHEREAS, the Governor of the State of Arkansas is vested with the authority to order to active duty the Militia of this State in case of tumult, riot or breach of the peace, or imminent danger thereof; and

WHEREAS, it has been made known to me, as Governor, from many sources, that there is imminent danger of tumult, riot and breach of the peace and the doing of violence to persons and property in Pulaski County, Arkansas;

NOW, THEREFORE, I, Orval E. Faubus, Governor of the State of Arkansas do hereby proclaim that a state of emergency presently exists and I do hereby order to active duty Major General Sherman T. Clinger, the Adjutant General of Arkansas, the State Militia units con-

The following documents can be found at 2 *Race Relations Law Reporter* 931–965 (1957). Reprinted with permission.

sisting of the Base Detachment of Adams Field and the State Headquarters Detachment at Camp Robinson, and any other units which
may be necessary to accomplish the mission of maintaining or restoring law and order and to preserve the peace, health, safety and security of the citizens of Pulaski County, Arkansas.

IN WITNESS WHEREOF, I have hereunto set my hand and cause the
Great Seal of the State of Arkansas to be affixed. Done in office in the
City of Little Rock this 2nd day of September, 1957.

s/ ORVAL E. FAUBUS

Governor

*Negro children attempting to enter the school were turned away by
the National Guard. The School Board then petitioned federal District
Judge Ronald Davies for instructions and also requested that he allow
integration to be postponed because of community tensions. Judge
Davies denied the request for a delay and ordered the Board to proceed with its desegregation plan. On September 9, with armed state
troops still barring entry to Central High School, Judge Davies issued
the following order:*

ORDER

DAVIES, DISTRICT JUDGE.

On the date hereof, the court having received a report from the
United States attorney for the Eastern District of Arkansas, made pursuant to the court's request, from which it appears that Negro students
are not being permitted to attend Little Rock Central High School
in accordance with the plan of integration of the Little Rock school
directors approved by this court and by the Court of Appeals for the
Eighth Circuit.

And the court being of the opinion that the public interest in the
administration of justice should be represented in these proceedings
and that it will be of assistance to the court to have the benefit of
views of counsel for the United States as *amici curiae,* and this court
being entitled at any time to call upon the law officers of the United
States to serve in that capacity, now, therefore,

IT IS ORDERED that the Attorney General of the United States or his designate and the United States attorney for the Eastern District of Arkansas or his designate are hereby requested and authorized to appear in these proceedings as *amici curiae* and to accord the court the benefit of their views and recommendations with the right to submit to the court pleadings, evidence, arguments and briefs and for the further purpose, under the direction of this court, to initiate such further proceedings as may be appropriate.

IT IS FURTHER ORDERED that the attorney general of the United States and the United States attorney for the Eastern District of Arkansas be, and they are hereby, directed to file immediately a petition against Orval E. Faubus, governor of the state of Arkansas; Maj. Gen. Sherman T. Clinger, adjutant general, Arkansas National Guard, and Lt. Col. Marion E. Johnson, unit commander, Arkansas National Guard, seeking such injunctive and other relief as may be appropriate to prevent the existing interferences with and obstructions to the carrying out of the orders heretofore entered by the court in this case.

Complying with this order, the Attorney General filed a petition requesting the court to enjoin Faubus and the National Guard commanders from interfering with desegregation at the high school. On September 20, a hearing was held. Faubus' attorneys denied that a federal court had jurisdiction over the governor of "a sovereign state" and then withdrew from the courtroom. After hearing the testimony of city officials and other witnesses, all of whom put the blame for unrest directly on Faubus, Judge Davies gave his decision.

DAVIES, DISTRICT JUDGE.

It is very clear to this court from the evidence and the testimony adduced upon the hearing today that the plan of integration adopted by the Little Rock school board and approved by this court and the court of appeals from the Eighth circuit has been thwarted by the governor of Arkansas by the use of national guard troops. It is equally demonstrable from the testimony here today that there would have been no violence in carrying out the plan of integration, and that there has been no violence.

The petition of the United States of America as amicus curiae for a preliminary injunction against Gov. Faubus, General Clinger and Colonel Johnson and all others named in the petition is granted; and such injunction shall issue without delay enjoining those respondents from obstructing or preventing by use of the national guard or otherwise attendance of Negro students at Little Rock high school under the plan of integration approved by this court and from otherwise obstructing or interfering with orders of this court in connection with the plan of integration. . . .

It is hereby ordered and decreed that defendant Orval E. Faubus, Governor of the State of Arkansas, Gen. Sherman T. Clinger, Adjutant General of the State of Arkansas, and Lieut. Colonel Marion E. Johnson of the Arkansas National Guard, their officers, agents, servants, employees, attorneys, all persons subject to their joint or several orders and directions, and all persons in active concert, participation or privity with them, be and they are hereby enjoined and restrained from hereafter (a) obstructing or preventing, by means of the Arkansas National Guard, or otherwise, Negro students, eligible under said plan of school integration to attend the Little Rock Central High School, from attending said school or (b) from threatening or coercing said students not to attend said school or (c) from obstructing or interfering in any way with the carrying out and effectuation of this court's orders . . . in this cause, or (d) from otherwise obstructing or interfering with the constitutional right of said Negro children to attend said school.

Provided that this order shall not be deemed to prevent Orval E. Faubus, as Governor of the State of Arkansas, from taking any and all action he may deem necessary or desirable for the preservation of peace and order, by means of the Arkansas National Guard, or otherwise, which does not hinder or interfere with the right of eligible Negro students to attend the Little Rock Central High School.

In the interim between Faubus' proclamation and the injunction, Arkansas Representative Brooks Hays had been trying to work out a compromise. Hays arranged for a meeting between Faubus and President Eisenhower, and on September 14, 1957, the two executives conferred for several hours. No settlement was reached, however.

After Judge Davies issued his injunction on September 20, Faubus withdrew the troops from around the school, though he refused to concede that the court order was valid.

The School Board planned to admit the colored children on September 23, but early that morning a mob had gathered, among whose leaders was a close personal friend of Faubus. The Negroes were sneaked into the back of the school, but by noon the police were losing control over the mob and the colored children were withdrawn. That night President Eisenhower issued the following proclamation:

PROCLAMATION 3204

OBSTRUCTION OF JUSTICE IN THE STATE OF ARKANSAS

By the President of The United States of America

A PROCLAMATION

WHEREAS certain persons in the State of Arkansas, individually and in unlawful assemblages, combinations, and conspiracies, have wilfully obstructed the enforcement of orders of the United States District Court for the Eastern District of Arkansas with respect to matters relating to enrollment and attendance at public schools, particularly at Central High School, located in Little Rock School District, Little Rock, Arkansas; and

WHEREAS such wilful obstruction of justice hinders the execution of the laws of that State and of the United States, and makes it impracticable to enforce such laws by the ordinary course of judicial proceedings; and

WHEREAS such obstruction of justice constitutes a denial of the equal protection of the laws secured by the Constitution of the United States and impedes the course of justice under those laws:

Now, THEREFORE, I, DWIGHT D. EISENHOWER, President of the United States, under and by virtue of the authority vested in me by the Constitution and statutes of the United States, including Chapter

22 *Federal Register* 7628.

15 of Title 10 of the United States Code, particularly sections 332, 333 and 334 thereof, do command all persons engaged in such obstruction of justice to cease and desist therefrom, and to disperse forthwith. . . .

DWIGHT D. EISENHOWER

The next morning the mob, in defiance of Eisenhower's proclamation, reassembled in front of the school. The President then issued Executive Order 10730.

EXECUTIVE ORDER 10730

Providing Assistance for the Removal of an Obstruction of Justice Within the State of Arkansas

WHEREAS on September 23, 1957, I issued Proclamation No. 3204 . . .

WHEREAS the command contained in that Proclamation has not been obeyed and wilful obstruction of enforcement of said court orders still exists and threatens to continue:

Now, THEREFORE, by virtue of the authority vested in me by the Constitution and Statutes of the United States, including Chapter 15 of Title 10, particularly sections 332, 333 and 334 thereof, and section 301 of Title 3 of the United States Code, it is hereby ordered as follows:

SECTION 1. I hereby authorize and direct the Secretary of Defense to order into the active military service of the United States as he may deem appropriate to carry out the purposes of this Order, any or all of the units of the National Guard of the United States and of the Air National Guard of the United States within the State of Arkansas to serve in the active military service of the United States for an indefinite period and until relieved by appropriate orders.

SECTION 2. The Secretary of Defense is authorized and directed to take all appropriate steps to enforce any orders of the United States District Court for the Eastern District of Arkansas for the removal of obstruction of justice in the State of Arkansas with respect to matters relating to enrollment and attendance at public schools in the Little Rock School District, Little Rock, Arkansas. In carrying out the provisions of this section, the Secretary of Defense is authorized to use the units, and members thereof, ordered into the active military service of the United States pursuant to Section 1 of this Order.

SECTION 3. In furtherance of the enforcement of the aforementioned orders of the United States District Court for the Eastern District of Arkansas, the Secretary of Defense is authorized to use such of the armed forces of the United States as he may deem necessary.

SECTION 4. The Secretary of Defense is authorized to delegate to the Secretary of the Army or the Secretary of the Air Force, or both, any of the authority conferred upon him by this Order.

DWIGHT D. EISENHOWER

THE WHITE HOUSE,
    September 24, 1957.

Pursuant to Executive Order 10730, Secretary of Defense Wilson issued the following order:

I, Charles E. Wilson, Secretary of Defense of the United States of America, by virtue of the direction to me from the President of the United States under executive order dated 24 September 1957, entitled "Providing Assistance for the removal of an Obstruction of Justice Within the State of Arkansas," hereby call into the Federal service all of the units and the members thereof of the Army National Guard and the Air National Guard of the state of Arkansas, to serve in the active military service of the United States for an indefinite period and until relieved by appropriate orders.

I order the members of such National Guard units to hold themselves in readiness for further orders as to the time and date of reporting to active duty by the Secretary of the Army acting for me.

Copies hereof shall be furnished forthwith to the Governor of Arkansas and to the commanding officers of the Army National Guard and the Air National Guard in the state of Arkansas.

I further direct that the Secretary of the Army take such action as he deems necessary to implement such executive order and this order, and I hereby vest in the Secretary of the Army the right to exercise any and all of the authority conferred upon me by sections 2 and 3 of the above mentioned executive order, as of 24 September 1957.

Acting under the direction of the Secretary of Defense, the Secretary of the Army sent troops from the 101st Airborne Division into Little Rock, and integration was carried out at bayonet point.

PART FOUR

Access to Judicial Power

7 / LIMITATIONS ON LAWSUITS

Custom, the Constitution, and public esteem have vested federal judges with great power, but under the common-law system judges cannot bring their power to bear on an issue until someone has brought a case before them. Courts, in Justice Jackson's phrase, lack a self-starter. A judge who acts within the legal framework can only decide a case when it has been brought before him in accordance with the jurisdictional rules which Congress has enacted. But even then the judicial process does not automatically go into operation. Having a federal question does not in itself mean that a litigant will get his case heard in the courts. Judges have long recognized that over-use can cheapen the value of judicial decisions, and that they are not obligated to decide disputes for everyone who has money enough to bring a lawsuit. The limitations imposed on access to the courts are often stated in the technical language of "legal interests" and "standing to sue," but fundamentally what is involved here is a concern for protecting the courts from involvement in controversies which, for various reasons, it would not be prudent for the judicial process to handle.

Chapter 2 discussed in some detail the jurisdiction of the federal courts. This chapter will focus on some of the more important standing rules which judges have formulated to regulate access to judicial power by those whose disputes meet the jurisdictional requirements.

Cases and Controversies

The first rule which a litigant must satisfy to obtain standing is that prescribed in the Constitution: federal jurisdiction reaches only "cases" and "controversies." These are technical terms. A case or controversy in the legal sense refers to a real dispute in which the interests of two or more persons are in collision. Federal judges have asserted time and again that they will not exert their power—and risk their prestige—to answer hypothetical, academic, or abstract questions, or hand down decisions where the judgment can have no practical effect.

Muskrat v. *United States* (1911) is one of the leading cases on the necessity of adverse interests. Congress had passed a statute authorizing Cherokee Indians to file a suit contesting the validity of earlier legislation which had restricted Cherokee land rights. The Supreme Court, however, ruled that no actual controversy was presented; for while the two parties each had real interests, there was no live disagreement between them, only an effort to get a ruling on the constitutionality of Indian regulations.

The case requirement is also one of the reasons assigned for the federal bar against advisory opinions. It has been the practice in many states for judges of the highest court to advise the governor or legislature, when so requested, as to their views on the constitutionality of proposed policy. Since the time of Chief Justice John Jay, however, federal judges have claimed that the absence of a case or controversy prevents them from performing a similar function. Nevertheless, there have been occasions on which judges have broken their own rule and offered advice, the opinion sent to President Monroe being the classic example. (See below, p. 250.)

More often judges have conferred in private with political leaders and have given informal rather than formal opinions. Roger Brooke Taney, for instance, continued to act as a confidant and adviser to President Jackson after his appointment as Chief Justice. During the New Deal period, when judges were voiding federal legislation on a wholesale scale, Secretary of Labor Frances Perkins talked to Justice Stone on a social occasion about how to develop a social security program that judges would uphold. "The taxing power of the Federal Government, my dear," Stone replied, "is sufficient for everything you want and need." In 1937, when the Senate was considering Roosevelt's Court-packing plan, Chief Justice Hughes sent an open letter to Senator Wheeler advising that increasing the number of justices would not allow the Court to sit in separate divisions to hear cases because of the constitutional command that there be "one supreme Court."

Perhaps the most successful advisory opinion ever rendered was that given by Chief Justice Taft to Calvin Coolidge just after Harding had died. Coolidge, somewhat awed by his new responsibilities, asked Taft what he should do. "I told him," the Chief Justice recounted a short time later, "to do nothing. I told him that I thought the public were glad to have him in the White House doing nothing. . . ."

Supreme Court justices have sometimes given the other branches of government the benefit of judicial advice in a more direct manner. The current statutes granting the Supreme Court wide discretion in controlling its docket were largely drafted by the justices on the Taft Court; and Taft and his associates openly lobbied for the bill's passage. There could have been no doubt in the minds of congressmen or the President that these regulations would pass judicial muster.

Judges have also used dicta in their opinions to guide future legislation. In 1922, for example, Chief Justice Taft, speaking for the Court in *Hill* v. *Wallace*, held unconstitutional a federal statute regulating transactions in grain futures. Such matters, Taft said, "cannot come within the regulatory power of Congress as such, unless they are regarded by Congress, from the evidence before it, as directly interfering with interstate commerce so as to be an obstruction or a burden thereon." Congress took the hint and a few months later passed the Grain Futures Act which declared that grain market manipulations were obstructing interstate commerce. The next year, again speaking through Taft, the Supreme Court sustained this second statute because "the Act only purports to regulate interstate commerce and sales of grain for future delivery on boards of trade because it finds that by manipulation they have become a constantly recurring burden and obstruction to that commerce."[1]

Legal Injury

Having a clash of interests is not sufficient in itself to activate judicial power. The plaintiff must, in the second place, show that his interest is a legally protected one. In other words, granted there is a clash and a real or threatened injury, is there injury to a *legal* right? Traditionally a legal right is one involving a property or pocketbook interest or some right specifically protected by a statutory or constitutional provision.

[1] *Board of Trade* v. *Olsen* (1923).

Special problems arise in establishing legal injury as a result of government policy. A litigant may usually challenge governmental action only where that action, if taken by a private person, would be the basis for a suit, or where a statute or constitutional clause sets up a protected interest. For example, since a business firm has no right at common law to be free from honest competition and no statutory or constitutional clause confers such a privilege, the Supreme Court has held that a private utility company has no standing to sue to prevent the federal government from selling electric power from a dam owned and operated by the United States.[2]

Direct Injury

Third, the injury complained of must also directly affect the plaintiff. Existing legal rules allow a litigant only to protect his own particular rights, not those of the public at large. To challenge governmental action, one must show that some tangible personal interest is at stake, not just a general interest in good government. For instance, the claim that the cost of a particular federal program might increase taxes has been held to be too remote and minute an injury to confer standing to attack the constitutionality of the program.

Nor, generally speaking, can a person use the federal courts to defend the rights of other people or set up the rights of others as a defense. In recent years, however, a modification of this doctrine has been developing in that organizations are sometimes permitted to assert the rights of their members where, as in loyalty-security matters, governmental policy lumps together the rights of all the group's members, and a decision regarding one will affect all.

Moreover, a denial of one party's constitutional rights which might have repercussions adversely affecting the rights of a second party, may be sufficient to give that second party standing. A private school was allowed in *Pierce* v. *Society of Sisters* (1925) to utilize the federal courts to enjoin enforcement of a state statute which infringed on parents' rights to send their children to schools of their own choice. Similarly, the Supreme Court in *Barrows* v. *Jackson* (1953) ruled that a white person, sued for breaking a restrictive real-estate covenant, could set up as a proper defense the right of Negroes to be free from state interference in purchasing property.

[2] *Alabama Power Co.* v. *Ickes* (1938).

Finality of Action

Fourth, if governmental action is involved, the action must be "sufficiently final" to be "ripe" for review. This rule is generally referred to as the doctrine of exhaustion of administrative remedies. Largely developed in litigation regarding independent regulatory commissions, the exhaustion doctrine means that an aggrieved person has no standing to contest an administrative decision until he has used all the procedures which the administrative agency has established to correct its own mistakes. For example, where a decision by an official can be appealed to a superior officer within the same agency, a petitioner must try this method before resorting to the courts.

The exhaustion rule allows administrative agencies to function without unnecessary outside interference, but the doctrine is not always applied. The Supreme Court has allowed petitioners to bypass administrative remedies in several different situations: (1) where irreparable injury might result; (2) where the agency is operating outside the scope of its authority; (3) where the futility of pursuing administrative remedies is obvious; (4) where the basic statute under which the agency operates is attacked as unconstitutional; (5) where the agency is being deliberately dilatory.

Conclusiveness of Judicial Decision

The fifth rule also involves finality, but finality of the court decision sought by the litigant. In line with the historic practice of English and colonial courts, federal judges have refused to take cases where the judicial decision, either at the trial or appellate level, would not be final as between the two litigants. In *Hayburn's Case* in 1792, for instance, the justices of the Supreme Court balked at enforcing provisions of a pension statute for Revolutionary War veterans because the statute would have allowed the Secretary of War to review judicial determinations as to who was eligible for a pension.

In 1948, a majority of the Court reaffirmed the rule of *Hayburn's Case* in *Chicago & Southern Airlines* v. *Waterman Steamship Co.* Rejecting a suggestion that a federal court could review an order of the Civil Aeronautics Board and that the President could then revise the court's decision, the majority said: "Judgments within the powers vested in the courts by the Judiciary Article of the Constitution may not lawfully be revised, overturned or refused faith and credit by another Department of Government. . . . It has . . . been the firm and unvarying practice of Constitutional Courts to render no judgments not binding and conclusive on the parties and none that are subject to later review or alteration by administrative action."

Political Questions

The sixth rule for standing which a litigant must meet is that he bring to the court a dispute which is appropriate for judicial settlement, what is called a justiciable rather than a political question. Because judges have tended to define "justiciable" and "political" in terms of each other, the distinction between the two cannot be fixed with any precision. Perhaps nomenclature is at the root of the difficulty. A political question in the technical sense has a very restricted meaning. Courts customarily decide questions of policy which are fraught with political implications. What judges call political questions usually raise questions whose settlement the Constitution gives to another branch of government, or problems in a field where judges have no special competence, or issues with which, as a practical matter, the judicial process could not cope.

While self-imposed, the political questions doctrine is an important limitation on judicial power; and since, as John P. Frank has noted, it is "more amenable to description by infinite itemization than by generalization," some examples will help illustrate the problems which the doctrine has been used to solve and those it also creates. The first explicit application of the theory was made by the Supreme Court in *Luther* v. *Borden* (1849). Stymied in efforts to reform the state government which was still largely operating under a charter of 1663, liberal elements in Rhode Island joined in a rebellion led by Thomas Dorr in 1841. For a time two rival governments existed in the state, and a private citizen sued a Charter government official for trespassing on his property. In his defense the official claimed he was executing a command of the lawful state government.

A decision would hinge on the question of which government had been legitimate, and the justices refused to stir up the embers of this controversy, which by the time the case had been heard by the Supreme Court had been long settled. First, Chief Justice Taney asked, how could federal courts determine which government had represented the people? Judges could not conduct an election nor would any of the other judicial fact-finding procedures be useful in ascertaining public preference. Fortunately, Taney continued, the Constitution, in providing that the federal government should guarantee every state a republican form of government and protect each from invasion or insurrection, had placed these responsibilities with Congress. Congress in turn had authorized the President to use force to put down revolutions. Although the President had not sent troops to Rhode Island, he had recognized the Charter government as legal. This decision was beyond the competence of courts to review. The Chief Justice concluded:

> It is said that this power of the President is dangerous to liberty, and may be abused. All power may be abused if placed in unworthy hands. . . . When citizens of the same State are in arms against each other, and the constituted authorities unable to execute the laws, the interposition of the United States must be prompt, or it is of little value. The ordinary course of proceedings in courts of justice would be utterly unfit for the crisis.

Similarly, the justices have held that the President and Congress have exclusive authority to decide whether a constitutional amendment has been properly ratified, whether the existence of referendum and recall destroys the republican status of a state government, or whether members of the House of Representatives can be elected from gerrymandered electoral districts. Especially in foreign affairs, judges have been quick to disclaim their competence and to emphasize that the other branches of government have plenary authority. Decisions on questions involving the recognition of foreign governments, the authority of foreign diplomats, the existence of treaties, or the beginning and ending of war, have all been refused as political rather than justiciable issues.

Perhaps the most candid statement of the practical considerations behind the doctrine was given by Chief Justice Chase in *Mississippi* v. *Johnson* (1867). Mississippi officials had asked the Court to forbid the President to enforce the Radical Republican Reconstruction program. In dismissing the suit, the Chief Justice wrote:

> Suppose . . . the injunction prayed for [were] allowed. If the President refuse obedience, it is needless to observe that the court is without power to enforce its process. If, on the other hand, the President complies with the order of the court . . . is it not clear that a collision may occur between the executive and legislative departments of the government? May not the House of Representatives impeach the President for such refusal? And in that case could this court interfere,

in behalf of the President, thus endangered by compliance with its mandate, and restrain by injunction the Senate of the United States from sitting as a court of impeachment? Would the strange spectacle be offered to the public wonder of an attempt by this court to arrest proceedings in that court?

Law and Diplomacy

None of these six rules is a precise formula, as numerous critics have pointed out. Kenneth C. Davis, for one, claims that the whole standing concept has been made unnecessarily complex. Standing, Davis says, involves only "the basically simple problem of whether or not the petitioner's asserted interest is in the circumstances deserving of legal protection." This may be a correct statement of the fundamental legal principle, but criticisms such as this overlook the crucial fact that the standing criteria partake as much of diplomacy as of law.

These rules are not dogmas. In part, they are means to keep the federal dockets free of trivial and officious litigation. They are, at the same time, means to assist federal judges in timing their decisions on substantive issues to obtain a maximum effect on public policy with a minimum of conflict with other governmental officials. The requirements for a case with direct, legal injury raising a justiciable question allow judges to avoid premature or unnecessary clashes with legislators or executive officers, just as the exhaustion of administrative remedies rule removes many potential conflicts with administrators. In similar fashion, the ban on advisory opinions and the requirement that a judicial decision be final protect the prestige of the courts.

These standing rules provide judges with a tactical flexibility which enables them to avoid conflict without appearing to depart from good legal form, and also permits them to decline to hear controversies which they do not find deserving, without appearing to indulge in subjective value judgments. Now flexibility is a necessary feature in any governmental process, but the question still may be asked whether Supreme Court justices have not sometimes become prisoners of these rules, or used them to evade the positive obligations which judicial review imposes.

Should, for example, the Supreme Court have refused to accord standing to federal employees who wished to challenge the Hatch Act's restrictions on their political activities? Should it have dismissed as political in nature the question whether a state has abridged the right to vote by gerrymandering electoral districts? Does it make sense in terms of logic, law, or politics to assign to the politicians elected from rotten boroughs the responsibility for proper districting?

SELECTED REFERENCES

Albertsworth, E. F., "Advisory Functions in Federal Supreme Court," 23 *Georgetown Law Journal* 643 (1935).

Annotation, "Standing to Sue," 96 L. Ed. 481.

Beth, Loren, "Technical and Doctrinal Aids to Constitutional Interpretation," 18 *University of Pittsburgh Law Review* 108 (1956).

Bischoff, Ralph F., "Status to Challenge Constitutionality," in Edmond Cahn (ed.), *Supreme Court and Supreme Law* (Bloomington: Indiana University Press, 1954), pp. 26–31.

Davis, Kenneth C., *Administrative Law* (Minneapolis: West Publishing Co., 1951), Chs. 15, 16.

Douglas, William O., *We the Judges* (New York: Doubleday, 1956), Ch. 2.

Frank, John P., "Political Questions," in Edmond Cahn (ed.), *Supreme Court and Supreme Law*, pp. 36–43.

Hart, Henry M. and Herbert Wechsler, *The Federal Courts and the Federal System* (Brooklyn: The Foundation Press, 1953), Ch. 2.

Jackson, Robert H., *The Supreme Court in the American System of Government* (Cambridge: Harvard University Press, 1955).

Note, "Federal Judicial Power: Exhaustion of Administrative Remedies," 2 *Race Relations Law Reporter* 561 (1957).

Note, "Federal Judicial Power: Exhaustion of State Judicial Remedies and the Doctrine of Equitable Abstention," 2 *Race Relations Law Reporter* 1215 (1957).

Perkins, Frances, *The Roosevelt I Knew* (New York: Viking Press, 1946).

Post, Charles G., *The Supreme Court and Political Questions* (Baltimore: The Johns Hopkins University Press, 1936).

Pritchett, C. Herman, *The American Constitution* (New York: McGraw-Hill Book Co., 1959), pp. 143–152.

Roche, John P., "Judicial Self-Restraint," 49 *American Political Science Review* 762 (1955).

1.
> *"We exceedingly regret every event that may cause em-*
> *barrassment to your administration . . ."*

GEORGE WASHINGTON'S REQUEST FOR AN ADVISORY OPINION

THOMAS JEFFERSON, *Secretary of State, sent the following letter to Chief Justice John Jay and the Associate Justices:*

Philadelphia, July 18, 1793.

Gentlemen:

THE WAR which has taken place among the powers of Europe produces frequent transactions within our ports and limits, on which questions arise of considerable difficulty, and of greater importance to the peace of the United States. These questions depend for their solution on the construction of our treaties, on the laws of nature and nations, and on the laws of the land, and are often presented under circumstances which do not give a cognizance of them to the tribunals of the country. Yet, their decision is so little analogous to the ordinary functions of the executive, as to occasion much embarrassment and difficulty to them. The President therefore would be much relieved if he found himself free to refer questions of this description to the opinions of the judges of the Supreme Court of the United States, whose knowledge of the subject would secure us against errors dangerous to the peace of the United States, and their authority insure the respect of all parties. He has therefore asked the attendance of such of the judges as could be collected in time for the occasion, to know, in the first place, their opinion, whether the public may, with propriety, be availed of their advice on these questions? And if they may, to present, for their advice, the abstract questions which have already occurred, or may soon occur, from which they will themselves

These documents are found at: Jared Sparks (ed.), *The Writings of George Washington* (Boston: Ferdinand Andrews, 1839), X, 542-545; and Henry P. Johnston (ed.), *The Correspondence and Public Papers of John Jay* (New York: Putnam's, 1890–93), III, 486–489.

strike out such as any circumstances might, in their opinion, forbid them to pronounce on. I have the honour to be with sentiments of the most perfect respect, gentlemen,

> Your most obedient and humble servant,
>
> Thos. Jefferson.

A number of questions on international law, treaties, and statutes of the United States were included in the correspondence. On July 20, 1793, the Justices wrote the President that they would like to postpone their answer. On August 8, 1793 they sent Washington this letter.

Sir:

We have considered the previous question stated in a letter written by your direction to us by the Secretary of State on the 18th of last month, [regarding] the lines of separation drawn by the Constitution between the three departments of this government. These being in certain respects checks upon each other, and our being judges of a court in the last resort, are considerations which afford strong arguments against the propriety of our extra-judicially deciding the questions alluded to, especially as the power given by the Constitution to the President, of calling on the heads of departments for opinions, seems to have been *purposely* as well as expressly united to the *executive* departments.

We exceedingly regret every event that may cause embarrassment to your administration, but we derive consolation from the reflection that your judgment will discern what is right, and that your usual prudence, decision, and firmness will surmount every obstacle to the preservation of the rights, peace, and dignity of the United States.

2.   *"The judges are deeply sensible of the mark of confidence bestowed on them . . ."*

JUSTICE JOHNSON* AND PRESIDENT MONROE

IN 1822, *after vetoing the Cumberland Road bill as an unconstitutional federal invasion of state authority, President Monroe solicited the opinions of several members of the Supreme Court as to the legality of federal improvements of roads and canals within individual states. Justice William Johnson sent the following reply. (The letter is undated.)*

JUDGE JOHNSON has had the honour to submit the President's argument on the subject of internal improvements to his brother-judges and is instructed to make the following report.

The judges are deeply sensible of the mark of confidence bestowed on them in this instance and should be unworthy of that confidence did they attempt to conceal their real opinion. Indeed to conceal or disavow it would be now impossible as they are all of opinion that the decision on the bank question [*McCulloch* v. *Maryland* (1819)] completely commits them on the subject of internal improvements as applied to post-roads and military roads. On the other points it is impossible to resist the lucid and conclusive reasoning contained in the argument.

The principle assumed in the case of the Bank is that the grant of the principal power carries with it the grant of all adequate and appropriate means of executing it. That the selection of those means must rest with the general government and as to that power and those means the Constitution makes the government of the U. S. supreme.

J. J. would take the liberty of suggesting to the President that it

Quoted in Donald G. Morgan, *Justice William Johnson: The First Dissenter* (Columbia: University of South Carolina Press, 1954), pp. 123–124. Reprinted with permission.

* Johnson, appointed to the Supreme Court by Jefferson, was a contemporary of John Marshall. Johnson served on the Court from 1804 to 1834.

would not be unproductive of good, if the Sec'y of State were to have
the opinion of this Court on the bank question printed and dispersed
through the Union.

J. J. is strongly impressed with the President's views of the difficulty
and delicacy attendant on any effort that might be made by the
U. S. to carry into effect any scheme of internal improvement through
the states, and as a question of policy or expediency sees plainly how
prudent it would be to prepare them for it by the most conciliatory
means.

3. *". . . ghosts that slay."*

A NOTE ON ADVISORY OPINIONS *Felix Frankfurter**

. . . SINCE RECONSTRUCTION days, the acutest controversies
which have come before our Supreme Court, and increasingly will
come, cluster around the Commerce Clause and Due Process. These
issues concern, in effect, a delimitation between the powers of the
Nation and those of the States and the eternal conflict between the
freedom of the individual and his control by society. The stuff of
these contests are facts, and judgment upon facts. Every tendency to
deal with them abstractedly, to formulate them in terms of sterile
legal questions, is bound to result in sterile conclusions unrelated to
actualities. The reports are strewn with wrecks of legislation considered *in vacuo* and torn out of the context of life which evoked the
legislation and alone made it intelligible. These are commonplaces. But
they are the heart of the matter of American constitutional law. A
failure scrupulously and persistently to observe these commonplaces
jeopardizes the traditional American constitutional system more than
all the loose talk about "usurpation."

Another commonplace, indispensable to the effective working of
our constitutional system, is rigorous regard in practice for the avowed
theory that legislation is for the legislature, that the court does not

37 *Harvard Law Review* 1002 (1924). Copyright 1924 the Harvard Law Review
Association. Reprinted with permission.
* Then Professor of Law, Harvard University.

sit in judgment upon the wisdom or fairness or utility of legislation. The Supreme Court is not a House of Lords with revisory power over legislation, although conservative scholars have suggested that the Supreme Court frankly assume the function implicit in some of its decisions. As part of the ritual of traditional theory, the Supreme Court professes to defer greatly to the legislature. Such deference is not merely a gesture of courtesy. It is the formulation of a basic truth in the distribution of governmental powers. For behind every act of legislation is the judgment of one of the coördinate branches of the government—no less than the courts bound by oath to support the Constitution—that what it has done is within the Constitution. . . . It is of profound importance if heeded, because the controversy between legislature and courts, in issues which matter most, is not at all a controversy about legal principles, but concerns the application of admitted principles to complicated and often elusive facts. The difference, then, in the crucial cases is apt to resolve itself not really to a difference about law, but to differences in knowledge of relevant facts and inferences drawn from such facts.

The bearing of all this upon resort to advisory opinions on modern constitutional questions is evident. The vice of the proposal, variously made, that opinions of the Supreme Court in advance of legislation would be "constructive," lies in the assumption, too often made by American political scientists, that constitutionality is a fixed quantity. A consideration of the history of the Due Process Clauses, of the persistent refusal of the Supreme Court to define "due process" or to generalize, of its empiric method of "pricking out a line in successive cases," in a word a study of the two thousand odd cases which have spun meaning out of the Delphic phrase "without due process of law," ought to furnish sobering reflection. Concepts like "liberty" and "due process" are too vague in themselves to solve issues. They derive meaning only if referred to adequate human facts. Facts and facts again are decisive. They are either present-day facts, or ancient facts clothed by the universalizing instinct of man to look like principles. Dean Pound has pointed out that concrete cases under the Due Process Clause are decided not by taking anything out of the Constitution but by putting Adam Smith into it. Not the least of constitutional controversies resolve themselves into the pressure of new facts against the resistance of inadequate or exploded facts persisting as legal assumptions. . . .

The advisory opinion deprives constitutional interpretation of the judgment of the legislature upon facts, of the effective defence of legislation as an application of settled legal principles to new situations, and of the means of securing new facts through the process of legislation within the allowable limits of trial and error. Legislation is an appeal to "judgment from experience as against a judgment from speculation." Unless we are to embrace fatalism, legislation to a considerable extent must necessarily be based on probabilities, on hopes and fears, and not on demonstration. To meet the intricate, stubborn, and subtle problems of modern industrialism, the legislature must be given ample scope for putting its prophecies to the test of proof. But to submit legislative proposals to the judicial judgment, instead of the deliberate decisions of the legislature, is to submit legislative doubts instead of legislative convictions. The whole focus of the judicial vision becomes thereby altered.

Moreover, legislation is thus deprived of its creative function. The history of modern legislation is rich in proof that facts may be established in support of measures although not previously in existence. The accidents of litigation may give time for the vindication of laws which *a priori* may run counter to deep prepossessions or speculative claims of injustice. The whole milieu of advisory opinions on proposed bills is inevitably different from that of litigation contesting legislation. However much provision may be made on paper for adequate arguments (and experience justifies little reliance) advisory opinions are bound to move in an unreal atmosphere. The impact of actuality and the intensities of immediacy are wanting. In the attitude of court and counsel, in the vigor of adequate representation of the facts behind legislation (lamentably inadequate even in contested litigation) there is thus a wide gulf of difference, partly rooted in psychologic factors, between opinions in advance of legislation and decisions in litigation after such proposals are embodied into law. Advisory opinions are rendered upon sterilized and mutilated issues. . . .

Perhaps the most costly price of advisory opinions is the weakening of legislative and popular responsibility. It is not merely the right of the legislature to legislate; it is its duty. Let legislatures inform themselves as best they can; but the burden of decision ought not to be shifted to the tribunal whose task is the most delicate in our whole scheme of government—the power of the judiciary to set limits to legislative activity within those ultimate but vague bounds which are undefined and *a priori* undefinable. . . .

It must be remembered that advisory opinions are not merely advisory opinions. They are ghosts that slay.

4.   *". . . it will be of some public service if they express their opinions, as individuals . . ."*

BROWDER V. GAYLE

FOLLOWING THE *decision of a three-judge federal district court, affirmed by the U.S. Supreme Court, that neither the state of Alabama nor the city of Montgomery could require racially segregated seating arrangements on local buses, Montgomery city officials sought instructions from the district court. Among the questions asked was whether, if the city leased its bus lines to a "private club" and this "private club" continued to require segregation, such action would constitute a violation of the Fourteenth Amendment.*

BEFORE RIVES, CIRCUIT JUDGE, and LYNNE and JOHNSON, DISTRICT JUDGES.

PER CURIAM.

The petition for instructions presented by the Board of Commissioners of the City of Montgomery, Alabama, on the 25th day of January, 1957, is dismissed for the reason that under the Constitution of the United States, Article III, §2, this Court's jurisdiction is confined to actual cases or controversies, and it has no power to give advisory opinions, nor to decide abstract, hypothetical, or contingent questions.

The Court being without jurisdiction, Judge Lynne feels that he

2 *Race Rel. L. Rep.* 412 (1957).

should express no individual opinion. Judges Rives and Johnson feel that it will be of some public service if they express their opinions, as individuals, of which they presently entertain no doubt, namely, that the word "private" as used in the third question is inappropriate, and that each of the three questions propounded should be answered "yes." . . .

5.   *"Courts ought not to enter this political thicket."*

COLEGROVE V. GREEN

AT THE *time of this case, Congress had set the size of the House of Representatives at 435, with each state's share to be automatically apportioned after every census. Although Congress has required that representatives must be elected from single-member districts, it has not, since 1929, regulated the relative size of districts within individual states. The rurally dominated legislature of Illinois had refused to redistrict the state and thereby increase the political power of the Chicago area. As a result, in the mid-1940's, the population of metropolitan districts ran as high as nine times that of rural, downstate districts. Protesting against this gerrymandering-by-default, three college professors from the Chicago area brought suit in 1946 in a federal district court to enjoin state officials from holding an election under the existing system. The special three-judge district court dismissed the suit and the professors appealed to the Supreme Court.*

MR. JUSTICE FRANKFURTER announced the judgment of the Court and an opinion in which Mr. Justice REED and Mr. Justice BURTON concur. . . .

We are of opinion that the petitioners ask of this Court what is beyond its competence to grant. This is one of those demands on judicial power which cannot be met by verbal fencing about "jurisdiction." It must be resolved by considerations on the basis of which this Court, from time to time, has refused to intervene in controversies.

328 U.S. 549, 66 S. Ct. 1198, 90 L. Ed. 1432 (1946).

It has refused to do so because due regard for the effective working of our Government revealed this issue to be of a peculiarly political nature and therefore not meet for judicial determination.

This is not an action to recover for damage because of the discriminatory exclusion of a plaintiff from rights enjoyed by other citizens. The basis for the suit is not a private wrong, but a wrong suffered by Illinois as a polity. . . . In effect this is an appeal to the federal courts to reconstruct the electoral process of Illinois in order that it may be adequately represented in the councils of the Nation. Because the Illinois legislature has failed to revise its Congressional Representative districts in order to reflect great changes, during more than a generation, in the distribution of its population, we are asked to do this, as it were, for Illinois.

Of course no court can affirmatively remap the Illinois districts so as to bring them more in conformity with the standards of fairness for a representative system. At best we could only declare the existing electoral system invalid. The result would be to leave Illinois undistricted and to bring into operation, if the Illinois legislature chose not to act, the choice of members for the House of Representatives on a state-wide ticket. The last stage may be worse than the first. The upshot of judicial action may defeat the vital political principle which led Congress, more than a hundred years ago, to require districting. . . . Assuming acquiescence on the part of the authorities of Illinois in the selection of its Representatives by a mode that defies the direction of Congress for selection by districts, the House of Representatives may not acquiesce. In the exercise of its power to judge the qualifications of its own members, the House may reject a delegation of Representatives-at-large. . . . Nothing is clearer than that this controversy concerns matters that bring courts into immediate and active relations with party contests. From the determination of such issues this Court has traditionally held aloof. It is hostile to a democratic system to involve the judiciary in the politics of the people. And it is not less pernicious if such judicial intervention in an essentially political contest be dressed up in the abstract phrases of the law.

The appellants urge with great zeal that the conditions of which they complain are grave evils and offend public morality. The Constitution of the United States gives ample power to provide against these evils. But due regard for the Constitution as a viable system precludes judicial correction. Authority for dealing with such problems resides elsewhere. Article I, section 4 of the Constitution provides that "The Times, Places and Manner of holding Elections for . . . Representatives, shall be prescribed in each State by the Legislature thereof; but the Congress may at any time by Law make or alter such Regulations . . ." The short of it is that the Constitution has conferred upon Congress exclusive authority to secure fair representation by the States in the popular House and left to that House determination whether States have fulfilled their responsibility. If Congress failed in exercising its powers, whereby standards of fairness are offended, the remedy ultimately lies with the people. Whether Congress faithfully discharges its duty or not, the subject has been committed to the exclusive control of Congress. An aspect of government from which the judiciary, in view of what is involved, has been excluded by the clear intention of the Constitution cannot be entered by the federal courts because Congress may have been in default in exacting from States obedience to its mandate. . . .

To sustain this action would cut very deep into the very being of Congress. Courts ought not to enter this political thicket. The remedy for unfairness in districting is to secure State legislatures that will apportion properly, or to invoke the ample powers of Congress. The Constitution has many commands that are not enforceable by courts because they clearly fall outside the conditions and purposes that circumscribe judicial action. Thus, "on Demand of the executive Authority," Art. IV, § 2, of a State it is the duty of a sister State to deliver up a fugitive from justice. But the fulfillment of this duty cannot be judicially enforced. Commonwealth of Kentucky v. Dennison. . . . The duty to see to it that the laws are faithfully executed cannot be brought under legal compulsion. State of Mississippi v. Johnson. . . . Violation of the great guaranty of a republican form of government in States cannot be challenged in the courts. Pacific States Telephone & Telegraph Co. v. Oregon. . . . The Constitution has left the performance of many duties in our governmental scheme to depend on the fidelity of the executive and legislative action and, ultimately, on the vigilance of the people in exercising their political rights. Dismissal of the complaint is affirmed.

Access to Judicial Power

MR. JUSTICE JACKSON took no part in the consideration or decision of this case.

MR. JUSTICE RUTLEDGE. I concur in the result. . . . Assuming that the controversy is justiciable, I think the cause is of so delicate a character, in view of the considerations above noted, that the jurisdiction should be exercised only in the most compelling circumstances.

As a matter of legislative attention, whether by Congress or the General Assembly, the case made by the complaint is strong. But the relief it seeks pitches this Court into delicate relation to the functions of state officials and Congress, compelling them to take action which heretofore they have declined to take voluntarily or to accept the alternative of electing representatives from Illinois at large in the forthcoming elections.

The shortness of the time remaining makes it doubtful whether action could, or would, be taken in time to secure for petitioners the effective relief they seek. To force them to share in an election at large might bring greater equality of voting right. It would also deprive them and all other Illinois citizens of representation by districts which the prevailing policy of Congress commands. . . .

If the constitutional provisions on which appellants rely give them the substantive rights they urge, other provisions qualify those rights in important ways by vesting large measures of control in the political subdivisions of the government and the state. There is not, and could not be except abstractly, a right of absolute equality in voting. At best there could be only a rough approximation. And there is obviously considerable latitude for the bodies vested with those powers to exercise their judgment concerning how best to attain this, in full consistency with the Constitution.

The right here is not absolute. And the cure sought may be worse than the disease.

I think, therefore, the case is one in which the Court may properly, and should, decline to exercise its jurisdiction. Accordingly, the judgment should be affirmed and I join in that disposition of the cause.

MR. JUSTICE BLACK, dissenting. . . .

It is contended, however, that a court of equity does not have the power [to invalidate Illinois' apportionment law], or even if it has the power, that it should not exercise it in this case. To do so, it is argued, would mean that the Court is entering the area of "political questions." I cannot agree with that argument. There have been cases . . . where this Court declined to decide a question because it was political. . . . Here we have before us a state law which abridges the Constitutional rights of citizens to cast votes in such way as to obtain the kind of Congressional representation the Constitution guarantees to them.

It is true that voting is a part of elections and that elections are "political." But as this Court said in Nixon v. Herndon . . . it is a mere "play on words" to refer to a controversy such as this as "political" in the sense that courts have nothing to do with protecting and vindicating the right of a voter to cast an effective ballot. . . .

In this case, no supervision over elections is asked for. What is asked is that this Court . . . declare a state apportionment bill invalid and . . . enjoin state officials from enforcing it. . . . What is involved here is the right to vote guaranteed by the Federal Constitution. It has always been the rule that where a federally protected right has been invaded the federal courts will provide the remedy to rectify the wrong done. Federal courts have not hesitated to exercise their equity power in cases involving deprivation of property and liberty. . . . There is no reason why they should do so where the case involves the right to choose representatives that make laws affecting liberty and property.

. . . It is true that declaration of invalidity of the State Act and the enjoining of State officials would result in prohibiting the State from electing Congressmen under the system of the old Congressional districts. But it would leave the State free to elect them from the State at large, which . . . is a manner authorized by the Constitution. It is said that it would be inconvenient for the State to conduct the election in this manner. But it has an element of virtue that the more convenient method does not have—namely, it does not discriminate against some groups to favor others, it gives all the people an equally effective voice in electing their representatives as is essential under a free government, and it is Constitutional.

MR. JUSTICE DOUGLAS and MR. JUSTICE MURPHY join in this dissent.

In Gomillion *v.* Lightfoot *(1960) the Supreme Court, speaking through Justice Frankfurter, held that its doctrine that redistricting is a political question did not extend so far as to preclude a judicial decision that deliberate gerrymandering designed to deny qualified Negro electors a right to vote was a violation of the 14th and 15th amendments.*

                    "We have no power per se to review and annul acts of
6.   *Congress . . ."*

MASSACHUSETTS V. MELLON

THE MATERNITY ACT *of 1921 provided for money out of the United States Treasury to be given to states which agreed to set up, under federal supervision, programs for care of mothers and infants. Invoking the Supreme Court's original jurisdiction, Massachusetts officials challenged the constitutionality of this statute. At about the same time a private citizen who had attacked the statute's validity in the lower federal courts appealed. The Supreme Court consolidated the two cases for purposes of argument and decision.*

MR. JUSTICE SUTHERLAND delivered the opinion of the Court. . . .

What, then is the nature of the right of the state here asserted and how is it affected by this statute? Reduced to its simplest terms, it is alleged that the statute constitutes an attempt to legislate outside the powers granted to Congress by the Constitution and within the field of local powers exclusively reserved to the states. Nothing is added to the force or effect of this assertion by the further incidental allegations that the ulterior purpose of Congress thereby was to induce the states to yield a portion of their sovereign rights; that the burden of the appropriations falls unequally upon the several states; and that there is imposed upon the states an illegal and unconstitutional option either to yield to the federal government a part of their reserved rights or lose their share of the moneys appropriated. But what burden is imposed upon the states, unequally or otherwise? Certainly there is none, unless it be the burden of taxation, and that falls upon their

262 U.S. 447, 43 S. Ct. 597, 67 L. Ed. 1078 (1923).

inhabitants, who are within the taxing power of Congress as well as that of the states where they reside. Nor does the statute require the states to do or to yield anything. If Congress enacted it with the ulterior purpose of tempting them to yield, that purpose may be effectively frustrated by the simple expedient of not yielding.

In the last analysis, the complaint of the plaintiff state is brought to the naked contention that Congress has usurped the reserved powers of the several states by the mere enactment of the statute, though nothing has been done and nothing is to be done without their consent; and it is plain that that question, as it is thus presented, is political, and not judicial in character, and therefore is not a matter which admits of the exercise of the judicial power. . . .

It follows that, in so far as the case depends upon the assertion of a right on the part of the state to sue in its own behalf, we are without jurisdiction. In that aspect of the case we are called upon to adjudicate, not rights of person or property, not rights of dominion over physical domain, not quasi sovereign rights actually invaded or threatened, but abstract questions of political power, of sovereignty, of government. . . .

We come next to consider whether the suit may be maintained by the state as the representative of its citizens. To this the answer is not doubtful. We need not go so far as to say that a state may never intervene by suit to protect its citizens against any form of enforcement of unconstitutional acts of Congress; but we are clear that the right to do so does not arise here. Ordinarily, at least, the only way in which a state may afford protection to its citizens in such cases is through the enforcement of its own criminal statutes, where that is appropriate, or by opening its courts to the injured persons for the maintenance of civil suits or actions. But the citizens of Massachusetts are also citizens of the United States. It cannot be conceded that a state, as parens patriæ, may institute judicial proceedings to protect citizens of the United States from the operation of the statutes thereof. While the state, under some circumstances, may sue in that capacity for the protection of its citizens . . . it is no part of its duty or power to enforce their rights in respect of their relations with the federal government. In that field it is the United States, and not the state, which represents them as parens patriæ, when such representation becomes appropriate; and to the former, and not to the latter, they must look for such protective measures as flow from that status.

Second. The attack upon the statute in the Frothingham Case is, generally, the same, but this plaintiff alleges, in addition that she is a taxpayer of the United States; and her contention, though not clear, seems to be that the effect of the appropriations complained of will be to increase the burden of future taxation and thereby take her property without due process of law. The right of a taxpayer to enjoin the execution of a federal appropriation act, on the ground that it is invalid and will result in taxation for illegal purposes, has never been passed upon by this court. In cases where it was presented, the question has either been allowed to pass sub silentio or the determination of it expressly withheld. . . . The interest of a taxpayer of a municipality in the application of its moneys is direct and immediate and the remedy by injunction to prevent their misuse is not inappropriate. It is upheld by a large number of state cases and is the rule of this court. . . . But the relation of a taxpayer of the United States to the federal government is very different. His interest in the moneys of the treasury—partly realized from taxation and partly from other sources—is shared with millions of others, is comparatively minute and indeterminable, and the effect upon future taxation, of any payment out of the funds, so remote, fluctuating and uncertain, that no basis is afforded for an appeal to the preventive powers of a court of equity.

The administration of any statute, likely to produce additional taxation to be imposed upon a vast number of taxpayers, the extent of whose several liability is indefinite and constantly changing, is essentially a matter of public and not of individual concern. If one taxpayer may champion and litigate such a cause, then every other taxpayer may do the same, not only in respect to the statute here under review, but also in respect of every other appropriation act and statute whose administration requires the outlay of public money, and whose validity may be questioned. The bare suggestion of such a result, with its attendant inconveniences, goes far to sustain the conclusion which we have reached, that a suit of this character cannot be maintained. It is of much significance that no precedent sustaining the right to maintain suits like this has been called to our attention, although, since the formation of the government, as an examination of the acts of Congress will disclose, a large number of statutes appropriating or involving the expenditure of moneys for nonfederal purposes have been enacted and carried into effect.

The functions of government under our system are apportioned. To the legislative department has been committed the duty of making laws, to the executive the duty of executing them, and to the judiciary the duty of interpreting and applying them in cases properly brought before the courts. The general rule is that neither department may invade the province of the other and neither may control, direct, or restrain the action of the other. . . . We have no power per se to review and annul acts of Congress on the ground that they are unconstitutional. That question may be considered only when the justification for some direct injury suffered or threatened, presenting a justiciable issue, is made to rest upon such an act. Then the power exercised is that of ascertaining and declaring the law applicable to the controversy. It amounts to little more than the negative power to disregard an unconstitutional enactment, which otherwise would stand in the way of the enforcement of a legal right. The party who invokes the power must be able to show, not only that the statute is invalid, but that he has sustained or is immediately in danger of sustaining some direct injury as the result of its enforcement, and not merely that he suffers in some indefinite way in common with people generally. If a case for preventive relief be presented, the court enjoins, in effect, not the execution of the statute, but the acts of the official, the statute notwithstanding. Here the parties plaintiff have no such case. Looking through forms of words to the substance of their complaint, it is merely that officials of the executive department of the government are executing and will execute an act of Congress asserted to be unconstitutional; and this we are asked to prevent. To do so would be, not to decide a judicial controversy, but to assume a position of authority over the governmental acts of another and coequal department, an authority which plainly we do not possess. . . .

7.

> "... *the moral stigma of a judgment which no longer affects legal rights does not present a case or controversy.*"

ST. PIERRE V. UNITED STATES

PER CURIAM. Petitioner, who it is alleged had in his testimony before a federal grand jury confessed to the commission of the crime of embezzlement, refused to divulge the name of the person whose money he had embezzled. For the refusal the district court sentenced him to five months' imprisonment for contempt of court, and the circuit court of appeals affirmed the judgment. . . . We granted certiorari . . . on a petition which raised important questions with respect to petitioner's constitutional immunity from self-incrimination. In the order allowing the writ we requested counsel to discuss the question whether the case had become moot.

On the argument it was conceded that petitioner had fully served his sentence before certiorari was granted. We are of opinion that the case is moot because, after petitioner's service of his sentence and its expiration, there was no longer a subject matter on which the judgment of this Court could operate. A federal court is without power to decide moot questions or to give advisory opinions which cannot affect the rights of the litigants in the case before it. . . . The sentence cannot be enlarged by this Court's judgment, and reversal of the judgment below cannot operate to undo what has been done or restore to petitioner the penalty of the term of imprisonment which he has served. Nor has petitioner shown that under either state or federal law further penalties or disabilities can be imposed on him as a result of the judgment which has now been satisfied. In these respects the case differs from that of an injunction whose command continues to operate in futuro even though obeyed. . . .

Petitioner also suggests that the judgment may impair his credibility as witness in any future legal proceeding. But the moral stigma of a judgment which no longer affects legal rights does not present a case or controversy for appellate review. Since the cause is moot, the writ will be

Dismissed.

319 U.S. 41, 63 S. Ct. 910, 87 L. Ed. 1199 (1943).

8.
> *"[A doctor has no] standing to secure an adjudication of*
> *his patients' constitutional right to life . . ."*

TILESTON V. ULLMAN

PER CURIAM.   This case comes here on appeal to review
a declaratory judgment of the Supreme Court of Errors of Connecticut
that §§ 6246 and 6562 of the General Statutes of Connecticut of 1930
—prohibiting the use of drugs or instruments to prevent conception,
and the giving of assistance or counsel in their use—are applicable
to appellant, a registered physician, and as applied to him are constitutional. . . .

The suit was tried and judgment rendered on the allegations of the
complaint which are stipulated to be true. Appellant alleged that the
statute, if applicable to him, would prevent his giving professional
advice concerning the use of contraceptives to three patients whose
condition of health was such that their lives would be endangered
by child-bearing, and that appellees, law enforcement officers of the
state, intend to prosecute any offense against the statute and "claim
or make claim" that the proposed professional advice would constitute
such offense. The complaint set out in detail the danger to the lives
of appellant's patients in the event that they should bear children, but
contained no allegations asserting any claim under the Fourteenth
Amendment of infringement of appellant's liberty or his property
rights. The relief prayed was a declaratory judgment as to whether
the statutes are applicable to appellant and if so whether they constitute a valid exercise of constitutional power "within the meaning
and intent of Amendment XIV of the Constitution of the United
States prohibiting a state from depriving any person of life without
due process of law". On stipulation of the parties the state superior
court ordered these questions of law reserved for the consideration
and advice of the Supreme Court of Errors. That court, which assumed
without deciding that the case was an appropriate one for a declaratory judgment, ruled that the statutes "prohibit the action proposed
to be done" by appellant and "are constitutional".

We are of the opinion that the proceedings in the state courts

318 U.S. 44, 63 S. Ct. 493, 87 L. Ed. 603 (1943).

present no constitutional question which appellant has standing to assert. The sole constitutional attack upon the statutes under the Fourteenth Amendment is confined to their deprivation of life—obviously not appellant's but his patients'. There is no allegation or proof that appellant's life is in danger. His patients are not parties to this proceeding and there is no basis on which we can say that he has standing to secure an adjudication of his patients' constitutional right to life, which they do not assert in their own behalf. . . . No question is raised in the record with respect to the deprivation of appellant's liberty or property in contravention of the Fourteenth Amendment, nor is there anything in the opinion or judgment of the Supreme Court of Errors which indicates or would support a decision of any question other than those raised in the superior court and reserved by it for decision of the Supreme Court of Errors. That court's practice is to decline to answer questions not reserved. . . .

Since the appeal must be dismissed on the ground that appellant has no standing to litigate the constitutional question which the record presents, it is unnecessary to consider whether the record shows the existence of a genuine case or controversy essential to the exercise of the jurisdiction of this Court.

Dismissed.

9.   *". . . like catching butterflies without a net . . ."*

ADLER V. BOARD OF EDUCATION

BEFORE NEW YORK's *comprehensive loyalty-security program for public-school teachers was actually put into operation, a group of people began a suit in a state court for a declaratory judgment and an injunction, claiming that the regulations violated freedom of speech and assembly. The trial court held the program unconstitutional, but the state Court of Appeals reversed. The case reached the U.S. Supreme Court on an appeal, and the New York program was upheld by six justices, Black and Douglas dissenting. Justice Frankfurter filed a separate opinion, dissenting on jurisdictional grounds.*

342 U.S. 485, 72 S. Ct. 380, 96 L. Ed. 517 (1952).

MR. JUSTICE FRANKFURTER, dissenting.

We are asked to pass on a scheme to counteract what are currently called "subversive" influences in the public school system of New York. The scheme is formulated partly in statutes and partly in administrative regulations, but all of it is still an unfinished blueprint. We are asked to adjudicate claims against its constitutionality before the scheme has been put into operation, before the limits that it imposes upon free inquiry and association, the scope of scrutiny that it sanctions, and the procedural safeguards that will be found to be implied for its enforcement have been authoritatively defined. I think we should adhere to the teaching of this Court's history to avoid constitutional adjudications on merely abstract or speculative issues and to base them on the concreteness afforded by an actual, present, defined controversy, appropriate for judicial judgment, between adversaries immediately affected by it. In accordance with the settled limits upon our jurisdiction I would dismiss this appeal. . . .

A New York enactment of 1949 precipitated this litigation. But that legislation is tied to prior statutes. By a law of 1917 "treasonable or seditious" utterances or acts barred employment in the public schools. . . . In 1939 a further enactment disqualified from the civil service and the educational system anyone who advocates the overthrow of government by force, violence or any unlawful means, or publishes material advocating such overthrow or organizes or joins any society advocating such doctrine. . . .

During the thirty-two years and ten years, respectively, that these laws have stood on the books, no proceedings, so far as appears, have been taken under them. In 1949 the Legislature passed a new act, familiarly known as the Feinberg Law, designed to reinforce the prior legislation. The Law begins with a legislative finding, based on "common report" of widespread infiltration by "members of subversive groups, and particularly of the communist party and certain of its affiliated organizations," into the educational system of the State and the evils attendant upon that infiltration. It takes note of existing laws and exhorts the authorities to greater endeavor of enforcement. The State Board of Regents, in which are lodged extensive powers over New York's educational system, was charged by the Feinberg Law with these duties. . . .

Accordingly, the Board of Regents adopted Rules for ferreting out violations. . . . An elaborate machinery was designed for annual reports on each employee with a view to discovering evidence of violations of these sections and to assuring appropriate action on such discovery. The Board also announced its intention to publish the required list of proscribed organizations and defined the significance of an employee's membership therein in proceedings for his dismissal. . . .

It thus appears that we are asked to review a complicated statutory scheme prohibiting those who engage in the kind of speech or conduct that is proscribed from holding positions in the public school system. The scheme is aligned with a complex system of enforcement by administrative investigation, reporting and listing of proscribed organizations. All this must further be related to the general procedures under the New York law for hearing and reviewing charges of misconduct against educational employees, modified as those procedures may be by the Feinberg Law and the Regents' Rules.

This intricate machinery has not yet been set in motion. Enforcement has been in abeyance since the present suit, among others, was brought to enjoin the Board of Education from taking steps or spending funds under the statutes and Rules on the theory that these transgressed various limitations which the United States Constitution places on the power of the States. The case comes here on the bare bones of the Feinberg Law only partly given flesh by the Regents' Rules. . . .

About forty plaintiffs brought the action initially; the trial court dismissed as to all but eight. The others were found without standing to sue under New York law. The eight who are here as appellants alleged that they were municipal taxpayers and were empowered, by virtue of N. Y. Gen. Municipal Law §51, to bring suit against municipal agencies to enjoin waste of funds. New York is free to determine how the views of its courts on matters of constitutionality are to be invoked. But its action cannot of course confer jurisdiction on this Court, limited as that is by the settled construction of Article III of the Constitution. . . . This is not a "pocketbook action." As taxpayers these plaintiffs cannot possibly be affected one way or the other by any disposition of this case, and they make no such claim. . . . In short, they have neither alleged nor shown that our decision on the issues they tender would have the slightest effect on their tax bills or even on the aggregate bill of all the City's taxpayers whom they claim to represent. . . .

This ends the matter for plaintiffs Krieger and Newman. But six of the plaintiffs advanced grounds other than that of being taxpayers in bringing this action. Two are parents of children in New York City schools. Four are teachers in these schools. On the basis of the record before us these claims, too, are insufficient, in view of our controlling adjudications, to support the jurisdiction of this Court.

The trial court found the interests of the plaintiffs as parents inconsequential. . . . I agree. Parents may dislike to have children educated in a school system where teachers feel restrained by unconstitutional limitations on their freedom. But it is like catching butterflies without a net to try to find a legal interest, indispensable for our jurisdiction, in a parent's desire to have his child educated in schools free from such restrictions. The hurt to parents' sensibilities is too tenuous or the inroad upon rightful claims to public education too argumentative to serve as the earthy stuff required for a legal right judicially enforceable. The claim does not approach in immediacy or directness or solidity that which our whole process of constitutional adjudication has deemed a necessary condition to the Court's settlement of constitutional issues.

An apt contrast is provided by *McCollum* v. *Board of Education* . . . where a parent did present an individualized claim of his own that was direct and palpable. There the parent alleged that Illinois imposed restrictions on the child's free exercise of faith and thereby on the parent's. The basis of jurisdiction in the *McCollum* case was not at all a parental right to challenge in the courts—or at least in this Court—educational provisions in general. The closely defined encroachment of the particular arrangement on a constitutionally protected right of the child, and of the parent's right in the child, furnished the basis for our review. The Feinberg Law puts no limits on any definable legal interest of the child or of its parents.

This leaves only the teachers. . . . These teachers do not allege that they have engaged in proscribed conduct or that they have any intention to do so. They do not suggest that they have been, or are, deterred from supporting causes or from joining organizations for fear of the Feinberg Law's interdict, except to say generally that the system complained of will have this effect on teachers as a group. They do not assert that they are threatened with action under the law, or that steps are imminent whereby they would incur the hazard of punishment for conduct innocent at the time, or under standards too vague to satisfy due process of law. They merely allege that the statutes and Rules permit such action against some teachers. . . . This suit is wanting in the necessary basis for our review.

This case proves anew the wisdom of rigorous adherence to the prerequisites for pronouncement by this Court on matters of constitutional law. The absence in these plaintiffs of the immediacy and solidity of interest necessary to support jurisdiction is reflected in the atmosphere of abstraction and ambiguity in which the constitutional issues are presented. The broad, generalized claims urged at the bar touch the deepest interests of a democratic society: its right to self-preservation and ample scope for the individual's freedom, especially the teacher's freedom of thought, inquiry and expression. No problem of a free society is probably more difficult than the reconciliation or accommodation of these too often conflicting interests. The judicial role in this process of accommodation is necessarily very limited and must be carefully circumscribed. . . .

10.

"*. . . appellants cannot obtain a decision from this Court by a feigned issue of taxation.*"

DOREMUS V. BOARD OF EDUCATION

MR. JUSTICE JACKSON delivered the opinion of the Court.

This action for a declaratory judgment on a question of federal constitutional law was prosecuted in the state courts of New Jersey.

342 U.S. 429, 72 S. Ct. 394, 96 L. Ed. 475 (1952). Federal and state statutes allow litigants to seek a court judgment declaring what their legal rights are in a given situation *after* an actual controversy has come into being but *before* injury has been suffered. Unless an additional remedy is sought (and litigants often also request an injunction), the court simply issues its declaration rather than a specific order; but this declaration is binding on the future conduct of all parties to the case.

It sought to declare invalid a statute of that State which provides for the reading, without comment, of five verses of the Old Testament at the opening of each public-school day. . . . No issue was raised under the State Constitution, but the Act was claimed to violate the clause of the First Amendment to the federal Constitution prohibiting establishment of religion.

No trial was held and we have no findings of fact, but the trial court denied relief on the merits on the basis of the pleadings and a pretrial conference, of which the record contains meager notes. The Supreme Court of New Jersey, on appeal, rendered its opinion that the Act does not violate the federal Constitution, in spite of jurisdictional doubts. . . .

Upon appeal to this Court, we considered appellants' jurisdictional statement but, instead of noting probable jurisdiction, ordered that "Further consideration of the question of the jurisdiction of this Court in this case and of the motion to dismiss or affirm is postponed to the hearing of the case on the merits." On further study, the doubts thus indicated ripen into a conviction that we should dismiss the appeal without reaching the constitutional question.

The view of the facts taken by the court below, though it is entitled to respect, does not bind us and we may make an independent examination of the record. Doing so, we find nothing more substantial in support of jurisdiction than did the court below. Appellants . . . assert a challenge to the Act in two capacities—one as parent of a child subject to it, and both as taxpayers burdened because of its requirements.

In support of the parent-and-school-child relationship, the complaint alleged that appellant Klein was parent of a seventeen-year-old pupil in Hawthorne High School, where Bible reading was practiced pursuant to the Act. That is all. There is no assertion that she was injured or even offended thereby or that she was compelled to accept, approve or confess agreement with any dogma or creed or even to listen when the Scriptures were read. On the contrary, there was a pretrial stipulation that any student, at his own or his parents' request, could be excused during Bible reading and that in this case no such excuse was asked. However, it was agreed upon argument here that this child had graduated from the public schools before this appeal was taken to this Court. Obviously no decision we could render now would protect any rights she may once have had, and this Court does not sit to decide arguments after events have put them to rest. . . .

The complaint is similarly niggardly of facts to support a taxpayer's grievance. Doremus is alleged to be a citizen and taxpayer of the State of New Jersey and of the Township of Rutherford, but any relation of that Township to the litigation is not disclosed to one not familiar with local geography. Klein is set out as a citizen and taxpayer of the Borough of Hawthorne in the State of New Jersey, and it is alleged that Hawthorne has a high school supported by public funds. In this school the Bible is read, according to statute. There is no allegation that this activity is supported by any separate tax or paid for from any particular appropriation or that it adds any sum whatever to the cost of conducting the school. No information is given as to what kind of taxes are paid by appellants and there is no averment that the Bible reading increases any tax they do pay or that as taxpayers they are, will, or possibly can be out of pocket because of it. . . .

This Court has held that the interests of a taxpayer in the moneys of the federal treasury are too indeterminable, remote, uncertain and indirect to furnish a basis for an appeal to the preventive powers of the Court over their manner of expenditure. *Alabama Power Co.* v. *Ickes . . . Massachusetts* v. *Mellon.* . . . The latter case recognized, however, that "The interest of a taxpayer of a municipality in the application of its moneys is direct and immediate and the remedy by injunction to prevent their misuse is not inappropriate." . . .

We do not undertake to say that a state court may not render an opinion on a federal constitutional question even under such circumstances that it can be regarded only as advisory. But, because our own jurisdiction is cast in terms of "case or controversy," we cannot accept as the basis for review, nor as the basis for conclusive disposition of an issue of federal law without review, any procedure which does not constitute such.

The taxpayer's action can meet this test, but only when it is a good-faith pocketbook action. It is apparent that the grievance which it is sought to litigate here is not a direct dollars-and-cents injury but is a religious difference. If appellants established the requisite special injury necessary to a taxpayer's case or controversy, it would not matter that their dominant inducement to action was more religious than mercenary. It is not a question of motivation but of possession of the requisite financial interest that is, or is threatened to be, injured by the unconstitutional conduct. We find no such direct and particular financial interest here. If the Act may give rise to a legal case or controversy on some behalf, the appellants cannot obtain a decision from this Court by a feigned issue of taxation.

The motion to dismiss the appeal is granted.

Mr. Justice DOUGLAS, with whom Mr. Justice REED and Mr. Justice BURTON concur, dissenting.

I think this case deserves a decision on the merits. There is no group more interested in the operation and management of the public schools than the taxpayers who support them and the parents whose children attend them. Certainly a suit by all the taxpayers to enjoin a practice authorized by the school board would be a suit by vital parties in interest. They would not be able to show, any more than the two present taxpayers have done, that the reading of the Bible adds to the taxes they pay. But if they were right in their contentions on the merits, they would establish that their public schools were being deflected from the educational program for which the taxes were raised. That seems to me to be an adequate interest for the maintenance of this suit by all the taxpayers. If all can do it, there is no apparent reason why less than all may not, the interest being the same. In the present case the issues are not feigned; the suit is not collusive; the mismanagement of the school system that is alleged is clear and plain.

If this were a suit to enjoin a federal law, it could not be maintained by reason of *Massachusetts* v. *Mellon*. . . . But New Jersey can fashion her own rules governing the institution of suits in her courts. If she wants to give these taxpayers the status to sue (by analogy to the right of shareholders to enjoin *ultra vires* acts of their corporation), I see nothing in the Constitution to prevent it. And where the clash of interests is as real and as strong as it is here, it is odd indeed to hold there is no case or controversy within the meaning of Art. III, § 2 of the Constitution.

8 / INTEREST GROUPS AND LITIGATION

Judicial power, we saw in the last chapter, has no self-starting mechanism; but this is a less important limitation on judicial policymaking than it might seem at first glance. If anything, federal court dockets are overcrowded with public policy questions. Scarcely a term goes by when the Supreme Court is not asked to decide significant questions concerning race relations, church-state problems, federalism, economic regulation, free speech, or government loyalty-security programs. A large share of these issues are brought to the courts by organized interest groups. When it is to their advantage, interest groups can function as a crank energizing judicial power.

Groups whose leaders feel that their interests are being threatened or inadequately protected by other branches of government are very apt to exploit avenues of access to the judicial process. The groups whose interests were hurt by the 1894 income tax law secured a quick invalidation of the tax in 1895. Successful counter-reaction was slower, and it was not until 1913 that the Sixteenth Amendment became a part of the Constitution. Similarly, business groups who had been defeated in Congress and the administrative process during the New Deal period took their lost cause to the judges.

One of the classic examples in American history of a group's ability to utilize judicial power when frustrated in the other governmental processes has been the NAACP's defense of Negro rights. The organization's success has been, by any standards, phenomenal, and Senator Russell of Georgia charged in 1958 that the Association's chief counsel, Thurgood Marshall, had "an almost occult power" over Supreme Court justices.

Occasionally, success in the judicial process has been the result of a fortuitous series of accidents, but in recent years groups have planned their forays into litigation just as meticulously as they have plotted their other political operations. NAACP leaders have frankly admitted the careful preparation of their lawsuits, and it is very likely that the Negro organization is more candid than unique in this respect. For example, a 1935 press release from the Edison Electric Institute explained the strategy of the public utilities in planning their attack on a regulatory statute:

> Utility executives were uncertain . . . how soon the court action would be started or which particular section or sections of the law would be chosen to bear the brunt of the attack. Until the attorneys had an opportunity to decide which company would lend itself most readily as the complainant there would be no decision.

Judicial involvement in public policymaking is probably most evident where the litigation is sponsored by an organized interest group, but the traditional view of the judge as an expert automaton who simply looks up and applies a predetermined rule of law cannot concede that the judiciary plays a significant role in the struggle among pressure groups to influence public policy. To admit this, it is feared, would be to picture judges as partisan politicians. In fact, however, a judge participates in the political process "not as a matter of choice but of function," as Peltason puts it. A judge's personality and philosophy will shape the manner of participation, but the very existence of power of the kind that judges wield makes it inevitable that political forces will focus on the judicial branch of government. And a judge must do precisely what his title implies: unless he can use one of the "standing" criteria to dismiss a case, he must *judge,* choose between the claims of opposing litigants. When one party is pressing the cause of the Negro or the AFL-CIO and the other the cause of white supremacy or the National Association of Manufacturers, a choice either way will materially affect both the values of the groups and the policies they are trying to influence.

Because judicial activities are shrouded in secrecy and mystery, it is more difficult to analyze the informal and formal channels of access to the courts than those leading to other branches of government; but the general criteria laid down by David Truman in *The Governmental Process* are of some use. His analysis suggests that the factors affecting access are the technical rules of the agency, the social status of the group seeking access, and the degree of organization and skill of the group's leadership.

Technical Rules

As Chapter 7 pointed out, if a potential litigant wishes to invoke federal judicial power, he must present a federal question and he must also have "standing to sue." Assuming the group has a federal question, it must also have a case; and to have a case it needs a litigant. If the interest the group wants secured is protected by a statute, the group's leaders can pressure the executive department to begin a criminal prosecution or a civil suit. This method has been especially important in antitrust law and in defending civil rights against infringements by state officials.

It is very probable, however, that the interest which the group wants advanced may be threatened rather than protected by a statute. In such a situation the group leaders may proceed to institute a test case. One of the means is to find a person who is willing to break the law and set up as a defense a claim that the statute is either unconstitutional or has no application in this sort of case. This procedure is a bit risky to the tester, unless, as has happened, the government agrees just to go through the motions of a prosecution to test the law. Such an agreement, of course, runs counter to the case requirement. But though judges may voice their suspicions, as Justice Frankfurter did about the Truman administration's prosecution of the CIO under the Taft-Hartley's ban against union participation in political campaigns, they can rarely be certain that a prosecution is not bona fide.

The ideal way for a group to challenge a law would be to arrange for a plaintiff and a defendant to have a friendly suit in which the group's lawyers could prepare the arguments for both sides. There is considerable reason to believe that in *Fletcher* v. *Peck* (1810), *Hylton* v. *United States* (1796), and *Dred Scott* v. *Sandford* (1857), not to mention *Carter* v. *Carter Coal Co.* (1936), where the president of the company sued to enjoin his firm from obeying one of the New Deal statutes, both parties *did* act in collusion. Again it is difficult for judges to detect co-operation between litigants, though the judicial record is probably better than these examples might indicate. To prevent a recurrence of the *Carter* situation, Congress in 1937 authorized the Justice Department to intervene in any suit between private parties in which the constitutionality of a federal statute is challenged.

A third way for a group to obtain "standing" is for it to persuade a member to act as plaintiff in a suit to enjoin an administrative official from enforcing a statute. In such a situation, the group may avail itself of a procedural device known as a "class action," a means whereby one or more persons, fairly representative of a larger group, can sue in their own behalf and in behalf "of all others similarly situated." Developed in English chancery courts and adopted in American practice, a class action is permitted by the Federal Rules of Civil Procedure where a number of persons have a common legal right and the group is "so numerous as to make it impractical to bring them all before the court."

The class action lightens the judge's load in that he has to make only one decision to settle the rights of perhaps thousands of persons. From the interest group's viewpoint, it also saves time and money. If, for instance, one Negro voter were to institute a class action against state election officials and could prove that they were refusing to allow qualified colored citizens to vote, the injunction would require the officials not only to cease discriminating against the plaintiff but against all other qualified Negro voters. Other advantages include the lessening of the chance of a plaintiff's compromising with the defendant—a plaintiff usually cannot do so under a class action without the permission of the court. The class action also diminishes the chances of a case being dismissed as moot. For example, by the time a desegregation suit brought by parents of teen-age children has gone up and down the court system, the children may well have graduated and the plaintiffs lost their standing. If the group wished to press for a decision, the litigation would have to begin all over again with the same possibility that delay might once more erode plaintiffs' standing. Under a class action, however, when one plaintiff loses his standing another can be substituted and the original litigation may proceed without interruption.

It may be that an interest group cannot obtain a plaintiff. As will be pointed out later, such recruiting is not always easy, but a group can still utilize judicial power to achieve its own aims by helping a stranger who is involved in litigation which raises issues touching on the group's interests. The American Civil Liberties Union, for example, often offers the assistance of its legal staff to aid defendants in criminal cases where the Union believes there has been a denial of a constitutional right. The ACLU will also pay the costs of appeal for defendants if it feels that they have a good case presenting an important issue. Supporting an existing case is usually less satisfactory than sponsoring one's own suit, however, since the litigant may only partially accept the group's advice, or the facts of the controversy may not be such as to give the group the best chance of winning, or the defendant's interests may not completely coincide with those of the group.

A fourth method which the technical rules of the judicial process allow a group is the *amicus curiae*, or friend of the court, brief. What happens here is that a group which perceives some interest of its own at stake in a case may petition a court to be allowed to file a brief expressing its views. A court may also on its own motion invite parties to appear as *amici*. Federal judges frequently ask Justice Department officials to participate in lawsuits, and the Supreme Court requested the attorneys general of Southern states to offer advice as to how the school segregation decisions should be implemented.

Social Status

Although social status is a nebulous criterion, it is still an important one. It is an accepted fact of political life that elected officials, with prejudices and predilections of their own as well as those of their constituents, are much more receptive to the pleas of some groups than to others. A politician is seldom too busy to listen with respect to the views of the president of the American Bar Association or the American Medical Association. And whether liberal or conservative, a legislator is likely to value the opinion of a Chamber of Commerce lobbyist over that of a representative from the Henry George Single Tax Plan.

Judges, like all other men, have personal and social biases. And while judges have usually striven for impartiality, their own environment and experiences cannot help but be important influences guiding their discretion. This is true whether the judge be a Marshall, who protected vested economic interests while promoting nationalism, a Brandeis, who favored economic experimentation and social reform, or a Frank Murphy, who was almost incapable of voting against an underdog. Justice Miller made this point in 1875 when he wrote about his colleagues:

> It is vain to contend with judges who have been at the bar the advocates for forty years of railroad companies, and all the forms of associated capital, when they are called upon to decide cases where such interests are in contest. All their training, all their feelings are from the start in favor of those who need no such influence.[1]

Miller was perhaps exaggerating. The fact that a judge is not free from prejudice does not necessarily mean that judges consciously choose a

[1] Quoted in Charles Fairman, *Mr. Justice Miller and the Supreme Court, 1862–1890* (Harvard University Press, 1939), p. 374.

constituency or that judicial behavior can be infallibly predicted on the basis of social background. Neither does it mean that judicial constituencies will be the same as those of legislators or administrators or that judges will always act to protect the interests of groups with social prestige and/or voting power. The symbol of the courts in this country is a blindfolded goddess of justice; and the words etched over the Supreme Court building, "Equal Justice under Law," embody an ideal of American life. Motivated by this ideal, judges will often go to great lengths to protect people who have neither status, nor wealth, nor votes. Indeed, in trying to formulate a new role for the Court in 1938, Harlan Fiske Stone wrote that judges had a special obligation to safeguard the rights of "insular minorities" who have no hope of securing a meaningful voice in political affairs. The success of the NAACP in the judicial process can be in large measure ascribed to the sympathy of liberal justices with the plight of the American Negro.

The determination of status is obviously a subjective affair. To one man the American Legion may be a dangerous group of reactionaries, to another the last hope of constitutional government. In recognition of this subjective element, interest groups seek access to the legislative and executive processes to influence the selection of judges. The Negro's coming of age as a major political force can be dated from the NAACP's role, however misguided, in the Senate's rejection of the nomination of John J. Parker to the Supreme Court.

Judges, however, are no more or less set in their thought patterns than other men, and groups which cannot influence judicial appointments are not completely barred from winning a judge's sympathy and respect. Informed books or law review articles which state the group's case in a reasoned, scholarly manner can have an impact on a judge's thinking. Equally as important are intelligent, well-prepared briefs.

Skills

Any discussion of how to "illuminate the judicial mind" immediately leads to the third of Truman's criteria, the degree of organization and skill of the group's leadership. While the tightness of a group's organization is a very important factor in determining access to administrators or legislators, it is less so in the judicial process and is largely overshadowed by the skill of the group's leaders. Law is a highly technical field with a language all its own. Since professional lawyers are the only people who can translate a group's interests into terms of "*stare decisis,*" "intent of the framers," or similar legal formulas, they assume a heavy share of the tactical and strategic leadership of a group. They must pick the right case at the right time and bring it before the right judge. Such decisions are as crucial to the outcome of litigation as the choice of time, location, and weapons is to the results of a military campaign.

The ability to co-operate with other groups is also important. Organizations with similar interests can be invited to participate in the case as *amici,* and together a co-ordinated plan of primary, secondary, and re-inforcing arguments can be drawn up, with each group utilizing its special skills and prestige. If the Solicitor General can be persuaded to enter the case as an *amicus* the group can enjoy the benefit of the expertise of the Justice Department's staff and the prestige of the United States government.

Once the field of battle has been chosen and allied forces co-ordinated, lawyers have a different kind of mission to perform. Daniel Webster's oratory, which often went on for days, could leave the justices shedding tears of sympathy. In 1895 Rufus Choate's plea for the Court to invalidate the income tax and "stop the Communist march" had obvious success. In 1935 George Wharton Pepper stirred judicial emotions with his closing argument for the Court to invalidate the Agricultural Adjustment Act: "I believe that I am standing here today to plead the cause of the America I have loved; and I pray Almighty God that not in my time may 'the land of the regimented' be accepted as a worthy substitute for 'the land of the free.' "

Most current interest groups rely on a staff of lawyers to prepare their arguments rather than on the oratorical brilliance of individual counsel. The NAACP has even gone so far as to have its lawyers practice before a board of Howard Law School professors, each of whom plays the part of an individual Supreme Court justice and questions and criticizes the argu-ment just as he envisions the particular justice doing.

Barratry

While the benefits of a favorable judicial decision may be great, litigation is an expensive and time-consuming business. An interest group with sufficient money to maintain an expert legal staff has a definite advantage over a private litigant with limited financial resources, or even over a wealthy man who does not have at his disposal a battery of lawyers who are particularly adept at arguing cases before the Supreme Court—and most lawyers have little experience before this tribunal. On the other hand, access to the judicial process does not mean either an automatic or final victory for a group's interests. Judges come and go and a new President may choose men with different talents and sympathies. Opposing groups quickly learn to mimic successful tactics or, where the judges' minds seem made up, to shift the arena of conflict back into the legislative or administrative process.

In addition there is the technical barrier which hampers a group's ability to get a plaintiff. Under the old common law as well as the statutory law of many states, it is a criminal offense for a lawyer to solicit lawsuits; the Canons of Professional Ethics also forbid a lawyer to stir up litigation. There are three separate offenses here: barratry, champerty, and mainte- nance. According to *American Jurisprudence*, barratry is the "habitual stirring up of quarrels and suits." Champerty describes a situation in which a person with no real interest in a particular piece of litigation assists one of the parties in return for a share of the expected proceeds. Maintenance is a more general term which encompasses "officious inter- meddling in a suit which in no way belongs to one, by maintaining or assisting either party, with money or otherwise, to prosecute or defend it."

Because of the NAACP's success in the judicial process, a number of southern officials have tried to drive the Negro organization out of busi- ness. Alabama, Arkansas, Georgia, Louisiana, South Carolina, Texas, and Virginia have carried on serious campaigns against the Association; and Florida and Tennessee have made some hostile moves. This counter attack has taken many forms such as prosecutions under corporation and tax laws, or employment of the contempt power and legislative investigations to harass the organization and force publication of its membership lists so that members can be exposed to private and often public reprisals. But one of the main weapons has been to accuse the NAACP of using fraud and bribery to obtain clients.

The NAACP freely admits that it has publicly advised Negroes that fed- eral judges will protect their constitutional rights, but denies paying or tricking litigants to institute suits. In its turn, the Association has charged that white southerners have put heavy economic pressure on Negroes to prevent their using the judicial process. Rather than try to fight this battle out in state legislatures, the NAACP has met the southern counterattack by resorting to the federal courts. In so doing, it has asserted two un- orthodox but far-reaching doctrines of law: (1) that an interest group has a constitutional right not only to utilize the judicial process to achieve its policy aims but also, barratry regulations to the contrary notwithstanding, to persuade individuals to do so; (2) that an interest group has "standing to sue" to protect the rights of its members, even where the names of the individual members cannot be revealed.

SELECTED REFERENCES

Horn, Robert A., *Groups and the Constitution* (Stanford: Stanford University Press, 1956).

Jacobs, Clyde, *Law Writers and the Courts* (Berkeley: University of California Press, 1954).

Murphy, Walter F., "The South Counter-Attacks: The Anti-NAACP Laws," 12 *Western Political Quarterly* 371 (1959).

Newland, Chester, "Legal Periodicals and the United States Supreme Court," 3 *Midwest Journal of Political Science* 58 (1959).

Note, "Private Attorneys General," 58 *Yale Law Journal* 574 (1949).

Note, "Class Actions," 1 *Race Relations Law Reporter* 991 (1956).

Note, "Inciting Litigation," 3 *Race Relations Law Reporter* 1257 (1958).

Note, "Freedom of Association," 4 *Race Relations Law Reporter* 207 (1959).

Peltason, Jack, *Federal Courts in the Political Process* (New York: Random House, 1955), Chs. 3, 5.

Rosenblum, Victor, *Law as a Political Instrument* (New York: Random House, 1955).

Schubert, Glendon A., Jr., *Constitutional Politics* (New York: Henry Holt, 1960), Ch. 3.

——, *Quantitative Analysis of Judicial Behavior* (Glencoe, Ill.: The Free Press, 1960), pp. 68–76.

Truman, David, *The Governmental Process* (New York; A. A. Knopf, 1951), Ch. 15.

Twiss, Benjamin, *Lawyers and the Constitution* (Princeton: Princeton University Press, 1942).

Vose, Clement E., "The National Consumers League and the Brandeis Brief," 1 *Midwest Journal of Political Science* 267 (1957).

——, *Caucasians Only: The Supreme Court, the NAACP and the Restrictive Covenant Cases.* (Berkeley: University of California Press, 1959).

> ". . . there is no incompatibility between the activity of
> organizations in litigation and the integrity or independ-
> ence of the judiciary."

1.

LITIGATION AS A FORM OF PRESSURE GROUP ACTIVITY   *Clement E. Vose**

ORGANIZATIONS SUPPORT legal action because individuals
lack the necessary time, money, and skill. . . . The form of group participation in court cases is set by such factors as the type of proceeding,
standing of the parties, legal or constitutional issues in dispute, the
characteristics of the organization, and its interest in the outcome.
Perhaps the most direct and open participation has been by organizations which have been obliged to protect their own rights and privileges. . . . The cases have sometimes placed organizations as parties,
but more often the organization supports a member or an officer in
litigation. One example must suffice.

The constitutional concept of religious freedom has been broadened
in recent years by the Supreme Court decisions in cases involving
members of the sect known as Jehovah's Witnesses. Most of the cases
began when a Jehovah's Witness violated a local ordinance or state
statute. Since 1938, the Witnesses, incorporated as the Watch Tower
Bible and Tract Society and represented by its counsel, Hayden
Cooper Covington, have won forty-four of fifty-five cases in the
United States Supreme Court. . . .

THE NAACP

Since 1909 the National Association for the Advancement of Colored
People has improved the legal status of Negroes immeasurably by the
victories it has won in more than fifty Supreme Court cases. During
its early years, the NAACP relied upon prominent volunteer lawyers
. . . to represent Negroes in the courts. Limited success coupled with

319 *The Annals of the American Academy of Political and Social Science* 20
(1958). Copyright 1958 the American Academy of Political and Social Science.
Reprinted with permission.
* Associate Professor of Government, Wesleyan University.

its failure to win gains from Congress led the NAACP in the 1930's to make court litigation fundamental to its program. A separate organization, the NAACP Legal Defense and Educational Fund, was incorporated for this purpose. The goal of the NAACP was to make Negroes "an integral part of the nation, with the same rights and guarantees that are accorded to other citizens, and on the same terms." This ambition meant that beginning in 1938 Thurgood Marshall as special counsel for the NAACP Legal Defense and Educational Fund held what was "probably the most demanding legal post in the country."

In aiming to establish racial equality before the law on a broad basis, the Legal Defense Fund has not functioned as a legal aid society. Limited resources have prevented the Fund from participating in all cases involving the rights of Negroes. As early as 1935 Charles Houston, an imaginative Negro lawyer who preceded Marshall as special counsel, set the tone of NAACP efforts when he declared that the legal campaign against inequality should be carefully planned "to secure decisions, rulings and public opinion on the broad principle instead of being devoted to merely miscellaneous cases."

By presenting test cases to the Supreme Court, the NAACP has won successive gains protecting the right of Negroes in voting, housing, transportation, education, and service on juries. Each effort has followed the development of new theories of legal interpretation and required the preparation of specific actions in the courts to challenge existing precedent. The NAACP Legal Defense Fund has accomplished these two tasks through the co-operation of associated and allied groups. First, as many as fifty Negro lawyers practicing in all parts of the country have been counsel in significant civil rights cases in the lower courts. Many of these men received their legal education at the Howard University Law School in Washington, D. C., and have shared membership in the National Bar Association since its founding in 1925. . . . Second, the NAACP has long benefited from its official advisory group, the National Legal Committee composed of leading Negro and white lawyers. . . . Third, other organizations with no direct connection with the Legal Defense Fund have sponsored a few cases. State and local chapters of the NAACP have often aided Negroes who were parties in cases, especially in the lower courts. The St. Louis

Association of Real Estate Brokers was the chief sponsor of the important restrictive covenant case of *Shelley* v. *Kraemer*. A Negro national college fraternity, Alpha Phi Alpha, sponsored quite completely the successful attack on discrimination in interstate railway dining cars. . . .

THE AMERICAN LIBERTY LEAGUE

The experience of the American Liberty League, organized in 1934 by conservative businessmen to oppose the New Deal, provides another variation on the theme of organizations in litigation. When the League proved unable to prevent enactment of economic regulation by Congress, a National Lawyers' Committee was formed to question the constitutionality of the legislation. In August 1935, the National Lawyers' Committee of fifty-eight members announced plans to prepare a series of reports to the public on whether particular federal laws were "consonant with the American constitutional system and American traditions." These reports "would be of a strictly professional nature and would in no case go into the question of social and economic advisability or the need for constitutional change to meet new conditions." This intention led the Committee during the next two years to conclude that a dozen New Deal statutes were unconstitutional.

The most celebrated Liberty League "brief" prepared by the National Lawyers' Committee questioned the constitutionality of the National Labor Relations Act. That analysis was prepared by a subcommittee of eight attorneys under the chairmanship of Earl F. Reed. It was then submitted to the other members and made public by Raoul E. Desverine, Chairman of the entire group, on Constitution Day, 1935. The reports of the Committee were given wide publicity through press releases, the distribution of pamphlets, and radio talks by leading conservative lawyers like James M. Beck. . . .

Members of the National Lawyers' Committee of the American Liberty League, but not the organization itself, participated in litigation. . . . Although the intention was to offer free legal services to citizens without funds to defend their constitutional rights, members of the National Lawyers' Committee actually represented major corporations which challenged the constitutionality of New Deal legislation

in the Supreme Court. Earl F. Reed simply adapted the Liberty
League report to apply to the specific facts of the case when he
represented the Jones and Laughlin Steel Corporation against the
National Labor Relations Board. Another member of the National
Lawyers' Committee, John W. Davis, represented the Associated Press
in a companion case.

AIDING THE GOVERNMENT DEFENSE

Judicial review in the United States constitutes an invitation for
groups whose lobbying fails to defeat legislation to continue opposition by litigation. The NAACP has taken advantage of this in questioning state segregation laws, and, especially before 1937, business groups
of various sizes—the American Liberty League, trade associations,
and corporations—contested the constitutionality of state and federal
regulatory legislation. This exploitation of judicial review has been
balanced by the practice of victorious groups in legislation continuing to support administrative agencies in charge of enforcement. When
statutes are challenged, organizations often support the Justice Department in Washington or a state Attorney General in defending them.
This is to say that when losers in legislation have brought test cases
in the courts, the legislative winners have aided the official legal
defense.

THE NATIONAL CONSUMERS' LEAGUE

The efforts of the National Consumers' League to defend the validity
of protective labor legislation affords an example of this private
organizational aid to the public defense of legislation. Organized by
society women in 1899 to improve the lot of women and children in
industry, the National Consumers' League sought first to boycott goods
produced under substandard conditions and then to persuade state
legislatures to control factory practices through legislation. When
employers in the hotel and laundry business organized to defeat
legislation in the courts, the National Consumers' League, in 1908,
organized a Committee on Legislation and Legal Defense of Labor
Laws to "assist in the defense of the laws by supplying additional
legal counsel and other assistance."

The leaders of the National Consumers' League, especially Mrs.

Florence Kelley and Miss Josephine Goldmark, learned to prod state Attorneys General in order to gain adequate defense for statutes under fire in the courts. They also made two positive contributions. First, arrangements were made to provide distinguished outside counsel—most importantly, Louis D. Brandeis; but also Felix Frankfurter, Newton D. Baker, and Dean Acheson—to supervise the preparation of briefs and to make oral arguments for a state. Second, the sociological material which was the mark of the Brandeis brief was prepared by Miss Josephine Goldmark and the staff of the National Consumers' League. The first four briefs that were successful were then collected with additional material and published by Miss Goldmark as *Fatigue and Efficiency*. Attorneys General in states whose labor laws were under attack could then invite Consumers' League attorneys to manage the defense or else use the sociological materials prepared by the League in the preparation of their own brief. As a result, the League contributed to the successful defense of state statutes in more than fifteen important cases.

Like most organizations with a long-range interest in litigation, the National Consumers' League believed that publicity was vital. . . . [B]ut the full Consumers' League program of child labor, maximum hour, and minimum wage regulation was not accommodated by the United States Supreme Court for three more decades. In that period the League stressed education on the subject and for this purpose distributed extra copies of its briefs to law schools, colleges, and public libraries.

No catalogue exists of government relations with private interests concerned with the conduct of litigation. The National Consumers' League experience suggests similar practices on other subjects at all government levels. At the municipal level, an attorney for a local milk producers association acted "of counsel" on the city's brief defending a favorable ordinance. At the state level, the segregation interest has been closely associated with various Attorneys General in the South. And a prominent attorney with national standing, John W. Davis, rendered free services to South Carolina in the School Segregation Cases. At the federal level, the Justice Department has often been urged by organizations to initiate action to enforce federal statutes.

ORGANIZATIONS AS "FRIENDS OF THE COURT"

The appearance of organizations as *amici curiae* has been the most noticed form of group representation in Supreme Court cases. . . . During the last decade *amici curiae* have submitted an average of sixty-six briefs and seven oral arguments in an average total of forty cases a term.

The frequent entrance of organizations into Supreme Court cases by means of the *amicus curiae* device has often given litigation the distinct flavor of group combat. This may be illustrated by the group representation in quite different cases. In 1943, when a member of the Jehovah's Witnesses challenged the constitutionality of a compulsory flag salute in the schools, his defense by counsel for the Watchtower Bible and Tract Society was supported by separate *amici curiae*, the American Civil Liberties Union and the Committee on the Bill of Rights of the American Bar Association. The appellant state board of education was supported by an *amicus curiae* brief filed by the American Legion. In 1951, in a case testing state resale price maintenance, the United States was an *amicus* against a Louisiana statute while the Commonwealth of Pennsylvania, the Louisiana State Pharmaceutical Association, American Booksellers, Inc., and the National Association of Retail Druggists entered *amici curiae* briefs in support of the statute. . . .

REGULATION OF ORGANIZATIONS IN THE COURTS

Judges, lawyers, legislators, and citizens have reacted to appearances that organizational activity in court cases touches the integrity of the judicial process. A number of limitations have resulted. But in protecting the legal system against these dangers, regulations may be too harsh on organizations and interfere unduly with the freedom of association their functioning represents. Especially is this true when the barriers against group participation in litigation are erected by legislative bodies, but it is not entirely absent when the rules are established by bar associations or by courts themselves. Some practices by organizations require control, but most of the practices of organizations in conducting litigation are perfectly compatible with an independent judiciary. . . .

During the trial of the leaders of the Communist party under the Smith Act in the Federal District Court for the Eastern District of New York located at Foley Square in New York City, picketing and parading outside the court was a daily occurrence. When the Senate Judiciary Committee was considering bills to limit this practice, it received many statements like the following: "Assuming under our form of representative government pressure groups must be tolerated in our legislative and executive branches, I feel there is no good reason why our courts should be subjected to such pressures." In accord with this view, Congress, in 1950, enacted legislation prohibiting any person from parading, picketing, or demonstrating in or near a federal courthouse with the intent of "interfering with, obstructing, or impeding" the administration of justice or of "influencing any judge, juror, witness, or court officer" in the discharge of his duty.

In 1953, the National Committee to Secure Justice in the Rosenberg Case addressed a petition claimed to have the support of 50,000 persons to the Supreme Court. . . . No rule prevents groups from such indecorous action but Justice Hugo Black has expressed the intense disapproval of the Supreme Court. In 1951, when granting a stay of execution to Willie McGhee, a Negro under the death penalty in Mississippi, Justice Black lamented the "growing practice of sending telegrams to judges in order to have cases decided by pressure." Declaring that he would not read them, he said that "the courts of the United States are not the kind of instruments of justice that can be influenced by such pressures." Justice Black gave an implied warning to the bar by noting that "counsel in this case have assured me they were not responsible for these telegrams."

The offer of the National Lawyers Committee of the American Liberty League to donate its services in test cases led a critic to make a formal complaint to the American Bar Association. The League was charged with unethical conduct for having "organized a vast free lawyers service for firms and individuals 'bucking' New Deal laws on constitutional grounds." The ABA Committee on Professional Ethics and Grievances ruled, in a formal opinion, that the activities of the Liberty League were perfectly proper, even laudable. The Committee found that neither the substance of the offer, to provide legal defense for "indigent citizens without compensation," nor the "proffer of service," even when broadcast over the radio, was offensive to the ethical code of the American bar. . . .

CONCLUSION

. . . Considering the importance of the issues resolved by American courts, the entrance of organizations into cases in these ways seems in order. Indeed the essential right of organizations to pursue litigation would appear to follow from the generous attitude of American society toward the freedom of individuals to form associations for the purpose of achieving common goals. Of course, traditional judicial procedures should be followed and the attorneys for organizations, as well as for individuals, must address their arguments to reason. If these standards of conduct are followed there is no incompatibility between the activity of organizations in litigation and the integrity or independence of the judiciary.

2.　　　　　　　 *". . . for the most part, briefs amici are repetitious at best and emotional explosions at worst."*

LOBBYISTS BEFORE THE COURT

Fowler V. Harper* and Edwin D. Etherington†

MANY PERSONS and groups do not hesitate to use their influence to persuade agencies of government to make decisions which they like. Of course, if reasonably regulated and ethically done, this is not only proper but often desirable even if the parties have axes of their own to grind. . . . The Supreme Court has not been immune. The lobbying device available for use before the Court is the brief amicus. When the nearly two hundred members of the Committee of Law Teachers Against Segregation in Legal Education filed their brief amicus curiae in the *Sweatt* case, they were using their influence in an effort to obtain

101 *University of Pennsylvania Law Review* 1172 (1953). Copyright 1953 University of Pennsylvania. Reprinted with permission.
* Professor of Law, Yale Law School.
† Attorney, former law clerk to Judge Henry Edgerton, U.S. Court of Appeals, District of Columbia Circuit; Vice President, New York Stock Exchange.

a decision to their liking. By the October, 1948 term amici briefs had become a genuine problem for the justices and their clerks. In that term there were 75 briefs filed in 57 cases. All but 14 were submitted with the consent of the parties and only 3 motions for leave to file were denied.

Even a cursory examination of these briefs indicates the time-wasting character of most of them. To be sure, a workmanlike brief such as that of the Committee of Law Teachers is a real help to the Court; but for the most part, briefs amici are repetitious at best and emotional explosions at worst. Indeed, the justices have, on occasion, been plagued with floods of post-card petitions and letters, visited by personal delegations and annoyed by alleged "briefs" submitted without pretense of party consent or motion for leave to file. The Daily Worker even went so far as to request its readers to file their personal "amicus briefs" in the *Dennis* case. It looked as if the situation were out of hand and the Supreme Court on the way to a serious loss of dignity. More and more the Court was being treated as if it were a political-legislative body, amenable and responsive to mass pressures from any source. The final straw appears to have been the case of the "Hollywood Ten" who declined to testify before the Un-American Activities Committee of the House. Some forty organizations got themselves "on record" on behalf of the defendants, including, among others, The American Civil Liberties Union, The Samuel Adams School of Social Studies, The National Union of Marine Cooks and Stewards, The Congress of American Women and the Conference of Studio Unions, The American Communications Association, The Methodist Federation for Social Action, The American Slav Congress, The American Jewish Congress, The National Council for the Arts, Sciences and Professions, The Progressive Party of America, and Alexander Meiklejohn et al. The American Writers Association filed on behalf of the United States. In addition, many other so-called briefs seem to have been submitted with complete indifference to the rule requiring consent of the parties or to the alternative practice of a petition for leave to file.

It is not surprising that the justices came finally to the conclusion that, in most cases, the "friends" of the Court were more trouble than they were worth. In November 1949, a new rule concerning briefs amicus curiae was announced. Except for governmental units which can still file such briefs as a matter of right, consent of all parties must be obtained, or if not, a motion must precede the brief describing the applicant's interest in the case and showing that the brief will cover matter not presented, or inadequately presented by the parties. Until the [1952] term, just one amicus brief has been admitted on motion for leave to file.

The experience of the American Jewish Congress which files briefs of genuine merit is illustrative of the effect of the new rule. The Congress, or more particularly its Commission on Law and Social Action, was very active in amicus argument prior to the rule change. In the 1947 and 1948 Terms, and early in the 1949 Term, it filed briefs in seven cases with consent of the parties: *Oyama v. California, Bernstein v. Van Heyghen Frères Société Anonyme, Bob-Lo Excursion Co. v. Michigan, Shelley v. Kraemer, Takahashi v. Fish and Game Commission, Stainback v. Mo Hock Ke Lok Po,* and *Lawson v. United States.* In another case, *Illinois ex rel. McCollum v. Board of Education,* the Congress drafted a brief which was filed on behalf of a number of Jewish organizations, and which Mr. Justice Frankfurter kept before him during oral argument and used extensively in a concurring opinion. In addition, when consent of the parties was withheld, the Congress moved for, and was granted, leave to file in *Terminiello v. Chicago* and sought the Court's permission to file in two others, *Sweatt v. Painter* and *Henderson v. United States.* The disposition of these motions requires explanation.

The *Sweatt* and *Henderson* cases came before the Court together with *McLaurin v. Oklahoma State Regents.* In May, 1949, the Congress filed a brief in support of the petition for certiorari in the *Sweatt* case, the Court having already noted probable jurisdiction over the appeal in the *Henderson* case. In October, the Congress filed its brief and a motion for leave to file in the *Henderson* case. On November 7, probable jurisdiction was noted in the *McLaurin* case, and certiorari was granted in the *Sweatt* case. The notation granting certiorari recited the filing of the amicus brief, but the Court never noted further action on the motion. The next week, November 14, the rule change was announced, and on January 9, 1950, the Court, consistent with its post-amendment practice, denied the motion for leave to file in the *Henderson* case.

Mr. Joseph B. Robinson, Staff Counsel for the Congress, feels that this pre-amendment activity would have been far less successful under the present rule. "It is safe to say that we would not have filed our brief and motion in the *Henderson* case if the rule had been changed a month earlier. It is also likely that if the rule had been in effect two years earlier, the *Terminiello* and *Sweatt* motions would have been denied, and the consent which we obtained in the other seven cases would not have been so easily obtained." Mr. Robinson may be too conservative; it is almost certain that consent could not have been obtained.

Since the adoption of the amendment, the American Jewish Congress has been able to obtain consent of the parties in two cases, in one of which, *Doremus v. Board of Education*, a brief was filed. In one other case, *Briggs v. Elliott*, involving a segregation issue, consent was denied by the attorney for the state of South Carolina, and the Congress believed it is hopeless to ask the Supreme Court to grant leave to file. "In other cases in which we might have filed amicus briefs, we have been deterred from taking any action by the unlikelihood of either obtaining consent or getting permission from the court."

The American Jewish Congress' difficulties are those felt by all similar organizations. The American Civil Liberties Union, the National Lawyers' Guild and the American Jewish Committee, which among them filed a number of creditable briefs during the 1948 and 1949 Terms, have moved for leave to file in fewer than ten cases since then, and not a single motion has been granted. During the past term, the Court has finally granted one motion, that of the United States Lines in *Warren v. United States*. The motion, which demonstrated very direct interest on the part of the United States Lines, appears to be the only motion for leave to file that has been successful in over two years.

The Court has thus gone from one extreme to the other in this matter. The new rule is much in disfavor with respectable organizations which have a legitimate interest in certain aspects of Supreme Court litigation. Indeed, it apparently does not sit well with some of the members of the Court itself. Justice Black has stated his dissatisfaction with the rule and Justice Frankfurter has twice reprimanded the Solicitor General for refusing consent to the filing of amici briefs. Justice Frankfurter's public letters to the Solicitor General suggest a wide diversity between the aim of the Court's Rule and its actual effects. "If all litigants," he says, "were to take the position of the Solicitor General, either no *amici* briefs (other than those that fall within the exceptions of Rule 27, 28 U.S.C.A.) would be allowed, or a fair sifting process for dealing with such applications would be nullified and an undue burden cast upon the Court. Neither alternative is conducive to the wise disposition of the Court's business. The practice of the Government amounts to an endeavor, I am bound to say, to transfer to the Court a responsibility that by the rule properly belongs to the Government." . . .

The amicus curiae has had a long and respected role in our own legal system and before that, in the Roman law. To be sure, participants are often a friend of one of the parties as well as the Court but the primary function of the amicus is to help the Court arrive at a just decision. Admittedly, the Supreme Court has a problem on its hands with which it must come to grips. Briefs amici are often valuable. They may be particularly valuable in connection with petitions for certiorari where the Court has to make a preliminary decision on the importance of the issues raised. Its task is to devise some way to preserve the advantages of briefs amici without first having to examine all such briefs to select those of merit. It is the absence of such a rule that has led the Court to exclude practically all by-standers who wish to lend their aid in the interest of justice. There is nothing wrong with lobbying, as such, if everything is aboveboard and on a level of decency, morally and intellectually. The Court might well assume some responsibility in making important distinctions.

3.   *"Effective advocacy of both public and private points of view . . . is . . . enhanced by group association . . ."*

NAACP V. ALABAMA

THE NAACP *had been chartered in Alabama in 1918. In 1956 the state attorney general brought suit to enjoin the Association from further operations, claiming that it had never complied with state corporation laws and that its assistance to Negroes seeking to end*

357 U.S. 449, 78 S. Ct. 1163, 2 L. Ed. 2d 1488 (1958).

segregation "was causing irreparable injury to the property and civil rights of residents and citizens of the State of Alabama for which criminal prosecution and civil actions afford no adequate relief. . . ." The trial judge issued an injunction forbidding the NAACP to carry on operations during the litigation, and also ordered the Association to produce a number of official records including its membership lists. The NAACP complied with the order except as to the membership lists. The judge held the Association in civil contempt and imposed a fine of $10,000 which would be increased to $100,000 if the lists were not surrendered within 5 days. The NAACP still refused. The state supreme court twice declined to review the case, and the U.S. Supreme Court granted certiorari.

MR. JUSTICE HARLAN delivered the opinion of the Court. . . .

The association both urges that it is constitutionally entitled to resist official inquiry into its membership lists, and that it may assert, on behalf of its members a right personal to them to be protected from compelled disclosure by the State of their affiliation with the Association as revealed by the membership lists. We think that petitioner argues more appropriately the rights of its members, and that its nexus with them is sufficient to permit that it act as their representative before this Court. In so concluding, we reject respondent's argument that the Association lacks standing to assert here constitutional rights pertaining to the members, who are not of course parties to the litigation.

To limit the breadth of issues which must be dealt with in particular litigation, this Court has generally insisted that parties rely only on constitutional rights which are personal to themselves. *Tileston* v. *Ullman.* . . . This rule is related to the broader doctrine that constitutional adjudication should where possible be avoided. . . . The principle is not disrespected where constitutional rights of persons who are not immediately before the Court could not be effectively vindicated except through an appropriate representative before the Court. . . .

If petitioner's rank-and-file members are constitutionally entitled to withhold their connection with the Association despite the production order, it is manifest that this right is properly assertable by the

Association. To require that it be claimed by the members themselves
would result in nullification of the right at the very moment of its
assertion. Petitioner is the appropriate party to assert these rights,
because it and its members are in every practical sense identical. The
Association, which provides in its constitution that "[a]ny person who
is in accordance with [its] principles and policies . . ." may become
a member, is but the medium through which its individual members
seek to make more effective the expression of their own views. The
reasonable likelihood that the Association itself through diminished
financial support and membership may be adversely affected if production is compelled is a further factor pointing towards our holding that
petitioner has standing to complain of the production order on behalf
of its members. . . .

We thus reach petitioner's claim that the production order in the
state litigation trespasses upon fundamental freedoms protected by
the Due Process Clause of the Fourteenth Amendment. Petitioner
argues that in view of the facts and circumstances shown in the record,
the effect of compelled disclosure of the membership lists will be to
abridge the rights of its rank-and-file members to engage in lawful
association in support of their common beliefs. It contends that governmental action which, although not directly suppressing association,
nevertheless carries this consequence, can be justified only upon some
overriding valid interest of the State.

Effective advocacy of both public and private points of view,
particularly controversial ones, is undeniably enhanced by group association, as this Court has more than once recognized by remarking
upon the close nexus between the freedoms of speech and assembly.
. . . It is beyond debate that freedom to engage in association for the
advancement of beliefs and ideas is an inseparable aspect of the
"liberty" assured by the Due Process Clause of the Fourteenth Amendment, which embraces freedom of speech. . . . Of course, it is immaterial whether the beliefs sought to be advanced by association pertain
to political, economic, religious or cultural matters, and state action
which may have the effect of curtailing the freedom to associate is
subject to the closest scrutiny.

The fact that Alabama, so far as is relevant to the validity of the
contempt judgment presently under review, has taken no direct action

. . . to restrict the right of petitioner's members to associate freely, does not end inquiry into the effect of the production order. . . . In the domain of these indispensable liberties, whether of speech, press, or association, the decisions of this Court recognize that abridgment of such rights, even though unintended, may inevitably follow from varied forms of governmental action. . . . Similar recognition of possible unconstitutional intimidation of the free exercise of the right to advocate underlay this Court's narrow construction of the authority of a congressional committee investigating lobbying and of an Act regulating lobbying, although in neither case was there an effort to suppress speech. . . . The governmental action challenged may appear to be totally unrelated to protected liberties. Statutes imposing taxes upon rather than prohibiting particular activity have been struck down when perceived to have the consequence of unduly curtailing the liberty of freedom of press assured under the Fourteenth Amendment. . . .

It is hardly a novel perception that compelled disclosure of affiliation with groups engaged in advocacy may constitute as effective a restraint on freedom of association as the forms of governmental action in the cases above were thought likely to produce upon the particular constitutional rights there involved. This Court has recognized the vital relationship between freedom to associate and privacy in one's associations. When referring to the varied forms of governmental action which might interfere with freedom of assembly, it said in *American Communications Assn. v. Douds* . . . "A requirement that adherents of particular religious faiths or political parties wear identifying arm-bands, for example, is obviously of this nature." Compelled disclosure of membership in an organization engaged in advocacy of particular beliefs is of the same order. Inviolability of privacy in group association may in many circumstances be indispensable to preservation of freedom of association, particularly where a group espouses dissident beliefs. . . .

We think that the production order, in the respects here drawn in question, must be regarded as entailing the likelihood of a substantial restraint upon the exercise by petitioner's members of their right to freedom of association. Petitioner has made an uncontroverted showing that on past occasions revelation of the identity of its rank-and-file members has exposed these members to economic reprisal, loss of employment, threat of physical coercion, and other manifestations of public hostility. Under these circumstances, we think it apparent that compelled disclosure of petitioner's Alabama membership is likely to affect adversely the ability of petitioner and its members to pursue their collective effort to foster beliefs which they admittedly have the right to advocate, in that it may induce members to withdraw from the Association and dissuade others from joining it because of fear of exposure of their beliefs shown through their associations and of the consequences of this exposure.

It is not sufficient to answer, as the State does here, that whatever repressive effect compulsory disclosure of names of petitioner's members may have upon participation by Alabama citizens in petitioner's activities follows not from *state* action but from *private* community pressures. The crucial factor is the interplay of governmental and private action, for it is only after the initial exertion of state power represented by the production order that private action takes hold.

We turn to the final question whether Alabama has demonstrated an interest in obtaining the disclosures it seeks from petitioner which is sufficient to justify the deterrent effect which we have concluded these disclosures may well have on the free exercise by petitioner's members of their constitutionally protected right of association. . . . It is not of moment that the State has here acted solely through its judicial branch, for whether legislative or judicial, it is still the application of state power which we are asked to scrutinize.

It is important to bear in mind that petitioner asserts no right to absolute immunity from state investigation, and no right to disregard Alabama's laws. As shown by its substantial compliance with the production order, petitioner does not deny Alabama's right to obtain from it such information as the State desires concerning the purposes of the Association and its activities within the State. Petitioner has not objected to divulging the identity of its members who are employed by or hold official positions with it. It has urged the rights solely of its ordinary rank-and-file members. . . .

Whether there was "justification" in this instance turns solely on the substantiality of Alabama's interest in obtaining the membership lists. . . . The issues in the litigation commenced by Alabama by its bill in equity were whether the character of petitioner and its activities in Alabama had been such as to make petitioner subject to the registration statute, and whether the extent of petitioner's activities without qualifying suggested its permanent ouster from the State. Without intimating the slightest view upon the merits of these issues, we are unable to perceive that the disclosure of the names of petitioner's rank-and-file members has a substantial bearing on either of them. As matters stand in the state court, petitioner (1) has admitted its presence and conduct of activities in Alabama since 1918; (2) has offered to comply in all respects with the state qualification statute, although preserving its contention that the statute does not apply to it; and (3) has apparently complied satisfactorily with the production order, except for the membership lists . . . whatever interest the State may have in obtaining names of ordinary members has not been shown to be sufficient to overcome petitioner's constitutional objections to the production order.

From what has already been said, we think it apparent that *Bryant v. Zimmerman* . . . cannot be relied on in support of the State's position, for that case involved markedly different considerations in terms of the interest of the State in obtaining disclosure. There, this Court upheld, as applied to a member of a local chapter of the Ku Klux Klan, a New York statute requiring any unincorporated association which demanded an oath as a condition to membership to file with state officials copies of its ". . . constitution, by-laws, rules, regulations and oath of membership, together with a roster of its membership and a list of its officers for the current year." . . . In its opinion, the Court took care to emphasize the nature of the organization which New York sought to regulate. The decision was based on the particular character of the Klan's activities, involving acts of unlawful intimidation and violence, which the Court assumed was before the state legislature when it enacted the statute, and of which the Court itself took judicial notice. Furthermore, the situation before us is significantly different from that in *Bryant*, because the organization there had made no effort to comply with any of the requirements of New York's statute but rather had refused to furnish the State with *any* information as to its local activities.

We hold that the immunity from state scrutiny of membership lists which the Association claims on behalf of its members is here so related to the right of the members to pursue their lawful private interest privately and to associate freely with others in so doing as to come within the protection of the Fourteenth Amendment. And we conclude that Alabama has fallen short of showing a controlling justification for the deterrent effect on the free enjoyment of the right to associate which disclosure of membership lists is likely to have. . . .

For the reasons stated, the judgment of the Supreme Court of Alabama must be reversed and the case remanded for proceedings not inconsistent with this opinion.

Reversed.

4.   *"The right of access to the courts is one of the great safe-guards of the liberties of the people . . ."*

NAACP V. PATTY

AS PART *of its "massive resistance" against the Supreme Court's school segregation decisions, the 1956 Extra Session of the Virginia Legislature adopted a number of statutes aimed at the NAACP.*

Chapters 31 and 32 required the registration of every person, firm, partnership, corporation, or association which engaged in any way in lobbying for or against racial legislation or which raised or spent money to pay the cost of litigation on behalf of any race. The required information—which was to be open to public inspection—included not only a complete financial statement, but also the names and addresses of all officers, contributors, and members within the state.

Chapter 35 defined barratry as "stirring up" litigation by "instigating" another person to bring a lawsuit by paying or arranging for payment of all or part of the costs of litigating. Certain exceptions were made, such as for legal aid societies, or where the attorney was related to the plaintiff by blood or marriage, or where the lawyer was entitled under law to a share in the proceeds. Violation of this statute by an individual was made a misdemeanor, and a corporation violating

159 F. Supp. 503, 3 *Race Rel. L. Rep.* 274 (1958).

the statute was liable to a fine of up to $10,000 and expulsion from the state.

Chapters 33 and 36 provided general rules for revoking lawyers' licenses as well as further prohibitions against offering inducements to a person to begin legal action before a state or Federal court or administrative agency.

The NAACP brought suit in a three-judge federal district court asking that state officials be enjoined from enforcing these statutes against the Negro group. (This decision was handed down five months before that in NAACP v. Alabama.)

BEFORE SOPER, CIRCUIT JUDGE, and HUTCHESON and HOFFMAN, DISTRICT JUDGES.

SOPER, CIRCUIT JUDGE. . . .

[T]he defendants urge that we should not exercise the power to restrain the enforcement of state statutes but should withhold action until the statutes have been construed by the Supreme Court of Appeals of Virginia. This contention is based on the policy defined in decisions of the Supreme Court of the United States that federal courts should avoid passing on constitutional questions in situations where an authoritative interpretation of state law may avoid the constitutional issues. Hence if the interpretation of a state statute is doubtful or a question of law remains undecided, the federal court should hold its proceedings in abeyance for a reasonable time pending construction of the statute by the state courts or until efforts to obtain such an adjudication have been exhausted.

These rulings, however, do not mean that the federal courts lose jurisdiction in cases where the state courts have not passed upon the statute under attack or that the federal court is powerless to take any action until a decision by the state court has been rendered. Such a conclusion could not be reached in the pending case since the federal statutes expressly confer jurisdiction upon the federal courts where civil rights have been violated . . . or where federal questions are involved. . . .

The policy laid down by the Supreme Court does not require a stay of proceedings in the federal courts in cases of this sort if the state statutes at issue are free of doubt or ambiguity. . . . Where the statute is free from ambiguity and there remains no reasonable interpretation which will render it constitutional, there are compelling reasons to bring about an expeditious and final ascertainment of the constitutionality of these statutes to the end that a multiplicity of similar actions may, if possible, be avoided.

This discussion brings us at last to a consideration of the attack made on the constitutionality of the statutes in their bearing upon the activities of the plaintiffs. The two registration statutes, Chapters 31 and 32, are free from ambiguities which require a prior interpretation by the courts of the state and hence the obligation to pass on the question of constitutionality cannot be avoided. . . .

The sort of registration required by Chapter 32 has a definite bearing upon the validity of the enactment since a statement of the business of the registrant in much detail is prescribed. . . .

Undoubtedly the burden of supplying these statements imposed upon persons who engage in [such] activities . . . constitutes a restriction upon the right of free speech which, as we have seen, the Association is entitled to exercise. Hence the question arises whether the statute is within the police powers which, in the past, have been properly exercised in many fields. The defendants point out that the promoting or opposing passage of legislation . . . may involve lobbying, which has long been recognized as a proper subject of regulation by the state and federal governments. Thus it was decided in United States v. Harriss, by a divided court, that the registration provisions of the Federal Regulation of Lobbying Act did not violate freedom of speech, provided the scope of the Act was limited to persons who had solicited or received contributions to influence or defeat the passage of legislation and who intended to accomplish this purpose through direct communication with members of Congress. The plain implication of the decision, as appears clearly from the dissenting opinions, is that unless the Act were so limited it would be an unwarranted interference with the right of free speech. The [earlier] lobbying statute of the State of Virginia . . . is likewise limited to those who employ a person to promote or oppose the passage of an act of the General Assembly and to a person accepting such employment. Such a person is required to register his name upon a legislative docket.

The terms of [Chapter 32] contain no such limitation. They apply to any person whose principal activities include "the promoting or opposing *in any manner* the passage of legislation by the General Assembly," excepting however, newspapers and similar publications, communications by radio and television, and persons engaged in a political election campaign. Hence the duty to register is imposed upon anyone who in concert with others merely speaks or writes on the subject, even if he has had no contact of any kind with the legislative body and has neither received nor spent any money to further his purpose. The discriminating and oppressive character of the provision is emphasized by the exemption of persons engaged in a political election campaign who are free to speak without registration, whereas, persons having no direct interest in elections as such and concerned only with securing equal rights for all persons are covered by the statute. Manifestly so broad a restriction cannot be held valid under the ruling of United States v. Harriss. (See p. 427.)

The terms of [Chapter 32] impinge directly upon the field of free speech for they apply to anyone, with the same exceptions, whose present activities include the "advocacy of racial integration or segregation" and so the same problem of the extent of regulatory power is presented. . . .

The defendants insist that Chapter 32 was enacted for the commendable purpose of protecting the public welfare and safety and therefore should be upheld. They point to the declaration of the policy in the preamble of the statute to eliminate all conditions which impede the peaceful co-existence of all persons in the state and which, according to the testimony of law enforcement officers, is threatened by the effort to establish integration of the races in the public schools. Great dependence is placed upon the decision of the Supreme Court in Bryant v. Zimmerman which is described as the leading case in this field most pertinent to the matter now before the court. The Supreme Court upheld a New York statute, aimed at the activities of the Ku Klux Klan, which required associations having an oath-bound membership to file lists of their members and officers with a State officer and made it a crime for members to attend meetings knowing that the registration requirement had not been complied with. It was held that the statute as applied to a member of the Ku Klux Klan would not violate the due process clause of the Fourteenth Amendment since the state, for its own protection, was entitled to the disclosure as a deterrent to violations of the law; and also that there was no denial of equal protection in excepting labor unions, Masons and other fraternal bodies from the statutes, since there was a tendency on the part of the Ku Klux Klan to shroud its acts in secrecy and engage in conduct inimical to the public welfare.

We do not think that these decisions justify the restriction upon public discussion which Chapter 32 imposes upon the plaintiffs in this case. Obviously the purpose and effect of a regulatory act must be examined in each case in light of the existing situation. In the present instance the executive and legislative officers of the state have publicly and forcibly announced their determination to impede and, if possible, to prevent the integration of the races by all lawful means; and the statutes passed at the Extra Session were clearly designed to cripple the agencies that have had the greatest success in promoting the rights of colored persons to equality of treatment in the past, and are possessed of sufficient resources to make an effort at this time to secure the enforcement of the Supreme Court's decree. The statute is not aimed, as the act considered in Bryant v. Zimmerman, at curbing the activities of an association likely to engage in violations of the law, but at bodies who are endeavoring to abide by and enforce the law and have not themselves engaged in acts of violence or disturbance of the public peace.

The Act is not saved, in so far as the plaintiffs are concerned, by making it applicable to advocates of both sides of the dispute so that it requires a disclosure of the names of persons who may be led to acts of violence by reason of their hostility to integration. Such a provision does not lead to equality of treatment under the circumstances known by the Legislature to prevail. Registration of persons engaged in a popular cause imposes no hardship while, as the evidence of this case shows, registration of names of persons who resist the popular will would lead not only to expressions of ill will and hostility but to the loss of members by the plaintiffs' Association.

Nor can the statute be sustained on the ground that breaches of peace may occur if integration in the public schools is enforced. The same contention was made in Buchanan v. Warley where the court struck down an ordinance of the City of Louisville which forbade colored persons to occupy houses in blocks occupied for the most part by white persons.

The terms of . . . the statute requiring registration of anyone whose activities cause or tend to cause racial conflicts or violence require little discussion. They are so vague and indefinite that the clause taken by itself does not satisfy the constitutional requirement that a criminal statute must give to a person of ordinary intelligence fair notice of the kind of conduct that constitutes the crime.

. . . Chapter 32 [also] requires the registration of anyone who engages in raising or expending funds for the employment of counsel or the payment of costs in connection with litigation on behalf of any race or color. In connection with other provisions contained in Chapters 31, 33, 35 and 36 relating to litigation, it constitutes an important part, perhaps the most important part, of the plan devised by the state authorities to impede or to prevent the integration of the races in the schools of the state; and it subjects the participant to all of the details of registration above described.

In its broad coverage the statute applies to any individual who employs and pays a lawyer to act for him in a law suit involving a racial question. It also covers the plaintiff corporations in their effort to raise the money which in the past has been used to assist the colored people in the prosecution of suits to secure their constitutional rights both before and after the decision in Brown v. Board of Education.

The right of access to the courts is one of the great safeguards of the liberties of the people and its denial or undue restriction is a violation of the due process clauses of the Fifth and Fourteenth Amendments. That the restriction is onerous in this instance cannot be denied, for it is not confined to identification of the collectors of the funds but requires the disclosure of every contributor and of every member of the Association whose annual dues may have been used in part to pay the expenses of litigation.

Undoubtedly a state may protect its citizens from fraudulent solicitation of funds by requiring a collector to establish his identity and his authority to act; and the state may also regulate the time and manner of the solicitation in the interest of public safety and convenience. . . .

The statute before us, however, presents a very different case. It requires not merely the identity of the collector of the funds but the disclosure of the name of every contributor. In effect, as applied to this case, it requires every person who desires to become a member of the Association and to exercise with it the rights of free speech and free assembly to be registered, and the size of his contribution to be shown. This seems to us far more onerous than the requirement of a license to speak, which was struck down as unconstitutional in Thomas v. Collins, especially as in this instance the disclosure is prescribed as part of a deliberate plan to impede the contributors in the assertion of their constitutional rights. In our opinion all [clauses of Chapter 32] as applied to the plaintiffs in this case are unconstitutional.

For like reasons Chapter 31 which covers much the same ground as . . . Chapter 32 must also be held invalid.

Chapters 33, 35 and 36 all relate to the improper practice of law. They are of prime importance since they furnish the basis for the contention of the prosecuting officers of the state that the plaintiff corporations are unlawfully engaged in the practice of law in Virginia and hence are not entitled to maintain these suits. . . .

We consider first Chapter 35 since it contains a carefully phrased definition of the crime of barratry and is free from ambiguity. Barratry is defined in § 1 as stirring up litigation; a barrator is one who stirs up litigation; and stirring up litigation means instigating a person to institute a suit at law or equity. . . .

The broad question is therefore raised as to whether it is within the power of the state to make it a crime for any corporation other than a general legal aid society to pay in whole or in part the expenses of litigation if it has only a general philanthropic or charitable interest in the litigation and does not have the kind of special interest described in the statute. Specifically, as applied to the facts of this case, the question is whether Virginia may make it a crime for organizations interested in the preservation of civil rights to contribute money for the prosecution of law suits instituted to promote this cause.

The right of the state to require high standards of qualification for those who desire to practice law within its borders and to revoke or suspend the license to practice law of attorneys who have been guilty of unethical conduct is unquestioned. Solicitation of business by an attorney is regarded as unethical conduct and a proper subject of disciplinary action; and it has been held that the state may prohibit a layman engaged in the business of collecting accounts from soliciting employment for this purpose, since a regulation which aims to bring the conduct of the business in harmony with the ethical practices of the legal profession is reasonable. . . .

It is manifest, however, that the activities of the plaintiff corporations are not undertaken for profit or for the promotion of ordinary business purposes but, rather, for the securing of the rights of citizens without any possibility of financial gain. . . . Indeed the exclusion of lawyers when acting for benevolent purposes and charitable societies, as distinguished from business corporations, from the restrictions imposed by the canons of Professional Ethics has long been recognized in the approval given by the courts to services voluntarily offered by members of the bar to persons in need, even when the attorneys have been selected by corporations organized to serve a cause in a controversial field. . . .

Chapter 35 in failing to recognize this settled rule, violates well-established constitutional principles in its bearing upon the plaintiff corporations. "A State cannot exclude a person from the practice of law or from any other occupation in a manner or for reasons that contravene the Due Process or Equal Protection Clause of the Fourteenth Amendment," Schware v. Board of Bar Examiners. In the first place, the statute obviously violates the equal protection clause, for it forbids the plaintiffs to defray the expenses of racial litigation, while at the same time it legalizes the activities of legal aid societies that serve all needy persons in all sorts of litigation. No argument has been offered to the court to sustain this discrimination. Moreover, Chapter 35 violates the due process clause, for it is designed to put the plaintiff corporations out of business by forbidding them to encourage and assist colored persons to assert rights established by the decisions of the Supreme Court of the United States. The activities of the plaintiffs as they appear in these cases do not amount to a solicitation of business or a stirring up of litigation of the sort condemned by the ethical standards of the legal profession. They comprise in substance public instruction of the colored people as to the extent of their rights, recommendation that appeals be made to the courts for relief, offer of assistance in prosecuting the cases when assistance is asked, and the payment of legal expenses for people unable to defend themselves; and the attorneys who have done the work have done so only when authorized by the plaintiffs. The evidence is uncontradicted that the initial steps which have led to the institution and prosecution of racial suits in Virginia with the assistance of the Association and the Fund have not been taken until the prospective plaintiffs made application to one or the other of the corporations for help. In our opinion the right of the plaintiff corporations to render this assistance cannot be denied. . . .

The majority opinion went on to say that the language of Chapters 33 and 36 was ambiguous, therefore no decision would be given regarding their constitutionality. An injunction would issue, however, against the enforcement of Chapters 31, 32, and 35. Judge Hutcheson dissented.

The Virginia attorney general appealed directly to the Supreme Court, and in Harrison v. NAACP *(1959), the High Bench in a 6-3 decision stated that the district court should have withheld a decision until after the Virginia courts had had an opportunity to interpret the statutes. The Supreme Court was applying in this case a doctrine known as "equitable abstention"—federal courts, whenever possible, should allow state tribunals to interpret ambiguous state statutes before federal judges decide on the constitutionality of such statutes.*

". . . Law Review articles, treatises, and so forth, prepared and disseminated by the lobbyists . . . command no
5.   *respect, have no standing as legal authorities. . . ."*

LOBBYING THROUGH LAW REVIEWS   *Wright Patman**

MR. PATMAN. Mr. Speaker, a proper functioning judiciary is respected. Indeed, a proper functioning judiciary is necessary to the protection of the rights of the individual. . . . Notwithstanding . . . I do not consider that Congress is required to bury its head and refuse

103 *Congressional Record* 14758 (daily ed., August 27, 1957).
* U.S. Congressman (Dem., Texas), 1928–.

to take note of the standards, methods, and factors relied upon by the Federal judiciary in reaching important decisions and results. . . .

A number of the Members of the Congress who are lawyers have expressed amazement at some recent decisions of our Federal judiciary. We all know that some of the recent decisions and results reached by our Federal judiciary are so important as to vitally affect our entire people. We wonder what factors were taken into account and relied upon to reach the announced decisions. Particularly the Supreme Court has been singled out for criticism in that connection. Many prominent lawyers have indicated that they are unable to determine what factors prompted the Supreme Court to decide certain cases as it did. . . .

Today we are finding that an additional factor is creeping in to influence the thinking and action of the Supreme Court of the United States. That factor is the Court's consideration of unknown, unrecognized and nonauthoritative text books, Law Review articles, and other writings of propaganda artists and lobbyists. In some instances it appears that the Court has considered and adopted such questionable writings in an ex parte fashion because counsels' arguments and briefs made no reference thereto. Apparently therefore the Court itself uncovered and utilized the articles written by these lobbyists without having notified counsel of its intention so to do. If as indicated such a procedure was followed a situation would be presented wherein counsel would have enjoyed no opportunity to meet the arguments of these theorists and lobbyists. In adopting and relying upon such pseudo legalistic papers disseminated by the lobbyist-authors thereof the result is that the theories advanced by these pretended authorities were presented and received by the Court in an ex parte fashion.

In other cases however it appears that some of the articles written by the lobbyists were mentioned or cited in the brief by counsel for defendants and later cited in the Court's opinion. In such instances it seems to me that here again the Court has acted in an ex parte fashion unless it gave affirmative notice to opposing counsel that it intended to use and rely upon the miscellaneous nonauthoritative writings of the lobbyists and theorists referred to hereinabove. This is true, it seems to me, because counsel is entitled to assume that the Court will not pay attention to citations or writings not theretofore accepted by the Court as authoritative. The Law Review articles, treatises, and so forth, prepared and disseminated by the lobbyists command no respect, have no standing as legal authorities and therefore warrant no consideration by opposing counsel. If the rule were otherwise counsel would be rendered helpless because their arguments would become diluted heavily with extraneous miscellaneous matter designed to overcome the various theories advanced by the lobbyists posing as legal authorities. . . .

One of the most devastating blows suffered by those provisions of our antitrust laws designed to nip monopolistic practices in the bud and before they arrive at full bloom was the decision by the Supreme Court of the United States in the case of *Standard Oil Company of Indiana* v. *Federal Trade Commission* . . . in 1951. In that case the Supreme Court cited a number of authorities it relied upon in arriving at its conclusion and decision against the Government and in favor of the Standard Oil Company of Indiana. Among those authorities were arguments which had been made by various persons in speeches, law review articles, and in testimony before committees. Prominent in the reasoning of the Court and important to its decision in that case in favor of the Standard Oil Company of Indiana was the Court's reasoning that the Robinson-Patman Act, the antitrust law under which that case had been brought, was inconsistent with the Sherman Antitrust Act. In that connection it cited an authority. In a footnote at page 249 appears the following:

> It has been suggested that, in theory, the Robinson-Patman Act as a whole is inconsistent with the Sherman and Clayton Acts. See Adelman, Effective Competition and the Antitrust Laws, 61 Harv. L. Rev. 1289, 1327-1350.

Writings by Adelman propagandizing against the application of the antitrust laws to monopolistic practices were reprinted and widely distributed by the Great Atlantic & Pacific Tea Co. Undoubtedly that propaganda assisted A. & P. in defending an antitrust case. Big business concerns contributed to a fund from which Adelman was paid to help in the preparation of writings on this subject.

Much of the lobbying directed to the Supreme Court in recent years has taken the form of law review articles, pamphlets and books presented as if they were objective works of unbiased, unprejudiced, nonpartisan writers. Actually, many of them have been carefully planned and devised by opponents of our public policy against monopoly with a "view to formulate future antitrust policy." In that connection recommendations were made for "coordination and re-vision" of our public policy against monopoly and our antitrust laws. Those recommendations in those works were directed principally to our Federal Judiciary and with a view to influencing the thinking and action of the Supreme Court of the United States. . . .

It appears the full impact of this lobbying of the Supreme Court by agitators against our antitrust laws was realized last year when the Court handed down its decision in the case of the *United States* v. *E. I. DuPont de Nemours & Company* . . . sometimes referred to as the Cellophane case. As many as 15 citations were made by members of the Court in the opinions and decisions of that case to law review articles and other writings as "authorities" from which it appears stemmed considerable reasoning by the Court providing a way for the decision against the Government and against the application of the antitrust laws in that case. Law review articles by one of the cochairmen of the Attorney General's Committee were cited by the Court in that case as was the report of the Attorney General's com-mittee. There were a number of citations to the latter.

It is not possible for us to appraise the extent and the significance of the damage which has been done by virtue of the fact that the report of the Attorney General's National Committee to Study the Antitrust Laws has been accepted and relied upon by the Supreme Court of the United States as an authority in deciding the more im-portant antitrust cases. One thing we do know—the Supreme Court in relying upon that report has accepted as an authority a collection of arguments compiled by a group, a majority of the members of which have opposed our public policy against monopoly and monopo-listic practices. It was the announced determination of that group to formulate future antitrust policy. It is clear that a part of its plan to effect that result was to re-educate the Supreme Court and the public into believing that certain monopolistic practices, including the practice of price discrimination, are merely competitive and that our antitrust laws which were designed to curb those practices are therefore anticompetitive. . . .

PART FIVE

Judicial Reasoning

9 / FACT FINDING IN THE COURTS

The decision of a case in court involves two processes: determining the facts, and then applying the appropriate rules of law to those facts. There can, of course, be lawsuits in which there is no dispute over the facts. In a criminal case, the defendant may plead guilty, and so relieve the prosecutor of any need to establish the facts of the law violation. In civil proceedings both parties may agree about the facts, and disagree only about the law applicable to the factual situation. But courts must be prepared to establish the facts in any controversy brought before them, and much of the peculiar character of judicial proceedings is attributable to their fact-finding methods.

As Jerome Frank in particular has pointed out, the importance of the factual determinations of trial courts is often inadequately appreciated, particularly by scholars who concentrate on the work of the appellate courts. The "upper-court myth," as he calls it, holds that the decisions of trial courts are controlled by legal rules supervised by the appellate courts, and that mistakes of trial courts can be remedied on appeal. But in fact appellate courts can normally challenge a finding of a trial court, where conflicting evidence has been offered, only if the record of the trial reveals that the finding was the product of the trial judge's incompetence, unfairness, or dishonesty.

315

The Adversary Process

At one time courts undertook to determine the truth or falsity of charges through trial by combat or by putting alleged wrongdoers in ducking stools. Modern courts conduct a trial of the facts by adversary process. Witnesses with direct knowledge bearing on the factual situation in dispute are called into court by one side or the other, and asked to give evidence. Witnesses for each side are cross-examined by counsel for the other side, in an effort to break down their testimony and show that it is not reliable or truthful or relevant. By providing each side with an opportunity to present proof of its contentions by oral or documentary evidence, and to cast doubt on the evidence presented by the other side, under the impartial supervision of a judge trained in this art of fact finding, it is assumed that the chances for determining the truth will be good.

Of course, the responsibility for determining the truth is often not given to the trained judge, but to a jury of untrained laymen, whose virtue is that they are a cross-section of the ordinary population, or "peers" of the defendant. The institution of the jury goes far back into English legal history, a history which cannot be recounted here. While it is easy to disparage the jury as a fact-finding instrument, no institution could have survived as long as the jury has unless it performed some useful functions.

Perhaps the major utility of the jury is to inject a popular, nonprofessional element into the administration of justice. Judges have their foibles, their prejudices, their professional biases. Long-continued exposure to the criminal population may harden their sensibilities. The system of legal punishment may itself be overrigorous and need in application the ameliorating influence of laymen who reflect the opinions of the time. Through the jury system the administration of justice is kept within the limits of public acceptance.

Because juries are composed of persons untrained in rigorous thought processes, the judicial system undertakes to protect them from the more obvious kinds of error. A body of rules of evidence has been built up, primarily to keep from the jury evidence which is not worthy of belief, or which would be likely to divert them from concentration on the facts relevant to the specific controversy before the court. For example, a jury is protected from hearsay evidence, i.e., testimony about facts of which the person testifying does not have personal knowledge.

Whether the responsibility for finding facts is placed on jury or judge, it is possible to be very skeptical about the typical trial as an instrument for fact finding. A lawyer may say that he is trying to bring out the truth in court, but what he is usually doing is to bring out only that evidence which will support his side of the controversy. The theory is that if each side follows this self-serving strategy, the truth will emerge. But it is only too clear that this result is often not achieved. It is significant that the judicial fact-finding process, a highly ritualized trial by battle of wits, is not used in any other area of human activity—in science, in scholarship, in business—where there is need to determine facts or to verify data. This suggests that the trial type of procedure is retained, in part at least, not because of its reliability in fact finding, but because its ritual ceremonialism is effective in winning consent for difficult societal decisions.

Private versus Public Issues

The fact-finding processes of the courts have typically been developed and employed for handling disputes involving a limited number of persons and fairly specific incidents or actions. Controversies over such matters as whether blows were struck, whether a contract was entered into, whether a speed limit was exceeded, whether certain words were uttered, whether a payment was made, whether a person was seen at a certain place and time—these are the sort of questions on which light can be thrown by having persons who were at the scene testify on what, to their direct knowledge, actually occurred.

While the adversary process presumably is best adapted to determining the facts in such "private" issues, it is even here increasingly on the defensive as more precise or scientific fact-finding methods become available. The fact of drunkenness, for example, may be established by tests of breath or blood, which courts have generally been willing to accept in evidence. On the other hand, such techniques as the lie detector or narcoanalysis have yet to win judicial acceptance. It is also worth noting that judges, in deciding on type and length of sentence in criminal cases, often make use of information secured entirely outside the protection of the adversary process.

Contrasting with these cases involving facts about individual action are the cases dealing with entire classes or groups, where the subject of controversy is the application or validity of social or economic legislation aimed at establishing social controls over conduct, or where public policies are attacked in court as violative of constitutional standards. In such disputes, the facts to be found often concern attitudes or opinions or social practices or economic conditions. When courts must find facts of such breadth, the typical practice of relying on testimony from the mouths of eyewitnesses or participants becomes inadequate or inappropriate. Can the supplying of information which a judge needs to make a wise decision in these areas be left to the litigants? It seems that different kinds of practices with respect to evidence—in fact, different kinds of evidence— must be available if judges are to decide such issues intelligently.

Judicial Notice and Judicial Research

To some degree the facts a judge needs to orient himself for a decision involving broad social issues may be supplied by the judge himself, through the process of "judicial notice." The practice of taking judicial notice of certain facts is long-established, but has operated characteristically within fairly narrow limits. The Model Code of Evidence of the American Law Institute provides that a judge may on his own motion take judicial notice, among other things, of "specific facts so notorious as not to be the subject of reasonable dispute, and . . . specific facts and propositions of generalized knowledge which are capable of immediate and accurate demonstration by resort to easily accessible sources of indisputable accuracy. . . ." In *Ohio Bell Telephone Co.* v. *Public Utilities Commission* (1937) the Supreme Court said it would take judicial notice of the fact that there had been an economic depression, and that market values decline during a depression. But the precise extent of the decline was beyond the scope of judicial notice, and would have to be proved by evidence.

Beyond judicial notice, a judge may undertake to develop his background knowledge of social or economic facts by off-the-bench research, just as he would read up on the legal points at issue in a trial. Justice Frankfurter made a significant comment from the bench to counsel during the first reargument of the school segregation cases:

> Can we not take judicial notice of writing by people who competently deal with these problems? Can I not take judicial notice of Myrdal's book without having him called as a witness? . . . How to inform the judicial mind, as you know, is one of the most complicated problems. It is better to have witnesses, but I did not know that we could not read the works of competent writers.

Such judicial research is not merely a practice of the latter-day Court. Alexander Bickel has noted how inadequate Justice Brandeis generally found the briefs and arguments of counsel to be, and that consequently he treated them "as only a starting-point for investigation." James M. Beck, who as Solicitor General handled the important case of *Myers* v. *United States* (1926) for the government, wrote to Chief Justice Taft after the decision expressing amazement that Taft had found and used extensive materials not located by counsel in the case.

Social and Economic Data

Judicial notice or judicial research can go only so far, however. These sources do not replace the need for evidence. Where social or economic practices are at issue, the evidence must be in a form suited to an understanding of these practices, and presented by persons who have a special claim to expertness in such matters. For example, in *Fay* v. *New York* (1947) the issue was whether the statutory standards for selection of so-called "blue-ribbon" juries were unconstitutionally narrow. The contention was made that laborers and craftsmen were systematically excluded from these special jury panels, and that the blue-ribbon juries were more likely to convict than the regular juries. On these two issues evidence was presented in the form of statistical analyses of occupations for the entire labor force in New York, compared with the occupations represented on the blue-ribbon panels, as well as extensive studies of the conviction records of special and general juries. The Supreme Court ultimately divided 5-4 in appraising the meaning of these statistics.

Again, significant use of factual evidence on educational facilities and practices as a basis for a conclusion of law was found in *Sweatt* v. *Painter* (1950). There the Supreme Court compared the University of Texas Law School, staffed by 19 professors, and having a student body of 850, a library of 65,000 volumes, a law review, and a moot court, with the state Negro law school and its faculty of 5, its student body of 23, and its library of 16,500 volumes. On the basis of these and other factual comparisons, the Court concluded that Texas was not offering Negro law students equal educational opportunities.

The most celebrated breakthrough in American jurisprudence involving new kinds of evidence was the brief prepared by Louis D. Brandeis and presented to the Supreme Court in the 1908 case of *Muller* v. *Oregon,* where he was defending the constitutionality of a state ten-hour law for women. This brief, the usefulness of which the Court specifically acknowledged in its opinion, gathered an enormous amount of information on foreign and American laws limiting hours for women, and official reports stressing the dangers to women from long hours of labor. Such laws and opinions "may not be, technically speaking, authorities," the Court said, but "they are significant of a widespread belief that woman's physical structure, and the functions she performs in consequence thereof, justify special legislation restricting or qualifying the conditions under which she should be permitted to toil."

In the Muller case the purpose of the facts brought to the Court's attention was to demonstrate that a state legislature had a "reasonable" basis for limiting women's hours of labor, and consequently that the law was constitutional. But, as Paul Freund has pointed out, a Brandeis brief is less useful where the objective is to overturn legislation on the ground that it is *un*reasonable, since some kind of sociological or economic data can be found to support any conceivable exercise of legislative discretion.

Social Science Expertise

Experts have long been permitted to offer "opinion" evidence in courts of law, but to qualify for this role they must first establish their expertness to the satisfaction of the court. An expert on ballistics, for example, will be permitted to testify about markings on a bullet or powder burns on a body. A psychiatrist or alienist will give his opinion on the sanity of a defendant.

Interesting developments are occurring as new fields of expertise endeavor to secure judicial recognition. Particularly significant are the efforts of the newly developing social sciences to qualify their findings as evidence worthy of judicial consideration. The segregation cases supply by all odds the most important recent illustration of the problems in attempting to present social science evidence in court. During the trial of the South Carolina case, *Briggs* v. *Elliott,* plaintiffs sought to present a political scientist to testify concerning the effects of segregation in the development of citizenship. The following colloquy took place:

> Judge Parker: "It seems to me that any lawyer or any man who has any experience in government would be just as well qualified as he would to express an opinion on that. He is not a scientist in the field of education. . . . Do you seriously contend he is qualified to testify as an educational expert? What do you say about that Mr. Marshall?"
>
> Mr. Marshall: ". . . we have been trying to . . . present as many experts in the field with as many different reasons why we consider that segregation in and of itself is injurious. . . ."

Judge Parker: "Are you going to offer any more witnesses along this line?"

Mr. Marshall: "No, sir. The other witnesses are *real* scientists."

Judge Parker: "Well, I'll take it for what it's worth. Go ahead."

In the subsequent oral argument before the Supreme Court, Justice Frankfurter expressed what must be a common judicial concern over the weight to be given to social science evidence. He said:

I do not mean that I disrespect it. I simply know its character. It can be a very different thing from, as I say, things that are weighed and measured and are fungible. We are dealing here with very subtle things, very subtle testimony.

Evidence on Community Standards

Prosecutions for obscenity offer a difficult problem for courts in determining what standards of judgment to apply. The test for obscenity, as stated by Justice Brennan in *Roth* v. *United States* (1957), is "whether to the average person, applying contemporary community standards, the dominant theme of the material taken as a whole appeals to prurient interest." But how does a court determine what are "contemporary community standards"? If a jury trial is involved, the members of the jury may themselves be regarded as a satisfactory cross-section of the community. It is customary in such cases for literary critics to express their opinions as experts on these matters, but efforts to present psychiatric or sociological experts to testify on the possible effect of alleged obscene publications have had a mixed reception.

In *Smith* v. *California* (1959), involving prosecution of the proprietor of a book store for having obscene books in his store, the trial judge blocked every effort made by the defendant to introduce evidence bearing on community standards. While the conviction was overturned by the Supreme Court on other grounds, Justice Frankfurter also thought that this refusal to permit experts to testify was a denial of due process. He wrote: "There is no external measuring rod for obscenity. Neither, on the other hand, is its ascertainment a merely subjective reflection of the taste or moral outlook of individual jurors or individual judges." Since the fact of obscenity depends upon community standards, a person charged with offering such material for sale has a right to enlighten the judgment of the tribunal, be it the jury or as in this case the judge, regarding the prevailing literary and moral community standards and to do so through qualified experts . . . community standards or the psychological or physiological consequences of questioned literature can as a matter of fact hardly be established except through experts.

Appellate judges in reviewing obscenity convictions must of necessity bring their own judgments to bear. Justice Harlan, dissenting in *Roth* v. *United States* (1957), wrote: "Many juries might find that Joyce's 'Ulysses' or Boccaccio's 'Decameron' was obscene, and yet the conviction of a defendant for selling either book would raise, for me, the gravest constitutional problems, for no such verdict could convince me, without more, that these books are 'utterly without redeeming social importance.' . . ."

When censorship cases involving books or motion pictures come before appellate courts, the judges customarily read the books or attend private showings of the movies. But when the movie, "Lady Chatterley's Lover," came before the Supreme Court in *Kingsley International Pictures Corp.* v. *Regents* (1959), Justice Black refused to see the picture. He believed that Supreme Court justices could have no standards other than their own private views on morality for deciding whether a picture could be shown, and he could not reconcile such uncertainty with the rule of law. He solved his problem by holding that censorship was unconstitutional on its face, thus avoiding the necessity of passing on the particular item attacked.

Where community opinion is relevant to a court's decision, one obvious method of securing evidence on the point would be by taking an opinion poll. These polls have gained a considerable acceptance in the fields of market analysis and voting studies. As for use in court, they have been accepted in evidence in a number of cases, but their status still remains questionable.

SELECTED REFERENCES

Botein, Bernard, "The Future of the Judicial Process," 15 *Record of the Association of the Bar of the City of New York* 152 (1960).

Davis, Kenneth C., "An Approach to Problems of Evidence in the Administrative Process," 55 *Harvard Law Review* 364 (1942).

——, "Judicial Notice," 55 *Columbia Law Review* 945 (1955).

Frank, Jerome, *Courts on Trial* (Princeton: Princeton University Press, 1950), Chs. 3–9, 15.

Garfinkel, Herbert, "Social Science Evidence and the School Segregation Cases," 21 *Journal of Politics* 37 (1959).

Greenberg, Jack, "Social Scientists Take the Stand," 54 *Michigan Law Review* 953 (1956).

Note, "Public Opinion Surveys as Evidence," 66 *Harvard Law Review* 498 (1952).

Silving, Helen, "Testing of the Unconscious in Criminal Cases," 69 *Harvard Law Review* 683 (1956).

Sorensen, Robert C. and Theodore C. Sorensen, "The Admissibility and Use of Opinion Research Evidence," 28 *New York University Law Quarterly Review* 1213 (1953).

Waterbury, Lester E., "Opinion Surveys in Civil Litigation," 17 *Public Opinion Quarterly* 71 (1953).

Wyzanski, Charles E., Jr., "A Trial Judge's Freedom and Responsibility," 65 *Harvard Law Review* 1281 (1952).

1.   *"The District Court gives more scope to a judge's initiative and discretion."*

THE IMPORTANCE OF THE TRIAL JUDGE   *Charles E. Wyzanski, Jr.**

Dear Lev:

I AM DEEPLY appreciative of your suggestion that my name be presented to the President and the Attorney General for their consideration whether to nominate me as a judge of the United States Court of Appeals for the First Circuit. . . . That you regard me as worthy of that high office is a great compliment. And were I to be appointed to a judgeship in that Court, I should regard it as both an honor and an opportunity for public service.

Yet I am persuaded that it is in both the public interest and my interest for me to decline to allow my name to be considered for the United States Court of Appeals. . . .

The District Court for the District of Massachusetts seems to me to offer at least as wide a field for judicial service as the Court of Appeals for the First Circuit. The District Court gives more scope to a judge's initiative and discretion. His width of choice in sentencing defendants is the classic example. But there are many other instances. In civil litigation a District Judge has a chance to help the lawyers frame the issues and develop the facts so that there may be a meaningful and complete record. He may innovate procedures promoting fairness, simplification, economy, and expedition. By instructions to juries and, in appropriate cases, by comments on the evidence he may help the jurors better to understand their high civic function. He is a teacher of parties, witnesses, petitioners for naturalization, and even casual visitors to his court. His conduct of a trial may fashion and sustain the moral principles of the community. More even than the rules of constitutional, statutory, and common law he applies, his character and

Letter to Senator Leverett Saltonstall, January 12, 1959.
* United States District Judge for the District of Massachusetts, 1942–.

personal distinction, open to daily inspection in his courtroom, constitute the guarantees of due process.

Admittedly, the Court of Appeals stands higher than the District Courts in the judicial hierarchy, and Congress by attaching a larger compensation to the office of Circuit Judge has expressed its view of the relative importance of the two courts. Yet not all informed persons would concur in that evaluation. My revered former chief, Judge Augustus N. Hand, always spoke of his service in the District Court as being more interesting as well as more revealing of his qualities, and more enjoyable, than his service in the Court of Appeals. . . .

Although less spectacular litigation may ordinarily be carried from the District Court to the Court of Appeals, statistics will show how small a percentage of a reasonably good trial judge's decrees are in fact appealed. The District Judge so often has the last word. Even where he does not, heed is given to his estimates of credibility, his determination of the facts, his discretion in framing or denying relief upon the facts he found. . . .

The District Judge is in more direct relation than is the judge of the Court of Appeals to the bar and its problems. It is within the proper function of a District Court not merely by rules and decisions, but by an informed, intelligent, and energetic handling of his calendar to effectuate prompt as well as unbiased justice. It is the vigor of the District Court more than the action of the Court of Appeals which governs the number of cases which are ripe for appeal, and the time between the beginning of an action and a final judgment in an appellate court. And, paradoxically, it is not infrequently the alertness of the District Judge and his willingness to help counsel develop uncertain points of law (even though the development of such points inevitably increases the risks of error by the trial judge and of reversal by the appellate court) which make a case significant in the progress of the law when it reaches a court of last resort.

While it may well be true that the highest *office* for a judge is to sit in judgment on other judges' errors, it is perhaps a more challenging *task* to seek, from minute to minute, to avoid one's own errors. And the zest of that task is enhanced by the necessity of reacting orally, instead of after the reflection permitted under the appellate judge's uninterrupted schedule of reading and writing.

I realize that the trial judge lacks the opportunity to benefit from the collegiate discussion open to an appellate judge. His ties with his brethren are less intimate. Consequently, he runs the perils of excessive individualism. Few there are who can gently chide him on his foibles, remind him of the grace of manners, or warn against the nigh universal sin of pride.

Yet perhaps the trial judge's relative loneliness brings him closer to the tragic plight of man. Was not Wallace Stevens speaking for the trial judge when he wrote

> "Life consists
> Of propositions about life. The human
> Reverie is a solitude in which
> We compose these propositions, torn by dreams"? . . .

Sincerely,
Charles E. Wyzanski, Jr.

> "*Our present trial method is . . . the equivalent of throwing pepper in the eyes of a surgeon when he is performing an operation.*"

2.

THE "FIGHT" THEORY VERSUS THE "TRUTH" THEORY *Jerome Frank**

WHEN WE say that present-day trial methods are "rational," presumably we mean this: The men who compose our trial courts, judges and juries, in each law-suit conduct an intelligent inquiry into all the practically available evidence, in order to ascertain, as near as may be, the truth about the facts of that suit. That might be called the "investigatory" or "truth" method of trying cases. Such a method can yield no more than a guess, nevertheless an educated guess.

Courts on Trial: Myth and Reality in American Justice (Princeton: Princeton University Press, 1950), pp. 80–85. Copyright 1950 Jerome Frank. Reprinted with permission of the publisher.
* Judge, U.S. Court of Appeals for the 2d Circuit, 1941–57.

The success of such a method is conditioned by at least these two factors: (1) The judicial inquirers, trial judges or juries, may not obtain all the important evidence. (2) The judicial inquirers may not be competent to conduct such an inquiry. Let us, for the time being, assume that the second condition is met—i.e., that we have competent inquirers—and ask whether we so conduct trials as to satisfy the first condition, i.e., the procuring of all the practically available important evidence.

The answer to that question casts doubt on whether our trial courts do use the "investigatory" or "truth" method. Our mode of trials is commonly known as "contentious" or "adversary." It is based on what I would call the "fight" theory, a theory which derives from the origin of trials as substitutes for private out-of-court brawls.

Many lawyers maintain that the "fight" theory and the "truth" theory coincide. They think that the best way for a court to discover the facts in a suit is to have each side strive as hard as it can, in a keenly partisan spirit, to bring to the court's attention the evidence favorable to that side. Macaulay said that we obtain the fairest decision "when two men argue, as unfairly as possible, on opposite sides," for then "it is certain that no important consideration will altogether escape notice."

Unquestionably that view contains a core of good sense. The zealously partisan lawyers sometimes do bring into court evidence which, in a dispassionate inquiry, might be overlooked. Apart from the fact element of the case, the opposed lawyers also illuminate for the court niceties of the legal rules which the judge might otherwise not perceive. The "fight" theory, therefore, has invaluable qualities with which we cannot afford to dispense.

But frequently the partisanship of the opposing lawyers blocks the uncovering of vital evidence or leads to a presentation of vital testimony in a way that distorts it. I shall attempt to show you that we have allowed the fighting spirit to become dangerously excessive.

This is perhaps most obvious in the handling of witnesses. Suppose a trial were fundamentally a truth-inquiry. Then, recognizing the inherent fallibilities of witnesses, we would do all we could to remove the causes of their errors when testifying. Recognizing also the importance of witnesses' demeanor as clues to their reliability, we would do

our best to make sure that they testify in circumstances most conducive to a revealing observation of that demeanor by the trial judge or
jury. In our contentious trial practice, we do almost the exact opposite.

No businessman, before deciding to build a new plant, no general
before launching an attack, would think of obtaining information on
which to base his judgment by putting his informants through the
bewildering experience of witnesses at a trial. "The novelty of the
situation," wrote a judge, "the agitation and hurry which accompanies
it, the cajolery or intimidation to which the witness may be subjected,
the want of questions calculated to excite those recollections which
might clear up every difficulty, and the confusion of cross-examination
. . . may give rise to important errors and omissions." "In the court
they stand as strangers," wrote another judge of witnesses, "surrounded
with unfamiliar circumstances giving rise to an embarrassment known
only to themselves."

In a book by Henry Taft . . . we are told: "Counsel and court find it
necessary through examination and instruction to induce a witness to
abandon for an hour or two his habitual method of thought and expression, and conform to the rigid ceremonialism of court procedure.
It is not strange that frequently truthful witnesses are . . . misunderstood, that they nervously react in such a way as to create the impression that they are either evading or intentionally falsifying. . . . An
honest witness testifies on direct examination. He answers questions
promptly and candidly and makes a good impression. On cross-examination, his attitude changes. He suspects that traps are being laid for
him. He hesitates; he ponders the answer to a simple question; he
seems to 'spar' for time by asking that questions be repeated; perhaps
he protests that counsel is not fair; he may even appeal to the court
for protection. Altogether the contrast with his attitude on direct
examination is obvious; and he creates the impression that he is
evading or withholding." Yet on testimony thus elicited courts every
day reach decisions affecting the lives and fortunes of citizens.

What is the role of the lawyers in bringing the evidence before the
trial court? . . . The lawyer considers it his duty to create a false impression, if he can, of any witness who gives such testimony. If such
a witness happens to be timid, frightened by the unfamiliarity of courtroom ways, the lawyer, in his cross-examination, plays on that weak-

ness, in order to confuse the witness and make it appear that he is concealing significant facts. Longenecker, in his book *Hints on the Trial of a Law Suit* . . . in writing of the "truthful, honest, over-cautious" witness, tells how "a skilful advocate by a rapid cross-examination may ruin the testimony of such a witness." The author does not even hint any disapproval of that accomplishment. Longenecker's and other similar books recommend that a lawyer try to prod an irritable but honest "adverse" witness into displaying his undesirable characteristics in their most unpleasant form, in order to discredit him with the judge or jury. . . . "And thus," adds Taft, "it may happen that not only is the value of his testimony lost, but the side which produces him suffers for seeking aid from such a source"—although, I would add, that may be the only source of evidence of a fact on which the decision will turn.

"An intimidating manner in putting questions," writes Wigmore, "may so coerce or disconcert the witness that his answers do not represent his actual knowledge on the subject. So also, questions which in form or subject cause embarrassment, shame or anger in the witness may unfairly lead him to such demeanor or utterances that the impression produced by his statements does not do justice to its real testimonial value." . . . Sir Frederic Eggleston recently said that . . . "the terrors of cross-examination are such that a party can often force a settlement by letting it be known that a certain . . . counsel has been retained."

The lawyer not only seeks to discredit adverse witnesses but also to hide the defects of witnesses who testify favorably to his client. If, when interviewing such a witness before trial, the lawyer notes that the witness has mannerisms, demeanor-traits, which might discredit him, the lawyer teaches him how to cover up those traits when testifying: He educates the irritable witness to conceal his irritability, the cocksure witness to subdue his cocksureness. In that way, the trial court is denied the benefit of observing the witness's actual normal demeanor, and thus prevented from sizing up the witness accurately.

Lawyers freely boast of their success with these tactics. They boast also of such devices as these: If an "adverse," honest witness, on cross-examination, makes seemingly inconsistent statements, the cross-examiner tries to keep the witness from explaining away the apparent inconsistencies. "When," writes Tracy, counseling trial lawyers, in a much-praised book, "by your cross-examination, you have caught the witness in an inconsistency, the next question that will immediately come to your lips is, 'Now, let's hear you explain.' Don't ask it, for he may explain and, if he does, your point will have been lost. If you have conducted your cross-examination properly (which includes interestingly), the jury will have seen the inconsistency and it will have made the proper impression on their minds. If, on re-direct examination the witness does explain, the explanation will have come later in the case and at the request of the counsel who originally called the witness and the jury will be much more likely to look askance at the explanation than if it were made during your cross-examination." Tracy adds, "Be careful in your questions on cross-examination not to open a door that you have every reason to wish kept closed." That is, don't let in any reliable evidence, hurtful to your side, which would help the trial court to arrive at the truth.

"In cross-examination," writes Eggleston, "the main preoccupation of counsel is to avoid introducing evidence, or giving an opening to it, which will harm his case. The most painful thing for an experienced practitioner . . . is to hear a junior counsel laboriously bring out in cross-examination of a witness all the truth which the counsel who called him could not" bring out "and which it was the junior's duty as an advocate to conceal." A lawyer, if possible, will not ask a witness to testify who, on cross-examination, might testify to true facts helpful to his opponent.

Nor, usually, will a lawyer concede the existence of any facts if they are inimical to his client and he thinks they cannot be proved by his adversary. If, to the lawyer's knowledge, a witness has testified inaccurately but favorably to the lawyer's client, the lawyer will attempt to hinder cross-examination that would expose the inaccuracy. He puts in testimony which surprises his adversary who, caught unawares, has not time to seek out, interview, and summon witnesses who would rebut the surprise testimony. . . .

These, and other like techniques, you will find unashamedly described in the many manuals on trial tactics written by and for eminently reputable trial lawyers. The purpose of these tactics—often effective—is to prevent the trial judge or jury from correctly evaluating the trustworthiness of witnesses and to shut out evidence the trial court ought to receive in order to approximate the truth.

In short, the lawyer aims at victory, at winning in the fight, not at aiding the court to discover the facts. He does not want the trial court to reach a sound educated guess, if it is likely to be contrary to his client's interests. Our present trial method is thus the equivalent of throwing pepper in the eyes of a surgeon when he is performing an operation. . . .

> ". . . It is not unfair to assume that the summarizing, emphasizing, and relating of the general to the specific by eminent experts illuminated the issues and perhaps informed . . . members of the bench whose interests might not have led them earlier to acquire such information."

3.

SOCIAL SCIENTISTS TAKE THE STAND   *Jack Greenberg**

. . . A RECENT example of the use of social science testimony for a conventional purpose is found in the [New Jersey] church-state case, *Tudor v. Board of Education,* in which Chief Justice Vanderbilt's opinion quotes extensively from the testimony of a social psychologist, an educational sociologist and an educator. The issue was whether the First Amendment to the federal Constitution (as incorporated into the Fourteenth) and Article I, paragraph 4 of the New Jersey Constitution forbade distribution of the Gideon Bible in New Jersey public schools. The Bibles had been given to the schools free of charge. Each child was asked to sign a card requesting one . . . the Supreme Court of New Jersey treated the question of coerciveness as a factual one. The school board urged that accepting a Bible was optional, therefore the program did not interfere with the free exercise of religion. But, the opinion retorted, this argument ignores reality. The testimony of the social scientists was quoted to show that the dis-

54 *Michigan Law Review* 953 (1956). Copyright 1956 Michigan Law Review. Reprinted and abridged with permission.
* Assistant Counsel, NAACP Legal Defense and Educational Fund.

Judicial Reasoning

tribution system tended, by psychological pressures, to compel children to accept Bibles. Quoted testimony also stated that the method of distribution created divisive tensions among children. This finding appears to be irrelevant, but it apparently contributed to the result as somewhat of a policy makeweight at least.

Further illustrations of the need for this type of testimony at the fact level can be found in the censorship field. In *Parmelee v. United States,* an action to confiscate and destroy certain books entitled *Nudism in Modern Life,* the court, noting the lack of social science evidence, wrote:

> . . . perhaps the most useful definition of obscene is that presented in . . . United States v. Kennerley, i.e., that it indicates "the present critical point in the compromise between candor and shame at which the community may have arrived here and now." But when we attempt to locate that critical point in the situation of the present case, we find nothing in the record to guide us except the book itself. The question is a difficult one, as to which the expert opinion of psychologists and sociologists would seem to be helpful if not necessary. . . . Lacking such assistance in the present case, we can compensate for it in some measure by noticing, judicially, evidence which is thus available to us.

But there are cases in which such testimony has been admitted. In *State v. Scope* the defendant was indicted for obscene libel for showing the movie, "Hollywood Peep Show." A psychiatrist testified for the state that the film was apt to injure teen-agers psychologically and would tend to rouse base emotions in normal adult males. The court held the testimony admissible. . . .

But in *Commonwealth v. Isenstadt* the Massachusetts Supreme Court took another view of admissibility. The defendant was tried for violating the obscenity law by selling the book *Strange Fruit.* He attempted to introduce the testimony of a writer and teacher of literature, a child psychiatrist and a professor of theology, to show that the book would "elevate rather than corrupt morals." The testimony was excluded on the ground that it concerned "nothing more than the reaction of normal human beings" and that "there is reason to believe that a jury, being composed of men drawn from the various segments of that public, would be as good a judge of the effects as experts in literature or psychiatry, whose . . . mental reactions . . . are likely to be entirely different from those of the general public." . . .

Public opinion analysts are the social scientists who have testified, and whose testimony has been suggested, most often. . . . Recently authority has held such testimony admissible on several occasions. In one case [*United States* v. *88 Cases of Bireley's Orange Juice* (1951)] the issue was whether Bireley's Orange Beverage was "economically adulterated" in that it allegedly appeared to the average consumer to be better than it was. The Government charged that it appeared to contain a great deal of orange juice, although it contained only 6 percent orange juice and was mostly water. The Government attempted to introduce a public opinion survey of 3,539 persons to establish what people thought the Bireley product contained. There was a hearsay objection. But the court concluded that [the objection] was unfounded. . . .

The understanding of "savings bank" was an issue in an action by New York State [*Franklin National Bank of Franklin Square* v. *New York* (1954)] to restrain a national bank from using the words "savings" in its publicity. Section 258 of the New York Banking Law forbade national banks to use the word "savings." Instead they were required to use terms like "thrift account" or "special interest" account. Defendant produced a poll to show the public understanding of "savings" which showed that "savings" would attract depositors more readily than the other terms. The court reviewed the polling technique in detail and the testimony concerning it. It concluded:

> Polls, as evidence, are not controlling, of course. Many are misleading; valueless. . . .
>
> A party endeavoring to establish the public state of mind on a subject, which state of mind can not be proved except by calling as witnesses so many of the public as to render the task impracticable, should be allowed to offer evidence concerning a poll which the party maintains reveals that state of mind. The evidence offered should include calling the planners, supervisors, and workers (or some of them) as witnesses so that the court may see and hear them; they should be ready to give a complete exposition of the poll and even its results; the work sheets, reports, surveys and all documents used in or prepared

during the poll taking and those showing its results should be offered in evidence, although the court may desire to draw its own conclusions. In this trial the learned counsel for defendant advanced proof of the kind to which I have just referred. I think that the proof as to the poll should be received in evidence.

When the case reached the United States Supreme Court the poll was not mentioned in Justice Jackson's opinion for the majority, but he assumed that the word "savings" was important to defendant: ". . . they must be deemed to have the right to advertise that fact by using the *commonly understood description* which Congress has specifically selected."

However, in most cases where polls have been introduced, objection apparently was not made, so there are few direct holdings that polls are admissible. . . .

There are, of course, problems of admissibility and weight of the evidence. In all cases where an expert testifies, he must first be qualified as especially able to make the judgment he proposes to offer. Therefore, there are the problems of whether his branch of social science is sufficiently certain to warrant an authoritative opinion and whether the expert is sufficiently versed in his field. What standard should be applied? There appears to be no reason why the standard should be any different from that for experts in general. . . .

In the public opinion poll cases there are problems of admissibility generally related to the hearsay rule. In a recent criminal case in Florida, *Irvin v. State*, the Negro defendant's attorneys engaged the Elmo Roper firm to ascertain what part of the populace in the county of trial believed defendant guilty, and whether the Negro community was so intimidated that a Negro juror would fear to vote for acquittal. The poll was excluded from evidence because the poll supervisors who testified about the polling methods were not present at every interview, and the dozen interviewers who actually asked the questions did not testify concerning each of their 1,500 interviews. The Supreme Court of Florida affirmed, holding poll evidence hearsay and also questioning the competency of evidence, noting pollsters' incorrect predictions in the 1948 presidential election.

. . . Courts are apparently growing more liberal in this area, and the hearsay objection may not remain too formidable. At any rate, if a

litigant wants to use the tedious process of putting on every inter-
viewer concerning every interview, he can probably get his poll into
evidence. He will either obviate the hearsay objection, or by weight
of sheer boredom persuade his opponent to stipulate much of the
testimony.

One of the main problems connected with poll testimony is the expense. The poll taken in *Irvin v. State* cost about $8,000; the defense
could afford it only because it was paid for by the Legal Defense
Fund of the National Association for the Advancement of Colored
People. Another problem is that interviewers may not want to testify,
especially if the case is controversial. But apart from expense and inconvenience, the relative infrequency of such testimony (and social
science testimony in general) has been due to unawareness that it can
be useful. . . .

TESTIMONY TO INFLUENCE SHAPING OF JUDGE-MADE LAW

. . . Before a new court-made rule of law can be formulated it is
often necessary to know what is occurring or may occur in society. A
variety of information drawn from sociology and elsewhere, although
not usually proved, is brought to bear along with the court's concepts
of justice and welfare. Such information is generally judicially noticed,
sometimes explicitly, sometimes tacitly. Legal analysis or experience
may expose these basic assumptions; whether they are well founded
may sometimes be proved or disproved with the help of social
science. . . .

The recently demolished legal keystone of racial segregation in
education, *Plessy v. Ferguson,* held in 1896:

> . . . the underlying fallacy of the plaintiff's argument [is] . . . the
> assumption that the enforced separation of the two races stamps the
> colored race with a badge of inferiority. . . . The argument also assumes
> that social prejudices may be overcome by legislation. . . . Legislation
> is powerless to eradicate racial instincts or to abolish distinctions based
> upon physical differences. . . .

This argument was, of course, rejected by the Supreme Court on
May 17, 1954 in the school cases. And when the Court made its decision it had before it records full of testimony by social scientists

relating to the assumptions made by *Plessy*. These witnesses were called by counsel for plaintiffs in the belief that live testimony, subject to cross-examination and rebuttal, could be more pertinent and compelling than quotations from books and articles. . . .

In those cases at least twenty social scientists from institutions all over the country testified. They exhaustively analyzed school segregation from different scientific points of view, on the basis of their learning and experience, and, in some instances, examination of plaintiff children. The four trial courts which heard this testimony split in their acceptance of it, two-to-two: Delaware and Kansas finding it true (although legally irrelevant in view of *Plessy*), Virginia and South Carolina, one judge dissenting, dismissing it as unproved and irrelevant. . . .

What role did the social science testimony play in the decision of the school cases? Although some have applauded or denounced the decisions as based principally on the testimony, a reading of the decisions reveals that the Supreme Court did not refer to the testimony, nor did it affirm or reverse the findings below on the effects of segregation. Indeed, in the District of Columbia case, it made its decision on a record devoid of testimony. . . .

But did it play any role? Of course, since the opinion does not say, we must speculate. Social scientists' research during recent decades deserves much of the credit for the general recognition of segregation's harm. Much of the testimony could only recapitulate what is already known, although in terms of *these* cases. But it is not unfair to assume that the summarizing, emphasizing, and relating of the general to the specific by eminent experts illuminated the issues and perhaps informed for the first time one or more members of the bench whose interests might not have led them earlier to acquire such information. Combined with a number of other factors the testimony undoubtedly contributed to the final result. . . .

Apart from admissibility, there is the problem of weight. Social science often deals with emotional and controversial areas of life. Often it may be difficult for the court, and for the social scientists, to separate uncertain controversy from positive fact finding. . . . This uncertainty is compounded by distrust of experts in general . . . they are frequently in conflict, often argumentative, and expensive. Besides all this, most judges come from a generation less versed in, and less sympathetic to, the newer scientific disciplines than the younger lawyers. Interestingly, when social scientists' conclusions have been accepted . . . some courts have written that they appeared correct apart from the evidence. . . .

As to the trustworthiness, the [school segregation] testimony was subjected to cross-examination and rebuttal by very capable defense counsel who, after the trial of the first school case, could not have been surprised. And even experts for the defense conceded it to be essentially correct. This is not to say that it had the precision of the physical sciences; it did not. Perhaps even, in time, some of the evidence upon which the testimony was based will, as happens in all sciences, be shown to have been wrong or insufficient. But it told us a very great deal about what is known of segregation's harm. True, the Constitution should not be wedded to any social science any more than to a school of economics. On the other hand, constitutional interpretation should consider all relevant knowledge. The Constitution turned on a moral judgment; but moral judgments are generated by awareness of facts. . . .

4.
"The problem with which we have here attempted to deal is admittedly on the frontiers of scientific knowledge."

THE EFFECTS OF SEGREGATION AND THE CONSEQUENCES OF DESEGREGATION: A SOCIAL SCIENCE STATEMENT

I

THE PROBLEM of the segregation of racial and ethnic groups constitutes one of the major problems facing the American people today. It seems desirable, therefore, to summarize the contri-

This statement, filed as an appendix to one of the NAACP's briefs in the school segregation cases, was drafted and signed by thirty-two prominent sociologists, anthropologists, psychologists, and psychiatrists who had worked and written in the field of race relations. It is reprinted at 37 *Minnesota Law Review* 427 (1953). Bibliographical references have been omitted.

butions which contemporary social science can make toward its resolution. There are, of course, moral and legal issues involved with
respect to which the signers of the present statement cannot speak
with any special authority and which must be taken into account in
the solution of the problem. There are, however, also factual issues
involved with respect to which certain conclusions seem to be justified
on the basis of the available scientific evidence. It is with these issues
only that this paper is concerned. . . .

In dealing with the question of the effects of segregation, it must be
recognized that these effects do not take place in a vacuum, but in a
social context. The segregation of Negroes and of other groups in the
United States takes place in a social milieu in which "race" prejudice
and discrimination exist. It is questionable in the view of some students of the problem whether it is possible to have segregation without substantial discrimination. Myrdal states: "Segregation . . . is
financially possible and, indeed, a device of economy only as it is combined with substantial discrimination." . . . The imbeddedness of segregation in such a context makes it difficult to disentangle the effects
of segregation *per se* from the effects of the context. . . .

II

At the recent Mid-century White House Conference on Children
and Youth, a fact-finding report on the effects of prejudice, discrimination and segregation on the personality development of children was
prepared as a basis for some of the deliberations. This report . . .
highlighted the fact that segregation, prejudices and discriminations,
and their social concomitants potentially damage the personality of all
children—the children of the majority group in a somewhat different
way than the more obviously damaged children of the minority group.

The report indicates that as minority group children learn the inferior status to which they are assigned . . . they often react with feelings of inferiority and a sense of personal humiliation. Many of them
become confused about their own personal worth. On the one hand,
like all other human beings they require a sense of personal dignity;
on the other hand, almost nowhere in the larger society do they find
their own dignity as human beings respected by others. Under these

conditions, the minority group child is thrown into a conflict with regard to his feelings about himself and his group. He wonders whether his group and he himself are worthy of no more respect than they receive. This conflict and confusion leads to self-hatred and rejection of his own group. . . .

. . . Not every child, of course, reacts with the same patterns of behavior. The particular pattern depends upon many interrelated factors. . . . Some children, usually of the lower socio-economic classes, may react by overt aggressions and hostility directed toward their own group or members of the dominant groups. Anti-social and delinquent behavior may often be interpreted as reactions to these racial frustrations. These reactions are self-destructive in that the larger society not only punishes those who commit them, but often interprets such aggressive and anti-social behavior as justification for continuing prejudice and segregation.

Middle class and upper class minority group children are likely to react to their racial frustrations and conflicts by withdrawal and submissive behavior. Or, they may react with compensatory and rigid conformity to the prevailing middle class values and standards and an aggressive determination to succeed in these terms in spite of the handicap of their minority status.

The report indicates that minority group children of all social and economic classes often react with a generally defeatist attitude and a lowering of personal ambitions. This, for example, is reflected in a lowering of pupil morale and a depression of the educational aspiration level among minority group children in segregated schools. In producing such effects, segregated schools impair the ability of the child to profit from the educational opportunities provided him. . . .

With reference to the impact of segregation and its concomitants on children of the majority group, the report indicates that the effects are somewhat more obscure. . . . The culture permits and, at times, encourages them to direct their feelings of hostility and aggression against whole groups of people the members of which are perceived as weaker than themselves. They often develop patterns of guilt feelings, rationalizations and other mechanisms which they must use in an attempt to protect themselves from recognizing the essential injustice of their unrealistic fears and hatreds of minority groups.

The report indicates further that confusion, conflict, moral cynicism, and disrespect for authority may arise in majority group children as a consequence of being taught the moral, religious and democratic principles of the brotherhood of man and the importance of justice and fair play by the same persons and institutions who, in their support of racial segregation and related practices, seem to be acting in a prejudiced and discriminatory manner. Some individuals may attempt to resolve this conflict by intensifying their hostility toward the minority group. Others may react by guilt feelings which are not necessarily reflected in more humane attitudes toward the minority group. Still others react by developing an unwholesome, rigid, and uncritical idealization of all authority figures—their parents, strong political and economic leaders. . . .

Conclusions similar to those reached by the Mid-century White House Conference Report have been stated by other social scientists who have concerned themselves with this problem. The following are some examples of these conclusions:

Segregation imposes upon individuals a distorted sense of social reality.

Segregation leads to a blockage in the communications and interaction between the two groups. Such blockages tend to increase mutual suspicion, distrust and hostility.

Segregation not only perpetuates rigid stereotypes and reinforces negative attitudes toward members of the other group, but also leads to the development of a social climate within which violent outbreaks of racial tensions are likely to occur. . . .

On the basis of this general fund of knowledge, it seems likely that feelings of inferiority and doubts about personal worth are attributable to living in an underprivileged environment only insofar as the latter is itself perceived as an indicator of low social status and as a symbol of inferiority. In other words, one of the important determinants in producing such feelings is the awareness of social status difference. While there are many other factors that serve as reminders of the differences in social status, there can be little doubt that the fact of enforced segregation is a major factor.

This seems to be true for the following reasons among others: (1) because enforced segregation results from the decision of the majority group without the consent of the segregated and is commonly so perceived; and (2) because historically segregation patterns in the United States were developed on the assumption of the inferiority of the segregated.

In addition, enforced segregation gives official recognition and sanction to these other factors of the social complex, and thereby enhances the effects of the latter in creating the awareness of social status differences and feelings of inferiority. The child who, for example, is compelled to attend a segregated school may be able to cope with ordinary expressions of prejudice by regarding the prejudiced person as evil or misguided; but he cannot readily cope with symbols of authority, the full force of the authority of the State—the school or the school board, in this instance—in the same manner. Given both the ordinary expression of prejudice and the school's policy of segregation, the former takes on greater force and seemingly becomes an official expression of the latter.

Not all of the psychological traits which are commonly observed in the social complex under discussion can be related so directly to the awareness of status differences—which in turn is, as we have already noted, materially contributed to by the practices of segregation. Thus, the low level of aspiration and defeatism so commonly observed in segregated groups is undoubtedly related to the level of self-evaluation: but it is also, in some measure, related among other things to one's expectations with regard to opportunities for achievement and, having achieved, to the opportunities for making use of these achievements. Similarly, the hypersensitivity and anxiety displayed by many minority group children about their relations with the larger society probably reflects their awareness of status differences; but it may also be influenced by the relative absence of opportunities for equal status contact which would provide correctives for prevailing unrealistic stereotypes.

The preceding view is consistent with the opinion stated by a large majority (90%) of social scientists who replied to a questionnaire concerning the probable effects of enforced segregation under conditions of equal facilities. This opinion was that, regardless of the facilities which are provided, enforced segregation is psychologically detrimental to the members of the segregated group. . . .

With reference to the probable effects of segregation under conditions of equal facilities on majority group members, many of the social scientists who responded to the poll . . . felt that the evidence is less convincing than with regard to the probable effects of such segregation on minority group members, and the effects are possibly less widespread. Nonetheless, more than 80% stated it as their opinion that the effects of such segregation are psychologically detrimental to the majority group members. . . .

III

Segregation is at present a social reality. Questions may be raised, therefore, as to what are the likely consequences of desegregation. . . .

The available scientific evidence indicates that much, perhaps all, of the observable differences among various racial and national groups may be adequately explained in terms of environmental differences. It has been found, for instance, that the differences between the average intelligence test scores of Negro and white children decrease, and the overlap of the distribution increases, proportionately to the number of years that the Negro children have lived in the North. Related studies have shown that this change cannot be explained by the hypothesis of selective migration. It seems clear, therefore, that fears based on the assumption of innate racial differences in intelligence are not well founded.

It may also be noted in passing that the argument regarding the intellectual inferiority of one group as compared to another is, as applied to schools, essentially an argument for homogeneous groupings of children by intelligence rather than by race. Since even those who believe that there are innate differences between Negroes and whites in America in average intelligence grant that considerable overlap between the two groups exists, it would follow that it may be expedient to group together the superior whites and Negroes, the average whites and Negroes, and so on. . . .

A second problem that comes up in an evaluation of the possible consequences of desegregation involves the question of whether segregation prevents or stimulates interracial tension and conflict and the corollary question of whether desegregation has one or the other effect.

The most direct evidence available on this problem comes from observations and systematic study of instances in which desegregation has occurred. Comprehensive reviews of such instances clearly establish the fact that desegregation has been carried out successfully in a variety of situations although outbreaks of violence had been commonly predicted. Extensive desegregation has taken place without major incidents in the armed services in both Northern and Southern installations and involving officers and enlisted men from all parts of the country, including the South. Similar changes have been noted in housing and industry. During the last war, many factories both in the North and South hired Negroes on a nonsegregated, nondiscriminatory basis. While a few strikes occurred, refusal by management and unions to yield quelled all strikes within a few days.

Relevant to this general problem is a comprehensive study of urban race riots which found that race riots occurred in segregated neighborhoods, whereas there was no violence in sections of the city where the two races lived, worked and attended school together.

Under certain circumstances desegregation not only proceeds without major difficulties, but has been observed to lead to the emergence of more favorable attitudes and friendlier relations between races. . . .

IV

The problem with which we have here attempted to deal is admittedly on the frontiers of scientific knowledge. Inevitably, there must be some differences of opinion among us concerning the conclusiveness of certain items of evidence, and concerning the particular choice of words and placement of emphasis in the preceding statement. We are nonetheless in agreement that this statement is substantially correct and justified by the evidence, and the differences among us, if any, are of a relatively minor order and would not materially influence the preceding conclusions.

5.   *". . . the behavioral sciences are so very young . . ."*

SCIENCE OR COMMON SENSE?   *Edmond Cahn**

A DANGEROUS MYTH.—In the Virginia [School Segrega-
tion] case and to a lesser extent in the other litigations, various
psychiatrists, psychologists, and social scientists gave expert testimony
concerning the harmful effects of segregation on Negro school children. In addition, some of appellants' witnesses prepared an elaborate
statement on the subject, which, signed by a total of thirty-two experts, was submitted to the Supreme Court as an appendix to appellants' brief. In the months since the utterance of the *Brown* and
Bolling opinions, the impression has grown that the outcome, either
entirely or in major part, was caused by the testimony and opinions
of the scientists, and a genuine danger has arisen that even lawyers
and judges may begin to entertain this belief. The word "danger" is
used advisedly, because I would not have the constitutional rights of
Negroes—or of other Americans—rest on any such flimsy foundation
as some of the scientific demonstrations in these records.

The moral factors involved in racial segregation are not new—like
the science of social psychology—but exceedingly ancient. What, after
all, is the most elementary and conspicuous fact about a primitive
community if not the physical proximity of human beings mingling
together? When the members of a community decide to exclude one
of their number from the group life without killing him outright,
what else can they do but force him to remove himself physically (as
in the case of Cain), ostracize him for what they consider the general
welfare (as the Athenians did), banish him from the cluster of community dwellings (as in outbreaks of leprosy or other plague), assign
him a fixed area or ghetto to occupy (as with the Jews in medieval
times), or lock him in a penitentiary (as we do with convicted crim-

"Jurisprudence," 30 *New York University Law Review* 150 (1955); also in *1954
Annual Survey of American Law* (New York: New York University School of Law,
1955), pp. 809–828. Copyright 1955 New York University School of Law. Reprinted with permission.

* Professor of Law, New York University.

inals)? Hardly anyone has been hypocritical enough to contend that no stigma or loss of status attaches to these forms of physical separation. Segregation does involve stigma; the community knows it does. It knows full well that if "Stone walls do not a prison make nor iron bars a cage," they certainly do hamper a person's freedom to move about and consort with whom he pleases. Possibly, as the poet said, the walls can be understood as a "hermitage" or retreat or monastery, but only for those who choose them without being compelled by the social group.

There are people who argue, sometimes quite sincerely, that racial segregation is not *intended* to humiliate or stigmatize. On first impression, the argument seems to have some slight mitigative value, for surely a deliberate insult is liable to cut deeper than one inflicted out of mere crudeness or insensibility. But the mitigation comes too late. An excuse that one did not intend to injure does not stand much chance of reception when the offender, having been informed of the damage he has done, continues and persists in the same old callous insults. As is observed in the ancient Babylonian Talmud, to shame and degrade a fellow-creature is to commit a kind of psychic mayhem upon him. Like an assailant's knife, humiliation slashes his self-respect and human dignity. He grows pale, the blood rushes from his face just as though it had been shed. That is why we are accustomed to say he feels "wounded."

Moreover, if affronts are repeated often enough, they may ultimately injure the victim's backbone. We hear there are American Negroes who protest they do not feel insulted by racially segregated public schools. If there are any such Negroes, then they are the ones who have been injured most grievously of all, because segregation has shattered their spines and deprived them of self-respect.

So one speaks in terms of the most familiar and universally accepted standards of right and wrong when one remarks (1) that racial segregation under government auspices inevitably inflicts humiliation, and (2) that official humiliation of innocent, law-abiding citizens is psychologically injurious and morally evil. Mr. Justice Harlan and many other Americans with responsive consciences recognized these simple, elementary propositions before, during, and after the rise of "separate but equal." For at least twenty years, hardly any cultivated person has questioned that segregation is cruel to Negro school children. The cruelty is obvious and evident. Fortunately, it is so very obvious that the Justices of the Supreme Court could see it and act on it even after reading the labored attempts by plaintiffs' experts to demonstrate it "scientifically."

Claims and Facts.—When scientists set out to prove a fact that most of mankind already acknowledges, they may provide a rather bizarre spectacle. Fifty years ago, certain biologists who were engaged in just this sort of enterprise, provoked George Bernard Shaw to denounce their "solemnly offering us as epoch-making discoveries their demonstrations that dogs get weaker and die if you give them no food; that intense pain makes mice sweat; and that if you cut off a dog's leg the three-legged dog will have a four-legged puppy." Then Mr. Shaw called the scientists a number of fearful names (beginning with "dolts" and "blackguards"), none of which would be remotely applicable to the psychologists and psychiatrists who testified in the desegregation cases. So far as I can judge, all of these are fine, intelligent, dedicated scholars. Yet one can honor them as they deserve without swallowing their claims.

Professor Kenneth B. Clark of the psychology department of City College acted as general social science consultant to the NAACP legal staff and served as liaison between the lawyers and the scientists. His endeavors having been long and arduous, perhaps it was natural that he should exaggerate whatever the experts contributed to the case. In an article written while the country was waiting for the Supreme Court's decisions, he asserted, "*Proof* of the arguments that segregation itself is inequality and that state imposed racial segregation inflicts injuries upon the Negro *had to come from the social psychologists and other social scientists.*" (Emphasis supplied.)

When Professor Clark wrote thus, he could not know that Chief Justice Warren's opinions would not mention either the testimony of the expert witnesses or the submitted statement of the thirty-two scientists. The Chief Justice cushioned the blow to some extent by citing certain professional publications of the psychological experts in a footnote, alluding to them graciously as "modern authority." In view of their devoted efforts to defeat segregation, this was the kind of gesture a magnanimous judge would feel impelled to make, and we are bound to take satisfaction in the accolade. Yet, once the courtesy had been paid, the Court was not disposed in the least to go farther or base its determination on the expert testimony.

As I have said, these developments Professor Clark could not have known when he staked so wide a claim for his profession. But he did know that circumstances in the Virginia litigation—the one he participated in most actively—had reflected very directly on his assertion. The Virginia school board had offered the testimony of three expert witnesses, and all three (psychiatrist Kelly, psychologist Buck, and Professor Clark's own former teacher, Professor Garrett of Columbia) had *admitted,* in one way or another, that racial segregation in the schools does injure Negro children's personalities. They admitted, as we have said, a fact of common experience. On the defendants' behalf, they testified as persuasively as they could against the Court's adopting what they called "disruptive" or "coercive" measures, and they spoke regretfully about the firmness of established regional customs. Buck summarized their attitude in two statements: "I feel that as an abstract idea, segregation is bad," and "I think the whole society is sick."

When we come to explain why the statement signed by the thirty-two social scientists went without mention by Chief Justice Warren, I find myself at a disadvantage. Only the reader's assistance can rescue me. I have examined the text of this statement, which has become easy of access by being reprinted in a law review. My personal, subjective reaction is that the text conveys little or no information beyond what is already known in "literary psychology" (by which I mean such psychological observations and insights as one finds continually in the works of poets, novelists, essayists, journalists, and religious prophets). The statement's vocabulary and style would not be called "literary"; I refer only to its substance. If my readers will inspect the statement for themselves, they will ascertain whether it impresses them as it did me. At that, my reaction may be due to a lack of technical training in scientific psychology and psychological testing.

The "Generally Accepted" Test.—When a scientist is engaged in demonstrating a fact of common knowledge (*e.g.,* that fire burns, that a cold causes snuffles, or that segregation degrades), it is not easy to pass a fair judgment on the validity of his proof. Our minds tend to supply his conclusion before he is ready to deduce it. Subconsciously we reinforce his evidence with the facts and feelings of our own experience, and if his reasoning should contain a flaw, we are too preoccupied with reaching the familiar destination to detect it. Moreover, in the present situation, men who specialize in conducting psychological tests might discover all sorts of weak assumptions and fallacies that mere lawyers would never notice. Under these several disadvantages, the most I can do here is present Professor Clark's evidence concerning the "generally accepted" test, together with the comments that suggest themselves to an untrained but interested observer.

Professor Clark testified as an expert in the South Carolina, Delaware, and Virginia litigations. The clearest description of the test appears in his testimony in the South Carolina case. He said:

> A. I made these tests on Thursday and Friday of this past week at your request, and I presented it to children in the Scott's Branch Elementary school, concentrating particularly on the elementary group. I used these methods which I told you about—the Negro and White dolls—which were identical in every respect save skin color. And, I presented them with a sheet of paper on which there were these drawings of dolls, and I asked them to show me the doll— May I read from these notes?
>
> JUDGE WARING: You may refresh your recollection.
>
> THE WITNESS: Thank you. I presented these dolls to them and I asked them the following questions in the following order: "Show me the doll that you like best or that you'd like to play with," "Show me the doll that is the 'nice' doll," "Show me the doll that looks 'bad'," and then the following questions also: "Give me the doll that looks like a white child," "Give me the doll that looks like a colored child," "Give me the doll that looks like a Negro child," and "Give me the doll that looks like you."
>
> By Mr. Carter:
> Q. "Like you?"
> A. "Like you." That was the final question, and you can see why. I wanted to get the child's free expression of his opinions and feelings before I had him identified with one of these two dolls. I found that of the children between the ages of six and nine whom I tested, which were a total of sixteen in number, that ten of those children chose the white doll as their preference; the doll which they liked best. Ten of them also considered the white doll a "Nice" doll. And, I think you

have to keep in mind that these two dolls are absolutely identical in every respect except skin color. Eleven of these sixteen children chose the brown doll as the doll which looked "bad." This is consistent with previous results which we have obtained testing over three hundred children, and we interpret it to mean that the Negro child accepts as early as six, seven or eight the negative stereotypes about his own group. And, this result was confirmed in Clarendon County where we found eleven out of sixteen children picking the brown doll as looking "bad," when we also must take into account that over half of these children, in spite of their own feelings,—negative feelings—about the brown doll, were eventually required on the last question to identify themselves with this doll which they considered as being undesirable or negative. It may also interest you to know that only one of these children, between six and nine, dared to choose the white doll as look- ing bad. The difference between eleven and sixteen was in terms of children who refused to make any choice at all and the children were always free not to make a choice. They were not forced to make a choice. These choices represent the children's spontaneous and free reactions to this experimental situation. Nine of these sixteen children considered the white doll as having the qualities of a nice doll. To show you that that was not due to some artificial or accidental set of cir- cumstances, the following results are important. Every single child, when asked to pick the doll that looked like the white child, made the correct choice. All sixteen of the sixteen picked that doll. Every single child, when asked to pick the doll that was like the colored child; every one of them picked the brown doll. My opinion is that a fundamental effect of segregation is basic confusion in the individuals and their con- cepts about themselves conflicting in their self images. That seemed to be supported by the results of these sixteen children, all of them knowing which of those dolls was white and which one was brown. Seven of them, when asked to pick the doll that was like themselves; seven of them picked the white doll. This must be seen as a concrete illustration of the degree to which the pleasures* which these children sensed against being brown forced them to evade reality—to escape the reality which seems too overburdening or too threatening to them. This is clearly illustrated by a number of these youngsters who, when asked to color themselves— For example, I had a young girl, a dark brown child of seven, who was so dark brown that she was almost

* Thus in original; probably should be "pressures."

black. When she was asked to color herself, she was one of the few children who picked a flesh color, pink, to color herself. When asked to color a little boy, the color she liked little boys to be, she looked all around the twenty-four crayons and picked up a white crayon and looked up at me with a shy smile and began to color. She said, "Well, this doesn't show." So, she pressed a little harder and began to color in order to get the white crayon to show. These are the kinds of results which I obtained in Clarendon County.

Q. Well, as a result of your tests, what conclusions have you reached, Mr. Clark, with respect to the infant plaintiffs involved in this case?

A. The conclusion which I was forced to reach was that these children in Clarendon County, like other human beings who are subjected to an obviously inferior status in the society in which they live, have been definitely harmed in the development of their personalities; that the signs of instability in their personalities are clear, and I think that every psychologist would accept and interpret these signs as such.

Q. Is that the type of injury which in your opinion would be enduring or lasting?

A. I think it is the kind of injury which would be as enduring or lasting as the situation endured, changing only in its form and in the way it manifests itself.

Mr. Carter: Thank you. Your witness.

General Comments.—We are not provided here with any proof of the numerical adequacy of the sampling or of its being a representative cross-section. We have no demonstration that abnormal or eccentric backgrounds of the individual children have been investigated. Among these 16 children (or 300, including the other groups mentioned) there would probably be a certain proportion with untypical private experiences. In such a strikingly small sample, the results could easily mislead.

Moreover, if one follows the arithmetic in Professor Clark's testimony—which is not easy for me—some of his interpretations seem to be predetermined. For example, if Negro children say a *brown* doll is like themselves, he infers that segregation has made them conscious of race; yet if they say a *white* doll is like themselves, he infers that segregation has forced them to evade reality.

Perhaps the main point is that this test does not purport to demonstrate the effects of *school* segregation, which is what the court was being asked to enjoin. If it disclosed anything about the effects of segregation on the children, their experiences at school were not differentiated from other causes. Considering the ages of the children, we may conjecture they had not been long at school.

Comment on the Opening Questions.—We do not know how the children took these questions. If Professor Clark had offered to give real dolls instead of showing pictures of dolls, the reaction might have been more serious. In any case, I do not think any certain inference follows from 10 out of 16 pointing to the picture of the white doll. Habituation with *dolls* (as distinguished from people) should be allowed for. Manufacturers and commercial fashions practically restrict a child's concept of what a "nice" doll would look like. Many white children of certain generations were taught to prefer "Topsy" or other colored dolls; some children would say that there is no really "nice" doll but a teddy-bear. At this point, the response seems uninformative.

Comment on the "Bad Doll" Question.—Here, it seems to me, the children were tricked. Perhaps that is how some of them felt. There had been no previous question about a "good doll," only about a "nice" one, which the children clearly understood meant one "you'd like to play with." What is a "bad doll"? Some children might consider this a term of preference for play purposes: all little "mothers" love to rebuke and punish naughty dolls. Other children, on hearing the question, would be simply bewildered by the sudden, unexpected introduction of moral or disciplinary references. Some may have responded by pointing to the brown doll because the question seemed to imply that a process of elimination was contemplated. But I hope the children asked themselves: Why must there be a "bad" doll at all? Why cannot both dolls be "nice"? We observe that five children declined to answer this question. Probably they felt it unfair or at least very confusing in the circumstances.

Comment on the Remaining Questions.—It is noteworthy that seven Negro children picked the white doll "when asked to pick the doll that was like themselves." Professor Clark leaps to infer that they were evading reality. This I doubt. Although his testimony does not make me clear on the point, I gather that these seven children were among the ten who had previously chosen the white doll as "nice." Were they wrong, then, to claim that the white doll was very much "like themselves" because they too were "nice"? No one can state positively what these children were thinking at the time; but if they did have perception enough to insist to themselves that the *"niceness"* was decisive and not the color, lo and behold! this would be wisdom indeed! "Out of the mouths of babes and sucklings—"? Perhaps, merely perhaps. In any event, I cannot see that the opposite interpretation (Professor Clark's) is so evident that it deserves to rank as scientific proof.

Aid from an Unexpected Quarter.—Fortunately, the outcome of the *Brown* and *Bolling* cases did not depend on the psychological experts' facing and answering the objections, queries, and doubts I have presented. It is possible that if the questions had been put to Professor Clark on cross-examination, he would have come forward with convincing answers. But, to all intents and purposes, the questions were not put. The doll test was not analyzed in suitable detail by any of the cross-examiners, probably because they, too, realized that segregation does degrade and injure Negro school schildren.

In the Virginia trial, the defense appeared particularly inept. Far from caring to concentrate on the doll test and its scientific validity, the lawyer for the defendants was preoccupied with other lines of cross-examination. He had a different set of values to display. Why concern himself with dissecting the experts' logic and the correctness of their inferences? Instead, questions were asked which would convey disparaging insinuations about a professor's parents, his ancestral religion, the source of his surname, the pigmentation of his skin, or the place of his birth. If these items did not discredit him satisfactorily, then one went on to inquire how many years he had spent in the South; if he had lived in the South, how long in Virginia; and so on— implying all the while that science, common sense, and human nature would not dare to cross Virginia county lines. And, of course, there would be continual hints that what the plaintiffs' witnesses really desired to achieve was miscegenation and a mixed race.

As any healthy-minded person reads the Virginia trial record, it is impossible not to contrast the altruism and sober dignity of the scientists with the behavior of defendants' counsel, who, by his manner of espousing the old order, exposed its cruelty and bigotry. Here was a living spectacle of what racial segregation can do to the human spirit. The segregated society, as defendants' own expert had said, was "sick"; and the tactics of cross-examination used by defendants' lawyer showed how very sick it was. I suggest that these pages of the record did not fail of notice in the deliberations of the United States Supreme Court.

Without Salt, No Science.—We may as well resign ourselves to letting the troglodytes remain troglodytes, and turn our attention back to our civilized friends, the social psychologists. As the courts' exclusionary rules of evidence tend to relax more and more, the scientists will appear more frequently to testify as expert witnesses. How much respect should the judges extend to their testimony?

The answer depends in large measure on the scientists. If I have been right in suggesting that their evidence in the desegregation cases seemed persuasive because it happened to coincide with facts of common knowledge, they surely cannot rely on having the same advantage in every future litigation. It is predictable that lawyers and scientists retained by adversary parties will endeavor more aggressively to puncture any vulnerable or extravagant claims. Judges may learn to notice where objective science ends and advocacy begins. At present, it is still possible for the social psychologist to "hoodwink a judge who is not over wise" without intending to do so; but successes of this kind are too costly for science to desire them.

For one thing: Merely translating a proposition of "literary" psychology into the terms of technical jargon can scarcely make it a scientific finding. For another: Just because social psychology is in a youthful and somewhat uncertain stage, the utmost rigor should be imposed on its *intermediate* processes.

The point is vital, involving as it does not only social psychology's prestige in the courts but—what is ultimately more valuable—its capacity to evolve and progress as a cumulative body of tested knowledge and approved method. Among the major impediments continually confronting this science are (1) the recurrent lack of agreement on substantive premises, and (2) the recurrent lack of extrinsic, empirical means for checking and verifying inferred results. As long as these disadvantages remain, and they are likely to remain in some measure for a very long time, social psychology will need, above all things, the use of scrupulous logic in its internal, intermediate processes. If the *premises* must be loose, the *reasoning* from them should be so much tighter; and if the final *results* cannot be validated precisely by external tests, then the *methods* of inference should be examined and re-examined all the more critically. It is meticulous standards that bring respect and credence to scientific testimony. When a social psychologist is called to serve as a "friend of the court," he should be able to assume our belief that his best friend, his premier loyalty, is always the objective truth.

Some of the Consequences.—Obviously, the *Brown* and *Bolling* opinions are susceptible of more than one interpretation. My views do not agree with those of some very able commentators, who consider that the opinions show important marks of the psychologists' influence. Granting this variety of interpretations, does it really matter whether the Supreme Court relies or does not rely on the psychologists' findings? Does it make any practical difference?

I submit it does. In the first place, since the behavioral sciences are so very young, imprecise, and changeful, their findings have an uncertain expectancy of life. Today's sanguine asseveration may be cancelled by tomorrow's new revelation—or new technical fad. It is one thing to use the current scientific findings, however ephemeral they may be, in order to ascertain whether the legislature has acted reasonably in adopting some scheme of social or economic regulation; deference here is shown not so much to the findings as to the legislature. It would be quite another thing to have our fundamental rights rise, fall, or change along with the latest fashions of psychological literature. Today the social psychologists—at least the leaders of the discipline—are liberal and egalitarian in basic approach. Suppose, a generation hence, some of their successors were to revert to the ethnic mysticism of the very recent past; suppose they were to present us with a collection of racist notions and label them "science." What then would be the state of our constitutional rights? Recognizing as we do how sagacious Mr. Justice Holmes was to insist that the Constitution be not tied to the wheels of any economic system whatsoever, we ought to keep it similarly uncommitted in relation to the other social sciences.

There is another potential danger here. It concerns the guarantee of "equal protection of the laws." Heretofore, no government official has contended that he could deny equal protection with impunity unless the complaining parties offered competent proof that they would sustain or had sustained some permanent (psychological or other kind of) damage. The right to equal protection has not been subjected to any such proviso. Under my reading of the *Brown* and *Bolling* opinions, this would remain the law. But if, in future "equal protection" cases, the Court were to hold that it was the expert testimony that determined the outcome of *Brown* and *Bolling*, the scope of the constitutional safeguard might be seriously restricted. Without cataloguing the various possibilities, one can discern at least that some of them would be ominous. It is not too soon to say so, for basic rights need early alarms. . . .

6.   *"Whether such a group exists within a community is a question of fact."*

HERNANDEZ V. TEXAS

MR. CHIEF JUSTICE WARREN delivered the opinion of the Court.

The petitioner, Pete Hernandez, was indicted for the murder of one Joe Espinosa by a grand jury in Jackson County, Texas. He was convicted and sentenced to life imprisonment. The Texas Court of Criminal Appeals affirmed the judgment of the trial court. . . . Prior to the trial, the petitioner, by his counsel, offered timely motions to quash the indictment and the jury panel. He alleged that persons of Mexican descent were systematically excluded from service as jury commissioners, grand jurors, and petit jurors, although there were such persons fully qualified to serve residing in Jackson County. The petitioner asserted that exclusion of this class deprived him, as a member of the class, of the equal protection of the laws guaranteed by the Fourteenth Amendment of the Constitution. After a hearing, the trial court denied the motions. . . .

In numerous decisions, this Court has held that it is a denial of the equal protection of the laws to try a defendant of a particular race or color under an indictment issued by a grand jury, or before a petit

347 U.S. 475, 74 S. Ct. 667, 98 L. Ed. 866 (1954).

jury, from which all persons of his race or color have, solely because of that race or color, been excluded by the State, whether acting through its legislature, its courts, or its executive or administrative officers. Although the Court has had little occasion to rule on the question directly, it has been recognized since Strauder v. State of West Virginia [1880] that the exclusion of a class of persons from jury service on grounds other than race or color may also deprive a defendant who is a member of that class of the constitutional guarantee of equal protection of the laws. The State of Texas would have us hold that there are only two classes—white and Negro—within the contemplation of the Fourteenth Amendment. The decisions of this Court do not support that view. . . .

Throughout our history differences in race and color have defined easily identifiable groups which have at times required the aid of the courts in securing equal treatment under the laws. But community prejudices are not static, and from time to time other differences from the community norm may define other groups which need the same protection. Whether such a group exists within a community is a question of fact. When the existence of a distinct class is demonstrated, and it is further shown that the laws, as written or as applied, single out that class for different treatment not based on some reasonable classification, the guarantees of the Constitution have been violated. The Fourteenth Amendment is not directed solely against discrimination due to a "two-class theory"—that is, based upon differences between "white" and Negro.

As the petitioner acknowledges, the Texas system of selecting grand and petit jurors by the use of jury commissions is fair on its face and capable of being utilized without discrimination. But as this Court has held, the system is susceptible to abuse and can be employed in a discriminatory manner. The exclusion of otherwise eligible persons from jury service solely because of their ancestry or national origin is discrimination prohibited by the Fourteenth Amendment. The Texas statute makes no such discrimination, but the petitioner alleges that those administering the law do.

The petitioner's initial burden in substantiating his charge of group discrimination was to prove that persons of Mexican descent constitute a separate class in Jackson County, distinct from "whites." One method by which this may be demonstrated is by showing the attitude of the community. Here the testimony of responsible officials and citizens contained the admission that residents of the community distinguished between "white" and "Mexican." The participation of persons of Mexican descent in business and community groups was shown to be slight. Until very recent times, children of Mexican descent were required to attend a segregated school for the first four grades. At least one restaurant in town prominently displayed a sign announcing "No Mexicans Served." On the courthouse grounds at the time of the hearing, there were two men's toilets, one unmarked, and the other marked "Colored Men" and "Hombres Aqui" ("Men Here"). No substantial evidence was offered to rebut the logical inference to be drawn from these facts, and it must be concluded that petitioner succeeded in his proof.

Having established the existence of a class, petitioner was then charged with the burden of proving discrimination. To do so, he relied on the pattern of proof established by Norris v. State of Alabama. . . . In that case, proof that Negroes constituted a substantial segment of the population of the jurisdiction, that some Negroes were qualified to serve as jurors, and that none had been called for jury service over an extended period of time, was held to constitute prima facie proof of the systematic exclusion of Negroes from jury service. This holding, sometimes called the "rule of exclusion," has been applied in other cases, and it is available in supplying proof of discrimination against any delineated class.

The petitioner established that 14% of the population of Jackson County were persons with Mexican or Latin American surnames, and that 11% of the males over 21 bore such names. The County Tax Assessor testified that 6 or 7 percent of the freeholders on the tax rolls of the County were persons of Mexican descent. The State of Texas stipulated that "for the last twenty-five years there is no record of any person with a Mexican or Latin American name having served on a jury commission, grand jury or petit jury in Jackson County." . . .

The petitioner met the burden of proof imposed in Norris v. Alabama. . . . To rebut the strong prima facie case of the denial of the equal protection of the laws guaranteed by the Constitution thus established, the State offered the testimony of five jury commissioners

that they had not discriminated against persons of Mexican or Latin
American descent in selecting jurors. They stated that their only objec-
tive had been to select those whom they thought were best qualified.
This testimony is not enough to overcome the petitioner's case. . . .

Circumstances or chance may well dictate that no persons in a certain class will serve on a particular jury or during some particular
period. But it taxes our credulity to say that mere chance resulted in
their being no members of this class among the over six thousand
jurors called in the past 25 years. The result bespeaks discrimination,
whether or not it was a conscious decision on the part of any individual jury commissioner. The judgment of conviction must be reversed. . . .

Reversed.

7.   ". . . *sometimes 'judicial notice' actually means judicial
ignorance.*"

REPOUILLE V. UNITED STATES

BEFORE L. HAND, AUGUSTUS N. HAND and FRANK, CIRCUIT
JUDGES.

L. HAND, CIRCUIT JUDGE.

The District Attorney . . . has appealed from an order, naturalizing
the appellee, Repouille. The ground of the objection in the district
court and here is that he did not show himself to have been a person
of "good moral character" for the five years which preceded the filing
of his petition. The facts were as follows: The petition was filed on
September 22, 1944, and on October 12, 1939, he had deliberately put
to death his son, a boy of thirteen, by means of chloroform. His reason
for this tragic deed was that the child had "suffered from birth from a
brain injury which destined him to be an idiot and a physical mon-
strosity malformed in all four limbs. The child was blind, mute, and
deformed. He had to be fed; the movements of his bladder and bowels
were involuntary, and his entire life was spent in a small crib." Re-

165 F. 2d 152 (1947). United States Circuit Court of Appeals, Second Circuit.

pouille had four other children at the time towards whom he has always been a dutiful and responsible parent. . . . The family was altogether dependent upon his industry for its support. He was indicted for manslaughter in the first degree; but the jury brought in a verdict of manslaughter in the second degree with a recommendation of the "utmost clemency"; and the judge sentenced him to not less than five years nor more than ten, execution to be stayed, and the defendant to be placed on probation, from which he was discharged in December, 1945. Concededly, except for this act he conducted himself as a person of "good moral character" during the five years before he filed his petition. Indeed, if he had waited before filing his petition from September 22, to October 14, 1944, he would have had a clear record for the necessary period, and would have been admitted without question.

Very recently we had to pass upon the phrase "good moral character" in the Nationality Act; and we said that it set as a test, not those standards which we might ourselves approve, but whether "the moral feelings, now prevalent generally in this country" would "be outraged" by the conduct in question: that is, whether it conformed to "the generally accepted moral conventions current at the time." In the absence of some national inquisition, like a Gallup poll, that is indeed a difficult test to apply; often questions will arise to which the answer is not ascertainable, and where the petitioner must fail only because he has the affirmative. Indeed, in the case at bar itself the answer is not wholly certain; for we all know that there are great numbers of people of the most unimpeachable virtue, who think it morally justifiable to put an end to a life so inexorably destined to be a burden to others, and—so far as any possible interest of its own is concerned— condemned to a brutish existence, lower indeed than all but the lowest forms of sentient life. Nor is it inevitably an answer to say that it must be immoral to do this, until the law provides security against the abuses which would inevitably follow, unless the practice were regulated. Many people—probably most people—do not make it a final ethical test of conduct that it shall not violate law; few of us exact of ourselves or of others the unflinching obedience of a Socrates. There being no lawful means of accomplishing an end, which they believe to be righteous in itself, there have always been conscientious persons who feel no scruple in acting in defiance of a law which is repugnant to their personal convictions, and who even regard as martyrs those who suffer by doing so. In our own history it is only necessary to recall the Abolitionists. It is reasonably clear that the jury which tried Repouille did not feel any moral repulsion at his crime. Although it was inescapably murder in the first degree, not only did they bring in a verdict that was flatly in the face of the facts and utterly absurd—for manslaughter in the second degree presupposes that the killing has not been deliberate—but they coupled even that with a recommendation which showed that in substance they wished to exculpate the offender. Moreover, it is also plain, from the sentence which he imposed, that the judge could not have seriously disagreed with their recommendation.

One might be tempted to seize upon all this as a reliable measure of current morals; and no doubt it should have its place in the scale; but we should hesitate to accept it as decisive, when, for example, we compare it with the fate of a similar offender in Massachusetts, who, although he was not executed, was imprisoned for life. Left at large as we are, without means of verifying our conclusion, and without authority to substitute our individual beliefs, the outcome must needs be tentative; and not much is gained by discussion. We can say no more than that, quite independently of what may be the current moral feelings as to legally administered euthanasia, we feel reasonably secure in holding that only a minority of virtuous persons would deem the practise morally justifiable, while it remains in private hands, even when the provocation is as overwhelming as it was in this instance. . . .

Order reversed; petition dismissed without prejudice to the filing of a second petition.

FRANK, CIRCUIT JUDGE (dissenting). . . .

The district judge found that Repouille was a person of "good moral character." Presumably, in so finding, the judge attempted to employ that statutory standard in accordance with our decisions, i. e., as measured by conduct in conformity with "the generally accepted moral conventions at the time." My colleagues, although their sources of information concerning the pertinent mores are not shown to be superior to those of the district judge, reject his finding. And they do so, too, while conceding that their own conclusion is uncertain, and (as they put it) "tentative." I incline to think that the correct statutory test (the test Congress intended) is the attitude of our ethical leaders. That attitude would not be too difficult to learn; indeed, my colleagues indicate that they think such leaders would agree with the district judge. But the precedents in this circuit constrain us to be guided by contemporary public opinion about which, cloistered as judges are, we have but vague notions. . . .

Seeking to apply a standard of this type, courts usually do not rely on evidence but utilize what is often called the doctrine of "judicial notice," which, in matters of this sort, properly permits informal inquiries by the judges. However, for such a purpose (as in the discharge of many other judicial duties), the courts are inadequately staffed, so that sometimes "judicial notice" actually means judicial ignorance.

But the courts are not utterly helpless; such judicial impotence has its limits. Especially when an issue importantly affecting a man's life is involved, it seems to me that we need not, and ought not, resort to our mere unchecked surmises, remaining wholly (to quote my colleagues' words) "without means of verifying our conclusions." . . .

I think, therefore, that, in any case such as this, where we lack the means of determining present-day public reactions, we should remand to the district judge with these directions: The judge should give the petitioner and the government the opportunity to bring to the judge's attention reliable information on the subject, which he may supplement in any appropriate way. All the data so obtained should be put of record. On the basis thereof, the judge should reconsider his decision and arrive at a conclusion. Then, if there is another appeal, we can avoid sheer guessing, which alone is now available to us, and can reach something like an informed judgment.

10 / PRECEDENTS AND LEGAL REASONING

After the facts of a controversy are found in court, the law applicable to the situation must be determined and applied. In fact finding the judge may share responsibility with the jury, but the judge alone determines the law. He must find the law, he must interpret the law, he must, if necessary (and it often is), make the law.

It is customary to say that there are three sources for the law applied by American judges: constitutions (federal and state), statutes (federal and state), and common law. In the sense used here, common law refers to that part of the law of England, the United States, and other English-speaking countries which is found in reported judicial decisions and in textbooks discussing those decisions, as distinguished from the law enacted by legislatures or constitutional conventions. The common law had its fount in English custom and tradition. In fact, the term itself derived from the medieval judicial theory that the law administered by the king's superior courts was the common custom of the realm, as contrasted with the customs of the localities in England.

The common law stands in contrast to the civil law of the European continent, which derives from the Roman tradition. The civil law is based on the codification of Roman law carried out in the Italian universities in

362

the twelfth and thirteenth centuries, and subsequently developed and interpreted by doctrinal writing, university teaching, and legislative additions. The civil law is thus a complete body of legislatively declared or prescribed texts as expounded by academicians, jurists, and commentators. The technique of deciding cases under the civil law is the deductive process of reasoning from the general to the particular, from the written texts and commentaries to the facts of the specific cases.

With the common law as a body of rules of law, developed in England and subsequently accepted in America, we are not here concerned. It is the technique by which the common law was developed and applied that is relevant to this discussion. The common law has for its model the inductive process, by which general principles are drawn from the decisions of particular controversies. These principles, once stated, become precedents which are controlling as the law to be applied in future controversies raising the same question. But applying the rule of precedents, or *stare decisis,* is no automatic process. Each new controversy requires that the precedents be re-examined in the light of the immediate controversy. In courts where the common-law tradition prevails, judges have a unique responsibility for providing the elements of both stability and change in the law.

Legal Reasoning

The basic technique employed by American courts in determining the law is reasoning by example. It makes some difference whether the source of the law applied is statute, constitution, or common law, and consequently the two following chapters are devoted to the special problems of statutory construction and constitutional interpretation. But the fundamental character of the judicial task is the same in each instance: a comparison of facts and decisions in a number of related controversies.

Let us take a common-law situation which presents the technique in its clearest form. A controversy comes before a judge in which facts A, B, C, and D are present. The judge reviews earlier reported cases in a search for similar situations. If he finds a case in which facts A, B, C, and D were present, then that case is a precedent and he will feel a strong obligation to decide the present case the same way the earlier case was decided. When a substantial number of cases involving such facts have been decided the same way, judges will say that a rule of law exists. A general rule has been built from a series of particular instances. Over a period of decades or centuries rules of law develop in this fashion covering a great variety of factual situations. Periodically, legislatures enact or revise some of these rules of law by adopting statutes.

But these rules of law are constantly being tested and questioned by new controversies. Seldom do the facts in one case exactly duplicate the facts of earlier cases. Thus there is nearly always an opportunity to contend that the rule of law applied previously is not applicable. For example, it may be argued that the facts in the earlier case were A, B, C, and D, while here they are A, B, C, and E. The judge then must decide whether the similarities are so close that the two cases can be controlled by the same rule; if so, the rule must be somewhat reformulated or enlarged in order to cover both the A-B-C-D and the A-B-C-E types of situations. Or the judge may decide that the replacement of D by E so changes the complex of facts that a different result is required, and in that event an entirely different rule may be applied or a new rule may be stated.

What goes on in a court of law, then, is not only a controversy about facts. The court is also a forum in which counsel argue the relevance of previous decisions to the current question, and the applicability of the rules of law enacted by earlier decisions. But since the rules of law are simply ways of explaining the decisions in previous cases, the emphasis is often less on the concept and more on demonstrating that the facts of the present case differ sufficiently from the earlier cases so that decisions reached there offer no precedent for the present decision.

Cardozo has well stated the case against the notion that adherence to precedents is simply a matter of a judge "match[ing] the colors of the case at hand against the colors of many sample cases spread out upon the desk. The sample nearest in shade supplied the applicable rule." If this were all there is to judging, he says, then the judge with the best card index of cases would be the wisest judge. "It is when the colors do not match, when the references in the index fail, when there is no decisive precedent, that the serious business of the judge begins. He must then fashion law for the litigants before him. In fashioning it for them, he will be fashioning it for others."

Counsel for the litigants urge on the judge precedents which they insist control his discretion in the present controversy and point out the proper decision. Precedents which are in apparent conflict with the result they are being paid to secure are explained away as inapplicable or for some other reason valueless as guides. The counsel and the judge as well must thus engage in a complicated process of comparing decisions in a search for similarities that are significant and essential enough to guide judicial judgments.

The Principle of the Case

In order for a previous decision to qualify as a precedent, the nonessentials of the decision must be stripped away so that the basic reason for the court's decision is revealed. This is generally referred to as establishing "the principle of the case," or the *ratio decidendi*. Many jurists have endeavored to explain how this task is performed but perhaps the five rules suggested by Arthur L. Goodhart are as useful as any.[1] His first two rules tell how the principle of the case is *not* to be found.

1. The principle of a case is not found in the reasons given in the opinion.
2. The principle is not found in the rule of law set forth in the opinion.

These first two rules suggest that the principle of a case is not established by the rationale of the judge's decision. It is not enough to know why the judge said he was deciding the case as he did, or what he thought was the rule of law being established. What is missing in these first two situations is any relation between the *facts* of the case and the decision. The principle of a case cannot be established without knowing the facts of the case.

But Goodhart's third rule indicates that there is still more to the problem than this.

3. The principle is not necessarily found by a consideration of all the ascertainable facts of the case and the judge's decision.

This is so, because not all the facts of a case are relevant to establishing the principle of the decision. A standard of relevance must be established. This is what we get in Goodhart's fourth rule.

4. The principle of the case is found by taking account (a) of the facts treated by the judge as material, and (b) his decision as based on them.

Here we finally have a rule on what to look for in the search for the *ratio decidendi*. But Goodhart goes on to give one final guide to relevance.

5. In finding the principle it is also necessary to establish what facts were held to be immaterial by the judge, for the principle may depend as much on exclusion as it does on inclusion.

[1] "Determining the Ratio Decidendi of a Case," 40 *Yale Law Journal* 161–183 (1930).

Dicta

Rule 4, as the basic positive guide, deserves further elaboration. In stressing the relationship between the judge's decision and the facts which he treated as material, Goodhart is merely reformulating what is generally referred to as the rule of dicta in judicial opinions. A dictum (or obiter dictum) is any expression in an opinion which is unnecessary to the decision reached in the case, or which relates to a factual situation other than the one which was actually before the court. The task of the judge is to decide the immediate case before him. Any comments which are not an integral part of the reasoning necessary to decide the case are consequently surplus verbiage and entitled to no consideration when the principle of that case is subsequently sought. The judicial opinion has value as a precedent only insofar as it is squarely based on the facts of the controversy being adjudicated.

One of the now classic examples of dictum in a Supreme Court decision is found in Chief Justice Taft's opinion in the case of *Myers* v. *United States* (1926). The Court was dealing there with a statute which prevented the President from removing a postmaster from office without securing the consent of the Senate. Taft wrote the Court's opinion holding that this legislation was an unconstitutional restriction on the President's removal power, but he did not confine his holding to the office of postmaster. Instead he specifically declared that the constitutional principles on which he based his decision applied uniformly to all presidential appointees, including the heads of the federal regulatory commissions.

In 1935 the Supreme Court had to decide a case involving presidential removal of precisely such an official, a member of the Federal Trade Commission. In *Humphrey's Executor* v. *United States* the Court declared that Taft's broader ruling was dictum, and not controlling in the case of an officer with quasi-legislative and quasi-judicial functions. Justice Sutherland wrote:

> The office of a postmaster is so essentially unlike the office now involved that the decision in the Myers case cannot be accepted as controlling our decision here. A postmaster is an executive officer restricted to the performance of executive functions. He is charged with no duty at all related to either the legislative or judicial power. The actual decision in the Myers case finds support in the theory that such an officer is merely one of the units in the executive department and hence inherently subject to the exclusive and illimitable power of removal by the chief executive, whose subordinate and aide he is. Putting

aside dicta, which may be followed if sufficiently persuasive but which are not controlling, the necessary reach of the decision goes far enough to include all purely executive officers. It goes no further. . . .

Distinguishing a Precedent

A second method for avoiding application of an earlier ruling which is apparently a precedent for the case in hand is to distinguish it. This process involves a demonstration that the principle of the earlier case is, when properly understood, inapplicable to the present problem. Since the facts of two cases are never the same, it is never impossible to find grounds for failing to follow the earlier decision.

Examples are numerous. In *Oyama* v. *California* (1948) the Supreme Court "assumed" the constitutionality of a California statute forbidding aliens ineligible for American citizenship (i.e., Japanese) to acquire agricultural land, though managing to render the act unenforceable on other grounds. Five months later in *Takahashi* v. *Commission* the Court had to consider the constitutionality of a similar California law banning alien Japanese from commercial fishing. Justice Reed thought that "the right to fish is analogous to the right to own land," but Justice Black for the majority managed to distinguish the two statutes. The *Oyama* decision, and the cases on which it relied, "could not in any event be controlling here. They rested solely upon the power of states to control the devolution and ownership of land within their borders, a power long exercised and supported on reasons peculiar to real property." In other words, land is different from fish.

If possible, there was even less effort made by Chief Justice Hughes in 1937 to explain how *Schechter* v. *United States* (1935) and *Carter* v. *Carter Coal Co.* (1936), both denying the federal government's power to regulate commerce, could be reconciled with the decision in *National Labor Relations Board* v. *Jones & Laughlin Steel Corp.* (1937), upholding the validity of the Wagner Act. He wrote:

> The question remains as to the effect upon interstate commerce of the labor practice involved. In the A.L.A. Schechter Poultry Corp. case . . . we found that the effect there was so remote as to be beyond the federal power. To find "immediacy or directness" there was to find it "almost everywhere," a result inconsistent with the maintenance of our federal system. In the Carter case . . . the Court was of the opinion that the provisions of the statute relating to production were invalid upon several grounds. . . . These cases are not controlling here.

Limiting a Precedent in Principle

Distinguishing a precedent presumably leaves it with full validity for the circumstances to which it was originally applied; it is simply found not applicable to the current controversy. But occasionally judicial consideration of a precedent may convince the court that the doctrine of the earlier opinion should actually be restated in a more limited way to conform with current understandings. *Carter* v. *Carter Coal Co.* suffered such a fate. As just noted, Chief Justice Hughes merely distinguished it in 1937, and yet it was quite obvious that portions of the opinion were in direct conflict with *Jones & Laughlin.* In 1941 the Supreme Court upheld another statute, the Fair Labor Standards Act, in *United States* v. *Darby Lumber Co.*, on grounds which were likewise in direct conflict with *Carter.* This time the Court thought it well to recognize that something had happened to the *Carter* reasoning and so, calling attention to its inconsistency with later decisions of the Court, gave notice that its doctrine was correspondingly "limited in principle."

Ignoring a Precedent

An embarrassing precedent can be handled by simply not mentioning it at all. This device may seem cowardly and also rather untidy, because it impairs the validity of the ignored precedent and leaves it a derelict on the stream of the law, a hazard to other judicial mariners.

For example, in *Lochner* v. *New York* (1905), the Supreme Court held unconstitutional a state ten-hour law for bakers. Then in *Bunting* v. *Oregon* (1917) a somewhat differently constituted Court upheld an Oregon ten-hour law for factory workers in a decision which never mentioned the completely incompatible *Lochner* case. The result of this silence was that when a Court majority decided to invalidate a District of Columbia minimum wage law for women in *Adkins* v. *Childrens Hospital* (1923) it was able to dig up the *Lochner* case as a precedent, contending that "the principles therein stated have never been disapproved." Chief Justice Taft, dissenting in *Adkins,* found this all very confusing, for he had always supposed that the *Lochner* decision had been "overruled sub silentio."

Again, in *United States* v. *Classic* (1941) Justice Stone held that federal primary elections were subject to congressional regulation, without referring in any way to the decision in *Grovey* v. *Townsend* (1935) which asserted that party primaries were outside the protection of the Constitution. This was a deliberate tactic to win the vote of Justice Roberts, who had written the *Grovey* opinion. Later, in *Smith* v. *Allwright* (1944), when Roberts' vote was not needed, the Court held that in fact *Grovey* had been dead ever since *Classic,* and drew this protest from Roberts:

> It is suggested that *Grovey* v. *Townsend* was overruled *sub silentio* in *United States* v. *Classic.* . . . If this Court's opinion in the Classic case discloses its method of overruling earlier decisions, I can only protest that, in fairness, it should rather have adopted the open and frank way of saying what it was doing than, after the event, characterize its past action as overruling *Grovey* v. *Townsend,* though those less sapient never realized the fact.

Overruling a Precedent

Lest it be thought that old precedents never die but just fade away, it should be recorded that occasionally a case is specifically overruled. This is perhaps more likely to happen when a precedent has become a notorious political as well as a legal liability. In the decade from 1937 to 1947, as the new Supreme Court liquidated many of the constitutional doctrines of the old Court, at least thirty-two previous decisions were overruled, and thirty of these cases turned on issues of constitutional interpretation. One of the most famous victims during this period of judicial reorientation was *Hammer* v. *Dagenhart* (1918), a decision in which the Court had by a 5-4 vote declared the federal Child Labor Act of 1916 unconstitutional. This ruling was based on such a tortured construction of the Court's previous decisions that its authority had always been slight, and in *United States* v. *Darby Lumber Co.* (1941) the justices welcomed the opportunity to dispose of it once and for all. Justice Stone said, for a unanimous Court:

> The conclusion is inescapable that Hammer v. Dagenhart was a departure from the principles which have prevailed in the interpretation of the commerce clause both before and since the decision and that such vitality, as a precedent, as it then had has long since been exhausted. It should be and now is overruled.

SELECTED REFERENCES

Cardozo, Benjamin N., *The Nature of the Judicial Process* (New Haven: Yale University Press, 1921).

Douglas, William O, "Stare Decisis," 49 *Columbia Law Review* 735 (1949).

Fuller, Lon L., "Reason and Fiat in Case Law," 59 *Harvard Law Review* 376 (1946).

Goodhart, Arthur L., "Case Law in England and America," 15 *Cornell Law Quarterly* 173 (1930).

——, "Determining the Ratio Decidendi of a Case," 40 *Yale Law Journal* 161 (1930).

——, "Precedent in English and Continental Law," 50 *Law Quarterly Review* 40 (1934).

Jackson, Robert H., "Decisional Law and Stare Decisis," 30 *American Bar Association Journal* 334 (1944).

Levi, Edward H., *An Introduction to Legal Reasoning* (Chicago: University of Chicago Press, 1948).

Murphy, Walter F., "Civil Liberties and the Japanese American Cases: A Study in the Uses of Stare Decisis," 11 *Western Political Quarterly* 3 (1958).

Pound, Roscoe, "The Theory of Judicial Decision," 36 *Harvard Law Review* 641 (1923).

Stone, Harlan F., "The Common Law in the United States," 50 *Harvard Law Review* 4 (1936).

Von Moschzisker, Robert, "Stare Decisis in Courts of Last Resort," 37 *Harvard Law Review* 409 (1924).

1.
"The basic pattern of legal reasoning is reasoning by example."

AN INTRODUCTION TO LEGAL REASONING   *Edward H. Levi**

. . . IT IS IMPORTANT that the mechanism of legal reasoning should not be concealed by its pretense. The pretense is that the law is a system of known rules applied by a judge. . . . In an important sense legal rules are never clear, and, if a rule had to be clear before it could be imposed, society would be impossible. The mechanism accepts the differences of view and ambiguities of words. It provides for the participation of the community in resolving the ambiguity by providing a forum for the discussion of policy in the gap of ambiguity. On serious controversial questions, it makes it possible to take the first step in the direction of what otherwise would be forbidden ends. The mechanism is indispensable to peace in a community.

The basic pattern of legal reasoning is reasoning by example. It is reasoning from case to case. It is a three-step process described by the doctrine of precedent in which a proposition descriptive of the first case is made into a rule of law and then applied to a next similar situation. The steps are these: similarity is seen between cases; next the rule of law inherent in the first case is announced; then the rule of law is made applicable to the second case. This is a method of reasoning necessary for the law, but it has characteristics which under other circumstances might be considered imperfections.

These characteristics become evident if the legal process is approached as though it were a method of applying general rules of law to diverse facts—in short, as though the doctrine of precedent meant that general rules, once properly determined, remained unchanged, and then were applied, albeit imperfectly, in later cases. If this were the doctrine, it would be disturbing to find that the rules change from

Reprinted from *An Introduction to Legal Reasoning* by Edward H. Levi, by permission of The University of Chicago Press. Copyright University of Chicago Press, 1948. Pp. 1–7.

* Dean of the Law School, University of Chicago.

case to case and are remade with each case. Yet this change in the rules is the indispensable dynamic quality of law. It occurs because the scope of a rule of law, and therefore its meaning, depends upon a determination of what facts will be considered similar to those present when the rule was first announced. The finding of similarity or difference is the key step in the legal process.

The determination of similarity or difference is the function of each judge. Where case law is considered, and there is no statute, he is not bound by the statement of the rule of law made by the prior judge even in the controlling case. The statement is mere dictum, and this means that the judge in the present case may find irrelevant the existence or absence of facts which prior judges thought important. It is not what the prior judge intended that is of any importance; rather it is what the present judge, attempting to see the law as a fairly consistent whole, thinks should be the determining classification. In arriving at his result he will ignore what the past thought important; he will emphasize facts which prior judges would have thought made no difference. It is not alone that he could not see the law through the eyes of another, for he could at least try to do so. It is rather that the doctrine of dictum forces him to make his own decision.

Thus it cannot be said that the legal process is the application of known rules to diverse facts. Yet it is a system of rules; the rules are discovered in the process of determining similarity or difference. But if attention is directed toward the finding of similarity or difference, other peculiarities appear. The problem for the law is: When will it be just to treat different cases as though they were the same? A working legal system must therefore be willing to pick out key similarities and to reason from them to the justice of applying a common classification. The existence of some facts in common brings into play the general rule. If this is really reasoning, then by common standards, thought of in terms of closed systems, it is imperfect unless some overall rule has announced that this common and ascertainable similarity is to be decisive. But no such fixed prior rule exists. It could be suggested that reasoning is not involved at all; that is, that no new insight is arrived at through a comparison of cases. But reasoning appears to be involved; the conclusion is arrived at through a process and was not immediately apparent. It seems better to say there is reasoning, but it is imperfect.

Therefore it appears that the kind of reasoning involved in the legal process is one in which the classification changes as the classification is made. The rules change as the rules are applied. More important, the rules arise out of a process which, while comparing fact situations, creates the rules and then applies them. But this kind of reasoning is open to the charge that it is classifying things as equal when they are somewhat different, justifying the classification by rules made up as the reasoning or classification proceeds. In a sense all reasoning is of this type, but there is an additional requirement which compels the legal process to be this way. Not only do new situations arise, but in addition people's wants change. The categories used in the legal process must be left ambiguous in order to permit the infusion of new ideas. And this is true even where legislation or a constitution is involved. The words used by the legislature or the constitutional convention must come to have new meanings. Furthermore, agreement on any other basis would be impossible. In this manner the laws come to express the ideas of the community and even when written in general terms, in statute or constitution, are molded for the specific case.

But attention must be paid to the process. A controversy as to whether the law is certain, unchanging, and expressed in rules, or uncertain, changing, and only a technique for deciding specific cases misses the point. It is both. . . .

Reasoning by example in the law is a key to many things. It indicates in part the hold which the law process has over the litigants. They have participated in the law making. They are bound by something they helped to make. Moreover, the examples or analogies urged by the parties bring into the law the common ideas of the society. The ideas have their day in court, and they will have their day again. This is what makes the hearing fair, rather than any idea that the judge is completely impartial, for of course he cannot be completely so. Moreover, the hearing in a sense compels at least vicarious participation by all the citizens, for the rule which is made, even though ambiguous, will be law as to them.

Reasoning by example shows the decisive role which the common ideas of the society and the distinctions made by experts can have in shaping the law. The movement of common or expert concepts into the law may be followed. The concept is suggested in arguing difference or similarity in a brief, but it wins no approval from the court. The idea achieves standing in the society. It is suggested again to a court. The court this time reinterprets the prior case and in doing so adopts the rejected idea. In subsequent cases, the idea is given further definition and is tied to other ideas which have been accepted by courts. It is now no longer the idea which was commonly held in the society. It becomes modified in subsequent cases. Ideas first rejected but which gradually have won acceptance now push what has become a legal category out of the system or convert it into something which may be its opposite. The process is one in which the ideas of the community and of the social sciences, whether correct or not, as they win acceptance in the community, control legal decisions. Erroneous ideas, of course, have played an enormous part in shaping the law. An idea, adopted by a court, is in a superior position to influence conduct and opinion in the community; judges, after all, are rulers. And the adoption of an idea by a court reflects the power structure in the community. But reasoning by example will operate to change the idea after it has been adopted.

Moreover, reasoning by example brings into focus important similarity and difference in the interpretation of case law, statutes, and the constitution of a nation. There is a striking similarity. It is only folklore which holds that a statute if clearly written can be completely unambiguous and applied as intended to a specific case. . . . Hence reasoning by example operates with all three. But there are important differences. What a court says is dictum, but what a legislature says is a statute. The reference of the reasoning changes. Interpretation of intention when dealing with a statute is the way of describing the attempt to compare cases on the basis of the standard thought to be common at the time the legislation was passed. While this is the attempt, it may not initially accomplish any different result than if the standard of the judge had been explicitly used. Nevertheless, the remarks of the judge are directed toward describing a category set up by the legislature. These remarks are different from ordinary dicta. They set the course of the statute, and later reasoning in subsequent cases is tied to them. As a consequence, courts are less free in applying a statute than in dealing with case law. The current rationale for this is the notion that the legislature has acquiesced by legislative silence in the prior, even though erroneous, interpretation of the court. . . .

Under the United States experience, contrary to what has sometimes been believed when a written constitution of a nation is involved, the court has greater freedom than it has with the application of a statute or case law. . . . The constitution sets up the conflicting ideals of the community in certain ambiguous categories. These categories bring along with them satellite concepts covering the areas of ambiguity. It is with a set of these satellite concepts that reasoning by example must work. But no satellite concept, no matter how well developed, can prevent the court from shifting its course, not only by realigning cases which impose certain restrictions, but by going beyond realignment back to the overall ambiguous category written into the document. The constitution, in other words, permits the court to be inconsistent. The freedom is concealed either as a search for the intention of the framers or as a proper understanding of a living instrument, and sometimes as both. But this does not mean that reasoning by example has any less validity in this field.

It may be objected that this analysis of legal reasoning places too much emphasis on the comparison of cases and too little on the legal concepts which are created. It is true that similarity is seen in terms of a word, and inability to find a ready word to express similarity or difference may prevent change in the law. The words which have been found in the past are much spoken of, have acquired a dignity of their own, and to a considerable measure control results. . . . Thus the connotation of the word for a time has a limiting influence—so much so that the reasoning may even appear to be simply deductive.

But it is not simply deductive. In the long run a circular motion can be seen. The first stage is the creation of the legal concept which is built up as cases are compared. The period is one in which the court fumbles for a phrase. Several phrases may be tried out; the misuse or misunderstanding of words itself may have an effect. The concept sounds like another, and the jump to the second is made. The second stage is the period when the concept is more or less fixed, although reasoning by example continues to classify items inside and out of the concept. The third stage is the breakdown of the concept, as reasoning by example has moved so far ahead as to make it clear that the suggestive influence of the word is no longer desired.

The process is likely to make judges and lawyers uncomfortable. It runs contrary to the pretense of the system. It seems inevitable, therefore, that as matters of kind vanish into matters of degree and then entirely new meanings turn up, there will be the attempt to escape to some overall rule which can be said to have always operated and which will make the reasoning look deductive. The rule will be useless. It will have to operate on a level where it has no meaning. Even when lip service is paid to it, care will be taken to say that it may be too wide or too narrow but that nevertheless it is a good rule. The statement of the rule is roughly analogous to the appeal to the meaning of a statute or of a constitution, but it has less of a function to perform. It is window dressing. Yet it can be very misleading. Particularly when a concept has broken down and reasoning by example is about to build another, textbook writers, well aware of the unreal aspect of old rules, will announce new ones, equally ambiguous and meaningless, forgetting that the legal process does not work with the rule but on a much lower level. . . .

2.   *"Stare decisis is the instrument of stability in a legal system."*

THE DEVELOPMENT OF THE DOCTRINE OF STARE DECISIS AND THE EXTENT TO WHICH IT SHOULD BE APPLIED *Robert A. Sprecher**

I

. . . THE DOCTRINE of *stare decisis et non quieta movere,* "to stand by the decisions and not to disturb settled points," developed during "the infancy of our law." Historians agree that Bracton's *Note Book,* containing one of the first collections of English decisions, gave

31 *American Bar Association Journal* 501 (1945). Copyright 1945 American Bar Association. Reprinted with permission.
* Practicing attorney.

early impetus to the doctrine. Bracton did not understand the modern implications of stare decisis, but he directed the attention of the legal profession to past decisions in "an attempt to bring back the law to its ancient principles." The first comprehensive law reports, the *Year Books,* not only constituted in and of themselves evidence of the importance of prior decisions, but they also contained progressively frequent reference to earlier cases and often a direct statement that certain cases were of some authority, such as the words of Chief Justice Priscot in 1454: "If this plea were now adjudged bad, as you maintain, it would assuredly be a bad example to the young apprentices who study the *Year Books,* for they would never have confidence in their books if now we were to adjudge the contrary of what has been so often adjudged in the Books."

Sir William Holdsworth has pointed out that the modern theory of stare decisis began to develop at the end of the fifteenth century when the changes in the system of pleading "concentrated the reporter's attention, not upon the oral debate in court as to what the pleading should be and what issue should be reached, but upon the decision of the court upon an issue reached by the written pleadings of the parties before the case had come into court." . . . In his great *Commentaries,* written in 1765, five hundred years after Bracton's *Note Book,* Blackstone was able to say that "it is an established rule to abide by former precedents, where the same points come again in litigation." The modern doctrine of the authority of decided cases was reached substantially by the end of the eighteenth century.

Under the modern doctrine, "a judicial precedent speaks in England with authority." "It is more than a model; it has become a fixed and binding rule." *Absolute authority* is said to exist in the following cases:

1. Every court is absolutely bound by the decisions of all courts superior to itself, and usually of all courts of coordinate jurisdiction.

2. The House of Lords is absolutely bound by its own prior decisions.

3. The Court of Appeal is probably bound by its own decisions, although there is some doubt.

However, Holdsworth has observed that the theory of precedents has been accepted in England only subject to reservations and conditions which modify its seemingly unyielding effect. The three important reservations and conditions, all of which ultimately rest on the declaratory theory of law, which is "the principle stated by Coke, Hale, and Blackstone, that these cases do not make law, but are only the best evidence of what the law is," are: (1) the rule laid down in a case need not be followed if it is "plainly unreasonable and inconvenient"—that is, if it is obviously contrary to a statute or to well established principle; (2) a judge has some freedom of choice in instances where courts of equal authority have handed down conflicting decisions; and (3) the authority of a decision is attached, not to the words used, nor to all the reasons given, but to the principle or principles necessary for the decision of the case.

The American doctrine of stare decisis approximated the English doctrine until the twentieth century and the advent of the socialization of the law, but "the modern and present trend is characterized by the overruling and distinguishing of precedents to an extent that would strike an English judge and lawyer as revolutionary."

The American doctrine has always embraced the three conditions of the English doctrine . . . but it has developed two additional conditions, foreign to English law, which are indeed revolutionary and which introduce an element of flexibility into the doctrine.

In the first place, the English doctrine of precedents is a policy voluntarily but rigidly accepted by courts of last resort to effectuate stability in the legal system, and it is enforced by those courts on lower courts in the system through the appeals procedure. The Supreme Court of the United States, on the other hand, has declared that whether stare decisis "shall be followed or departed from is a question entirely within the discretion of the court, which is again called upon to consider a question." . . . In place of the English hierarchy of absolute authority outlined above, the more flexible American doctrine functions approximately as follows:

1. The Supreme Court has never held itself to be rigidly bound by its own decisions, and other federal and state courts have followed that course in reference to their own decisions.

2. A decision of the United States Supreme Court is binding on federal matters on all other courts, federal or state.

3. While a decision of a federal court, other than the Supreme Court, may be persuasive in a state court on a federal matter, it is,

nevertheless, not binding since the state court owes obedience to only one federal court, namely, the Supreme Court. The converse is also true; a decision of a state court on a federal matter may be persuasive in the federal courts but it is not binding.

4. Decisions of the federal courts (other than the Supreme Court) are not binding upon other federal courts of coordinate rank, or of inferior rank, unless the latter owe obedience to the court rendering the decision.

The most important aspect of the flexibility of the American doctrine has been the attitude of the Supreme Court of the United States in cases involving the Federal Constitution, where correction through legislative action is practically impossible. The Court has often overruled its earlier constitutional decisions, and particularly so when the decision believed erroneous is the application of a constitutional principle rather than an interpretation of the Constitution to extract the principle itself.

The second revolutionary difference between the English and American theories of stare decisis is the adaptability of the latter to "the spirit of the times." The American doctrine is fully sensitive to social, economic, and political evolution or change. The fact that, consistent with the American doctrine of stare decisis, the judge functions in part as a law-maker is accepted in America as "one of the existing realities of life."

The discretionary application of the American doctrine furnishes the means of flexibility and the adaptability of the doctrine to the times furnishes some standard of flexibility. However, if flexibility were the only concern of a legal system, stare decisis, which is primarily an organ of stability, would be a useless appendage.

II

Clearly the first step in determining the extent to which the doctrine of stare decisis should be applied is to decide whether the doctrine is to be applied at all, and the answer to that question has largely been supplied by the history of the development of our legal system. . . .

Lacking universal truths to serve as the ultimate source of judgment, a legal system is faced with the alternatives of permitting judges to function arbitrarily and according to individual whim or impulse, or of imposing upon judges from without some objective standard. . . . Even the earliest judges, the Homeric kings, unwilling to admit that they were unfettered in their judgments, pointed to divine inspiration as their source of law, and when they were superseded by a juristical aristocracy to whom the knowledge of the laws was confided from generation to generation, a true objective standard was imposed upon the judges—a standard defined by tribal customs. . . . Anglo law became committed to the objective method when Sir Edward Coke reminded James I that the medieval doctrine of the supremacy of the law took precedence over the divine right of monarchy by quoting to him the words of Bracton: "The King is subject not to men, but to God and the law." The political philosophy of a government of laws rather than of men was embodied in the Constitution of the United States and became a living doctrine in the decisions of Chief Justice Marshall. Cardozo recognized that "the destruction of all rules and the substitution in every instance of the individual sense of justice" might result in "a benevolent despotism if the judges were benevolent men" but "it would put an end to the reign of law."

Once it has been decided that judges are to be restricted in their function of judging by some objective standard, the next problem is to select a standard. The standard must be one which compromises progress and stability. "Law must be stable, and yet it cannot stand still." . . .

Stare decisis is the instrument of *stability* in a legal system. The concept of stability has several important ramifications which may be considered as separate beneficial results of the application of the doctrine, although each is an aspect of stability and each merges almost imperceptibly into the next.

Stare decisis furnishes a legal system with *certainty* and *predictability*. It enables lawyers to advise their clients with a reasonable degree of confidence that certain acts will produce certain consequences. The accuracy with which lawyers can predict legal results measures the esteem with which the legal profession is regarded by the public. Stare decisis enables all members of society to chart and plan future conduct with reasonable knowledge of the risks involved and the probable results to be obtained.

Stare decisis clothes a legal system with *reliability*. When individuals have relied upon authoritative rules of conduct, they are assured that those rules will not be changed so as to make past conduct illegal. Without adherence to precedent, property and contract rights would never be settled. . . . "But the more deplorable consequence will inevitably be that the administration of justice will fall into disrepute. Respect for tribunals must fall when the bar and the public come to understand that nothing that has been said in prior adjudication has force in a current controversy."

Stare decisis assures all persons of *equality and uniformity of treatment*. It guarantees a government of laws and not of men, and that all men will be treated equally under the law. It prevents judges from exercising partiality or prejudice, either through corruption or ignorance. It minimizes the possibility that an inexperienced judge will fall into errors of injustice.

Stare decisis is an instrument of *convenience and expediency*. "The labor of judges would be increased almost to the breaking point if every past decision could be reopened in every case, and one could not lay one's own course of bricks on the secure foundation of the courses laid by others who had gone before him." . . .

Stare decisis preserves the judicial *experience* of the past. This does not mean blind adherence to precedent, but acceptance of rules and principles, the justice and wisdom of which time has not impaired. . . .

> "Growth without innovation is the conventional ideal of
3.   the common law."

THE COMMON LAW METHOD   *Robert A. Leflar**

THE KEY to understanding here is that the common law consists not only of detailed rules but of principles, standards, doctrines and traditions, which in longtime effectiveness far outweigh the little rules. Some courts once laid down a rule that an autoist approach-

---

"The Task of the Appellate Court," 33 *Notre Dame Lawyer* 548 (1958). Copyright 1958 University of Notre Dame. Reprinted with permission.

* Distinguished Professor of Law, University of Arkansas, and former Associate Justice, Arkansas Supreme Court.

ing a railroad track must not only stop, look and listen, but must get out of his car and look down the track if his view be otherwise obscured, before crossing it, else be deemed guilty of contributory negligence if his car is struck by a negligently operated train. The rule was preposterous, because it failed to take into account the possibility that in some circumstances a train might come into sight, and even reach the crossing, while the driver was returning to and restarting his car. It was out of keeping with the facts of life as they relate to driving automobiles on modern highways. Soon the earlier case was overruled, and the courts returned to the true common law guide for such cases, which is a standard of reasonable care, the care which an ordinary prudent man would exercise under the same or similar circumstances. The amount and types of diligence necessary for compliance with the standard of reasonable care under the circumstances vary on similar sets of facts, sometimes from jury to jury but more significantly from generation to generation. Thus in automobile cases conditions of transportation and transportation values change, and applications of the standard have changed with them. Little rules as to what constitutes reasonable care in this or that situation have come and gone, been asserted and then retracted, but the common law standard has remained. . . .

In the criminal law we have a doctrine that there can be no guilt without a guilty mind. It is said that *mens rea* must be present before the criminal defendant may be found guilty. Where did that requirement come from? In most states it was never enacted by the legislature. It is derived from the common law. The legislature may have provided flatly that "the doing of x act shall be a felony." D is proved to have done x act, but shows that he did it in his sleep, or was unaware of facts which gave his act x character. He may have married a second wife while he had a first wife living, which the statute defines as bigamy, but he honestly believed his first wife was dead. The courts say that such a man is not guilty of bigamy. But they also say that for some other crimes a guilty mind is not required. If D is color-blind so that he thinks red is green, and he runs a stoplight, he will be held guilty despite his moral innocence. When we deal with types of conduct upon which a mass of other people must rely objectively with no opportunity to gauge the actor's inner innocence, we say he acts at his peril even for purposes of the criminal law. The distinction makes sense, and our criminal law achieves a nice balance of fairness with efficiency by means of it, but we need to remember that both the rule and the distinction were made up by the courts. . . .

A good illustration of current growth in the common law may be taken from the field of defamation. When I was a law student the rule was that a tort occurred at each time and each place a libel or slander was published, and publication occurred each time the defendant caused it to be read or heard by any person. With radio and television, and the great national magazines, that meant an almost uncountable number of publications with separate torts in each state where the magazine was circulated or the broadcast heard, and repeated torts each time a newsstand copy was perused or a library reader saw the offending article. New and separate actions could be brought almost interminably, and adjudication of one claim would leave the others still unsettled. To meet this situation the courts, not the legislatures, in the 1940's devised the single publication rule, which is that publication to the whole mass of readers or listeners is one transaction occurring one time and constituting one tort. That was not the law anywhere in America thirty years ago, but it is now in several states. . . .

Areas of growth in the law in our own time, comparable in importance but even greater in size, arise from the new complexities of a twentieth century economy. Labor law serves as an example. When cases concerning organized labor began to come to the courts a century or so ago, the courts sought to solve them without innovation, by precedents and analogies from a past which envisioned laborers altogether as individuals, not as a corporate group in any sense. The effort was not successful, and what the courts then did with labor cases is history only, and not the law of today. A fresh start had to be made when the essentially corporate character of our new economy became evident to most students of it. To bring the law governing the activities and relationships of organized labor into line with its function in our society became a major task, after that false start, and aid from legislative enactments was required where some special areas were concerned. But the courts too were able to make the adjustment. They found better precedents and better analogies, and the standard techniques of the law enabled them in time to develop the rules we have today which, though still in flux, serve reasonably well to resolve the disputes which the relationships of big labor with big industry bring to the courts. So it has been with the old decisions relating to business combinations and restraint of trade; they represented attitudes characteristic of another economic era, and because they did not fit our times they have fallen by the wayside. . . .

From what I have been saying one who did not know better might think that the common law as administered by the courts is a body of adjudication that always keeps abreast of the needs of society, that responds like a delicate seismograph connected with some intricate machine which promptly translates its perceptions of movement in society into law appropriate to the new conditions when legislatures have failed to act as promptly as they might have. We know that nothing is further from the fact. Despite the history I have just recited, judicial lawmaking is a slow and cumbersome process, a case-by-case approach which, as Holmes observed, often does no more than carry us from tuft to tuft across the morass, seldom presenting problems whole, but in little pieces only, so that the broad complete solutions which a legislature can achieve are almost never possible. Judicial timidity also takes its toll from progress, for it is often easier to see the past than the present, and a judge who craves easy certainty finds it more readily if he does not look too much beyond the lawbooks in his chambers. Every one of us can think of rules of law that have been obsolete for a long time, yet are still followed in the courts. One that every doctor and psychologist in America can tell us about is that which governs the relation between insanity and crime. The rule we follow is one that was laid down by the judges in the English House of Lords, in a series of questions and answers in *McNaghten's Case,* in 1843. It sets up a test of the defendant's ability to distinguish between right and wrong with respect to the act done. This is a test based on capacity to reason, yet many scientists today tell us that diseases of the mind take many forms, destruction of the reasoning powers being incident only to some of them. The insanity that we talk about in our criminal law is not the insanity of the psychiatric studies. A few courts, New Hampshire back in 1871, the District of Columbia four years ago, have had the courage to break away from the time-honored *McNaghten* rule, but most courts have not. The same story could be told concerning the courts' slow and reluctant recognition of new types of interests . . . the courts' unwillingness to discard old rules of evidence which bar relevant testimony at trials, thus working toward concealment rather than ascertainment of the truth; their frequent insistence upon retaining old procedural forms and practices which slow down without aiding the processes of justice—these things are the common substance of standard complaints, too often justified, concerning the law and its administration.

One thing stands out above all else from this—our courts have made most of our law, the mass of our common law. Courts do make law. It is their business to make law. At least that is true of appellate courts. They do not merely decide single cases, but lay down precedent which is a guide to future decision in the same jurisdiction and persuasive in other jurisdictions, and, therefore, is "law" in the sense that it is a basis for Holmesian prophecy as to what a court will do in the next case of the same sort that comes along. A basis for prophecy, we can say, but not a basis for mathematical calculation, since judges who make law can, if they will, make new law and make it different from the old. One of the complaints we have against them is that sometimes they do not make new law when we think they should.

Someone may say that this system of judge-made law does not fit in with the ideal of a government by law and not by men. This objection assumes that appellate judges are men, which can be conceded. . . . But who is to make our laws, if not men? It is only a question of which men. That is part of the answer. The rest of the answer to the objection, and the main part of the answer, is that this system of judicial lawmaking is the Anglo-American system, the system that our nation has known and followed since its beginnings, the system that we are talking about when we boast that ours is a land of law and not of tyranny. It is our system and it always has been. The Germans and French and Italians have a different system, based upon legislated codes rather than upon judge-made common law. The Russian system is closer to the continental European system than to ours. A good many of the newer nations in the world, coming fresh upon the problems of modern civilization, have chosen to set up codes modeled on those of continental Europe. But English-speaking countries in general have preferred to follow the common law way. That of course does not prove that it is the better way, and certainly does not prove that it is perfect, but it does prove that it is not un-American, for whatever that signifies. It also proves that it is a system under which a nation such as ours can live for almost two hundred years and grow great in the process, while at the same time achieving a considerable world reputation for its justice under law. . . .

The greatest single, limiting factor set up by judicial tradition upon judicial freedom is without doubt the doctrine of precedent, stare decisis. No common law court disregards this doctrine. That obviously does not mean that our appellate courts undertake to follow their prior decisions in every subsequent case. We know they do not. The doctrine of stare decisis does not call for that.

Stare decisis is common law doctrine, not constitutional law. . . . Appellate courts make a general practice of following their past decisions. To a lesser extent courts also make a practice of following their past dicta, their nonessential statements about what the law is, distinguishable from the *ratio decidendi* which actually control their cases. Cardozo speaks of "static" and "dynamic" precedents, those which are limited narrowly and those which the courts choose to expand and extend. The static ones look mostly to the past, the dynamic are springboards for growth in law because they speak in terms of the present and the future. Also there are precedents upon which people rely in entering upon life's transactions, and others upon which reliance is seldom placed until there is a case in court involving them. Precedents which lay down rules of property, or which state the effect of commercial transactions, are of the first sort. For special reasons rules of criminal law are placed in this category too. Courts seldom overturn these precedents. To be contrasted are the cases which state rules to govern civil liability for bad conduct, either negligent or intentional. The allegedly negligent auto driver does not assert reliance upon a judicial precedent as his reason for driving as he did. A change in the rule of case law will not be unfair to him if he was not measuring his conduct by it in the first place. . . .

The strength of a particular case as precedent varies, according to the availability of alternative grounds for decision, the field of law in which the case falls, the breadth of the principle it represents, the judicial reputation of the man who wrote the opinion, the comparability of the surrounding facts in successive cases, and a dozen other factors. This variability characterizes the strength as precedent of both *ratio decidendi* and dictum. Strong precedents are seldom overruled expressly, though this does happen; they are more likely to be "distinguished" if they are not to be followed. Sometimes the process of distinguishing them leaves life in them, and sometimes it practically takes the life out of them. Distinguishing them, however, preserves the link of continuity with them, avoids the sharp break with the past that an outright overruling involves.

Continuity is the hallmark of judicial respectability, the formality that satisfies convention. If the form of continuity is preserved, regardless of what judicial advance be made, the court has stayed within the convention of precedent. If precedent is openly rejected, innovation is apparent. Growth without innovation is the conventional ideal of the common law. The doctrine of precedents does not oppose growth, nor favor it either. Rather, it aids and abets growth, leaves open the opportunity for it. . . .

Today we hear courts criticized because, it is said, they are deciding cases not on law but on sociology. If that implies that our courts are breaking away altogether from the doctrine of precedents and the techniques that are part of the doctrine, and are claiming freedom to decide cases without regard to it, we have a serious criticism. If it means, however, only that the courts are taking sociology into account in reaching their decisions in areas where law governs social relationships, then the courts are being criticized for doing what they have always done in our system. Perhaps the fact is that they are merely indiscreet in being unsubtle about what they are doing by open use of the word "sociology," where older courts used verbiage that had more sound of law books to it. . . .

4.   *"Necessarily this is a problem in probabilities."*

WIENER V. UNITED STATES

MR. JUSTICE FRANKFURTER delivered the opinion of the Court. . . .

. . . The facts are not in dispute. By the War Claims Act of 1948 . . . Congress established that Commission with "jurisdiction to receive and adjudicate according to law" . . . claims for compensating internees,

357 U.S. 349, 78 S. Ct. 1275, 2 L. Ed. 2d 1377 (1958).

prisoners of war, and religious organizations . . . who suffered personal injury or propery damage at the hands of the enemy in connection with World War II. The Commission was to be composed of three persons, at least two of whom were to be members of the bar, to be appointed by the President, by and with the advice and consent of the Senate. The Commission was to wind up its affairs not later than three years after the expiration of the time for filing claims, originally limited to two years but extended by legislation. . . . This limit on the Commission's life was the mode by which the tenure of the Commissioners was defined, and Congress made no provision for removal of a Commissioner.

Having been duly nominated by President Truman, the petitioner was confirmed on June 2, 1950, and took office on June 8, following. On his refusal to heed a request for his resignation, he was, on December 10, 1953, removed by President Eisenhower in the following terms: "I regard it as in the national interest to complete the administration of the War Claims Act of 1948, as amended, with personnel of my own selection." The following day, the President made recess appointments to the Commission, including petitioner's post. After Congress assembled, the President, on February 15, 1954, sent the names of the new appointees to the Senate. The Senate had not confirmed these nominations when the Commission was abolished. . . . Thereupon, petitioner brought this proceeding in the Court of Claims for recovery of his salary as a War Claims Commissioner from December 10, 1953, the day of his removal by the President, to June 30, 1954, the last day of the Commission's existence. A divided Court of Claims dismissed the petition. . . . We brought the case here . . . because it presents a variant of the constitutional issue decided in *Humphrey's Executor* v. *United States*. . . .

Controversy pertaining to the scope and limits of the President's power of removal fills a thick chapter of our political and judicial history. The long stretches of its history, beginning with the very first Congress, with early echoes in the Reports of this Court, were laboriously traversed in *Myers* v. *United States* . . . and need not be retraced. President Roosevelt's reliance upon the pronouncements of the Court in that case in removing a member of the Federal Trade Commission on the ground that "the aims and purposes of the Administration with respect to the work of the Commission can be carried out most effectively with personnel of my own selection" reflected contemporaneous professional opinion regarding the significance of the *Myers* decision. Speaking through a Chief Justice who himself had been President, the Court did not restrict itself to the immediate issue before it, the President's inherent power to remove a postmaster, obviously an executive official. As of set purpose and not by way of parenthetic casualness, the Court announced that the President had inherent constitutional power of removal also of officials who have "duties of a quasi-judicial character . . . whose decisions after hearing affect interests of individuals, the discharge of which the President can not in a particular case properly influence or control." . . .

The assumption was short-lived that the *Myers* case recognized the President's inherent constitutional power to remove officials, no matter what the relation of the executive to the discharge of their duties and no matter what restrictions Congress may have imposed regarding the nature of their tenure. The versatility of circumstances often mocks a natural desire for definitiveness. Within less than ten years a unanimous Court, in *Humphrey's Executor* v. *United States* . . . narrowly confined the scope of the *Myers* decision to include only "all purely executive officers." . . . The Court explicitly "disapproved" the expressions in *Myers* supporting the President's inherent constitutional power to remove members of quasi-judicial bodies. . . . Congress had given members of the Federal Trade Commission a seven-year term and also provided for the removal of a Commissioner by the President for inefficiency, neglect of duty or malfeasance in office. In the present case, Congress provided for a tenure defined by the relatively short period of time during which the War Claims Commission was to operate— that is, it was to wind up not later than three years after the expiration of the time for filing of claims. But nothing was said in the Act about removal.

This is another instance in which the most appropriate legal significance must be drawn from congressional failure of explicitness. Necessarily this is a problem in probabilities. . . .

Humphrey's case . . . drew a sharp line of cleavage between officials who were part of the Executive establishment and were thus removable by virtue of the President's constitutional powers, and those who are members of a body "to exercise its judgment without the leave or hindrance of any other official or any department of the government" . . . as to whom a power of removal exists only if Congress may fairly be said to have conferred it. This sharp differentiation derives from the difference in functions between those who are part of the Executive establishment and those whose tasks require absolute freedom from Executive interference. "For it is quite evident," again to quote *Humphrey's Executor*, "that one who holds his office only during the pleasure of another, cannot be depended upon to maintain an attitude of independence against the latter's will." . . .

Thus, the most reliable factor for drawing an inference regarding the President's power of removal in our case is the nature of the function that Congress vested in the War Claims Commission. . . . The ground of President Eisenhower's removal of petitioner was precisely the same as President Roosevelt's removal of Humphrey. Both Presidents desired to have Commissioners, one on the Federal Trade Commission, the other on the War Claims Commission, "of my own selection." . . . The terms of removal in the two cases are identic and express the assumption that the agencies of which the two Commissioners were members were subject in the discharge of their duties to the control of the Executive. An analysis of the Federal Trade Commission Act left this Court in no doubt that such was not the conception of Congress in creating the Federal Trade Commission. The terms of the War Claims Act of 1948 leave no doubt that such was not the conception of Congress regarding the War Claims Commission.

The history of this legislation emphatically underlines this fact. The short of it is that the origin of the Act was a bill, H. R. 4044, 80th Cong., 1st Sess., passed by the House that placed the administration of a very limited class of claims by Americans against Japan in the hands of the Federal Security Administrator and provided for a Commission to inquire into and report upon other types of claims. . . . The Federal Security Administrator was indubitably an arm of the President. When the House bill reached the Senate, it struck out all but the enacting clause, rewrote the bill, and established a Commission with "jurisdiction to receive and adjudicate according to law" three classes of claims, as defined by § § 5, 6 and 7. The Commission was established as an adjudicating body with all the paraphernalia by which legal claims are put to the test of proof, with finality of determination "not subject to review by any other official of the United States or by any court, by mandamus or otherwise." . . . Awards were to be paid out of a War Claims Fund in the hands of the Secretary of the Treasury, whereby such claims were given even more assured collectability than adheres to judgments rendered in the Court of Claims. . . . With minor amendment . . . this Senate bill became law.

When Congress has for distribution among American claimants funds derived from foreign sources, it may proceed in different ways. Congress may appropriate directly; it may utilize the Executive; it may resort to the adjudicatory process. . . . The final form of the legislation, as we have seen, left the widened range of claims to be determined by adjudication. . . . The fact that it chose to establish a Commission to "adjudicate according to law" the classes of claims defined in the statute did not alter the intrinsic judicial character of the task with which the Commission was charged. The claims were to be "adjudicated according to law," that is, on the merits of each claim, supported by evidence and governing legal considerations, by a body that was "entirely free from the control or coercive influence, direct or indirect," *Humphrey's Executor* v. *United States* . . . of either the Executive or the Congress. If, as one must take for granted, the War Claims Act precluded the President from influencing the Commission in passing on a particular claim, *a fortiori* must it be inferred that Congress did not wish to have hang over the Commission the Damocles' sword of removal by the President for no reason other than that he preferred to have on that Commission men of his own choosing. . . .

The judgment is

Reversed.

5.   *"We do not write upon a clean slate."*

GREEN V. UNITED STATES

GREEN AND WINSTON, *two Communist leaders convicted under the Smith Act, were released on bail pending appeal. When the Supreme Court affirmed their convictions the two men jumped bail and hid out for four-and-a-half years. After they surrendered, the*

356 U.S. 165, 78 S. Ct. 632, 2 L. Ed. 2d 672 (1958).

trial judge found them guilty of contempt and sentenced them to three years in prison. Green and Winston appealed, claiming, among other things, that this contempt conviction, since it was imposed without grand jury indictment or jury trial, violated fundamental constitutional rights. The Court of Appeals upheld the contempt conviction, and the Supreme Court granted certiorari.

MR. JUSTICE HARLAN delivered the opinion of the Court. . . .

. . . The statements of this Court in a long and unbroken line of decisions involving contempts ranging from misbehavior in court to disobedience of court orders establish beyond peradventure that criminal contempts are not subject to jury trial as a matter of constitutional right. Although appearing to recognize this, petitioners nevertheless point out that punishment for criminal contempts cannot in any practical sense be distinguished from punishment for substantive crimes . . . and that contempt proceedings have traditionally been surrounded with many of the protections available in a criminal trial. But this Court has never suggested that such protections included the right to grand jury indictment. . . . And of course the summary procedures followed by English courts prior to adoption of the Constitution in dealing with many contempts of court did not embrace the use of either grand or petit jury. . . . It would indeed be anomalous to conclude that contempts subject to sentences of imprisonment for over one year are "infamous crimes" under the Fifth Amendment although they are neither "crimes" nor "criminal prosecutions" for the purpose of jury trial within the meaning of Art. III, § 2, and the Sixth Amendment.

We are told however that the decisions of this Court denying the right to jury trial in criminal contempt proceedings are based upon an "historical error" reflecting a misunderstanding as to the scope of the power of English courts at the early common law to try summarily for contempts, and that this error should not here be extended to a denial of the right to grand jury. But the more recent historical research into English contempt practices predating the adoption of our Constitution reveals no such clear error and indicates if anything that the precise nature of those practices is shrouded in much obscurity. And whatever the breadth of the historical error said by contemporary scholarship to have been committed by English courts of the late-Seventeenth and Eighteenth Centuries in their interpretation of English precedents involving the trials of contempts of court, it at least seems clear that English practice by the early Eighteenth Century comprehended the use of summary powers of conviction by courts to punish for a variety of contempts committed within and outside court. Such indeed is the statement of English law of this period found in Blackstone . . . who explicitly recognized use of a summary power by English courts to deal with disobedience of court process. It is noteworthy that the Judiciary Act of 1789, first attempting a definition of the contempt power, was enacted by a Congress with a Judiciary Committee including members of the recent Constitutional Convention, who no doubt shared the prevailing views in the American Colonies of English law as expressed in Blackstone. . . . Against this historical background, this Court has never deviated from the view that the constitutional guarantee of trial by jury for "crimes" and "criminal prosecutions" was not intended to reach to criminal contempts. . . .

We do not write upon a clean slate. The principle that criminal contempts of court are not required to be tried by a jury under Article III or the Sixth Amendment is firmly rooted in our traditions. . . .

Affirmed.

MR. JUSTICE FRANKFURTER, concurring. . . .

. . . Law is a social organism, and evolution operates in the sociological domain no less than in the biological. The vitality and therefore validity of law is not arrested by the circumstances of its origin. What Magna Carta has become is very different indeed from the immediate objects of the barons at Runnymede. The fact that scholarship has shown that historical assumptions regarding the procedure for punishment of contempt of court were ill-founded, hardly wipes out a century and a half of the legislative and judicial history of federal law based on such assumptions. . . .

Whatever the conflicting views of scholars in construing more or less dubious manuscripts of the Fourteenth Century, what is indisputable is that from the foundation of the United States the constitutionality of the power to punish for contempt without the intervention of a jury has not been doubted. The First Judiciary Act

conferred such a power on the federal courts in the very act of their
establishment . . . and of the Judiciary Committee of eight that reported the bill to the Senate, five members including the chairman,
Senator, later to be Chief Justice, Ellsworth, had been delegates to
the Constitutional Convention. In the First Congress itself no less
than nineteen members, including Madison who contemporaneously
introduced the Bill of Rights, had been delegates to the Convention.
And when an abuse under this power manifested itself, and led
Congress to define more explicitly the summary power vested in the
courts, it did not remotely deny the existence of the power but merely
defined the conditions for its exercise more clearly, in an Act "declaratory of the law concerning contempts of court." . . .

Nor has the constitutionality of the power been doubted by this
Court throughout its existence. In at least two score cases in this
Court, not to mention the vast mass of decisions in the lower federal
courts, the power to punish summarily has been accepted without
question. It is relevant to call the roll of the Justices, not including
those now sitting, who thus sustained the exercise of this power:

Washington	Gray	Pitney
Marshall	Blatchford	McReynolds
Johnson	Lamar	Brandeis
Livingston	Fuller	Clarke
Todd	Brewer	Taft
Story	Brown	Sutherland
Duval	Shiras	Butler
Clifford	H. E. Jackson	Sanford
Swayne	White	Stone
Miller	Peckham	Roberts
Davis	McKenna	Cardozo
Field	Holmes	Reed
Strong	Day	Murphy
Bradley	Moody	Jackson
Hunt	Lurton	Rutledge
Waite	Hughes	Vinson
Harlan	Van Devanter	Minton
Matthews	J. R. Lamar	

To be sure, it is never too late for this Court to correct a misconception in an occasional decision, even on a rare occasion to change
a rule of law that may have long persisted but also have long been
questioned and only fluctuatingly applied. To say that everybody on

the Court has been wrong for 150 years and that that which has been deemed part of the bone and sinew of the law should now be extirpated is quite another thing. Decision-making is not a mechanical process, but neither is this Court an originating lawmaker. The admonition of Mr. Justice Brandeis that we are not a third branch of the legislature should never be disregarded. Congress has seen fit from time to time to qualify the power of summary punishment for contempt that it gave the federal courts in 1789 by requiring in explicitly defined situations that a jury be associated with the court in determining whether there has been a contempt. . . . It is for Congress to extend this participation of the jury, whenever it see fit to do so, to other instances of the exercise of the power to punish for contempt. It is not for this Court to fashion a wholly novel constitutional doctrine . . . in the teeth of an unbroken legislative and judicial history from the foundation of the Nation.

MR. JUSTICE BLACK, with whom THE CHIEF JUSTICE and MR. JUSTICE DOUGLAS concur, dissenting.

The power of a judge to inflict punishment for criminal contempt by means of a summary proceeding stands as an anomaly in the law. In my judgment the time has come for a fundamental and searching reconsideration of the validity of this power which has aptly been characterized by a State Supreme Court as, "perhaps, nearest akin to despotic power of any power existing under our form of government." Even though this extraordinary authority first slipped into the law as a very limited and insignificant thing, it has relentlessly swollen, at the hands of not unwilling judges, until it has become a drastic and pervasive mode of administering criminal justice usurping our regular constitutional methods of trying those charged with offenses against society. . . .

I would reject those precedents which have held that the federal courts can punish an alleged violation outside the courtroom of their decrees by means of a summary trial, at least as long as they can punish by severe prison sentences or fines as they now can and do. I would hold that the defendants here were entitled to be tried by a jury after indictment by a grand jury and in full accordance with all the procedural safeguards required by the Constitution for "all criminal prosecutions." I am convinced that the previous cases to the contrary are wrong—wholly wrong for reasons which I shall set out in this opinion.

Ordinarily it is sound policy to adhere to prior decisions but this practice has quite properly never been a blind, inflexible rule. Courts are not omniscient. Like every other human agency, they too can profit from trial and error, from experience and reflection. As others have demonstrated, the principle commonly referred to as *stare decisis* has never been thought to extend so far as to prevent the courts from correcting their own errors. Accordingly, this Court has time and time again from the very beginning reconsidered the merits of its earlier decisions even though they claimed great longevity and repeated reaffirmation. . . . Indeed, the Court has a special responsibility where questions of constitutional law are involved to review its decisions from time to time and where compelling reasons present themselves to refuse to follow erroneous precedents; otherwise its mistakes in interpreting the Constitution are extremely difficult to alleviate and needlessly so. . . .

If ever a group of cases called for reappraisal it seems to me that those approving summary trial of charges of criminal contempt are the ones. The early precedents which laid the groundwork for this line of authorities were decided before the actual history of the procedures used to punish contempt was brought to light, at a time when "[w]holly unfounded assumptions about 'immemorial usage' acquired a factitious authority and were made the basis of legal decisions." [Frankfurter and Landis, Power to Regulate Contempts, 37 Harv. L. Rev. 1010, 1011.] These cases erroneously assumed that courts had always possessed the power to punish all contempts summarily and that it inhered in their very being without supporting their suppositions by authority or reason. Later cases merely cite the earlier ones in a progressive cumulation while uncritically repeating their assumptions about "immemorial usage" and "inherent necessity."

No justified expectations would be destroyed by the course I propose. There has been no heavy investment in reliance on the earlier cases; they do not remotely lay down rules to guide men in their commercial or property affairs. . . . Apparently even the majority recognizes the need for some kind of reform by engrafting the requirement that punishment for contempt must be "reasonable"—

that irrepressible, vague and delusive standard which at times threatens to engulf the entire law, including the Constitution itself, in a sea of judicial discretion. . . .

Summary trial of criminal contempt, as now practiced, allows a single functionary of the state, a judge, to lay down the law, to prosecute those whom he believes have violated his command (as interpreted by him), to sit in "judgment" on his own charges, and then within the broadest kind of bounds to punish as he sees fit. . . . No official, regardless of his position or the purity and nobleness of his character, should be granted such autocratic omnipotence. Indeed if any other officer were presumptuous enough to claim such power I cannot believe the courts would tolerate it for an instant under the Constitution. . . .

. . . The myth of immemorial usage has been exploded by recent scholarship as a mere fiction. Instead it seems clear that until at least the late Seventeenth or early Eighteenth Centuries the English courts, with the sole exception of the extraordinary and ill-famed Court of Star Chamber whose arbitrary procedures and gross excesses brought forth many of the safeguards included in our Constitution, neither had nor claimed power to punish contempts committed out of court by summary process. Fox, The History of Contempt of Court; Frankfurter and Landis, Power to Regulate Contempts, 37 Harv. L. Rev. 1010, 1042–1052; Beale, Contempt of Court, Criminal and Civil, 21 Harv. L. Rev. 161. Prior to this period such contempts were tried in the normal and regular course of the criminal law, including trial by jury. . . .

Then in 1765 Justice Wilmot declared in an opinion prepared for delivery in the Court of King's Bench (but never actually handed down) that courts had exercised the power to try all contempts summarily since their creation in the forgotten past. Although this bald assertion has been wholly discredited by the painstaking research of the eminent authorities referred to above, and even though Wilmot's opinion was not published until some years after our Constitution had been adopted, nor cited as authority by any court until 1821, his views have nevertheless exerted a baleful influence on the law of contempt both in this country and in England. . . .

Professors Frankfurter and Landis in their fine article . . . unequivocally declare:

. . . the Clayton Act [providing for jury trial of certain charges of criminal contempt] does nothing new. It is as old as the best traditions of the common law. . . .

Down to the early part of the eighteenth century cases of contempt even in and about the common-law courts when not committed by persons officially connected with the court were dealt with by the ordinary course of law, *i.e.*, tried by jury, except when the offender confessed or when the offense was committed "in the actual view of the court." . . .

[U]ntil 1720 there is no instance in the common-law precedents of punishment otherwise than after trial in the ordinary course and not by summary process. . . .

Those who claim that the delegates who ratified the Constitution and its contemporaneous Amendments intended to exempt the crime of contempt from the procedural safeguards expressly established by those great charters for the trial of "all crimes" carry a heavy burden indeed. There is nothing in the Constitution or any of its Amendments which even remotely suggests such an exception. And as the Government points out in its brief, it does not appear that there was a word of discussion in the Constitutional Convention or in any of the state ratifying conventions recognizing or affirming the jurisdiction of courts to punish this crime by summary process, a power which in all particulars is so inherently alien to the method of punishing other public offenses provided by the Constitution. . . .

In the last analysis there is no justification in history, in necessity, or most important in the Constitution for trying those charged with violating a court's decree in a manner wholly different from those accused of disobeying any other mandate of the state. It is significant that neither the Court nor the Government makes any serious effort to justify such differentiation except that it has been sanctioned by prior decisions. . . .

MR. JUSTICE BRENNAN, with whom THE CHIEF JUSTICE and MR. JUSTICE DOUGLAS join, dissenting.

I dissent because I do not believe that the evidence was sufficient to establish beyond a reasonable doubt the petitioners' guilt of the criminal contempt charged. . . .

11 / STATUTORY INTERPRETATION

The great bulk of the law applied by American courts today is statute law. Congress, the state legislatures, and city councils originate a tremendous mass of enactments which courts must interpret and apply. This predominance of statute law is a characteristic of only the past century. Earlier, the judge-made principles of the common law had been relied on to control social and economic relationships; but the industrial-urban developments of the later nineteenth century required legislation both to break the bonds of the past and to provide new controls over the rapidly developing abuses of the laissez-faire social order. This shift can be seen with startling clarity in the statistics of the Supreme Court's business. According to Felix Frankfurter's calculations, as late as 1875 more than 40 per cent of the controversies before the Court were common-law litigation, while by 1925 only 5 per cent fell in this category.

The Rule of Strict Construction

Judges were initially unhappy about the trend which challenged their legislative primacy. This institutional competition was sharpened because judges tended to represent the *status quo* and to favor the more conservative forces in society, whereas legislators were more influenced by the new currents of opinion. Consequently the judicial tactic in dealing with statutory construction was at first to adopt rules which would hamper the effectiveness of statutes as much as possible and limit the impact of new legislation.

The bias of the courts was perhaps most clearly seen in the rule that legislation in derogation of the common law would be strictly construed, but strict construction was also practiced on any legislation which imposed new or drastic burdens or special penalties. Almost every significant piece of "progressive" legislation went through a period of judicial sabotage which took the form, not only of outright attacks on the constitutionality of the legislation, but also of interpretations which denied to the law the power and scope the legislature had intended to convey. For example, the powers of the Interstate Commerce Commission were interpreted so narrowly by the Supreme Court after the Commission was set up by the Act of 1887, that by 1896 the agency was practically out of business. It took a series of new statutes and a change in judicial attitudes in the twentieth century to undo this damage.

While strict construction motivated by judicial jealousy of legislatures has long been outgrown, it remains an established rule in at least one area, the interpretation of penal statutes. Criminal statutes must be sufficiently specific in their terms to define and give adequate notice of the kind of conduct they forbid or penalize. As the Supreme Court said in *Connally* v. *General Construction Co.* (1926): "A statute which either forbids or requires the doing of an act in terms so vague that men of common intelligence must necessarily guess at its meaning and differ as to its application, violates the first essential of due process of law."

Implementation of this principle of certainty and notice requires the courts to resolve any ambiguities of language in criminal statutes in favor of the accused. This rule, as Chief Justice Marshall remarked in *United States* v. *Wiltberger* (1820), "is founded on the tenderness of the law for the rights of individuals; and on the plain principle that the power of punishment is vested in the legislative, not in the judicial department. It is the legislature, not the Court, which is to define a crime, and ordain its punishment."

The Problem of Ambiguity

The task of statutory interpretation might seem, on first consideration, to pose fewer problems than the task of reasoning from case law. There is no need to search among many precedents for the principle of the case. There is no need to look for dicta so that they may be excluded from consideration. The court starts with a text, which is the end result of a legislature's effort to state a rule of law in language which will make the legislative meaning clear and plain.

However, it is demanding too much of words to insist that they convey a single clear command to those charged with their interpretation and implementation. The task of draftsmanship is difficult enough when only a single person is endeavoring to give precise form to his thoughts. It is infinitely more difficult when many legislators with widely differing points of view are involved, and when their task is to find formulas on which a majority of the participants can agree. Given the legislative problem, a considerable amount of ambiguity in the product is a necessity, not a consequence of bad draftsmanship.

Legislatures are not efficient fact-finding bodies. They must act on the basis of necessarily imperfect knowledge. Their members know different things and have different purposes. Sometimes the ambiguity is a result of compromises required to obtain a majority. Sometimes the legislators are subjected to such pressure that something must be done, but no one is sure just what. Then an ambiguous statute will be an expedient way of shifting the pressure to the courts.

An interesting example of this latter tactic was supplied by the Submerged Lands Act of 1953, which Congress passed in order to transfer to the ocean and Gulf Coast states the subsurface oil and mineral rights which the Supreme Court held in 1947 to belong to the national government. Congress was clear that it wanted the states to possess these rights in the three miles adjacent to shore. But the Gulf states claimed that their boundaries extended into the water for three leagues (about ten miles). Uncertain whether this claim should be recognized, Congress wrote the three-mile provision into the statute, and then added this proviso:

> Nothing in this section is to be construed as questioning or in any manner prejudicing the existence of any State's seaward boundary beyond three geographical miles if it was so provided by its constitution or laws prior to or at the time such State became a member of the Union, or if it has been heretofore approved by Congress.

Attempting to give effect to this rather Delphic language, the Supreme Court in 1960 concluded that by these tests the boundaries of Texas and Florida extended three leagues, but the other three Gulf states were entitled to only three miles.[1]

Given the inevitable condition of legislative ambiguity, it follows that the opportunities for judicial use of discretion in statutory interpretation are very wide. For this reason, judges must assume unusual responsibilities

[1] *United States* v. *Louisiana, Texas, Mississippi, Alabama, and Florida.*

when they construe statutes. In reasoning about case law they are at least operating *intra muros* and dealing with the work of their own kind. But in assigning meaning to statutes they are crossing a jurisdictional line and must step warily lest they be accused of usurping the legislative role.

Administrative Interpretation

Many statutes are entrusted to particular administrative agencies for enforcement. This is particularly true of tax and business regulatory laws. The Internal Revenue Service, the National Labor Relations Board, and the Interstate Commerce Commission are examples of agencies which administer important statutes, and are constantly interpreting these statutes as a basis for their decisions and actions.

Where such administrative interpretations are available, the task of the judiciary tends to be lightened. It is true that the initial judicial reaction to the establishment of administrative regulatory agencies was hostile, but more recently the courts, under the leadership of the Supreme Court, have come to welcome the assistance they receive from trained administrative tribunals, and have tended to give great weight to their statutory interpretations.

Of course judges retain full authority to reverse any administrative interpretations of statutes with which they disagree, but on occasion they have gone so far in accepting the administrative judgment that they have been accused of abdicating their functions of judicial review. In *NLRB* v. *Hearst Publications* (1944), where the question was whether street-corner newsboys were "employees" of the newspapers as that term was used in the Wagner Act, the Supreme Court stressed the superior capacities of the NLRB to decide the issue. "Everyday experience in the administration of the statute gives it familiarity with the circumstances and backgrounds of employment relationships in various industries," and so the Court accepted the Board's interpretation. But Justice Roberts dissented: "The question who is an employee, so as to make the statute applicable to him, is a question of the meaning of the Act and, therefore, is a judicial and not an administrative question."

Legislative Intent

It is a generally accepted principle that judges, in interpreting the written law, should give effect to the spirit and intent of the law. By so doing courts seem to recognize their subordinate position and their obligation to help the legislature achieve its purposes. However, the intent of a legislature is often so obscure that a court in searching for it will find it necessary to fall back on its own judgment as to what the legislature ought to have intended. As Monroe Smith wrote in his lecture on Jurisprudence:

> . . . the possibilities of lawfinding under cover of interpretation are very great. A distinguished German jurist, Windscheid, has remarked that in interpreting legislation modern courts may and habitually do "think over again the thought which the legislator was trying to express," but that the Roman jurist went further and "thought out the thought which the legislator was trying to think."[2]

There have been wide differences of opinion as to the practices a court might employ in attempting to discover legislative intent. In England, the rule is that courts must examine nothing but the words of the statute itself. They can take no note of any discussions in Parliament during the passage of the act, nor any statements of members of the government in presenting the bill, nor any committee deliberations on the bill. The early American practice tended to follow the English example. But with the later proliferation of social and economic regulatory legislation, the courts found it increasingly useful to look at the legislative reports and debates in order to understand legislative purposes. Today it is accepted practice to place considerable stress on the legislative history of an act in determining its meaning, and members of Congress, recognizing the important role of legislative history, often take pains to get statements into the *Congressional Record* which will support their view of the intent of the legislative language being adopted.

Legislative Ratification of Judicial Interpretation

Legislative intention is not sought simply by looking into the antecedents of a statute. After a congressional act is on the books and has been judicially interpreted, the subsequent action of Congress may be studied by courts for clues as to legislative approval or disapproval of the judicial interpretation. In this search, both legislative action and nonaction may be cited as relevant evidence of legislative intent. For example, after a statute has been judicially interpreted in a certain way, efforts may

---

[2] Quoted by T. R. Powell in "The Logic and Rhetoric of Constitutional Law," 15 *Journal of Philosophy, Psychology, and Scientific Method* 654 (1918).

be made in Congress by those opposed to this interpretation to amend the statute so as to give it a different meaning from the one asserted by the courts. If this effort should fail, it may be argued with some justification that Congress has, by implication, ratified the judicial interpretation.

However, so many statutes are continually being interpreted by the courts that it is impossible for them all to receive this kind of congressional consideration. What conclusion can legitimately be drawn from the fact that a particular statute is given a consistent meaning over a period of years and the fact that this interpretation is never even considered in Congress? Does this prove that Congress has ratified the judicial interpretation by non-action? Or suppose that a statute, over a long period, is interpreted by an administrative agency to give that agency certain powers, and that this interpretation is never questioned in Congress. Does this amount to legislative ratification of the interpretation and foreclose the courts from considering whether this meaning of the statute is the proper one?

An excellent example of this latter situation is found in the case of *Kent* v. *Dulles* (1958). The Supreme Court had to decide whether the State Department had statutory authority to deny passports to American citizens who were allegedly Communists or engaged in activities which would further the international Communist movement. The basic Passport Act was a very broad statute simply authorizing the Secretary of State to grant and issue passports "under such rules as the President shall designate and prescribe." The State Department had refused passports to Communists from 1919 to 1933, and again from 1947 on. Congress had adopted no legislation during this period restricting the State Department's passport power, and had in fact enacted several statutes, such as the Internal Security Act of 1950, which explicitly tightened passport controls. But, on the other hand, it had adopted no statute specifically authorizing the State Department to do what it had done in the Kent case and others like it.

Under these circumstances the Court majority refused to conclude that Congress had, by implication, authorized the Secretary of State "to withhold passports to citizens because of their beliefs or associations." The right to travel, the Court held, was a basic constitutional right protected by the due process clause of the Fifth Amendment. If this right were to be limited, there must be a clear and specific statutory foundation laid for the limitation. The Court refused to read legislative intent into a combination of administrative practice and legislative silence.

Interpretation to Avoid Constitutional Questions

A rule of interpretation frequently utilized by judges, and one highly recommended by the Supreme Court, requires that wherever possible legislation be interpreted in such a way as to avoid constitutional questions. Involved here is a recognition of the need to use very cautiously the judicial power of declaring legislative acts unconstitutional, particularly acts of Congress, a policy to be discussed in more detail in the next chapter. When Justice Brandeis in the case of *Ashwander* v. *Tennessee Valley Authority* (1936) listed for the Court's benefit the "series of rules under which it has avoided passing upon a large part of all the constitutional questions pressed upon it for decision," the seventh rule went as follows:

> When the validity of an act of the Congress is drawn in question, and even if a serious doubt of constitutionality is raised, it is a cardinal principle that this Court will first ascertain whether a construction of the statute is fairly possible by which the question may be avoided.

Often, of course, judges will be in disagreement as to how far they may legitimately go in interpreting a statute so as to make it constitutional. The principle of judicial self-restraint may give conflicting advice. The rule that a judge should not declare a statute invalid if he can avoid it may be challenged by the rule that a judge should give to the words of a statute their normal and intended meaning. For a court to rewrite a statute in order to make it constitutional may be a more unwarranted exercise of judicial power than to take the legislation at its face value and judge it accordingly.

One of the many notable instances of judicial difference on this issue occurred in *United States* v. *CIO* (1948). The Supreme Court was dealing with a prosecution of a labor organization under the Taft-Hartley Act for publishing a newspaper in which support was expressed for a particular candidate for Congress. The Court majority held that if the statute applied to such publications, "the gravest doubt would arise in our minds as to its constitutionality," and consequently held that the act had not intended to outlaw union expenditures for such publications. Justice Rutledge replied for a four-judge minority that:

> By reading [such expenditures] out of the section, in order not to pass upon its validity, the Court in effect abdicates its function in the guise of applying the policy against deciding questions of constitution-

ality unnecessarily. I adhere to that policy. But I do not think it justifies invasion of the legislative function by rewriting or emasculating the statute. This in my judgment is what has been done in this instance. Accordingly I dissent from the construction given to the statute and from the misapplication of the policy. I also think the statute patently invalid.

SELECTED REFERENCES

Beaney, William M., "Civil Liberties and Statutory Construction," 8 *Journal of Public Law* 66 (1959).

Bickel, Alexander M. and Harry H. Wellington, "Legislative Purpose and the Judicial Process: The Lincoln Mills Case," 71 *Harvard Law Review* 1 (1957).

Carr, Robert K., *The Supreme Court and Judicial Review* (New York: Farrar and Rinehart, 1942), Ch. 9.

Frank, Jerome, *Law and the Modern Mind* (New York: Brentano's, 1930), Chs. 3, 4.

———, "Words and Music: Some Remarks on Statutory Interpretation," 47 *Columbia Law Review* 1259 (1947).

Mantel, Howard N., "The Congressional Record: Fact or Fiction of the Legislative Process," 12 *Western Political Quarterly* 981 (1959).

Miller, Arthur S., "Statutory Language and the Purposive Use of Ambiguity," 42 *Virginia Law Review* 23 (1956).

Pound, Roscoe, "Common Law and Legislation," 21 *Harvard Law Review* 383 (1908).

Radin, Max, "A Case Study in Statutory Interpretation: Western Union Co. vs. Lenroot," 33 *California Law Review* 219 (1945).

———, "Statutory Interpretation," 43 *Harvard Law Review* 863 (1930); and criticism by James M. Landis, "A Note on 'Statutory Interpretation,'" 43 *ibid.* 886 (1930).

Symposium on Statutory Construction, 3 *Vanderbilt Law Review* 365 (1950).

1. *"... judges are not unfettered glossators."*

SOME REFLECTIONS ON THE READING OF STATUTES *Felix Frankfurter*

. . . ANYTHING that is written may present a problem of meaning, and that is the essence of the business of judges in construing legislation. The problem derives from the very nature of words. They are symbols of meaning. But unlike mathematical symbols, the phrasing of a document, especially a complicated enactment, seldom attains more than approximate precision. If individual words are inexact symbols, with shifting variables, their configuration can hardly achieve invariant meaning or assured definiteness. Apart from the ambiguity inherent in its symbols, a statute suffers from dubieties. It is not an equation or a formula representing a clearly marked process, nor is it an expression of individual thought to which is imparted the definiteness a single authorship can give. A statute is an instrument of government partaking of its practical purposes but also of its infirmities and limitations, of its awkward and groping efforts. . . . The imagination which can draw an income tax statute to cover the myriad transactions of a society like ours, capable of producing the necessary revenue without producing a flood of litigation, has not yet revealed itself. Moreover, government sometimes solves problems by shelving them temporarily. The legislative process reflects that attitude. Statutes as well as constitutional provisions at times embody purposeful ambiguity or are expressed with a generality for future unfolding. . . .

The intrinsic difficulties of language and the emergence after enactment of situations not anticipated by the most gifted legislative imagination, reveal doubts and ambiguities in statutes that compel judicial construction. The process of construction, therefore, is not an exercise in logic or dialectic: The aids of formal reasoning are not irrelevant; they may simply be inadequate. The purpose of construc-

2 *Record of the Association of the Bar of the City of New York* 213 (1947). Copyright 1947 the Association of the Bar of the City of New York. Reprinted with permission.

tion being the ascertainment of meaning, every consideration brought to bear for the solution of that problem must be devoted to that end alone. To speak of it as a practical problem is not to indulge a fashion in words. It must be that, not something else. Not, for instance, an opportunity for a judge to use words as "empty vessels into which he can pour anything he will"—his caprices, fixed notions, even statesmanlike beliefs in a particular policy. Nor, on the other hand, is the process a ritual to be observed by unimaginative adherence to well-worn professional phrases. . . .

. . . The area of free judicial movement is considerable. . . . The difficulty is that the legislative ideas which laws embody are both explicit and immanent. And so the bottom problem is: What is below the surface of the words and yet fairly a part of them? Words in statutes are not unlike words in a foreign language in that they too have "associations, echoes, and overtones." Judges must retain the associations, hear the echoes, and capture the overtones. . . .

Even within their area of choice the courts are not at large. They are confined by the nature and scope of the judicial function in its particular exercise in the field of interpretation. They are under the constraints imposed by the judicial function in our democratic society. As a matter of verbal recognition certainly, no one will gainsay that the function in construing a statute is to ascertain the meaning of words used by the legislature. To go beyond it is to usurp a power which our democracy has lodged in its elected legislature. . . . A judge must not rewrite a statute, neither to enlarge nor to contract it. . . .

This duty of restraint, this humility of function as merely the translator of another's command, is a constant theme of our Justices. . . . In short, judges are not unfettered glossators. They are under a special duty not to over-emphasize the episodic aspects of life and not to undervalue its organic processes—its continuities and relationships. For judges at least it is important to remember that continuity with the past is not only a necessity but even a duty. . . .

Let me descend to some particulars.

The text.—Though we may not end with the words in construing a disputed statute, one certainly begins there. . . . The Court no doubt must listen to the voice of Congress. But often Congress cannot be heard clearly because its speech is muffled. Even when it has spoken, it is as true of Congress as of others that what is said is what the listener hears. Like others, judges too listen with what psychologists used to call the apperception mass, which I take it means in plain English that one listens with what is already in one's head. One more caution is relevant when one is admonished to listen attentively to what a statute says. One must also listen attentively to what it does not say.

We must, no doubt, accord the words the sense in which Congress used them. . . . we assume that Congress uses common words in their popular meaning, as used in the common speech of men. The cases speak of the "meaning of common understanding," "the normal and spontaneous meaning of language," "the common and appropriate use," "the natural straightforward and literal sense," and similar variants. . . .

Sometimes Congress supplies its own dictionary. It did so in 1871 in a statute defining a limited number of words for use as to all future enactments. . . . Or there may be indications from the statute that words in it are the considered language of legislation. "If Congress has been accustomed to use a certain phrase with a more limited meaning than might be attributed to it by common practice, it would be arbitrary to refuse to consider that fact when we come to interpret a statute." . . . Or words may acquire scope and function from the history of events which they summarize or from the purpose which they serve. . . . Words of art bring their art with them. They bear the meaning of their habitat whether it be a phrase of technical significance in the scientific or business world, or whether it be loaded with the recondite connotations of feudalism. . . . The peculiar idiom of business or of administrative practise often modifies the meaning that ordinary speech assigns to language. And if a word is obviously transplanted from another legal source, whether the common law or other legislation, it brings the old soil with it.

The context.—Legislation is a form of literary composition. But construction is not an abstract process equally valid for every composition, not even for every composition whose meaning must be judicially ascertained. The nature of the composition demands awareness of certain presuppositions. . . . And so, the significance of an enactment,

its antecedents as well as its later history, its relation to other enactments, all may be relevant to the construction of words for one purpose and in one setting but not for another. Some words are confined
to their history; some are starting points for history. Words are intellectual and moral currency. They come from the legislative mint with
some intrinsic meaning. Sometimes it remains unchanged. Like currency, words sometimes appreciate or depreciate in value.

Frequently the sense of a word cannot be got except by fashioning
a mosaic of significance out of the innuendoes of disjointed bits of
statute. Cardozo phrased this familiar phenomenon by stating that
"the meaning of a statute is to be looked for, not in any single section,
but in all the parts together and in their relation to the end in
view." . . .

You may have observed that I have not yet used the word "intention." All these years I have avoided speaking of the "legislative
intent" and I shall continue to be on my guard against using it. The
objection to "intention" was indicated in a letter by Mr. Justice Holmes
which the recipient kindly put at my disposal:

> Only a day or two ago—when counsel talked of the intention of a
> legislature, I was indiscreet enough to say I don't care what their inten-
> tion was. I only want to know what the words mean. . . .

Legislation has an aim; it seeks to obviate some mischief, to supply an
inadequacy, to effect a change of policy, to formulate a plan of government. That aim, that policy is not drawn, like nitrogen, out of the
air; it is evinced in the language of the statute, as read in the light of
other external manifestations of purpose. That is what the judge must
seek and effectuate. . . .

The difficulty in many instances where a problem of meaning arises
is that the enactment was not directed towards the troubling question.
The problem might then be stated, as once it was by Mr. Justice
Cardozo, "which choice is it the more likely that Congress would have
made?" . . . But the purpose which a court must effectuate is not that
which Congress should have enacted, or would have. It is that which
it did enact, however inaptly, because it may fairly be said to be imbedded in the statute, even if a specific manifestation was not thought

of, as is often the very reason for casting a statute in very general terms.

Often the purpose or policy that controls is not directly displayed in the particular enactment. Statutes cannot be read intelligently if the eye is closed to considerations evidenced in affiliated statutes, or in the known temper of legislative opinion. Thus, for example, it is not lightly to be presumed that Congress sought to infringe on "very sacred rights." This improbability will be a factor in determining whether language, though it should be so read if standing alone, was used to effect such a drastic change. . . .

Nor can canons of construction save us from the anguish of judgment. Such canons give an air of abstract intellectual compulsion to what is in fact a delicate judgment, concluding a complicated process of balancing subtle and elusive elements. . . . Insofar as canons of construction are generalizations of experience, they all have worth. In the abstract, they rarely arouse controversy. Difficulties emerge when canons compete in soliciting judgment, because they conflict rather than converge. For the demands of judgment underlying the art of interpretation, there is no vade-mecum. . . .

The quality of legislative organization and procedure is inevitably reflected in the quality of legislative draftsmanship. Representative Monroney told the House last July that "ninety-five percent of all the legislation that becomes law passes the Congress in the shape that it came from our committees. Therefore if our committee work is sloppy, if it is bad, if it is inadequate, our legislation in ninety-five percent of the cases will be bad and inadequate as well." . . . But what courts do with legislation may in turn deeply affect what Congress will do in the future. Emerson says somewhere that mankind is as lazy as it dares to be. Loose judicial reading makes for loose legislative writing. It encourages the practise illustrated in a recent cartoon in which a senator tells his colleagues "I admit this new bill is too complicated to understand. We'll just have to pass it to find out what it means." . . .

But there are more fundamental objections to loose judicial reading. In a democracy the legislative impulse and its expression should come from those popularly chosen to legislate, and equipped to devise policy, as courts are not. The pressure on legislatures to discharge their responsibility with care, understanding and imagination should be stiffened, not relaxed. Above all, they must not be encouraged in irresponsible or undisciplined use of language. In the keeping of legislatures perhaps more than any other group is the well-being of their fellow-men. Their responsibility is discharged ultimately by words. . . .

2.   *". . . it is not easy to find the intent of the legislature."*

THE APPLICATION OF STATUTES   *Edward H. Levi*

IT IS CUSTOMARY to think of case-law reasoning as inductive and the application of statutes as deductive. The thought seems erroneous but the emphasis has some meaning. With case law the concepts can be created out of particular instances. This is not truly inductive, but the direction appears to be from particular to general. . . .

The application of a statute seems to be in great contrast. The words are given. They are not to be taken lightly since they express the will of the legislature. The legislature is the law-making body. It looks like deduction to apply the word to the specific case.

The difference is seen immediately when it is realized that the words of a statute are not dictum. The legislature may have had a particular case uppermost in mind, but it has spoken in general terms. Not only respect but application is due to the general words the legislature used. The rules for statutory construction make the same point. They are words which tell one how to operate a given classification system. The problem is to place the species inside the genus and the particular case inside the species. The words used by the legislature are treated as words of classification which are to be applied. Yet the rules themselves show that there may be some ambiguity in the words used. The words are to be construed in the light of the meaning given to other words in the same or related statute. The specification of particular instances indicates that similar but unmentioned instances are not to be included. But the specification of particular instances, when in ad-

Reprinted from *An Introduction to Legal Reasoning* by Edward H. Levi, by permission of The University of Chicago Press. Copyright University of Chicago Press, 1948. Pp. 19–24.

dition a word of a general category is used, may be the indication that other like instances are also intended. . . .

Thus in the application of a statute the intent of the legislature seems important. The rules of construction are ways of finding out the intent. The actual words used are important but insufficient. The report of congressional committees may give some clue. Prior drafts of the statute may show where meaning was intentionally changed. Bills presented but not passed may have some bearing. Words spoken in debate may now be looked at. Even the conduct of the litigants may be important in that the failure of the government to have acted over a period of time on what it now suggests as the proper interpretation throws light on the common meaning. But it is not easy to find the intent of the legislature.

Justice Reed has given us some Polonius-sounding advice on the matter [*United States* v. *American Trucking Association* (1940)]:

> There is, of course, no more persuasive evidence of the purpose of a statute than the words by which the legislature undertook to give expression to its wishes. Often these words are sufficient in and of themselves to determine the purpose of the legislature. In such cases we have followed their plain meaning. When that meaning has led to absurd or futile results, however, this Court has looked beyond the words to the purpose of the act. Frequently, however, even when the plain meaning did not produce absurd results but merely an unreasonable one "plainly at variance with the policy of legislation as a whole" this Court has followed that purpose rather than the literal words. When aid to construction of the meaning of words, as used in the statute, is available, there certainly can be no "rule of law" which forbids the use, however clear the words may appear on superficial examination. The interpretation of the meaning of statutes, as applied to justiciable controversies, is exclusively a judicial function. This duty requires one body of public servants, the judges, to construe the meaning of what another body, the legislators, has said. Obviously there is danger that the courts' conclusion as to legislative purpose will be unconsciously influenced by the judges' own views or by factors not considered by the enacting body. A lively appreciation of the danger is the best assurance of escape from its threat but hardly justifies an acceptance of a literal interpretation dogma which withholds from the courts available information for reaching a correct conclusion. Emphasis should be laid too upon the

necessity for appraisal of the purposes as a whole of Congress in analyzing the meaning of clauses of sections of general acts. A few words of general connotation appearing in the text of statutes should not be given a wide meaning, contrary to settled policy, "except as a different purpose is plainly shown."

The words of advice force one to reexamine whether there is any difference between case-law and statutory interpretation. . . . One important difference can be noted immediately. Where case law is considered, there is a conscious realignment of cases; the problem is not the intention of the prior judge. But with a statute the reference is to the kind of things intended by the legislature. . . . The difficulty is that what the legislature intended is ambiguous. In a significant sense there is only a general intent which preserves as much ambiguity in the concept used as though it had been created by case law.

This is not the result of inadequate draftsmanship, as is so frequently urged. Matters are not decided until they have to be. For a legislature perhaps the pressures are such that a bill has to be passed dealing with a certain subject. But the precise effect of the bill is not something upon which the members have to reach agreement. . . . There is a related and an additional reason for ambiguity. As to what type of situation is the legislature to make a decision? Despite much gospel to the contrary, a legislature is not a fact-finding body. There is no mechanism, as there is with a court, to require the legislature to sift facts and to make a decision about specific situations. There need be no agreement about what the situation is. The members of the legislative body will be talking about different things; they cannot force each other to accept even a hypothetical set of facts. The result is that even in a non-controversial atmosphere just exactly what has been decided will not be clear.

Controversy does not help. Agreement is then possible only through escape to a higher level of discourse with greater ambiguity. This is one element which makes compromise possible. Moreover, from the standpoint of the individual member of the legislature there is reason to be deceptive. He must escape from pressures at home. Newspapers may have created an atmosphere in which some legislation must be passed. Perhaps the only chance to get legislation through is to have it

mean something not understood by some colleagues. . . . And if all
this were not sufficient, is cannot be forgotten that to speak of legislative intent is to talk of group action, where much of the group may
be ignorant or misinformed. Yet the emphasis should not be on this
fact, but on the necessity that there be ambiguity before there can be
any agreement about how unknown cases will be handled.

But the court will search for the legislative intent, and this does
make a difference. Its search results in an initial filling up of the gap.
The first opinions may not definitely set the whole interpretation. A
more decisive view may be edged toward, but finally there is likely to
be an interpretation by the court which gives greater content to the
words used. In building up this interpretation, the reference will be
to the kind of examples that the words used, as commonly understood,
would call to mind. Reasoning by example will then proceed from
that point. There is a difference then from case law in that the legislature has compelled the use of one word. The word will not change
verbally. It could change in meaning, however, and if frequent appeals
as to what the legislature really intended are permitted, it may shift
radically from time to time. When this is done, a court in interpreting
legislation has really more discretion than it has with case law. For it
can escape from prior cases by saying that they have ignored the legislative intent.

There is great danger in this. Legislatures and courts are cooperative
lawmaking bodies. It is important to know where the responsibility
lies. If legislation which is disfavored can be interpreted away from
time to time, then it is not to be expected, particularly if controversy
is high, that the legislature will ever act. It will always be possible to
say that new legislation is not needed because the court in the future
will make a more appropriate interpretation. If the court is to have
freedom to reinterpret legislation, the result will be to relieve the legislature from pressure. The legislation needs judicial consistency.
Moreover, the court's own behavior in the face of pressure is likely to
be indecisive. In all likelihood it will do enough to prevent legislative
revision and not much more. Therefore it seems better to say that once
a decisive interpretation of legislative intent has been made, and in
that sense a direction has been fixed within the gap of ambiguity, the

court should take that direction as given. In this sense a court's interpretation of legislation is not dictum. The words it uses do more than to decide the case. They give broad direction to the statute.

The doctrine which is suggested here is a hard one. In many controversial situations, legislative revision cannot be expected. It often appears that the only hope lies with the courts. Yet the democratic process seems to require that controversial changes should be made by the legislative body. This is not only because there is a mechanism for holding legislators responsible. It is also because courts are normally timid. Since they decide only the case before them, it is difficult for them to compel any controversial reform unless they are willing to hold to an unpopular doctrine over a sustained period of time. . . . When courts enter the area of great controversy, they require unusual protection. They must be ready to appeal to the constitution.

Where legislative interpretation is concerned, therefore, it appears that legal reasoning does attempt to fix the meaning of the word. When this is done, subsequent cases must be decided upon the basis that the prior meaning remains. It must not be re-worked. Its meaning is made clear as examples are seen, but the reference is fixed. It is a hard doctrine against which judges frequently rebel. . . .

". . . the language being plain, and not leading to absurd or wholly impracticable consequences, it is the sole evidence of the ultimate legislative intent."

3.

INTERPRETATION OF THE MANN ACT

THE MANN ACT *was passed by Congress on June 25, 1910. The statute, which according to its terms "shall be known and referred to as the 'White Slave Traffic Act,'" provides in its essential portion:*

Any person who shall knowingly transport or cause to be transported, or aid or assist in obtaining transportation for, or in transporting, in interstate or foreign commerce or in any territory or in the District of Columbia, any woman or girl for the purpose of prostitution or debauchery, or for any other immoral purpose, or with the intent and purpose to induce, entice or compel such woman or girl to become a prostitute, or to give herself up to debauchery, or to engage in any other immoral practice . . . shall be deemed guilty of a felony.

The Supreme Court upheld the constitutionality of the act in Hoke *v.* United States (1913), *as a regulation of interstate commerce. The argument against the act was that it was "a subterfuge and an attempt to interfere with the police power of the States to regulate the morals of their citizens," but the Court replied that the act was concerned with "a domain which the States cannot reach and over which Congress alone has power."*

CAMINETTI V. UNITED STATES

Four men were convicted under the Mann Act, two for taking their mistresses across a state line and two for inducing and coercing a young girl under eighteen to go from Oklahoma to Kansas with the intent of getting her to engage in immoral practices.

Mr. Justice Day delivered the opinion of the Court. . . .

It is contended that the Act of Congress is intended to reach only "commercialized vice" or the traffic in women for gain, and that the conduct for which the several petitioners were indicted and convicted, however reprehensible in morals, is not within the purview of the statute when properly construed in the light of its history and the purposes intended to be accomplished by its enactment. In none of the cases was it charged or proved that the transportation was for gain or for the purpose of furnishing women for prostitution for hire, and it is insisted that, such being the case, the acts charged and proved, upon which conviction was had, do not come within the statute.

It is elementary that the meaning of a statute must, in the first instance, be sought in the language in which the act is framed, and if that is plain, and if the law is within the constitutional authority of the law-making body which passed it, the sole function of the courts is to enforce it according to its terms. . . .

Where the language is plain and admits of no more than one mean-

242 U.S. 470, 37 S. Ct. 192, 61 L. Ed. 442 (1917).

ing the duty of interpretation does not arise and the rules which are to aid doubtful meanings need no discussion. . . . There is no ambiguity in the terms of this act. It is specifically made an offense to knowingly transport or cause to be transported, etc., in interstate commerce, any woman or girl for the purpose of prostitution or debauchery, or for "any other immoral purpose," or with the intent and purpose to induce any such woman or girl to become a prostitute or to give herself up to debauchery, or to engage in any other immoral practice.

Statutory words are uniformly presumed, unless the contrary appears, to be used in their ordinary and usual sense, and with the meaning commonly attributed to them. To cause a woman or girl to be transported for the purposes of debauchery, and for an immoral purpose, to-wit, becoming a concubine or mistress . . . or to transport an unmarried woman, under eighteen years of age, with the intent to induce her to engage in prostitution, debauchery and other immoral practices . . . would seem by the very statement of the facts to embrace transportation for purposes denounced by the act, and therefore fairly within its meaning.

While such immoral purpose would be more culpable in morals and attributed to baser motives if accompanied with the expectation of pecuniary gain, such considerations do not prevent the lesser offense against morals of furnishing transportation in order that a woman may be debauched, or become a mistress or a concubine from being the execution of purposes within the meaning of this law. To say the contrary would shock the common understanding of what constitutes an immoral purpose. . . .

But it is contended that though the words are so plain that they cannot be misapprehended when given their usual and ordinary interpretation, and although the sections in which they appear do not in terms limit the offense defined and punished to acts of "commercialized vice," or the furnishing or procuring of transportation of women for debauchery, prostitution or immoral practices for hire, such limited purpose is to be attributed to Congress and engrafted upon the act in view of the language of § 8 and the report which accompanied the law upon its introduction into and subsequent passage by the House of Representatives.

In this connection, it may be observed that while the title of an act cannot overcome the meaning of plain and unambiguous words used in its body . . . the title of this act embraces the regulation of interstate commerce "by prohibiting the transportation therein for immoral purposes of women and girls, and for other purposes." It is true that § 8 of the act provides that it shall be known and referred to as the "White-slave traffic Act," and the report accompanying the introduction of the same into the House of Representatives set forth the fact that a material portion of the legislation suggested was to meet conditions which had arisen in the past few years, and that the legislation was needed to put a stop to a villainous interstate and international traffic in women and girls. Still, the name given to an act by way of designation or description, or the report which accompanies it, cannot change the plain import of its words. . . .

Reports to Congress accompanying the introduction of proposed laws may aid the courts in reaching the true meaning of the legislature in cases of doubtful interpretation. . . . But, as we have already said, and it has been so often affirmed as to become a recognized rule, when words are free from doubt they must be taken as the final expression of the legislative intent, and are not to be added to or subtracted from by considerations drawn from titles or designating names or reports accompanying their introduction, or from any extraneous source. In other words, the language being plain, and not leading to absurd or wholly impracticable consequences, it is the sole evidence of the ultimate legislative intent. . . .

The judgment in each of the cases is

Affirmed.

Mr. Justice McReynolds took no part in the consideration or decision of these cases.

Mr. Justice McKenna, with whom concurred the Chief Justice and Mr. Justice Clarke, dissenting.

Undoubtedly in the investigation of the meaning of a statute we resort first to its words, and when clear they are decisive. The principle has attractive and seemingly disposing simplicity, but that it is not easy of application or, at least, encounters other principles, many cases demonstrate. The words of a statute may be uncertain in their signification or in their application. If the words be ambiguous, the problem they present is to be resolved by their definition; the subject-matter and the lexicons become our guides. But here, even, we are not exempt from putting ourselves in the place of the legislators. If the words be clear in meaning but the objects to which they are addressed be uncertain, the problem then is to determine the uncertainty. And for this a realization of conditions that provoked the statute must inform our judgment. . . . The transportation which is made unlawful is of a woman or girl "to become a prostitute or to give herself up to debauchery, or to engage in any other immoral practice." Our present concern is with the words "any other immoral practice," which, it is asserted, have a special office. The words are clear enough as general descriptions; they fail in particular designation. . . . "Immoral" is a very comprehensive word. It means a dereliction of morals. In such sense it covers every form of vice, every form of conduct that is contrary to good order. It will hardly be contended that in this sweeping sense it is used in the statute. But if not used in such sense, to what is it limited and by what limited? If it be admitted that it is limited at all, that ends the imperative effect assigned to it in the opinion of the court. But not insisting quite on that, we ask again, By what is it limited? By its context, necessarily, and the purpose of the statute.

For the context I must refer to the statute; of the purpose of the statute Congress itself has given us illumination. It devotes a section to the declaration that the "Act shall be known and referred to as the 'White-slave traffic Act.'" And its prominence gives it prevalence in the construction of the statute. It cannot be pushed aside or subordinated by indefinite words in other sentences, limited even there by the context. . . . The designation "White-slave traffic" has the sufficiency of an axiom. If apprehended, there is no uncertainty as to the conduct it describes. It is commercialized vice, immoralities having a mercenary purpose, and this is confirmed by other circumstances.

The author of the bill was Mr. Mann, and in reporting it from the House Committee on Interstate and Foreign Commerce he declared for the Committee that it was not the purpose of the bill to interfere with or usurp in any way the police power of the States, and further that it was not the intention of the bill to regulate prostitution or the places where prostitution or immorality was practiced, which were said to be matters wholly within the power of the States and over which the federal government had no jurisdiction. And further explaining the bill, it was said that the sections of the act had been "so drawn that they are limited to cases in which there is the act of transportation in interstate commerce of women for purposes of prostitution." And again:

"The White Slave Trade. . . . The legislation is needed to put a stop to a villainous interstate and international traffic in women and girls. . . . It does not attempt to regulate the practice of voluntary prostitution, but aims solely to prevent panderers and procurers from compelling thousands of women and girls against their will and desire to enter and continue in a life of prostitution." House Report No. 47, 61st Cong., 2d sess., pp. 9, 10.

In other words, it is vice as a business at which the law is directed, using interstate commerce as a facility to procure or distribute its victims. . . .

This being the purpose, the words of the statute should be construed to execute it, and they may be so construed even if their literal meaning be otherwise. . . .

MORTENSEN V. UNITED STATES

Mr. & Mrs. Hans Mortensen, operators of a house of ill-fame in Grand Island, Nebraska, took two of their prostitutes along on their vacation to Yellowstone National Park and Salt Lake City. On their return to Grand Island, the girls renewed their activities in the Mortensens' employ. Shortly thereafter the Mortensens were indicted and convicted under the Mann Act for bring the girls back to Nebraska. There was no charge that any immoral acts had occurred during the vacation or that the Mortensens had used any pressure to persuade the girls to return.

MR. JUSTICE MURPHY delivered the opinion of the Court. . . .

The primary issue before us is whether there was any evidence from which the jury could rightly find that petitioners transported the girls from Salt Lake City to Grand Island for an immoral purpose in violation of the Mann Act.

The penalties of § 2 of the Act are directed at those who knowingly

322 U.S. 369, 64 S. Ct. 1037, 88 L. Ed. 1331 (1944).

transport in interstate commerce "any woman or girl for the purpose of prostitution or debauchery, or for any other immoral purpose, or with the intent and purpose to induce, entice, or compel such woman or girl to become a prostitute or to give herself up to debauchery, or to engage in any other immoral practice." The statute thus aims to penalize only those who use interstate commerce with a view toward accomplishing the unlawful purposes. To constitute a violation of the Act, it is essential that the interstate transportation have for its object or be the means of effecting or facilitating the proscribed activities. . . . An intention that the women or girls shall engage in the conduct outlawed by § 2 must be found to exist before the conclusion of the interstate journey and must be the dominant motive of such interstate movement. And the transportation must be designed to bring about such result. Without that necessary intention and motivation, immoral conduct during or following the journey is insufficient to subject the transporter to the penalties of the Act. . . .

It may be assumed that petitioners anticipated that the two girls would resume their activities as prostitutes upon their return to Grand Island. But we do not think it is fair or permissible under the evidence adduced to infer that this interstate vacation trip, or any part of it, was undertaken by petitioners for the purpose of, or as a means of effecting or facilitating, such activities. The sole purpose of the journey from beginning to end was to provide innocent recreation and a holiday for petitioners and the two girls. . . . What Congress has outlawed by the Mann Act, however, is the use of interstate commerce as a calculated means for effectuating sexual immorality. In ordinary speech an interstate trip undertaken for an innocent vacation purpose constitutes the use of interstate commerce for that innocent purpose. Such a trip does not lose that meaning when viewed in light of a criminal statute outlawing interstate trips for immoral purposes.

The fact that the two girls actually resumed their immoral practices after their return to Grand Island does not, standing alone, operate to inject a retroactive illegal purpose into the return trip to Grand Island. Nor does it justify an arbitrary splitting of the round trip into two parts so as to permit an inference that the purpose of the drive to Salt Lake City was innocent while the purpose of the homeward journey to Grand Island was criminal. The return journey under the circumstances of this case cannot be considered apart from its integral relation with the innocent round trip as a whole. There is no evidence of any change in the purpose of the trip during its course. If innocent when it began it remained so until it ended. . . .

To punish those who transport inmates of a house of prostitution on an innocent vacation trip in no way related to the practice of their commercial vice is consistent neither with the purpose nor with the language of the Act. Congress was attempting primarily to eliminate the "white slave" business. . . . To accomplish its purpose the statute enumerates the prohibited acts in broad language capable of application beyond that intended by the legislative framers. But even such broad language is conditioned upon the use of interstate transportation for the purpose of, or as a means of effecting or facilitating, the commission of the illegal acts. Here the interstate round trip had no such purpose and was in no way related to the subsequent immoralities in Grand Island. In short, we perceive no statutory purpose or language which prohibits petitioners under these circumstances from using interstate transportation for a vacation or for any other innocent purpose.

The judgment of the court below is

Reversed.

MR. CHIEF JUSTICE STONE:

MR. JUSTICE BLACK, MR. JUSTICE REED, MR. JUSTICE DOUGLAS and I think the judgment should be affirmed.

Courts have no more concern with the policy and wisdom of the Mann Act than of the Labor Relations Act or any other which Congress may constitutionally adopt. Those are matters for Congress to determine, not the courts. . . .

The fact that petitioners, who were engaged in an established business of operating a house of prostitution in Nebraska, took some of its women inmates on a transient and innocent vacation trip to other states, is in no way incompatible with the conclusion that petitioners, in bringing them back to Nebraska, purposed and intended that they should resume there the practice of commercial vice, which in fact they did promptly resume in petitioners' establishment. The record is without evidence that they engaged or intended to engage in any other activities in Nebraska, or that anything other than the practice of their profession was the object of their return. . . .

CLEVELAND V. UNITED STATES

Six members of a fundamentalist Mormon sect practicing polygamy were convicted under the Mann Act for transporting their several wives across state lines.

MR. JUSTICE DOUGLAS delivered the opinion of the Court. . . .

The Act makes an offense the transportation in interstate commerce of "any woman or girl for the purpose of prostitution or debauchery, or for any other immoral purpose." The decision turns on the meaning of the latter phrase, "for any other immoral purpose." . . .

It is argued that the *Caminetti* decision gave too wide a sweep to the Act; that the Act was designed to cover only the white slave business and related vices; that it was not designed to cover voluntary actions bereft of sex commercialism; and that in any event it should not be construed to embrace polygamy which is a form of marriage and, unlike prostitution or debauchery or the concubinage involved in the *Caminetti* case, has as its object parenthood and the creation and maintenance of family life. . . .

While *Mortensen* v. *United States* . . . rightly indicated that the Act was aimed "primarily" at the use of interstate commerce for the conduct of the white slave business, we find no indication that a profit motive is a *sine qua non* to its application. Prostitution, to be sure, normally suggests sexual relations for hire. But debauchery has no such implied limitation. In common understanding the indulgence which that term suggests may be motivated solely by lust. And so we start with words which by their natural import embrace more than commercialized sex. What follows is "any other immoral purpose." Under the *ejusdem generis* rule of construction the general words are confined to the class and may not be used to enlarge it. But we could not give the words a faithful interpretation if we confined them more narrowly than the class of which they are a part.

That was the view taken by the Court in [earlier] cases. We do not stop to reexamine the *Caminetti* case to determine whether the Act was properly applied to the facts there presented. But we adhere to its holding . . . that the Act, while primarily aimed at the use of inter-

329 U.S. 14, 67 S. Ct. 13, 91 L. Ed. 12 (1946).

state commerce for the purposes of commercialized sex, is not restricted to that end.

We conclude, moreover, that polygamous practices are not excluded from the Act. They have long been outlawed in our society. As stated in *Reynolds* v. *United States* . . .

> Polygamy has always been odious among the northern and western nations of Europe, and, until the establishment of the Mormon Church, was almost exclusively a feature of the life of Asiatic and of African people. At common law, the second marriage was always void (2 Kent, Com. 79), and from the earliest history of England polygamy has been treated as an offence against society.

. . . Polygamy is a practice with far more pervasive influences in society than the casual, isolated transgressions involved in the *Caminetti* case. The establishment or maintenance of polygamous households is a notorious example of promiscuity. . . . We could conclude that Congress excluded these practices from the Act only if it were clear that the Act is confined to commercialized sexual vice. Since we cannot say it is, we see no way by which the present transgressions can be excluded. These polygamous practices have long been branded as immoral in the law. Though they have different ramifications, they are in the same genus as the other immoral practices covered by the Act. . . .

It is also urged that the requisite criminal intent was lacking since petitioners were motivated by a religious belief. That defense claims too much. If upheld, it would place beyond the law any act done under claim of religious sanction. But it has long been held that the fact that polygamy is supported by a religious creed affords no defense in a prosecution for bigamy. *Reynolds* v. *United States.* . . . Whether an act is immoral within the meaning of the statute is not to be determined by the accused's concepts of morality. Congress has provided the standard. The offense is complete if the accused intended to perform, and did in fact perform, the act which the statute condemns. . . .

Affirmed.

Mr. Justice Black and Mr. Justice Jackson think that the cases should be reversed. They are of opinion that affirmance requires extension of the rule announced in the *Caminetti* case and that the correctness of that rule is so dubious that it should at least be restricted to its particular facts.

MR. JUSTICE RUTLEDGE, concurring. . . .

MR. JUSTICE MURPHY, dissenting.

Today another unfortunate chapter is added to the troubled history of the White Slave Traffic Act. It is a chapter written in terms that misapply the statutory language and that disregard the intention of the legislative framers. It results in the imprisonment of individuals whose actions have none of the earmarks of white slavery, whatever else may be said of their conduct. . . .

It is not my purpose to defend the practice of polygamy or to claim that it is morally the equivalent of monogamy. But it is essential to understand what it is, as well as what it is not. Only in that way can we intelligently decide whether it falls within the same genus as prostitution or debauchery.

There are four fundamental forms of marriage: (1) monogamy; (2) polygyny, or one man with several wives; (3) polyandry, or one woman with several husbands; and (4) group marriage. The term "polygamy" covers both polygyny and polyandry. Thus we are dealing here with polygyny, one of the basic forms of marriage. Historically, its use has far exceeded that of any other form. It was quite common among ancient civilizations and was referred to many times by the writers of the Old Testament; even today it is to be found frequently among certain pagan and non-Christian peoples of the world. We must recognize, then, that polygyny, like other forms of marriage, is basically a cultural institution rooted deeply in the religious beliefs and social mores of those societies in which it appears. It is equally true that the beliefs and mores of the dominant culture of the contemporary world condemn the practice as immoral and substitute monogamy in its place. To those beliefs and mores I subscribe, but that does not alter the fact that polygyny is a form of marriage built upon a set of social and moral principles. . . .

The Court states that polygamy is "a notorious example of promiscuity." The important fact, however, is that, despite the differences that may exist between polygamy and monogamy, such differences do not place polygamy in the same category as prostitution or debauchery. When we use those terms we are speaking of acts of an entirely different nature, having no relation whatever to the various forms of marriage. It takes no elaboration here to point out that marriage, even when it occurs in a form of which we disapprove, is not to be compared with prostitution or debauchery or other immoralities of that character.

The Court's failure to recognize this vital distinction and its insistence that polygyny is "in the same genus" as prostitution and debauchery do violence to the anthropological factors involved. Even etymologically, the words "polygyny" and "polygamy" are quite distinct from "prostitution," "debauchery" and words of that ilk. There is thus no basis in fact for including polygyny within the phrase "any other immoral purpose" as used in this statute. . . .

4.   *"Judicial construction, constitutional or statutory, always is subject to hazards of judicial reconstruction."*

UNITED STATES V. HARRISS

SECTION 305 *of the Federal Regulation of Lobbying Act requires "every person receiving any contributions or expending any money" to influence passage or defeat of congressional legislation to file the name and address of each person who makes a contribution of $500 or more or to whom $10 or more is paid as well as the sum total of all contributions and expenditures. Section 308 requires "any person who shall engage himself for pay or for any consideration" to influence congressional legislation to register under oath and give the name of employers or clients by whom he is or is to be paid, a full accounting of expenses and expenditures, the legislation with which he is concerned, and citations to any material which he has "caused to be published."*

A group of lobbyists were charged with failing to register and to report expenditures. The district judge dismissed the charges on the grounds that the statute was an unconstitutional abridgment of First Amendment freedoms of speech, assembly, and petition. The government appealed.

347 U.S. 612, 74 S. Ct. 808, 98 L. Ed. 989 (1954).

MR. CHIEF JUSTICE WARREN delivered the opinion of the Court. . . .

I

The constitutional requirement of definiteness is violated by a criminal statute that fails to give a person of ordinary intelligence fair notice that his contemplated conduct is forbidden by the statute. The underlying principle is that no man shall be held criminally responsible for conduct which he could not reasonably understand to be proscribed.

On the other hand, if the general class of offenses to which the statute is directed is plainly within its terms, the statute will not be struck down as vague even though marginal cases could be put where doubts might arise. . . . And if this general class of offenses can be made constitutionally definite by a reasonable construction of the statute, this Court is under a duty to give the statute that construction. . . .

. . . The key section of the Lobbying Act is § 307, entitled "Persons to Whom Applicable". . . .

> The provisions of this title shall apply to any person (except a political committee as defined in the Federal Corrupt Practices Act, and duly organized State or local committees of a political party), who by himself, or through any agent or employee or other persons in any manner whatsoever, directly or indirectly, solicits, collects, or receives money or any other thing of value to be used principally to aid, or the principal purpose of which person is to aid, in the accomplishment of any of the following purposes:
>
> (a) The passage or defeat of any legislation by the Congress of the United States.
>
> (b) To influence, directly or indirectly, the passage or defeat of any legislation by the Congress of the United States.

This section modifies the substantive provisions of the Act, including § 305 and § 308. In other words, unless a "person" falls within the category established by § 307, the disclosure requirements of § 305 and § 308 are inapplicable. Thus coverage under the Act is limited to those persons (except for the specified political committees) who solicit, collect, or receive contributions of money or other thing of value, and then only if the principal purpose of either the persons or the contributions is to aid in the accomplishment of the aims set forth in § 307(a) and (b). In any event, the solicitation, collection, or receipt of money or other thing of value is a prerequisite to coverage under the Act.

The Government urges a much broader construction—namely, that under § 305 a person must report his expenditures to influence legislation even though he does not solicit, collect, or receive contributions as provided in § 307. Such a construction, we believe, would do violence to the title and language of § 307 as well as its legislative history. If the construction urged by the Government is to become law, that is for Congress to accomplish by further legislation.

We now turn to the alleged vagueness of the purposes set forth in § 307(a) and (b). As in United States v. Rumely . . . which involved the interpretation of similar language, we believe this language should be construed to refer only to " 'lobbying in its commonly accepted sense' "—to direct communication with members of Congress on pending or proposed federal legislation. The legislative history of the Act makes clear that, at the very least, Congress sought disclosure of such direct pressures, exerted by the lobbyist[s] themselves or through their hirelings or through an artificially stimulated letter campaign. It is likewise clear that Congress would have intended the Act to operate on this narrower basis, even if a broader application to organizations seeking to propagandize the general public were not permissible.

There remains for our consideration the meaning of "the principal purpose" and "to be used principally to aid." The legislative history of the Act indicates that the term "principal" was adopted merely to exclude from the scope of § 307 those contributions and persons having only an "incidental" purpose of influencing legislation. Conversely, the "principal purpose" requirement does not exclude a contribution which in substantial part is to be used to influence legislation through direct communication with Congress or a person whose activities in substantial part are directed to influencing legislation through direct communication with Congress. If it were otherwise—if an organization, for example, were exempted because lobbying was only one of its main activities—the Act would in large measure be reduced to a mere exhortation against abuse of the legislative process. In construing the Act narrowly to avoid constitutional doubts, we must also avoid a construction that would seriously impair the effectiveness of the Act in coping with the problem it was designed to alleviate.

To summarize, therefore, there are three prerequisites to coverage under § 307: (1) the "person" must have solicited, collected, or received contributions; (2) one of the main purposes of such "person," or one of the main purposes of such contributions, must have been to influence the passage or defeat of legislation by Congress; (3) the intended method of accomplishing this purpose must have been through direct communication with members of Congress. And since § 307 modifies the substantive provisions of the Act, our construction of § 307 will of necessity also narrow the scope of § 305 and § 308. . . . Thus § 305 is limited to those persons who are covered by § 307; and when so covered, they must report all contributions and expenditures having the purpose of attempting to influence legislation through direct communication with Congress. Similarly, § 308 is limited to those persons (with the stated exceptions) who are covered by § 307 and who, in addition, engage themselves for pay or for any other valuable consideration for the purpose of attempting to influence legislation through direct communication with Congress. Construed in this way, the Lobbying Act meets the constitutional requirement of definiteness.

II

Thus construed, § § 305 and 308 also do not violate the freedoms guaranteed by the First Amendment—freedom to speak, publish, and petition the Government.

Present-day legislative complexities are such that individual members of Congress cannot be expected to explore the myriad pressures to which they are regularly subjected. Yet full realization of the American ideal of government by elected representatives depends to no small extent on their ability to properly evaluate such pressures. Otherwise the voice of the people may all too easily be drowned out by the voice of special interest groups seeking favored treatment while masquerading as proponents of the public weal. This is the evil which the Lobbying Act was designed to help prevent.

Toward that end, Congress has not sought to prohibit these pressures. It has merely provided for a modicum of information from those who for hire attempt to influence legislation or who collect or spend funds for that purpose. It wants only to know who is being hired, who is putting up the money, and how much. . . .

The judgment below is reversed and the cause is remanded to the District Court for further proceedings not inconsistent with this opinion.

Reversed.

MR. JUSTICE CLARK took no part in the consideration or decision of this case.

MR. JUSTICE DOUGLAS with whom MR. JUSTICE BLACK concurs, dissenting. . . .

MR. JUSTICE JACKSON, dissenting. . . .

The clearest feature of this case is that it begins with an Act so mischievously vague that the Government charged with its enforcement does not understand it, for some of its important assumptions are rejected by the Court's interpretation. The clearest feature of the Court's decision is that it leaves the country under an Act which is not much like any Act passed by Congress. . . .

The Act passed by Congress would appear to apply to all persons who (1) solicit or receive funds for the purpose of lobbying, (2) receive and expend funds for the purpose of lobbying, or (3) merely expend funds for the purpose of lobbying. The Court at least eliminates this last category from coverage of the Act, though I should suppose that more serious evils affecting the public interest are to be found in the way lobbyists spend their money than in the ways they obtain it. . . .

Also, Congress enacted a statute to reach the raising and spending of funds for the purpose of influencing congressional action *directly or indirectly.* The Court entirely deletes "indirectly" and narrows "directly" to mean "direct communication with members of Congress." These two constructions leave the Act touching only a part of the practices Congress deemed sinister.

Finally, as if to compensate for its deletions from the Act, the Court expands the phrase "the principal purpose" so that it now refers to any contribution which "in substantial part" is used to influence legislation.

I agree, of course, that we should make liberal interpretations to save legislative Acts, including penal statutes which punish conduct traditionally recognized as morally "wrong." Whoever kidnaps, steals, kills, or commits similar acts of violence upon another is bound to know that he is inviting retribution by society, and many of the statutes which define these long-established crimes are traditionally and perhaps necessarily vague. But we are dealing with a novel offense that has no established bounds and no such moral basis. The criminality of the conduct dealt with here depends entirely upon a purpose to influence legislation. . . .

The First Amendment forbids Congress to abridge the right of the people "to petition the Government for a redress of grievances." If this right is to have an interpretation consistent with that given to other First Amendment rights, it confers a large immunity upon activities of persons, organizations, groups and classes to obtain what they think is due them from government. Of course, their conflicting claims and propaganda are confusing, annoying and at times, no doubt, deceiving and corrupting. But we may not forget that our constitutional system is to allow the greatest freedom of access to Congress, so that the people may press for their selfish interests, with Congress acting as arbiter of their demands and conflicts.

In matters of this nature, it does not seem wise to leave the scope of a criminal Act, close to impinging on the right of petition, dependent upon judicial construction for its limitations. Judicial construction, constitutional or statutory, always is subject to hazards of judicial reconstruction. One may rely on today's narrow interpretation only at his peril, for some later Court may expand the Act to include, in accordance with its terms, what today the Court excludes. . . . The *ex post facto* provision of our Constitution has not been held to protect the citizen against a retroactive change in decisional law. . . . As long as this statute stands on the books, its vagueness will be a contingent threat to activities which the Court today rules out, the contingency being a change of views by the Court as hereafter constituted. . . .

12 / CONSTITUTIONAL INTERPRETATION

Interpretation of the Constitution is the highest and most difficult responsibility which American judges are called on to perform. The special role of the Supreme Court as the keeper of the Constitution has been recognized ever since it was so forcefully asserted by Chief Justice Marshall in *Marbury* v. *Madison* (1803), a decision which also established the supremacy of the Court's interpretation of the Constitution over that of the Congress, at least insofar as the judicial process was concerned.

What *Marbury* v. *Madison* did not do was to suggest that there was any room for judicial discretion in the constitutional interpretations announced by the Court. Marshall's opinion seemed to assume that the meaning of the Constitution was self-evident and that a judicial declaration on any such point was consequently indisputable. He wrote: "If an act of the legislature, repugnant to the Constitution, is void, does it, notwithstanding its invalidity, bind the courts . . . ?" The question might more appropriately have been stated: "In case the legislature passes a statute which it regards as constitutional but which the Supreme Court regards as unconstitutional, whose view is to prevail?" But Marshall begged this question, and simply assumed the superior right or ability of the Court to make constitutional interpretations.

433

The Avoidance of Constitutional Questions

However, even in the era of mechanical jurisprudence, when constitutional interpretation was alleged to allow no use of judicial discretion, the Supreme Court recognized that it should not construe the Constitution in deciding a controversy unless there was absolutely no alternative way to dispose of the case. Some of the techniques used by the Court to achieve escape from the task of constitutional interpretation have already been brought out. The strict enforcement of the rules of litigability and the doctrine of political questions, as discussed in Chapter 7, are methods of avoiding constitutional questions. In Chapter 11 we noted that one of the rules of statutory interpretation is to adopt meanings which will be least likely to subject the statute to charges of invalidity. These devices do not exhaust the judicial techniques for avoiding constitutional issues, however.

One of the significant restraints which the Court imposes on itself is that of not anticipating a question of constitutional law in advance of the necessity of deciding it. A variation on this theme is the rule that, even though a constitutional question is properly presented by the record, the Court will not pass upon it if there is also present some other ground (for example, a matter of statutory interpretation) on which the case can be decided. Appeals from the highest court of a state challenging its decision of a question under the federal Constitution will be dismissed if the judgment can be sustained on an independent state ground.

An excellent illustration of the Court's fertility in devising escapes from the necessity of deciding constitutional questions is found in its handling of the federal loyalty-security program for federal employees. The Court decided six cases involving this program between 1955 and 1959, and in any of them it could have made the decision turn on one of the serious constitutional charges that had been brought against this controversial program. Yet the Court accomplished the remarkable feat of deciding against the government in every one of these cases without ever resting a ruling on constitutional grounds. *Peters* v. *Hobby* (1955), *Service* v. *Dulles* (1957), and *Vitarelli* v. *Seaton* (1959) turned on errors in administrative procedure. *Cole* v. *Young* (1956) was disposed of by the statutory interpretation route. In *Taylor* v. *McElroy* (1959) the suit was held moot because the employee had been restored to his job after the Supreme Court accepted the case. *Greene* v. *McElroy* (1959), in which the Court got closest to expressing its views on the constitutional issue of right to confront accusers in the security hearings, was actually decided on the ground that neither the President nor Congress had authorized security procedures which dispensed with the confrontation safeguard.

There was an interesting interchange during the Supreme Court argument in the Peters case between Thurman Arnold, counsel for Peters, and Justice Frankfurter which well illustrates the Court's policy. Arnold in his brief had not questioned the procedure of the federal Loyalty Review Board in handling Peters' case, but had confined himself to the constitutional charges against the security system. When Justice Harlan asked him about the procedural point, Arnold replied: "Frankly, Your Honor, I had not anticipated that problem." He went on to say that he would not like to win the case on that ground, but Justice Frankfurter cut in: "The question is not whether you want to win the case on that ground or not. This Court reaches constitutional issues last, not first."

Meaning from History

In spite of its best efforts at avoidance, the Supreme Court must of necessity come to grips with constitutional questions in many of the cases it decides. It must consequently determine the meaning of the Constitution according to some supportable theory of interpretation.

One proposition sometimes invoked is that the meaning of the Constitution should be determined by reference to the intention of the men who made it. There is a very considerable plausibility to this argument, but the difficulties of determining the intention of the Framers are sufficiently indicated in the subsequent discussion of this point by William Anderson. (Reprinted below, p. 440.)

Slightly different from an approach through the intention of the Framers is the effort to establish the meaning of the words used in the Constitution. This is the method of interpretation suggested by Justice Holmes in his comment: "We ask, not what this man meant, but what those words would mean in the mouth of a normal speaker of English, using them in the circumstances in which they were used." W. W. Crosskey's massive treatise on the Constitution uses this method. By extensive research on word usage during the period of the Constitutional Convention, Crosskey built up a specialized dictionary on the basis of which he argued for a radical revision of the meaning of some key provisions in the Constitution.

The legitimacy of such meanings is as difficult to establish as the intention of the Framers, however. Moreover, both methods of interpretation are essentially backward-looking. They assume a fixed meaning for the words of the Constitution which can be changed only by the process of constitutional amendment. Both reject the legitimacy of amendment by consensus or usage or historical development. Both ignore the wise advice of Chief Justice Marshall in *McCulloch* v. *Maryland*, when he said: "We must never forget, that it is a constitution we are expounding," one which is "intended to endure for ages to come, and consequently, to be adapted to the various crises of human affairs." In *Missouri* v. *Holland* (1920), Holmes put the same kind of plea for a "living" constitution in even more effective form:

> . . . when we are dealing with words that also are a constituent act, like the Constitution of the United States, we must realize that they have called into life a being the development of which could not have been foreseen completely by the most gifted of its begetters. It was enough for them to realize or to hope that they had created an organism; it has taken a century and has cost their successors much sweat and blood to prove that they created a nation. The case before us must be considered in the light of our whole experience and not merely in that of what was said a hundred years ago.

The problems of the Framers' intentions do not all go back to 1787. The Fourteenth Amendment, drafted and adopted in the period between 1866 and 1868, has been the subject of controversy as bitter as any relating to the original Constitution. The principal issue has been whether the drafters of the Amendment intended by its terms to make applicable as against the states all of the provisions which the Bill of Rights had originally applied to the national government. The Supreme Court has consistently denied that the Amendment had any such purpose, but a minority of the justices have not been convinced, and in the 1947 case of *Adamson* v. *California* Justice Black dramatically restated the historical case for the minority view.

Polls of Other Jurisdictions

For guidance in constitutional interpretation the Court may turn to the practices of other jurisdictions to see what their standards have been in dealing with comparable problems. Particularly since a number of our constitutional concepts came from England, the Court has often sought to use English experience to deepen its understanding. The due process provision, which goes back to Magna Carta, has occasioned many such inquiries. In the case of *Murray's Lessee* v. *Hoboken Land and Improve-ment Co.* (1856) the Court announced that one of its tests for deter-mining whether a particular procedure constituted due process of law would be whether it was consistent with the settled usages and modes of proceeding in the common and statute law of England. *Hurtado* v. *California* (1884) ruled that grand-jury indictment was not required by due process, since this practice was not even known at the time of Magna Carta or for centuries thereafter.

Not only historical data, but also current practices in the various American states and in the English-speaking countries are regarded by the Court as relevant when confronted with a difficult problem of deter-mining constitutional norms. Since the Court rejected the idea that the due process clause of the Fourteenth Amendment imposes on the states all the protections of the Bill of Rights, it had to develop some other standard for determining the meaning of due process. Justice Cardozo supplied such a standard in *Palko* v. *Connecticut* (1937): the concept of "ordered liberty." Any restriction on individual freedom which was inconsistent with a system of ordered liberty was to be considered by the Court as contrary to due process.

This standard, of course, is rather vague. When faced with the problem of applying it in passing on particular restrictive practices, the justices have often sought the corroboration of a survey of actual practices. Thus in *Betts* v. *Brady* (1942), where the Court had to decide whether due process required that counsel be supplied for a defendant in a non-capital case, Justice Roberts canvassed the practices of the English common law, the provisions of the colonial and early state constitutions, the statutes in force in the thirteen original states at the time of the adoption of the Bill of Rights, and the constitutions presently in force in the states. This survey demonstrated, he concluded, that "in the great majority of the states, it has been the considered judgment of the people, their representatives and their courts that appointment of counsel is not a fundamental right, essential to a fair trial. On the contrary, the matter has generally been deemed one of legislative policy."

Again, in *Wolf* v. *Colorado* (1949), Justice Frankfurter surveyed cur-rent practices in all the states and in ten jurisdictions within the British Commonwealth in seeking to determine whether due process would pre-vent the use in a state court of evidence obtained by an illegal search and seizure. In an appendix to his opinion he arranged all the states into nine different categories according to their positions on this issue. But the use of such methods has not won the unanimous approval of the

Court's members. Justice Murphy, dissenting in the Wolf case, said: "I cannot believe that we should decide due process questions by simply taking a poll of the rules in various jurisdictions."

Balancing of Interests

The judicial function is often referred to as a balancing of interests; in fact, the symbolic figure of justice is a blindfolded goddess with a pair of scales. In a minor lawsuit one may think of this process as involving a weighing of facts, but where a constitutional issue has to be determined, the balancing process is more likely to be concerned with weighing the competing values of a free society. The conflict between freedom and order is a never-ending one, and is continually presenting issues for resolution by the balancing process.

There is some disagreement whether judges can properly function in a balancing role. In the case of *Saia* v. *New York* (1948), the Supreme Court was considering whether a municipality could refuse to permit a religious group to use loud-speakers for their services in a public park. Justice Douglas, in denying this power to the municipal officials, remarked that "Courts must balance the various community interests in passing on the constitutionality of local regulations of the character involved here." But Justice Jackson disagreed strongly with this idea of the judicial role. "It is for the local communities to balance their own interests—that is politics—and what courts should keep out of. Our only function is to apply constitutional limitations."

However, the balancing concept retains a strong appeal for judges in describing and rationalizing their decisional processes. The "constitutional limitations" of which Jackson speaks are abstract political principles. When applied to specific factual situations, judges often find that they must choose between conflicting principles, each of which states a proper constitutional goal. It was partly to resolve this conflict that the so-called "preferred position" rule was developed by the Court in the late 1930's and applied during the subsequent decade. This doctrine, though more fully articulated by Justice Harlan F. Stone, was based in part on Justice Cardozo's dictum in *Palko* v. *Connecticut* (1937) that First Amendment liberties were on "a different plane of social and moral values." Freedom of thought and speech, he said, was "the matrix, the indispensable condition, of nearly every other form of freedom. . . . Neither liberty nor justice could exist if they were sacrificed." In the Saia case, Justice Douglas specifically noted that in the balancing process the courts "should be mindful to keep the freedoms of the First Amendment in a preferred position."

Some members of the Court have objected to the "preferred position" rule as an attempt to rig the judicial scales, and have contended that all constitutional freedoms must stand on the same footing. More significant, however, have been the disputes over what may legitimately be thrown into the scales—what is to be balanced against what? One of the classic arguments on this point occurred in *Barenblatt* v. *United States* (1959), where Justice Harlan, over Justice Black's protest, balanced an individual's right to keep silent before a congressional investigating committee against the nation's right to self-preservation.

SELECTED REFERENCES

Braden, George D., "The Search for Objectivity in Constitutional Law," 57 *Yale Law Journal* 571 (1948).

Cahill, Fred V., Jr., *Judicial Legislation* (New York: Ronald Press, 1952), Ch. 3.

Cahn, Edmond (ed.), *Supreme Court and Supreme Law* (Bloomington: Indiana University Press, 1954), Ch. 3.

Carr, Robert K., *The Supreme Court and Judicial Review* (New York: Farrar and Rinehart, 1942), Ch. 5.

Crosskey, William W., *Politics and the Constitution in the History of the United States* (Chicago: University of Chicago Press, 1953), Ch. 1.

Curtis, Charles P., Jr., *Lions under the Throne* (Boston: Houghton, Mifflin, 1947).

Douglas, William O., "Stare Decisis," 49 *Columbia Law Review* 735 (1949).

———, *We the Judges* (New York: Doubleday, 1956).

McCloskey, Robert G. (ed.), *Essays in Constitutional Law* (New York: Alfred A. Knopf, 1957), Chs. 1–3, 12.

Murphy, Walter F., "The Constitution: Interpretation and Intent," 45 *American Bar Association Journal* 592 (1959).

Powell, Thomas R., *Vagaries and Varieties in Constitutional Interpretation* (New York: Columbia University Press, 1956), Chs. 1, 2.

Pritchett, C. Herman, *The American Constitution* (New York: McGraw-Hill, 1959), Ch. 4.

White, Thomas R., "Construing the Constitution: The New 'Sociological' Approach," 43 *American Bar Association Journal* 1085 (1957).

1.
> ". . . *intentions are highly subjective and personal things. They are not like badges pinned to a coat lapel.*"

THE INTENTION OF THE FRAMERS: A NOTE ON CONSTITUTIONAL INTERPRETATION   *William Anderson**

. . . THE FIRST difficulty in discussing "the intention of the framers" is to determine what individual persons are to be included under the rubric of "the framers." . . . Most users of the phrase appear to think entirely of the men who formulated the original written Constitution in 1787. They seemingly forget that the present Constitution, while it still includes most of the original document, has been profoundly changed through the adoption of 22 Amendments and through the making of numerous other constitutional decisions. These decisions have come not only from the Supreme Court but also from Congress and the Executive, from the arbitrament of arms, and in a sense from the acceptance of the people. . . .

Let us consider first the evidences concerning the intentions of the *original framers.*

The so-called Federal Convention of 1787 consisted at the maximum of 55 members, but that total number of members probably was not present on any one day. Members came and went. Some were present for only relatively short periods of time. At the end, apparently just over 40 members were participating.

The records of what men did and said in the Convention are mainly unofficial and decidedly incomplete. Apparently a number of members spoke very little during the proceedings. Some did not serve on any committee. Clearly if a member attends but little, says little or nothing for the record, serves on no committee, and leaves little or no other record in the form of private letters, memoranda, or a diary, it is hard to reconstruct his intentions. As the other end of the scale were a

49 *American Political Science Review* 340 (1955). Copyright 1955 American Political Science Association. Reprinted with permission.

* Professor Emeritus of Political Science, University of Minnesota.

number of members who attended regularly, spoke often, served on committees, and in other ways contributed to the work of the Convention and to the record of what it did. The records as to the views and intentions of these more active and vocal members are in some instances fairly substantial, but in other cases, like that of Gouverneur Morris, one of the principal final stylists of the Constitution, they are disappointingly incomplete.

The original intentions of the members, whatever they were, did not remain steadfast throughout the Convention. As the discussion developed, new topics were taken up, new ideas and arguments were presented, and the interrelations of various problems of government were brought out. Decisions were made one day and changed or rescinded the next. On such matters as the election and the position of the chief executive, intentions were changed almost from day to day. Also, having first voted to authorize Congress to legislate in all cases in which the several states would be incompetent, the Convention later did not include this language in the Constitution. What did the framers intend on this major point? Can we be sure that even at the end, when agreement was voted on certain verbal formulations, there was full concurrence also in intentions? . . .

At the end of the deliberations 39 members signed the Constitution, but four active participating members (Elbridge Gerry, Luther Martin, George Mason and Edmund Randolph) refused to do so. As to the 39 signers, it is perhaps safe to say that they all thought it best to put the proposed Constitution up to the people for approval, and thus avoid the delays and uncertainties that would accompany any attempt to get a better constitution drafted. That there was a considerable area of agreement not only upon general objectives as set forth in the Preamble but also upon the general plan of the Constitution—a consensus that it was at least better than the scheme of the Articles of Confederation—we must assume. Otherwise not enough members would have been likely to sign the document. Whether every member of the Convention who signed it had read the completed document or heard it read is unknown. Some of the more casual participants may well have accepted it upon the reassurance of others. In any case no one will ever know how much each signer actually knew about the document, how many of his own wishes or intentions upon specific points were embodied in it, or how fully the members were in agreement upon the meanings of the words in the document.

We know that some of the men who signed it had definite reservations about some parts of the Constitution. Alexander Hamilton was one of these. Apparently a number of members thought there should have been a bill of rights, but Hamilton thought otherwise. George Washington advised that men should put aside any personal objections, support the Constitution as drafted, and then try to improve it by amendments after its adoption. To what extent these unsatisfied members agreed with others on the meaning of what the Constitution actually provided is not clear.

On the basis of the record as we have it, therefore, I cannot understand how anyone can assert positively that all the signers agreed fully even upon the words in the Constitution, much less upon what the words meant. How their individual views deviated from the general plan will never be known from the present record. The signers who spoke in the state ratifying conventions put up a fairly united front in favor of adopting the Constitution, but even such collaborating members as Hamilton and Madison in *The Federalist* essays clearly had divergent ideas about the nature of the Union, the respective powers of the national and state governments, and national taxes—to name only a few important subjects.

. . . But what about those who refused to sign? Are they to be counted among the framers whose intentions scholars should try to ascertain? At the end they were opponents and not friends of the proposal. It did not express their wishes or intentions. . . .

In each state convention to which the Constitution was submitted, there were a few persons who had also served in the Federal Convention. What they said in the state conventions, though intended to persuade the other delegates, and obviously conciliatory toward the opposition, may be taken generally as some additional evidence of what these framers intended. Unfortunately, the records of the debates in the state conventions are far from being complete.

What other members of the state conventions said, being contemporary comment, has some evidential value, but is valuable mainly as revealing what men of that time thought about the provisions of the

proposed Constitution, as noted above, and not about the intentions of
the framers. . . .

. . . An entirely different status must, naturally, be accorded to those
Federalist essays that were written for the New York papers by two
brilliant young members of the Federal Convention—Alexander Hamilton and James Madison. (John Jay was not a Convention member.)
The essays written in advocacy of the Constitution by these two men,
like the post-Convention utterances of other former members thereof,
must be accorded very great weight as evidence of the intentions of
the framers—unless one can substantiate the charge that these men
shifted their positions after the Convention. What might have caused
such a shift? One possibility would be forgetfulness as to what was decided or intended, but such a charge has not been seriously pressed.
Another would be duplicity, arising from a desire so strong to have
the Constitution adopted that deception was practiced on the public
and on the members of the state conventions as to the real meaning
of the Constitution and the true intentions of the members of the
Convention. . . . It seems to me that on the whole the *Federalist*
essays are still the best explication of what several of the leading
members of the Convention intended to accomplish, and an excellent
interpretation of the areas of agreement reached by the Convention's
majority.

. . . my conclusions are that intentions are the intentions (purposes,
choices, acts of will, desires for a certain outcome) of individual human beings. Every man, being a different and distinct individual, un-
avoidably has intentions that are somewhat different from those of
everyone else. Such a thing as a solid, completely unified intention of
all the members in any group would be hard if not impossible to find.

Furthermore, intentions are highly subjective and personal things.
They are not like badges pinned to a coat lapel. They lie deep in the
hearts and minds of men. They are not always clearly stated by those
who have them, nor even capable of clear and specific formulation.
The words used to convey them seldom do so perfectly.

As I read the evidence, there was no single "intention of the framers" as to the Constitution as a whole, beyond perhaps the generalities
of the Preamble and the intention to submit the Constitution to the
people for adoption as a measure that might result in more effective

government. There were broad areas of general agreement among the majority on such matters as national supremacy, three branches of government, and a comprehensive national taxing power. When one tries to spell out precisely what was agreed upon on any specific point, however, the evidence is incomplete and contradictory. . . .

. . . Twenty-two amendments to the Constitution have been adopted and put into effect. . . . Thus in addition to the men of 1787 who sat down together in Philadelphia presumably to revise the Articles but actually to make a new Constitution, there have been unnumbered "framers" in later years who have impressed some of their words and intentions upon the Constitution. The original document has been overlaid with a thick and growing encrustation of constitutional rules and principles by these later framers. Just what they intended is also not always clear. What the framers of the 14th Amendment intended has become a subject for debate almost as keen as the debate over the intention of the original framers. In cases of obvious conflict, which shall be given priority, the earlier or the later framers? Can there be much doubt that in cases of conflict the later framers should prevail?

And these later additions to the Constitution raise their own questions of verbal interpretation. What is meant by the phrases "due process of law" and "equal protection of the laws," in the 14th Amendment? Here are phrases of great potential amplitude from which lawyers and judges have been able to extract various procedural and substantive restrictions on the powers of the states without reaching agreement on what the phrases mean or their framers intended.

What, then, were the intentions of the framers of these amendments? . . . I simply am unable to imagine what types and quantities of records would be needed to clinch any important point in the several major problems that arise. Neither can I imagine how any known method of psychoanalysis, content analysis, or plain crystal-ball gazing applied to such records or to the people who left them could give thoroughly reliable and irrefutable answers concerning the intentions of these later framers. The transition that needs to be made from the enduring and objective facts of the written words used to the fleeting, largely unexpressed, and subjective facts of the intentions of framers who passed away many years ago is beyond human capacity to make. . . .

2.

> ". . . the Fourteenth Amendment was [not] a covert way
> of imposing upon the States all the rules which it seemed
> important to Eighteenth Century statesmen to write into
> the Federal Amendments . . ."

ADAMSON V. CALIFORNIA

A DEFENDANT charged with murder in a California court declined to take the witness stand in his own defense. The reason was that he had previously been convicted on burglary, larceny, and robbery charges, and if he had taken the stand the fact of these previous convictions could have been revealed to the jury. As authorized by California law, the prosecutor and the judge commented on, and called the attention of the jury to, this failure on the part of the defendant to take the stand in his own behalf. The conviction was appealed on the ground that the California law compelled self-incrimination and violated the due process clause of the Fourteenth Amendment.

MR. JUSTICE REED delivered the opinion of the Court. . . .
Generally, comment on the failure of an accused to testify is forbidden in American jurisdictions. This arises from state constitutional or statutory provisions similar in character to the federal provisions. . . . California, however, is one of a few states that permit limited comment upon a defendant's failure to testify. That permission is narrow. The California law . . . authorizes comment by court and counsel upon the "failure of the defendant to explain or to deny by his testimony any evidence or facts in the case against him." This does not involve any presumption, rebuttable or irrebuttable, either of guilt or of the truth of any fact, that is offered in evidence. . . . It allows inferences to be drawn from proven facts. Because of this clause, the court can direct the jury's attention to whatever evidence there may be that a defendant could deny and the prosecution can argue as to inferences that may be drawn from the accused's failure to testify. . . . However sound may be the legislative conclusion that an accused

332 U.S. 46, 67 S. Ct. 1672, 91 L. Ed. 1903 (1947).

should not be compelled in any criminal case to be a witness against himself, we see no reason why comment should not be made upon his silence. It seems quite natural that when a defendant has opportunity to deny or explain facts and determines not to do so, the prosecution should bring out the strength of the evidence by commenting upon defendant's failure to explain or deny it. . . .

It is true that if comment were forbidden, an accused in this situation could remain silent and avoid evidence of former crimes and comment upon his failure to testify. We are of the view, however, that a state may control such a situation in accordance with its own ideas of the most efficient administration of criminal justice. The purpose of due process is not to protect an accused against a proper conviction but against an unfair conviction. When evidence is before a jury that threatens conviction, it does not seem unfair to require him to choose between leaving the adverse evidence unexplained and subjecting himself to impeachment through disclosure of former crimes. . . .

Affirmed.

MR. JUSTICE FRANKFURTER, concurring.

Less than ten years ago, Mr. Justice Cardozo announced as settled constitutional law that while the Fifth Amendment, "which is not directed to the states, but solely to the federal government," provides that no person shall be compelled in any criminal case to be a witness against himself, the process of law assured by the Fourteenth Amendment does not require such immunity from self-crimination: "in prosecutions by a state, the exemption will fail if the state elects to end it." *Palko* v. *Connecticut.* . . . The matter no longer called for discussion; a reference to *Twining* v. *New Jersey* . . . decided thirty years before the *Palko* case, sufficed.

Decisions of this Court do not have equal intrinsic authority. The *Twining* case shows the judicial process at its best—comprehensive briefs and powerful arguments on both sides, followed by long deliberation, resulting in an opinion by Mr. Justice Moody which at once gained and has ever since retained recognition as one of the outstanding opinions in the history of the Court. After enjoying unquestioned prestige for forty years, the *Twining* case should not now be diluted, even unwittingly, either in its judicial philosophy or in its particulars. As the surest way of keeping the *Twining* case intact, I would affirm this case on its authority. . . .

For historical reasons a limited immunity from the common duty to testify was written into the Federal Bill of Rights, and I am prepared to agree that, as part of that immunity, comment on the failure of an accused to take the witness stand is forbidden in federal prosecutions. It is so, of course, by explicit act of Congress. . . . But to suggest that such a limitation can be drawn out of "due process" in its protection of ultimate decency in a civilized society is to suggest that the Due Process Clause fastened fetters of unreason upon the States. . . .

Between the incorporation of the Fourteenth Amendment into the Constitution and the beginning of the present membership of the Court—a period of seventy years—the scope of that Amendment was passed upon by forty-three judges. Of all these judges, only one, who may respectfully be called an eccentric exception, ever indicated the belief that the Fourteenth Amendment was a shorthand summary of the first eight Amendments theretofore limiting only the Federal Government, and that due process incorporated those eight Amendments as restrictions upon the powers of the States. Among these judges were not only those who would have to be included among the greatest in the history of the Court, but—it is especially relevant to note—they included those whose services in the cause of human rights and the spirit of freedom are the most conspicuous in our history. It is not invidious to single out Miller, Davis, Bradley, Waite, Matthews, Gray, Fuller, Holmes, Brandeis, Stone and Cardozo (to speak only of the dead) as judges who were alert in safeguarding and promoting the interests of liberty and human dignity through law. . . . they did not find that the Fourteenth Amendment, concerned as it was with matters fundamental to the pursuit of justice, fastened upon the States procedural arrangements which, in the language of Mr. Justice Cardozo, only those who are "narrow or provincial" would deem essential to "a fair and enlightened system of justice." *Palko* v. *Connecticut*. . . .

The short answer to the suggestion that the provision of the Fourteenth Amendment, which ordains "nor shall any State deprive any person of life, liberty, or property, without due process of law," was a way of saying that every State must thereafter initiate prosecutions through indictment by a grand jury, must have a trial by a jury of twelve in criminal cases, and must have trial by such a jury in common law suits where the amount in controversy exceeds twenty dollars, is that it is a strange way of saying it. It would be extraordinarily strange for a Constitution to convey such specific commands in such a roundabout and inexplicit way. After all, an amendment to the Constitution should be read in a " 'sense most obvious to the common understanding at the time of its adoption.' . . . For it was for public adoption that it was proposed." . . . Those reading the English language with the meaning which it ordinarily conveys, those conversant with the political and legal history of the concept of due process, those sensitive to the relations of the States to the central government as well as the relation of some of the provisions of the Bill of Rights to the process of justice, would hardly recognize the Fourteenth Amendment as a cover for the various explicit provisions of the first eight Amendments. Some of these are enduring reflections of experience with human nature, while some express the restricted views of Eighteenth-Century England regarding the best methods for the ascertainment of facts. The notion that the Fourteenth Amendment was a covert way of imposing upon the States all the rules which it seemed important to Eighteenth Century statesmen to write into the Federal Amendments, was rejected by judges who were themselves witnesses of the process by which the Fourteenth Amendment became part of the Constitution. . . . at the time of the ratification of the Fourteenth Amendment the constitutions of nearly half of the ratifying States did not have the rigorous requirements of the Fifth Amendment for instituting criminal proceedings through a grand jury. It could hardly have occurred to these States that by ratifying the Amendment they uprooted their established methods for prosecuting crime and fastened upon themselves a new prosecutorial system. . . .

And so, when, as in a case like the present, a conviction in a State court is here for review under a claim that a right protected by the Due Process Clause of the Fourteenth Amendment has been denied, the issue is not whether an infraction of one of the specific provisions of the first eight Amendments is disclosed by the record. The relevant question is whether the criminal proceedings which resulted in conviction deprived the accused of the due process of law to which the United States Constitution entitled him. Judicial review of that guaranty of the Fourteenth Amendment inescapably imposes upon this Court an exercise of judgment upon the whole course of the proceedings in order to ascertain whether they offend those canons of decency and fairness which express the notions of justice of English-speaking peoples even toward those charged with the most heinous offenses. These standards of justice are not authoritatively formulated anywhere as though they were prescriptions in a pharmacopoeia. But neither does the application of the Due Process Clause imply that judges are wholly at large. The judicial judgment in applying the Due Process Clause must move within the limits of accepted notions of justice and is not to be based upon the idiosyncrasies of a merely personal judgment. The fact that judges among themselves may differ whether in a particular case a trial offends accepted notions of justice is not disproof that general rather than idiosyncratic standards are applied. An important safeguard against such merely individual judgment is an alert deference to the judgment of the State court under review.

MR. JUSTICE BLACK, dissenting. . . .

This decision reasserts a constitutional theory spelled out in *Twining* v. *New Jersey* . . . that this Court is endowed by the Constitution with boundless power under "natural law" periodically to expand and contract constitutional standards to conform to the Court's conception of what at a particular time constitutes "civilized decency" and "fundamental liberty and justice." Invoking this *Twining* rule, the Court concludes that although comment upon testimony in a federal court would violate the Fifth Amendment, identical comment in a state court does not violate today's fashion in civilized decency and fundamentals and is therefore not prohibited by the Federal Constitution as amended.

The *Twining* case was the first, as it is the only, decision of this Court which has squarely held that states were free, notwithstanding the Fifth and Fourteenth Amendments, to extort evidence from one accused of crime. I agree that if *Twining* be reaffirmed, the result reached might appropriately follow. But I would not reaffirm the

Twining decision. I think that decision and the "natural law" theory of the Constitution upon which it relies degrade the constitutional safeguards of the Bill of Rights and simultaneously appropriate for this Court a broad power which we are not authorized by the Constitution to exercise. . . . My reasons for believing that the *Twining* decision should not be revitalized can best be understood by reference to the constitutional, judicial, and general history that preceded and followed the case. . . .

The first ten amendments were proposed and adopted largely because of fear that Government might unduly interfere with prized individual liberties. The people wanted and demanded a Bill of Rights written into their Constitution. The amendments embodying the Bill of Rights were intended to curb all branches of the Federal Government in the fields touched by the amendments—Legislative, Executive, and Judicial. The Fifth, Sixth, and Eighth Amendments were pointedly aimed at confining exercise of power by courts and judges within precise boundaries, particularly in the procedure used for the trial of criminal cases. Past history provided strong reasons for the apprehensions which brought these procedural amendments into being and attest the wisdom of their adoption. For the fears of arbitrary court action sprang largely from the past use of courts in the imposition of criminal punishments to suppress speech, press, and religion. Hence the constitutional limitations of courts' powers were, in the view of the Founders, essential supplements to the First Amendment, which was itself designed to protect the widest scope for all people to believe and to express the most divergent political, religious, and other views.

But these limitations were not expressly imposed upon state court action. In 1833, *Barron* v. *Baltimore* . . . was decided by this Court. It specifically held inapplicable to the states that provision of the Fifth Amendment which declares: "nor shall private property be taken for public use, without just compensation." In deciding the particular point raised, the Court there said that it could not hold that the first eight amendments applied to the states. This was the controlling constitutional rule when the Fourteenth Amendment was proposed in 1866.

My study of the historical events that culminated in the Fourteenth

Amendment, and the expressions of those who sponsored and favored, as well as those who opposed its submission and passage, persuades me that one of the chief objects that the provisions of the Amendment's first section, separately, and as a whole, were intended to accomplish was to make the Bill of Rights, applicable to the states. With full knowledge of the import of the *Barron* decision, the framers and backers of the Fourteenth Amendment proclaimed its purpose to be to overturn the constitutional rule that case had announced. This historical purpose has never received full consideration or exposition in any opinion of this Court interpreting the Amendment. . . .

. . . In my judgment that history conclusively demonstrates that the language of the first section of the Fourteenth Amendment, taken as a whole, was thought by those responsible for its submission to the people, and by those who opposed its submission, sufficiently explicit to guarantee that thereafter no state could deprive its citizens of the privileges and protections of the Bill of Rights. Whether this Court ever will, or whether it now should, in the light of past decisions, give full effect to what the Amendment was intended to accomplish is not necessarily essential to a decision here. However that may be, our prior decisions, including *Twining*, do not prevent our carrying out that purpose, at least to the extent of making applicable to the states, not a mere part, as the Court has, but the full protection of the Fifth Amendment's provision against compelling evidence from an accused to convict him of crime. And I further contend that the "natural law" formula which the Court uses to reach its conclusion in this case should be abandoned as an incongruous excrescence on our Constitution. I believe that formula to be itself a violation of our Constitution, in that it subtly conveys to courts, at the expense of legislatures, ultimate power over public policies in fields where no specific provision of the Constitution limits legislative power. . . .

I cannot consider the Bill of Rights to be an outworn 18th Century "strait jacket" as the *Twining* opinion did. Its provisions may be thought outdated abstractions by some. And it is true that they were designed to meet ancient evils. But they are the same kind of human evils that have emerged from century to century wherever excessive power is sought by the few at the expense of the many. In my judgment the people of no nation can lose their liberty so long as a Bill of

Rights like ours survives and its basic purposes are conscientiously interpreted, enforced and respected so as to afford continuous protection against old, as well as new, devices and practices which might thwart those purposes. I fear to see the consequences of the Court's practice of substituting its own concepts of decency and fundamental justice for the language of the Bill of Rights as its point of departure in interpreting and enforcing that Bill of Rights. If the choice must be between the selective process of the *Palko* decision applying some of the Bill of Rights to the States, or the *Twining* rule applying none of them, I would choose the *Palko* selective process. But rather than accept either of these choices, I would follow what I believe was the original purpose of the Fourteenth Amendment—to extend to all the people of the nation the complete protection of the Bill of Rights. To hold that this Court can determine what, if any, provisions of the Bill of Rights will be enforced, and if so to what degree, is to frustrate the great design of a written Constitution.

Conceding the possibility that this Court is now wise enough to improve on the Bill of Rights by substituting natural law concepts for the Bill of Rights, I think the possibility is entirely too speculative to agree to take that course. I would therefore hold in this case that the full protection of the Fifth Amendment's proscription against compelled testimony must be afforded by California. This I would do because of reliance upon the original purpose of the Fourteenth Amendment. . . .

Mr. Justice Douglas joins in this opinion.

Mr. Justice Murphy, with whom Mr. Justice Rutledge concurs, dissenting.

While in substantial agreement with the views of Mr. Justice Black, I have one reservation and one addition to make.

I agree that the specific guarantees of the Bill of Rights should be carried over intact into the first section of the Fourteenth Amendment. But I am not prepared to say that the latter is entirely and necessarily limited by the Bill of Rights. Occasions may arise where a proceeding falls so far short of conforming to fundamental standards of procedure as to warrant constitutional condemnation in terms of a lack of due process despite the absence of a specific provision in the Bill of Rights. . . .

> *"I cannot believe that we should decide due process*
> *questions by simply taking a poll of the rules in various*
> 3.   *jurisdictions . . ."*

WOLF V. COLORADO

A COLORADO *doctor was found guilty of conspiracy to commit abortions on the basis of records seized in his office by police officers who had no warrant for the search. Evidence thus secured was admissible in Colorado courts under the rulings of the state supreme court. The conviction was appealed on the ground that the state practice was in violation of the due process clause of the Fourteenth Amendment.*

MR. JUSTICE FRANKFURTER delivered the opinion of the Court. . . .

Unlike the specific requirements and restrictions placed by the Bill of Rights (Amendments I to VIII) upon the administration of criminal justice by federal authority, the Fourteenth Amendment did not subject criminal justice in the States to specific limitations. The notion that the "due process of law" guaranteed by the Fourteenth Amendment is shorthand for the first eight amendments of the Constitution and thereby incorporates them has been rejected by this Court again and again, after impressive consideration. . . . Only the other day the Court reaffirmed this rejection after thorough reexamination of the scope and function of the Due Process Clause of the Fourteenth Amendment. *Adamson* v. *California.* . . . The issue is closed.

For purposes of ascertaining the restrictions which the Due Process Clause imposed upon the States in the enforcement of their criminal law, we adhere to the views expressed in *Palko* v. *Connecticut.* . . .

Due process of law thus conveys neither formal nor fixed nor narrow requirements. It is the compendious expression for all those rights which the courts must enforce because they are basic to our free society. But basic rights do not become petrified as of any one time, even though, as a matter of human experience, some may not too

338 U.S. 25, 69 S. Ct. 1359, 93 L. Ed. 1782 (1949).

rhetorically be called eternal verities. It is of the very nature of a free society to advance in its standards of what is deemed reasonable and right. Representing as it does a living principle, due process is not confined within a permanent catalogue of what may at a given time be deemed the limits or the essentials of fundamental rights.

To rely on a tidy formula for the easy determination of what is a fundamental right for purposes of legal enforcement may satisfy a longing for certainty but ignores the movements of a free society. It belittles the scale of the conception of due process. The real clue to the problem confronting the judiciary in the application of the Due Process Clause is not to ask where the line is once and for all to be drawn but to recognize that it is for the Court to draw it by the gradual and empiric process of "inclusion and exclusion." *Davidson* v. *New Orleans.* . . .

The security of one's privacy against arbitrary intrusion by the police—which is at the core of the Fourth Amendment—is basic to a free society. It is therefore implicit in "the concept of ordered liberty" and as such enforceable against the States through the Due Process Clause. The knock at the door, whether by day or by night, as a prelude to a search, without authority of law but solely on the authority of the police, did not need the commentary of recent history to be condemned as inconsistent with the conception of human rights enshrined in the history and the basic constitutional documents of English-speaking peoples.

Accordingly, we have no hesitation in saying that were a State affirmatively to sanction such police incursion into privacy it would run counter to the guaranty of the Fourteenth Amendment. But the ways of enforcing such a basic right raise questions of a different order. How such arbitrary conduct should be checked, what remedies against it should be afforded, the means by which the right should be made effective, are all questions that are not to be so dogmatically answered as to preclude the varying solutions which spring from an allowable range of judgment on issues not susceptible of quantitative solution.

In *Weeks* v. *United States* . . . this Court held that in a federal prosecution the Fourth Amendment barred the use of evidence secured through an illegal search and seizure. This ruling was made

for the first time in 1914. It was not derived from the explicit requirements of the Fourth Amendment; it was not based on legislation expressing Congressional policy in the enforcement of the Constitution.
The decision was a matter of judicial implication. Since then it has
been frequently applied and we stoutly adhere to it. But the immediate
question is whether the basic right to protection against arbitrary
intrusion by the police demands the exclusion of logically relevant
evidence obtained by an unreasonable search and seizure because, in
a federal prosecution for a federal crime, it would be excluded. As a
matter of inherent reason, one would suppose this to be an issue as to
which men with complete devotion to the protection of the right of
privacy might give different answers. When we find that in fact most
of the English-speaking world does not regard as vital to such protection the exclusion of evidence thus obtained, we must hesitate to
treat this remedy as an essential ingredient of the right. The contra-
riety of views of the States is particularly impressive in view of the
careful reconsideration which they have given the problem in the
light of the *Weeks* decision.

I. Before the *Weeks* decision 27 States had passed on the admissibility of evidence obtained by unlawful search and seizure.
   (a) Of these, 26 States opposed the *Weeks* doctrine. . . .
   (b) Of these, 1 State anticipated the *Weeks* doctrine. . . .

II. Since the *Weeks* decision 47 States all told have passed on the
Weeks doctrine. . . .
   (a) Of these, 20 passed on it for the first time.
       (1) Of the foregoing States, 6 followed the *Weeks*
           doctrine. . . .
       (2) Of the foregoing States, 14 rejected the *Weeks*
           doctrine. . . .
   (b) Of these, 26 States reviewed prior decisions contrary to the
       Weeks doctrine.
       (1) Of these, 10 States have followed *Weeks,* overruling
           or distinguishing their prior decisions. . . .
       (2) Of these, 16 States adhered to their prior decisions
           against *Weeks.* . . .
   (c) Of these, 1 State repudiated its prior formulation of the
       Weeks doctrine.

III. As of today 31 States reject the *Weeks* doctrine, 16 States are in agreement with it. . . .

IV. Of 10 jurisdictions within the United Kingdom and the British Commonwealth of Nations which have passed on the question, none has held evidence obtained by illegal search and seizure inadmissible. . . .

The jurisdictions which have rejected the *Weeks* doctrine have not left the right to privacy without other means of protection. Indeed, the exclusion of evidence is a remedy which directly serves only to protect those upon whose person or premises something incriminating has been found. We cannot, therefore, regard it as a departure from basic standards to remand such persons, together with those who emerge scatheless from a search, to the remedies of private action and such protection as the internal discipline of the police, under the eyes of an alert public opinion, may afford. Granting that in practice the exclusion of evidence may be an effective way of deterring unreasonable searches, it is not for this Court to condemn as falling below the minimal standards assured by the Due Process Clause a State's reliance upon other methods which, if consistently enforced, would be equally effective. . . .

We hold, therefore, that in a prosecution in a State court for a State crime the Fourteenth Amendment does not forbid the admission of evidence obtained by an unreasonable search and seizure. . . .

Affirmed.

Mr. Justice Black, concurring. . . .

. . . I agree with what appears to be a plain implication of the Court's opinion that the federal exclusionary rule is not a command of the Fourth Amendment but is a judicially created rule of evidence which Congress might negate. . . .

Mr. Justice Douglas, dissenting. . . .

Mr. Justice Murphy, with whom Mr. Justice Rutledge joins, dissenting. . . .

. . . Of course I agree with the Court that the Fourteenth Amendment prohibits activities which are proscribed by the search and seizure clause of the Fourth Amendment. . . . It is difficult for me to understand how the Court can go this far and yet be unwilling to make the step which can give some meaning to the pronouncements it utters.

Imagination and zeal may invent a dozen methods to give content to the commands of the Fourth Amendment. But this Court is limited to the remedies currently available. It cannot legislate the ideal system. If we would attempt the enforcement of the search and seizure clause in the ordinary case today, we are limited to three devices: judicial exclusion of the illegally obtained evidence; criminal prosecution of violators; and civil action against violators in the action of trespass.

Alternatives are deceptive. Their very statement conveys the impression that one possibility is as effective as the next. In this case their statement is blinding. For there is but one alternative to the rule of exclusion. That is no sanction at all.

This has been perfectly clear since 1914, when a unanimous Court decided *Weeks* v. *United States*. . . . "If letters and private documents can thus be seized and held and used in evidence against a citizen accused of an offense," we said, "the protection of the Fourth Amendment declaring his right to be secure against such searches and seizures is of no value, and, so far as those thus placed are concerned, might as well be stricken from the Constitution." . . .

Today the Court wipes those statements from the books with its bland citation of "other remedies." Little need be said concerning the possibilities of criminal prosecution. Self-scrutiny is a lofty ideal, but its exaltation reaches new heights if we expect a District Attorney to prosecute himself or his associates for well-meaning violations of the search and seizure clause during a raid the District Attorney or his associates have ordered. But there is an appealing ring in another alternative. A trespass action for damages is a venerable means of securing reparation for unauthorized invasion of the home. . . .

But what an illusory remedy this is, if by "remedy" we mean a positive deterrent to police and prosecutors tempted to violate the Fourth Amendment. The appealing ring softens when we recall that in a trespass action the measure of damages is simply the extent of the injury to physical property. If the officer searches with care, he can avoid all but nominal damages—a penny, or a dollar. Are punitive damages possible? Perhaps. But a few states permit none, whatever the circumstances. In those that do, the plaintiff must show the real ill will or malice of the defendant, and surely it is not unreasonable to assume that one in honest pursuit of crime bears no malice toward the search victim. If that burden is carried, recovery may yet be defeated by the rule that there must be physical damages before punitive damages may be awarded. In addition, some states limit punitive damages to the actual expenses of litigation. . . . Even assuming the ill will of the officer, his reasonable grounds for belief that the home he searched harbored evidence of crime is admissible in mitigation of punitive damages. . . . The bad reputation of the plaintiff is likewise admissible. If the evidence seized was actually used at a trial, that fact has been held a complete justification of the search, and a defense against the trespass action. . . . And even if the plaintiff hurdles all these obstacles, and gains a substantial verdict, the individual officer's finances may well make the judgment useless—for the municipality, of course, is not liable without its consent. . . .

The conclusion is inescapable that but one remedy exists to deter violations of the search and seizure clause. That is the rule which excludes illegally obtained evidence. Only by exclusion can we impress upon the zealous prosecutor that violation of the Constitution will do him no good. And only when that point is driven home can the prosecutor be expected to emphasize the importance of observing constitutional demands in his instructions to the police. . . .

I cannot believe that we should decide due process questions by simply taking a poll of the rules in various jurisdictions, even if we follow the *Palko* "test." Today's decision will do inestimable harm to the cause of fair police methods in our cities and states. Even more important, perhaps, it must have tragic effect upon public respect for our judiciary. For the Court now allows what is indeed shabby business: lawlessness by officers of the law. . . .

MR. JUSTICE RUTLEDGE, dissenting. . . .

On June 19, 1961, a majority of 5 justices voted in Mapp v. Ohio *to reverse* Wolf v. Colorado *and to apply the exclusionary rule to state courts. Speaking for the new majority, Justice Clark said that experience had indicated that the "other remedies" referred to in Frankfurter's opinion in the* Wolf *case were "worthless and futile." Clark added: "While in 1949 . . . almost two-thirds of the States were opposed to the use of the exclusionary rule, now, despite the* Wolf *case, more than one-half of those since passing on upon it, by their own legislative or judicial decision, have wholly or partly adhered to the* Weeks *[exclusionary] rule."*

4.
> "Such a result reduces 'balancing' to a mere play on words ..."

BARENBLATT V. UNITED STATES

LLOYD BARENBLATT, *formerly an instructor in psychology at Vassar, refused to tell a subcommittee of the House Committee on Un-American Activities whether he was or ever had been a member of the Communist party or had joined supposedly Communist-dominated groups while at the University of Michigan. He did not claim the Fifth Amendment privilege against self-incrimination, but instead argued that the First Amendment bars congressional inquiry into matters of belief and association. He was convicted of contempt of Congress in a district court. The court of appeals upheld the conviction. The Supreme Court granted certiorari.*

MR. JUSTICE HARLAN delivered the opinion of the Court....

Our function, at this point, is purely one of constitutional adjudication in the particular case and upon the particular record before us, not to pass judgment upon the general wisdom or efficacy of the activities of this Committee in a vexing and complicated field.

The precise constitutional issue confronting us is whether the Subcommittee's inquiry into petitioner's past or present membership in the Communist Party transgressed the provisions of the First Amendment, which of course reach and limit congressional investigations. . . .

The Court's past cases establish sure guides to decision. Undeniably, the First Amendment in some circumstances protects an individual from being compelled to disclose his associational relationships. However, the protections of the First Amendment, unlike a proper claim of the privilege against self-incrimination under the Fifth Amendment, do not afford a witness the right to resist inquiry in all circumstances. Where First Amendment rights are asserted to bar governmental interrogation resolution of the issue always involves a balancing by the courts of the competing private and public interests at stake in the particular circumstances shown. These principles were recognized

360 U.S. 109, 79 S. Ct. 1081, 3 L. Ed. 2d 1115 (1959).

in [*Watkins* v. *United States*], where, in speaking of the First Amendment in relation to congressional inquiries, we said . . . "It is manifest that despite the adverse effects which follow upon compelled disclosure of private matters, not all such inquiries are barred. . . . The critical element is the existence of, and the weight to be ascribed to, the interest of the Congress in demanding disclosures from an unwilling witness." . . . In light of these principles we now consider petitioner's First Amendment claims.

The first question is whether this investigation was related to a valid legislative purpose, for Congress may not constitutionally require an individual to disclose his political relationships or other private affairs except in relation to such a purpose. . . .

That Congress has wide power to legislate in the field of Communist activity in this Country, and to conduct appropriate investigations in aid thereof, is hardly debatable. The existence of such power has never been questioned by this Court, and it is sufficient to say, without particularization, that Congress has enacted or considered in this field a wide range of legislative measures, not a few of which have stemmed from recommendations of the very Committee whose actions have been drawn in question here. In the last analysis this power rests on the right of self-preservation, "the ultimate value of any society," *Dennis* v. *United States*. . . . Justification for its exercise in turn rests on the long and widely accepted view that the tenets of the Communist Party include the ultimate overthrow of the Government of the United States by force and violence, a view which has been given formal expression by the Congress.

On these premises, this Court in its constitutional adjudications has consistently refused to view the Communist Party as an ordinary political party, and has upheld federal legislation aimed at the Communist problem which in a different context would certainly have raised constitutional issues of the gravest character. . . . On the same premises this Court has upheld under the Fourteenth Amendment state legislation requiring those occupying or seeking public office to disclaim knowing membership in any organization advocating overthrow of the Government by force and violence, which legislation none can avoid seeing was aimed at membership in the Communist Party. . . . Similarly, in other areas, this Court has recognized the close nexus between the Communist Party and violent overthrow of government. . . . To suggest that because the Communist Party may also sponsor peaceable political reforms the constitutional issues before us should now be judged as if that Party were just an ordinary political party from the standpoint of national security, is to ask this Court to blind itself to world affairs which have determined the whole course of our national policy since the close of World War II. . . .

We think that investigatory power in this domain is not to be denied Congress solely because the field of education is involved. Nothing in the prevailing opinions in *Sweezy* v. *New Hampshire* . . . stands for a contrary view. The vice existing there was that the questioning of Sweezy, who had not been shown ever to have been connected with the Communist Party, as to the contents of a lecture he had given at the University of New Hampshire, and as to his connections with the Progressive Party, then on the ballot as a normal political party in some 26 States, was too far removed from the premises on which the constitutionality of the State's investigation had to depend to withstand attack under the Fourteenth Amendment. . . . This is a very different thing from inquiring into the extent to which the Communist Party has succeeded in infiltrating into our universities, or elsewhere, persons and groups committed to furthering the objective of overthrow. . . .

Nor can we accept the further contention that this investigation should not be deemed to have been in furtherance of a legislative purpose because the true objective of the Committee and of the Congress was purely "exposure." So long as Congress acts in pursuance of its constitutional power, the judiciary lacks authority to intervene on the basis of the motives which spurred the exercise of that power. . . . These principles of course apply as well to committee investigations into the need for legislation as to the enactments which such investigations may produce. . . . Thus, in stating in the *Watkins* case . . . that "there is no congressional power to expose for the sake of exposure," we at the same time declined to inquire into the "motives of committee members," and recognized that their "motives alone would not vitiate an investigation which had been instituted by a House of Congress if that assembly's legislative purpose is being served." Having scrutinized this record we cannot say that the unanimous panel of the Court of Appeals which first considered this case was wrong in concluding that "the primary purposes of the inquiry were in aid of legislative processes." . . .

Finally, the record is barren of other factors which in themselves might sometimes lead to the conclusion that the individual interests at stake were not subordinate to those of the state. There is no indication in this record that the Subcommittee was attempting to pillory witnesses. Nor did petitioner's appearance as a witness follow from indiscriminate dragnet procedures, lacking in probable cause for belief that he possessed information which might be helpful to the Subcommittee. And the relevancy of the questions put to him by the Subcommittee is not open to doubt.

We conclude that the balance between the individual and the governmental interests here at stake must be struck in favor of the latter, and that therefore the provisions of the First Amendment have not been offended. . . .

Affirmed.

MR. JUSTICE BLACK, with whom THE CHIEF JUSTICE, and MR. JUSTICE DOUGLAS concur, dissenting. . . .

I do not agree that laws directly abridging First Amendment freedoms can be justified by a congressional or judicial balancing process. There are, of course, cases suggesting that a law which primarily regulates conduct but which might also indirectly affect speech can be upheld if the effect on speech is minor in relation to the need for control of the conduct. With these cases I agree. Typical of them are *Cantwell* v. *Connecticut* . . . and *Schneider* v. *Irvington*. . . . Both of these involved the right of a city to control its streets. In *Cantwell*, a man had been convicted of breach of the peace for playing a phonograph on the street. He defended on the ground that he was disseminating religious views and could not, therefore, be stopped. We upheld his defense, but in so doing we pointed out that the city did have substantial power over conduct on the streets even where this power might to some extent affect speech. . . . But even such laws governing conduct, we emphasized, must be tested, though only by a balancing process, if they indirectly affect ideas. On one side of the balance, we pointed out, is the interest of the United States in seeing that its fundamental law protecting freedom of communication is not abridged; on the other the obvious interest of the State to regulate conduct within its boundaries. In *Cantwell* we held that the need to control the streets could not justify the restriction made on speech. We stressed the fact that where a man had a right to be on a street, "he had a right peacefully to impart his views to others." . . . Similar views were expressed in *Schneider,* which concerned ordinances prohibiting the distribution of handbills to prevent littering. We forbade application of such ordinances when they affected literature designed to spread ideas. There were other ways, we said, to protect the city from littering which would not sacrifice the right of the people to be informed. In so holding, we, of course, found it necessary to "weigh the circumstances." . . . But we did not in *Schneider,* any more than in *Cantwell,* even remotely suggest that a law directly aimed at curtailing speech and political persuasion could be saved through a balancing process. Neither these cases, nor any others, can be read as allowing legislative bodies to pass laws abridging freedom of speech, press and association merely because of hostility to views peacefully expressed in a place where the speaker had a right to be. . . .

To apply the Court's balancing test under such circumstances is to read the First Amendment to say "Congress shall pass no law abridging freedom of speech, press, assembly and petition, unless Congress and the Supreme Court reach the joint conclusion that on balance the interests of the Government in stifling these freedoms is greater than the interest of the people in having them exercised." This is closely akin to the notion that neither the First Amendment nor any other provision of the Bill of Rights should be enforced unless the Court believes it is *reasonable* to do so. Not only does this violate the genius of our *written* Constitution, but it runs expressly counter to the injunction to Court and Congress made by Madison when he introduced the Bill of Rights. "If they [the first ten amendments] are incorporated into the Constitution, independent tribunals of justice will consider themselves in a peculiar manner the guardians of those rights; they will be an impenetrable bulwark against *every* assumption of power in the Legislative or Executive; they will be naturally led to resist *every* encroachment upon rights expressly stipulated for in the Consti-

tution by the declaration of rights." Unless we return to this view of
our judicial function, unless we once again accept the notion that the
Bill of Rights means what it says and that this Court must enforce
that meaning, I am of the opinion that our great charter of liberty
will be more honored in the breach than in the observance.

But even assuming what I cannot assume, that some balancing is
proper in this case, I feel that the Court after stating the test ignores
it completely. At most it balances the right of the Government to
preserve itself, against Barenblatt's right to refrain from revealing
Communist affiliations. Such a balance, however, mistakes the factors
to be weighed. In the first place, it completely leaves out the real
interest in Barenblatt's silence, the interest of the people as a whole
in being able to join organizations, advocate causes and make political
"mistakes" without later being subjected to governmental penalties
for having dared to think for themselves. It is this right, the right to
err politically, which keeps us strong as a Nation. For no number of
laws against communism can have as much effect as the personal
conviction which comes from having heard its arguments and rejected
them, or from having once accepted its tenets and later recognized
their worthlessness. Instead, the obloquy which results from investigations such as this not only stifles "mistakes" but prevents all but the
most courageous from hazarding any views which might at some later
time become disfavored. This result, whose importance cannot be
overestimated, is doubly crucial when it affects the universities, on
which we must largely rely for the experimentation and development
of new ideas essential to our country's welfare. It is these interests of
society, rather than Barenblatt's own right to silence, which I think
the Court should put on the balance against the demands of the
Government, if any balancing process is to be tolerated. Instead they
are not mentioned, while on the other side the demands of the Government are vastly overstated and called "self-preservation." It is
admitted that this Committee can only seek information for the purpose of suggesting laws, and that Congress' power to make laws in
the realm of speech and association is quite limited, even on the
Court's test. Its interest in making such laws in the field of education,
primarily a state function, is clearly narrower still. Yet the Court styles

this attenuated interest self-preservation and allows it to overcome the need our country has to let us all think, speak, and associate politically as we like and without fear of reprisal. Such a result reduces "balancing" to a mere play on words and is completely inconsistent with the rules this Court has previously given for applying a "balancing test," where it is proper: "[T]he courts should be *astute* to examine the *effect* of the challenged legislation. Mere *legislative preferences or beliefs* . . . may well support regulation directed at other personal activities, but be insufficient to justify such as diminishes the exercise of rights so vital to the maintenance of democratic institutions." *Schneider* v. *Irvington.* . . .

MR. JUSTICE BRENNAN dissenting. . . .

> *"The consideration . . . here is . . . fully exploring the complex moral foundation that underlies the Constitution."*

5.

LABELS AND LIBERTARIANS *Donald Meiklejohn**

. . . THE "BALANCING" view . . . urges that the highest constitutional values, including the First Amendment freedoms, must be "weighed against" other social values, such as national security, quiet in parks on Sunday afternoons, orderly traffic on city streets, and the peaceful settlement of industrial disputes. Should . . . judicial thinkers adhere exclusively to this balancing process . . . ? Or is there a different approach, not necessarily appropriate to all constitutional questions, but appropriate at least to the "civil liberties," which must be prior to and indeed define the limits of "balancing"?

Little more than a suggestion for a complete argument for such a view can be offered within the compass of this discussion. The start can be made effectively, I think, in terms of the reasoning . . . in

66 *Ethics* 51 (1955). Copyright 1955 The University of Chicago Press. Reprinted with permission.

* Chairman of the Social Science Section, The College of the University of Chicago.

Stone's conception of the political process, as set forth in a footnote to his opinion in the Carolene Products case.[1] In that footnote, Stone urged that special attention should be accorded to the political processes in which the popular will is formed, and in particular to those processes in which minorities are hindered in their efforts to secure representation in public policy. This surely is good libertarian doctrine. But is it to be subjected, itself, to the "balancing process"? Surely it cannot be. Balancing means adjustment among contending claims and can be valid only if the rules are equitably maintained. The freedoms of the First Amendment, as Cardozo so well pointed out in his Palko opinion, are indispensable elements in the rules governing the democratic political process. They are what the Founding Fathers, and we, as we follow them, have declared to be the conditions of all the particular political decisions to be made. Of course, within the framework of the process so established, particular social values must be balanced, one against another. But an umpire's decision respecting competing players cannot intelligibly proceed by balancing himself against them; his job is to weigh one of them against the other. Nor does the weighing process require that neither can be right entirely; the essential condition of ordered liberty is simply that each participant receive due consideration. . . .

. . . it may be useful to outline in general terms the constitutional philosophy underlying Cardozo's and Stone's opinions as I interpret them.

The "balancing" view instructs us, as I understand it, to weigh the First Amendment against other provisions of the Constitution. The contending view, which I am trying to outline here, takes the First Amendment at its face value, as defining principles which the American community does not propose to balance away by any others. Manifestly the First Amendment cannot be maintained in a completely literal sense, as if any speaking or publication or assembling might claim immunity from control. Yet the "reasonable" approach here is not to nibble away at the edges of these freedoms. It is rather to analyze them in the context of our basic conceptions of political society; it is to see why they are so uncompromisingly asserted in the First Amendment. And such analysis, which is familiar enough, shows their

[1] *United States* v. *Carolene Products Co.* (1938). See below, p. 635.

indispensability as elements of political freedom in the community's rendering of its collective judgments. Without them, the community does not achieve that wise and representative quality in its judgments which is the heart of self-government. With them, and only with them, can the community claim to express, as well as to discover, its own reflective will. . . .

. . . The Founding Fathers' affirmation that the national security is thoroughly consistent with political freedom is adequately accepted in prevailing judicial discussion. On the surface, at least, the issue is how to define the speech that is permissible, and essential to self-government: it is how to define and relate such terms as "discussion," "advocacy," and "incitement."

World War I cases dealing with speech and security initiated the course of constitutional theorizing which came to accept, in the 1930's, the distinction drawn in the 1917 Masses[2] case by Learned Hand between advocacy and incitement—that distinction which Hand termed, not "scholastic," but a hard-won safeguard of liberty. As the libertarians extended and refined their doctrine in the Hughes Court, the protections of the First Amendment were extended very far toward the boundary where incitatory expression moves into action—where, to quote from Holmes's Schenck[3] opinion a phrase far more instructive than the danger test, "words are used with the effect of force." But now and primarily in terms of Vinson's Douds[4] and Hand's Dennis[5] opinions the line is redrawn. Advocacy now is assimilated to incitement; the probability of dangerous action in an indefinite future (why wait till the bombs fall?) is introduced into the assessment.

The libertarian cause today must, it seems to me, be defined in terms of restoring the "analytic" mode of constitutional reasoning, so that *all* speech is protected which deserves to be protected because of its relation to political freedom. This means distinguishing the speech which is "advocacy"—that is, takes a stand—from speech which, narrowly, "incites." It may be conceded that what incites in one context need not be incitement in another—reference to circumstances still is

[2] *Masses Publishing Co.* v. *Patten* (1917).
[3] *Schenck* v. *United States* (1919).
[4] *American Communications Ass'n* v. *Douds* (1950).
[5] *Dennis* v. *United States* (1951). See below, p. 679.

indispensable. But the reasoning is not cast adrift on the entire range of external conditions. Those conditions are relevant only as they show that "incitement" is or is not involved.

The distinction between advocacy and incitement is, as Judge Hand said, no merely "scholastic distinction." It is the distinction between contributing to a common thinking process and combining in a common action. The former is the indispensable constituent in the formation of a group of people whose members can be said to retain their freedom as the group acts; without a chance to participate in the group's thinking a member is not free. This is the sense of Stone's footnote in the Carolene case. In other words, advocacy on public issues is essential to the political process which is the heart of democratic self-government. It may, I think, safely be said that when Holmes wrote in his Gitlow[6] dissent that "every idea is an incitement," he actually was referring to advocacy, to speech in which the speaker is proposing a plan of action. On the other hand, authentic incitement that urges a mob to lynch or march or burn does not enhance but rather corrupts the process of self-government and makes the listeners the servants of the speaker. That is why, quite as much as for the protection of property or security, incitements may and must be abated.

. . . The consideration proper here is not balancing; it is analysis, or interpretation. It is fully exploring the complex moral foundation that underlies the Constitution.

There are, indeed, occasions of many sorts where unrestricted speaking is no essential part of democratic self-government: Murphy's opinion in the Chaplinsky[7] case is perhaps the most succinct example. A military camp in a battle area, an area under martial law, as well as a sickroom are not available for unlimited discussion; at the other extreme, the Congress is declared to be always available for such discussion—subject, of course, to parliamentary rules of order. Of course, there are people now who interpret the cold war as putting the whole United States in a crisis area where discussion must be restricted; but surely this judgment can be met on its own ground as simply mistaken in fact. The crucial question to ask, which Brandeis defined in his Whitney[8] opinion, is whether there is a chance for false doctrines to be

[6] *Gitlow* v. *New York* (1925).
[7] *Chaplinsky* v. *New Hampshire* (1942).
[8] *Whitney* v. *California* (1927).

countered and corrected by true ones, whether there is available for Truth a "fair and open encounter." It is our maintenance of that encounter today that has done very much to expose Communists here and abroad to the discredited condition which they deserve. Rather than balance, libertarians need to read and act upon the Brandeis argument, as Douglas did in the Dennis case:

> To courageous self-reliant men, with confidence in the power of free and fearless reasoning applied through the processes of popular government, no danger flowing from speech can be deemed clear and present unless the incidence of the evil apprehended is so imminent that it may befall before there is opportunity for free discussion. If there be time to expose through discussion the falsehood and fallacies, to avert the evil by the processes of education, the remedy to be applied is more speech, not enforced silence. Only an emergency can justify suppression. Such must be the rule if authority is to be reconciled with freedom. Such, in my opinion, is the command of the Constitution. It is therefore always open to Americans to challenge a law abridging free speech and assembly by showing there was no emergency justifying it.

The balancing theory of the pragmatists is rooted deep in their awareness of the fallibility of men (is not the balancing goddess blind?) and in the externality of men's different purposes to one another. But fallibility and externality are themselves intelligible only in terms of the common standards by which thinking men live and act together. Those standards do not admit balancing, for they are what make possible our common enterprise in freedom.

PART SIX

The Decisional Process

13 / ORGANIZATION OF THE DECISIONAL PROCESS

Decision-making is an extremely broad concept. For use as an instrument of political analysis, however, it may be defined as the process by which responsibility for settling a problem is accepted, the value of past solutions is assessed, present alternatives are discovered and their future results predicted, and a choice is made among these alternatives. Technical legal rules, the judge's formal training as a lawyer, the degree to which he accepts the general societal notion of the judicial function, his experience on and off the bench, as well as his personal and more specific concept of the judicial role—all of these limit the types of problems for which courts will accept responsibility, channelize investigation of past solutions, and restrict the range of alternative solutions from which choice may be made. In similar fashion, these influences on decision-making in the context of a law-court tradition may broaden or narrow a judge's ability to evaluate the results of alternatives and will certainly restrict his choice among those alternatives which are available. This chapter concentrates on the structure of judicial decision-making, the mechanics and form of that process.

Trial-Court Procedures

A district judge often feels obliged to give a decision almost as a reflex action. During the course of a trial, one lawyer may object to the argument or conduct of his opponent and ask the judge for an immediate ruling. Judges, especially if a jury is present, do not like to recess the court to research and meditate on procedural points, though they are sometimes forced to do so by the complexity of the issues. In contrast to the necessity of quick decisions while the trial is in progress, the judge has some opportunity to research and reflect on the instructions which he will give to the jurors at the close of the trial. The judge may also ask the lawyers on each side to assist him by drafting proposed instructions. Since the final decision in the case is the jury's, these instructions are not normally published, though they are kept with the records of the trial so that they may be reviewed in the event of an appeal. The sole record of the jury's deliberative process is the verdict itself.

Since proceedings before a judge sitting without a jury are much less formal, the trial judge has to make relatively fewer rulings on procedural technicalities. After hearing the evidence and argument, and reading any briefs submitted, he will decide the case either immediately or after deliberation that may last as long as several weeks. His decision will usually be accompanied by a short written opinion which will consist of at least two parts, findings of fact and conclusions of law, though it may also include a statement explaining the reasoning by which he arrived at these results. The West Publishing Company, the commercial firm which prints the *Federal Supplement*, the only generally available volumes of federal district court decisions, publishes only those opinions which it feels will be of wide interest to the legal profession. This means that a large percentage of district court opinions can be found only in the files of individual courthouses.

Supreme Court Decision-Making

Decision-making at the appellate level follows a more leisurely pace than that of trial courts. The procedures of the various courts of appeals and the Supreme Court are essentially similar, but the Supreme Court has its own peculiarities because of its role in the American political system. The Supreme Court's term begins on the first Monday in October and runs until sometime in June, though the heavy burden of their docket sometimes forces the justices to stay in session until early July and even then to carry cases over to the next term. Generally, the Court sits for two-week periods to hear argument and announce decisions and then adjourns for two weeks to allow the justices to research, think, and write their opinions.

During the weeks the Court is sitting, the justices meet at a few minutes before noon on Mondays through Thursdays in the robing room behind the courtroom. At high noon the maroon velvet curtains part and the justices take their places behind the bench as the crier gavels the court to attention and chants:

> The Honorable, the Chief Justice and Associate Justices of the Supreme Court of the United States! Oyez, Oyez, Oyez! All persons having business before the Honorable, the Supreme Court of the United States are admonished to draw near and give their attention, for the Court is now sitting. God save the United States and this Honorable Court.

On Tuesdays through Thursdays the justices hear oral argument from noon to four-thirty, with half an hour recess for lunch at two o'clock. Counsel for each side will usually have an hour or less to present his argument, though in especially important cases such as the steel seizure dispute or the school segregation controversy the Court will grant additional time. The attorney stands at a lectern facing the justices in their high-backed leather chairs. A white light flashes when he has five minutes left, and when his time is up a red light goes on. Argument stops immediately. The story is told that Chief Justice Hughes once called time on a lawyer in the middle of the word *if*.

Oral argument can be an arduous experience for a lawyer. The justices may stare impassively at the draperies, chat among themselves, write notes, read, send young page boys for law books, or even occasionally nap, apparently totally uninterested in what is being said to them. On the other hand, they may suddenly shift moods and turn a dull presentation into a lively discussion by a rapid series of piercing questions and cross-examinations. Trying to race along with nine different minds, sometimes going off in nine different directions, is strenuous mental exercise. When he was Solicitor General and before his own appointment to the Court, Stanley Reed once fainted dead away in the middle of arguing a case, and many other lawyers have experienced obvious intellectual blackouts.

Mondays during the weeks the Court is sitting are set aside for the announcement of decisions in cases previously argued. Except during the last weeks of the term, however, there is usually some time left for oral argument. Fridays are reserved for the conference. The justices meet at eleven o'clock and may continue in session all day and perhaps have to meet the next day to complete their discussion.

Essentially there are two different kinds of decisions which the Court must make. The first concerns what cases shall be heard and decided. As Chapter 2 pointed out, the Supreme Court has wide discretion in exercising its jurisdiction. The writ of certiorari is usually granted only if four justices think the issues important enough to warrant taking up the Court's limited time, but occasionally certiorari has been granted when one or two justices have felt very strongly about a case's significance.

In recent years the Court has been receiving more than fifteen hundred certiorari petitions a term, and it is obvious that the justices cannot give detailed consideration, much less discussion, to each case. Fortunately, so the justices say, most of these requests are frivolous and can be quickly disposed of. Law clerks are often used to summarize certiorari petitions for the justices, and the Chief Justice's handling of the conference can accelerate their disposition.

If certiorari is granted, the case is put on the docket and scheduled for oral argument. Before the date set for argument the record of the case is printed and each side submits written briefs explaining its contentions in some detail. Once again it is impossible for the justices to read all the material. The briefs are examined with great care; but since it is not unusual for a trial record in a complicated case to run to several thousand pages, the justices have to learn what parts can be skipped or perused and what parts closely studied. The Supreme Court Rules require that the briefs contain specific page citations to those parts of the record being discussed, but there are limits to specificity. In *Sacher* v. *United States*, for example, several lawyers had been convicted of contempt for their general conduct during a trial whose record took up 13,000 pages.

On Fridays after oral argument the justices meet in conference to decide the cases just argued. The conference room is locked to all except the justices, and the junior member of the Court, referred to around Washington as "the highest-paid doorkeeper in town," answers any knocks on the door. Before discussion begins each justice shakes hands with every other justice. The Chief Justice presides and has the difficult and delicate duty of allowing adequate discussion of each case while still getting through the docket, and of encouraging meaningful intellectual exchanges without letting the conference degenerate into personal argument. The Chief Justice gives his views first, and then each justice speaks in order of seniority. When the discussion is called to a close, the justices vote in reverse order of seniority.

The Chief Justice, if he voted with the majority, assigns the task of writing the opinion of the Court. If the Chief was in the minority the senior associate justice makes the assignment. Before John Marshall, the Court had generally followed the British practice whereby each judge who had the time or inclination wrote his own opinion. There was seldom an institutional opinion of the Court. Marshall, realizing that the appearance of monolithic unity of reasoning as well as of result would give greater impact to judicial decisions, made it standard practice to designate one judge, usually himself, to act as spokesman for the whole Court.

Writing Opinions

The opinion-assigning function is a source of power for the Chief Justice since he can designate the judge who, he believes, will write the opinion which he thinks the situation calls for. On the other hand, since every justice is still theoretically free to file his own concurring or dissenting opinion, the desire to mass the Court, or at least a majority, behind a single expression of views can inhibit the power of the Court's spokesman. Opinions are circulated among the justices, and the resulting process is often one of negotiation and compromise as one judge objects to a certain phrase or to a line of reasoning, another to other parts. The opinion writer then has to reconcile these comments or risk the disintegration of the majority into concurring factions. This is an important consideration since an opinion which is not endorsed by a majority of the Court stands only as the expression of individual views, respected but not necessarily to be followed under the doctrine of *stare decisis*. Chided about his opinion in a case in 1931, Justice Stone explained to a friend:

> I should have preferred to have written your opinion than the one which will actually appear in the books. Had I done so, I should have been in a minority of two or three, instead of a majority of six. Someone else would have written the opinion [of the Court]. . . . I proceed upon the theory, which I am willing to admit may be a mistaken one, that the large objective should be kept constantly in mind and reached by whatever road is open, provided only that untenable distinctions are not taken, and that I am not in the process, committed incidentally to the doctrine of which I disapprove or which would hinder the Court's

coming out ultimately in the right place. All of this proves that the university professor is the only free man who can develop legal doctrine in his own way and travel the road he chooses in accounting for his conclusions.[1]

Dissenting and concurring opinions, if written, are also circulated among the justices, and changes may be made by each author to meet points raised by other drafts. The very existence of the dissenting opinion —not considered proper form in civil-law countries like France—restricts the maneuvering room of the Court's spokesman. He cannot compromise with other justices to the point where his writing loses cohesion or force and becomes an easy target for the dissenter. Even where there is no dissent, the author faces a similar problem when he considers the effect on his own reputation and the prestige of the Court of a disjointed opinion which may be mercilessly dissected in scholarly journals, newspaper editorials, the *Congressional Record,* or Presidential press conferences. Sometimes the justices simply cannot arrive at a mutually satisfactory opinion and have to revert to the older practice of seriatim expressions of views. In any event, when the opinion or opinions are completed, the Chief Justice brings the case up again at conference, and if no further changes are desired the decision will be announced the next Monday the Court is in session.

In writing his opinion, the dissenter has the less difficult job. Although he too is under pressure to persuade other justices to join in his protest, he writes without the authority—and therefore the responsibility—of speaking for one of the co-ordinate branches of the federal government on a matter of public policy. As Justice Cardozo said:

> The spokesman of the Court is cautious, timid, fearful of the vivid word, the heightened phrase. He dreams of an unworthy brood of scions, the spawn of careless *dicta,* disowned by the *ratio decidendi.* . . . The result is to cramp and paralyze. One fears to say anything when the peril of misunderstanding puts a warning finger to the lips. Not so, however, the dissenter. . . . Deep conviction and warm feeling are saying their last say with knowledge that the cause is lost. . . . The dissenter speaks to the future, and his voice is pitched to a key that will carry through the years.[2]

[1] Quoted in Alpheus T. Mason, *Harlan Fiske Stone* (New York: Viking Press, 1956), p. 308.

[2] "Law and Literature," 14 *Yale Review* 699, 715–716 (1925).

SELECTED REFERENCES

Bickel, Alexander, *The Unpublished Opinions of Mr. Justice Brandeis* (Cambridge: Harvard University Press, 1957).

Braden, George, "The Value of Law Clerks," 24 *Mississippi Law Journal* 295 (1953).

Cardozo, Benjamin N., "Law and Literature," 14 *Yale Review* 699 (1925).

Frank, Jerome, *Law and the Modern Mind* (New York: Brentano's, 1930).

Frankfurter, Felix, "Chief Justices I Have Known," 39 *Virginia Law Review* 883 (1953).

Lewis, Anthony, "How the Supreme Court Reaches Decisions," *New York Times Magazine*, December 1, 1957, pp. 51 ff.

McElwain, Edwin, "The Business of the Supreme Court as Conducted by Chief Justice Hughes," 63 *Harvard Law Review* 5 (1949).

Rehnquist, William H., "Who Writes Decisions of the Supreme Court?" *U.S. News and World Report*, December 13, 1957, pp. 74–75.

Stern, Robert L. and Eugene Gressman, *Supreme Court Practice* (2d ed.; Washington, D.C.: Bureau of National Affairs, 1954).

1.   *" 'What is the milk in the coconut?' "*

HIGH DRAMA IN THE HIGH COURT   *Anthony Lewis**

GRANDIOSE, INTIMATE; ritualistic, informal; austere, human. These paradoxical terms pass through the mind of the observer as he surveys the scene in the Supreme Court of the United States.

That drama—the process of the Court at work—does not ordinarily attract much public attention. It is only the critical moments, like the extraordinary sessions on Little Rock this summer that bring general awareness of the fascination and the significance of the courtroom spectacle.

The disclosure of the justices' mood in the oral arguments on the Little Rock case made plain how significant for the final result the courtroom proceedings may be. But watching the justices at work is not only education, but entertainment. The Supreme Court offers, from time to time, as good a public show as anything in Washington except an occasional Senate session.

Grandiose is the word for the external setting. The W. P. A. guide to Washington called the Supreme Court building a "great marble temple" which "by its august scale and mighty splendor seems to bear little relation to the functional purposes of government."

Shortly before the justices moved into the building in 1935 from their old chamber in the Capitol, Justice Stone wrote his sons: "The place is almost bombastically pretentious, and thus it seems to me wholly inappropriate for a quiet group of old boys such as the Supreme Court. . . ." He told his friends that the justices would be "nine black beetles in the Temple of Karnak."

Justice Brandeis would never set foot in the office assigned him in the new building. Prof. Paul A. Freund, his former law clerk, explains: "He [felt] that the authority of the Court must come from the intrinsic strength of its work and not from the trappings or imprimatur of

The New York Times Magazine, October 26, 1958, pp. 10, 19–20. Copyright 1958 *The New York Times.* Reprinted with permission.

* Pulitzer Prize-winning reporter who covers the Supreme Court for the *Times.*

power. . . . A marble palace, he thought, would not be conducive to the spirit of humility befitting those whose title to govern rests on the power of reason."

Passing the columns and statues of the huge pseudo-classic facade, the visitor walks a cold marble corridor to the courtroom. Here again the impression is one of austere pomp—pillars, red velvet hangings, an enormously high ceiling, friezes carved high on the walls.

The ritual opening of every day's session adds to the atmosphere of awe. The justices gather in the robing room in back of the red draperies behind the bench. People sitting near the front of the room can hear the hum of their talk.

Then a buzzer sounds at the marshal's desk to the right of the bench, the court crier smashes his gavel loudly on the desk, spectators rise and the justices file in. As they stand in black robes at their places, the crier intones the traditional phrases ending, "God save the United States and this honorable Court."

In such a setting the remarkable thing is how informal—almost cozy, one might say at times—an oral argument before the Supreme Court of the United States can be.

An Alabama labor lawyer had talked for about fifteen minutes last winter when Justice Felix Frankfurter peered over the bench and asked: "Is that all there is to this case?"

"No, sir," said the lawyer. "There's a heap to this case."

"As you state it," the justice came back, "it's so simple that I'm suspicious. . . . What is the milk in the coconut?"

The milk turned out to be an assertion by the lawyer that unions covered by Federal labor law had a right to be free of damage suits by employes who had been kept out of plants by violent picketing. He lost his case, 6 to 2.

Oral argument is both the most important and the most interesting aspect of the relatively small portion of the Court's work that is in public view. It can win or lose cases, it exposes the personalities of court and counsel and it conveys a continuing sense of the Court as an institution. . . .

In more spacious times a Daniel Webster could go on for days. And citations of God and country were good form. As recently as 1935 one of the greatest of modern Supreme Court advocates, former

Senator George Wharton Pepper, Republican of Pennsylvania, concluded his attack on the constitutionality of the New Deal's Agricultural Adjustment Act with these words:

"Indeed, may it please your honors, I believe I am standing here to plead the cause of the America I have loved; and I pray Almighty God that not in my time may 'the land of the regimented' be accepted as a worthy substitute for 'the land of the free.'"

It is difficult to think of anyone who could carry off that style of argument today. The lawyer is well advised to be simple and direct. And, perhaps surprisingly, he might well emphasize the facts rather than the law of his case. The justices of the Supreme Court, so remote from trials, seem lonesome for concrete details.

Rule forty-four of the Supreme Court says: "The court looks with disfavor on any oral argument that is read from a prepared text." Informality, even spontaneity, is preferred, but any lawyer knows that to be effectively spontaneous he must be really well prepared on his case.

It would be nice to report that the average Supreme Court argument is well prepared, informative, persuasive. Unhappily, it is just as likely to be a dreary, wandering affair. The American bar simply does not have England's great tradition of oral advocacy. . . .

Some lawyers grieve because they are interrupted by a question before they finish their first polished sentence. But they might better take the interest of the justice as a compliment and be resilient enough to satisfy it. For, as Justice Frankfurter has written, the Court is "not designed as a dozing audience for the reading of soliloquies but as a questioning body, utilizing oral arguments as a means for exposing the difficulties of a case with a view to meeting them."

[When] the Court was considering whether the Army could lawfully give a man a less than honorable discharge because of doubtful pre-induction associations, Government counsel sought to minimize the difference between an "honorable" discharge and a discharge "under honorable conditions" given one man.

"What is the difference?" Chief Justice Earl Warren asked.

"Legally, they mean the same thing," counsel answered. He said the honorable discharge was merely an extra "accolade."

The Chief Justice was not satisfied. He asked what portion of dischargees "get the accolade." Counsel answered with a list of annual discharge figures, not percentages, and the Chief Justice repeated each figure aloud.

"So 95 per cent get the accolade?" the Chief Justice finally asked, with evident sarcasm. Counsel agreed.

The opinion, when it came down some months later, referred to the "accolade" of honorable discharges. The Government lost the case.

That same argument had more dramatic moments. At one point Justice Hugo L. Black was probing the Government's assertion that Army discharges were not subject to judicial review at all. He asked: "Suppose the Army said it had given this discharge because it didn't like the man's religion. Would there be a remedy in a court of law?"

Government counsel said no. Justice Frankfurter, furious at the Government's handling of the case, told the lawyer sharply: "You need not take this extreme position."

Justice William J. Brennan Jr. asked whether a completely arbitrary discharge would not present a constitutional question. Again counsel said no.

"Are you going to argue that, too?" Justice Frankfurter asked angrily. "What is there you are not going to argue?"

Some time later Government counsel disclosed for the first time in his argument that the Justice Department did not defend the legality of the less than honorable discharges, but said only that they were not judicially reviewable.

To a man the nine justices leaped forward in their chairs and shouted questions simultaneously. When counsel confirmed that they had heard him correctly, everyone in the courtroom knew that the case was as good as decided.

In the same way, one series of questions put to Richard C. Butler, counsel for the Little Rock School Board, exposed the root problem in that case and the answer the Court inevitably was going to give. This series was the one that ended with the Chief Justice asking:

"Can we defer a program of this kind merely because there are those elements in the community that would commit violence to prevent it from going into effect?"

The justices' questioning techniques, and the importance they place on questions, vary widely.

The Chief Justice, who carries special weight because of his position, is likely to be bland and polite unless he thinks he is getting an evasive answer; then he can be relentless. Justice Black's voice is gentle, but his questions are powerful and dangerous to handle. Justice Frankfurter, the most frequent speaker from the bench, is sharp and witty, offering observations as well as questions. For example, he told one lawyer . . .

"You think there's nothing in the point. But I'm sometimes surprised at how often a majority of my colleagues thinks there is something to a point when I do not, or vice versa."

Things were not always so informal. . . . Senator Pepper recalled in 1956 that, when he came down to make his first argument in 1892, he was at first refused admission to the bar of the Supreme Court because he was not properly dressed. Justice Horace Gray whispered to one of his colleagues: "Who is that beast who dares to come in here with a gray coat?"

Young Mr. Pepper borrowed a morning coat, and all was well.

Nowadays they still have quill pens at the counsel tables. (Lawyers take them home as souvenirs for their children.) But just about the only men to appear in striped trousers and cutaways are the Solicitor General and his staff.

The Solicitor General's office is a special case, anyway. It includes an extraordinarily able group of lawyers who appear more regularly before the Supreme Court than anyone else and hence know it better.

The Solicitor General, now J. Lee Rankin, carries a special responsibility for frank dealings between the Executive Branch and the Court. But frankness isn't all. Professor Freund recalls the occasion when Justice Holmes complimented a Solicitor General on his candor. As the gentleman began to preen himself, Justice Holmes added: "You know, candor is one of the most effective instruments of deception."

When all is said and done, can oral argument really make the difference in a Supreme Court case?

Those who heard Senator Pepper argue the A. A. A. case say his argument alone won it—and drew from the Court one of its most bitterly criticized anti-New Deal opinions. Today it would be a rare thing for eloquence to win a case, but almost everyone agrees that

incompetence can easily lose one. And the justices themselves have
said publicly that the shaping of issues in argument helps to determine the analysis followed by the Court's opinion writer—which may
be as important as the result. . . .

And though oral argument of a case may take just an hour or two,
those hours come at a significant time. On Friday of each argument
week, at their regular conference, the justices cast tentative votes on
the cases heard that week. Rarely will they have had much time to
study the briefs since the argument. Thus the oral presentation will
be what is freshest in their minds when they decide. . . .

2.   *". . . I found that I must either submit to circumstances*
                 or become . . . a cypher in our consultations . . ."

JUSTICE WILLIAM JOHNSON* TO THOMAS JEFFERSON

WHILE I was on our state-bench I was accustomed to
delivering seriatim opinions in our appellate court, and was not a
little surprised to find our Chief Justice in the Supreme Court delivering all the opinions in cases in which he sat, even in some instances
when contrary to his own judgment and vote. But I remonstrated in
vain; the answer was he is willing to take the trouble and it is a mark
of respect to him. I soon however found out the real cause. Cushing
was incompetent. Chase could not be got to think or write—Patterson
[sic] was a slow man and willingly declined the trouble, and the other
two judges [Marshall and Bushrod Washington] you know are commonly estimated as one judge. . . .

Some case soon occurred in which I differed from my brethren,
and I thought it a thing of course to deliver my opinion. But, during
the rest of the session I heard nothing but lectures on the indecency
of judges cutting at each other, and the loss of reputation which the

Letter of December 10, 1822, quoted in Donald G. Morgan, *Justice William
Johnson: The First Dissenter* (Columbia: University of South Carolina Press,
1954), pp. 181–182. Reprinted with permission.

* Johnson, appointed to the Supreme Court by Jefferson, was a contemporary of
John Marshall. Johnson served on the Court from 1804 to 1834.

Virginia appellate court had sustained by pursuing such a course. At length I found that I must either submit to circumstances or become such a cypher in our consultations as to effect no good at all. I therefore bent to the current, and persevered until I got them to adopt the course they now pursue, which is to appoint someone to deliver the opinion of the majority, but leave it to the discretion of the rest of the judges to record their opinions or not ad libitum [at pleasure].

3.   *" 'Just between ourselves . . .' "*

THE MINNESOTA MORATORIUM CASE   *Alpheus T. Mason**

. . . NOW, EVEN in rural areas, law and order ran neck and neck with riot and anarchy. Formerly prosperous Midwestern states such as Minnesota had seen annual cash income of farmers fall in 1932 to an average of $141. That same year more than one-half of the state's farms were mortgaged or foreclosed. . . . "In isolated instances mobs of farmers took the law into their own hands and prevented foreclosure sales by force." These sporadic outbreaks indicated the trend and force of feeling among the debtors, and Minnesota's wheat growers made every effort to impress their plight on the state's lawmakers. "When the legislature assembled, a caravan of two or three thousand farmers descended upon St. Paul from southern Minnesota, in an astonishing array of antediluvian automobiles, and swarmed over the capitol, making demands and threats and uttering dire predictions." Three weeks later the Governor addressed an uproarious gathering on the steps of the capitol: "I want to say to the people of Minnesota that if the legislature—the Senate in particular—does not make ample provision for the sufferers in this state . . . I shall invoke the powers that I hold. I shall declare martial law. A lot of people who are now fighting the measures because they happen to possess considerable wealth will be brought in by provost guards. . . ."

The Governor ordered sheriffs "to refrain from proceeding with all foreclosure sales until after the legislative sessions." In due course, a

Harlan Fiske Stone: Pillar of the Law (New York: Viking Press, 1956), pp. 360–365. Copyright 1956 The Viking Press. Reprinted with permission.

* McCormick Professor of Jurisprudence, Princeton University.

bill modeled on New York's postwar Emergency Housing Act, giving courts power to postpone mortgage foreclosures, was passed without a dissenting vote. Debtors now hastened to bring their holdings under its protection, while creditors challenged in the courts this statutory readjustment of the terms of their contracts.

The first test case under the Act concerned one Blaisdell and his wife, who were struggling to pay off a mortgage on their fourteen-room house by letting rooms and keeping boarders. The state's highest court did not question the legislature's action in bowing to desperation. "The members of the legislature," it observed, "come from every community of the state and from all the walks of life. They are familiar with conditions generally in every calling, occupation, profession, and business in the state. Not only they, but the courts, must be guided by what is common knowledge. It is common knowledge that in the last few years land values have shrunk enormously. Loans made a few years ago upon the basis of then going values cannot possibly be replaced on the basis of present values. . . ."

On November 8 and 9, 1933, in faraway Washington, the case was argued in the Supreme Court, and on January 8, 1934, the Justices sustained the Act, 5 to 4. [*Home Building and Loan Association* v. *Blaisdell.*] Chief Justice Hughes, taking advantage of his prerogative, assigned this strategic majority opinion to himself.

The Minnesota statute seemed to fly in the face of the Constitution's categorical imperative—that no state shall pass any law "impairing the obligation of contracts" (Article I, Section 10). Nevertheless the Chief Justice upheld the act by distinguishing between the *obligation* of contract and the *remedy* given by the legislature to enforce that obligation. In short, he tried to demonstrate that the moratorium did not really impair the *obligation* of Minnesota mortgages; the statute only modified the remedy. Article I, Section 10, is qualified, Hughes argued, "by the measure of control which the state retains over remedial processes," and the mortgage contracts themselves are subject to the "reservation of the reasonable exercise of the protective power of the state," which is "read into all contracts as a postulate of the legal order."

The Chief Justice went out of his way to consider the relation of emergency to power. "Emergency does not create power," he said. "Emergency does not increase granted power or remove or diminish the restrictions imposed upon power granted or reserved." Specific constitutional requirements, such as the representation of each state by two senators, are plainly distinguishable, he noted, from the constitutional provisions against impairing the obligation of contracts. The former provision is not affected by emergency; the latter is. "While emergency does not create power, emergency may furnish the occasion for the exercise of power."

It was this line of reasoning that opened the way for . . . attack. . . . Sutherland's jurisprudence knew no such loopholes. . . . "I can only interpret what is said," the dissenter remarked scornfully, "as meaning that while an emergency does not diminish a restriction upon power it furnishes an occasion for diminishing it; and this, as it seems to me, is merely to say the same thing by the use of another set of words, with the effect of affirming that which has just been denied." Sutherland was especially vehement in opposing Hughes' "adaptative" theory of the fundamental law. Invoking historical evidence, he concluded: "The foregoing leaves no reasonable ground upon which to base a denial that the clause of the Constitution now under consideration was meant to foreclose state action impairing the obligation of contracts *primarily and especially* in respect of such action aimed at giving relief to *debtors in time of emergency*." War constituted an emergency, justifying legislative modification of rent leases, to be sure, but ruinous economic depression was not a comparable holocaust. This was no occasion for slackening the stubborn "strength of the fabric" woven by the Fathers. The aging justice had seen "economic emergencies" before: "The present exigency is nothing new. From the beginning of our existence as a nation, periods of depression, of industrial failure, of financial distress, of unpaid and unpayable indebtedness, have alternated with years of plenty."

Two hundred billion dollars of private credit had been destroyed, a total national income had been reduced from over eighty billions to under forty billions. But to this Supreme Court Justice all such cataclysmic economic chaos was nothing new. Now, as always, recovery must be achieved by "self-denial and painful effort." As the snapper to his forthright dissent, the former Utah Senator challenged: "If the provisions of the Constitution be not upheld when they pinch as well as when they comfort, they may as well be abandoned."

Cardozo and Stone read the Chief Justice's first draft with misgivings so serious that each considered writing a concurring opinion. The former actually prepared a draft, and Stone submitted a long memorandum. . . . The opening paragraph of Cardozo's undelivered concurrence quoted Marshall's famous dictum: "We must never forget that it is *a constitution* we are expounding," a constitution "intended to endure for ages to come, and, consequently, to be adapted to the various *crises* of human affairs." Cardozo also included the bold note Holmes struck in 1920: "The case before us must be considered in the light of our whole experience and not merely in that of what was said a hundred years ago." The Minnesota statute, Cardozo admitted, "may be inconsistent with things" which the men of 1787 believed or took for granted, but "their beliefs to be significant must be adjusted to the world they knew. It is not . . . inconsistent with what they would say today. . . ." For them as for us, Cardozo suggested, "the search was for a broader base, for a division that would separate the lawful and forbidden lines more closely in correspondence with the necessities of government."

Cardozo did not undertake to square the Minnesota statute with the literal requirements of Article I, Section 10. He did not rest his case in favor of the moratorium on "the distinction between right and remedy with all its bewildering refinements." The more general provisions of the Fourteenth Amendment were seen as pointing the way "toward a rational compromise between private rights and public welfare." "A promise exchanged between individuals," he concluded, "was not to paralyze the state in its endeavor at times of direful crises to keep its life-blood flowing."

Cardozo's attack on Justice Sutherland's deep-freeze dogmas was equally forthright. "A gospel of laissez faire—of individual initiative—of thrift and industry and sacrifice—may be inadequate in the great society that we live in to point the way to salvation, at least for economic life. The state when it acts today by statutes like the one before us is not furthering the selfish good of individuals or classes as ends of ultimate validity. It is furthering its own good by maintaining the economic structure on which the good of all depends." The Chief Justice took over this idea almost verbatim.

Stone also threatened to speak out independently if certain of his points were rejected. "I have taken more than the usual time to study your opinion," he wrote, December 13, 1933, "because of the great importance to the public and to the court of the questions involved." Like Cardozo, he wished to elevate the tone of the opinion and focus the argument on the merits of the case: "I am not inclined to join in so much of the [opinion] . . . as states that the relief afforded could only be of a temporary character. . . . I think we should be meticulous in not making pronouncements with respect to cases other than that before us. Moreover, the statement itself, without definition, has not very much meaning. . . . It seems to me that we should leave ourselves absolutely unhampered by pronouncements which might be taken to affect situations not presented to us in this case."

Continuing, Stone wrote: "I think the part of the opinion which discusses what the Court has sometimes treated as a distinction between obligation and remedy is somewhat confusing and, to some extent, obscures the point with which we have to deal in the present case. The distinction . . . comes to nothing more than a question of degree, and the net result of the cases seems to be unreasonable. Our present case has no complications of this character, since the statute does cut down both obligation and remedy to a material extent, and the sole question is whether private parties, by their contract, may tie the hands of the state so that it is powerless to deal with a problem vital to the Government itself. I think the opinion would gain in power and directness if the discussion of the right-remedy phase were very much condensed or relegated to a footnote."

Why not, Stone suggested, erect the opinion on more realistic foundations? "We are . . . confronted with a problem permeating the entire economic structure, of which Chief Justice Marshall probably never had any conception. A generation or more ago the state was concerned principally with problems affecting the moral and physical well-being of society. When its concern for public morality had led a state to a judgment different from that which had formerly prevailed, this Court could not say that it exceeded constitutional limitations in curtailing a grant to indulge in public lotteries, even though lotteries had long been accepted as legitimate activity. Today, when the whole economic structure of society is threatened with widespread foreclosures, the state has afforded a measure of relief which tends to prevent the impending ruin of mortgagees, as well as mortgagors, and to preserve the stake of the former as well as of the latter in land mortgages, viewed as a form of investment security. . . . It is, I think, desirable to emphasize the special character of the mortgage situation as affects both mortgagors and mortgagees, to show that, looked at collectively, the legislation protects the interest of both and harms neither. Once conceded, as it must be, that the contract clause is not an absolute and unyielding restriction upon the state, such legislation is demonstrated to be so reasonable in character as to be plainly within state competency."

The Chief Justice's opinion, as finally announced, included long passages from the Cardozo draft opinion and from Stone's memoranda. But he kept intact the legalistic logomachy about emergency power, thus exposing himself to Sutherland's broadside. From Cardozo came the verbal formulation of the Court's recognition of "the necessity of finding ground for a rational compromise between individual rights and the public welfare"—the passage that commentators praised as embodying juristic statesmanship. But Hughes retained the stultifying arguments to which Stone and Cardozo objected. So equivocal a result dissatisfied Stone. "Probably if I had been doing the writing, I should have presented the matter in somewhat different form," he remarked to a friend. "Just between ourselves I feel it was too long and discursive." . . .

4.   *"It is a delicate matter."*

JUSTICE ROBERT H. JACKSON TO CHIEF JUSTICE HARLAN F. STONE

I HOPE YOU will forgive me for intruding into the matter of assignments, the difficulties of which I feel you generally resolve with wisdom and always with fairness, but I wonder if you have not overlooked some of the ugly factors in our national life which go to the wisdom of having Mr. Justice Frankfurter act as the voice of the Court in the matter of *Smith* v. *Allwright*. It is a delicate matter. We

Quoted in Alpheus T. Mason, *Harlan Fiske Stone: Pillar of the Law* (New York: Viking Press, 1956), p. 614. Reprinted with permission.

must reverse a recent, well-considered, and unanimous decision. We deny the entire South the right to a white primary, which is one of its most cherished rights. It seems to me very important that the strength which an all but unanimous decision would have may be greatly weakened if the voice that utters it is one that may grate on Southern sensibilities. Mr. Justice Frankfurter unites in a rare degree factors which unhappily excite prejudice. In the first place, he is a Jew. In the second place, he is from New England, the seat of the abolition movement. In the third place, he has not been thought of as a person particularly sympathetic with the Democratic party in the past. I know that every one of these things is a consideration that to you is distasteful and they are things which I mention only with the greatest reluctance and frank fear of being misunderstood. I have told Mr. Justice Frankfurter that in my opinion it is best for this Court and for him that he should not be its spokesman in this matter and that I intend to bring my view of it to your attention. With all humility I suggest that the Court's decision, bound to arouse bitter resentment, will be much less apt to stir ugly reactions if the news that the white primary is dead, is broken to it, if possible, by a Southerner who has been a Democrat and is not a member of one of the minorities which stir prejudices kindred to those against the Negro.

I have talked with some of them [other members of the Court] who are still in the building, and they feel as I do.

I rely on the good understanding which I have always felt existed between us and upon our mutual anxiety for the welfare and prestige of the Court to excuse my intrusion in a matter which, having spoken my piece, is solely for your judgment.

After receiving this note, Chief Justice Stone re-assigned the opinion of the Court to Justice Stanley Reed, who had been a Kentucky Democrat before his appointment to the bench.

5.   *"This is how clerks are made."*

THE COURT: AN INDICTMENT ANALYZED   *Alexander M. Bickel**

. . . THE LAW CLERKS have been characterized as a "second team," as "ghost writers," and, more insinuatingly, as wielders of "unorthodox influence." The charge has also been made that the influence they exert comes from the political Left.

The short answer is: First, that the law clerks are in no respect any kind of a powerful kitchen cabinet, though they are not to be dismissed as just messenger boys either; second, that their political views and emotional preferences, while they enliven the lunch hour, make no discernible difference to anything in their work; and third, that as a group the law clerks will no more fit any single political label than will any other eighteen young Americans who are not picked on a political basis. . . .

To begin with, who are they and how do they get there? Their positions are created by statute. There are two to each associate justice, three for the Chief Justice, and incidentally, one each for judges of the lower Federal courts. The justices, except for Justice Douglas who has been making do with one, normally take their full complement.

The clerks are recent law school graduates, usually young men in their mid-twenties. Their records at their respective schools are always among the best. That is ordinarily the principal factor in their selection. And their careers are almost certain to have included service on their schools' law reviews. These reviews are a singular species of scholarly publication, being student-edited and largely student-written. . . .

A law clerk is normally appointed by his justice on the strength of the recommendation of a law school dean or other professor. Of course, there will generally have been a personal interview, and the justice may well have laid down some specifications, such as that his clerks

The New York Times Magazine, April 27, 1958, pp. 16, 64–69. Copyright 1958 *The New York Times.* Reprinted with permission.

* Associate Professor of Law, Yale University; former law clerk to Mr. Justice Frankfurter.

come from the region of his own origin. Tenure is one year, sometimes two, very infrequently longer.

Over the long run, the large, nationally known law schools, such as Harvard, Yale, Columbia, Pennsylvania, Chicago, tend to be most heavily represented. But the smaller schools are by no means excluded. . . .

This is how clerks are made. What they are made to do is not quite so simply described. For one thing, there are variations from office to office, and from time to time in the same office, and from case to case with the same clerk. For another, there can be no up-to-date particulars, for such particulars involve live issues and live judges, and the judicial process requires a degree of privacy incomparably stricter than is fitting in the legislative or executive process. . . .

Law clerks . . . generally assist their respective justices in searching the law books and other sources for materials relevant to the decision of cases before the court. The task of legal research has become enormous for everyone in the profession. The day of the single, unassisted practitioner is over, and so is the day of the unassisted judge.

The clerks often present the fruits of their searches to their justices along with their recommendations. They go over drafts of opinions and may suggest changes. They tend to see a lot of their justices, and talk a great deal with them. And the talk is mostly about law and cases. They listen a good deal also, being the only properly available sounding board for the justices aside from other members of the court.

The process of selection described above is sufficient, I should think, to explode the assertion that the political views of the Left tend to predominate among the clerks. Only on the hysterical assumption that our universities are staffed by Machiavellian radicals and that our brightest young men are incapable of thinking for themselves can such an assertion be maintained.

But the indication, also given above, of the tasks performed by the clerks cannot be said to prove anything one way or another about their influence on the disposition of cases that come before the court. And of course the parties to such cases and their counsel might well be disturbed to think that influence of this sort is exerted. Yet we can surely start with the presumption, as far as specific results are concerned, that it is likely to be beyond the power of these inexperienced young men,

as it would be beyond the power of wiser and older heads, to turn
the minds of the generally strong, experienced and able lawyers and
statesmen who sit on the Supreme Court.

Nothing that is known about the present court and nothing in the
historical record—nothing that isn't either unfounded rumor or remote
hearsay—speaks against this presumption. But what history does reveal
and what reflection can confirm and generalize is that law clerks are,
nevertheless, more than just youthful runners of research errands. . . .

We take our judicial law . . . not merely from nine men but from a
profession—with all that that implies in intellectual discipline, and in
standards rooted in tradition. The role that the profession as a whole
plays—by subjecting the court's work to informed criticism and appraisal and by producing disinterested scholarship—can be plainly,
sometimes spectacularly, traced in the development of all branches of
our law. . . .

The process of law-making is not arrested nor is it characterized by
the decision of any single case. It lives by testing and enlarging general ideas, and it is forever rethinking last year's case and projecting
future, as yet unformed, cases. It is to be observed not so much in the
specific disposition of a cause—though that is important, to be sure—
as in the opinion that explains and justifies and generalizes the result.

In the early days, it is fair to say, the nexus between the court and
the profession—the company in which a justice made law—was chiefly
an intimate, well-informed, specialized, largely resident Supreme Court
bar. Such a bar no longer exists. Today fewer and fewer lawyers—
aside from the handful, albeit the very distinguished handful, in the
Office of the Solicitor General of the United States—appear regularly
before the Supreme Court and regularly scrutinize its work. Most
lawyers who come there now pay the court only episodic attention.

I don't mean that the practising bar as a whole has lost touch with
the work of the court; certainly not the organized bar. But there has
been a change. The place of an intimate Supreme Court bar has been
taken by the academic branch of the profession. . . .

But, of course, the law teachers of the country are spread over the
forty-eight states. What they lack in continual attendance at the Supreme Court they make up, however, through the law reviews and
through the justices' law clerks—two institutions which, by what can

hardly be deemed mere historical accident, have also come to maturity only since the turn of the century.

The role of the law reviews is readily apparent. It is there that those who make it their business to analyze and appraise the work of the court do their analyzing and appraising. And it is there that under their guidance—perhaps auspices is a better word because on most law reviews the reins are exceedingly loose—students publish basic research of the most painstaking sort.

Concerning the role of the law clarks it is necessary to start with a disclaimer. Of course, no law teacher whose student is about to commence a term as law clerk to a justice gives him instructions to convey certain ideas to the justice. To believe that this could happen is to take a naïvely depreciating view of everyone concerned, not least of all the clerk.

And yet the clerks, arriving every year, *are* a conduit from the law schools to the court. They bring with them, and they convey with varying degrees of explicitness, the intellectual atmosphere from which they are newly come. They complement the law reviews on the justice's desk with the additional, rather more inchoate ideas and arguments and puzzlements that fill the classrooms and corridors of any university worthy of the name. And that is performing no trivial function. . . .

In this fashion, the law schools and the law reviews, and through them the law clerks—the law clerks, and through them the law schools and the law reviews—make their limited yet important contribution. We should, I suggest, draw much assurance from that contribution, for it serves to enhance the intellectual integrity of the judicial process, and is in its modest way one of the influences that keep judicial law rationally responsive to the needs of the day. . . .

It remains to say that the relationship between the court and its professional company is not a one-way street. It should be apparent that the institution of clerking has also the attributes of any craft's apprentice system. Great judges project their influence into the future—in ways that are beyond the printed word—through their law clerks. . . .

In any event, in the past, the relationship again has been with the universities more than with any other of the walks of a lawyer's professional life. Over half of Brandeis' twenty-one law clerks became teachers of law. . . . Of course, many clerks become important practitioners or judges. Thus Brandeis' first clerk, Chief Judge Calvert Magruder of the Federal Court of Appeals in Boston, is one of the two or three most distinguished judges in the country. All this, though it merely serves to invoke the golden past, deserves mention just the same, as exemplifying the finest traditions of an apprentice system which might be thought not to need additional excuses for existing. These, however, it has.

6.   *". . . 'lead us not into temptation.' "*

THE INFLUENCE OF THE CHIEF JUSTICE IN THE DECISIONAL PROCESS
*David J. Danelski**

THE CHIEF JUSTICE of the United States has a unique opportunity for leadership in the Supreme Court. He presides in open court and over the secret conferences where he usually presents each case to his associates, giving his opinion first and voting last. He assigns the Court's opinion in virtually all cases when he votes with the majority; and when the Court is divided, he is in a favorable position to seek unity. But his office does not guarantee leadership. His actual influence depends upon his esteem, ability, and personality and how he performs his various roles.

IN CONFERENCE

The conference is the matrix of leadership in the Court.[1] The Court member who is able to present his views with force and clarity and

This is an abridged version of a paper delivered at the 1960 annual meeting of the American Political Science Association.

* Member of the Illinois and Washington bars; Assistant Professor of Political Science, University of Illinois.

[1] This study is based largely on private papers of members of the Supreme Court from 1921 to 1946. The theory of conference leadership is derived primarily from the work of Robert F. Bales. See his "Task Roles and Social Roles in Problem-Solving Groups" in Maccoby *et al., Readings in Social Psychology* (New York, 1958), pp. 437–447.

defend them successfully is highly esteemed by his associates. When perplexing questions arise, they turn to him for guidance. He usually makes more suggestions than his colleagues, gives more opinions, and orients the discussion more frequently, emerging as the Court's task leader. In terms of personality, he is apt to be somewhat reserved; and, in concentrating on the decision of the Court, his response to the emotional needs of his associates is apt to be secondary.

Court members frequently disagree in conference and argue their positions with enthusiasm, seeking to persuade their opponents and the undecided brethren. And always, when the discussion ends, the vote declares the victor. All of this gives rise to antagonism and tension, which, if allowed to get out of hand, would make intelligent, orderly decision of cases virtually impossible. However, the negative aspects of conference interaction are more or less counterbalanced by activity which relieves tension, shows solidarity, and makes for agreement. One Court member usually performs more such activity than the others. He invites opinions and suggestions. He attends to the emotional needs of his associates by affirming their value as individuals and as Court members, especially when their views are rejected by the majority. Ordinarily he is the best-liked member of the Court and emerges as its social leader. While the task leader concentrates on the Court's decision, the social leader concentrates on keeping the Court socially cohesive. In terms of personality, he is apt to be warm, receptive, and responsive. Being liked by his associates is ordinarily quite important to him; he is also apt to dislike conflict.

As presiding officer of the conference, the Chief Justice is in a favorable position to assert task and social leadership. His presentation of cases is an important task function. His control of the conference's process makes it easy for him to invite suggestions and opinions, seek compromises, and cut off debate which appears to be getting out of hand, all important social functions.

It is thus possible for the Chief Justice to emerge as both task and social leader of the conference. This, however, requires the possession of a rare combination of qualities plus adroit use of them. Normally, one would expect the functions of task and social leadership to be performed by at least two Court members, one of whom might or might not be the Chief Justice. As far as the Chief Justice is concerned, the following leadership situations are possible:

	Task Leadership	*Social Leadership*
I	+	+
II	−	+
III	+	−
IV	−	−

In situation I, the Chief Justice is a "great man" leader, performing both leadership functions. The consequences of such leadership, stated as hypotheses, are: (1) conflict tends to be minimal; (2) social cohesion tends to increase; (3) satisfaction with the conference tends to increase; (4) production, in terms of number of decisions for the time spent, tends to increase. The consequences in situations II and III are the same as in I, particularly if the Chief Justice works in coalition with the associate justice performing complementary leadership functions. However, in situation IV, unless the task and social functions are adequately performed by associate justices, consequences opposite to those in situations I, II, and III tend to occur. . . .

Situation II prevailed in the Taft Court (1921–1930): Chief Justice Taft was social leader, and his good friend and appointee, Justice Van Devanter, was task leader. Evidence of Van Devanter's esteem and task leadership is abundant. Taft, for example, frequently asserted that Van Devanter was the ablest member of the Court. If the Court were to vote, he said, that would be its judgment too. The Chief Justice admitted that he did not know how he could get along without Van Devanter in conference, for Van Devanter kept the Court consistent with itself, and "his power of statement and his immense memory make him an antagonist in conference who generally wins against all opposition." At times, Van Devanter's ability actually embarrassed the Chief Justice, and he wondered if it might not be better to have Van Devanter run the conference himself. "Still," said Taft, "I must worry along until the end of my ten years, content to aid in the deliberation when there is a difference of opinion." In other words, Taft was content to perform the social functions of leadership. And he did this well. His humor soothed over the rough spots in conference. "We are very happy with the present Chief," said Holmes in 1922. "He is good-humored, laughs readily, not quite rapid enough, but keeps things moving pleasantly."

Situation I prevailed in the Hughes Court (1930–1941): task and social leadership were combined in Chief Justice Hughes. He was the most esteemed member of his Court. This was due primarily to his performance in conference. Blessed with a photographic memory, he would summarize comprehensively and accurately the facts and issues in each case he presented. When he finished, he would look up and say with a smile: "Now I will state where I come out." Then he would outline his views as to how the case should be decided. Sometimes that is all the discussion a case received, and the justices proceeded to vote for the disposition suggested by the Chief. Where there was discussion, the other Court members gave their views in order of seniority without interruption, stating why they concurred or dissented from the views of the Chief Justice. After they had their say, Hughes would review the discussion, pointing out his agreement and disagreement with the views expressed. Then he would call for a vote.

As to the social side of Hughes' leadership, there is the testimony of Justice Roberts: never in the eleven years Roberts sat with Hughes in conference did he see him lose his temper. Never did he hear him pass a personal remark or even raise his voice. Never did he witness him interrupting or engaging in controversy with an associate. Despite Hughes' popular image of austerity, several of his associates have said that he had a keen sense of humor which aided in keeping differences in conference from becoming discord. Moreover, when discussion showed signs of deteriorating into wrangling, Hughes would cut it off. On the whole, he was well-liked. Justice Roberts said: "Men whose views were as sharply opposed as those of Van Devanter and Brandeis, or those of Sutherland and Cardozo, were at one in their admiration and affectionate regard for their presiding officer." Roberts could have well added Justices Holmes, Black, Reed, Frankfurter, Douglas, McReynolds, and perhaps others.

Situation IV prevailed during most of Stone's Chief Justiceship (1941–1946). When Stone was promoted to the center chair, Augustus Hand indicated in a letter to Hughes that Stone did not seem a sure bet as task leader because of "a certain inability to express himself orally and maintain a position in a discussion." Hand proved to be correct. Stone departed from the conference role cut out by Hughes. When he presented cases, he lacked the apparent certitude of his predecessor; and, at times, his statement indicated that he was still groping for a solution. In that posture, cases were passed on to his associates for discussion. Court members spoke out of turn, and Stone did little to control their debate. Instead, according to Justice Reed, he would join in the debate with alacrity, "delighted to take on all comers around the conference table." "Jackson," he would say, "that's damned nonsense." "Douglas, *you* know better than that."

In other words, Stone was still acting like an associate justice. Since he did not assume the Chief Justice's conference role as performed by Hughes, task leadership began to slip from his grasp. Eventually, Justice Black emerged as the leading contender for task leadership. Stone esteemed Black, but distrusted his unorthodox approach; thus no coalition occurred as in the Taft Court. Justices Douglas, Murphy, Rutledge, and, to a lesser degree, Reed acknowledged Black's leadership which he was able to reinforce by generally speaking before them in conference. Justices Roberts, Frankfurter, and Jackson, however, either looked to Stone for leadership or competed for it themselves.

The constant vying for task leadership in the Stone conference led to serious conflict, ruffled tempers, severe tension, and antagonism. A social leader was badly needed. Stone was well-liked by his associates and could have performed this function well, but he did not. He did not use his control over the conference process to cut off debates leading to irreconcilable conflict. He did not remain neutral when controversies arose so that he could later mediate them. As his biographer, Alpheus T. Mason, wrote: "He was totally unprepared to cope with the petty bickering and personal conflict in which his Court became engulfed." At times, when conference discussion became extremely heated, Justice Murphy suggested that further consideration of certain cases be postponed. Undoubtedly others also performed social functions of leadership, but in this regard, Stone was a failure.

A consideration of the personalities of the task and social leaders on the Court from 1921 to 1946 is revealing. Of his friend, task leader Van Devanter, William D. Mitchell said: "Many thought him unusually austere, but he was not so with his friends. He was dignified and reserved." Of task leader Black, his former law clerk, John P. Frank, wrote: "Black has firm personal dignity and reserve. . . . [He] is a very, very tough man. When he is convinced, he is cool hard steel. . . . His temper is usually in close control, but he fights, and his words may occasionally have a terrible edge. He can be a rough man in an argument." On the other hand, social leader Taft was a warm, genial, responsive person who disliked conflict of any kind. Stone had a similar personality. He, too, according to Justice Jackson, "dreaded conflict." Hughes' personality contained elements conducive to both task and social leadership. He was "an intense man," said Justice Roberts; when he was engrossed in the work of the Court, "he had not time for lightness and pleasantry." Nonetheless, added Roberts, Hughes' relations with "his brethren were genial and cordial. He was considerate, sympathetic, and responsive."

The consequences of the various Court leadership configurations from 1921 to 1946 may be summarized as follows:

	TAFT (II)	HUGHES (I)	STONE (IV)
Conflict	Present but friendly.	Present but bridled by CJ.	Considerable; unbridled and at times unfriendly.
Cohesion	Good; teamwork and compromise.	Fair; surface personal cordiality; less teamwork than in Taft Court.	Poor; least cohesion in 25-year period; personal feuds in the Court.
Satisfaction	Considerable.	Mixed; Stone dissatisfied prior to 1938; Frankfurter, Roberts, and others highly satisfied.	Least in 25-year period; unrelieved tension and antagonism.
Production	Fair; usually one four- to five-hour conference a week with some items carried over.	Good; usually one conference a week.	Poor; frequently more than one conference a week; sometimes three and even four.

Except in production, the Taft Court fared better than the Courts under his two successors. The consequences of leadership in the Stone Court were predictable from the hypotheses, but Hughes' "great man" leadership should have produced consequences more closely approximating those in the Taft Court. The difference in conflict, cohesion, and satisfaction in the two Courts can be perhaps attributed to the fact that Taft was a better social leader than Hughes.

OPINION ASSIGNMENT

The Chief Justice's power to assign opinions is significant because his designation of the Court's spokesman may be instrumental in:

(1) Determining the value of a decision as a precedent, for the grounds of a decision frequently depend upon the justice assigned the opinion.
(2) Making a decision as acceptable as possible to the public.
(3) Holding the Chief Justice's majority together when the conference vote is close.
(4) Persuading dissenting associates to join in the Court's opinion.

The Chief Justice has maximal control over an opinion when he assigns it to himself; undoubtedly Chief Justices have retained many important cases for that reason. The Chief Justice's retention of "big cases" is generally accepted by his associates. In fact, they expect him to speak for the Court in those cases so that he may lend the prestige of his office to the Court's pronouncement.

When the Chief Justice does not speak for the Court, his influence lies primarily in his assignment of important cases to associates who generally agree with him. From 1925 to 1930, Taft designated his fellow conservatives, Sutherland and Butler, to speak for the Court in about half of the important constitutional cases[2] assigned to associate justices. From 1932 to 1937, Hughes, who agreed more with Roberts, Van Devanter, and Sutherland than the rest of his associates during this period, assigned 44 per cent of the important constitutional cases to Roberts and Sutherland. From 1943 to 1945, Stone assigned 55.5 per cent of those cases to Douglas and Frankfurter. During

[2] "Important constitutional cases" were determined by examination of four recent leading works on the Constitution. If a case was discussed in any two of the works, it was considered an "important constitutional case."

that period, only Reed agreed more with Stone than Frankfurter, but Douglas agreed with Stone less than any other justice except Black. Stone had high regard for Douglas' ability, and this may have been the Chief Justice's overriding consideration in making these assignments.

It is possible that the Chief Justice might seek to influence dissenting justices to join in the Court's opinion by adhering to one or both of the following assignment rules:

> *Rule 1:* Assign the case to the justice whose views are the closest to the dissenters on the ground that his opinion would take a middle approach upon which both majority and minority could agree.

> *Rule 2:* Where there are blocs on the Court and a bloc splits, assign the opinion to a majority member of the dissenters' bloc on the grounds that (a) he would take a middle approach upon which both majority and minority could agree and (b) the minority justices would be more likely to agree with him because of general mutuality of agreement.

There is some evidence that early in Taft's Chief Justiceship he followed Rule 1 occasionally and assigned himself cases in an effort to win over dissenters. An analysis of his assignments from 1925 to 1930, however, indicates that he apparently did not adhere to either of the rules with any consistency. The same is true for Stone's assignments from 1943 to 1945. In other words, Taft and Stone did not generally use their assignment power to influence their associates to unanimity. However, an analysis of Hughes' assignments from 1932 to 1937 indicates that he probably did. He appears to have followed Rule 1 when either the liberal or conservative blocs dissented intact. When the liberal bloc dissented, Roberts, who was then a center judge, was assigned 46 per cent of the opinions. The remaining 54 per cent were divided among the conservatives, apparently according to their degree of conservatism: Sutherland, 25 per cent; Butler, 18 per cent; McReynolds, 11 per cent. When the conservative bloc dissented, Hughes divided 63 per cent of those cases between himself and Roberts.

Hughes probably also followed Rule 2. When the left bloc split, Brandeis was assigned 22 per cent of the cases he could have received compared with his 10 per cent average for unanimous cases.

When the right bloc split, Sutherland was assigned 16 per cent of the decisions he could have received compared with his 11 per cent average for unanimous cases. He received five of the six cases assigned the conservatives when their bloc split.

Of course, there are other considerations underlying opinion assignment by the Chief Justice, such as equality of distribution, ability, and expertise. It should be noted that opinion assignment may also be a function of social leadership.

UNITING THE COURT

One of the Chief Justice's most important roles is that of Court unifier. Seldom has a Chief Justice had a more definite conception of that role than Taft. His aim was unanimity, but he was willing to admit that at times dissents were justifiable and perhaps even a duty. Dissents were proper, he thought, in cases where a Court member strongly believed the majority erred in a matter involving important principle or where a dissent might serve some useful purpose, such as convincing Congress to pass certain legislation. But, in other cases, he believed a justice should be a good member of the team, silently acquiesce in the views of the majority, and not try to make a record for himself by dissenting.

Since Taft's conception of the function of the dissent was shared by most of his associates, his efforts toward unity were well received. Justices joining the Taft Court were indoctrinated in the "no dissent unless absolutely necessary" tradition, most of them learning it well. Justice Butler gave it classic expression on the back of one colleague's opinions in 1928:

> I voted to reverse. While this sustains your conclusion to affirm, I still think reversal would be better. But I shall in silence acquiesce. Dissents seldom aid in the right development or statement of the law. They often do harm. For myself I say: "lead us not into temptation."

Hughes easily assumed the role of Court unifier which Taft cut out for him, for his views as to unanimity and dissent were essentially the same as Taft's. Believing that some cases were not worthy of dissent, he would join in the majority's disposition of them, though he initially voted the other way. For example, in a 1939 case involving statutory construction, he wrote to an associate: "I choke a little at swallowing your analysis, still I do not think it would serve any useful purpose to expose my views."

Like Taft, Hughes mediated differences of opinion between contending factions, and in order to get a unanimous decision, he would try to find common ground upon which all could stand. He was willing to modify his own opinions to hold or increase his majority; and if this meant he had to put in some disconnected thoughts or sentences, in they went. In cases assigned to others, he would readily suggest the addition or subtraction of a paragraph in order to save a dissent or a concurring opinion.

When Stone was an associate justice, he prized the right to dissent and occasionally rankled under the "no dissent unless absolutely necessary" tradition of the Taft and Hughes Courts. As Chief Justice, he did not believe it appropriate for him to dissuade Court members from dissenting in individual cases by persuasion or otherwise. A Chief Justice, he thought, might admonish his associates generally to exercise restraint in the matter of dissents and seek to find common ground for decision, but beyond that he should not go. And Stone usually went no further. His activity or lack of it in this regard gave rise to new expectations on the part of his associates as to their role and the role of the Chief Justice regarding unanimity and dissent. In the early 1940's, a new tradition of freedom of individual expression displaced the tradition of the Taft and Hughes Courts. This explains in part the unprecedented number of dissents and separate opinions during Stone's Chief Justiceship.

Nonetheless, Stone recognized that unanimity was desirable in certain cases. He patiently negotiated a unanimous decision in the Nazi Saboteurs case[3]. It should be pointed out, however, that this case was decided early in his Chief Justiceship before the new tradition was firmly established. By 1946, when he sought unanimity in the case of General Yamashita[4], the new tradition of freedom was so well established that Stone not only failed to unite his Court, but the dissenters, Murphy and Rutledge, apparently resented his attempt to do so.

The unprecedented number of dissents and concurrences during

[3] *Ex parte Quirin* (1942).
[4] *In re Yamashita* (1946).

Stone's Chief Justiceship can be only partly attributed to the displac-
ing of the old tradition of loyalty to the Court's opinion. A major
source of difficulty appears to have been the free-and-easy expression
of views in conference. Whether the justices were sure of their
grounds or not, they spoke up and many times took positions from
which they could not easily retreat; given the heated debate which
sometimes occurred in the Stone conference, the commitment was not
simply intellectual. What began in conference frequently ended with
elaborate justification as concurring or dissenting opinions in the
United States Reports. This, plus Stone's passiveness in seeking to attain unanimity, is probably the best explanation for what Pritchett
characterized as "the multiplication of division" in the Stone Court.

CONCLUSION

Interpersonal influence in the Supreme Court is an important aspect
of the judicial process which has been given little attention. Of course,
the "why" of the Court's decisions cannot be explained solely or even
predominantly in those terms. Yet interpersonal influence is a variable
worthy of consideration. Take, for example, the Court's about-face in
the flag salute cases. With task leader Hughes presiding in 1940, not
a single justice indicated in conference that he would dissent in the
Gobitis[5] case. Subsequently, Stone registered a solo dissent, but such
militant civil libertarians as Black, Douglas, and Murphy remained
with Hughes. Only three years later, the Court reversed itself in the
Barnette[6] case with Black, Douglas, and Murphy voting with Stone.
One might seriously ask whether the presence of Hughes in the first
case and not in the second had something to do with the switch. Much
more work has to be done in this area, but it appears that in future
analyses of the Court's work, task and social leadership will be useful
concepts.

The importance of the Chief Justice's power to assign opinions is
obvious. Equally if not more important is his role in unifying the
Court. Taft's success in this regard greatly contributed to the Court's
prestige, for unanimity reinforces the myth that the law is certain. In
speaking of the Court in 1927, Hughes said that "no institution of our

---

[5] *Minersville School District* v. *Gobitis* (1940).
[6] *West Virginia* v. *Barnette* (1943). See below, p. 638.

government stands higher in public confidence." As Court unifier, he sought to maintain that confidence after his appointment in 1930. That the Court's prestige is correlated with unanimity was demonstrated in Stone's Chief Justiceship: as dissent rose, the Court's prestige declined.

Thus the activity of the Chief Justice can be very significant in the judicial process. If he is the Court's task leader, he has great influence in the allocation of political values which are inevitably involved in many of the Court's decisions. More than any of his associates, his activity is apt to affect the Court's prestige; this is important, for ultimately the basis of the Court's power is its prestige.

14 / MOTIVATION IN THE
DECISIONAL PROCESS

It should be evident from the preceding chapters that judicial decision-making is far from being a matter of mechanical application of precise technical rules. The structure of the decisional process, just as the technical legal rules themselves, has an important effect in channelizing the thinking of judges. The social and political roles of courts would undergo serious modifications if, for instance, trial judges recessed their courts for meticulous research on every procedural point disputed by opposing counsel, or if all judges agreed (as has been sometimes proposed by responsible critics) to stop registering dissenting votes, or if appellate judges ceased to confer and simply filed separate opinions in each case. But as significant as it is, the structure of the decisional process gives only rough form to actual decision-making. No set of procedures can free the judge from his burden of making a highly personalized choice among intangibles.

Measuring the Immeasurable

Judicial fact-finding is a difficult task, partaking more of art than of science. The discovery of precedents is easy—in fact, too easy; because of legal encyclopedias, annotations, court digests, and case indexes and cross-indexes, numerous prior decisions can usually be found to support either side of an issue in litigation. But no research apparatus can decide for a judge the exact applicability or the vitality of past decisions. Similarly, there is no simple formula to determine whether jurisdictional and standing requirements have been met; nor has anyone yet shown how a judge can unerringly determine the meaning of a constitutional or statutory clause. For the judge at least, as Holmes once remarked, certainty is generally an illusion. "We are not final," Justice Robert H. Jackson once reminded his colleagues, "because we are infallible, but we are infallible only because we are final."

Arriving at a judicial decision involves a weighing of values and an exercise of discretion. And if these intellectual activities do not present sufficiently perplexing problems, other factors operate to keep the work of the judge basically that of choosing among probabilities. For, when the more legally oriented questions about a case have been answered, two fundamental queries remain: what is the effect of the decision on the litigants and what is the effect of the decision on public policy? Legal rules are supposed to be means, not ends. They should not be allowed to obscure the judicial goals of settling disputes fairly and peacefully and of formulating, or at least furthering, wise and workable public policy.

It might well have been easier in the narrowest technical sense, for instance, for the Supreme Court in 1954 to have sustained the constitutionality of racial segregation in public grammar and high schools. Precedents from the late 1890's and early 1900's supporting segregation could have been relied on, and those later cases ruling against segregation distinguished as pertaining only to higher education or to transportation in interstate commerce. The doctrine of the presumption of constitutionality could have been invoked, and the preferred freedoms doctrine held not applicable since no attack on speech or voting rights was involved. Yet it is doubtful whether the justices could, in good conscience, have blinded themselves to the effects on domestic and foreign relations of the United States that an apartheid policy would have had if officially sanctioned in mid-twentieth century by the nation's highest tribunal of justice. Other policy questions, while usually less emotionally explosive, are no more facilely answered, since, as Justice Frankfurter once said, they frequently involve clashes of rights rather than of wrongs.

Moreover, as will be discussed in detail in Chapters 15-17, the justices must consider the limitations on their power. It may be imprudent to make a decision which interest groups can persuade Congress to reverse or the President to refuse to implement, or which will excite efforts to curb the Court. Such a decision can be doubly imprudent not only because of the immediate adverse effect on the particular policy involved, but also because of the serious harm that may be done to the judiciary's future capacity to do good in other decisions. Yet a judge's conscience may demand a decision which invites retaliation. To recognize these situations and to perceive where the danger of serious injury to judicial power is real and where it is only apparent requires great discernment; to know which course of action is proper requires great wisdom; and to make the proper decision, one way or the other, requires great courage.

Judicial Self-Analysis

The solution of these political, legal, and moral problems will depend to a large extent on the personality of the individual judge. The societal values which he wishes to protect, the role which he sees himself fulfilling, as well as less rational motivations, all inevitably color a judge's general outlook on life and his more specific reactions to particular situations. In the 1920's and 1930's critics from the realist school of jurisprudence like Jerome Frank were ready to dismiss legal rules as mere rationalizations in their attempts to stress the importance of the motivational factor in decision-making. "Efforts to eliminate the personality of the judge," Frank wrote, "are doomed to failure. The correct course is to recognize the necessary existence of this personal element and to act accordingly."

While the realists undoubtedly underestimated the value of legal rules, they have won a limited victory in the field of self-analysis. No longer are sophisticated judges confident that it is the Constitution or Congress or the "Law" which speaks within them. A wise judge knows that it is he himself who decides and that his decision is influenced by motivations which he not only does not fully understand, but often of which he is not even conscious. Today a judge is very apt to confess his own humanity and examine his predilections as best he can, hoping that even though he may not completely eradicate his biases he will still be better able to recognize them for what they are and so deprive them of much of their strength. Occasionally a judge will use an opinion as a means of exposing, insofar as he is able, the inner conflicts which he has experienced in arriving at a decision. More often, unfortunately, such battles are not recorded in public papers.

Motivation and Methodology

Published opinions have great value both as guides for future action by private citizens and government officials, and as explanations and justifications of a particular line of policy. They are, however, still of only limited use in understanding the thinking of individual judges or the more general functioning of the judicial process. Opinions shed much light on the work of judges, but they also diffuse that light, leaving a large part of judicial behavior and motivation a set of vague, shadowy motions which do not quite come into proper focus. Several factors aggravate this problem: the veil of secrecy which surrounds judicial deliberation; the intra-court bargaining and negotiation which often precede announcement of opinions; and the frequent inability—or unwillingness—of judges to explain the real reasons which lie behind decisions.

Candid autobiographical writing, especially if the judge has some training in psychology, might seem to be an obvious means of creating better understanding of judicial motivation. But, as Justice Frankfurter has noted, "The power of searching analysis of what it is that they are doing seems rarely to be possessed by judges, either because they are lacking in the art of critical exposition or because they are inhibited from practising it." Undoubtedly the old myth of the judicial role still has sufficient strength to make many judges fear to speak openly of their work lest the prestige of courts suffer. To this extent, at least, the realists' demand for candor has not been altogether successful. It is interesting that Jerome Frank's most penetrating work on law and psychology was done before rather than after he became a federal judge, and that Felix Frankfurter's writing took on a noticeably idealistic tone after his appointment to the bench.

To overcome these obstacles in the path of understanding the judiciary, scholars have had to go beyond scrutiny of official opinions. One of the oldest methods has been that of biographical studies of individual judges. This approach can yield two advantages: it may allow the student to perceive more clearly the personal values of the judge; and, since judges sometimes keep their correspondence and memoranda, it may give a sharp picture of the inner workings of a court and provide information as to the motivation of other judges. Several biographies, especially Mason's *Harlan Fiske Stone* and Fairman's *Mr. Justice Miller*, have achieved outstanding success on both counts. Most judicial biographies, however, have fallen far short of these high accomplishments. One of the main reasons has been that many judges either did not keep, or edited or destroyed or limited access to, their private papers pertaining to their judicial careers. Perhaps the full potential of the biographical method will not be achieved until psychologists acquire legal and political skills and become interested in the judicial process.

Some writers have relied on a more general historical approach, describing a line of court decisions and their impact on Congress, the President, state governments, and public policy. Warren's *The Supreme Court in United States History* and Swisher's *American Constitutional Development* are among the more successful of such efforts. Other scholars have used studies in depth of a single case or a related series of cases. Westin's *The Anatomy of a Constitutional Law Case* is a good example of such a depth inquiry. Vose's *Caucasians Only: The Supreme Court, the NAACP, and the Restrictive Covenant Cases* takes a different approach, examining the judicial process by analyzing the attempts of an interest group to attain its policy aims through litigation.

While invaluable for understanding the judicial process, historical and depth studies have usually borne only indirectly on problems of judicial motivation. One of the newest and most controversial methods of attacking the motivational problem is the use of statistical procedures. Employing techniques developed in other fields of political science, such studies have tried to overcome the opinion problems by concentrating on the votes of individual judges on specific issues. The fact that the American judicial tradition permits justices rather freely to indicate disagreement with their colleagues yields extremely interesting data on judicial attitudes. As one commentator has pointed out:

A unanimous judicial decision throws little light upon what Walton Hamilton calls "deliberation in process." It tells nothing of the conflicts around the judicial conference table, the alternative lines of argument developed, the accommodations and the compromises which went into the final result. A unanimous opinion is a composite and quasi-anonymous product, largely valueless for purposes of understanding the values and motivation of individual justices.

A nonunanimous opinion admits the public to the Supreme Court's inner sanctum. In such a case the process of deliberation has failed to produce a conclusion satisfactory to all participants. Having carried the argument as far as they usefully can, the justices find it necessary finally to take a vote, state and support the winning and losing positions, and place the arguments before the world for judgment. In informing the public of their divisions and their reasons, the justices also supply information about their attitudes and their values which is available in no other way. For the fact of disagreement demonstrates that the members of the Court are operating on different assumptions, that their inarticulate major premises are dissimilar, that their value systems are differently constructed and weighted, that their political, economic, and social views contrast in important respects.[1]

The data on Supreme Court voting behavior can be analyzed, tabulated, and charted in a variety of ways, as a school of judicial "quantifiers" has demonstrated. Their approaches have ranged from simple counting and preparation of "box scores" on justices all the way to highly refined mathematical analysis. Symbolic logic, vector analysis, and game theory have also been employed in the search for more objective measures of judicial behavior. A considerable controversy has developed over the use of such methods. The differences between the generalizers who quantify and those who do not (qualifiers) are suggested by Joseph Tanenhaus:

> In the first place, the quantifier tends to place greater emphasis on systematic and objective classification. He seeks to devise procedures which will permit trained analysts to come up with highly comparable results. On the other hand, the qualifier tends to feel that such striving for reliability sacrifices too much that is vital. In his view the richest ore is mined by those who devote their energies to nuances too elusive for systematic objectivity.
>
> In the second place, the quantifier is more disposed than the qualifier to study the voting behavior of judges as distinguished from the opinions they father. To the qualifier, a judge's vote grossly oversimplifies the hard choice he is frequently obliged to make among competing principles, values and interests. And what is more, each of a judge's votes is counted equally by the quantifiers, although some decisions are obviously more important than others.[2]

Despite these objections, the quantifiers persist in their belief that their methods can be usefully employed to support or deflate hypotheses about judicial motivation and behavior. They point out that a Supreme Court justice votes far more frequently than he writes opinions. Second, while not all the literary, psychological, and diplomatic problems of opinions are completely eliminated by concentrating on the objective facts

[1] C. Herman Pritchett, *The Roosevelt Court* (New York: Macmillan, 1948), p. xii.
[2] "Supreme Court Attitudes toward Federal Administrative Agencies," 22 *Journal of Politics* 502 (1960).

of voting, they are certainly reduced. Third, voting statistics tend to show rather consistent behavior patterns which compensate in some degree for differences in importance between cases. Fourth, these statistics often show that judges may be stating one doctrine as official dogma while they are really practicing quite another policy. Whatever the final outcome of this debate, there can be little doubt that statistical methodology, if imaginatively blended with other forms of analysis, can offer fruitful insights into judicial behavior.

SELECTED REFERENCES

Barnard, Jessie, "Dimensions and Axes of Supreme Court Decisions," 34 *Social Forces* 19 (1955).

Beveridge, Albert J., *The Life of John Marshall* (Boston: Houghton Mifflin, 1916), 4 vols.

Fairman, Charles, *Mr. Justice Miller and the Supreme Court, 1862–1890* (Cambridge: Harvard University Press, 1939).

Frank, Jerome, *Law and the Modern Mind* (New York: Brentano's, 1930).

Frankfurter, Felix, "The Judicial Process and the Supreme Court," 98 *Proceedings of the American Philosophical Society* 233 (1954).

Kort, Fred, "Predicting Supreme Court Decisions Mathematically," 51 *American Political Science Review* 1 (1957); a reply by Franklin M. Fisher and a rejoinder by Kort are at 52 *ibid*. 321, 339 (1958).

Lasswell, Harold D., "Self-Analysis and Judicial Thinking," 40 *International Journal of Ethics* 354 (1930).

Mason, Alpheus T., *Harlan Fiske Stone: Pillar of the Law* (New York: Viking Press, 1956).

Murphy, Walter F., Book Review, 73 *Harvard Law Review* 1236 (1960).

Pritchett, C. Herman, *The Roosevelt Court: A Study in Judicial Politics and Values* (New York: Macmillan, 1948).

———, *Civil Liberties and the Vinson Court* (Chicago: University of Chicago Press, 1954).

Robinson, Edward S., *Law and the Lawyers* (New York: Macmillan, 1935).

Schroeder, Theodore, "The Psychologic Study of Judicial Opinions," 6 *California Law Review* 89 (1918).

Schubert, Glendon A., *Quantitative Analysis of Judicial Behavior* (Glencoe, Ill.: The Free Press, 1960).

Snyder, Eloise C., "The Supreme Court as a Small Group," 36 *Social Forces* 232 (1958).

Swisher, Carl B., *Roger Brooke Taney* (New York: Macmillan, 1935).

——, *American Constitutional Development* (2d ed.; Boston: Houghton Mifflin, 1954).

Tanenhaus, Joseph, "Supreme Court Attitudes toward Federal Administrative Agencies," 22 *Journal of Politics* 502 (1960).

Vose, Clement C., *Caucasians Only: The Supreme Court, the NAACP, and the Restrictive Covenant Cases* (Berkeley: University of California Press, 1959).

Warren, Charles, *The Supreme Court in United States History* (rev. ed.; Boston: Little, Brown, 1926), 2 vols.

Westin, Alan F., *The Anatomy of a Constitutional Law Case* (New York: Macmillan, 1958).

1.
"... 'my practice is therein the same with that of your other worships.' "

THE JUDGMENT INTUITIVE: THE FUNCTION OF THE "HUNCH" IN JUDICIAL DECISION *Joseph C. Hutcheson, Jr.**

MANY YEARS ago, at the conclusion of a particularly difficult case both in point of law and of fact, tried to a court without a jury, the judge, a man of great learning and ability, announced from the Bench that since the narrow and prejudiced modern view of the obligations of a judge in the decision of causes prevented his resort to the judgment aleatory by the use of his "little, small dice" he would take the case under advisement, and, brooding over it, wait for his hunch.

To me, a young, indeed a very young lawyer, picked, while yet the dew was on me and I had just begun to sprout, from the classic gardens of a University, where I had been trained to regard the law as a system of rules and precedents, of categories and concepts, and the judge had been spoken of as an administrator, austere, remote, "his intellect a cold logic engine," who, in that rarefied atmosphere in which he lived coldly and logically determined the relation of the facts of a particular case to some of these established precedents, it appeared that the judge was making a jest, and a very poor one, at that.

I had been trained to expect inexactitude from juries, but from the judge quite the reverse. I exalted in the law its tendency to formulize. I had a slot machine mind. I searched out categories and concepts and, having found them, worshiped them. . . .

I knew that judges "are the depositories of the laws like the oracles, who must decide in all cases of doubt and are bound by an oath to decide according to the law of the land," but I believed that creation and evolution were at an end, that in modern law only deduction had

14 *Cornell Law Quarterly* 274 (1929). Copyright 1929 Cornell University. Reprinted with permission.

* U.S. District Judge, Southern District of Texas, 1918–30; Judge, U.S. Court of Appeals for Fifth Circuit, 1931–; Chief Judge, Fifth Circuit, 1949–59.

place, and that the judges must decide "through being long personally accustomed to and acquainted with the judicial decisions of their
predecessors."

I recognized, of course, that in the preparation of the facts of a
case there was room for intuition, for feeling; that there was a sixth
sense which must be employed in searching out the evidence for clues,
in order to assemble facts and more facts, but all of this before the
evidence was in. I regarded the solution of the problem when the evidence was all in as a matter for determination by the judge by pure
reason and reflection, and while I knew that juries might and did arrive at their verdicts by feeling, I repudiated as impossible the idea
that good judges did the same.

I knew, of course, that some judges did follow "hunches,"— "guesses"
I indignantly called them. I knew my Rabelais, and had laughed over
without catching the true philosophy of old Judge Bridlegoose's trial,
and roughly, in my youthful, scornful way, I recognized four kinds of
judgments; first the cogitative, of and by reflection and logomancy;
second, aleatory, of and by the dice; third, intuitive, of and by feeling
or "hunching;" and fourth, asinine, of and by an ass; and in that same
youthful, scornful way I regarded the last three as only variants of
each other, the results of processes all alien to good judges.

As I grew older, however, and knew and understood better the
judge to whom I have in this opening referred; as I associated more
with real lawyers, whose intuitive facilities were developed and made
acute by the use of a trained and cultivated imagination; as I read
more after and came more under the spell of those great lawyers and
judges whose thesis is that "modification is the life of the law," I
came to see that "as long as the matter to be considered is debated in
artificial terms, there is danger of being led by a technical definition
to apply a certain name and then to deduce consequences which have
no relation to the grounds on which the name was applied;" that "the
process of inclusion and exclusion so often applied in developing a
rule, cannot end with its first enunciation. The rule announced must
be deemed tentative. For the many and varying facts to which it will
be applied cannot be foreseen." . . .

I came to see that instinct in the very nature of law itself is change, adaptation, conformity, and that the instrument for all of this change, this adaptation, this conformity, for the making and the nurturing of the law as a thing of life, is the power of the brooding mind, which in its very brooding makes, creates and changes jural relations, establishes philosophy, and drawing away from the outworn past, here a little, there a little, line upon line, precept upon precept, safely and firmly, bridges for the judicial mind to pass the abysses between that past and the new future. . . .

And so, after eleven years on the Bench following eighteen at the Bar, I, being well advised by observation and experience of what I am about to set down, have thought it both wise and decorous to now boldly affirm that "having well and exactly seen, surveyed, over-looked, reviewed, recognized, read and read over again, turned and tossed about, seriously perused and examined the preparatories, pro-ductions, evidences, proofs, allegations, depositions, cross speeches, contradictions . . . and other such like confects and spiceries, both at the one and the other side, as a good judge ought to do, I posit on the end of the table in my closet all the pokes and bags of the defendants —that being done I thereafter lay down upon the other end of the same table the bags and satchels of the plaintiff."

Thereafter I proceed "to understand and resolve the obscurities of these various and seeming contrary passages in the law, which are laid claim to by the suitors and pleading parties," even just as Judge Bridlegoose did, with one difference only. "That when the matter is more plain, clear and liquid, that is to say, when there are fewer bags," and he would have used his "other large, great dice, fair and goodly ones," I decide the case more or less off hand and by rule of thumb. While when the case is difficult or involved, and turns upon a hairs-breadth of law or of fact, that is to say, "when there are many bags on the one side and on the other" and Judge Bridlegoose would have used his "little small dice," I, after canvassing all the available material at my command, and duly cogitating upon it, give my imagination play, and brooding over the cause, wait for the feeling, the hunch—that in-tuitive flash of understanding which makes the jump-spark connection between question and decision, and at the point where the path is darkest for the judicial feet, sheds its light along the way.

And more, "lest I be stoned in the street" for this admission, let me hasten to say to my brothers of the Bench and of the Bar, "my practice is therein the same with that of your other worships."

For let me premise here, that in feeling or "hunching" out his decisions, the judge acts not differently from, but precisely as the lawyers do in working on their cases, with only this exception; that the lawyer, having a predetermined destination in view,—to win his law suit for his client—looks for and regards only those hunches which keep him in the path that he has chosen, while the judge, being merely on his way with a roving commission to find the just solution, will follow his hunch wherever it leads him, and when, following it, he meets the right solution face to face, he ceases his labors. . . .

Further, at the outset, I must premise that I speak now of the judgment or decision, the solution itself, as opposed to the apologia for that decision; the decree, as opposed to the logomachy, the effusion of the judge by which that decree is explained or excused. I speak of the judgment pronounced, as opposed to the rationalization by the judge on that pronouncement. . . .

There is nothing unreal or untrue about this picture of the judge, nor is there anything in it from which a just judge should turn away. It is true, and right that it is true, that judges really do try to select categories or concepts into which to place a particular case so as to produce what the judge regards as a righteous result, or, to avoid any confusion in the matter of morals, I will say a "proper result."

This is true. I think we should go further, and say it ought to be true. No reasoning applied to practical matters is ever really effective unless motivated by some impulse. . . .

The purely contemplative philosopher may project himself into an abstract field of contemplation where he reasons, but practical men, and in that judges must be included, must have impulses. The lawyer has them, and because he has them his work is tremendously important. If a lawyer merely reasoned abstractly and without motive he would do the judge no good. But the driving impulse to bring about his client's success not only makes him burrow industriously for precedents, and as industriously bring them forth, but also makes him belabor and cudgel the brains of the listening judge to bring him into agreement.

It is this factor in our jurisprudence, and only this, that clients have lawyers and that lawyers are advocates, which has made and will continue to make it safe for judges not only to state, but sometimes to make the law. . . . If the judge sat upon the Bench in a purely abstract relation to the cause, his opinion in difficult cases would be worth nothing. He must have some motive to fire his brains, to "let his mind be bold." . . .

And having travailed and reached his judgment, he struggles to bring up and pass in review before his eager mind all of the categories and concepts which he may find useful directly or by analogy, so as to select from them that which in his opinion will support his desired result.

For while the judge may be, he cannot appear to be, arbitrary. He must at least appear reasonable, and unless he can find a category which will at least "semblably" support his view, he will feel uncomfortable. . . .

But whether or not the judge is able in his opinion to present reasons for his hunch which will pass jural muster, he does and should decide difficult and complicated cases only when he has the feeling of the decision, which accounts for the beauty and the fire of some, and the labored dullness of many dissenting opinions. . . .

2.   *"Humility . . . means an alert self-scrutiny . . ."*

HALEY V. OHIO

JOHN HALEY, *a fifteen-year-old Negro, was arrested about midnight on a charge of murder and questioned by relays of police for five hours until he agreed to sign a confession prepared by detectives. At no time during the period of interrogation or for three days thereafter was Haley allowed to see a lawyer, a friend, or a relative. On the basis of this confession and other evidence Haley was convicted of murder and sentenced to life imprisonment. The Ohio Supreme Court dismissed Haley's appeal but the U.S. Supreme Court granted certiorari.*

332 U.S. 596, 68 S. Ct. 302, 92 L. Ed. 224 (1948).

MR. JUSTICE DOUGLAS announced the judgment of the Court and an opinion in which MR. JUSTICE BLACK, MR. JUSTICE MURPHY, and MR. JUSTICE RUTLEDGE join. . . .

The trial court, after a preliminary hearing on the voluntary character of the confession, allowed it to be admitted in evidence over petitioner's objection that it violated his rights under the Fourteenth Amendment. The court instructed the jury to disregard the confession if it found that he did not make the confession voluntarily and of his free will.

But the ruling of the trial court and the finding of the jury on the voluntary character of the confession do not foreclose the independent examination which it is our duty to make here. *Ashcraft* v. *Tennessee.* . . . If the undisputed evidence suggests that force or coercion was used to exact the confession, we will not permit the judgment of conviction to stand, even though without the confession there might have been sufficient evidence for submission to the jury. *Malinski* v. *New York.* . . .

We do not think the methods used in obtaining this confession can be squared with that due process of law which the Fourteenth Amendment commands.

What transpired would make us pause for careful inquiry if a mature man were involved. And when, as here, a mere child—an easy victim of the law—is before us, special care in scrutinizing the record must be used. Age 15 is a tender and difficult age for a boy of any race. He cannot be judged by the more exacting standards of maturity. That which would leave a man cold and unimpressed can overawe and overwhelm a lad in his early teens. This is the period of great instability which the crisis of adolescence produces. A 15-year-old lad, questioned through the dead of night by relays of police, is a ready victim of the inquisition. Mature men possibly might stand the ordeal from midnight to 5 a. m. But we cannot believe that a lad of tender years is a match for the police in such a contest. He needs counsel and support if he is not to become the victim first of fear, then of panic. He needs someone on whom to lean lest the overpowering presence of the law, as he knows it, crush him. No friend stood at the side of this 15-year-old boy as the police, working in relays, questioned him hour after hour, from midnight until dawn. No lawyer stood guard to make sure that the police went so far and no farther, to see to it that they stopped short of the point where he became the victim of coercion. No counsel or friend was called during the critical hours of questioning . . . not even a gesture towards getting a lawyer for him was ever made.

This disregard of the standards of decency is underlined by the fact that he was kept incommunicado for over three days during which the lawyer retained to represent him twice tried to see him and twice was refused admission. A photographer was admitted at once; but his closest friend—his mother—was not allowed to see him for over five days after his arrest. It is said that these events are not germane to the present problem because they happened after the confession was made. But they show such a callous attitude of the police towards the safeguards which respect for ordinary standards of human relationships compels that we take with a grain of salt their present apologia that the five-hour grilling of this boy was conducted in a fair and dispassionate manner. When the police are so unmindful of these basic standards of conduct in their public dealings, their secret treatment of a 15-year-old boy behind closed doors in the dead of night becomes darkly suspicious.

The age of petitioner, the hours when he was grilled, the duration of his quizzing, the fact that he had no friend or counsel to advise him, the callous attitude of the police towards his rights combine to convince us that this was a confession wrung from a child by means which the law should not sanction. Neither man nor child can be allowed to stand condemned by methods which flout constitutional requirements of due process of law. . . .

The course we followed in *Chambers* v. *Florida* . . . *White* v. *Texas* . . . *Ashcraft* v. *Tennessee* . . . and *Malinski* v. *New York* . . . must be followed here. The Fourteenth Amendment prohibits the police from using the private, secret custody of either man or child as a device for wringing confessions from them.

Reversed.

MR. JUSTICE FRANKFURTER, joining in reversal of judgment. . . .

The doubts and difficulties derive from the very nature of the problem before us. They arise frequently when this Court is obliged to give definiteness to "the vague contours" of Due Process or, to change the figure, to spin judgment upon State action out of that gossamer concept. Subtle and even elusive as its criteria are, we cannot escape that duty of judicial review. The nature of the duty, however, makes it especially important to be humble in exercising it. Humility in this context means an alert self-scrutiny so as to avoid infusing into the vagueness of a Constitutional command one's merely private notions. Like other mortals, judges, though unaware, may be in the grip of prepossessions. The only way to relax such a grip, the only way to avoid finding in the Constitution the personal bias one has placed in it, is to explore the influences that have shaped one's unanalyzed views in order to lay bare prepossessions.

A lifetime's preoccupation with criminal justice, as prosecutor, defender of civil liberties, and scientific student, naturally leaves one with views. Thus, I disbelieve in capital punishment. But as a judge I could not impose the views of the very few States who through bitter experience have abolished capital punishment upon all the other States, by finding that "due process" proscribes it. Again, I do not believe that even capital offenses by boys of fifteen should be dealt with according to the conventional criminal procedure. It would, however, be bald judicial usurpation to hold that States violate the Constitution in subjecting minors like Haley to such a procedure. If a State, consistently with the Fourteenth Amendment, may try a boy of fifteen charged with murder by the ordinary criminal procedure, I cannot say that such a youth is never capable of that free choice of action which, in the eyes of the law, makes a confession "voluntary." Again, it would hardly be a justifiable exercise of judicial power to dispose of this case by finding in the Due Process Clause Constitutional outlawry of the admissibility of all private statements made by an accused to a police officer, however much legislation to that effect might seem to me wise. . . .

But whether a confession of a lad of fifteen is "voluntary" and as such admissible, or "coerced" and thus wanting in due process, is not a matter of mathematical determination. Essentially it invites psychological judgment—a psychological judgment that reflects deep, even if inarticulate, feelings of our society. Judges must divine that feeling as best they can from all the relevant evidence and light which they can bring to bear for a confident judgment of such an issue, and with every endeavor to detach themselves from their merely private views. . . .

This brings me to the precise issue on the record before us. . . . The answer, as has already been intimated, depends on an evaluation of psychological factors, or, more accurately stated, upon the pervasive feelings of society regarding such psychological factors. Unfortunately, we cannot draw upon any formulated expression of the existence of such feelings. Nor are there available experts on such matters to guide the judicial judgment. Our Constitutional system makes it the Court's duty to interpret those feelings of society to which the Due Process Clause gives legal protection. Because of their inherent vagueness the tests by which we are to be guided are most unsatisfactory, but such as they are we must apply them. . . .

It is suggested that Haley's guilt could easily have been established without the confession elicited by the sweating process of the night's secret interrogation. But this only affords one more proof that in guarding against misuse of the law enforcement process the effective detection of crime and the prosecution of criminals are furthered and not hampered. Such constitutional restraints of decency derive from reliance upon the resources of intelligence in dealing with crime and discourage the too easy temptations of unimaginative crude force, even when such force is not brutally employed. . . .

Unhappily we have neither physical nor intellectual weights and measures by which judicial judgment can determine when pressures in securing a confession reach the coercive intensity that calls for the exclusion of a statement so secured. Of course, the police meant to exercise pressures upon Haley to make him talk. That was the very purpose of their procedure. In concluding that a statement is not voluntary which results from pressures such as were exerted in this case to make a lad of fifteen talk when the Constitution gave him the right to keep silent and when the situation was so contrived that appreciation of his rights and thereby the means of asserting them were effectively withheld from him by the police, I do not believe I express a merely personal bias against such a procedure. Such a finding, I believe, reflects those fundamental notions of fairness and justice in the determination of guilt or innocence which lie embedded in the feelings of the American people and are enshrined in the Due Process Clause of the Fourteenth Amendment. To remove the inducement to resort to such methods this Court has repeatedly denied use of the fruits of illicit methods. . . .

Mr. Justice Burton, with whom The Chief Justice, Mr. Justice Reed and Mr. Justice Jackson concur, dissenting. . . .

3.   *" 'The First Amendment has erected a wall between church and state.' "*

CATHOLICS ON THE COURT
Harold W. Chase,* Margaret Jane Green,† and Robert Mollan†

. . . There have been six Catholics on the Supreme Court, two of whom have served as Chief Justice:

Roger Taney	1836-1864	(Chief Justice)
Edward White	1894-1921	(Chief Justice)
Joseph McKenna	1896-1925	
Pierce Butler	1922-1939	
Frank Murphy	1940-1949	
William Brennan	1956-	

The first three Catholic Justices had little opportunity to deal with cases involving the provisions of the First Amendment pertaining to freedom of religion. . . . Although Taney, despite his long tenure on the Court, had no occasion to participate in cases involving the issue of separation of church and state, White and McKenna did have two cases. They went along with their seven Protestant brethren in 1899 in deciding that the First Amendment and the concept of separation of church and state did not bar the Commissioners of the District of Columbia from granting public money to a private Catholic hospital, where the hospital agreed to accept poor patients sent there by the Commissioners. Again, while White and McKenna were on the Court,

The New Republic, September 26, 1960, pp. 13 ff. Copyright 1960 *The New Republic.* Reprinted with permission.

* Associate Professor, Department of Political Science, University of Minnesota.
† Teaching Assistants, Department of Political Science, University of Minnesota.

in 1908, the Court unanimously held that the First Amendment safe-guarded the right of the Sioux Indians to use tribal funds to contract with the Bureau of Catholic Indian Missions to educate some Sioux in a Catholic school on a reservation.

While Justice Butler was on the bench, a unanimous court decided than an Oregon law *requiring* children between the ages of eight and sixteen to attend public schools was unconstitutional. Likewise, Butler went along with a unanimous Court in finding that public money de-rived from taxation could be used to buy books for school children in private as well as in public schools, provided the books were the same as those in the public schools and not religious in character.

In a series of cases involving conscientious objectors Butler was part of the majority of the Court which decided that citizenship could be withheld from aliens who for religious reasons were conscientious ob-jectors. He also wrote the opinion for a unanimous Court which held students could be required at the state university to take ROTC, their religious scruples notwithstanding.

On the basis of these decisions, one could charge that White, McKenna and Butler did not manifest an appreciation of the constitu-tional requirement of separation of church and state. As a matter of fact, in virtually all of the cases they did not see that this was at issue. But, if the charge is true, it applies equally to their Protestant con-temporaries on the Court.

During Justice Frank Murphy's tenure, a whole host of cases deal-ing with the issues of freedom of religion were decided by the Supreme Court. Before dealing with Murphy's record in these cases, it is per-tinent to stress that Murphy was no apostate Catholic. He took his religion seriously. . . .

Most of the cases involving religion which Justice Murphy helped to decide were brought to the Court by Jehovah's Witnesses, a re-ligious sect which is particularly offensive to Catholics for its unceas-ing and bitter attack on the Catholic Church, Catholic doctrine and the Pope. Yet Murphy went along with the Court in declaring uncon-stitutional a number of local ordinances employed to keep Jehovah's Witnesses from speaking, holding meetings, distributing literature and using loudspeakers. In a concurring opinion in one of those cases, Murphy made clear his reasons for his position: "I believe that nothing enjoys a higher estate in our society than the right given by the First and Fourteenth Amendments freely to practice and proclaim one's religious convictions. The right extends to the aggressive and disputatious as well as the meek and acquiescent." . . .

In the widely-discussed flag salute cases, Murphy, along with seven non-Catholic Justices, decided originally that the children of Jehovah's Witnesses could be required to salute the flag despite their religious scruples against doing so. Several years later when the Court dealt with the issue for a second time, Murphy joined a new majority which decided that the Court had previously been wrong. In a concurring opinion he made clear the reasons for his change of heart: . . . "There is before us the right of freedom to believe, freedom to worship one's Maker according to the dictates of one's conscience, a right which the Constitution specifically shelters. Reflection has convinced me that as a judge I have no loftier duty or responsibility than to uphold that spiritual freedom to its farthest reaches."

In two cases where the majority decided to abridge the freedom of Jehovah's Witnesses, Murphy dissented. One involved city ordinances imposing license taxes upon the sale of printed matter; significantly, a majority of the Court later adopted Murphy's view as its own. The other case, *Prince* v. *Massachusetts,* dealt with the violation by Jehovah's Witnesses of a state statute forbidding children to sell magazines in the street and public places and forbidding anyone to help them do so. . . .

In view of Murphy's stand in the Jehovah's Witnesses cases, his participation in the majority opinion in the controversial *Everson*[1] case may seem contradictory. The majority, consisting of Murphy and four non-Catholics, speaking through Justice Black, decided that it was constitutional for local school districts to distribute public money to parents of school children in order to reimburse them for the cost of bus transportation to and from Catholic parochial schools as well as public schools. The majority agreed that, "The First Amendment has erected a wall between church and state. That wall must be kept high and impregnable. We could not approve of the slightest breach. New Jersey has not breached it here." The reasoning for such an assertion was: "This Court has said that parents may, in the discharge of their

[1] *Everson* v. *Ewing Township* (1947).

duty under state compulsory education laws, send their children to a religious rather than a public school if the school meets the secular educational requirements which the state has power to impose. It appears that these parochial schools meet New Jersey's requirements. The state contributes no money to the schools. It does not support them. Its legislation, as applied, does no more than provide a general program to help parents get their children, regardless of their religion, safely and expeditiously to and from accredited schools." . . .

But any conclusions which may be drawn about Murphy's acceptance of the majority opinion in *Everson* must be tempered by his position in the *McCollum*[2] case. In *McCollum*, Murphy joined with the majority that found tax-supported public schools could not conduct religious instruction in school buildings during hours set apart for secular teaching. In contrast, when no Catholics were on the bench, the Court later found constitutional programs which provided for religious instruction on released time, that is, "programs which permit public schools to release students during the school day so that they may leave the school buildings and school grounds and go to religious centers for religious instruction or devotional exercises."

It is clear from the record that Justice Murphy afforded the widest latitude to the exercise of freedom of religion to all comers. It is also clear that with one possible exception, the *Everson* case, he insisted upon separation of church and state. Of course, there are those who would maintain that Murphy's position is best explained by the fact that the Catholics must while in the minority guard against any abridgment of freedom of religion lest the majority apply restraints on the Catholics themselves. But this is putting Murphy in the position of being damned if he did and damned if he didn't. . . .

Since Murphy's death, the only Catholic who has served on the Court is Justice William Brennan. In approximately four years on the bench Brennan has had no occasion to participate in an important case involving religious issues.

Here then is the record of the Catholic Justices in cases dealing with church and state. But it is sometimes suggested that in cases not dealing with religion *per se*, Catholic Justices have taken positions on substantive issues which reflect an adherence to Catholic doctrine.

[2] *McCollum* v. *Board of Education* (1948). See below, p. 577.

For example, there are those who think that Justice Butler's lone dissent in the famous sterilization case is an instance in point. There the Court upheld the constitutionality of a Virginia law permitting sterilization of mental defectives. Butler did not explain his dissenting vote, thus leaving the way open to the interpretation that because he was a Catholic it was impossible for him to go along with the rest of the Court in approving a birth control measure of any kind.

Against this, however, one may balance some of the decisions in which Justice Brennan has participated. In cases involving a federal law punishing the mailing of "obscene" materials and a state law making the sale or advertising of "obscene" materials a crime, the Court necessarily had to meet head-on the problem of defining "obscenity." The standard rejected was that obscenity "be judged merely by the effect of an isolated excerpt upon particularly susceptible persons." The more permissive standard adopted by Brennan and the majority was "whether to the average person, applying contemporary community standards, the dominant theme of the material taken as a whole appeals to prurient interests."

It could be argued, perhaps, that Brennan's Catholicism restrained him from going as far as the dissenters in the case, Justices Douglas and Black, who would be even more permissive in obscenity cases. But, although the United States Catholic Bishops in their statement of 1957 approved the principle enunciated by Brennan—that obscenity is not protected by the First Amendment—they indicated that the Court's definition of obscenity was unsatisfactory: "Between the legally punishable and the morally good there exists a wide gap. . . ." And surely Brennan's recent agreement with the other members of the Court that the portrayal of adultery in the motion picture, *Lady Chatterley's Lover*, is not obscenity does not square with the church view. . . .

From this study of the Catholic Justices, the most obvious conclusion is that the ideas of the Catholic Justices as a group are not distinguishable from the ideas of non-Catholics. Indeed, the record of Justice Murphy alone is enough to belie the contention that every devout Catholic must necessarily feel compelled to give precedence to Catholic doctrine over the constitutional doctrine of separation of church and state.

4. *"These are . . . 'relational statistics' . . ."*

LIBERTARIAN MOTIVATIONS ON THE VINSON COURT *C. Herman Pritchett*

JUSTICE FRANKFURTER is fond of quoting an old English saying that "the devil himself knoweth not the mind of men." The mind of a man who happens to be a judge is the center of many contending impulses when he is making it up, and an external reconstruction of the process is quite impossible. However, the rules of the game require that judges supply clues to their thought processes in the form of written opinions. In every major case decided by the Supreme Court, one or more of its members provided a written justification for the decision announced. The individualistic tradition of Anglo-Saxon jurisprudence, moreover, permits justices who do not agree with the views of their brethren to say so, and to give their reasons for dissenting. Thus the Supreme Court on decision day takes on the aspect of a small legislature in which votes are cast pro and con on significant issues of public policy, with accompanying explanations much more coherent and systematic and better-reasoned than are customarily available in explanation of votes cast, say, in the United States Senate.

While it has not been usual to do so, these judicial votes can be subjected to the same kinds of analysis as have been traditionally employed for the study of legislative voting behavior. Thus Table I undertakes to throw light on the attitudes of members of the recent Court toward civil liberties claims by recording their votes as favoring or opposing the claimed liberties in some 84 nonunanimous cases decided during the six terms from October, 1946 to June, 1952.

Such a table is useful, however, only if the analyst has some tenable hypothesis about the nature of the relations between a justice's decisions and his personal convictions. It would be naive to assume that justices in deciding cases are completely free to vote their own preferences, or that a voting record necessarily mirrors a justice's inner convictions. On the other hand, it would be even more naive to assume

47 *American Political Science Review* 321 (1953). Copyright 1953 American Political Science Association. Reprinted with permission.

that a Supreme Court justice merely "looks up the law" on a subject and applies it to the case in hand.

TABLE I. VOTING RECORDS OF JUSTICES IN NONUNANIMOUS CIVIL LIBERTIES DECISIONS, 1946–51 TERMS

| | *No. Cases* | *For Free Speech Claims* | *For Alien Claims* | *For Criminal Defendants' Claims* | | *Total* |
				Federal	*State*	
No. Cases		**23**	**18**	**17**	**26**	**84**
Murphy	42	100%	100%	100%	100%	100%
Rutledge	43	100	100	85	100	95
Douglas	72	100	64	87	96	89
Black	83	96	100	53	88	86
Frankfurter	82	50	76	82	42	60
Majority	84	26	33	53	37	37
Jackson	82	23	44	59	13	32
Clark	23	13	0	33	38	22
Burton	84	17	28	18	15	19
Minton	36	19	18	0	17	17
Vinson	84	13	33	0	12	14
Reed	84	22	6	12	12	13

A workable hypothesis on Supreme Court decision-making must be formulated with an appreciation of the operating conditions under which the judge makes his choices. In many respects his situation is quite comparable with that of any individual who must make decisions on important matters within an institutional framework which brings to him questions for decision and provides mechanisms for making those decisions effective. Appellate courts share with legislatures the problem of decision-making in a collectivity of equals, in contrast to the conditions of decision-making in a hierarchy. We may tend to think of legislators as having greater freedom than judges in arriving at policy choices, but upon reflection it becomes obvious that legislators no more than judges are able to vote as free agents. They must think about what is good for their party. They must give some account to the probable effect of their vote on the prospects for reelection. They may decide to vote for something they do not want in order to get support for something they want very much. They may decide to vote for less than they want because their practical judgment tells them that is all they can get.

A Supreme Court justice finds himself in much the same situation, though operating within a judicial rather than a legislative context does make for some differences. He does not have a constituency of electors or a party position to consider. But the rules and traditions of the Court supply institutional preferences with which his own preferences must compete. One of these institutional preferences, for example, is *stare decisis,* the rule of precedent. The individual judge may think that the precedents are wrong, or outmoded. If so, he may follow his personal preference and state his reasons for voting to change the law. He is free to do that. He is not free to ignore the precedents, to act as though they did not exist. He has free choice, but among limited alternatives and only after he has satisfied himself that he has met the obligations of consistency and respect for settled principles which his responsibility to the Court imposes upon him. His private views as an individual help to form and may be incorporated into his public views as a justice, but they are not the same thing.

What this means, in more concrete terms, is that when a civil liberties case comes to the Supreme Court, the justices are not asked whether they are more or less in favor of civil liberties. They are asked how the Court, consistently with its role as the highest judicial body in a federal system, should dispose of a proceeding, the basic facts in which have been found and the form of which has been given by lower judicial bodies. Under these circumstances some justices may not even choose to think of the civil liberties issue in the case. They may see the controlling problem as adherence or non-adherence to the precedents. They may think of the issue as judicial respect for legislative action. As participants in the judicial process they have a perfect right to choose from among the alternatives presented the ones which determine their view of the case.

Thus it is that a statistical table or "box score" such as Table I cannot be accepted as an index of personal attachment to libertarian values on the part of the justices. These votes were cast, not in their personal but in their judicial capacity, and represented their resolution of situations where many legitimate values may have been competing for attention. What the table does establish is the degree to which each member of the Court found it possible or desirable as a judge to prefer libertarian values over others present in the proceedings. These are what Mark DeWolfe Howe calls "relational statistics," and while Howe is a bitter critic of the statistical method as applied to judicial decisions, he is willing to admit that if interpreted on this basis box scores may be acceptable. But he adds the warning that relational statistics "have significance only when discriminating account is taken of all the values which are brought into relationship."

Obviously it is impossible to identify all the values which each justice may have related to the decision of a case. But our working hypothesis is that a decision involving civil liberties questions will be primarily influenced by the interaction of two factors. One is the direction and intensity of a justice's libertarian sympathies, which will vary according to his weighting of the relative claims of liberty and order in our society. Theoretically, positions on a liberty-order attitude scale could range from an individualist anarchism at one extreme to rigid authoritarianism on the other. The orthodoxy required for a Supreme Court appointment ensures, however, that the spread of opinion among members of that body will be much narrower.

The second factor is the conception which the justice holds of his judicial role and the obligations imposed on him by his judicial function. Every justice in deciding a case must give some thought to what is appropriate for him as a judge to do. The pressures which bear upon him are many, and they are mostly toward a pattern of conformity—conformity with precedents, conformity with the traditions of the law, conformity with public expectations as to how a judge should act, conformity toward established divisions of authority in a federal system based on the principle of separation of powers. While no justice can be oblivious to these pressures, they are not self-enforcing, and he is free to make his own interpretations of their requirements in guiding his own judicial conduct. The attitude scale involved may be thought of as ranging from an expansionist to a contractionist judicial philosophy, from broad to narrow judicial review, from judicial activism to judicial restraint.

Any attempt to rank justices on these two scales in an absolute fashion would be hopeless, but it should not be as difficult to locate them relatively to each other, and particularly by reference to their deviation from the Court's majority position at any one time. Table I shows that five members of the Vinson Court—Murphy, Rutledge, Douglas, Black, and Frankfurter—voted for libertarian claims substantially more often than the Court majority. In the terms of our hypothesis, the extremely high rate of support for libertarian claims registered by the first four of these justices suggests that they are strongly positive on both scales; their personal preferences must be strongly libertarian, and they must have a conception of their judicial function which permits or even requires them to give judicial effect to their libertarian preferences. Without assuming any absolute identity of views on their part, the motivation of these four justices can be characterized as libertarian activism.

5.   *"Hughberts has a pure strategy . . ."*

GAME THEORY AND JUDICIAL BEHAVIOR   *Glendon A. Schubert, Jr.*[*]

. . . THE JUDICIAL process is tailor-made for investigation by the theory of games. Whatever may be their obligations as officers of courts, attorneys frequently play the role of competing gamesmen, and the model of the two-person zero-sum game certainly can be applied to many trials. The two examples that I should like to describe briefly, however, involve the application of game theory to the analysis of the behavior of Supreme Court justices. . . .

The first of these I shall call the Hughberts Game. During the 1936 Term, the Court was divided between a three-justice liberal bloc and a four-justice conservative bloc, with Hughberts (Hughes and Roberts) in the middle. If we assume that, in the face of Roosevelt's attack upon the Court, the Chief Justice—with the support of Roberts—wished to maximize both his own authority within the Court and the degree of unanimity in the Court's decisions, while at the same time directing the Court to as liberal a course of decision as possible in order to forestall the possibility of the more drastic reforms proposed by the Presi-

"The Study of Judicial Decision-Making as an Aspect of Political Behavior," 52 *American Political Science Review* 1007 (1958). Copyright 1958 American Political Science Association. Reprinted with permission.
[*] Professor of Political Science, Michigan State University.

dent, game theory can tell us how Hughberts should vote if he—I shall consider Hughes and Roberts to be a single player from now on—were to behave rationally in order to realize these objectives. A game must have a payoff which can be expressed in numerical terms, and for this purpose I have used the Shapley-Shubik empirical power index in order to be able to compare the Court's actual voting behavior with the imputed utilities (*i.e.*, the payoff) postulated by the game model. Simply stated, the Shapley-Shubik index measures the extent to which each justice shared in the power of decision, which is defined as the probability of his having been pivotal in the winning coalition. [L. S. Shapley and Martin Shubik, "A Method for Evaluating the Distribution of Power in a Committee System," 48 *American Political Science Review* 787 (1954).]

The left bloc and the right bloc are each defined as players in the game, which is three-person and zero-sum. Hughberts has a pure strategy, which in essence requires that he form a coalition with the Left when possible, that he form a coalition with the Right when splintering or non-participation makes it impossible for him to form a winning coalition with the Left, and that he always join the coalition of the Left and the Right when the other players do not choose to adopt conflicting strategies. In fact, the voting behavior of Hughes and Roberts conforms very closely to the prescriptions of the game model (Figure 1). In terms of the empirical payoff, the four-justice right bloc, the three-justice left bloc, and the two-justice center bloc are all approximately equal in power:

The Left		Hughberts		The Right	
Brandeis	.1312	Hughes	.1600	Van Devanter	.0957
Cardozo	.1264	Roberts	.1536	Sutherland	.0864
Stone	.1054			Butler	.0742
				McReynolds	.0672
Totals	.3630		.3136		.3235
Expected power:	.3333		.3333		.3333
Difference:	+ .0297		− .0197		− .0098

It is easy to demonstrate that in a three-person simple majoritarian game, equality of power is imputed among the players. It is by no means a self-evident proposition, however, that among nine justices

HUGHBERTS
(2 votes)

+   −

THE LEFT
(3 votes)

THE RIGHT
(4 votes)

	+	−
+ **+**	(3/9, 2/9, 4/9) [96] 2 (R) 1 (Bu, M) 1 (M) 1 (M)[St] 1 (Su)	(3/7, 0, 4/7) [0]
+ **−**	(3/5, 2/5, 0) [6] 1 [St, V]	(0, 1/3, 2/3) [4] 1 (H) 1 [St] 1 (R) 1 [Br, St]
− **+**	(0, 1/3, 2/3) [5] 3 [St] 1 (Br) 1 (H, Br)[St]	(3/5, 2/5, 0) [8] 1 (M) 1 (V)[St]
− **−**	(3/7, 0, 4/7) [0]	(3/9, 2/9, 4/9) [76] 2 (Bu, M) 1 (Bu) 1 (Br, R) 1 (M) 1 (M)[St]

Fig. 1. Payoff Matrix for the Hughberts Game

Legend: The symbols + and − designate the players' strategies:

+ = voting for affirmance of the lower court's decision

− = voting for reversal of the lower court's decision

The imputations for partitioning of the payoff among the players, according to the intersection of strategies, are given within parentheses at the top of each cell.

The number of decisions falling within each cell is given in brackets. The number of decisions, in each cell, in which there were deviations from the blocs, are itemized. Justices who defected from their respective blocs are shown in parentheses, and those who failed to participate in particular decisions are shown in brackets, according to the following key:

Br = Brandeis   H = Hughes   M = McReynolds
C = Cardozo   R = Roberts   Bu = Butler
St = Stone   Su = Sutherland
                                    V = Van Devanter

(Mr. Justice Cardozo did not deviate from the voting position attributed to the left bloc in any of the 195 decisions of the 1936 Term.)

each casting a single and equal vote, two justices can be just as powerful as four justices.

I shall call the other example the Certiorari Game. Do Supreme Court justices combine into a bloc with the deliberate objective of forcing upon the rest of the Court the consideration of an issue which the bloc wants decided in a particular way? The data for the game consist of the decisions of the Supreme Court, both jurisdictional and on the merits, in Federal Employers' Liability Act evidentiary cases since 1942. The basic assumption is that a certiorari bloc was functioning throughout this period, although the number of justices affiliating with the bloc varied at different times and an antagonist player (Frankfurter) in opposition to the certiorari bloc entered the game (as such) only during the latter stages of the play. In order to simplify the discussion, let us confine our attention to the first period of the game, comprising the 1942–1948 Terms.

At that time, the certiorari bloc consisted of Murphy, Rutledge, Black, and Douglas. If we assume that the objective of the bloc was to maximize the number of decisions favorable to workmen's claims, game theory can prescribe how the bloc should behave rationally in order to accomplish this objective. Four justices are adequate to grant certiorari, but not (normally) to decide cases on the merits. It is assumed that, during this period, the remaining five justices had no fixed predisposition either towards or against the claimants. The only question in these cases is whether the trial court correctly evaluated the evidence; the cases turn, in other words, on questions of fact rather than law. Typically, they fall into two categories: (a) the trial court directs a judgment for the defendant railroad, on the ground that the evidence is insufficient for the case to go to a jury, or else the court directs a judgment for the defendant notwithstanding a jury verdict for the plaintiff; or (b) the trial judge enters a judgment for the plaintiff on the basis of a jury verdict. In either event, the decision of the trial court has been affirmed or reversed by a court of appeals, and either the plaintiff workman or the defendant railroad has petitioned the Supreme Court for certiorari. It is assumed that, since these cases turn only on the evaluation of evidence, there is an equal chance that any of the five uncommitted justices will vote either for or against a claimant if the court of appeals has disagreed with the trial court.

Therefore, since the certiorari bloc needs to pick up only one additional favorable vote on the merits, the chances of its doing so should be 31/32, for the only permutation of the five uncommitted members on which the bloc could lose would be for all five of the other justices to vote against the claimant. The certiorari bloc has a pure strategy: never to vote in favor of petitions filed by railroads, always to vote to grant certiorari in cases in which review is sought by workers *and* in which an appellate court has reversed a judgment in favor of the plaintiff, and always to vote for the petitioner on the merits. *If* the certiorari bloc follows its pure strategy, the Court should decide 97 percent of the cases in favor of the claimants. If the bloc departs from its pure strategy, it can expect to win a smaller proportion of victories on the merits, because it has played irrationally.

As a matter of fact, the payoff to the certiorari bloc during this period was 92 percent (12 pro decisions and 1 con) in cases in which the bloc adhered to its pure strategy; of the 11 cases in which the bloc departed from its pure strategy by voting to grant certiorari for petitioners who had been two-time losers in the courts below, 8 were pro and 3 were con, for a payoff of only 73 percent. In later periods of the game, the bloc adhered much more closely to its pure strategy, and consequently enjoyed greater success. During the present period, the bloc consists of five justices, so the expected payoff is 100 percent. As a matter of fact, the bloc lost one of the fourteen cases decided on the merits during the 1956 and 1957 Terms, perhaps because the bloc, a little power drunk, became careless and granted certiorari in a case so frivolous that even the bloc members joined in the unanimous decision against the claimant. An alternative explanation for this deviant decision might be that the certiorari bloc was not being irrational, but rather that it *deliberately* accepted jurisdiction with the expectation that the decision would go unanimously against the workman, for the public relations objective of countering criticism that it *always* favored workmen. . . .

"Identification of the operative variable may be attempted through the use of Guttman Scalogram Analysis."

6.

SUPREME COURT BEHAVIOR AND CIVIL RIGHTS   *S. Sidney Ulmer**

. . . ONE CANNOT, of course, expect a collegial court of nine justices to decide all cases unanimously. Differences in interpretation of Constitution and statute there most assuredly will be. But when the reactions of the justices are markedly different over a long series of cases one is led to suspect that individual characteristics are important decision-shaping factors. Analysis reveals that in twenty-two non-unanimous civil liberties cases decided in the 1956 term, Douglas and Black voted *for the civil liberty claim twenty-one times.* Clark, on the other hand voted for the civil liberty claim in one case and *against the claim in twenty-one.* In the 1957 term out of forty-one non-unanimous civil liberties cases Douglas voted *for the claim in forty instances.* Clark, with the same number of opportunities voted *against the claim in thirty-nine cases.*

Certainly discrepancies of this nature are not alone due to mere differences as to the meaning of Constitution or statute. Indeed it is reasonable in this context to suggest that the *attitude* of the judge toward civil liberty claims was the factor shaping the individual decisions. Llewellyn and the legal realists have often noted that the important factor in judicial decision-making is the reaction of the judge to the fact-stimuli of life around him. This observation would seem pertinent in the area of civil liberties decisions if anywhere.

We shall hypothesize, therefore, that the responses of the justices in civil liberties cases are in terms of *one dominant variable: deprivation of a claimed civil liberty.* This hypothesis assumes that the justice will make his decision not by asking "What does the law require?" but by asking himself such questions as: "Shall I allow any deprivation of a claimed civil liberty? Shall I allow deprivation to the extent of X? to

13 *Western Political Quarterly* 288 (1960). Copyright 1960 University of Utah. Reprinted with permission.

* Assistant Professor, Department of Political Science, Michigan State University.

the extent of Y? to the extent of Z?" Since the civil liberties cases have been selected in terms of one common factor: *deprivation of a claimed civil liberty,* verification of response to *one dominant variable* will constitute strong support for the hypothesis. Failure to verify *one dominant operative variable* will nullify the hypothesis.

Identification of the operative variable may be attempted through the use of Guttman Scalogram Analysis. This research tool was developed by Louis Guttman in the early 1940's to cope with a basic problem in opinion research. The problem is to determine if questions asked on a single issue have a single meaning for the respondents. Only if such a single meaning is present can respondents be ranked along an attitude continuum in order of favorableness. Scalogram analysis is designed to detect the presence or absence of this single meaning or dominant variable in terms of which responses are made and respondents may be ranked. Such a variable is identified if a "scale" exists. A perfect scale is said to exist if the questions and responses can be arranged in such a way that "persons who answer a given question favorably all have higher ranks than persons who answer the same question unfavorably." From the rank or scale score of the respondent we know exactly which questions he favored and can therefore say that a response to any question defines the respondent's attitude. Perfect scales, however, are not expected in practice. The difference between a perfect scale and a given scale pattern is measured by a coefficient of reproducibility (CR). Guttman has arbitrarily classified any pattern with a CR of less than .90 as non-scale type.

The attitude of a respondent toward a primary operating variable is measured relatively by his rank order. It is denoted numerically by his scale score. Thus, the complete behavior of a respondent to a series of questions can be indicated by a numerical score within the margin of error denoted by the CR.

As applied to Supreme Court cases, certain slight modifications in Guttman's techniques are necessary. The cases are conceptualized as posing a series of questions to a population composed of nine Supreme Court justices. The votes in the cases represent responses to the questions. The questions concern the degree of allowable deprivation to which specific civil liberties may be subjected. Each subsequent case

FIGURE 1. SCALOGRAM ANALYSIS: CIVIL LIBERTY CASES — UNITED STATES SUPREME COURT — 1956 TERM

	Douglas	Black	Warren	Brennan	Frankfurter	Harlan	Whittaker	Burton	Clark	Reed	Vote
Scale Score	22	22	20	19	14	12	11	5	0	0	
as Percentage of First Rank	100	100	90.9	81.7	63.6	54.5	50	22.7	0	0	
Jencks v. United States	+	+	+	+	+	+	n	+	−	n	7-1
Yates v. United States	+	+	+	n	+	+	n	+	−	n	6-1
Schneiderman v. United States	+	+	+	n	+	+	n	+	−	n	6-1
Richmond v. United States	+	n	+	n	+	+	n	+	−	n	6-1
Roviaro v. United States	+	+	+	+	+	+	n	+	−	n	6-1
Watkins v. United States	+	+	+	+	+	+	n	n	−	n	6-1
Kremen v. United States	+	+	+	+	+	+	n	−	−	n	6-2
Kinsella v. Krueger	+	+	+	+	+	+	n	−	−	n	6-2
Reid v. Covert	+	+	+	+	+	+	n	−	−	n	6-2
Sweezy v. New Hampshire	−	+	+	+	+	+	n	−	−	n	6-2
Chessman v. Teets	+	+	+	+	+	+	n	−	−	−	6-3
Gold v. United States	+	+	+	+	+	+	n	−	−	−	6-3
Fikes v. Alabama	+	+	+	+	+	−	n	+	+	−	6-3
Paoli v. United States	+	+	−	+	−	−	−	−	−	n	4-5
Konigsberg v. State Bar	+	+	+	+	−	−	+	+	−	n	5-3
Petition of Groban	+	+	+	+	−	−	−	−	−	n	4-5
Kingsley Books v. Brown	+	+	+	+	−	−	n	−	−	−	4-5
Nilva v. United States	+	+	+	+	−	−	n	−	−	n	4-5
Pollard v. United States	+	+	+	+	−	−	−	−	−	−	4-5
Breithaupt v. Abram	+	+	+	+	−	−	n	−	−	n	3-6
Roth v. United States	+	+	−	+	−	−	n	−	−	−	3-6
Alberts v. California	+	+	−	−	−	−	n	−	−	n	2-7
Number of Participations	22	21	22	19	22	22	5	21	22	6	182
Inconsistencies	1	1	1	1	1	1	1	1	1		5

Legend: + for the civil liberty claim
− against the civil liberty claim
n nonparticipation

$$\text{Coefficient of Reproducibility} = 1 - \frac{5}{182} = .973$$

Note: Case titles have been shortened in some instances.

in the list is conceptualized as less deprivational than the one preceding it. The non-unanimous civil liberties cases for the 1956 term, when analyzed, form a scale with properties well within the requirements of scale theory. The existence of the scale indicates: (1) a structured attitude continuum along which response is highly consistent, and (2) the presence of one dominant operating variable. The variable hypothesized is the one in terms of which the cases were originally selected: *deprivation of a claimed civil liberty.* Thus, the data for the 1956 term supports the general hypothesis. The scalogram in Figure 1 ranks the justices in order of favorableness toward civil liberty claims. Douglas and Black turn out to be most favorable toward such claims with Burton and Clark least favorable. Reed's ranking is of little significance due to his large number of nonparticipations. Consistency of the justices in these cases is measured by the coefficient of reproducibility of .973. This indicates that 97.3 percent of the over-all response can be accounted for by one operating variable.

There were only five inconsistent votes out of 182 cast. . . . It should be noted that this scale can be used as a predictive device. As long as the same justices sit and the same types of questions are raised, one can predict from the 1956 scale that the relative ranking in terms of favorableness toward civil liberty claims will be maintained. . . .

PART SEVEN

Limits on Judicial Power

15 / POLITICAL CHECKS ON
JUDICIAL POWER

In previous chapters we have discussed some of the elements of judicial power and decision-making, but an analysis of either topic would be incomplete without an examination of the limitations on the judiciary. The nature and scope of restrictions on the power of judges will substantially affect the behavior of other office-holders, interest groups, and of the judges themselves. Groups whose interests have been thwarted in the judicial process can perhaps utilize these limitations to overcome a court decision, as can legislators or administrators who are jealous of judicial power, or who genuinely fear that a judicial policy is dangerous to the national interest, or who simply are reacting to political pressures. Recognition of their own limitations may move judges to avoid or change a decision on certain issues; and dissenting judges can appeal to the other branches of government to correct what they consider to be the errors of their colleagues.

Executive Limitations

The most obvious limitation on judicial power is that of enforcement. Federal judges have at their command no physical force other than that supplied by Congress and the President. Even the marshals of the various courts are appointed by the President and are subject to immediate dismissal at his pleasure. John Marshall and Roger Brooke Taney both had experiences with Presidents who refused to execute judicial decrees. Jefferson, so Marshall thought, was ready to defy the expected decision, in *Marbury* v. *Madison*, that Marbury should have his commission. Marshall shrewdly avoided this difficulty; but in 1807 the Chief Justice was less tactful. When presiding over the treason trial of Aaron Burr as part of his circuit-riding duties, Marshall ordered Jefferson to produce some correspondence between the President and one of the prosecution witnesses. Jefferson, however, refused to obey the subpoena and instructed the marshal of the court not to try to enforce it.

Marshall had a somewhat similar experience with Andrew Jackson. During the late 1820's Georgia had been asserting jurisdiction over the Cherokee lands within the state, despite the fact that the Indians were protected by a treaty with the United States government. In 1831 state authorities convicted two missionaries who had violated a Georgia statute requiring white persons living among the Cherokees to secure a license and take an oath of allegiance to the state. The missionaries appealed to the United States Supreme Court, and in *Worcester* v. *Georgia* the justices reversed the convictions. Local officials indignantly denounced the decision, and the state judges acted as if the case had never been appealed. The two missionaries went to jail and stayed there until pardoned by the governor.

According to one account, Andrew Jackson, when told of the Supreme Court action, said, "Well, John Marshall has made his decision, now let him enforce it." While the story is probably apocryphal, Jackson made no overt move to coerce the Georgia authorities. There were, however, a number of sound political reasons for his not doing so. Among them was the fact that this was the time of South Carolina's efforts to nullify the tariff, and Jackson did not want to drive Georgia into the nullification camp. Allowing the state to ignore a Supreme Court decision was a price Jackson was willing to pay.

Taney had a more direct clash with executive power. Lincoln, in the early days of the Civil War before Congress had authorized him to do so, had suspended the writ of habeas corpus and substituted trial by military tribunals for regular judicial proceedings for border-state civilians suspected of aiding the Confederacy. In May, 1861, John Merryman, a notorious Maryland secessionist, was arrested and locked up in Fort McHenry. Merryman's lawyer petitioned the nearest circuit court for habeas corpus. Taney, who presided over the circuit court at Baltimore, issued the writ against General George Cadwalader, ordering him to bring the prisoner into court for a hearing. The next day, however, the general sent an aide to explain that under presidential instructions he could not deliver the prisoner.

Taney rejected this explanation and directed the marshal of the court to arrest Cadwalader for contempt. The general prevented this move by refusing to permit the marshal to enter the fort. Taney then ruled that Merryman could not legally be tried by court martial; and noting that he was deciding the case as Chief Justice of the United States rather than as a circuit judge, he delivered a blistering opinion which he sent to the President. "He certainly does not faithfully execute the laws," Taney wrote about Lincoln, "if he takes upon himself legislative power, by suspending the writ of habeas corpus, and the judicial power also, by arresting and imprisoning a person without due process of law."

For the time being, Lincoln ignored the Chief Justice, but his message of July 4, 1861, contained an answer to Taney in the famous questions: ". . . are all the laws *but one* to go unexecuted, and the government itself go to pieces lest that one be violated? Even in such a case, would not the official oath be broken if the government should be overthrown, when it was believed that disregarding the single law, would tend to preserve it?" Later that year, Merryman was indicted for treason and his case remitted to the circuit court. He was released under bond and was never tried.

These may have been exceptional cases, but the thread connecting court decisions with executive enforcement has often been thin. Franklin D. Roosevelt had a radio address prepared to explain why he was not going to comply with an expected Supreme Court decision that the statute taking the United States off a strict gold standard was unconstitutional. Since the justices held the act valid by a 5–4 decision, the speech never had to be given. In 1952, President Truman undoubtedly considered retaining control of the steel mills in defiance of the Court. If he had done so, only pressures from Congress or from within the Democratic party could have vindicated the Court. In 1958, during the Little Rock crisis, it seemed that Eisenhower was more than willing to compromise with Governor Faubus on school integration. Eisenhower took no action to assist the district court for days after Faubus had used force to compel disobedience to the court order. Had the President not finally concluded that Faubus was bargaining in bad faith, the school segregation cases might have become a monument to judicial futility.

There are other ways in which a President can influence or limit judicial power. Every Chief Executive tries to shape judicial behavior through his appointments, though life tenure makes this a rather unsure method. He may also, as Jefferson, Jackson, Lincoln, and Theodore and Franklin Roosevelt did with varying degrees of success, throw the prestige of the White House onto the policymaking scales and openly compete with the judges on their strongest ground.

A President may also approach one or more of the justices and bargain informally. Charles Evans Hughes' biographer claims that at the beginning of the New Deal Roosevelt tried to sound out several justices on the possibility of a modus vivendi between the White House and the Court. Furthermore, a President may take advantage of personal friendship to persuade a judge to vote the "right" way, as President-elect Buchanan did with Justice Grier in the Dred Scott Case. Or a President may appeal publicly but subtly to the patriotism of the justices.

Congressional Checks

The President, as chief legislator and as head of his party, may also attempt to utilize congressional authority against the judges. The congressional checks on judicial power are far more extensive than those of the President acting alone, though the fact that they are possessed by almost 550 men makes their exercise more difficult.

The first congressional restriction on judicial power is that of the purse strings. While the Constitution states that a judge's salary shall not be lowered during his term of office, there is no way in which judges can compel Congress to appropriate money, except by an appeal to the electorate. In spite of the constitutional barrier, Congress could harass the judiciary by cutting appropriations for staff as well as for buildings and equipment, or forbid any money to be spent out of the treasury to assist the execution of a specific decision. In 1947, for instance, the House of Representatives came within one vote of refusing to appropriate money to pay back salaries to three government employees who, the Supreme Court ruled, had been illegally discharged.

Among the more important legislative checks on judges is the authority to enact a law explicitly rejecting a court interpretation of a previous statute, or to propose a constitutional amendment to reverse a decision, or even to strike at the source of judicial power. The statutory method has been increasingly employed in the last few decades, due partly to the Supreme Court's tendency since 1937 to base decisions on statutory rather than constitutional interpretation, and due also to the fact that many interest groups have become adept at pressuring Congress to pass what appear to be minor adjustments in existing law. The procedure of constitutional amendment is much more cumbersome, of course. While hundreds of amendments to reverse court decisions have been introduced, only four have been formally proposed and ratified: the Eleventh Amendment, reversing *Chisholm* v. *Georgia,* the Thirteenth and Fourteenth, in part reversing the Dred Scott Case; and the Sixteenth, overturning the Income-Tax cases.

The weakest spot in the judicial armor is that of jurisdiction. Congress, the justices have claimed, may not enlarge or curtail the original jurisdiction of the Supreme Court as specified in the Constitution; but there is no doubt that in almost all other respects Congress has plenary authority over both judicial procedure and jurisdiction. Congress withheld full jurisdiction over federal questions from district and circuit courts until 1875. Before that time, state courts were the only tribunals which could handle many questions of federal law, with an avenue of appeal open to the U.S. Supreme Court. Moreover, there were persistent efforts in Congress throughout John Marshall's tenure to repeal Section 25 of the Judiciary Act of 1789 which gave the Court appellate jurisdiction over state decisions. *Ex parte McCardle* (1868) marked the first time, however, that Congress revoked the Supreme Court's jurisdiction as a curb on judicial power. As we have seen, Congress in the Norris-La Guardia Act of 1932 blocked management's ability to obtain anti-union injunctions from federal judges by removing the authority of federal judges to issue injunctions in labor disputes.

Congress also has a major responsibility in the organization and staffing of federal courts. Senators play an important role in the appointing process. As for judicial organization, the Constitution specifies only that there shall be "one supreme Court" and "such inferior Courts as the Congress may from time to time ordain and establish." This leaves Congress a rather wide range of discretion. In addition, the size of the Supreme Court is not set by the Constitution, allowing a possibility of "Court-packing."

The number of justices was set at six by the Act of 1789, but the lame-duck Federalists in 1801 tried to deprive Jefferson of one appointment by providing that the next vacancy on the bench should not be filled. The Jeffersonians simply repealed this provision in 1802. As the country expanded and it became necessary to add new circuits, the size of the Court was increased. In 1837 the number of justices was set at nine. In 1864, to give the nationalists on the bench a more comfortable majority over the states-righters, the Court was increased to ten. Then in 1866, as a means of curbing Andrew Johnson's power, Congress provided that the next three Supreme Court vacancies should not be filled. When Grant became President, however, Congress increased the size of the Court to nine.

Meanwhile, in February, 1870, before Grant had made any appointments, the Court by a 4–3 vote held the Legal Tender acts unconstitutional,[1] a decision which would have tremendously increased debtors' obligations and caused a general contraction of the currency. The administration had advance warning of the decision from Chief Justice Chase, however, and the day the decision was announced Grant nominated two new justices, one of whom had voted in favor of the constitutionality of paper money while a state judge. The other, as a railroad lawyer, was also thought to be a proponent of paper currency. Within sixteen months, the two new justices had aligned with the three previous dissenters to reverse the first decision on the Legal Tender acts.[2]

Although the Senate and the President continually fenced over individual appointments, increasing the size of the Court as a means of influencing judicial decisions was not tried again until F.D.R.'s 1937 proposal that he be allowed to appoint one new justice for every justice who, having reached the age of seventy, did not retire, as long as the number of justices did not exceed fifteen. For once Roosevelt badly bungled the political management of his scheme, and the Court bill was buried in the Senate after 168 days of maneuvering.

In 1953, Senator John Marshall Butler of Maryland introduced a constitutional amendment drafted by the American Bar Association, under which Congress would have surrendered its authority to control the size and jurisdiction of the Supreme Court. The amendment passed the Senate over liberal opposition in 1954, but was quietly shelved in the House. Four years later it was Butler who joined with Senator William Jenner to lead the Republican half of a southern Democratic–conservative Republican attempt to curb the Supreme Court's appellate jurisdiction.

Congress can also influence judicial policy by its powers of impeachment and removal. Jefferson tried to use these means to break Federalist judicial power. With John Marshall as the real target, Jefferson's followers were successful in removing one district judge, but failed to get the Senate to convict Justice Chase in 1805. This defeat led Jefferson to remark that impeachment was "a scarecrow," an evaluation that remains essentially accurate in characterizing the value of impeachment as a partisan political weapon.

[1] *Hepburn* v. *Griswold* (1870).
[2] *Knox* v. *Lee* (1871).

There are, however, other effective ways of removal. Congress may simply abolish a court and make no provision for further duties or salaries for the incumbent judges. Thus, in 1802, the Jeffersonians abolished the circuit courts which the Adams administration had set up in 1801 and staffed with sixteen deserving Federalists. Under the Judiciary Act of 1802 Supreme Court justices were once again compelled to ride the circuit. To delay, if not avoid, a Supreme Court decision declaring the removal of the circuit judges unconstitutional, Jefferson's forces also adopted legislation postponing the next sitting of the justices for fourteen months. In similar fashion, Radical Republicans proposed in 1861 that the Supreme Court be abolished as fitting revenge for the Dred Scott and Merryman decisions.

A more subtle means of removal is for Congress to encourage judges to retire by liberal retirement benefits. The first retirement act, that of 1869, permitting judges over seventy with ten years' judicial service to retire at full pay, was designed to ease Justices Grier and Nelson off the bench. Congress reneged on this promise after Holmes' retirement in 1932; but, to encourage Justice Van Devanter and some of his elderly colleagues to retire, Congress in 1937 passed a new statute protecting judges' retirement benefits.

Various plans have been proposed for compulsory retirement at seventy or seventy-five. Roosevelt's Court bill would have encouraged retirements and the Butler Amendment would have required retirement after seventy-five. So far no mandatory retirement system has been adopted for federal judges, though under a 1958 statute the chief judges of courts of appeals and of district courts in districts with more than one judge are relieved of all administrative responsibility at seventy.

State Checks

State officials have a less direct check on federal power, but their influence on the executive or on important segments of Congress may be considerable. If nothing else, state protests may focus public attention on a court decision and serve as a rallying point for groups seeking reversal.

"Interposition" or "nullification" is another political device that may be used against federal judicial power. Although the classic exposition of the doctrine was given by John C. Calhoun during the tariff controversy that raged from 1828 to 1833, the antecedents of interposition can be traced to the Kentucky and Virginia Resolutions of 1798–99 and even beyond to Virginia's protests in 1791 against the federal government's assumption of state debts. Although it was southern in origin, states from every part of the country have invoked the doctrine when it was to their advantage. The more famous state efforts to resist judicial power were those of Pennsylvania in 1809, Virginia in 1815, Ohio in 1819, Georgia in 1831–32, and Wisconsin in 1859. Except in the case of Georgia, each of these attempts failed. The doctrine has been repeatedly rejected by each branch of the federal government, and was denounced by Madison as "a colossal heresy" and "an inlet to anarchy." Interposition, however, was revived in 1955 as one of the means of resisting the school segregation cases, and resolutions declaring these decisions void were adopted by Alabama, Arkansas, Florida, Georgia, Louisiana, Mississippi, South Carolina, and Virginia.

Nullification, whether in the form of legislative resolutions or a governor's use of force, is only one of the means that Southern officials employed to resist desegregation. Some state statutes tried to justify open retention of segregation as a valid means of protecting the public health and safety. Other statutes abolished race as the overt basis for school segregation and substituted pupil placement laws under which pupils are assigned to racially segregated schools supposedly on the basis of non-racial factors. The various southern resistance plans are being gradually struck down by federal judges, but there is no doubt that these devices have postponed desegregation. There is doubt, however, whether an equally long and far more fruitful postponement could not have been obtained by good-faith compliance with the school cases.

A more subtle, but nonetheless effective, means of resisting federal judicial power has been used where state officials have obeyed a specific Supreme Court decision but have quietly ignored the underlying doctrines of law and policy. In 1927, for example, the Supreme Court held in *Tumey* v. *Ohio* that a defendant convicted before a justice of the peace who received a share of the fine had been denied due process. Ohio abided by the decision as far as Tumey was concerned, but waited almost thirty years before changing its justice-of-the-peace system.

Judges and Politicians

It might seem from these limitations that federal judges could be throttled at the whim of other politicians, but this clearly has not been the case. At least four reasons could be offered for the continuance of judicial power despite these serious checks. First, courts are protected by their magic; only rarely can a hand be laid on a judge without a public outcry of sacrilege. Second, elected officials often need a judicial blessing to legitimize political decisions on the margin of constitutionality. Third, while judges inevitably offend some powerful interest groups, they usually manage by doing so to please other groups who can also pressure elected officials. Though the relative strength of these sets of groups varies from situation to situation, the technical rules of the legislative process give a great advantage to those interests which only want to preserve the *status quo*. Fourth, federal legislators and administrators compete with each other and with state officials for political power as well as with federal judges. An elected politician who takes a long view of his own power position can seldom be certain that in crippling judicial power he might not also be transferring power to one of his other rivals.

SELECTED REFERENCES

Alsop, Joseph and Turner Catledge, *The 168 Days* (New York: Doubleday Doran, 1938).

Barker, Lucius, "The Offshore Oil Controversy since 1953," 1958 *Wisconsin Law Review* 107.

Beveridge, Albert J., *The Life of John Marshall* (Boston: Houghton Mifflin, 1919), III, Chs. 2, 4, 9.

Elliott, Sheldon D., "Court Curbing Proposals in Congress," 33 *Notre Dame Lawyer* 597 (1958).

Fairman, Charles, "The Retirement of Federal Judges," 51 *Harvard Law Review* 397 (1938).

Longaker, Richard, "Andrew Jackson and the Judiciary," 71 *Political Science Quarterly* 341 (1956).

Mason, Alpheus T., *Harlan Fiske Stone: Pillar of the Law* (New York: Viking Press, 1956), IV.

McKay, Robert, "Georgia versus the United States Supreme Court," 4 *Journal of Public Law* 285 (1955).

Murphy, Walter F., "Desegregation in Education: A Generation of Future Litigation," 15 *Maryland Law Review* 221 (1955).

Note, "Interposition versus Judicial Power," 1 *Race Relations Law Reporter* 465 (1956).

Note, "Congressional Reversal of Supreme Court Decisions: 1945–1957," 71 *Harvard Law Review* 1324 (1958).

Peltason, Jack, *Federal Courts in the Political Process* (New York: Random House, 1955), Ch. 6.

Pollak, Louis H., "The Supreme Court under Fire," 6 *Journal of Public Law* 428 (1957).

Pritchett, C. Herman, *Congress versus the Supreme Court, 1957–1960* (Minneapolis: University of Minnesota Press, 1961).

Ratner, Sidney, "Was the Supreme Court Packed by President Grant?" 50 *Political Science Quarterly* 343 (1935).

Rauh, Joseph L., "The Truth about Congress and the Court," 22 *The Progressive* 30 (Nov., 1958).

Silver, David M., *Lincoln's Supreme Court*, Illinois Studies in the Social Sciences, Vol. 38 (1956).

Sorauf, Frank J., *"Zorach* v. *Clauson:* The Impact of a Supreme Court Decision," 53 *American Political Science Review* 777 (1959).

ten Broek, Jacobus, "Partisan Politics and Federal Judgeship Impeachment since 1903," 23 *Minnesota Law Review* 185 (1939).

U.S. Senate, Committee on the Judiciary, Hearings on S. 2646, *Limitation of Appellate Jurisdiction of the United States Supreme Court*, Part 1, 85th Cong., 1st Sess., 1957; Part 2, 85th Cong., 2d Sess., 1958.

Vanlandingham, Kenneth, "Pecuniary Interests of Justices of the Peace in Kentucky: The Aftermath of Tumey v. Ohio," 45 *Kentucky Law Journal* 607 (1957).

Warren, Charles, "Legislative and Judicial Attacks on the Supreme Court of the United States," 47 *American Law Review* 1, 161 (1913).

———, *The Supreme Court in United States History* (Rev. ed., Boston: Little, Brown, 1926), 2 vols.

1.
"I know no safe depository of the ultimate powers of the society but the people themselves . . ."

THOMAS JEFFERSON TO WILLIAM C. JARVIS, SEPTEMBER 28, 1820

I THANK YOU, Sir, for the copy of your *Republican* which you have been so kind as to send me. . . . I have not yet had time to read it seriously, but in looking over it cursorily I see much in it to approve, and shall be glad if it shall lead our youth to the practice of thinking on such subjects and for themselves. That it will have this tendency may be expected, and for that reason I feel an urgency to note what I deem an error in it. . . . You seem . . . to consider the judges as the ultimate arbiters of all constitutional questions; a very dangerous doctrine indeed, and one which would place us under the despotism of an oligarchy. Our judges are as honest as other men, and not more so. They have, with others, the same passions for party, for power, and the privilege of their corps. Their maxim is *"boni judicis est ampliare jurisdictionem"* [the task of a good judge is to expand his jurisdiction], and their power is the more dangerous as they are in office for life, and not responsible, as the other functionaries are, to the elective control. The constitution has erected no such single tribunal, knowing that to whatever hands confided, with the corruptions of time and party, its members would become despots. It has more wisely made all the departments co-equal and co-sovereign within themselves. If the legislature fails to pass laws for a census, for paying the judges and other officers of government, for establishing a militia, for naturalization as prescribed by the constitution, or if they fail to meet in congress, the judges cannot issue their mandamus to them; if the President fails to supply the place of a judge, to appoint other civil or military officers, to issue requisite commissions, the judges cannot force him. They can issue their mandamus or distringas to no executive or legislative officer to enforce the fulfillment of their official duties, any more than the president or legislature may issue

A. A. Lipscomb (ed.), *The Writings of Thomas Jefferson* (Washington: Thomas Jefferson Memorial Association, 1903), XV, 276–279.

orders to the judges or their officers. Betrayed by the English example, and unaware, as it should seem, of the control of our constitution in this particular, they have at times overstepped their limit by undertaking to command executive officers in the discharge of their executive duties; but the constitution, in keeping three departments distinct and independent, restrains the authority of the judges to judiciary organs, as it does the executive and legislative to executive and legislative organs. The judges certainly have more frequent occasion to act on constitutional questions, because the laws of *meum* and *tuum* and of criminal action, forming the great mass of the system of law, constitute their particular department. When the legislative or executive functionaries act unconstitutionally, they are responsible to the people in their elective capacity. The exemption of the judges from that is quite dangerous enough. I know no safe depository of the ultimate powers of the society but the people themselves; and if we think them not enlightened enough to exercise their control with a wholesome discretion, the remedy is not to take it from them, but to inform their discretion by education. This is the true corrective of abuses of constitutional power. . . . My personal interest in such questions is entirely extinct, but not my wishes for the longest possible continuance of our government on its pure principles; if the three powers maintain their mutual independence on each other it may last long, but not so if either can assume the authorities of the other. . . .

2.   *"The Congress, the Executive, and the Court must each . . . be guided by its own opinion of the Constitution."*

ANDREW JACKSON'S VETO OF THE BANK BILL

ON JULY 4, 1832, *Congress passed an Act to continue the Bank of the United States. On July 10, 1832, President Andrew Jackson vetoed the bank bill as unwise, unfair, and unconstitutional. The*

James D. Richardson (ed.), *A Compilation of the Messages and Papers of the Presidents* (Washington: Bureau of National Literature and Art, 1908), II, 581-582.

portion of his veto message dealing with the argument that the constitutionality of the Bank had been definitively settled by the decision of the United States Supreme Court in McCulloch v. *Maryland, 4 Wheaton 316 (1819), is reprinted here. This part of the message was largely drafted by Roger Brooke Taney, who was soon to succeed John Marshall as Chief Justice of the United States.*

IT IS maintained by the advocates of the bank that its constitutionality in all its features ought to be considered as settled by precedent and by the decision of the Supreme Court. To this conclusion I can not assent. Mere precedent is a dangerous source of authority, and should not be regarded as deciding questions of constitutional power except where the acquiescence of the people and the States can be considered as well settled. So far from this being the case on the subject, an argument against the bank might be based on precedent. One Congress, in 1791, decided in favor of a bank; another, in 1811, decided against it. One Congress, in 1815, decided against a bank; another, in 1816, decided in its favor. Prior to the present Congress, therefore, the precedents drawn from that source were equal. If we resort to the States, the expressions of legislative, judicial, and executive opinions against the bank have been probably to those in its favor as 4 to 1. There is nothing in precedent, therefore, which, if its authority were admitted, ought to weigh in favor of the act before me.

If the opinion of the Supreme Court covered the whole ground of this act, it ought not to control the coordinate authorities of this Government. The Congress, the Executive, and the Court must each for itself be guided by its own opinion of the Constitution. Each public officer who takes an oath to support the Constitution swears that he will support it as he understands it, and not as it is understood by others. It is as much the duty of the House of Representatives, of the Senate, and of the President to decide upon the constitutionality of any bill or resolution which may be presented to them for passage or approval as it is of the supreme judges when it may be brought before them for judicial decision. The opinion of the judges has no more authority over Congress than the opinion of Congress has over the judges, and on that point the President is independent of both. The authority of the Supreme Court must not, therefore, be permitted to control the Congress or the Executive when acting in their legislative capacities, but to have only such influence as the force of their reasoning may deserve.

3.

". . . if the policy . . . is to be irrevocably fixed by decisions of the Supreme Court . . . the people will have ceased, to be their own rulers . . ."

ABRAHAM LINCOLN'S FIRST INAUGURAL ADDRESS, MARCH 4, 1861

. . . A MAJORITY, held in restraint by constitutional checks, and limitations, and always changing easily, with deliberate changes of popular opinions and sentiments, is the only true sovereign of a free people. Whoever rejects it, does, of necessity, fly to anarchy or to despotism. Unanimity is impossible; the rule of a minority, as a permanent arrangement, is wholly inadmissible; so that rejecting the majority principle, anarchy, or despotism in some form, is all that is left.

I do not forget the position assumed by some, that constitutional questions are to be decided by the Supreme Court; nor do I deny that such decisions must be binding in any case, upon the parties to a suit, as to the object of that suit, while they are also entitled to a very high respect and consideration, in all parallel cases, by all other departments of government. And while it is obviously possible that such decision may be erroneous in any given case, still the evil effect following it, being limited to that particular case, with the chance that it may be over-ruled, and never become a precedent for other cases, can better be borne than could the evils of a different practice. At the same time the candid citizen must confess that if the policy of the government, upon vital questions, affecting the whole people, is to be irrevocably fixed by decisions of the Supreme Court, the instant they are made, in ordinary litigation between parties, in personal actions, the people will have ceased, to be their own rulers, having to that extent, practically resigned their government, into the hands of that eminent tri-

James D. Richardson (ed.), *A Compilation of the Messages and Papers of the Presidents* (Washington: Bureau of National Literature and Art, 1908), VI, 9.

bunal. Nor is there, in this view, any assault upon the court, or the judges. It is a duty, from which they may not shrink, to decide cases properly brought before them; and it is no fault of theirs, if others seek to turn their decisions to political purposes.

4.   *"We must find a way to take an appeal from the Supreme Court to the Constitution itself."*

REORGANIZING THE FEDERAL JUDICIARY   *Franklin D. Roosevelt*

IN 1933 you and I knew that we must never let our economic system get completely out of joint again—that we could not afford to take the risk of another great depression.

We also became convinced that the only way to avoid a repetition of those dark days was to have a government with power to prevent and to cure the abuses and the inequalities which had thrown that system out of joint.

We then began a program of remedying those abuses and inequalities—to give balance and stability to our economic system—to make it bombproof against the causes of 1929.

Today we are only part way through that program—and recovery is speeding up to a point where the dangers of 1929 are again becoming possible, not this week or month perhaps, but within a year or two.

National laws are needed to complete that program. Individual or local or State effort alone cannot protect us in 1937 any better than 10 years ago. . . . The American people have learned from the depression. For in the last three national elections an overwhelming majority of them voted a mandate that the Congress and the President begin the task of providing that protection—not after long years of debate, but now.

The courts, however, have cast doubts on the ability of the elected Congress to protect us against catastrophe by meeting squarely our modern social and economic conditions.

We are at a crisis in our ability to proceed with that protection. It is a quiet crisis. There are no lines of depositors outside closed banks.

Speech of March 9, 1937. Senate Report No. 711, 75th Cong., 1st Sess., pp. 41–44.

But to the farsighted it is far-reaching in its possibilities of injury to America.

I want to talk with you very simply about the need for present action in this crisis—the need to meet the unanswered challenge of one-third of a nation ill-nourished, ill-clad, ill-housed.

Last Thursday I described the American form of government as a three-horse team provided by the Constitution to the American people so that their field might be plowed. The three horses are, of course, the three branches of government—the Congress, the executive, and the courts. Two of the horses are pulling in unison today; the third is not. Those who have intimated that the President of the United States is trying to drive that team overlook the simple fact that the President, as Chief Executive, is himself one of the three horses.

It is the American people themselves who are in the driver's seat.

It is the American people themselves who want the furrow plowed.

It is the American people themselves who expect the third horse to pull in unison with the other two.

I hope that you have reread the Constitution of the United States. Like the Bible, it ought to be read again and again.

It is an easy document to understand when you remember that it was called into being because the Articles of Confederation under which the Original Thirteen States tried to operate after the Revolution showed the need of a National Government with power enough to handle national problems. In its preamble the Constitution states that it was intended to form a more perfect Union and promote the general welfare; and the powers given to the Congress to carry out those purposes can be best described by saying that they were all the powers needed to meet each and every problem which then had a national character and which could not be met by merely local action.

But the framers went further. Having in mind that in succeeding generations many other problems then undreamed of would become national problems, they gave to the Congress the ample broad powers "to levy taxes . . . and provide for the common defense and general welfare of the United States."

That, my friends, is what I honestly believe to have been the clear and underlying purpose of the patriots who wrote a Federal Constitution to create a National Government with national power, intended as they said, "to form a more perfect union . . . for ourselves and our posterity." . . .

But since the rise of the modern movement for social and economic progress through legislation, the Court has more and more often and more and more boldly asserted a power to veto laws passed by the Congress and State legislatures in complete disregard of this original limitation.

In the last four years the sound rule of giving statutes the benefit of all reasonable doubt has been cast aside. The Court has been acting not as a judicial body, but as a policy-making body.

When the Congress has sought to stabilize national agriculture, to improve the conditions of labor, to safeguard business against unfair competition, to protect our national resources, and in many other ways to serve our clearly national needs, the majority of the Court has been assuming the power to pass on the wisdom of these acts of the Congress—and to approve or disapprove the public policy written into these laws.

That is not only my accusation. It is the accusation of most distinguished justices of the present Supreme Court. I have not the time to quote to you all the language used by dissenting justices in many of these cases. But in the case holding the Railroad Retirement Act unconstitutional, for instance, Chief Justice Hughes said in a dissenting opinion that the majority opinion was "a departure from sound principles," and placed "an unwarranted limitation upon the commerce clause." And three other justices agreed with him.

In the case holding the A.A.A. unconstitutional, Justice Stone said of the majority opinion that it was a "tortured construction of the Constitution." And two other justices agreed with him.

In the case holding the New York Minimum Wage Law unconstitutional, Justice Stone said that the majority were actually reading into the Constitution their own "personal economic predilections," and that if the legislative power is not left free to choose the methods of solving the problems of poverty, subsistence, and health of large numbers in the community, then "government is to be rendered impotent." And two other justices agreed with him. . . .

In the face of such dissenting opinions, it is perfectly clear that as Chief Justice Hughes has said, "We are under a Constitution, but the Constitution is what the judges say it is."

The Court in addition to the proper use of its judicial functions has improperly set itself up as a third House of the Congress—a super-legislature, as one of the justices has called it—reading into the Constitution words and implications which are not there, and which were never intended to be there.

We have, therefore, reached the point as a Nation where we must take action to save the Constitution from the Court and the Court from itself. We must find a way to take an appeal from the Supreme Court to the Constitution itself. We want a Supreme Court which will do justice under the Constitution—not over it. In our courts we want a government of laws and not of men.

I want—as all Americans want—an independent judiciary as proposed by the framers of the Constitution. That means a Supreme Court that will enforce the Constitution as written—that will refuse to amend the Constitution by the arbitrary exercise of judicial power—amendment by judicial say-so. It does not mean a judiciary so independent that it can deny the existence of facts universally recognized. . . .

What is my proposal? It is simply this: Whenever a judge or justice of any federal court has reached the age of seventy and does not avail himself of the opportunity to retire on a pension, a new member shall be appointed by the President then in office, with the approval, as required by the Constitution, of the Senate of the United States.

That plan has two chief purposes: By bringing into the judicial system a steady and continuing stream of new and younger blood, I hope, first, to make the administration of all federal justice speedier and therefore less costly; secondly, to bring to the decision of social and economic problems younger men who have had personal experience and contact with modern facts and circumstances under which average men have to live and work. This plan will save our National Constitution from hardening of the judicial arteries. . . .

Those opposing this plan have sought to arouse prejudice and fear by crying that I am seeking to "pack" the Supreme Court and that a baneful precedent will be established.

What do they mean by the words "packing the Court"?

Let me answer this question with a bluntness that will end all honest misunderstanding of my purposes.

If by that phrase "packing the Court" it is charged that I wish to place on the bench spineless puppets who would disregard the law and would decide specific cases as I wished them to be decided, I make this answer: That no President fit for his office would appoint, and no Senate of honorable men fit for their office would confirm, that kind of appointees to the Supreme Court.

But if by that phrase the charge is made that I would appoint and the Senate would confirm justices worthy to sit beside present members of the Court who understand those modern conditions; that I will appoint justices who will not undertake to override the judgment of the Congress on legislative policy; that I will appoint justices who will act as justices and not as legislators—if the appointment of such justices can be called "packing the Courts"—then I say that I, and with me the vast majority of the American people, favor doing just that thing— now. . . . Our difficulty with the Court today rises not from the Court as an institution but from human beings within it. But we cannot yield our constitutional destiny to the personal judgment of a few men who, being fearful of the future, would deny us the necessary means of dealing with the present.

This plan of mine is no attack on the Court; it seeks to restore the Court to its rightful and historic place in our system of constitutional government and to have it resume its high task of building anew on the Constitution "a system of living law." . . .

5. *"Without jurisdiction the court cannot proceed at all in any cause."*

EX PARTE MC CARDLE

IN 1866 AND 1867 *the Supreme Court declared unconstitutional military trials for civilians in areas where regular civil courts were open, and also voided a federal statute requiring a "test oath" for admission to certain public professions. These decisions threatened to*

7 Wallace 506, 19 L. Ed. 264 (1869).

outlaw the military rule which the Radical Republicans had established in the South. William McCardle, a Mississippi editor, who was being held for trial before a military commission, appealed to the Supreme Court. Ironically, he utilized an 1867 statute intended to protect officials administering the Reconstruction program. To avert a decision that most of the Reconstruction program was unconstitutional, Congress in 1868 repealed—over Johnson's veto—the 1867 act which gave the Supreme Court appellate jurisdiction in the case. The Court heard the McCardle *case in time to decide it prior to repeal of the statute; but over bitter protests from two justices the majority delayed a decision until after the repeal.*

ARGUMENT OF COUNSEL. . . .

Mr. Sharkey, for the appellant:

The prisoner alleged an illegal imprisonment. The imprisonment was justified under certain acts of Congress. The question then presents a case arising under "the laws of the United States"; and by the very words of the Constitution the judicial power of the United States extends to it. By words of the Constitution, equally plain, that judicial power is vested in one Supreme Court. This court, then, has its jurisdiction directly from the Constitution, not from Congress. The jurisdiction being vested by the Constitution alone, Congress cannot abridge or take it away. The argument which would look to Congressional legislation as a necessity to enable this court to exercise "the judicial power" (any and every judicial power) "of the United States," renders a power, expressly given by the Constitution, liable to be made of no effect by the inaction of Congress. Suppose that Congress never made any exceptions or any regulations in the matter. What, under a supposition that Congress must define when, and where, and how, the Supreme Court shall exercise it, becomes of this "judicial power of the United States," so expressly, by the Constitution, given to this court? It would cease to exist. But this court is coexistent and co-ordinate with Congress, and must be able to exercise the whole judicial power of the United States, though Congress passed no act on the subject. . . .

Now, can Congress thus interfere with cases on which this high tribunal has passed, or is passing, judgment? Is not legislation like this an exercise by the Congress of judicial power? . . .

Messrs. L. Trumbull and M. H. Carpenter, contra:

1. The Constitution gives to this court appellate jurisdiction in any case like the present one was, only with such exceptions and under such regulations as Congress makes.

2. It is clear, then, that this court had no jurisdiction of this proceeding—*an appeal from the Circuit Court*—except under the act of February 5th, 1867. . . .

3. The act conferring the jurisdiction having been repealed, the jurisdiction ceased; and the court had thereafter no authority to pronounce any opinion or render any judgment in this cause. . . .

The Chief Justice [CHASE] delivered the opinion of the court.

The first question necessarily is that of jurisdiction; for, if the act of March, 1868, takes away the jurisdiction defined by the act of February, 1867, it is useless, if not improper, to enter into any discussion of other questions.

It is quite true, as was argued by the counsel for the petitioner, that the appellate jurisdiction of this court is not derived from acts of Congress. It is, strictly speaking, conferred by the Constitution. But it is conferred "with such exceptions and under such regulations as Congress shall make." . . .

The source of that jurisdiction, and the limitations of it by the Constitution and by statute, have been on several occasions subjects of consideration here. In the case of *Durousseau* v. *The United States,* particularly, the whole matter was carefully examined, and the court held, that while "the appellate powers of this court are not given by the judicial act, but are given by the Constitution," they are, nevertheless, "limited and regulated by that act, and by such other acts as have been passed on the subject." The court said, further, that the judicial act was an exercise of the power given by the Constitution to Congress "of making exceptions to the appellate jurisdiction of the Supreme Court." "They have described affirmatively," said the court, "its jurisdiction, and this affirmative description has been understood to imply a negation of the exercise of such appellate power as is not comprehended with it."

The principle that the affirmation of appellate jurisdiction implies the negation of all such jurisdiction not affirmed having been thus established, it was an almost necessary consequence that acts of Congress, providing for the exercise of jurisdiction, should come to be spoken of as acts granting jurisdiction, and not as acts making exceptions to the constitutional grant of it.

The exception to appellate jurisdiction in the case before us, however, is not an inference from the affirmation of other appellate jurisdiction. . . . The provision of the act of 1867, affirming the appellate jurisdiction of this court in cases of *habeas corpus* is expressly repealed. It is hardly possible to imagine a plainer instance of positive exception.

We are not at liberty to inquire into the motives of the legislature. We can only examine into its power under the Constitution; and the power to make exceptions to the appellate jurisdiction of this court is given by express words.

What, then, is the effect of the repealing act upon the case before us? We cannot doubt as to this. Without jurisdiction the court cannot proceed at all in any cause. Jurisdiction is power to declare the law, and when it ceases to exist, the only function remaining to the court is that of announcing the fact and dismissing the cause. And this is not less clear upon authority than upon principle. . . .

It is quite clear, therefore, that this court cannot proceed to pronounce judgment in this case, for it has no longer jurisdiction of the appeal; and judicial duty is not less fitly performed by declining ungranted jurisdiction than in exercising firmly that which the Constitution and the laws confer.

Counsel seem to have supposed, if effect be given to the repealing act in question, that the whole appellate power of the court, in cases of *habeas corpus,* is denied. But this is an error. The act of 1868 does not except from that jurisdiction any cases but appeals from Circuit Courts under the act of 1867. It does not affect the jurisdiction which was previously exercised.

The appeal of the petitioner in this case must be

Dismissed for want of jurisdiction.

6.   *"To limit the appellate jurisdiction of the Supreme Court . . ."*

S. 2646, 85TH CONGRESS, 1ST SESSION (1957); INTRODUCED BY SENATOR WILLIAM JENNER (REPUBLICAN, INDIANA)

A BILL TO limit the appellate jurisdiction of the Supreme Court in certain cases.

Be it enacted by the Senate and House of Representatives of the United States of America in Congress assembled, That (a) chapter 81 of title 28 of the United States Code is amended by adding at the end thereof the following new section:

§ 1258. Limitation on appellate jurisdiction of the Supreme Court.

Notwithstanding the provisions of sections 1253, 1254, and 1257 of this chapter, the Supreme Court shall have no jurisdiction to review, either by appeal, writ of certiorari, or otherwise, any case where there is drawn into question the validity of—

(1) any function or practice of, or the jurisdiction of, any committee or subcommittee of the United States Congress, or any action or proceeding against a witness charged with contempt of Congress;

(2) any action, function, or practice of, or the jurisdiction of, any officer or agency of the executive branch of the Federal Government in the administration of any program established pursuant to an Act of Congress or otherwise for the elimination from service as employees in the executive branch of individuals whose retention may impair the security of the United States Government;

(3) any statute or executive regulation of any State the general purpose of which is to control subversive activities within such State;

(4) any rule, bylaw, or regulation adopted by a school board, board of education, board of trustees, or similar body, concerning subversive activities in its teaching body; and

(5) any law, rule, or regulation of any State, or of any board of bar examiners, or similar body, or of any action or proceeding

taken pursuant to any such law, rule, or regulation pertaining to the admission of persons to the practice of law within such State.

(b) The analysis of such chapter is amended by adding at the end thereof the following new item:

1258. Limitation on the appellate jurisdiction of the Supreme Court.

Amended in the Judiciary Committee, this bill was defeated in the Senate on August 20, 1958, by a 49–41 vote.

7.   *"Do the courts of the States stand . . . in the relation of the inferior to the Supreme Court of the United States?"*

A DISCOURSE ON THE CONSTITUTION AND GOVERNMENT OF THE UNITED STATES   *John C. Calhoun*

. . . NOW, AS there is nothing in the constitution which vests authority in the government of the United States, or any of its departments, to enforce its decision against that of the separate government of a State; and nothing in this clause [Art. III, Sec. 2, U.S. Con.] which makes the several States amenable to its process, it is manifest that there is nothing in it, which can possibly give the judicial power authority to enforce the decision of the government of the United States, against that of a separate State. . . .

It is, in the last place, contended,—that the Supreme Court of the United States has the right to decide on the constitutionality of all laws; and, in virtue of this, to decide, in the last resort, all questions involving a conflict between the constitution of the United States and laws and treaties made in pursuance thereof, on the one side, and the constitutions and laws of the several States on the other.

It is admitted, that the court has the right, in all questions of a judicial character which may come before it, where the laws and treaties of the United States, and the constitution and laws of a State are in conflict or brought in question, to decide which is, or is not consistent with the constitution of the United States. But it is denied that

Richard Crallé (ed.), *The Works of John C. Calhoun* (Charleston: Walker and James, 1851), I, 259–260, 263–265, 321–325, 338.

this power is peculiar to it; or that its decision, in the last resort, is binding on any but the parties to it, and its co-departments. So far from being peculiar to it, the right appertains, not only to the Supreme Court of the United States, but to all courts of the several States, superior and inferior. . . . Now, as the constitution of the United States is, within its sphere, supreme over all others appertaining to the system, it necessarily results, that where any law conflicts with it, it is the duty of the court, before which the question arises, to pronounce the constitution to be paramount. If it be the Supreme Court of the United States, its decision,—being that of the highest judicial tribunal, in the last resort, of the parties to the case or controversy,—is, of course, final as it respects them,—but only as it respects them. It results, that its decision is not binding as between the United States and the several States, as neither can make the other defendant in any controversy between them. . . .

[Calhoun moves to a discussion of Sec. 25 of the Judiciary Act of 1789.] The question is thus narrowed down to a single point;—Has Congress the authority . . . to make a law providing for an appeal from the courts of the several States to the Supreme Court of the United States?

There is, on the face of the two clauses [the jurisdictional clauses of Art. III], nothing whatever to authorize the making of such a law. Neither of them names or refers, in the slightest manner to the States, or to the courts of the States; or gives the least authority, apparently, to legislate over or concerning either. The object of the former of these two clauses, is simply to extend the judicial power, so as to make it commensurate with the other powers of the government. . . . While the latter simply provides, in what cases the Supreme Court of the United States shall have original, and in what, appellate jurisdiction. . . .

Such being the plain meaning and intent of these clauses,—the question is;—How can Congress derive from them, authority to make a law providing for an appeal from the highest courts of the several States, in the cases specified in the 25th sect. of the Judiciary Act, to the Supreme Court of the United States?

To this question no answer can be given, without assuming that the State courts,—even the highest,—stand in the relation of inferior courts to the Supreme Court of the United States, wherever a question touching their authority comes before them. Without such an assumption, there is not, and cannot be a shadow of authority to warrant an appeal from the former to the latter. But does the fact sustain the assumption? Do the courts of the States stand, as to such questions, in the relation of the inferior to the Supreme Court of the United States? If so, it must be by some provision of the constitution of the United States. It cannot be a matter of course. How can it be reconciled with the admitted principle, that the federal government and those of the several States, are each supreme in their respective spheres? Each, it is admitted, is supreme, as it regards the other, in its proper sphere; and, of course, as has been shown, coequal and co-ordinate.

If this be true, then, the respective departments of each must be necessarily and equally so;—as the whole includes the parts. The State courts are the representatives of the reserved rights, vested in the governments of the several States, as far as it relates to the judicial power. Now, as these are reserved *against* the federal government,— as the very object and intent of the reservation, was to place them beyond the reach of its control,—how can the courts of the States be inferior to the Supreme Court of the United States; and, of course, subject to have their decisions re-examined and reversed by it, without, at the same time, subjecting the portion of the reserved rights of the governments of the several States, vested in it, to the control of the federal government? . . .

I have now shown that the 25th section of the judiciary act is unauthorized by the constitution; and that it rests on an assumption which would give to Congress the right to enforce, through the judiciary department, whatever measures it might think proper to adopt; and to put down all resistance by force. The effect of this is to make the government of the United States the sole judge . . . as to the extent of its powers, and to place the States and their separate governments and institutions at its mercy. . . .

8.   *"We pledge ourselves to use all lawful means to bring about a reversal of this decision . . ."*

THE SOUTHERN MANIFESTO

THE UNWARRANTED decision of the Supreme Court in the public school cases is now bearing the fruit always produced when men substitute naked power for established law.

The Founding Fathers gave us a Constitution of checks and balances because they realized the inescapable lesson of history that no man or group of men can be safely entrusted with unlimited power. They framed this Constitution with its provisions for change by amendment in order to secure the fundamentals of government against the dangers of temporary popular passion or the personal predilections of public officeholders.

We regard the decision of the Supreme Court in the school cases as a clear abuse of judicial power. It climaxes a trend in the federal judiciary undertaking to legislate, in derogation of the authority of Congress, and to encroach upon the reserved rights of the States and the people.

The original Constitution does not mention education. Neither does the 14th amendment nor any other amendment. The debates preceding the submission of the 14th amendment clearly show that there was no intent that it should affect the system of education maintained by the States.

The very Congress which proposed the amendment subsequently provided for segregated schools in the District of Columbia.

When the amendment was adopted in 1868, there were 37 States of the Union. Every one of the 26 States that had any substantial racial differences among its people, either approved the operation of segregated schools already in existence or subsequently established such schools by action of the same law-making body which considered the 14th amendment. . . .

"A Declaration of Constitutional Principles," signed by 19 southern Senators and 77 Representatives on March 12, 1956. 102 *Congressional Record* 4460; 1 *Race Relations Law Reporter* 435 (1956).

This interpretation [the "separate but equal" principle], restated time and again, became a part of the life of the people of many of the States and confirmed their habits, customs, traditions, and way of life. It is founded on elementary humanity and common sense, for parents should not be deprived by Government of the right to direct the lives and education of their own children.

Though there has been no constitutional amendment or act of Congress changing this established legal principle almost a century old, the Supreme Court of the United States, with no legal basis for such action, undertook to exercise their naked judicial power and substituted their personal political and social ideas for the established law of the land.

This unwarranted exercise of power by the Court, contrary to the Constitution, is creating chaos and confusion in the States principally affected. It is destroying the amicable relations between the white and Negro races that have been created through 90 years of patient effort by the good people of both races. It has planted hatred and suspicion where there has been heretofore friendship and understanding.

Without regard to the consent of the governed, outside agitators are threatening immediate and revolutionary changes in our public-school system. If done, this is certain to destroy the system of public education in some of the States.

With the gravest concern for the explosive and dangerous condition created by this decision and inflamed by outside meddlers:

We reaffirm our reliance on the Constitution as the fundamental law of the land.

We decry the Supreme Court's encroachments on rights reserved to the States and to the people, contrary to established law, and to the Constitution.

We commend the motives of those States which have declared the intention to resist forced integration by any lawful means.

We appeal to the States and people who are not directly affected by these decisions to consider the constitutional principles involved against the time when they too, on issues vital to them, may be the victims of judicial encroachment.

Even though we constitute a minority in the present Congress, we have full faith that a majority of the American people believe in the dual system of government which has enabled us to achieve our greatness and will in time demand that the reserved rights of the States and of the people be made secure against judicial usurpation.

We pledge ourselves to use all lawful means to bring about a reversal of this decision which is contrary to the Constitution and to prevent the use of force in its implementation.

In this trying period, as we all seek to right this wrong, we appeal to our people not to be provoked by the agitators and troublemakers invading our States and to scrupulously refrain from disorder and lawless acts.

9.   *". . . a question of contested power has arisen . . ."*

ALABAMA'S NULLIFICATION RESOLUTION

WHEREAS THE Constitution of the United States was formed by the sanction of the several states, given by each in its sovereign capacity; and

WHEREAS the states being the parties to the constitutional compact, it follows of necessity that there can be no tribunal above their authority to decide, in the last resort, whether the compact made by them be violated; and, consequently, they must decide themselves in the last resort, such questions as may be of sufficient magnitude to require their interposition; and

WHEREAS a question of contested power has arisen: The Supreme Court of the United States asserts, for its part, that the states did, in fact, in 1868 upon the adoption of the Fourteenth Amendment, prohibit unto themselves the power to maintain racially separate public institutions; the State of Alabama, for its part, asserts that it and its sister states have never surrendered such right; and

WHEREAS this assertion upon the part of the Supreme Court of the United States, accompanied by threats of coercion and compulsion

Act No. 42, 1956 Special Session of the Alabama Legislature. 1 *Race Relations Law Reporter* 437 (1956).

against the sovereign states of this Union, constitutes a deliberate, palpable, and dangerous attempt by the court to prohibit to the states certain rights and powers never surrendered by them; and

WHEREAS the question of contested power asserted in this resolution is not within the province of the court to determine, but that as in other cases in which one party to a compact asserts an infraction thereof, the judgment of all other equal parties to the compact must be sought to resolve the question; be it

RESOLVED By the Legislature of Alabama, Both Houses Thereof Concurring:

That until the issue between the State of Alabama and the General Government is decided by the submission to the states, pursuant to Article V of the Constitution, of a suitable constitutional amendment that would declare, in plain and unequivocal language, that the states do surrender their power to maintain public schools and other public facilities on a basis of separation as to race, the Legislature of Alabama declares the decisions and orders of the Supreme Court of the United States relating to separation of races in the public schools are, as a matter of right, null, void, and of no effect; and the Legislature of Alabama declares to all men as a matter of right, this State is not bound to abide thereby; we declare, further, our firm intention to take all appropriate measures honorably and constitutionally available to us, to avoid this illegal encroachment upon our rights, and to urge upon our sister states their prompt and deliberate efforts to check further encroachment by the General Government, through judicial legislation, upon the reserved powers of all states. . . .

This resolution became an Act on February 2, 1956 without approval of the Governor.

10. *". . . there is a considerable latitude of modes of compliance with a decision . . ."*

THE IMPACT OF A COURT DECISION: AFTERMATH OF THE MC COLLUM CASE

*Gordon Patric**

IN 1948 *the U. S. Supreme Court ruled in* McCollum v. Board of Education *that it was a violation of the First Amendment's ban against establishment of religion for a local school board to allow use by religious organizations of public school facilities during regular school hours for the purpose of giving religious instruction to students who wished to receive instruction.*

. . . MC COLLUM WAS remanded to the Illinois Supreme Court and ultimately a writ of mandamus was served on Champaign School Board Number 71. The writ read:

> [I]t is hereby ordered that (1) the Board of Education of Community Unit School District Number 4, Champaign County, Illinois, immediately adopt and enforce rules and regulations prohibiting all instruction in the teaching of religious education in the manner heretofore conducted by said School District Number 71 . . . in all public school houses and buildings in said district when occupied by public schools; and (2) to prohibit within said original School District Number 71 the use of the state's public school machinery to help enroll pupils in the religious classes of sectarian groups.

The weekday religious education program in Champaign ended, but the Protestant pastors who had sponsored it substituted another. Their new program was established after school hours on public school property. The supporters of this new program paid the local school officials a rental fee and went ahead with the new arrangement. This was much less successful than the first Champaign plan. It faltered and was dissolved in 1950. Enrollments had lagged, attendance had fallen off, and the sponsors of the program had difficulties in getting

6 *Journal of Public Law* 455 (1957). Copyright 1957 Emory University School of Law. Reprinted with permission.

* Assistant Professor of Political Science, Loyola University (Chicago).

instructors. But these local developments were only one small part of the pattern of compliance which evolved from the *McCollum* decision.

DIVERSITIES IN INTERPRETION AND COMPLIANCE . . .

A. *Weekday programs involving public school time and property*

A large number of weekday programs were terminated as a result of the Court's holding in *McCollum*. Some were closed down immediately. Some continued for weeks or even until the end of the school year the following June. In some of these cases, the initiative for ending the programs was supplied by school or other public officials; in others, churchmen supplied the initiative. In the cities of Elgin and Rockford, programs which had provided weekday religious instruction to about thirty-seven hundred school children were ended. The Elgin program was completely terminated—after eleven years of operation. On March 9, 1948, the day after the Supreme Court of the United States reversed the courts of Illinois, Rockford school authorities expressed unwillingness to break up their on-premises plan prior to a directive from the Illinois Superintendent of Public Instruction. The sponsoring churchmen, on the other hand, were certain that their weekday classes would have to be withdrawn from public school buildings. This was done; plans were considered for a substitute weekday program, but failed to materialize.

On-premises programs were overturned in the city of Peoria and several smaller communities in central Illinois. Shortly after the *McCollum* decision, the elaborate on-premises weekday system in the city of Peoria and outlying communities collapsed. Prior to the ruling, this was probably the largest weekday program in central Illinois. . . . The central Illinois communities of Cornell and Carlock also decided to end their programs of instruction in the public schools. A few miles southeast of Peoria, at Pekin, the result was the same, but was achieved more slowly. The superintendent of the Pekin public schools ruled that the weekday classes could continue on school time and property until June 1948, the end of the school year. . . .

In Granite City, in southern Illinois, the sponsoring Protestant pastors and school officials decided not to launch a substitute program.

Enforcement of *McCollum* with reference to on-premises programs was also extensive in North Dakota and in Michigan. In Michigan religious classes which had been held during school time were withdrawn from about five hundred public school buildings. The directors of the North Dakota Inter-Church Council agreed that on-premises weekday religious instruction had to end in North Dakota. Before the decision, that body had established, directed and co-ordinated weekday classes which were then being held on school time and grounds in several parts of the state. . . .

The issue remained in doubt, for the time being at least, in some communities. This was true in the town of Kewanee. There the school authorities asked for a decision from the sponsoring clergymen, whose spokesman insisted that discontinuance was out of the question. He explained that the ministers wanted to drop the on-premises program and erect a constitutional one in its place.

On the other hand, no changes were made as a result of the decision in some of the communities which had programs of religious instruction held in school buildings during classroom time. For example, no changes whatsoever were made in the northern Illinois communities of Zion and Polo. Zion officials accomplished this simply by postponing any decision as to change. Some of the elementary school officials declared that they wanted to wait and observe the effects of the decision elsewhere before making any changes. The position of the president of the local school board was that religious classes conducted in Zion public school buildings partially on school time were not affected since "they were no expense to the taxpayer." The Polo program was more than twenty-five years old. Here the response was definite. After the decision, the participating Polo ministers declared that their arrangement was going to continue. Lay leaders in the area felt the same way.

On-premises weekday classes in West Salem, a southern Illinois community, also survived the *McCollum* decision. The sponsoring clergymen and their friends insisted that no changes be made. None were, and the weekday plan in West Salem still exists on an on-premises basis.

Shortly after the *McCollum* decision, Virginia's Attorney General . . . ruled that religion classes on public school time and premises could continue in Virginia. The decision met with general agreement from state public education officials and Protestant leaders of the Virginia Council of Churches. This response meant that in counties such as Alleghany, Augusta, Fairfax and Shenandoah, on-premises weekday classes were not ended. The Attorney General held that the *McCollum* decision pertained to another practice: that it made unconstitutional the handling by public school authorities of any of the administrative matters involved in the conduct of a program of weekday religious instruction.

Between closing of on-premises classes after learning of the Court's decision and no action as a result of that decision, individuals responsible for local programs took a variety of other actions in a number of instances. The sponsors in Oak Park and River Forest found it necessary to make a transition in these Chicago suburbs. After the *McCollum* decision, they held classes in local churches after school hours. Their revised program had no connection with public school schedules and facilities.

The weekday program in Oregon, Illinois, was only temporarily suspended while local Protestant ministers were disengaging their weekday classes from the use of public school facilities. A new program was launched in which the weekday classes were scheduled in local churches during school hours.

In the city of Decatur, classes were removed from public schools within two weeks after the *McCollum* decision. Later, local clergymen who had participated in the former program and school officials agreed that religious instruction could be given in school buildings before the beginning of the school day. This result was also reached in Sterling and Rock Falls. . . . Here, too, the pastors behind the local weekday program came forward later with the proposal that weekday classes be conducted in the school buildings before school began in the morning. . . .

B. Implementation and programs utilizing public school time only

. . . Immediately after the decision of the Court, the Chicago Board of Education declared that *McCollum* did not apply to the program there. It had been the practice in Chicago since 1929 to permit public school pupils to receive religious instruction during school hours in neighborhood churches or other centers. School authorities in New York took the same position. New York City Superintendent of Schools, William Jansen, declared that no changes were going to be made as a result of the *McCollum* decision; that public school pupils were still going to be allowed religious instruction on released time. . . .

Several groups opposed this stand. They stood for sweeping interpretation and an extended application of the *McCollum* decision. Frank E. Karelson, Jr., Vice-President of the Public Education Association, argued to this effect two days after *McCollum* was decided. Rabbi William F. Rosenblum, President of the Synagogue Council of America, and Henry Epstein, Chairman of the National Community Relations Advisory Council, said the same thing in behalf of their organizations. So did spokesmen for the American Civil Liberties Union. But New York school authorities did not change their stand and as a result these groups, which opposed released-time instruction, and other groups joined to support two Brooklyn women, Mrs. Tessim Zorach and Mrs. Esta Gluck, when they later brought suit challenging the constitutionality of the program in New York City. . . .

Thus, indications are that in those states where legislators favored religious instruction on public school time before *McCollum,* and where state officials did not view it as unconstitutional after the decision, changes in weekday programs were unlikely to occur because of the decision.

However, there were a few instances in which weekday religion programs involving only public school time were ended because of the *McCollum* decision. The Court's ruling was the reason the public school superintendent at Bethalto and Cottage Hills, Illinois, terminated the weekday programs there. In New Orleans, Louisiana, a rather extensive weekday program involving only public school time was abolished. There Protestant leaders of the city's Church Council, the co-ordinating body for several local Protestant denominations, gave up their weekday classes. Roman Catholic authorities in New Orleans had launched an identical program about 1937 but made no changes in it whatsoever. It appears that the advocates of weekday religion— those who helped to establish the programs prior to the decision or those who were not then opposed to them—decided that only on-premises weekday programs had to be ended or altered because of the *McCollum* decision.

C. *Extensive enforcement advocated by the opponents of weekday religion*

Some of the opponents of weekday religion, and many of the people who changed their weekday policies following the *McCollum* decision, agreed with the advocates that on-premises programs were the ones affected by the decision. After the ruling, Lutheran leaders of the Missouri Synod in North Dakota urged the state school officials to help end on-premises programs. The school officials did this after first persuading the Protestant leaders of the Inter-Church Council, which sponsored the programs, that they had to end. In Michigan, on the other hand, the state public education officials took the initiative and declared that on-premises programs had to be abolished because of the *McCollum* decision.

As noted above, many opponents of weekday religion have insisted upon extensive enforcement of the *McCollum* decision. This was the stand taken by some of the American Civil Liberties Union members in regard to the weekday program in St. Louis, Missouri. They and local school authorities agreed that the Supreme Court's decision required the abolition of a weekday plan which occupied public school time. Their theory was that the program had entailed coercion since the pupils who did not take the classes had to remain at the schools. In Portland, Oregon, Jewish groups were able to introduce a change in the school-time weekday classes sponsored by Protestant groups and Roman Catholics. These Jewish groups insisted that the *McCollum* decision prevented Portland school officials from distributing enrollment cards for weekday classes in public school facilities. . . .

CONCLUSION

. . . When it came to putting the Court's decision into effect, which people were most influential? In most instances, decisions were made by state governmental officials (principally attorneys general and public education authorities), local public school officials, Protestant churchmen, and other religious groups. These, of course, were the people most closely associated with weekday religion programs. . . . After the decision, these same people interpreted the Court's ruling and were usually responsible for putting it into effect—particularly where there was no local pressure for maximum compliance. In general, the advocates of weekday religion and those who neither favored the decision nor sought compliance with it were most influential in determining the pattern of compliance. On the other hand, the groups which supported the Court's ruling exercised much less influence. In only a few instances (e.g., St. Louis, Missouri and Portland, Oregon), were local opponents of religious instruction able to secure enforcement of the *McCollum* decision with regard to other than on-premises programs. . . .

. . . If any single generalization can be made from this discussion, it is that the impact nation-wide of a Supreme Court decision is by no means uniform. The various patterns of compliance adopted in the local situations where the decision was sought to be enforced indicate that there is a considerable latitude of modes of compliance with a decision of the highest court of the land.

In 1952 the Supreme Court by a 6–3 vote in Zorach v. Clauson *upheld the constitutionality of the New York released-time plan under which school authorities permitted students to leave school property during regular class hours and attend privately run religious instruction. The three dissenters claimed there was no substantial difference between the Illinois and New York situations; in both the coercive power of the state was being used to aid religious education. One of the dissenters said in private that the adverse reaction to the McCollum case had been a major factor in the Zorach decision.*

16 / CHECKS WITHIN THE JUDICIAL BUREAUCRACY

The limitations which the judicial system imposes on trial judges are evident. First, in all important criminal cases as well as in many civil suits, the litigants have a right to trial by jury. While a judge may shield the jurors from some untrustworthy evidence and give them detailed explanations of "the law," the final decision on the facts of a case is theirs. Moreover, under existing legal rules, a judge is not supposed to overturn a jury's verdict if it appears that reasonable men could reasonably have arrived at such a conclusion.

A second check on trial judges—aside from those imposed by their own consciences, community expectations, and newspaper publicity—is the right of appeal. The losing litigant may as a matter of right appeal a federal district judge's decision to the appropriate court of appeals, though of course this does not apply to verdicts of acquittal in criminal prosecutions. In turn, decisions of courts of appeals are reversible by the Supreme Court. Because appellate judges must reach their decisions on a cold written record, they often evidence some reluctance to overturn the judgment of a colleague who presided over the actual trial, but nonetheless reversals of lower-court decisions are quite common.

Checks on Appellate Courts

While the checks which higher courts exercise on lower courts through the process of appellate review are well known, it is not so generally realized that the lower levels of the judicial bureaucracy have their own very effective means for frustrating directions and commands from the higher courts. This should not be surprising, for the fact of bureaucratic resistance is well known in the administrative hierarchy. Practicing politicians as well as students of politics have long recognized the check on presidential power imposed by the federal administrative machinery. High policy must be interpreted; it can sometimes be changed or even frustrated by the bureaucrats who apply laws and executive orders. Officials down the line have interests, loyalties, and ambitions which go beyond and often clash with the allegiance accorded a given tenant of the White House. Each bureaucrat has his own ideas about proper public policy, particularly in his field of special competence. Internal friction or drag is thus an inherent part of the executive process, a factor to be weighed in choosing among policy alternatives, much the same as congressional, or judicial, or pressure-group resistance.

Less obviously, but not necessarily less significantly, a similar bureaucratic factor must be reckoned with in the execution of Supreme Court decisions. Except in disputes between states or the rare litigation involving diplomats, the Supreme Court usually does not render either the initial or the final decision in a case. If it reverses a state decision, the Court remands the case to state courts for disposition "not inconsistent with this opinion"; and it frequently gives only slightly more precise directions in overruling federal tribunals. The Supreme Court typically formulates general policy. Lower-court judges apply that policy, and working in its interstices inferior judges may materially modify the High Court's doctrine.

Much of this lower-court leeway is created by the opinion-writing compromises among the justices. Because of the divergent lines of reasoning which may appear in a single opinion, a trial judge who wishes to hew strictly to the Supreme Court's policy may be left in doubt as to what was dogma and what was dicta. This discretion is further increased by the sheer volume of judicial business. About ninety thousand pieces of litigation are begun each year in federal courts and another million and a half in state tribunals. There is simply no way that nine men could review more than a minute fraction of these cases, even if asked to do so.

State-Court Checks

As might be expected, state judges have a wider field in which to operate. Two technical rules help to enlarge their area of discretion. The first, already mentioned, is that when the Supreme Court reverses a state decision, it seldom directs the state courts to arrive at a particular result; usually the High Bench only orders the state tribunals to proceed in the case in a manner "not inconsistent with this opinion." Second, the Supreme Court will review only those state cases which were based on a substantial federal question. The Court has reiterated time and again its practice of not reviewing state decisions which have sufficient independent grounding in state law so that a reversal of the determinations of federal issues would not affect the final outcome of the case. Whether this doctrine is one of administrative convenience or is a constitutional limitation has been questioned, but as long as it is followed a state appellate judge who is a skillful opinion writer can, when so minded, do much to prevent Supreme Court review, even of federal questions.

Considering the perennial friction between state and national interests and outlooks, the different elements weighed in the appointment of state and federal judges, their allegiances (former if not current) to opposing political parties or to separate levels of party hierarchy, the different ambitions of the judges, and their varying conceptions of the role of the judiciary in a federal and democratic system, the wonder is that occasions of open conflict are the exception rather than the rule. Perhaps the use of the vague remand prescription acts as a psychological safety valve in allowing some of the pressure of resentment against reversal to be released in construing Supreme Court instructions.

An additional safety valve is criticism of Supreme Court decisions, a practice in which judges who have been reversed engage only slightly less bitterly than disappointed litigants. The most serious recent verbal attack came when the 1958 Conference of State Chief Justices issued a sharp accusation that justices of the Supreme Court were usurping state judicial power by confusing their own policy views with constitutional commands. The Conference chose to launch this attack at the strategic moment when congressional assaults against the Supreme Court had reached a climax.

Both these devices permit exercise of power as well as escape of pressure. Criticism may persuade the Court of the error of its ways, or help convince Congress of a need for remedial legislation. The interpreting authority may even be stretched to accomplish a *de facto* overturning of Supreme Court decisions. A *Harvard Law Review* study published in 1954 reported that in eleven terms, some forty-six Supreme Court reversals of state decisions required additional litigation. "In slightly less than half of these cases the party successful in the Supreme Court was unsuccessful in the state court following the remand." This study also indicated that the evasion had usually been accomplished by interpretation rather than by defiance. Whether or not the party who won in the Supreme Court lost at the later remand to the trial court is not an infallible indication of state-court evasion, of course. But it is interesting that winning before the High Bench would have changed the outcome of litigation in only 50 per cent of the cases examined.

The line between evasion and defiance is always difficult to draw, and when in 1954 the Supreme Court declared Jim Crow legally dead, the attitude of many segregationist state judges shifted perceptibly. Yet the manner in which southern judicial resistance has been expressed is significant. These judges have criticized the school segregation decisions on and off the bench; they were among the leaders of the movement in the 1958 Conference of State Chief Justices to reprimand the Supreme Court. They have given moral support and perhaps, one may guess, legal advice to southern political leaders. But when pressed, no state supreme court has yet failed to concede that the school segregation cases are the law of the land and binding on lower courts. Resistance of state supreme courts (and, though not universally, of state lower courts) has taken three specific forms: (1) refusing to expand the school decision to other areas; (2) upholding the constitutionality of state efforts to evade compliance; and (3), in line with the state chief justices' censure, balking at Supreme Court decisions in related areas of race and of federal-state relations.

Federal Court Checks

There are both similarities and differences between the political relations of state courts and lower federal courts to the Supreme Court. Formal state-federal competition is absent, but it is often replaced by a local-national clash which can be almost equally abrasive. This, in turn, is affected by the varying considerations involved in the appointment of lower and Supreme Court judges. Even if Eisenhower's judicial probation-promotion policy is continued, High Court members are likely to be different types of men from those usually selected for the lower bench.

When the normal friction between trial and appellate judges is added to these other factors, a substantial reservoir of potential conflict has been built up. On the other hand, several forces act to soften this strife. First, and this bond unites federal with state judges as well as the three levels of federal judges with each other, they are all participants in the cult of the robe. They share the same holy mysteries and dispense the same sacred doctrine. No matter how fierce their inter-court rivalries, common possession of this magic sets judges apart from the rest of men and gives them interests and outlooks as *judges*. Second, district, circuit, and Supreme Court judges are all *federal* officials, and therefore, in a sense, joint competitors, whether they like it or not, with state judges for power.

The concept of an independent judiciary, which can increase the number of collisions between state and national tribunals, is balanced within the national system by appellate court supervision which, if it does not prevent conflict, does help keep that conflict from coming out into the open. A state judge owes his appointment to local political groups and can be removed, if at all, only by state action. Federal district and circuit judges are made even more independent by their life tenure, but their inferior position in the hierarchical chain of national authority subjects them to more strict Supreme Court surveillance. Under its power as supervisor of the administration of federal justice, the Supreme Court can set more exacting standards for lower courts of the United States than for state tribunals.

This makes federal-court defiance less likely than state, but district and circuit judges are not mere pawns in the judicial game. They, too, can lash out in caustic criticism. In 1958, for example, the Court of Appeals for the Ninth Circuit reversed the conviction of a pair of Communist leaders on the basis of the Supreme Court's narrow interpretations of the Smith Act in *Yates* v. *United States*. Judge Chambers remarked tartly that the court would have upheld the validity of the convictions on the basis of past practice had not the Supreme Court changed the law. "One may as well recognize that the Yates decision leaves the Smith Act, as to any further prosecutions under it, a virtual shambles—unless the American Communist Party should witlessly set out to reconstitute itself again with a new 'organization.' "

The reactions of a number of lower federal judges to the state chief justices' censure of the Supreme Court were no more subtle. The *U.S. News and World Report* polled all district and circuit judges, asking if they agreed or disagreed with the report of the state chief justices. Only 128 of 351 answered, and of these 59 expressed approval, 50 disapproval, and 19 voiced no opinion.

Another channel of criticism, more discreet but also more directly aimed at securing remedial congressional action, is the judicial conference, at either the national or circuit level. Several times in recent years the Judicial Conference of the United States has endorsed bills to reverse Supreme Court decisions allowing relatively liberal opportunities for state prisoners to seek habeas corpus in federal courts; and the Judicial Conference of the District of Columbia recommended to Congress in 1958 that it adopt legislation to reverse Supreme Court decisions holding confessions inadmissible in evidence in federal courts if the police delayed unnecessarily in bringing the accused before a magistrate to be informed of the nature of the charge against him and of his constitutional rights to silence and to consult with a lawyer.

Lower-court judges are often asked to decide problems on which the Supreme Court has not yet passed judgment. In deciding such cases these judges can do, once removed, what Supreme Court justices occasionally do in analogous situations. For the High Court's question, "What would the Founding Fathers or Congress have willed had they foreseen the case at bar?" the lower courts can substitute, "What would the Supreme Court have visualized the Framers or Congress as willing had the Supreme Court foreseen this case?" This kind of speculation comes close to giving oneself a blank check.

Further complications enter when judges sense shifts in Supreme Court policy. "It is a little difficult," Charles Curtis once observed, "for the lower court to have to follow the Supreme Court of the next succeeding year." Two schools of thought tell lower courts how to handle such problems. One, represented by the late Jerome Frank, feels that "when a lower court perceives a pronounced new doctrinal trend in Supreme Court decisions, it is its duty, cautiously to be sure, to follow not to resist it." In a footnote to this statement, Frank added: "To use mouthfilling words, cautious extrapolation is in order."

But prediction is a risky enterprise and guesses, no matter how informed, can be and have been wrong. In 1949, for example, Judge Frank thought that the Supreme Court had turned into an "impotent zombi" its 1922 decision that professional baseball was beyond the scope of congressional regulatory power, and consequently outside the reach of the Sherman Act. In 1953, however, the Supreme Court continued baseball's antitrust immunity, though not affirming all that the earlier case had implied.

Recognition of the prediction risk lies behind the views of a more conservative school of thought which holds that inferior judges should follow doubtful precedents until the Supreme Court specifically voids them. As Chief Judge Calvert Magruder of the First Circuit has said: "We should always express a respectful deference to controlling decisions of the Supreme Court, and do our best to follow them. We should leave it to the Supreme Court to overrule its own cases."

Magruder was taking an instrumental rather than an ideological position, however. He admitted that when a new situation arises a lower court has two choices: either to concentrate on previous Supreme Court opinions and milk available dicta for possible guidance, or to strike out afresh and give its own opinion of what the law should be. And Magruder confessed that he himself had used both methods. He conceded further that on one occasion where he was using the second method, "it was necessary to deal somewhat roughly, though very respectfully," with an explicit Supreme Court decision which he thought "shaky."

Perhaps the most significant portion of Judge Magruder's address was his open acknowledgment that lower-court jurists, although mindful of their obligation to the Supreme Court, were sometimes simply unwilling to follow the justices in their interpretation of the law. As an example the judge cited a 1957 decision of his court limiting the definition of a seaman under the Jones Act. The Supreme Court had summarily reversed the Court of Appeals, but, Magruder frankly stated, were the issue to come up once more, "I am afraid that we shall again 'stick our necks out' and say, as a matter of law, that the man is not a seaman, thereby courting another probable reversal by the Supreme Court."

The power of prediction evidently confers considerable latitude on its user. He may be discerning what he believes the future does hold, what he hopes the future will hold, or what he judges the future should hold. Such guessing can influence the Supreme Court, or Congress, and it can also embarrass both by creating not just one but, by the time certiorari is granted and the case heard on review, a whole series of *faits accomplis*. On the other hand, refusal to accord official recognition to changing doctrine can also confer power by concealing or at least giving good form to serious disagreement with the newly developing Supreme Court policy. In South Carolina, District Judge George Bell Timmerman, Sr., father of the governor, twice after 1954 insisted on applying the rule of *Plessy* v. *Ferguson* to bus segregation, asserting that the school cases had only involved education and not transportation. "One's education and personality," Timmerman said disdainfully, "is not developed on a city bus."

The authority to make findings of fact gives trial judges extensive power which appellate tribunals can only partly control. And in the school segregation cases, the Supreme Court broadened the scope of this inherent authority by specifically directing the exercise of the widest sort of judicial discretion, guided only by the flexible formula "with all deliberate speed." This is obviously a grant of vast power, and the High Bench has relied on the courts of appeals to supervise its exercise. Such a policy constitutes a manifestation of faith as well as an invitation for assumption of power. And occasionally a judge will seize the full implications of this invitation. Flying directly in the face of the desegregation ruling, and even after one reversal by the Court of Appeals, District Judge William H. Atwell declined to order Dallas, Texas, to set a date for integration because this would cause "civil wrongs." Lest his own feelings be mistaken, Atwell declared: "I believe that it will be seen that the [Supreme] Court based its decision on no law but rather on what the Court regarded as more authoritative, modern psychological knowledge. . . . It will be recalled that in 1952, Mr. Justice Frankfurter said it was not competent to take judicial notice of 'Claims of social scientists.' "

This is not to deny that most federal judges are trying their best to carry out desegregation in a sincere and workable manner, but even the most imaginative member of the realist school of jurisprudence could hardly conceive of a more fertile field for free play of judicial predilections, conscious and subconscious. As a reaction against this freedom and its resultant responsibility, there is evidence of a growing resentment among lower-court judges in southern and border states, a feeling that they have been left to engage in a violent emotional battle against prevailing white mores while the justices in Washington refuse to stoop to such conflict by daintily denying certiorari in segregation cases.

It is possible that the Court of Appeals for the Eighth Circuit in the August, 1958, phase of the Little Rock campaign was trying to force the Supreme Court's hand when it took the somewhat unusual step of staying its own order to preserve the *status quo*. If the case had not been immediately reviewed by the Supreme Court, the stay would have allowed Central High School to transfer its Negro students and to reopen as a segregated institution. This would have been an immense victory for Governor Faubus' obstructionist tactics.

If the Court of Appeals was trying to compel the High Bench to reiterate its principles and re-enter the fight, the circuit judges succeeded wonderfully well. Both the opinion of the Chief Justice and Frankfurter's concurrence spelled out the Court's constitutional authority and interpretation, as well as its policy intentions, in a far more powerful form than had either of the two previous school decisions.

Counterchecks

The lower courts can and do check the Supreme Court, but the Supreme Court can act to counter lower-court power. While it cannot fire and hire new personnel as the President can sometimes do, the Court can review and reverse inferior judges. This is important beyond any effect on a particular case. Judges do not enjoy the prospect of public correction and reprimand any more than other men. The Supreme Court can put added bite to this psychological whip by sarcasm and scathing criticism of its own. Alternatively, the Court may resort to more diplomatic means and try reasoned persuasion.

In a more subtle fashion, the Supreme Court may nip evasions by means of gratuitous legal advice, a method which almost touches the tabu against advisory opinions. It will be recalled from Chapter 7, for instance, that in its September, 1958, Little Rock opinion the Court managed to warn federal judges and state officials, as well as potential plaintiffs, that it would not look with favor on projected private-school plans.

When confronted with systematic evasion the Supreme Court could, as a last resort, invoke its inherent power to punish for contempt in order to coerce either state or federal judges. But this is as unlikely to be used as is the impeachment and removal power of Congress. More probably, the Court would do as it did in the second restrictive covenant cases[1] and what it indicated it would do in its Little Rock opinion: cast technicalities aside and bring the full weight of its constitutional authority to bear on the substantive issues in the dispute. Or, if the case had originated in a federal court, it might make the final determination of the problems itself. Faced with such counter-measures, lower-court judges would no doubt retreat in an effort both to save face and to salvage as much as possible, realizing that the battle could be continued in the administrative and legislative processes much more easily if a final showdown in the judicial process were avoided.

In such a fashion this aspect of judicial decision-making comes full circle. The Supreme Court must take into account the reaction of inferior judges, and lower courts must attempt to divine the counter-reaction of the Supreme Court. Meanwhile, both must keep a wary eye on public opinion and maneuverings within the other branches of government to ascertain how these will affect the policy concerned. Judges have not solved the dilemmas caused by this feedback process, nor have adminis-

[1] *Barrows* v. *Jackson* (1953).

trators. And if power can be checked only by power, it may be healthy for the continued existence of limited government if neither judicial nor administrative officers ever fully resolve these conflicts.

SELECTED REFERENCES

Bickel, Alexander, *The Unpublished Opinions of Mr. Justice Brandeis* (Cambridge: Harvard University Press, 1957).

Frank, Jerome, *Courts on Trial* (Princeton: Princeton University Press, 1950), Chs. 3, 15, 17.

Magruder, Calvert, "The Trials and Tribulations of an Intermediate Appellate Court," 44 *Cornell Law Quarterly* 1 (1958).

Mason, Alpheus T., *Harlan Fiske Stone* (New York: Viking Press, 1956), III-VI.

Murphy, Walter F., "Lower Court Checks on Supreme Court Power," 53 *American Political Science Review* 1017 (1959).

Note, "Final Disposition of State Court Decisions Reversed and Remanded by the Supreme Court, October Term, 1931 to October Term, 1940," 55 *Harvard Law Review* 1357 (1942).

Note, "State Court Evasion of United States Supreme Court Mandates," 56 *Yale Law Journal* 574 (1947).

Note, "Evasion of Supreme Court Mandates in Cases Remanded to State Courts since 1941," 67 *Harvard Law Review* 1251 (1954).

Note, "Interposition vs. Judicial Power," 1 *Race Relations Law Reporter* 465 (1956).

Truman, David, *The Governmental Process* (New York: A. A. Knopf, 1951), Chs. 13–14.

Warren, Charles, "Federal and State Court Interference," 43 *Harvard Law Review* 345 (1930).

1.　　　　　*"The police may not arrest upon mere suspicion but only on 'probable cause.'"*

CONFESSIONS AND POLICE DETENTION

MALLORY *v.* UNITED STATES

IN 1954 *District of Columbia police arrested Andrew Mallory, a mentally retarded nineteen-year-old Negro, for rape. In spite of Rule 5(a) of the Federal Rules of Criminal Procedure which commands that a person be brought "without unnecessary delay" before a magistrate who will examine the reasons for the arrest and inform the accused of his rights, police interrogated Mallory intermittently for over seven hours without bringing him before a magistrate. At the end of this period, Mallory confessed to the crime. The trial was delayed over a year because the prosecutor doubted the accused understood the nature of the proceedings. At the trial the confession, the only important prosecution evidence, was admitted and Mallory was convicted and sentenced to death. The Court of Appeals affirmed the conviction, but the Supreme Court granted certiorari.*

MR. JUSTICE FRANKFURTER delivered the opinion of the Court. . . .

The case calls for the proper application of Rule 5(a) of the Federal Rules of Criminal Procedure. That Rule provides:

"(a) Appearance Before the Commissioner. An officer making an arrest under a warrant issued upon a complaint or any person making an arrest without a warrant shall take the arrested person without unnecessary delay before the nearest available commissioner or before any other nearby officer empowered to commit persons charged with offenses against the laws of the United States. . . ."

In McNabb v. United States . . . we spelled out the important reasons of policy behind this body of legislation:

354 U.S. 449, 77 S. Ct. 1356, 1 L. Ed. 2d 1479 (1957).

"The purpose of this impressively pervasive requirement of criminal procedure is plain. . . . The awful instruments of the criminal law cannot be entrusted to a single functionary. The complicated process of criminal justice is therefore divided into different parts, responsibility for which is separately vested in the various participants upon whom the criminal law relies for its vindication. Legislation such as this, requiring that the police must with reasonable promptness show legal cause for detaining arrested persons, constitutes an important safeguard—not only in assuring protection for the innocent but also in securing conviction of the guilty by methods that commend themselves to a progressive and self-confident society. For this procedural requirement checks resort to those reprehensible practices known as the 'third degree' which, though universally rejected as indefensible, still find their way into use. It aims to avoid all the evil implications of secret interrogation of persons accused of crime." . . .

The requirement of Rule 5(a) is part of the procedure devised by Congress for safeguarding individual rights without hampering effective and intelligent law enforcement. Provisions related to Rule 5(a) contemplate a procedure that allows arresting officers little more leeway than the interval between arrest and the ordinary administrative steps required to bring a suspect before the nearest available magistrate. . . .

The scheme for initiating a federal prosecution is plainly defined. The police may not arrest upon mere suspicion but only on "probable cause." The next step in the proceeding is to arraign the arrested person before a judicial officer as quickly as possible so that he may be advised of his rights and so that the issue of probable cause may be promptly determined. The arrested person may, of course, be "booked" by the police. But he is not to be taken to police headquarters in order to carry out a process of inquiry that lends itself, even if not so designed, to eliciting damaging statements to support the arrest and ultimately his guilt.

The duty enjoined upon arresting officers to arraign "without unnecessary delay" indicates that the command does not call for mechanical or automatic obedience. Circumstances may justify a brief delay between arrest and arraignment, as for instance, where the story volunteered by the accused is susceptible of quick verification through third parties. But the delay must not be of a nature to give opportunity for the extraction of a confession.

The circumstances of this case preclude a holding that arraignment was "without unnecessary delay." Petitioner was arrested in the early afternoon and was detained at headquarters within the vicinity of numerous committing magistrates. Even though the police had ample evidence from other sources than the petitioner for regarding the petitioner as the chief suspect, they first questioned him for approximately a half hour. When this inquiry of a nineteen-year-old lad of limited intelligence produced no confession, the police asked him to submit to a lie-detector test. He was not told of his rights to counsel or to a preliminary examination before a magistrate, nor was he warned that he might keep silent and "that any statement made by him may be used against him." After four hours of further detention at headquarters, during which arraignment could easily have been made in the same building in which the police headquarters were housed, petitioner was examined by the lie-detector operator for another hour and a half before his story began to waver. Not until he had confessed, when any judicial caution had lost its purpose, did the police arraign him.

We cannot sanction this extended delay, resulting in confession, without subordinating the general rule of prompt arraignment to the discretion of arresting officers in finding exceptional circumstances for its disregard. . . . It is not the function of the police to arrest, as it were, at large and to use an interrogating process at police headquarters in order to determine whom they should charge before a committing magistrate on "probable cause." . . .

Following the McNabb precedent, the Court held the confession inadmissible in evidence and reversed the conviction.

PORTER *v.* UNITED STATES

District of Columbia police arrested Charles Porter at 10:30 P.M., Tuesday, July 31, 1956, on a charge of assault with a dangerous weapon. The prisoner was not brought before a magistrate that night.

258 F. 2d 685 (1958).
United States Court of Appeals for the District of Columbia.

At 11:15 P.M., Tuesday, he made a written statement admitting fighting with the victim, whom he accused of seeing his wife. He repeated this statement orally at about 9 A.M., Wednesday. At about 10 A.M., Wednesday, Porter was taken before a magistrate under Rule 5(a), but before his actual appearance police learned the victim had died. They took Porter back to the station and questioned him further. At 12:45 P.M., Wednesday, Porter made a second written statement containing additional admissions. At 3:30 P.M., Wednesday, seventeen hours after his arrest, Porter was arraigned before a magistrate. Porter was later convicted and appealed, arguing that at least the second written statement was inadmissible under the McNabb and Mallory decisions.

Before: REED, ASSOCIATE JUSTICE OF THE SUPREME COURT, retired,* and BAZELON, and BURGER, CIRCUIT JUDGES.

REED, ASSOCIATE JUSTICE. . . .

First. Under these circumstances, was the admission in evidence of either the first or second statement . . . an error, requiring reversal? Or, stated differently, was the production of the prisoner for preliminary appearance "without unnecessary delay"? . . .

A few words will suffice on the question of the admission of the first statement. . . . No objection was made by defense counsel. The statement was given almost immediately. It was without pressure of any kind except the mere fact of detention. To say it was inadmissible would be to say no statement to police is admissible after arrest—a step that the Supreme Court . . . has declined to adopt. . . . The arrest was past the ordinary hours for appearances. . . . There is no rule of law in federal courts that bars the admissibility of extra-judicial statements of prisoners to the police after arrest and before the time has expired of permissible detention between arrest and appearance before a magistrate.

While we have no doubt that the second [written] statement was made within the period of necessary delay, in advance of the required appearance before a magistrate, a different conclusion is rea-

* Under federal law a retired justice may be asked to sit on a court of appeals to help dispose of a backlog of cases. Reed, it should be noted, had been on the Supreme Court when *McNabb* v. *United States* (1943) first ruled confessions secured during "unnecessary delay" inadmissible in federal courts. Reed had dissented against this ruling.

sonably possible. The result might well depend upon a court's weighing of the interests of society in law enforcement through the disclosure of the actual facts surrounding an alleged criminal act and the protection of a prisoner from being induced, even though without unconstitutional coercion, to make a clean breast of his participation in the action charged. . . .

As for the prisoner's appearance before the magistrate after the charge of manslaughter, we conclude that also was without unnecessary delay. Surely a man arrested Tuesday night at eleven o'clock for assault need not be taken before a magistrate until the next morning. No one will assert, without specific proof, that the personnel of our police departments are so regardless of court rulings on interrogation as to require every prisoner to be taken before a magistrate at midnight for every kind of offense or before the opening of the courts in the morning.

Promptly at usual court hours, though the seriousness of decedent's injuries was already known to the police, but not his death, the prisoner was presented before the court. When the judge heard of the death, he directed the return of the prisoner by the United States Marshal to the City Homicide Squad. On his return, with the probability of a charge of some degree of homicide, what more natural than that the police would take a statement before selecting a charge of murder or manslaughter. It is to be noted that the statement was made after a question as to whether the prisoner wanted to do so. . . . We do not think there was unnecessary delay. . . .

BAZELON, CIRCUIT JUDGE, dissenting. . . .

. . . Rule 5 is the mechanism for effectuating the individual's constitutional rights to be free from restraint except upon probable cause, to be bailed from confinement in proper cases, and not to be compelled to incriminate himself. Whether there is probable cause to detain an arrested person requires a judicial determination. Even if there is such a cause he is entitled, within recognized limitations, to be free on bail pending trial. And he must be informed of his right to counsel and of his right to refuse to make any statement lest he incriminate himself. Without such protection our citizens would be subject to police control rather than due process of law. There would be a police state. . . .

While the phrase "without unnecessary delay" may connote something less than immediacy, it "allows arresting officers little more leeway than the interval between arrest and the ordinary administrative steps required to bring a suspect before the nearest available magistrate." *Mallory* v. *United States.* . . . That the police in the present case thought the "ordinary administrative steps" had been completed is plain from the fact that the prisoner had been taken to court for the Rule 5 commitment proceedings at 10:00 A.M., some twelve hours after his arrest. . . .

The real purpose in delaying the arraignment is disclosed in the Government's alternative contention that it was proper to bring appellant back to police headquarters, without arraigning him, for the purpose of putting in writing the oral statements which appellant had made shortly after 9:00 A.M. . . . This, of course, is a callous admission that the arraignment was postponed and appellant "taken to police headquarters in order to carry out a process of inquiry that lends itself . . . to eliciting damaging statements to support the arrest and ultimately his guilt." *Mallory* v. *United States.* . . . Since this is exactly what the law forbids, the ensuing confession was inadmissible in evidence.

The other confessions discussed in the majority opinion—a written one taken from appellant the night of his arrest and an oral one shortly after 9:00 o'clock the next morning—are not before us. Both were received in evidence without objection and neither was attacked on appeal. Yet the majority considers them and concludes that they were admissible under *Mallory* v. *United States.* . . . I consider that conclusion clearly erroneous.

I hold to the view that confessions obtained through police interrogation of an arrested person before he has been arraigned under Rule 5 are inadmissible. . . .

The majority also asserts that appellant's arrest occurred "past the ordinary hours for appearances" and concludes that this circumstance gave the police a license not only to postpone his arraignment until the opening of court the next day but also to question him in the interval. There are no "ordinary hours for appearances." . . . The United States Commissioner is available for night time arraignments when the Government sees fit to have a prisoner arraigned without delay. Recently a rotation system was established among the sixteen Municipal

Court judges whereby at least one of them is available for arraignment of arrested persons at any hour of the day or night. . . .

TESTIMONY OF HON. ALEXANDER HOLTZOFF, U.S. DISTRICT JUDGE,
BEFORE SENATE SUBCOMMITTEE ON CONSTITUTIONAL RIGHTS

I am appearing at this hearing in response to your gracious written invitation. . . . I would have deemed it inappropriate as a judge to appear here on my own initiative, but I feel that it would be equally inappropriate for me to fail to respond to your request for my views. . . .

Until recently, the test of the admissibility of a confession was solely whether it was voluntary. By voluntary is meant that it was not obtained, in whole or in part, either by duress or by inducements. Duress, of course, is not limited only to physical force or physical abuse, but includes as well mental or moral pressure, such as a prolonged grilling, or similar methods. . . . For a similar reason the law excludes confessions obtained by inducements. On the other hand, a voluntary confession freely and willingly made, no matter when or under what circumstances, has always been regarded as admissible in the federal courts, until recently. The sole test of admissibility was invariably whether the confession was voluntary. To exclude voluntary confessions on any ground whatsoever is in my humble judgment detrimental to the cause of justice and permits guilty persons to escape conviction. The rule has worked well. On the one hand, it safeguards defendants against possible oppression, and on the other hand, it protects the public by permitting the use of the strongest kind of evidence.

An entirely different rule of law disconnected from the question of confessions, provides that a person who is arrested must be brought before a committing magistrate without unnecessary delay. It should be emphasized that this is not a constitutional requirement. Preliminary hearings before committing magistrates are not required by the Constitution and do not constitute any part of constitutional due process. They were unknown in common law. . . . The federal requirement . . .

U.S. Senate, Subcommittee on Constitutional Rights of the Committee on the Judiciary, *Hearings on Confessions and Police Detention,* 85th Cong., 2d Sess. (1958), pp. 2–6.

is merely a rule of procedure embodied in rule 5 of the Federal Rules of Criminal Procedure.

Until recently there was no connection between the test of admissibility of a confession and the requirement that an arrested person be taken before a committing magistrate without unnecessary delay. As a matter of fact, there is no inherent or logical relation between them. The Federal Rules of Criminal Procedure were drafted by an Advisory Committee appointed by the Supreme Court of the United States. The Committee considered and rejected a proposal that if an arrested person is not brought before a committing magistrate without unnecessary delay, then a confession or any statement made by him during the period of undue delay should be rendered inadmissible on that ground alone. The Advisory Committee, of which I was a member as well as secretary, was of the opinion that this proposal, which was rejected, would impose too great a penalty for failure to comply with a mere procedural requirement, and further than that would visit the penalty on the public rather than on the official who failed to comply with the rule. Recently, the rule of evidence governing the admissibility of confessions in the federal courts was changed by judicial decisions, and it has been held that even a voluntary confession should be excluded at the trial if the arrested person was not brought before a committing magistrate without unnecessary delay and the confession was made during such period of delay. This is a new rule of evidence which, of course, it is within the power of the Supreme Court to evolve by judicial decisions. It is equally within the power of the Congress to change this principle by legislation. The new doctrine often unnecessarily blocks the work of the police and other investigative agencies and at times leads to acquitting the guilty. It is not necessary for the proper and legitimate protection of the accused. . . .

As to confessions, it would be very helpful indeed if we could revert back to the time honored rule that the sole test of admissibility of a confession is whether it is voluntary. That would protect the public. The Congress has power to accomplish this result in legislation.

Now, I would like to say this, if I may, Mr. Chairman. I am fully cognizant of the fact that I am expressing views that are not in accord with some recent statements of the Supreme Court. And I want to go on record as doing so with sincere respect for that august tribunal. As a judge, I deplore the attacks that have been made on it recently. . . .

On the other hand, it is no disrespect to the Court to utter courteously and objectively views that are not in accord with some of its expressions. To deny this right to anyone would not be in accord with the American tradition as evidenced in the first amendment. In fact, there have been great Americans at various times in our history who expressed disagreement with specific decisions of the Supreme Court. The names of such men as Thomas Jefferson, Andrew Jackson, Abraham Lincoln, Theodore Roosevelt, and Franklin Roosevelt come to mind in this connection.

We must bear in mind that the purpose of the criminal law is to protect the public. On the one hand, it is essential that no innocent person be convicted of a crime, and that oppressive methods be not used even against the guilty.

On the other hand, it is equally indispensable that victims of crimes and potential victims of possible future crimes receive adequate protection. The victim of the crime must not become a forgotten man. . . .

In 1958 both houses of Congress passed bills to reverse the effect of the McNabb-Mallory *decisions. The House and Senate versions, however, differed in important respects; and although a conference committee agreed on a compromise measure, the conference report was shelved on a point of order—a point pressed by a threat of a filibuster by Senator Wayne Morse (Dem., Oregon).*

2.   *"[We] reject the assumption that the courts of Georgia would allow this man to go to his death . . ."*

GEORGIA V. THE SUPREME COURT

WILLIAMS *v.* GEORGIA

AUBREY WILLIAMS, *a Negro, was convicted of murder in March, 1953. In May, 1953, the U.S. Supreme Court reversed the conviction of another Negro in* Avery *v.* Georgia, *holding that the*

349 U.S. 375, 75 S. Ct. 814, 99 L. Ed. 1161, 1 *Race Rel. L. Rep.* 29 (1955).

method of jury selection had denied the defendant equal protection of the law. The same method of jury selection had been used in Williams *as in* Avery, *that is, the names of prospective white jurors had been placed on white cards and those of Negroes on yellow cards. Six months after the* Avery *decision,* Williams' *attorney invoked the* Avery *rule to claim that the jury which had convicted his client had been illegally impaneled. The Georgia courts dismissed this appeal on the grounds that under state law a defendant had to challenge a jury when it was "put on" him. The U.S. Supreme Court granted certiorari.*

MR. JUSTICE FRANKFURTER delivered the opinion of the Court. . . .

On oral argument here . . . the State, with commendable regard for its responsibility, agreed that the use of yellow and white tickets in this case was, in light of this Court's decision in Avery, a denial of equal protection, so that a new trial would be required but for the failure to challenge the array. We need only add that it was the system of selection and the resulting danger of abuse which was struck down in Avery and not an actual showing of discrimination on the basis of comparative numbers of Negroes and whites on the jury lists. The question now before us, in view of the State's concession, is whether the ruling of the Georgia Supreme Court rests upon an adequate nonfederal ground, so that this Court is without jurisdiction to review the Georgia court.

A state procedural rule which forbids the raising of federal questions at late stages in the case, or by any other than a prescribed method, has been recognized as a valid exercise of state power. The principle is clear enough. But the unique aspects of the never-ending new cases that arise require its individual application to particular circumstances. Thus, we would have a different question from that before us if the trial court had no power to consider Williams' constitutional objection at the belated time he raised it. But, where a State allows questions of this sort to be raised at a late stage and be determined by its courts as a matter of discretion, we are not concluded from assuming jurisdiction and deciding whether the state court action in the particular circumstances is, in effect, an avoidance of the federal right.

A state court may not, in the exercise of its discretion, decline to entertain a constitutional claim while passing upon kindred issues raised in the same manner.

The Georgia courts have indicated many times that motions for new trial after verdict are not favored, and that extraordinary motions for new trial after final judgment are favored even less. But the Georgia statute provides for such motion, and it has been granted in "exceptional" or "extraordinary" cases. The general rule is that the granting or denying of an extraordinary motion for new trial rests primarily in the discretion of the trial court, and the appellate court will not reverse except for a clear abuse of discretion. In practice, however, the Georgia appellate courts have not hesitated to reverse and grant a new trial in exceptional cases. . . .

We conclude that the trial court and the State Supreme Court declined to grant Williams' motion though possessed of power to do so under state law. Since his motion was based upon a constitutional objection, and one the validity of which has in principle been sustained here, the discretionary decision to deny the motion does not deprive this Court of jurisdiction to find that the substantive issue is properly before us.

But the fact that we have jurisdiction does not compel us to exercise it. . . . In the instant case, there is an important factor which has intervened since the affirmance by the Georgia Supreme Court which impels us to remand for that court's further consideration. This is the acknowledgment by the State before this Court that, as a matter of substantive law, Williams has been deprived of his constitutional rights. . . . We think that orderly procedure requires a remand to the State Supreme Court for reconsideration of the case. Fair regard for the principles which the Georgia courts have enforced in numerous cases and for the constitutional commands binding on all courts compels us to reject the assumption that the courts of Georgia would allow this man to go to his death as the result of a conviction secured from a jury which the State admits was unconstitutionally impaneled. . . .

MR. JUSTICE CLARK, with whom MR. JUSTICE REED and MR. JUSTICE MINTON join, dissenting. . . .

WILLIAMS v. STATE

DUCKWORTH, CHIEF JUSTICE.

"The powers not delegated to the United States by the Constitution, nor prohibited by it to the States, are reserved to the States respectively, or to the people." Constitution of the United States, 10th Amendment. . . . Even though executives and legislators, not being constitutional lawyers, might often overstep the foregoing unambiguous constitutional prohibition of federal invasion of State jurisdiction, there can never be an acceptable excuse for judicial failure to strictly observe it. This court bows to the Supreme Court on all federal questions of law but we will not supinely surrender sovereign powers of this State. In this case the opinion of the majority of that court recognizes that this court decided the case according to established rules of law, and that no federal jurisdiction existed which would authorize that court to render a judgment either affirming or reversing the judgment of this court, which are the only judgments by that court that this court can constitutionally recognize.

The Supreme Court . . . undertakes to remand the case for further consideration, and in their opinion has pointed to Georgia law vesting in the trial judge discretion in ruling upon an extraordinary motion for new trial and apparently concluded therefrom that this court should reverse the trial court because that discretion was not exercised in the way the Supreme Court would have exercised it. We know and respect the universally recognized rule that the exercise of discretion never authorizes a violation or defiance of law. In this case, as pointed out by us, that law is that the question sought to be raised must be raised before trial and not otherwise.

Not in recognition of any jurisdiction of the Supreme Court to influence or in any manner to interfere with the functioning of this court on strictly State questions, but solely for the purpose of completing the record in this court in a case that was decided by us in 1953, and to avoid further delay, we state that our opinion in *Williams* v. *State* . . . is supported by sound and unchallenged law, conforms

88 S.E. 2d 376, 1 *Race Rel. L. Rep.* 400 (1955).
Supreme Court of Georgia.

with the State and federal constitutions, and stands as the judgment of all seven of the Justices of this Court.

Judgment of affirmance rendered May 10, 1954, adhered to. All the Justices concur.

WILLIAMS *v.* GEORGIA

After this rebuff by the Georgia Supreme Court, Williams' attorneys again petitioned the U.S. Supreme Court for review.

Petition for certiorari to the Supreme Court of Georgia denied.

350 U.S. 950, 76 S. Ct. 326, 100 L. Ed. 828, 1 *Race Rel. L. Rep.* 298 (1956).

THE NEW YORK TIMES, MARCH 31, 1956 (p. 30)

GEORGIA SLAYER DIES

REIDSVILLE, GA., March 30 (AP)—Aubrey Lee Williams, a Negro whose case stirred up a states' rights quarrel between Georgia and the United States Supreme Court, died in the electric chair today for the slaying of an Atlanta liquor store operator. He was convicted of shooting Harry Furst in an $800 robbery October 4, 1952. . . .

3.   *". . . 'With all deliberate speed' . . ."*

VIRGIL HAWKINS GOES TO LAW

FLORIDA *ex rel.* HAWKINS *v.* BOARD OF CONTROL

IN 1949 *a Negro named Virgil Hawkins, having been refused admission to the University of Florida Law School because of his race, brought suit in a state court asking for a writ of mandamus to compel university officials to admit him. (A mandamus is a court order to a public officer commanding him to carry out some specific and nondiscretionary or ministerial act whose performance is imposed*

347 U.S. 971, 74 S. Ct. 783, 98 L. Ed. 1112, 1 *Race Rel. L. Rep.* 13

on the official by law as part of his duty.) In 1952, the Florida Supreme Court dismissed the suit, and Hawkins sought review by the U.S. Supreme Court.

PER CURIAM:

The petition for writ of certiorari is granted. The judgment is vacated and the case remanded for consideration in light of the Segregation Cases decided May 17, 1954 and conditions that now prevail.

FLORIDA *ex rel.* HAWKINS *v.* BOARD OF CONTROL

After the U.S. Supreme Court's order was entered, the Hawkins case went back to the Florida Supreme Court.

ROBERTS, J. . . .

It is our opinion that, both under the equitable principles applicable to mandamus proceedings and the express command of the United States Supreme Court in its "implementation decision" [the 1955 order remanding the school segregation cases back to the courts in which they began with instructions for the trial judges to fashion decrees which would carry out desegregation in light of local problems "with all deliberate speed"] the exercise of a sound judicial discretion requires this court to withhold, for the present, the issuance of a peremptory writ of mandamus in this cause, pending a subsequent determination of law and fact as to the time when the relator should be admitted to the University of Florida Law School; and, to that end and for that purpose, Honorable John H. Murphree, Circuit Judge, is hereby appointed as a commissioner of this court to take testimony from the relator and respondents and such witnesses as they may produce, material to the issues alleged in the third defense of the respondents, as follows:

> That the admission of students of the negro race to the University of Florida, as well as to other state institutions of higher learning established for white students only, presents grave and serious problems affecting the welfare of all students and the institutions them-

83 So. 2d 20, 1 *Race Rel. L. Rep.* 89 (1955).
Supreme Court of Florida.

selves, and will require numerous adjustments and changes at the institutions of higher learning; and respondents cannot satisfactorily make the necessary changes and adjustments until all questions as to time and manner of establishing the new order shall have been decided on the further consideration thereof by the United States Supreme Court. . . .

and with directions to file a transcript of such testimony without recommendations or findings of fact to this court within four months from the date hereof; such testimony to be limited in scope to conditions that may prevail, and that may lawfully be taken into account, in respect to the College of Law of the University of Florida.

We adopt this procedure pursuant to the directive of the "implementation decision" to the effect that we retain jurisdiction "during this period of transition" so that we "may properly take into account the public interest" as well as the "personal interest" of the relator in the elimination of such obstacles as otherwise might impede a systematic and effective transition to the accomplishment of the results ordered by the Supreme Court of the United States. Based upon such evidence as may be offered at the hearing above directed, this court will thereupon determine an effective date for the issuance of a peremptory writ of mandamus.

It is so ordered.

DREW, C. J., HOBSON and THORNAL, JJ., concur.

TERRELL, J., concurs specially.

THOMAS and SEBRING, JJ., concur in part and dissent in part.

TERRELL, J., concurring with ROBERTS, J.:

I agree with the opinion of Mr. Justice Roberts. . . .

There is an intangible aspect to the integrated school question that speaks louder for equity. . . . It has to do with the diverse moral, cultural and I. Q. or preparation response of the white and Negro races. It may also be said to embrace the economy of the Negro teachers. [On a]ccount of the differential these factors present, it is a matter of common knowledge that whites and Negroes in mass are totally unprepared in mind and attitude for change to non-segregated schools. The degree of one's culture and manners may resolve these differentials, but they will not resolve under the impact of court decrees or statutes. Closing cultural gaps is a long and tedious process and is not one for court decrees or legislative acts. . . . There is no known yardstick to measure the equity that this observation may provoke. Innate deficiencies in self-restraint and cultural acuteness always engender stresses, especially when they are infected with a racial element that is difficult to control. . . .

SEBRING, J., concurring in part and dissenting in part. . . .

. . . this Court, in reaching its conclusion in the case at bar, that the facilities offered by the State of Florida to the relator Hawkins afforded him the equal educational opportunities guaranteed by the Federal Constitution, relied heavily, if not entirely, upon the principle stated in Plessy v. Ferguson . . . respecting the effect of the Fourteenth Amendment upon state laws and regulations requiring segregation of races in state supported institutions. . . . But now that the Supreme Court of the United States had expressly repudiated the long-standing principle established in Plessy v. Ferguson . . . so far as it relates to public education, the only federal judicial guide that we have as to what the States must do in order to provide "equal educational opportunities" to its citizens, within the purview of the Fourteenth Amendment to the Federal Constitution, is that laid down in Brown v. Board of Education, . . . which expressly holds "that in the field of public education the doctrine of 'separate but equal' has no place."

That it is our judicial duty to give effect to this new pronouncement cannot be seriously questioned. For . . . all Florida judges have taken a solemn oath to "support, protect and defend" [the federal Constitution]. . . .

. . . While it is elementary that the opinion and judgment dated May 31, 1955, is binding only upon the parties that were actually involved in the cases in which it was entered, it cannot be doubted that in the rendition of its opinion and judgment the court laid down certain principles and rules which we must follow in the instant case in determining the nature of the relief that should be afforded the relator:

> The opinions of [May 17, 1954] declaring the fundamental principle that racial discrimination in public education is unconstitutional, *are incorporated herein by reference.* All provisions of federal, state, or local law requiring or permitting such discrimination must yield to this principle. . . .

When these principles and rules are applied to the facts revealed by the pleadings in the instant case, it is clear that no lawful reason has been shown by the respondents as to why the relator should not be admitted to the College of Law of the University of Florida on the same basis as any white student. . . .

THOMAS, J.

In view of the decision of the Supreme Court of the United States cited in the mandate of that court issued in this case, I think this court has no alternative but to grant the motion for a peremptory writ notwithstanding the answer so I concur in the conclusion of Sebring, J. that such should be the disposition of this controversy now.

FLORIDA *ex rel.* HAWKINS *v.* BOARD OF CONTROL

Disappointed at this further delay, Hawkins again petitioned the U.S. Supreme Court to review the case.

PER CURIAM:

The petition for certiorari is denied.

On May 24, 1954, we issued a mandate in this case to the Supreme Court of Florida. We directed that the case be reconsidered in light of our decision in the Segregation Cases decided May 17, 1954, Brown v. Board of Education. In doing so, we did not imply that decrees involving graduate study present the problems of public elementary and secondary schools. We had theretofore, in three cases, ordered the admission of Negro applicants to graduate schools without discrimination because of color. Thus, our second decision in the Brown case, which implemented the earlier one, had no application to a case involving a Negro applying for admission to a state law school. Accordingly, the mandate of May 24, 1954 is recalled and is vacated. In lieu thereof, the following order is entered:

PER CURIAM:

The petition for writ of certiorari is granted. The judgment is vacated and the case is remanded on the authority of the Segregation

350 U.S. 413, 76 S. Ct. 464, 100 L. Ed. 486, 1 *Race Rel. L. Rep.* 297 (1956).

Cases decided May 17, 1954. As this case involves the admission of a Negro to a graduate professional school, there is no reason for delay. He is entitled to prompt admission under the rules and regulations applicable to other qualified candidates.

FLORIDA *ex rel.* HAWKINS *v.* BOARD OF CONTROL

Once again the case went back to the Florida Supreme Court.

ROBERTS, J. . . .

. . . it is unthinkable that the Supreme Court of the United States would attempt to convert into a writ of right that which has for centuries at common law and in this state been considered a discretionary writ; nor can we conceive that that court would hold that the highest court of a sovereign state does not have the right to control the effective date of its own discretionary process. . . . We will not assume that the court intended such a result.

It is a "consummation devoutly to be wished" that the concept of "states' rights" will not come to be of interest only to writers and students of history. Such concept is vital to the preservation of human liberties *now.* . . . We think the great majority of persons would agree that if the death knell of this fundamental principle of Jeffersonian democracy is to be tolled, the bell should be rung by the people themselves as the Constitution contemplates. President Lincoln's words of warning are just as true today as they were almost a century ago, when he said in his first inaugural address on March 4, 1861:

> If the policy of the government upon vital questions affecting the whole people is to be irrevocably fixed by decisions of the Supreme Court . . . the people will have ceased to be their own rulers, having to that extent practically resigned their government into the hands of that eminent tribunal. . . .

But . . . despite these recent decisions, we cannot attribute to the Supreme Court an intention to abrogate the rule which denies to fed-

93 So. 2d 354, 2 *Race Rel. L. Rep.* 358 (1957).
Supreme Court of Florida.

eral courts the right to regulate or control long-established rules of practice and procedure adopted by state courts for the administration of justice therein. . . . A fortiori, we cannot assume that the Supreme Court intended to deprive the highest court of an independent sovereign state of one of its traditional powers, that is, the right to exercise a sound judicial discretion as to the date of the issuance of its process in order to prevent a serious public mischief. . . .

We come now to the question of whether the facts, as developed under the guidance of this court's commissioner, require the immediate admission of the Relator to the University of Florida Law School, provided he meets the entrance requirements. It might be noted that the Relator had due notice and an opportunity to be heard at the hearings scheduled by the commissioner. He did not appear nor did he present any testimony in support of his right to immediate admission. Moreover, the history of this controversy leads us to believe that the Relator does not, in fact, have a genuine interest in obtaining a legal education. He was given an opportunity to secure a legal education outside this state under the Regional Education Plan, but declined; he was given an opportunity to attend the University of Florida Law School, temporarily, if law facilities were not available at the Florida Agricultural & Mechanical University, but declined; he was then given an opportunity to attend the law school at the Florida Agricultural & Mechanical University, but declined. . . .

The survey conducted under the guidance of the court's commissioner shows, among others, that a substantial number of students and a substantial number of the parents of students state that they expect to take action—which apparently is positive action—to persuade Negro students to leave the University or make it so unpleasant for them that they will move out of a dormitory room or out of a class or out of a cafeteria or otherwise stop using the facilities of the University of Florida, should integration occur. It was also shown that 41 percent of the parents of students now in our white universities would cause them to drop out of those schools or transfer to another school; and that 62 percent of the parents of white 1956 high school graduates would send their children elsewhere than to our white state institutions, if we have enforced integration. There would be loss of revenue to our white institutions from grants, from activities on the part of the alumni of those institutions in support of their financial affairs, and from students moving out of dormitories (many of which are being paid for out of revenue certificates), if we have integration. Those institutions would lose the support of 52 percent of their alumni, if integration occurs, which would seriously impair the financial support to be expected from our state legislature. Integration would unquestionably result in the abandonment of substantially all of the graduate work now being offered at the Florida Agricultural & Mechanical University because it would be an unnecessary duplication of the same courses offered at the University of Florida or at Florida State University.

Our study of the results of the survey material to the question here, and other material evidence, leads inevitably to the conclusion that violence in university communities and a critical disruption of the university system would occur if negro students are permitted to enter the state white universities at this time, including the Law School of the University of Florida, of which it is an integral part. This court has an opportunity to prevent the incidents of violence which are, even now, occurring in various parts of this country as a result of the states' efforts to enforce the Supreme Court's decision in the Brown case. . . .

In the exercise of what we sincerely believe to be sound judicial discretion, we have decided that the relator's motion for a peremptory writ should be denied, but without prejudice to the right of relator to renew his motion when he is prepared to present testimony showing that his admission can be accomplished without doing great public mischief. For the reasons stated, the entry of a final judgment is deferred until further order of the court.

It is so ordered.

THORNAL and O'CONNELL, JJ., concur.

TERRELL, C. J., and HOBSON, J., concur specially.

THOMAS and DREW, JJ., dissent.

TERRELL, C. J., concurring.

1 concur in the opinion of Mr. Justice Roberts, particularly with that part relating to the power of this and other states to control their process when public mischief is imminent. This doctrine is all the more compelling when long settled rules relating to the administration of justice and the prevention of violence are brought in question.

Historically, individuals, as well as states, have interposed action to thwart the inroads of federal authority not so much for delay as to preserve what was deemed to be the most precious of American ideals. . . .

Some anthropologists and historians much better informed than I am point out that segregation is as old as the hills. The Egyptians practiced it on the Israelites; the Greeks did likewise for the barbarians; the Romans segregated the Syrians; the Chinese segregated all foreigners; segregation is said to have produced the caste system in India and Hitler practiced it in his Germany, but no one ever discovered that it was in violation of due process until recently and to do so some of the same historians point out that the Supreme Court abandoned the Constitution, precedent and common sense and fortified its decision solely with the writings of Gunnar Myrdal, a Scandinavian sociologist. What he knew about constitutional law we are not told nor have we been able to learn.

Such is in part the predicate on which the states are resisting integration. They contend that since the Supreme Court has tortured the Constitution, particularly the welfare clause, the interstate commerce clause, the Ninth and Tenth Amendments, the provisions relating to separation of state and federal powers, and the powers not specifically granted to the federal government being reserved to states, they have a right to torture the court's decision. Whatever substance there may be to this contention, it is certain that forced integration is not the answer to the question. . . .

. . . Violence has arisen everywhere and continues to arise [on] account of attempts to comply with the federal courts' orders and the end is not yet. These "states are the natural guardians of the public against violence"; they know the reasons for it; they are fully aware that such tensions are grounded in the attempt of the federal courts at a form of enforced integration that is contrary to every precept that activates the need for law in this country. . . . If Florida is not authorized to meet and solve the problem by which it is confronted in a sane and sensible manner, then all the law I have been taught governing state and federal power has been pitched down the drain. . . .

HOBSON, J., concurring specially. . . .

In the interest of both races, that is to say, the common weal, the writ of mandamus should, in the exercise of sound judicial discretion, be withheld until the Supreme Court of the United States in this case, after consideration of those matters which it has not heretofore had an opportunity to weigh and evaluate, unequivocally directs that relator be admitted to the College of Law at the University of Florida. . . . And since I am bound by the paramount federal law, if such ruling should be made by a fully informed Supreme Court, I could not fail to comply without stultifying my oath of office.

THOMAS, J., dissenting. . . .

DREW, J., dissenting. . . .

. . . The Constitution of the United States of America, Article VI, provides that "This Constitution . . . shall be the supreme Law of the Land; and the Judges in every State shall be bound thereby, any Thing in the Constitution or Laws of any State to the Contrary notwithstanding." The oath of office I have taken requires that I "support, protect and defend" it. The Supreme Court of the United States has been established by long tradition as the final interpreter of the Constitution of the United States. Such an interpretation has been made in this case.

I cannot conclude that any discretion remains in this Court to lawfully postpone the issuance of a peremptory writ. . . .

Courts are the mere instruments of the law and can will nothing. . . . The power vested in the judiciary should never be exercised for the sole purpose of giving effect to the will of the judge. . . . I conceive it to be my plain duty to give effect to the law which has been established by the United States Supreme Court. . . .

FLORIDA *ex rel.* HAWKINS *v.* BOARD OF CONTROL

Following this new defeat in the state supreme court, Hawkins again sought review by the U.S. Supreme Court.

Petition for Writ of Certiorari to the Supreme Court of Florida denied without prejudice to the petitioner's seeking relief in an appropriate United States District Court.

355 U.S. 839, 78 S. Ct. 20, 2 L. Ed. 2d 49, 2 *Race Rel. L. Rep.* 1093 (1957).

HAWKINS *v.* BOARD OF CONTROL

Hawkins took the hint in the Supreme Court's 1957 memorandum order and brought suit in a federal district court in Florida, asking for an injunction against university officials. The district judge held a hearing but refused to permit Hawkins to present evidence. The injunction request was denied. Hawkins appealed.

Before HUTCHESON, CHIEF JUDGE, BORAH, TUTTLE, JJ.

PER CURIAM. . . .

The question presented to us is whether the court erred in entering its order complained of.

Rule 65 (b) Federal Rules of Civil Procedure requires that a motion for a preliminary injunction "shall be set for hearing. . . ." Hearing requires a trial of an issue of fact. Trial of an issue of fact necessitates an opportunity to present evidence. Since appellant was not given the opportunity to present evidence in his behalf, the order denying the preliminary injunction must be set aside.

In his complaint appellant alleges that he had been striving since 1949 to obtain admission to the state law school in question. Much of this time has been consumed in litigation to vindicate this asserted right. He prayed that the court advance this case on its docket and order a speedy hearing on the merits in order that, if entitled thereto, he might be admitted to the next term of the law school. In these circumstances this request should be granted and the cause should be expedited to the end that a trial may be had on the merits at the earliest practicable date.

The order of the trial court denying the preliminary injunction is REVERSED and the cause is REMANDED for further proceedings in accordance with this opinion. . . .

253 F. 2d 752, 3 *Race Rel. L. Rep.* 462 (1958).
United States Court of Appeals for the Fifth Circuit.

FLORIDA *ex rel.* HAWKINS *v.* BOARD OF CONTROL

Following the Court of Appeals decision in 1958, Hawkins' case went back to the district court.

DEVANE, DISTRICT JUDGE. . . .

In the complaint filed by plaintiff in this court plaintiff . . . sought an order from this court directing the Board of Control to admit him as a law student at the University of Florida Law School. The greater part of his complaint is devoted to allegations stating his claimed rights in that respect, but as also pointed out above, he expanded the litigation in this court to make it a *class action* not only in behalf of himself, but of other persons similarly situated who had made applications for admission to various schools of the University of Florida. . . .

. . . After extended argument on the motions filed by defendants, counsel for plaintiff read into the record a stipulation on behalf of plaintiff abandoning plaintiff's prayer for an order of this court directing the Board of Control and the Registrar of the University of Florida to permit him to enter said University as a law student and announced that plaintiff sought in this case only an order of this Court enjoining defendants from enforcing any policy, custom or usage of limiting admission to the University of Florida to white persons only. . . .

The Court has carefully considered all the testimony submitted by the respective parties and finds and holds that . . . this court has no alternative but to hold plaintiff is entitled to maintain this class action against defendants. When it comes to the relief that should be granted, the Court finds and holds upon the evidence submitted with reference to plaintiff's right to enter the University of Florida Law School that plaintiff failed completely to establish any such right under the law applicable to cases of this character and he will be denied the right to enter the law school.

When it comes to the relief that should be granted upon the class action feature of the case, the Court finds and holds that the evidence submitted by defendants clearly shows that the injunctive relief granted by this Court should be and it will be limited to enjoining

3 *Race Rel. L. Rep.* 657 (1958).
U.S. District Court, Northern District, Tallahassee Division, Florida.

the defendants from enforcing any policy, custom or usage of limiting admission to the *graduate* schools and *graduate* professional schools *of the* University of Florida to white persons only. . . .

4.   *". . . the Supreme Court too often has tended to adopt the role of policy-maker without proper judicial restraint."*

RESOLUTIONS OF THE STATE CHIEF JUSTICES

IN AUGUST, *1958, the Conference of State Chief Justices adopted by a 36–8 vote the following report of its special committee set up to study the effect of recent U.S. Supreme Court decisions.*

. . . WE BELIEVE that strong state and local governments are essential to the effective functioning of the American system of federal government; that they should not be sacrificed needlessly to leveling, and sometimes deadening, uniformity; and that in the interest of active, citizen participation in self-government—the foundation of our democracy—they should be sustained and strengthened.

As long as this country continues to be a developing country and as long as the conditions under which we live continue to change, there will always be problems of the allocation of power depending upon whether certain matters should be regarded as primarily of national concern or as primarily of local concern. These adjustments can hardly be effected without some friction. How much friction will develop depends in part upon the wisdom of those empowered to alter the boundaries and in part upon the speed with which such changes are effected. Of course, the question of speed really involves the exercise of judgment and the use of wisdom, so that the two things are really the same in substance.

We are now concerned specifically with the effect of judicial decisions upon the relations between the federal government and the state governments. Here we think that the overall tendency of decisions of the Supreme Court over the last 25 years or more has been to press the extension of federal power and to press it rapidly. . . .

The extent to which the Supreme Court assumes the function of policy-maker is also of concern to us in the conduct of our judicial business. We realize that in the course of American history the Supreme Court has frequently—one might, indeed, say customarily—exercised policy-making powers going far beyond those involved, say, in making a selection between competing rules of law.

We believe that in the fields with which we are concerned, and as to which we feel entitled to speak, the Supreme Court too often has tended to adopt the role of policy-maker without proper judicial restraint. We feel this is particularly the case in both of the great fields we have discussed—namely, the extent and extension of the federal power, and the supervision of state action by the Supreme Court by virtue of the Fourteenth Amendment. In the light of the immense power of the Supreme Court and its practical non-reviewability in most instances no more important obligation rests upon it, in our view, than that of careful moderation in the exercise of its policy-making role.

We are not alone in our view that the Court, in many cases arising under the Fourteenth Amendment, has assumed what seems to us primarily legislative powers. . . . We do not believe that either the framers of the original Constitution or the possibly somewhat less gifted draftsmen of the Fourteenth Amendment ever contemplated that the Supreme Court would, or should, have the almost unlimited policy-making powers which it now exercises. It is strange, indeed, to reflect that under a constitution which provides for a system of checks and balances and of distribution of power between national and state governments one branch of one government—the Supreme Court—should attain the immense, and in many respects, dominant, power which it now wields.

We believe that the great principle of distribution of powers among the various branches of government and between levels of government has vitality today and is the crucial base of our democracy. We further believe that in construing and applying the Constitution and laws made in pursuance thereof, this principle of the division of power based upon whether a matter is primarily of national or of local concern should not be lost sight of or ignored, especially in fields which which bear upon the meaning of a constitutional or statutory provision, or the validity of state action presented for review. For, with due allowance for the changed conditions under which it may or must operate, the principle is as worthy of our consideration today as it was of the consideration of the great men who met in 1787 to establish our nation as a nation.

It has long been an American boast that we have a government of laws and not of men. We believe that any study of recent decisions of the Supreme Court will raise at least considerable doubt as to the validity of that boast. We find first that in constitutional cases unanimous decisions are comparative rarities and that multiple opinions, concurring or dissenting, are common occurrences. We find next that divisions in result on a 5 to 4 basis are quite frequent. We find further that on some occasions a majority of the Court cannot be mustered in support of any one opinion and that the result of a given case may come from the divergent views of individual justices who happen to unite on one outcome or the other of the case before the Court.

We further find that the Court does not accord finality to its own determinations of constitutional questions, or for that matter of others. We concede that a slavish adherence to *stare decisis* could at times have unfortunate consequences; but it seems strange that under a constitutional doctrine which requires all others to recognize the Supreme Court's rulings on constitutional questions as binding adjudications of the meaning and application of the Constitution, the Court itself has so frequently overturned its own decisions thereon, after the lapse of periods varying from one year to seventy-five, or even ninety-five years. . . . The Constitution expressly sets up its own procedures for amendment, slow or cumbersome though they may be.

These frequent differences and occasional overrulings of prior decisions in constitutional cases cause us grave concern as to whether individual views of the members of the court as from time to time constituted, or of a majority thereof, as to what is wise or desirable do not unconsciously override a more dispassionate consideration of what is or is not constitutionally warranted. We believe that the latter is the correct approach, and we have no doubt that every member of the Supreme Court intends to adhere to that approach, and believes that he does so. It is our earnest hope which we respectfully express, that that great Court exercise to the full its power of judicial self-restraint by adhering firmly to its tremendous, strictly judicial powers and by eschewing, so far as possible, the exercise of essentially legislative powers when it is called upon to decide questions involving the validity of state action, whether it deems such action wise or unwise. The value of our system of federalism, and of local self-government in local matters which it embodies, should be kept firmly in mind, as we believe it was by those who framed our Constitution.

At times the Supreme Court manifests, or seems to manifest, an impatience with the slow workings of our federal system. That impatience may extend to an unwillingness to wait for Congress to make clear its intention to exercise the powers conferred upon it under the Constitution, or the extent to which it undertakes to exercise them, and it may extend to the slow processes of amending the Constitution which that instrument provides. The words of Elihu Root on the opposite side of the problem, asserted at a time when demands were current for recall of judges and judicial decisions, bear repeating: "If the people of our country yield to impatience which would destroy the system that alone makes effective these great impersonal rules and preserves our constitutional government, rather than endure the temporary inconvenience of pursuing regulated methods of changing the law, we shall not be reforming. We shall not be making progress, but shall be exhibiting that lack of self-control which enables great bodies of men to abide the slow process of orderly government rather than to break down the barriers of order when they are struck by the impulse of the moment." . . .

We believe that what Mr. Root said is sound doctrine to be followed toward the Constitution, the Supreme Court, and its interpretation of the Constitution. Surely, it is no less incumbent upon the Supreme Court, on its part, to be equally restrained and to be as sure as is humanly possible that it is adhering to the fundamentals of the Constitution with regard to the distribution of powers and the separation of powers, and with regard to the limitations of judicial power which are implicit in such separation and distribution, and that it is not merely giving effect to what it may deem desirable. . . .

17 / JUDICIAL SELF-RESTRAINT

The restraints on judicial power discussed in the two previous chapters have been largely external in the sense of being imposed on a judge. Restraints which are internalized, enforced by inner compulsion, are generally more rigidly followed than those restrictions imposed only by outside force. Certainly one can say that as a group federal judges have conducted themselves according to the highest ethical standards. There have been many errors of judgment, frequent failures at accurate self-analysis, and occasional emotional lapses; but instances of moral turpitude or deliberate perversion of what judges honestly believe to be the correct legal rule have been singularly rare.

There is a broad societal consensus on general principles of judicial ethics, and this consensus has effectively infused judicial behavior with restraints of conscience. There is, however, no such consensus on the more complex questions concerning judicial decision-making and policy-making. Here, whether out of pure concern for popular government, fear of political reprisal, or some combination of these and other factors, judges have tried to construct theories to limit themselves and their colleagues.

Self-Restraint and the Judicial Role

The view that a judge takes of his own role in society will, of course, be fundamental to any theory of judicial limitations. It has been asserted that some judges are "goal-oriented," that they are concerned more with the proper result in a case and less with the meticulously correct technical means to achieve that result. Justice Murphy in dissent in *Falbo* v. *United States* (1944) summed up this approach when he said: "The law knows no finer hour than when it cuts through formal concepts and transitory emotions to protect unpopular citizens against discrimination and persecution."

Other judges have been more "functionally oriented," more concerned with the procedural aspects of court operations than with the end result of those operations. Dissenting in *Uveges* v. *Pennsylvania* (1948), Justice Frankfurter complained of what he considered the majority's overeagerness to find error in the state judicial proceeding: "After all, this is the Nation's ultimate judicial tribunal, not a super-legal-aid bureau." Later, in *Terminiello* v. *Chicago* (1949), he protested: "This is a court of review, not a tribunal unbounded by rules. We do not sit like a kadi under a tree dispensing justice according to considerations of individual expediency."

Neither of these approaches is without serious theoretical and practical difficulties, and each leads the judge to evaluate his conduct in terms of another concept, that of judicial self-restraint. Self-restraint is a broad term, but it does take on a definite meaning in the context of American constitutional development. Closely related to the idea of "avoidance of constitutional questions" discussed in Chapter 12, the essence of the self-restraint notion is that judges should accord maximum respect to decisions of legislators and administrators and should never invalidate those decisions simply because judges would prefer alternative lines of policy. One of the oldest expressions of this doctrine is the so-called "presumption rule," which holds that a statute is presumed constitutional and places the burden of proof on the litigant who challenges the validity of legislation.

Self-Restraint and Economic Regulation

The background for current concern over judicial self-restraint is the post-Civil War struggle among group interests over freedom of corporation activities from popular control. The specific constitutional issue was the extent to which the Fifth and Fourteenth Amendments, which forbade the federal and state governments to deprive persons of their rights to life, liberty, or property "without due process of law," barred legislation regulating prices, rates, wages, hours, and other conditions of labor.

Initially, the attitude of a majority of the Supreme Court justices was that, where a business was open for use by the public, its owners subjected themselves to reasonable public regulation. Whether a rate was reasonable was principally a legislative rather than a judicial question. As Chief Justice Waite said in *Munn* v. *Illinois* (1877): "We know that this is a power which may be abused; but that is no argument against its existence. For protection against abuses by legislatures the people must resort to the polls, not to the courts."

Waite's approach, however, was soon to be abandoned. By the turn of the century the Supreme Court was ruling that the reasonableness of rates was primarily a judicial rather than a legislative question, and that freedom of business from government regulation was the proper constitutional rule and restraint the exception. When questions of labor legislation came up during this period, federal judges were equally ready to follow their own laissez-faire economic theories. In defense of this increased judicial role, Justice Brewer asserted in 1893 that:

> The great body of judges are as well versed in the affairs of life as any, and they, who unravel all the mysteries of accounting between partners, settle the business of the largest corporations and extract the truth from the mass of sciolistic verbiage that falls from the lips of expert witnesses in patent cases, will find no difficulty in determining what is right and wrong between employer and employees, and whether proposed rates of freight and fare are reasonable as between the public and the owners; while, as for speed, is there anything quicker than a writ of injunction?

It was against this background that Oliver Wendell Holmes argued for a return to a policy of self-restraint. Skeptical of all social and economic dogmas and sensitive to the fallibility of judges, Holmes pleaded with his brethren to allow "the dominant forces" in society to fight their interest struggles in the legislative process. He urged his colleagues to withhold their veto power if it appeared that the law in question had a reasonable basis, even if it was not the wisest possible solution. "It must be remembered," Holmes reminded the justices, "that legislators are ultimate guardians of the liberties and welfare of the people in quite as great a degree as the courts."

During the first third of the twentieth century, Holmes' philosophy sometimes won out in the Court, but more often it lost. Writing in 1930, Professor Frankfurter stated that the Supreme Court had invalidated more legislation since 1920 than it had in the preceding fifty years. "Merely as a matter of arithmetic," the future justice wrote, "this is an impressive mortality rate." Most of the statutes declared unconstitutional involved governmental regulation of business, and the great crisis over judicial activism came during the conflict over the New Deal.

Each of the justices disapproved of many of Roosevelt's policies, although this disapproval differed measurably in intensity. The chief cause of division among the justices centered on the role the Court should play in thwarting the New Deal. Dissenting in *Nebbia* v. *New York* (1934), a decision in which a bare majority had sustained a state statute setting minimum retail prices for milk, Justice McReynolds had voiced the theory of the four most conservative members of the Court when he said that "this Court must have regard to the wisdom of the enactment."

McReynolds, Sutherland, Van Devanter, and Butler picked up some additional votes in later cases. During the next twenty-six months, the Court invalidated New Deal legislation in eleven decisions, and state economic regulation fared no better. Protesting against this use of judicial power, Harlan F. Stone in his dissent in *United States* v. *Butler* (1936) intimated that the majority had adopted a "tortured" construction of the Constitution because the statute offended their personal economic beliefs. Judges, Stone warned, should be "concerned only with the power to enact statutes, not with their wisdom." The remedy for unwise laws was the ballot box. "Courts," Stone chided his colleagues, "are not the only agency of government which must be assumed to have capacity to govern."

The events of 1936–37 moved some of the justices to reconsider their opposition to the New Deal, and within a few years federal judges had almost entirely withdrawn from their former role as censors of state and federal economic legislation. Only where state regulation threatened to interfere with interstate commerce were judges likely to intervene. Speaking for a unanimous Court in *Williamson* v. *Lee Optical Co.* (1955), Justice Douglas summed up the history of the previous eighteen years: "The day is gone when this Court uses the Due Process Clause of the Fourteenth Amendment to strike down state laws, regulatory of business and industrial conditions, because they may be unwise, improvident, or out of harmony with a particular school of thought."

Self-Restraint and Political Freedom

The triumph of self-restraint in economic affairs marked only the beginning of a new phase in the struggle over the judicial role. Holmes himself had been somewhat more willing to invalidate legislation which touched areas of civil rather than economic freedom; and Stone, almost immediately after his victory over the Court's Old Guard, began to try to set some tentative limits to self-restraint. If the primary check on political power was to be the ballot box, then, Stone reasoned, judges would have special responsibility to keep the political processes open—to protect the right to vote, to speak freely, and to form political organizations. Moreover, courts would have a similar responsibility to protect the rights of "insular minorities" which had no hope of achieving political status.

It was in this context that Stone formulated the theory of "preferred freedom." Accepting Cardozo's view in *Palko* v. *Connecticut* that the First Amendment rights to freedom of expression, press, assembly, and religion were the core of constitutional government, Stone asserted that these freedoms stood in a preferred position when in conflict with other rights of individuals or with governmental authority. In such instances Stone would have relaxed the usual presumption of legislative constitutionality.

This preferred position theory became the focal point of a renewed struggle over self-restraint. On the one hand were Justices Black and Douglas who wanted to move beyond Stone's argument and to presume unconstitutional legislation touching First Amendment rights. As Justice Black wrote in *Milk Wagon Drivers Union* v. *Meadowmoor Dairies* (1941):

> I view the guaranties of the First Amendment as the foundation upon which our governmental system rests and without which it could not continue to endure as conceived and planned. Freedom to speak and write about public questions is as important to the life of our government as is the heart to the human body. In fact, this privilege is the heart of our government. If that heart be weakened, the result is debilitation; if it be stilled, the result is death.

On the other hand, Justice Frankfurter, after some initial hesitation, has argued that the preferred position theory "expresses a complicated process of constitutional adjudication by a deceptive formula." Frankfurter has conceded that "those liberties of the individual which history has attested as the indispensable conditions of an open as against a closed society come to this Court with a momentum for respect lacking when appeal is made to liberties which derive merely from shifting economic arrangements." But he has labeled any doctrine which establishes preferences among constitutional provisions and challenges the normal presumption of validity as "mischievous." Reasonableness, Frankfurter believes, is the test of constitutionality whether the challenged action involves freedom of speech or contract, and humility is the proper judicial attitude in all cases.

Self-Restraint and Judicial Motivation

This conflict has made itself felt in the decision of such cases as those involving compulsory flag salutes, soapbox orators, group libel laws, traffic in obscenity, free speech for Communists, or the extent to which religious liberty includes the right to proselytize with immunity from public regulation. The preferred position theory has been attacked on the ground that it transforms into a legal doctrine what is really little more than a rationalization of policy choices—in the cases just suggested, choices for unfettered freedom. This judicial position, it is charged, repeats the identical error of the pre-1937 Court, except that then the judges were according business freedom a preferred position.

Black and Douglas answer that it is the Constitution itself which has set up this preference. For, while the Fourth Amendment offers protection only against "unreasonable" searches and seizures, and the Fifth Amendment only prohibits a taking of life, liberty, or property "without due process of law," the First Amendment is literally absolute in its terms: "Congress shall make *no* law . . ." But Frankfurter and his followers rebut that this is a narrow argument which reads an inflexible interpretation into a Constitution designed, as John Marshall said, to meet all the exigencies of government and "to endure for ages to come."

For its part, however, strict self-restraint poses two immediately apparent difficulties. The first is that of reconciliation with judicial review. Rigidly applied, the "reasonableness" test of constitutionality would practically mean the end of judicial review, since almost no legislation can be said to be totally devoid of basis in reason. Yet no justice has advocated that the Court surrender its authority to interpret the Constitution. "The duty of deference," Frankfurter admitted in *Stein* v. *New York* (1953), "can not be allowed imperceptibly to slide into abdication." Somewhere, sometime, somehow, all the justices have agreed, courts must draw a line between permissible and forbidden governmental action.

And this means preferring a judicial interpretation of what the Constitution reasonably permits over the interpretation of legislators or administrators.

The second difficulty involves problems of motivation and self-analysis. As Chapter 14 pointed out, judges who have a sophisticated understanding of psychology have to ask themselves whether in overriding—or sustaining—a legislative judgment they are not satisfying their own policy preferences.

In *Louisiana* v. *Resweber* (1947), where a condemned man had failed to die in the electric chair because of its faulty mechanism, Frankfurter supplied the fifth vote for the Supreme Court's decision that a second, and long-delayed, effort to execute the prisoner would not be double jeopardy or cruel and unusual punishment, and thus a violation of due process. Explaining his position, Frankfurter said:

> I cannot rid myself of the conviction that were I to hold that Louisiana would transgress the Due Process Clause if the State were allowed, in the precise circumstances before us, to carry out the death sentence, I would be enforcing my private view rather than that consensus of society's opinion which, for purposes of due process, is the standard enjoined by the Constitution.

But Frankfurter offered no explanation as to how he found standards outside of his own value system, or how he discovered the consensus of society on an issue which had never arisen before under such circumstances. Modern psychology, in questioning the possibility of complete rationality and in demonstrating that one may take as much satisfaction from self-denial as from self-gratification, has placed a heavy burden on judges.

This problem of motivation has gnawed at the judicial conscience and temper, stirring both deep introspection and sharp recriminations. Cases involving civil liberties, due process, and state action have been especially bothersome. As we saw in *Adamson* v. *California* (1947), Justices Black and Douglas want the Court to hold that the first eight amendments are incorporated in the Fourteenth and thus limit both judicial and state discretion. On the other hand, Frankfurter reverses his stand on preferred freedoms and asserts in this context that some rights really are more fundamental than others, and only those more fundamental rights are included in the Fourteenth Amendment. Just which rights are more or less fundamental Frankfurter leaves to a case-by-case determination by judges, thus increasing the scope of judicial discretion.

These approaches to the judicial function as well as the theories of self-restraint and preferred position differ significantly both for the microcosm of judicial behavior and the macrocosm of public policy formulation. But neither these differences nor the mutual recriminations about deciding cases on the basis of personal value judgments should obscure the fact that each group of justices has tried to build a theory that is sufficiently comprehensive to explain and justify a limited judicial role, and sufficiently objective to be used by other judges. Each of these approaches and theories has its defects; but, for whatever motivation, each of them also attempts to impose very real restrictions on the exercise of judicial power.

SELECTED REFERENCES

Black, Charles, *The People and the Court* (New York: Macmillan, 1960).

Braden, George, "The Search for Objectivity in Constitutional Law," 57 *Yale Law Journal* 571 (1948).

Brewer, David J., "The Nation's Safeguard," 16 *Report of the New York State Bar Association* 37 (1893).

Corwin, Edward S., *Liberty against Government* (Baton Rouge: Louisiana State University Press, 1948).

Douglas, William O., *The Right of the People* (New York: Doubleday, 1958), Ch. 1.

Frankfurter, Felix, "The United States Supreme Court Molding the Constitution," 32 *Current History* 235 (May 1930).

Jackson, Robert H., *The Supreme Court in the American System of Government* (Cambridge: Harvard University Press, 1955).

Mason, Alpheus T., *The Supreme Court from Taft to Warren* (Baton Rouge: Louisiana State University Press, 1958).

Mendelson, Wallace, *Capitalism, Democracy, and the Supreme Court* (New York: Appleton-Century-Crofts, 1960).

Pritchett, C. Herman, "Libertarian Motivations on the Vinson Court," 47 *American Political Science Review* 321 (1953).

Roche, John P., "Judicial Self-Restraint," 49 *American Political Science Review* 762 (1955).

Thomas, Helen Shirley, *Felix Frankfurter: Scholar on the Bench* (Baltimore: Johns Hopkins University Press, 1960), Chs. 4, 6, 7, 10.

1.   *"Self-restraint belongs in the domain of will and not of judgment."*

THE STONE-SUTHERLAND DEBATE DURING THE NEW DEAL CRISIS

UNITED STATES *v.* BUTLER

IN THE *Agricultural Adjustment Act of 1933 Congress had attempted to meet the farm crisis by a plan of payments to farmers for reducing crop acreage. The program was to be financed by a tax on processors. Butler, a processor, refused to pay the tax. When the case reached the Supreme Court the statute was declared unconstitutional by a 6–3 vote. For the majority, Justice Roberts wrote a long opinion holding that even though Congress did have power to tax and spend for the general welfare and even though Art. VI of the Constitution gave precedence to federal over state laws, the tax was invalid because it in effect regulated matters which were properly concerns of the states.*

MR. JUSTICE STONE, dissenting. . . .

1. The power of courts to declare a statute unconstitutional is subject to two guiding principles of decision. . . . One is that courts are concerned only with the power to enact statutes, not with their wisdom. The other is that while unconstitutional exercise of power by the executive and legislative branches of government is subject to judicial restraint, the only check upon our own exercise of power is our own sense of self-restraint. For the removal of unwise laws from the statute books appeal lies not to the courts but to the ballot and to the processes of democratic government.

2. The constitutional power of Congress to levy an excise tax upon the processing of agricultural products is not questioned. The present levy is held invalid . . . because the use to which its proceeds are put is disapproved. . . .

297 U.S. 1, 56 S. Ct. 312, 80 L. Ed. 477 (1936).

It is with these preliminary and hardly controverted matters in mind that we should direct our attention to the pivot on which the decision of the Court is made to turn. It is that a levy unquestionably within the taxing power of Congress may be treated as invalid because it is a step in a plan to regulate agricultural production and is thus a forbidden infringement of state power. The levy is not any less an exercise of taxing power because it is intended to defray an expenditure for the general welfare rather than for some other support of government. . . .

It is upon the contention that state power is infringed by purchased regulation of agricultural production that chief reliance is placed. It is insisted that, while the Constitution gives to Congress, in specific and unambiguous terms, the power to tax and spend, the power is subject to limitations which do not find their origin in any express provision of the Constitution and to which other expressly delegated powers are not subject. . . .

The limitation now sanctioned must lead to absurd consequences. The government may give seeds to farmers, but may not condition the gift upon their being planted in places where they are most needed or even planted at all. The government may give money to the unemployed, but may not ask that those who get it shall give labor in return, or even use it to support their families. It may give money to sufferers from earthquake, fire, tornado, pestilence or flood, but may not impose conditions—health precautions designed to prevent the spread of disease or induce the movement of population to safer or more sanitary areas. All that, because it is purchased regulation infringing state powers, must be left for the states, who are unable or unwilling to supply the necessary relief. . . .

That the governmental power of the purse is a great one is not now for the first time announced. Every student of the history of government and economics is aware of its magnitude and of its existence in every civilized government. Both were well understood by the framers of the Constitution. . . . The suggestion that it must now be curtailed by judicial fiat because it may be abused by unwise use hardly rises to the dignity of argument. So may judicial power be abused. . . .

A tortured construction of the Constitution is not to be justified by recourse to extreme examples of reckless congressional spending which might occur if courts could not prevent [them]. Courts are not the only agency of government that must be assumed to have capacity to govern. Congress and the courts both unhappily may falter or be mistaken in the performance of their constitutional duty. But interpretation of our great charter of government which proceeds on any assumption that the responsibility for the preservation of our institutions is the exclusive concern of any one of the three branches of government, or that it alone can save them from destruction, is far more likely, in the long run, "to obliterate the constituent members" . . . than the frank recognition that language, even of a constitution, may mean what it says: that the power to tax and spend includes the power to relieve a nation-wide economic maladjustment by conditional gifts of money.

MR. JUSTICE BRANDEIS and MR. JUSTICE CARDOZO join in this opinion.

WEST COAST HOTEL *V.* PARRISH

Justice Roberts read Stone's Butler *opinion in draft form and was so stung by its effect that he asked the Chief Justice to persuade Stone to tone it down. The next term—after Roosevelt's landslide victory in 1936—Roberts (and to a lesser extent Hughes) began changing sides in the famous "switch in time that saved nine." In the Parrish case, Roberts supplied the fifth vote to sustain the constitutionality of a state minimum wages and hours law, the same kind of regulation which had been declared unconstitutional fourteen years earlier in* Adkins v. Children's Hospital *and only a year earlier in* Morehead v. New York.

Correctly reading the Parrish *decision as the beginning of the Court's capitulation in the New Deal fight, Sutherland tried to answer Stone's* Butler *dissent.*

MR. JUSTICE SUTHERLAND, dissenting:

MR. JUSTICE VAN DEVANTER, MR. JUSTICE MCREYNOLDS, MR. JUSTICE BUTLER and I think the judgment of the court below should be reversed.

300 U.S. 379, 57 S. Ct. 578, 81 L. Ed. 703 (1937).

The principles and authorities relied upon to sustain the judgment, were considered in Adkins v. Children's Hospital and Morehead v. New York, and their lack of application to cases like the one in hand was pointed out. A sufficient answer to all that is now said will be found in the opinions of the court in those cases. . . .

Under our form of government, where the written Constitution, by its own terms, is the supreme law, some agency, of necessity, must have the power to say the final word as to the validity of a statute assailed as unconstitutional. The Constitution makes it clear that the power has been intrusted to this court when the question arises in a controversy within its jurisdiction; and so long as the power remains there, its exercise cannot be avoided without betrayal of the trust.

It has been pointed out many times . . . that this judicial duty is one of gravity and delicacy, and that rational doubts must be resolved in favor of the constitutionality of the statute. But whose doubts, and by whom resolved? Undoubtedly it is the duty of a member of the court, in the process of reaching a right conclusion, to give due weight to the opposing views of his associates; but in the end, the question which he must answer is not whether such views seem sound to those who entertain them, but whether they convince him that the statute is constitutional or engender in his mind a rational doubt upon that issue. The oath which he takes as a judge is not a composite oath, but an individual one. And in passing upon the validity of a statute, he discharges a duty imposed upon *him*, which cannot be consummated justly by an automatic acceptance of the views of others which have neither convinced, nor created a reasonable doubt in, his mind. If upon a question so important he thus surrenders his deliberate judgment, he stands forsworn. He cannot subordinate his convictions to that extent and keep faith with his oath or retain his judicial and moral independence.

The suggestion that the only check upon the exercise of the judicial power, when properly invoked, to declare a constitutional right superior to an unconstitutional statute is the judge's own faculty of self-restraint is both ill considered and mischievous. Self-restraint belongs in the domain of will and not of judgment. The check upon the judge is that imposed by his oath of office, by the Constitution and by his own conscientious and informed convictions; and since he had

634   *Limits on Judicial Power*

the duty to make up his own mind and adjudge accordingly, it is hard to see how there could be any other restraint. This court acts as a unit. It cannot act in any other way; and the majority . . . establishes the controlling rule as the decision of the court. . . . But it is the right of those in the minority to disagree, and sometimes, in matters of grave importance, their imperative duty to voice their disagreement at such length as the occasion demands—always, of course, in terms which, however forceful, do not offend the proprieties or impugn the good faith of those who think otherwise.

It is urged that the question involved should now receive fresh consideration . . . because of "the economic conditions which have supervened"; but the meaning of the Constitution does not change with the ebb and flow of economic events. We frequently are told in more general words that the Constitution must be construed in the light of the present. If by that is meant that the Constitution is made up of living words that apply to every new condition which they include, the statement is quite true. But to say, if that be intended, that the words of the Constitution mean today what they did not mean when written—that is, that they do not apply to a situation now to which they would have applied then—is to rob that instrument of the essential element which continues it in force as the people have made it until they, and not their official agents, have made it otherwise. . . .

The judicial function is that of interpretation; it does not include the power of amendment under the guise of interpretation. To miss the point of difference between the two is to miss all that the phrase "supreme law of the land" stands for and to convert what was intended as inescapable and enduring mandates into mere moral reflections.

If the Constitution, intelligently and reasonably construed in the light of these principles, stands in the way of desirable legislation, the blame must rest upon that instrument, and not upon the court for enforcing it according to its terms. The remedy in that situation—and the only true remedy—is to amend the Constitution. . . .

2.   *". . . more exacting judicial scrutiny . . ."*

UNITED STATES V. CAROLENE PRODUCTS COMPANY

IN THIS *apparently unimportant case, the Supreme Court by a 6–1 vote sustained the constitutionality of a federal statute prohibiting the shipment in interstate commerce of "filled milk." In his opinion for the majority, however, Justice Stone laid the groundwork for his preferred freedoms doctrine. To the statement that even in the absence of specific legislative findings of fact "the existence of facts supporting the legislative judgment is to be presumed," Stone appended the following footnote. (Actually the second and third paragraphs of the footnote were drafted by Stone's clerk, Louis Lusky, and the first paragraph was added by Charles Evans Hughes.)*

THERE MAY BE narrower scope for operation of the presumption of constitutionality when legislation appears on its face to be within a specific prohibition of the Constitution, such as those of the first ten amendments, which are deemed equally specific when held to be embraced within the Fourteenth. . . .

It is unnecessary to consider now whether legislation which restricts those political processes which can ordinarily be expected to bring about a repeal of undesirable legislation, is to be subjected to more exacting judicial scrutiny under the general prohibitions of the Fourteenth Amendment than are most other types of legislation. . . .

Nor need we inquire whether similar considerations enter into the review of statutes directed at particular religious . . . or national . . . or racial minorities . . .: whether prejudice against discrete and insular minorities may be a special condition, which tends seriously to curtail the operation of those political processes ordinarily to be relied upon to protect minorities, and which may call for a correspondingly more searching judicial inquiry. . . .

304 U.S. 144, 58 S. Ct. 778, 82 L. Ed. 1234 (1938).

3.
"*. . . we act in these matters not by authority of our competence but by force of our commissions.*"

THE FLAG SALUTE CONTROVERSY

JUSTICE FRANKFURTER TO JUSTICE STONE

IN 1940, *the Supreme Court had before it the case of* Minersville School District *v.* Gobitis *(310 U.S. 586, 60 S. Ct. 1010, 84 L. Ed. 1375). A local Pennsylvania school board had required all children attending public schools to participate in a flag salute ceremony. Such a salute ran counter to the religious beliefs of Jehovah's Witnesses, and a Jehovah's Witness father obtained an injunction from a federal district court against the board's enforcing its order against his children. The Supreme Court granted certiorari after the Court of Appeals upheld the district judge. By an 8–1 vote, the Supreme Court reversed the lower courts and sustained the constitutionality of the flag salute requirement. Before the decision was announced, Justice Frankfurter, author of the majority opinion, wrote a memorandum to Justice Stone, the sole dissenter.*

May 27, 1940

Dear Stone:

Were No. 690 *[Minersville School District* v. *Gobitis]* an ordinary case I should let the opinion speak for itself. But that you should entertain doubts has naturally stirred me to an anxious re-examination of my own views, even though I can assure you that nothing has weighed as much on my conscience, since I have come on this Court, as has this case. . . . After all, the vulgar intrusion of law in the domain of conscience is for me a very sensitive area. For various reasons . . . a good part of my mature life has thrown whatever weight it has had against foolish and harsh manifestations of coercion and for the amplest expression of dissident views, however absurd or offensive

This letter is reprinted in Alpheus T. Mason, *Security through Freedom* (Ithaca: Cornell University Press, 1955), pp. 217–220. It is reprinted with the permission of the author, the publisher, and Mr. Justice Frankfurter.

these may have been to my own notions of rationality and decency. . . .

But no one has more clearly in his mind than you, that even when it comes to these ultimate civil liberties . . . we are not in the domain of absolutes. Here, also, we have an illustration of what the Greeks thousands of years ago recognized as a tragic issue, namely, the clash of rights, not the clash of wrongs. For resolving such clash we have no calculus. But there is for me, and I know also for you, a great make-weight for dealing with this problem, namely, that we are not the primary resolvers of the clash. We are not exercising an independent judgment; we are sitting in judgment upon the judgment of the legis-lature. I am aware of the important distinction which you so skillfully adumbrated in your footnote 4 (particularly the second paragraph of it) in the *Carolene Products Co.* case. I agree with that distinction; I regard it as basic. I have taken over that distinction in its central aspect . . . in the present opinion by insisting on the importance of keeping open all those channels of free expression by which undesir-able legislation may be removed, and keeping unobstructed all forms of protests against what are deemed invasions of conscience. . . .

What weighs with me strongly in this case is my anxiety that, while we lean in the direction of the libertarian aspect, we do not exercise our judicial power unduly, and as though we ourselves were legislators by holding too tight a rein on the organs of popular government. In other words, I want to avoid the mistake comparable to that made by those whom we criticized when dealing with the control of property. I hope I am aware of the different interests that are compendiously summarized by opposing "liberty" to "property." But I also know that the generalizations implied in these summaries are also inaccurate and hardly correspond to the complicated realities of an advanced society. I cannot rid myself of the notion that it is not fantastic, although I think foolish and perhaps worse, for school authorities to believe . . . that to allow exemption to some of the children goes far towards dis-rupting the whole patriotic exercise. . . .

For time and circumstances are surely not irrelevant considerations in resolving the conflicts that we do have to resolve in this particular case. . . . You may have noticed that in my opinion I did not rely on the prior adjudications by this Court of this question. I dealt with the matter as I believe it should have been dealt with, as though it were a new question. But certainly it is relevant to make the adjustment that we have to make within the framework of the present circumstances and those that are clearly ahead of us. . . . this case would have a tail of implications as to legislative power that is certainly debatable and might easily be invoked far beyond the size of the immediate kite, were it to deny the very minimum exaction, however foolish as to the Gobitis children, of expression of faith in the heritage and purposes of our country.

For my intention . . . was to use this opinion as a vehicle for preaching the true democratic faith of not relying on the Court for the impossible task of assuring a vigorous, mature, self-protecting and tolerant democracy by bringing the responsibility for a combination of firmness and toleration directly home where it belongs—to the people and their representatives themselves.

I have tried in this opinion really to act on what will, as a matter of history, be a lodestar for due regard between legislative and judicial powers, to wit, your dissent in the *Butler* case. . . . The duty of compulsion [in the flag salute requirement] being as minimal as it is for an act, the normal legislative authorization of which certainly cannot be denied, and all channels of affirmative free expression being open to both children and parents, I cannot resist the conviction that we ought to let the legislative judgment stand and put the responsibility for its exercise where it belongs. . . .

Faithfully yours,

Felix Frankfurter

WEST VIRGINIA STATE BOARD OF EDUCATION *v.* BARNETTE

This case involved the constitutionality of a West Virginia statute, which, after the Gobitis decision, had set up a flag salute requirement similar to that in Minersville. Two important changes had taken place in the Court in the meantime, however. Justices Black, Douglas, and Murphy, in a separate opinion in another case concerning Jehovah's Witnesses, had confessed that they had erred in the first flag salute case. Second, two members of the Gobitis majority, McReynolds and Hughes, had retired, and the two new members of the Court, Jackson

319 U.S. 624, 63 S. Ct. 1178, 87 L. Ed. 1628 (1943).

and Rutledge, were thought to be hostile to the compulsory flag salute. Jehovah's Witnesses brought a suit to enjoin enforcement of the flag salute regulation. Noting the changes on the Supreme Court, a special three judge federal district court granted the injunction. State officials appealed.

MR. JUSTICE JACKSON delivered the opinion of the Court. . . .

The freedom asserted by these appellees does not bring them into collision with rights asserted by any other individual. It is such conflicts which most frequently require intervention of the State to determine where the rights of one end and those of another begin. But the refusal of these persons to participate in the ceremony does not interfere with or deny rights of others to do so. Nor is there any question in this case that their behavior is peaceable and orderly. The sole conflict is between authority and rights of the individual. The State asserts power to condition access to public education on making a prescribed sign and profession and at the same time to coerce attendance by punishing both parent and child. The latter stand on a right of self-determination in matters that touch individual opinion and personal attitude. . . .

There is no doubt that, in connection with the pledges, the flag salute is a form of utterance. Symbolism is a primitive but effective way of communicating ideas. The use of an emblem or flag to symbolize some system, idea, institution, or personality, is a short cut from mind to mind. Causes and nations, political parties, lodges and ecclesiastical groups seek to knit the loyalty of their followings to a flag or banner, a color or design. The State announces rank, function, and authority through crowns and maces, uniforms and black robes; the church speaks through the Cross, the Crucifix, the altar and shrine, and clerical raiment. Symbols of State often convey political ideas just as religious symbols come to convey theological ones. Associated with many of these symbols are appropriate gestures of acceptance or respect: a salute, a bowed or bared head, a bended knee. A person gets from a symbol the meaning he puts into it, and what is one man's comfort and inspiration is another's jest and scorn. . . .

It is also to be noted that the compulsory flag salute and pledge requires affirmation of a belief and an attitude of mind. . . . It is now a commonplace that censorship or suppression of expression of opinion is tolerated by our Constitution only when the expression presents a clear and present danger of action of a kind the State is empowered to prevent and punish. It would seem that involuntary affirmation could be commanded only on even more immediate and urgent grounds than silence. But here the power of compulsion is invoked without any allegation that remaining passive during a flag salute ritual creates a clear and present danger that would justify an effort even to muffle expression. To sustain the compulsory flag salute we are required to say that a Bill of Rights which guards the individual's right to speak his own mind, left it open to public authorities to compel him to utter what is not in his mind. . . .

The *Gobitis* opinion reasoned that this is a field "where courts possess no marked and certainly no controlling competence," that it is committed to the legislatures as well as the courts to guard cherished liberties and that it is constitutionally appropriate to "fight out the wise use of legislative authority in the forum of public opinion and before legislative assemblies rather than to transfer such a contest to the judicial arena," since all the "effective means of inducing political changes are left free." . . .

The very purpose of a Bill of Rights was to withdraw certain subjects from the vicissitudes of political controversy, to place them beyond the reach of majorities and officials and to establish them as legal principles to be applied by the courts. One's right to life, liberty, and property, to free speech, a free press, freedom of worship and assembly, and other fundamental rights may not be submitted to vote; they depend on the outcome of no elections. . . .

Nor does our duty to apply the Bill of Rights to assertions of official authority depend upon our possession of marked competence in the field where the invasion of rights occurs. True, the task of translating the majestic generalities of the Bill of Rights, conceived as part of the pattern of liberal government in the eighteenth century, into concrete restraints on officials dealing with the problems of the twentieth century, is one to disturb self-confidence. . . . But we act in these matters not by authority of our competence but by force of our commissions. We cannot, because of modest estimates of our competence in such specialties as public education, withhold the judgment that history authenticates as the function of this Court when liberty is infringed. . . .

The case is made difficult not because the principles of its decision are obscure but because the flag involved is our own. Nevertheless, we apply the limitations of the Constitution with no fear that freedom to be intellectually and spiritually diverse or even contrary will disintegrate the social organization. To believe that patriotism will not flourish if patriotic ceremonies are voluntary and spontaneous instead of a compulsory routine is to make an unflattering estimate of the appeal of our institutions to free minds. . . . freedom to differ is not limited to things that do not matter much. That would be a mere shadow of freedom. The test of its substance is the right to differ as to things that touch the heart of the existing order.

If there is any fixed star in our constitutional constellation, it is that no official, high or petty, can prescribe what shall be orthodox in politics, nationalism, religion, or other matters of opinion or force citizens to confess by word or act their faith therein. . . .

The decision of this Court in *Minersville School District* v. *Gobitis* and the holdings of those few *per curiam* decisions which preceded and foreshadowed it are overruled, and the judgment enjoining enforcement of the West Virginia Regulation is

Affirmed.

MR. JUSTICE ROBERTS and MR. JUSTICE REED adhere to the views expressed by the Court in *Minersville School District* v. *Gobitis* . . . and are of the opinion that the judgment below should be reversed.

MR. JUSTICE BLACK and MR. JUSTICE DOUGLAS, concurring. . . .

MR. JUSTICE FRANKFURTER, dissenting.

One who belongs to the most vilified and persecuted minority in history is not likely to be insensible to the freedoms guaranteed by our Constitution. Were my purely personal attitude relevant I should wholeheartedly associate myself with the general libertarian views in the Court's opinion, representing as they do the thought and action of a lifetime. But as judges we are neither Jew nor Gentile, neither Catholic nor agnostic. We owe equal attachment to the Constitution and are equally bound by our judicial obligations whether we derive our citizenship from the earliest or the latest immigrants to these shores. As a member of this Court I am not justified in writing my private notions of policy into the Constitution, no matter how deeply I may cherish them or how mischievous I may deem their disregard. The duty of a judge who must decide which of two claims before the Court shall prevail, that of a State to enact and enforce laws within its general competence or that of an individual to refuse obedience because of the demands of his conscience, is not that of the ordinary person. It can never be emphasized too much that one's own opinion about the wisdom or evil of a law should be excluded altogether when one is doing one's duty on the bench. The only opinion of our own even looking in that direction that is material is our opinion whether legislators could in reason have enacted such a law. In the light of all the circumstances, including the history of this question in this Court, it would require more daring than I possess to deny that reasonable legislators could have taken the action which is before us for review. . . .

Not so long ago we were admonished that "the only check upon our own exercise of power is our own sense of self-restraint. For the removal of unwise laws from the statute books appeal lies not to the courts but to the ballot and to the processes of democratic government." . . .

The admonition that judicial self-restraint alone limits arbitrary exercise of our authority is relevant every time we are asked to nullify legislation. The Constitution does not give us greater veto power when dealing with one phase of "liberty" than with another, or when dealing with grade school regulations than with college regulations that offend conscience. . . . In neither situation is our function comparable to that of a legislature or are we free to act as though we were a super-legislature. Judicial self-restraint is equally necessary whenever an exercise of political or legislative power is challenged. There is no warrant in the constitutional basis of this Court's authority for attributing different rôles to it depending upon the nature of the challenge to the legislation. Our power does not vary according to the particular provision of the Bill of Rights which is invoked. The right not to have property taken without just compensation has, so far as the scope of judicial power is concerned, the same constitutional dignity as the right to be protected against unreasonable searches and seizures, and the latter has no less claim than freedom of the press or freedom of speech or religious freedom. In no instance is this Court the primary protector of the particular liberty that is invoked. . . .

When Mr. Justice Holmes, speaking for this Court, wrote that "it must be remembered that legislatures are ultimate guardians of the liberties and welfare of the people in quite as great a degree as the courts" . . . he went to the very essence of our constitutional system and the democratic conception of our society. He did not mean that for only some phases of civil government this Court was not to supplant legislatures and sit in judgment upon the right or wrong of a challenged measure. He was stating the comprehensive judicial duty and rôle of this Court in our constitutional scheme whenever legislation is sought to be nullified on any ground, namely, that responsibility for legislation lies with legislatures, answerable as they are directly to the people, and this Court's only and very narrow function is to determine whether within the broad grant of authority vested in legislatures they have exercised a judgment for which reasonable justification can be offered. . . .

The reason why from the beginning even the narrow judicial authority to nullify legislation has been viewed with a jealous eye is that it serves to prevent the full play of the democratic process. The fact that it may be an undemocratic aspect of our scheme of government does not call for its rejection or its disuse. But it is the best of reasons, as this Court has frequently recognized, for the greatest caution in its use. . . .

Under our constitutional system the legislature is charged solely with civil concerns of society. If the avowed or intrinsic legislative purpose is either to promote or to discourage some religious community or creed, it is clearly within the constitutional restrictions imposed on legislatures and cannot stand. But it by no means follows that legislative power is wanting whenever a general non-discriminatory civil regulation in fact touches conscientious scruples or religious beliefs of an individual or a group. Regard for such scruples or beliefs undoubtedly presents one of the most reasonable claims for the exertion of legislative accommodation. . . . But the real question is, who is to make such accommodations, the courts or the legislature? . . .

That claims are pressed on behalf of sincere religious convictions does not of itself establish their constitutional validity. Nor does waving the banner of religious freedom relieve us from examining into the power we are asked to deny the states. Otherwise the doctrine of separation of church and state, so cardinal in the history of this nation and for the liberty of our people, would mean not the disestablishment of a state church but the establishment of all churches and of all religious groups.

The subjection of dissidents to the general requirement of saluting the flag, as a measure conducive to the training of children in good citizenship, is very far from being the first instance of exacting obedience to general laws that have offended deep religious scruples. Compulsory vaccination . . . food inspection regulations . . . the obligation to bear arms . . . testimonial duties . . . compulsory medical treatment . . . these are but illustrations of conduct that has often been compelled in the enforcement of legislation of general applicability even though the religious consciences of particular individuals rebelled at the exaction.

Law is concerned with external behavior and not with the inner life of man. It rests in large measure upon compulsion. Socrates lives in history partly because he gave his life for the conviction that duty of obedience to secular law does not presuppose consent to its enactment or belief in its virtue. The consent upon which free government rests is the consent that comes from sharing in the process of making and unmaking laws. The state is not shut out from a domain because the individual conscience may deny the state's claim. The individual conscience may profess what faith it chooses. It may affirm and promote that faith—in the language of the Constitution, it may "exercise" it freely—but it cannot thereby restrict community action through political organs in matters of community concern, so long as the action is not asserted in a discriminatory way either openly or by stealth. One may have the right to practice one's religion and at the same time owe the duty of formal obedience to laws that run counter to one's beliefs. . . .

. . . . West Virginia does not compel the attendance at its public schools of the children here concerned. West Virginia does not so compel, for it cannot. This Court denied the right of a state to require its children to attend public schools. . . .

Parents have the privilege of choosing which schools they wish their children to attend. And the question here is whether the state may make certain requirements that seem to it desirable or important for the proper education of those future citizens who go to schools maintained by the states, or whether the pupils in those schools may be relieved from those requirements if they run counter to the consciences of their parents. Not only have parents the right to send children to schools of their own choosing but the state has no right to bring such schools "under a strict governmental control" or give "affirmative direction concerning the intimate and essential details of such schools, entrust their control to public officers, and deny both owners and patrons reasonable choice and discretion in respect of teachers, curriculum, and textbooks." . . . Why should not the state likewise have constitutional power to make reasonable provisions for the proper instruction of children in schools maintained by it? . . .

We are told that symbolism is a dramatic but primitive way of communicating ideas. Symbolism is inescapable. Even the most sophisticated live by symbols. But it is not for this Court to make psychological judgments as to the effectiveness of a particular symbol in inculcating concededly indispensable feelings, particularly if the state happens to see fit to utilize the symbol that represents our heritage and our hopes. . . . The significance of a symbol lies in what it represents. To reject the swastika does not imply rejection of the Cross. And so it bears repetition to say that it mocks reason and denies our whole history to find in the allowance of a requirement to salute our flag on fitting occasions the seeds of sanction for obeisance to a leader. To deny the power to employ educational symbols is to say that the state's educational system may not stimulate the imagination because this may lead to unwise stimulation. . . .

One's conception of the Constitution cannot be severed from one's conception of a judge's function in applying it. The Court has no reason for existence if it merely reflects the pressures of the day. Our system is built on the faith that men set apart for this special function, freed from the influences of immediacy and from the deflections of worldly ambition, will become able to take a view of longer range than the period of responsibility entrusted to Congress and legislatures. We are dealing with matters as to which legislators and voters have conflicting views. Are we as judges to impose our strong convictions on where wisdom lies? . . .

Of course patriotism can not be enforced by the flag salute. But neither can the liberal spirit be enforced by judicial invalidation of illiberal legislation. Our constant preoccupation with the constitutionality of legislation rather than with its wisdom tends to preoccupation of the American mind with a false value. The tendency of focussing attention on constitutionality is to make constitutionality synonymous with wisdom, to regard a law as all right if it is constitutional. Such an attitude is a great enemy of liberalism. Particularly in legislation affecting freedom of thought and freedom of speech much which should offend a free-spirited society is constitutional. Reliance for the most precious interests of civilization, therefore, must be found outside of their vindication in courts of law. Only a persistent positive translation of the faith of a free society into the convictions and habits and actions of a community is the ultimate reliance against unabated temptations to fetter the human spirit.

4.   *"This is conduct that shocks the conscience."*

ROCHIN V. CALIFORNIA

SUSPECTING *Antonio Rochin of illegal possession of narcotics, Los Angeles police broke into his home and tried to seize him. Rochin, however, swallowed the evidence. Failing in their efforts to pry his mouth open and recover the narcotics, police took Rochin to a hospital where a stomach pump was used to force him to vomit the evidence. On the basis of evidence thus obtained Rochin was convicted. The state supreme court refused to review the conviction, and Rochin sought and obtained certiorari from the U.S. Supreme Court.*

MR. JUSTICE FRANKFURTER delivered the opinion of the Court. . . .

. . . The power to define crimes belongs to Congress only as an appropriate means of carrying into execution its limited grant of legis-

342 U.S. 165, 72 S. Ct. 205, 96 L. Ed. 183 (1952).

lative powers. . . . Broadly speaking, crimes in the United States are what the laws of the individual States make them, subject to the limitations . . . in the original Constitution, prohibiting bills of attainder and *ex post facto* laws, and of the Thirteenth and Fourteenth Amendments. . . . Accordingly, in reviewing a State criminal conviction under a claim of right guaranteed by the Due Process Clause of the Fourteenth Amendment, from which is derived the most far-reaching and most frequent federal basis of challenging State criminal justice, "we must be deeply mindful of the responsibilities of the States for the enforcement of criminal laws, and exercise with due humility our merely negative function in subjecting convictions from state courts to the very narrow scrutiny which the Due Process Clause of the Fourteenth Amendment authorizes." *Malinski* v. *New York.* . . .

However, this Court too has its responsibility. Regard for the requirements of the Due Process Clause "inescapably imposes upon this Court an exercise of judgment upon the whole course of the proceedings [resulting in a conviction] in order to ascertain whether they offend those canons of decency and fairness which express the notions of justice of English-speaking peoples even toward those charged with the most heinous offenses." *Malinski* v. *New York.* . . . These standards of justice are not authoritatively formulated anywhere as though they were specifics. Due process of law is a summarized constitutional guarantee of respect for those personal immunities which, as Mr. Justice Cardozo twice wrote for the Court, are "so rooted in the traditions and conscience of our people as to be ranked as fundamental." . . . or are "implicit in the concept of ordered liberty." *Palko* v. *Connecticut.* . . .

The vague contours of the Due Process Clause do not leave judges at large. We may not draw on our merely personal and private notions and disregard the limits that bind judges in their judicial function. Even though the concept of due process of law is not final and fixed, these limits are derived from considerations that are fused in the whole nature of our judicial process. . . .

Due process of law thus conceived is not to be derided as resort to a revival of "natural law." To believe that this judicial exercise of judgment could be avoided by freezing "due process of law" at some fixed stage of time or thought is to suggest that the most important aspect of constitutional adjudication is a function for inanimate machines and not for judges, for whom the independence safeguarded by Article III of the Constitution was designed and who are presumably guided by established standards of judicial behavior. Even cybernetics has not yet made that haughty claim. To practice the requisite detachment and to achieve sufficient objectivity no doubt demands of judges the habit of self-discipline and self-criticism, incertitude that one's own views are incontestable and alert tolerance toward views not shared. But these are precisely the presuppositions of our judicial process. They are precisely the qualities society has a right to expect from those entrusted with ultimate judicial power.

Restraints on our jurisdiction are self-imposed only in the sense that there is from our decisions no immediate appeal short of impeachment or constitutional amendment. But that does not make due process of law a matter of judicial caprice. The faculties of the Due Process Clause may be indefinite and vague, but the mode of their ascertainment is not self-willed. In each case "due process of law" requires an evaluation based on a disinterested inquiry pursued in the spirit of science, on a balanced order of facts exactly and fairly stated, on the detached consideration of conflicting claims . . . on a judgment not *ad hoc* and episodic but duly mindful of reconciling the needs both of continuity and of change in a progressive society.

Applying these general considerations to the circumstances of the present case, we are compelled to conclude that the proceedings by which this conviction was obtained do more than offend some fastidious squeamishness or private sentimentalism about combatting crime too energetically. This is conduct that shocks the conscience. Illegally breaking into the privacy of the petitioner, the struggle to open his mouth and remove what was there, the forcible extraction of his stomach's contents—this course of proceeding by agents of government to obtain evidence is bound to offend even hardened sensibilities. They are methods too close to the rack and the screw to permit of constitutional differentiation. . . .

Reversed.

Mr. Justice Minton took no part in the consideration or decision of this case.

MR. JUSTICE BLACK, concurring.

Adamson v. *California* . . . sets out reasons for my belief that state as well as federal courts and law enforcement officers must obey the Fifth Amendment's command that "No person . . . shall be compelled in any criminal case to be a witness against himself." . . .

What the majority hold is that the Due Process Clause empowers this Court to nullify any state law if its application "shocks the conscience," offends "a sense of justice" or runs counter to the "decencies of civilized conduct." The majority emphasize that these statements do not refer to their own consciences or to their senses of justice and decency. For we are told that "we may not draw on our merely personal and private notions"; our judgment must be grounded on "considerations deeply rooted in reason and in the compelling traditions of the legal profession." We are further admonished to measure the validity of state practices, not by our reason, or by the traditions of the legal profession, but by "the community's sense of fair play and decency"; by the "traditions and conscience of our people"; or by "those canons of decency and fairness which express the notions of justice of English-speaking peoples." These canons are made necessary, it is said, because of "interests of society pushing in opposite directions."

If the Due Process Clause does vest this Court with such unlimited power to invalidate laws, I am still in doubt as to why we should consider only the notions of English-speaking peoples to determine what are immutable and fundamental principles of justice. Moreover, one may well ask what avenues of investigation are open to discover "canons" of conduct so universally favored that this Court should write them into the Constitution? All we are told is that the discovery must be made by an "evaluation based on a disinterested inquiry pursued in the spirit of science, on a balanced order of facts."

Some constitutional provisions are stated in absolute and unqualified language such, for illustration, as the First Amendment stating that no law shall be passed prohibiting the free exercise of religion or abridging the freedom of speech or press. Other constitutional provisions do require courts to choose between competing policies, such as the Fourth Amendment which, by its terms, necessitates a judicial decision as to what is an "unreasonable" search or seizure. There is, however, no express constitutional language granting judicial power to invalidate *every* state law of *every* kind deemed "unreasonable" or contrary to the Court's notion of civilized decencies; yet the constitutional philosophy used by the majority has, in the past, been used to deny a state the right to fix the price of gasoline . . . and even the right to prevent bakers from palming off smaller for larger loaves of bread. . . . What paralyzing role this same philosophy will play in the future economic affairs of this country is impossible to predict. Of even graver concern, however, is the use of the philosophy to nullify the Bill of Rights. I long ago concluded that the accordion-like qualities of this philosophy must inevitably imperil all the individual liberty safeguards specifically enumerated in the Bill of Rights. . . .

MR. JUSTICE DOUGLAS, concurring.

The evidence obtained from this accused's stomach would be admissible in the majority of states where the question has been raised. So far as the reported cases reveal, the only states which would probably exclude the evidence would be Arkansas, Iowa, Michigan, and Missouri. Yet the Court now says that the rule which the majority of the states have fashioned violates the "decencies of civilized conduct." To that I cannot agree. It is a rule formulated by responsible courts with judges as sensitive as we are to the proper standards for law administration.

As an original matter it might be debatable whether the provision in the Fifth Amendment that no person "shall be compelled in any criminal case to be a witness against himself" serves the ends of justice. Not all civilized legal procedures recognize it. But the choice was made by the Framers, a choice which sets a standard for legal trials in this country. . . . I think that words taken from his lips, capsules taken from his stomach, blood taken from his veins are all inadmissible provided they are taken from him without his consent. They are inadmissible because of the command of the Fifth Amendment.

That is an unequivocal, definite and workable rule of evidence for state and federal courts. But we cannot in fairness free the state courts from that command and yet excoriate them for flouting the "decencies of civilized conduct" when they admit the evidence. That is to make the rule turn not on the Constitution but on the idiosyncrasies of the judges who sit here. . . .

5.
"*Modern community living requires modern scientific methods of crime detection . . .*"

BREITHAUPT V. ABRAM, WARDEN

PAUL BREITHAUPT *was involved in an auto accident in which three people were killed. A liquor bottle was found in his car and his breath smelled of liquor. At the hospital to which Breithaupt was taken, and while he was still unconscious, police asked the doctor to take a blood sample from Breithaupt and to test its alcoholic content. The doctor complied and the test indicated that Breithaupt had been driving while drunk. He was convicted of involuntary manslaughter and did not appeal. While in prison he tried to get a writ of habeas corpus, which state courts denied. He sought and obtained certiorari from the U.S. Supreme Court.*

MR. JUSTICE CLARK delivered the opinion of the Court. . . .
Petitioner . . . urges that the conduct of the state officers here offends that "sense of justice" of which we spoke in *Rochin* v. *California.* . . . But we see nothing comparable here to the facts in *Rochin.*
Basically the distinction rests on the fact that there is nothing "brutal" or "offensive" in the taking of a sample of blood when done, as in this case, under the protective eye of a physician. To be sure, the driver here was unconscious when the blood was taken, but the absence of conscious consent, without more, does not necessarily render the taking a violation of a constitutional right; and certainly the test as administered here would not be considered offensive by even the most delicate. Furthermore, due process is not measured by the yardstick of personal reaction or the sphygmogram of the most sensitive person, but by that whole community sense of "decency and fairness" that has been woven by common experience into the fabric of acceptable conduct. It is on this bedrock that this Court has established the concept of due process. The blood test procedure has become routine in our everyday life. It is a ritual for those going into the military service as well as those applying for marriage licenses. Many colleges require such tests before permitting entrance and literally millions of

352 U.S. 432, 77 S. Ct. 408, 1 L. Ed. 2d 448 (1957).

us have voluntarily gone through the same, though a longer, routine in becoming blood donors. Likewise, we note that a majority of our States have either enacted statutes in some form authorizing tests of this nature or permit findings so obtained to be admitted in evidence. We therefore conclude that a blood test taken by a skilled technician is not such "conduct that shocks the conscience," *Rochin* . . . nor such a method of obtaining evidence that it offends a "sense of justice," *Brown* v. *Mississippi*. . . . This is not to say that the indiscriminate taking of blood under different conditions or by those not competent to do so may not amount to such "brutality" as would come under the *Rochin* rule. . . .

. . . Modern community living requires modern scientific methods of crime detection lest the public go unprotected. The increasing slaughter on our highways, most of which should be avoidable, now reaches the astounding figures only heard of on the battlefield. . . . As against the right of an individual that his person be held inviolable, even against so slight an intrusion as is involved in applying a blood test of the kind to which millions of Americans submit as a matter of course nearly every day, must be set the interests of society in the scientific determination of intoxication, one of the great causes of the mortal hazards of the road. . . .

Affirmed.

MR. CHIEF JUSTICE WARREN, with whom MR. JUSTICE BLACK and MR. JUSTICE DOUGLAS join, dissenting.

The judgment in this case should be reversed if *Rochin* v. *California* . . . is to retain its vitality and stand as more than an instance of personal revulsion against particular police methods. I cannot agree with the Court when it says, "we see nothing comparable here to the facts in *Rochin*." It seems to me the essential elements of the cases are the same and the same result should follow. . . . I cannot accept an analysis that would make physical resistance by a prisoner a prerequisite to the existence of his constitutional rights. . . . Only personal reaction to the stomach pump and the blood test can distinguish them. . . .

MR. JUSTICE DOUGLAS, with whom MR. JUSTICE BLACK joins, dissenting.

The Court seems to sanction in the name of law enforcement the assault made by the police on this unconscious man. If law enforcement were the chief value in our constitutional scheme, then due process would shrivel and become of little value in protecting the rights of the citizen. But those who fashioned the Constitution put certain rights out of the reach of the police and preferred other rights over law enforcement. . . .

As I understand today's decision there would be a violation of due process if the blood had been withdrawn from the accused after a struggle with the police. But the sanctity of the person is equally violated and his body assaulted where the prisoner is incapable of offering resistance as it would be if force were used to overcome his resistance. In both cases evidence is used to convict a man which has been obtained from him on an involuntary basis. . . . Under our system of government, police cannot compel people to furnish the evidence necessary to send them to prison. . . .

And if the decencies of a civilized state are the test, it is repulsive to me for the police to insert needles into an unconscious person in order to get the evidence necessary to convict him, whether they find the person unconscious, give him a pill which puts him to sleep, or use force to subdue him. The indignity to the individual is the same in one case as in the other, for in each is his body invaded and assaulted by the police who are supposed to be the citizen's protector. . . .

6.
"Every constitutional question involves a weighing of competing values."

THE SEARCH FOR OBJECTIVITY[1] IN CONSTITUTIONAL LAW *George D. Braden**

I

ONE OF THE first recent efforts by justices to make explicit a philosophy of self-imitation appeared in Chief Justice Stone's now famous footnote in the otherwise little noticed *Carolene Products*

57 *Yale Law Journal* 571 (1948). Copyright 1948 the Yale Law Journal Co. Reprinted with permission.

[1] By "objectivity" I mean that quality of a rule of law which enables it to be applied to similar situations with similar results regardless of the identity of the judges who apply it.

* Former clerk to a U.S. Circuit Judge, and Associate Professor of Law, Yale Law School; currently a counsel for the General Electric Company.

case. . . . Stone's thesis appears to be something like this: "I am first of all a man of reason. I believe in reason and its power in the market place of discourse. I am also a democrat. I believe that our governments are to be run by the governed. Therefore I shall use my great power as a Supreme Court justice sparingly, but I shall use it when it is necessary to preserve the democratic process or to protect those injured by unreason under circumstances where political processes cannot be relied on to protect them." . . .

Here then is a statement of a basic formula for constitutional decisions in certain areas. It is not a statement which can be found in the Constitution or in the Court's gloss on the Constitution. It is rather one man's explanation of why he finds the Due Process and Commerce Clauses to be limitations on government in some instances and not in others. Put another way, it is simply a part of one man's set of values for his society which he holds strongly enough to be willing to enforce when the opportunity arises.

An analysis of this philosophy reveals some shortcomings. In the first place, it is open-ended. What are "discrete and insular minorities"? Racial and religious groups, yes. Public utilities? Had Chief Justice Stone sat on the Court in the days of Granger legislation against the railroads, would he have held the railroads to be such a minority? In the second place, such a philosophy based on reason may work in reverse in that a justice unable to see any validity in any argument advanced in support of a legislative act may conclude that it is irrational legislation and hence aimed at a "minority." Third, it is not a complete blueprint. It says that delicate weighing is required when the legislative assertion of necessity is attacked in the name of protection of political processes or of minorities, but it does not give the balance point on the scales. . . . A working philosophy can not be completely blueprinted; it must grow by experience. But Chief Justice Stone's philosophy is so abstract that it contains virtually nothing to show how it works in individual cases. Would he have dissented in *Colegrove* v. *Green*, where the Court refused to remedy unbalanced representation in Congress? With regard to minorities, did he scrutinize severely "legislation directed at" or "legislation affecting" minorities? Did he require some objective mark of minority status, such as color, to bring his philosophy into effective operations?

This is not an objective theory of judicial review. The Chief Justice never claimed that it was. A man who said "the only check upon our own exercise of power is our own sense of self-restraint" could hardly believe in any self-executing objective standard of constitutionality. . . .

II

Mr. Justice Frankfurter has likewise come forth with a well-considered philosophy of judicial restraint in areas of limitations on government, but he departs from Chief Justice Stone in presenting his as objective and impersonal. His starting point is the necessity for judicial self-restraint. . . . He is apparently prepared to accept as a minimum of power the protection of political processes, the first half of Chief Justice Stone's thesis. In his exhaustive statement of his creed in the second flag salute case, he notes that the "channels of affirmative free expression" were open to the Jehovah's Witnesses, the opponents of compulsory flag saluting. "Had we before us any act of the state putting the slightest curbs upon such free expression, I should not lag behind any member of this Court in striking down such an invasion of the right to freedom of thought and freedom of speech protected by the Constitution." Inasmuch as the Fourteenth Amendment, under which the flag salute case was brought, says nothing about freedom of thought or speech, Mr. Justice Frankfurter must have some reason for reading such freedom into the Due Process Clause. That his reason apparently is much the same as the Chief Justice's is fairly inferred from these quoted statements and from his concluding words in his opinion for the Court in the first flag salute case. There he exalts the role of the legislature, provided that "all the effective means of inducing political changes are left free from interference."

It is equally apparent that Mr. Justice Frankfurter does not accept Chief Justice Stone's protection of minorities. The fact that the two men opposed each other in both flag salute cases is enough in itself to establish this. If Mr. Justice Frankfurter stopped with his thesis in those two cases it might be possible to state that he has a personal philosophy even narrower than that of Chief Justice Stone, possessing the best qualities of the latter's without some of the shortcomings noted above. But he does not stop there. He casts his theory in such a way as to make it objective. First, he makes reference to "specific" prohibitions in the Constitution, using as an example the Bill of Rights, adding that each is as important as the next one. Inasmuch as the First Amendment protects political processes, he could rely on this "specific" provision were it not for the problem of getting the First Amendment into the Fourteenth. He is not willing to import all the Bill of Rights into the Fourteenth, and must therefore provide a basis for discriminating between parts of the Bill of Rights, rejecting some and accepting others for purposes of enforcing the Due Process Clause of the Fourteenth Amendment. It is in setting forth the criterion for discrimination that his objective theory takes shape.

This objective criterion is most frequently expressed in words of Mr. Justice Cardozo. For example, on one occasion Mr. Justice Frankfurter relies on his predecessor's words when he says, "We are dealing with principles of liberty and justice 'so rooted in the traditions and conscience of our people as to be ranked as fundamental'—something without which 'a fair and enlightened system of justice would be impossible.'" . . . On occasion he quotes from others, and sometimes phrases the criterion in his own words. It all adds up to fundamental notions of justice and liberty.

The important point, of course, is Mr. Justice Frankfurter's assertion that these are not *his* fundamental notions. In the *Willie Francis*[2] case, he says, in a concurring opinion, "We cannot escape acknowledging that [the problem before us] involves the application of standards of fairness and justice very broadly conceived. They are not the application of merely personal standards but the impersonal standards of society which alone judges, as the organs of Law, are empowered to enforce." . . .

Mr. Justice Frankfurter's thesis would thus appear to be somewhat as follows: "I do not let any personal views of my own govern my decisions. I decide cases only on the basis of the consensus of society's opinion of what are fundamental standards of fair play and justice. Naturally, I must have a constitutional provision through which this consensus of opinion can express itself."

[2] *Louisiana* v. *Resweber* (1947). See above, p. 628.

Many questions come to mind at once. What is this consensus? Is it qualitative or quantitative? Is it nationwide or broken into statewide segments? If nationwide, is it determined by a majority of states or a majority of people? What is it a consensus of? Abstract notions of fair play and justice? Or an opinion on the third degree, or flag-saluting, or racial segregation? Or an opinion on the given case before the Court? And how does a justice, who knows what he is looking for, find it? By a Gallup Poll? By editorials in leading papers? By the number of committees of substantial citizens who support the notion? By the number of briefs *amici curiae* filed? By the number of states which follow a given course? . . .

Aside from all these theoretical difficulties with Mr. Justice Frankfurter's objective standard, there is the practical problem of applying it to concrete cases. That he is aware of this is clear from his acknowledgement that "judges among themselves may differ," and his belief that "alert deference to the judgment of the State court under review" will keep the differences under control. He has said this cannot be "blind acceptance." He must, therefore, be saying that even though judges can agree on what is society's opinion, he reserves the privilege of applying it his way. But he cannot do that except by his own view of how best to enforce the objective rules he finds. By "the gradual process of judicial inclusion and exclusion," he will clothe society's abstraction with reality. The reality is his, not society's.

It seems fair to conclude that Mr. Justice Frankfurter has postulated an objective standard of constitutionality that breaks down upon dissection. What, then, has Mr. Justice Frankfurter propounded? . . . tentatively, it can be argued that his objective standard is a way of expressing two things: his own set of values for his society and his own conception of the safe limits of his function. Some things he believes in strongly enough to use his power to protect them. Others he may believe in but not strongly enough to risk the charge of abuse of office. These are not all the factors to be taken into account. Justices are not such uncomplicated mechanisms. But these are certainly two key factors which are more significant than his own words about the "impersonal standards of society which alone judges, as the organs of Law, are empowered to enforce."

III

Mr. Justice Black also searches for an "impersonal standard" by which he can decide issues of constitutional limitations on government. But his method is the antithesis of Mr. Justice Frankfurter's. In *Adamson* v. *California,* they both staged a full-dress review of their theories. . . . Mr. Justice Black's thesis is that he enforces the Bill of Rights because that is what the Constitution specifically provides for. He further asserts that a study of the history of the Fourteenth Amendment convinces him that the Bill of Rights was carried into the Fourteenth Amendment. Thus, he asserts an objective standard of constitutionality covering both state and national government.

Many technical difficulties have to be surmounted by Mr. Justice Black before he can defend his thesis as an objective standard. Whether his history is accurate is a question of importance that need not be dealt with here. . . . What apparently does cause him trouble is the argument that he could hardly want to be so literal as to insist on every prohibition in the Bill of Rights. The argument is put thus: "Even the boldest innovator would shrink from suggesting to more than half the States that they no longer initiate prosecutions without indictment by grand jury, or that thereafter all the States of the Union must furnish a jury of twelve for every case involving a claim above twenty dollars." Mr. Justice Black appears to hedge against such a literal transference when he says, "Whether this Court ever will, or whether it now should, in the light of past decisions, give full effect to what the [Fourteenth] Amendment was intended to accomplish is not necessarily essential to a decision here." To the extent that he means this hedge to be effective, his thesis differs not one whit from Mr. Justice Frankfurter's. They both put into the Fourteenth Amendment what they want to.

Mr. Justice Black's thesis has still other loopholes. First, he may not find in the Bill of Rights "specific" protection for everything he may want to protect. For example, there is no equal protection clause in the Bill of Rights. Would he deny equal protection where national action was in question? Or would he read equal protection backwards from the Fourteenth into the Fifth? What "specific" provision other than equal protection could he find that would forbid racial discrimination? Second, he may have to twist "specific" provisions in order to get under them when reliance on "due process" would be simpler. For example, in *Tot* v. *United States*, a Congressional statutory presumption was invalidated for lack of due process in that the presumed fact had no "reasonable relation to the circumstances of life as we know them." Mr. Justice Black concurred but apparently relied on the Sixth Amendment, which requires a public trial, and confronting an accused with the witnesses against him. . . .

In theory Mr. Justice Black's thesis is objective in that he cannot go outside the "specific" prohibitions of the Bill of Rights and herein it differs from Mr. Justice Frankfurter's thesis inasmuch as the "consensus of society's opinion" is not a definite and unchanging catalog which can be observed by a third person. As a practical matter the two can arrive at the same result. For example, Willie Francis was not protected from electrocution after an initial failure. Mr. Justice Frankfurter said this was because the "consensus of society's opinion" would not protect Willie. Mr. Justice Black presumably thought Willie was not twice put in jeopardy or subjected to cruel and unusual punishment. Whether the Bill of Rights was in or out of the Fourteenth Amendment was of no significance in deciding Willie's fate. . . .

IV

. . . Each theory collapses, on analysis, into little more than a front for policy-making. . . . Perhaps Mr. Justice Frankfurter measures his power, finds it precarious, and retreats. If so, that is the cause of the retreat, not "society's opinion." Perhaps Mr. Justice Black is stymied by an inability to maneuver around "specific" words. If so, it is a lack of ingenuity, a fear of criticism, or a judgment of the reaction to the transparency of his maneuver which stops him, not the "specific" words.

There is no objectivity in constitutional law because there are no absolutes. Every constitutional question involves a weighing of competing values. . . . Hence the justice who wants to tell the world how he decides cases must do what Chief Justice Stone did in a limited way and what Mr. Justice Black almost by accident did in a less limited way. He must say: "This is what I believe is important in our civilization and I shall do all I can to preserve it." And forthwith set forth his creed. If this is too shocking to society or if the many limitations on the Court's power are not in themselves believed to be sufficient to restrain the imposition of "idiosyncratic" values, then society must take away the Court's power. There is no middle ground.

PART EIGHT

Conclusion

18 / DEMOCRACY AND JUDICIAL REVIEW

Perhaps the most obvious paradox on the surface of the American political system is that a supposedly democratic scheme of government allows federal judges, appointed for life and directly answerable to no electorate, to play not only a large part, but on occasions a major part, in the formation of public policy. This contradiction is sometimes denied, sometimes ignored, sometimes dismissed with a "well, it works" shrug. But sometimes, as in the intra-Court disputes over self-restraint, it is faced up to by judges. The purpose of this chapter is to discuss some of the problems which this paradox raises and to analyze some of the ways in which judges have coped with those problems.

Checks and Balances

Granted the abstract conflict between judicial review and democracy, the question might be asked whether there are factors which ease this conflict, at least in the specific context of American government. First, it might be answered, the judiciary is not the only non-democratic branch of the federal government. For all its other virtues, the Senate, where 200,000 Nevadans have the same number of representatives as 14,000,-000 New Yorkers, and where archaic rules and the threat of a filibuster jeopardize almost every important piece of legislation, is hardly a show-place of majority rule. Nor does the House of Representatives, with its constituent districts heavily gerrymandered to overweight rural as against urban interests and with its often dictatorial Rules Committee, usually dominated by men from "safe" one-party districts, provide a forum which by any known formula directly represents a majority of the population.

While the President and Vice President come closest to being chosen by a true majority of the voters, the Electoral College is blatantly un-democratic in theory. Nor do American political parties offer the electorate a clear-cut choice between alternative lines of policy, or act as disciplin-ing agencies to hold public officials responsible for their conduct in office.

Viewed, then, as one part of a political system in which the members of no single institution are necessarily directly accountable to a majority of the voters in the country as a whole, and in which the institutions have mutually overlapping and checking power, judicial authority becomes less incongruent with the type of democratic theory which tries to blend popular sovereignty with limited government. And the American concept of politics, both in theory and practice, shows a distinct preference for limited government over absolute majoritarianism.

Even Thomas Jefferson, who later in his life was to wage a bitter vendetta with John Marshall and the federal judiciary, advocated a strong judicial role in restricting popular power. For example, Jefferson recom-mended in 1784 that the Virginia constitution be amended to make it paramount over ordinary legislation, "so that all acts contrary to it may be adjudged null. . . ." In 1786 he accepted as a matter of course the authority of judges to declare statutes unconstitutional. In 1789 he wrote Madison regarding the proposed bill of rights for the federal Constitution:

> In the arguments in favor of a declaration of rights, you omit one which has great weight with me; the legal check which is put in the hands of the judiciary. This is a body, which, if rendered independent and kept strictly to their own department, merits great confidence for their learning and integrity. In fact, what degree of confidence would be too much for a body composed of such men as Wythe, Blair and Pendleton? On characters like these, the *"civium ardor prava jubentium"* [popular frenzy] would make no impression.

Madison put Jefferson's suggestion to use. In the congressional debate over the adoption of the Bill of Rights, he answered the argument that these rights would only be "paper barriers" in the following manner:

If they [the proposed amendments] are incorporated into the Constitution, independent tribunals of justice will consider themselves in a peculiar manner the guardians of these rights; they will be an impenetrable bulwark against any assumption of power in the Legislative or Executive; they will be naturally led to resist every encroachment upon rights expressly stipulated for in the Constitution by the declaration of rights.

A second factor making judicial review less incompatible with democratic government is that, although judges wield great power, they do not possess unbounded power. Self-restraint is among the more important limitations on courts, but Harlan Stone was simply wrong when he said in 1936 that the only restriction on judges was their own sense of restraint. Even if they were to disregard all the ethical ideals of the judicial office and all the internal restraints of conscience, a majority of Supreme Court justices who acted with the single goal of maximizing their power would still run into serious institutional limitations, and not only from their colleagues and from lower-court judges. To retain that segment of their prestige—and power—which stems from the law-court tradition, these justices would have to operate primarily within that framework. Sophisticated judges can manipulate their technical and procedural limitations for expansionist purposes, but they cannot fully elude the restraints which the law-court tradition imposes on judicial freedom of action.

Moreover, elected politicians at every political level are responsive to the pressures of various interest groups; and groups whose aims have been thwarted in the judicial process seldom hesitate to seek redress in another governmental forum. In addition, politicians have interests of their own as legislators and as administrators. Politics makes men wary of potential rivals for power, even those in black robes. A court that is perceived to be encroaching on legislative or executive prerogatives is quite likely to expose itself to serious attack; and as already seen, there are numerous ways by which judges can be curbed. Since prestige is such a vital component of judicial power, even the threat of a legislative or executive attack can cause damage.

As men who have generally had a good deal of practical political experience, judges undoubtedly recognize such restrictions and realize that they must weigh them in their decision-making. This does not mean, of course, that judges are obliged to take a straw poll or consult with other public officials before deciding cases. On the contrary, if there is any one lesson that stands out in American legal history it is that judges have considerable leeway in shaping policy. But judges are not completely free either to violate the ideal concept of their office or to voice all of their deeply felt principles. If they wish to affect policy and not merely to tilt at windmills, they must be reasonably certain that their decisions will be supported with sufficient strength in other governmental quarters so as to block frequent or major reversals.

Validation and Invalidation

Some proponents of judicial power make an additional argument: In practice, courts have seldom frustrated the current popular will, at least as reified through congressional legislation. Except for occasional instances, as in 1895 when the Court invalidated the income tax by a 5–4 vote, or in 1918 when by the same slim margin it struck down the federal Child Labor Law, constitutional decisions, these proponents argue, have usually not run counter to the interests dominant in Congress at the time. In less than forty cases in all Supreme Court history has a federal statute been voided within four years of its passage, and twelve of these were struck down during the New Deal period.

The New Deal era, this argument concedes, was an exceptional time, but it lasted for only a few years. It was doubly exceptional in that Roosevelt did not get to make a Supreme Court appointment until six months after his second inauguration, while throughout Court history vacancies have occurred on the average of one every twenty-two months. Since several of the crucial decisions were by 5–4 or 6–3 votes, one or two additional sympathetic justices might have turned a massive conflict into a minor skirmish.

There are many objections to this line of reasoning. Constitutional decisions are not the only means of judicial policy-making. Statutory interpretation can be an equally effective instrument, just as offering dicta can cast a constitutional pall over projected legislation. But this thesis does point up what was said in Chapter 5: one of the principal functions of judges has been to stamp political compromises with the seal of constitutional legitimacy. And insofar as they perform this function, courts can hardly be acting in opposition to the more popularly chosen branches of government. It is only when they declare political compromises illegitimate or misinterpret those compromises that problems arise.

Minorities Rule

If the view is taken that most legislation involves only issues between minorities rather than between a majority and a minority, judicial review becomes something less than the antithesis of democratic government (and democratic government becomes something other than majority rule). Starting with the proposition that "generally speaking, policy at the national level is the outcome of conflicts, bargaining, and agreement among minorities," Robert Dahl asserts that the American political process is neither one of minority rule nor majority rule, but can be described more accurately as *"minorities* rule, where one aggregation of minorities achieves policies opposed by another aggregation." Dahl sees the Supreme Court, with its frequent new appointments, as part of a dominant national alliance, and he contends that the justices usually will support—and historically have supported—the policies of that alliance. Indeed, Dahl claims that, while judges can fashion specific policy within the general coalition agreement or occasionally—at great risk—make broad policy where the alliance has not yet arrived at a consensus, they are generally both unable and unwilling to contradict the policies of the alliance.

Dahl's thesis has two drawbacks which are immediately evident. First, he assumes that the appointment process is a relatively sure business, an assumption which Presidents from Jefferson to Eisenhower would dispute. Second, judges continue to act as if one of the significant issues constantly before them were that of reconciling majority rule and judicial review. This belief, as we saw in Chapter 16, has resulted in the division within the Supreme Court over self-restraint and preferred freedoms.

The Inescapable Duty

No matter what theory of the judicial function judges follow, as long as access to the courts remains open and as long as judges have some measure of the power which they have historically possessed, it is inevitable that individuals and groups will attempt to utilize the judicial process to achieve their policy aims. Nor is it probable that judges will— or can—always refuse to intercede in matters of public policy, if for no other reason than that abstention can itself be a means of assisting one side. Legislative and executive officials, responding both to political pressures and to putative threats to their own power interests, are likely to watch federal judicial power with suspicion and to continue to try to influence the trend of court policy-making.

By the very fact that their courts are one of the agencies of government, judges cannot avoid being participants in the struggle for political power. They may meet that struggle in a non-partisan way, as partisanship is defined in terms of loyalty to region, faction, or party. They may bring to bear all the objectivity, all the learning, all the humility which intelligent men, aware of their own emotional attachments, can muster. They may require that policy questions be presented in a neat, technically impeccable framework. They may refuse to lay down any more doctrine than the minimal amount necessary to decide a specific case. Yet there are times, as Justices Jackson and Frankfurter, two of the most fervent believers in self-restraint, have conceded, when a judge cannot escape the duty to judge, to choose between competing values.

SELECTED REFERENCES

Alfange, Dean, *The Supreme Court and the National Will* (New York: Doubleday Doran, 1937).

Black, Charles L., Jr., *The People and the Court* (New York: Macmillan, 1960).

Boudin, Louis B., *Government by Judiciary* (New York: Wm. Godwin, 1932), 2 vols.

Carr, Robert K., *The Supreme Court and Judicial Review* (New York: Farrar and Rinehart, 1942).

Corwin, Edward S., *Court over Constitution: A Study of Judicial Review as an Instrument of Popular Government* (Princeton: Princeton University Press, 1938).

Dahl, Robert A., "Decision-Making in a Democracy: The Supreme Court as a National Policy-Maker," 6 *Journal of Public Law* 279 (1957).

Douglas, William O., *The Right of the People* (New York: Doubleday, 1958), Ch. 1.

Mason, Alpheus T., *The Supreme Court from Taft to Warren* (Baton Rouge: Louisiana State University Press, 1958).

Meiklejohn, Alexander, *Free Speech and Its Relation to Self-Government* (New York: Harper, 1948).

———, *Political Freedom: The Constitutional Powers of the People* (New York: Harper, 1960).

Mendelson, Wallace, "Mr. Justice Frankfurter—Law and Choice," 10 *Vanderbilt Law Review* 333 (1957).

Rosenblum, Victor G., *Law as a Political Instrument* (New York: Random House, 1955).

Swisher, Carl Brent, "Dred Scott One Hundred Years After," 19 *Journal of Politics* 175 (1957).

———, *The Supreme Court in Modern Role* (New York: New York University Press, 1958).

Thomas, Helen Shirley, *Felix Frankfurter: Scholar on the Bench* (Baltimore: Johns Hopkins University Press, 1960), Chs. 4, 5, 12, 13.

1. *". . . it would be most irksome to be ruled by a bevy of Platonic Guardians . . ."*

THE BILL OF RIGHTS   *Learned Hand**

. . . THE AUTHORITY of courts to annul statutes (and *a fortiori,* acts of the Executive) may, and indeed must, be inferred, although it is nowhere expressed, for without it we should have to refer all disputes between the "Departments" and states to popular decision, patently an impractical means of relief, whatever Thomas Jefferson may have thought. However, this power should be confined to occasions when the statute or order was outside the grant of power to the grantee, and should not include a review of how the power has been exercised. This distinction in the case of legislation demands an analysis of its component factors. These are an estimate of the relevant existing facts and a forecast of the changes that the proposed measure will bring about. In addition it involves an appraisal of the values that the change will produce, as to which there are no postulates specific enough to serve as guides on concrete occasions. In the end all that can be asked on review by a court is that the appraisals and the choice shall be impartial. The statute may be far from the best solution of the conflicts with which it deals; but if it is the result of an honest effort to embody that compromise or adjustment that will secure the widest acceptance and most avoid resentment, it is "Due Process of Law" and conforms to the First Amendment. . . .

I am well aware that the decisions do not so narrowly circumscribe the power of courts to intervene under the authority of the First Amendment and the "Due Process Clause." I have not tried to say how far those decisions have in fact extended the scope of these

The Bill of Rights (Cambridge: Harvard University Press, 1958), pp. 66–72. Copyright 1958 the President and Fellows of Harvard College. Reprinted with permission.

* United States District Judge for the Southern District of New York, 1909–24; Circuit Judge, United States Court of Appeals for the Second Circuit, 1924–39; Chief Judge of the Second Circuit, 1939–51.

clauses. Frankly, I should despair of succeeding. On the contrary I
have been only trying to say what is the measure of judicial intervention that can be thought to be implicit, though unexpressed, in the
Constitution. . . . Even though until about a century ago it was the
accepted role of courts to confine themselves to occasions when Congress or the states had stepped over their borders, why should we now
retreat, if it has become the custom to go further and correct patent
deviations from a court's notions of justice? . . . Ours is no different
from other constitutions, and it has by now been modified to protect
the basic privileges of any free society by means of an agency made
irresponsive to the pressure of public hysteria, public panic and public
greed.

There may be much to be said for the existence of some such organ
in a democratic state, especially if its power be confined to a suspensive veto, like that for example of the present British House of Lords.
The recuperative powers of a government that has no such curb are
indeed great, but in the interval between the damage and the restora-
tion great permanent injury may be done, and in any event the suffering of individuals will never be repaired. Those who advocate such
relief at times concede too scanty importance to the provisions very
carefully devised at least in the federal Constitution to check hasty
and ill-considered legislation. The veto and independent tenure of the
President, unlike that of the ministry in most democracies are obvious
curbs upon sudden swings of popular obsession; so too is the Senate,
whose control is in the hands of a small minority of the population,
representing a facet of public opinion quite different from that of the
urban sections. However, I am not going to discuss whether it might
not be desirable to have a third chamber, but on the contrary I shall
assume for argument that it would be. The question still remains
whether the courts should be that chamber. Let me try to sum up the
case on both sides: and first that of those who wish to give the courts
power to review the merits.

I agree that they have the better argument so far as concerns Free
Speech. The most important issues here arise when a majority of the
voters are hostile, often bitterly hostile, to the dissidents against whom
the statute is directed; and legislatures are more likely than courts to
repress what ought to be free. It is true that the periods of passion

or panic are ordinarily not very long, and that they are usually succeeded by a serener and more tolerant temper; but, as I have just
said, serious damage may have been done that cannot be undone. . . .
This is a substantial and important advantage of wide judicial review.

When one comes to the other interests covered by the "Bill of
Rights" it seems to me impossible to be sure on which side the advantage lies. Judges are perhaps more apt than legislators to take a long
view, but that varies so much with the individual that generalization
is hazardous. We are faced with the ever present problem in all popular government: how far the will of immediate majorities should
prevail. Even assuming, as I am, that a suspensive veto would be
desirable, the power to annul a statute is much more than that. It
does not send back the challenged measure for renewed deliberation;
it forbids it by making a different appraisal of the values, which . . .
is the essence of legislation. Moreover, judges are seldom content
merely to annul the particular solution before them; they do not, indeed they may not, say that taking all things into consideration, the
legislators' solution is too strong for the judicial stomach. On the contrary they wrap up their veto in a protective veil of adjectives such
as "arbitrary," "artificial," "normal," "reasonable," "inherent," "fundamental," or "essential," whose office usually, though quite innocently,
is to disguise what they are doing and impute to it a derivation far
more impressive than their personal preferences which are all that in
fact lie behind the decision. If we do need a third chamber it should
appear for what it is, and not as the interpreter of inscrutable principles.

Another supposed advantage of the wider power of review seems
to be that by "the moral radiation of its decision" a court may point
the way to a resolution of the social conflicts involved better than any
likely to emerge from a legislature. In other words, courts may light
the way to a saner world and ought to be encouraged to do so. I
should indeed be glad to believe it, and it may be that my failure to
observe it is owing to some personal defect of vision; but . . . for a
judge to serve as communal mentor appears to me a very dubious
addition to his duties. . . .

So much for the advantages that may result from a judicial review.
In what respect is it inexpedient? In the first place it is apparent, I

submit, that in so far as it is made part of the duties of judges to take sides in political controversies, their known or expected convictions or predilections will, and indeed should, be at least one determinant in their appointment and an important one. There has been plenty of past experience that confirms this; indeed, we have become so used to it that we accept it as a matter of course. No doubt it is inevitable . . . that the personal proclivities of an interpreter will to some extent interject themselves into the meaning he imputes to a text, but in very much the greater part of a judge's duties he is charged with freeing himself as far as he can from all personal preferences, and that becomes difficult in proportion as these are strong. The degree to which he will secure compliance with his commands depends in large measure upon how far the community believes him to be the mouthpiece of a public will, conceived as the resultant of many conflicting strains that have come, at least provisionally, to a consensus. . . .

This consideration becomes especially important in appellate courts. It is often hard to secure unanimity about the borders of legislative power, but that is much easier than to decide how far a particular adjustment diverges from what the judges deem tolerable. On such issues experience has over and over again shown the difficulty of securing unanimity. This is disastrous because disunity cancels the impact of monolithic solidarity on which the authority of a bench of judges so largely depends. People become aware that the answer to the controversy is uncertain, even to those best qualified, and they feel free, unless especially docile, to ignore it if they are reasonably sure that they will not be caught. . . . Moreover, it certainly does not accord with the underlying presuppositions of popular government to vest in a chamber, unaccountable to anyone but itself, the power to suppress social experiments which it does not approve. Nothing, I submit, could warrant such a censorship except a code of paramount law that not only measured the scope of legislative authority but regulated how it should be exercised.

Each of us must in the end choose for himself how far he would like to leave our collective fate to the wayward vagaries of popular assemblies. No one can fail to recognize the perils to which the last forty years have exposed such governments. We are not indeed forced to choose between absolutism and the kind of democracy that so often prevailed in Greek cities during the sixth to fourth centuries before our era. The Founding Fathers were acutely, perhaps overacutely aware of the dangers that had followed that sort of rule. . . . For myself it would be most irksome to be ruled by a bevy of Platonic Guardians, even if I knew how to choose them, which I assuredly do not. If they were in charge, I should miss the stimulus of living in a society where I have, at least theoretically, some part in the direction of public affairs. . . .

2. *". . . democracies need not elect all the officers who exercise crucial authority . . ."*

THE DEMOCRATIC CHARACTER OF JUDICIAL REVIEW *Eugene V. Rostow**

THE IDEA that judicial review is undemocratic is not an academic issue of political philosophy. Like most abstractions, it has far-reaching practical consequences. . . . The attack on judicial review as undemocratic rests on the premise that the Constitution should be allowed to grow without a judicial check. The proponents of this view would have the Constitution mean what the President, the Congress, and the state legislatures say it means. In this way, they contend, the electoral process would determine the course of constitutional development, as it does in countries with plenipotentiary parliaments.

But the Constitution of the United States does not establish a parliamentary government, and attempts to interpret American government in a parliamentary perspective break down in confusion or absurdity. One may recall, in another setting, the anxious voice of the *Washington Post* urging President Truman to resign because the Republican Party had won control of the Congress in the 1946 elections.

It is a grave oversimplification to contend that no society can be democratic unless its legislature has sovereign powers. The social quality of democracy cannot be defined by so rigid a formula. Government and politics are after all the arms, not the end, of social life. The

66 *Harvard Law Review* 193 (1952). Copyright 1952 Harvard Law Review Association. Reprinted with permission.

* Professor of Law and Dean of the Law School, Yale University.

purpose of the Constitution is to assure the people a free and democratic society. The final aim of that society is as much freedom as possible for the individual human being. The Constitution provides society with a mechanism of government fully competent to its task, but by no means universal in its powers. The power to govern is parcelled out between the states and the nation and is further divided among the three main branches of all governmental units. By custom as well as constitutional practice, many vital aspects of community life are beyond the direct reach of government—for example, religion, the press, and, until recently at any rate, many phases of educational and cultural activity. The separation of powers under the Constitution serves the end of democracy in society by limiting the roles of the several branches of government and protecting the citizen, and the various parts of the state itself, against encroachments from any source. The root idea of the Constitution is that man can be free because the state is not.

The power of constitutional review, to be exercised by some part of the government, is implicit in the conception of a written constitution delegating limited powers. A written constitution would promote discord rather than order in society if there were no accepted authority to construe it, at the least in cases of conflicting action by different branches of government or of constitutionally unauthorized governmental action against individuals. The limitation and separation of powers, if they are to survive, require a procedure for independent mediation and construction to reconcile the inevitable disputes over the boundaries of constitutional power which arise in the process of government. British Dominions operating under written constitutions have had to face the task pretty much as we have, and they have solved it in similar ways. Like institutions have developed in other federal systems. . . .

Whether another method of enforcing the Constitution could have been devised, the short answer is that no such method has developed. The argument over the constitutionality of judicial review has long since been settled by history. The power and duty of the Supreme Court to declare statutes or executive action unconstitutional in appropriate cases is part of the living Constitution. "The course of constitutional history," Mr. Justice Frankfurter recently remarked, has cast responsibilities upon the Supreme Court which it would be "stultification" for it to evade. The Court's power has been exercised differently at different times: sometimes with reckless and doctrinaire enthusiasm; sometimes with great deference to the status and responsibilities of other branches of the government; sometimes with a degree of weakness and timidity that comes close to the betrayal of trust. But the power exists, as an integral part of the process of American government. . . . Whether or not this was the intention of the Founding Fathers, the unwritten Constitution is unmistakable.

If one may use a personal definition of the crucial word, this way of policing the Constitution is not undemocratic. True, it employs appointed officials, to whom large powers are irrevocably delegated. But democracies need not elect all the officers who exercise crucial authority in the name of the voters. Admirals and generals can win or lose wars in the exercise of their discretion. The independence of judges in the administration of justice has been the pride of communities which aspire to be free. Members of the Federal Reserve Board have the lawful power to plunge the country into depression or inflation. The list could readily be extended. Government by referendum or town meeting is not the only possible form of democracy. The task of democracy is not to have the people vote directly on every issue, but to assure their ultimate responsibility for the acts of their representatives, elected or appointed. For judges deciding ordinary litigation, the ultimate responsibility of the electorate has a special meaning. It is a responsibility for the quality of the judges and for the substance of their instructions, never a responsibility for their decisions in particular cases. It is hardly characteristic of law in democratic society to encourage bills of attainder, or to allow appeals from the courts in particular cases to legislatures or to mobs. Where the judges are carrying out the function of constitutional review, the final responsibility of the people is appropriately guaranteed by the provisions for amending the Constitution itself, and by the benign influence of time, which changes the personnel of courts. Given the possibility of constitutional amendment, there is nothing undemocratic in having responsible and independent judges act as important constitutional mediators. Within the narrow limits of their capacity to act, their great task is to help maintain a pluralist equilibrium in society. They can do much to keep it from being dominated by the states or the Federal Government, by Congress or the President, by the purse or the sword.

In the execution of this crucial but delicate function, constitutional review by the judiciary has an advantage thoroughly recognized in both theory and practice. The power of the courts, however final, can only be asserted in the course of litigation. Advisory opinions are forbidden, and reefs of self-limitation have grown up around the doctrine that the courts will determine constitutional questions only in cases of actual controversy, when no lesser ground of decision is available, and when the complaining party would be directly and personally injured by the assertion of the power deemed unconstitutional. Thus the check of judicial review upon the elected branches of government must be a mild one, limited not only by the detachment, integrity, and good sense of the justices, but by the structural boundaries implicit in the fact that the power is entrusted to the courts. Judicial review is inherently adapted to preserving broad and flexible lines of constitutional growth, not to operating as a continuously active factor in legislative or executive decisions.

The division and separation of governmental powers within the American federal system provides the community with ample power to act, without compromising its pluralist structure. The Constitution formalizes the principle that a wide dispersal of authority among the institutions of society is the safest foundation for social freedom. It was accepted from the beginning that the judiciary would be one of the chief agencies for enforcing the restraints of the Constitution. . . .

It is error to insist that no society is democratic unless it has a government of unlimited powers, and that no government is democratic unless its legislature has unlimited powers. Constitutional review by an independent judiciary is a tool of proven use in the American quest for an open society of widely dispersed powers. In a vast country, of mixed population, with widely different regional problems, such an organization of society is the surest base for the hopes of democracy. . . .

3.
"*The Supreme Court can contribute toward realization of free government . . .*"

THE SUPREME COURT: TEMPLE AND FORUM   *Alpheus T. Mason*

IT IS . . . RELEVANT to ask whether a politically irresponsible body, such as the Supreme Court, can block the will of the majority in the name of minorities and still remain a democratic institution. When the minority rights protected are those of property, the answer is probably "no." Between 1890 and 1937, the Supreme Court actually retarded the growth of democracy. When, on the other hand, judicial review serves to give a minority, otherwise barred, access to the political process, it implements rather than limits free government. The Court's function is not to determine what decisions can be made by political processes, but to prevent the mechanism from breaking down. Under this theory the legislature can control the wages and hours of workers; it cannot limit the right to vote with respect to race or color. Congress can regulate agricultural production; it cannot control the content of newspapers. The state can demand that children attend school; it cannot compel them to participate in ceremonies that violate their religious convictions. Judicial hands-off in economic matters is perfectly consistent with judicial activism to preserve the integrity and effective operation of the political process.

An appointive body, such as the Supreme Court, exercising political control in a system of government whose powers are supposed to derive from the people, has, as we have seen, sometimes been considered an alien offshoot from an otherwise democratic polity. The dilemma was once resolved by invoking the fiction that the Court had no power—that it merely applied the Constitution which, in some mystical way, is always the highest expression of the people's will. Though this ancient theory still shows signs of vitality, it is not altogether satisfying. The real problem is to protect individuals and minorities without thereby destroying capacity in the majority to govern. Majorities—and this is the key point of democratic theory—are

48 *Yale Review* 524 (1959). Copyright 1959 Yale University Press. Reprinted with permission.

always in flux. Tomorrow's majority may have a different composition as well as different goals. Defense of the political rights of minorities thus becomes, not the antithesis of majority rule, but its very foundations. The Supreme Court can contribute toward realization of free government by guaranteeing all minority groups free access to the political process and the instruments of political change, while at the same time allowing the majority government—as long as the political process is open and untrammeled—to rule.

In a free society, no organ of government can be defended solely in terms of its symbolic value. The Supreme Court is but one among several agencies empowered, within limits, to govern. The suggestion that any organ of government is beyond public scrutiny, more particularly that the judiciary should enjoy freedom from critical examination greater than any other agency can claim, is to be deplored. Nothing of the sort was envisioned by the framers of the Constitution. Implicit in the system of government they established is the basic premise that unchecked power in any hands whatsoever is intolerable. The freedom the judiciary has from political responsibility and control makes its processes more rather than less appropriate for critical exploration.

The Supreme Court is a forum. Its contribution consists in what it does, in the deliberative process that precedes judgment. An act of judgment based on reason can have a moral force far exceeding that of the purse or sword. Thus the Court's worth consists not only in its restraining power, but also in the part it plays in making vocal and audible the ideals and values that might otherwise be silenced. The Court explores and passes judgment on living issues, on complexities which are at any given moment puzzling and dividing us. . . .

4. *"Courts are not representative bodies."*

DENNIS V. UNITED STATES

     ELEVEN LEADERS *of the Communist Party were convicted under the Smith Act, which makes it a crime to advocate, or conspire to advocate, the duty, necessity, advisability, or propriety of violent*

341 U.S. 494, 71 S. Ct. 857, 95 L. Ed. 1137 (1951).

overthrow of the government. The Supreme Court in a limited grant of certiorari agreed to review these convictions only on the question of the constitutionality of the Smith Act. By a 6–2 division the Court upheld the statute's constitutionality, but the majority could not agree on an institutional opinion and filed three sets of views.

            MR. JUSTICE FRANKFURTER, concurring in affirmance of the judgment. . . .

    . . . The demands of free speech in a democratic society as well as the interest in national security are better served by candid and informed weighing of the competing interests, within the confines of the judicial process, than by announcing dogmas too inflexible for the non-Euclidian problems to be solved.

    But how are competing interests to be assessed? Since they are not subject to quantitative ascertainment, the issue necessarily resolves itself into asking, who is to make the adjustment?—who is to balance the relevant factors and ascertain which interest is in the circumstances to prevail? Full responsibility for the choice cannot be given to the courts. Courts are not representative bodies. They are not designed to be a good reflex of a democratic society. Their judgment is best informed, and therefore most dependable, within narrow limits. Their essential quality is detachment, founded on independence. History teaches that the independence of the judiciary is jeopardized when courts become embroiled in the passions of the day and assume primary responsibility in choosing between competing political, economic and social pressures.

    Primary responsibility for adjusting the interests which compete in the situation before us of necessity belongs to the Congress. The nature of the power to be exercised by this Court has been delineated in decisions not charged with the emotional appeal of situations such as that now before us. We are to set aside the judgment of those whose duty it is to legislate only if there is no reasonable basis for it.

    We must assure fairness of procedure, allowing full scope of governmental discretion but mindful of its impact on individuals in the context of the problem involved. And, of course, the proceedings in a particular case before us must have the warrant of substantial proof. Beyond these powers we must not go; we must scrupulously observe the narrow limits of judicial authority even though self-restraint is alone set over us. Above all we must remember that this Court's power of judicial review is not "an exercise of the powers of a super-legislature."

. . . Some members of the Court—and at times a majority—have done more. They have suggested that our function in reviewing statutes restricting freedom of expression differs sharply from our normal duty in sitting in judgment on legislation. It has been said that such statutes "must be justified by clear public interest, threatened not doubtfully or remotely, but by clear and present danger. The rational connection between the remedy provided and the evil to be curbed, which in other contexts might support legislation against attack on due process grounds, will not suffice." It has been suggested, with the casualness of a footnote, that such legislation is not presumptively valid, and it has been weightily reiterated that freedom of speech has a "preferred position" among constitutional safeguards. . . .

. . . Free-speech cases are not an exception to the principle that we are not legislators, that direct policy-making is not our province. How best to reconcile competing interests is the business of legislatures, and the balance they strike is a judgment not to be displaced by ours, but to be respected unless outside the pale of fair judgment.

On occasion we have strained to interpret legislation in order to limit its effect on interests protected by the First Amendment. . . . But in no case has a majority of this Court held that a legislative judgment, even as to freedom of utterance, may be overturned merely because the Court would have made a different choice between the competing interests had the initial legislative judgment been for it to make. . . .

. . . Not every type of speech occupies the same position on the scale of values. There is no substantial public interest in permitting certain kinds of utterances: "the lewd and obscene, the profane, the libelous, and the insulting or 'fighting' words—those which by their very utterance inflict injury or tend to incite an immediate breach of the peace." . . .

These general considerations underlie decision of the case before us.

On the one hand is the interest in security. The Communist Party was not designed by these defendants as an ordinary political party.

. . . On the other hand is the interest in free speech. The right to exert all governmental powers in aid of maintaining our institutions and resisting their physical overthrow does not include intolerance of opinions and speech that cannot do harm although opposed and perhaps alien to dominant, traditional opinion. The treatment of its minorities, especially their legal position, is among the most searching tests of the level of civilization attained by a society. It is better for those who have almost unlimited power of government in their hands to err on the side of freedom. We have enjoyed so much freedom for so long that we are perhaps in danger of forgetting how much blood it cost to establish the Bill of Rights. . . .

. . . Freedom of expression is the well-spring of our civilization—the civilization we seek to maintain and further by recognizing the right of Congress to put some limitation upon expression. Such are the paradoxes of life. For social development of trial and error, the fullest possible opportunity for the free play of the human mind is an indispensable prerequisite. The history of civilization is in considerable measure the displacement of error which once held sway as official truth by beliefs which in turn have yielded to other truths. Therefore the liberty of man to search for truth ought not to be fettered, no matter what orthodoxies he may challenge. Liberty of thought soon shrivels without freedom of expression. . . .

It is not for us to decide how we would adjust the clash of interests which this case presents were the primary responsibility for reconciling it ours. Congress has determined that the danger created by advocacy of overthrow justifies the ensuing restriction on freedom of speech. The determination was made after due deliberation, and the seriousness of the congressional purpose is attested by the volume of legislation passed to effectuate the same ends.

Can we then say that the judgment Congress exercised was denied it by the Constitution? Can we establish a constitutional doctrine which forbids the elected representatives of the people to make this choice? Can we hold that the First Amendment deprives Congress of what it deemed necessary for the Government's protection?

To make validity of legislation depend on judicial reading of events still in the womb of time—a forecast, that is, of the outcome of forces at best appreciated only with knowledge of the topmost secrets of nations—is to charge the judiciary with duties beyond its equipment. . . .

Civil liberties draw at best only limited strength from legal guaranties. Preoccupation by our people with the constitutionality, instead of with the wisdom, of legislation or of executive action is preoccupation with a false value. Even those who would most freely use the judicial brake on the democratic process by invalidating legislation that goes deeply against their grain, acknowledge, at least by paying lip service, that constitutionality does not exact a sense of proportion or the sanity of humor or any absence of fear. Focusing attention on constitutionality tends to make constitutionality synonymous with wisdom. When legislation touches freedom of thought and freedom of speech, such a tendency is a formidable enemy of the free spirit. Much that should be rejected as illiberal, because repressive and envenoming, may well be not unconstitutional. The ultimate reliance for the deepest needs of civilization must be found outside their vindication in courts of law; apart from all else, judges, howsoever they may conscientiously seek to discipline themselves against it, unconsciously are too apt to be moved by the deep undercurrents of public feeling. A persistent, positive translation of the liberating faith into the feelings and thoughts and actions of men and women is the real protection against attempts to straitjacket the human mind. Such temptations will have their way, if fear and hatred are not exorcised. The mark of a truly civilized man is confidence in the strength and security derived from the inquiring mind. We may be grateful for such honest comforts as it supports, but we must be unafraid of its uncertitudes. Without open minds there can be no open society. And if society be not open the spirit of man is mutilated and becomes enslaved.

MR. JUSTICE BLACK, dissenting. . . .

My basic disagreement with the Court is not as to how we should explain or reconcile what was said in prior decisions but springs from a fundamental difference in constitutional approach. Consequently, it would serve no useful purpose to state my position at length.

At the outset I want to emphasize what the crime involved in this case is, and what it is not. These petitioners were not charged with an attempt to overthrow the Government. They were not charged with overt acts of any kind designed to overthrow the Government. They were not even charged with saying anything or writing anything designed to overthrow the Government. The charge was that they agreed to assemble and to talk and publish certain ideas at a later date: the indictment is that they conspired to organize the Communist Party and to use speech or newspapers and other publications in the future to teach and advocate the forcible overthrow of the Government. No matter how it is worded, this is a virulent form of prior censorship of speech and press, which I believe the First Amendment forbids. . . .

So long as this Court exercises the power of judicial review of legislation, I cannot agree that the First Amendment permits us to sustain laws suppressing freedom of speech and press on the basis of Congress' or our own notions of mere "reasonableness." Such a doctrine waters down the First Amendment so that it amounts to little more than an admonition to Congress. The Amendment as so construed is not likely to protect any but those "safe" or orthodox views which rarely need its protection. . . .

Public opinion being what it now is, few will protest the conviction of these Communist petitioners. There is hope, however, that in calmer times, when present pressures, passions and fears subside, this or some later Court will restore the First Amendment liberties to the high preferred place where they belong in a free society.

5.   *". . . in the end, judgment cannot be escaped . . ."*

SWEEZY V. NEW HAMPSHIRE

PAUL SWEEZY, *a classical Marxist, had refused to answer certain questions about his lectures and political activities put to him by the New Hampshire Attorney General, who had been authorized by the state legislature to serve as a one-man investigating committee to inquire into subversion. For this refusal Sweezy was subsequently convicted of contempt. The state supreme court affirmed the conviction and the U.S. Supreme Court granted certiorari and reversed the con-*

354 U.S. 234, 77 S. Ct. 1203, 1 L. Ed. 2d 1311 (1957).

viction. Although the Court voted 6–2 to reverse, the justices were unable to agree on their reasoning, and there was no opinion of the Court.

           MR. JUSTICE FRANKFURTER, whom MR. JUSTICE HARLAN joins, concurring in the result. . . .

The questions that petitioner refused to answer regarding the university lecture, the third given by him in three years at the invitation of the faculty for humanities, were:

"What was the subject of your lecture?"

"Didn't you tell the class at the University of New Hampshire on Monday, March 22, 1954, that Socialism was inevitable in this country?"

"Did you advocate Marxism at that time?"

"Did you express the opinion, or did you make the statement at that time that Socialism was inevitable in America?"

"Did you in this last lecture on March 22 or in any of the former lectures espouse the theory of dialectical materialism?"

"I have in the file here a statement from a person who attended your class, and I will read it in part because I don't want you to think I am just fishing. 'His talk this time was on the inevitability of the Socialist program. It was glossed-over interpretation of the materialist dialectic.' Now, again I ask you the original question."

In response to the first question of this series, petitioner had said at the hearing:

"I would like to say one thing in this connection, Mr. Wyman. I stated under oath at my last appearance that, and I now repeat it, that I do not advocate or in any way further the aim of overthrowing constitutional government by force and violence. I did not so advocate in the lecture I gave at the University of New Hampshire. In fact I have never at any time so advocated in a lecture anywhere. Aside from that I have nothing I want to say about the lecture in question."

The New Hampshire Supreme Court, although recognizing that such inquiries "undoubtedly interfered with the defendant's free exercise" of his constitutionally guaranteed right to lecture, justified the interference on the ground that it would occur "in the limited area in which the legislative committee may reasonably believe that the overthrow of existing government by force and violence is being or has been taught, advocated or planned, an area in which the interest of the State justifies this intrusion upon civil liberties." According to the court, the facts that made reasonable the committee's belief that petitioner had taught violent overthrow in his lecture were that he was a Socialist with a record of affiliation with groups cited by the Attorney General of the United States or the House Un-American Activities Committee and that he was co-editor of an article stating that, although the authors hated violence, it was less to be deplored when used by the Soviet Union than by capitalist countries.

When weighed against the grave harm resulting from governmental intrusion into the intellectual life of a university, such justification for compelling a witness to discuss the contents of his lecture appears grossly inadequate. Particularly is this so where the witness has sworn that neither in the lecture nor at any other time did he ever advocate overthrowing the Government by force and violence. . . .

. . . The problems that are the respective preoccupations of anthropology, economics, law, psychology, sociology and related areas of scholarship are merely departmentalized dealing, by way of manageable division of analysis, with interpenetrating aspects of holistic perplexities. For society's good—if understanding be an essential need of society—inquiries into these problems, speculations about them, stimulation in others of reflection upon them, must be left as unfettered as possible. Political power must abstain from intrusion into this activity of freedom, pursued in the interest of wise government and the people's well-being, except for reasons that are exigent and obviously compelling.

These pages need not be burdened with proof, based on the testimony of a cloud of impressive witnesses, of the dependence of a free society on free universities. This means the exclusion of governmental intervention in the intellectual life of a university. . . .

Petitioner stated, in response to questions at the hearing, that he did not know of any Communist interest in, connection with, influence over, activity in, or manipulation of the Progressive Party. He refused to answer, despite court order, the following questions on the ground that, by inquiring into the activities of a lawful political organization, they infringed upon the inviolability of the right to privacy in his political thoughts, actions and associations:

"Was she, Nancy Sweezy, your wife, active in the formation of the Progressive Citizens of America?"

"Was Nancy Sweezy then working with individuals who were then members of the Communist Party?"

"Was Charles Beebe active in forming the Progressive Citizens of America?"

"Did he work with your present wife—Did Charles Beebe work with your present wife in 1947?"

"Did it [a meeting at the home of one Abraham Walenko] have anything to do with the Progressive Party?"

The Supreme Court of New Hampshire justified this intrusion upon his freedom on the same basis that it upheld questioning about the university lecture, namely, that the restriction was limited to situations where the Committee had reason to believe that violent overthrow of the Government was being advocated or planned. . . .

For a citizen to be made to forego even a part of so basic a liberty as his political autonomy, the subordinating interest of the State must be compelling. Inquiry pursued in safeguarding a State's security against threatened force and violence cannot be shut off by mere disclaimer, though of course a relevant claim may be made to the privilege against self-incrimination (the New Hampshire Constitution guarantees this privilege). But the inviolability of privacy belonging to a citizen's political loyalties has so overwhelming an importance to the well-being of our kind of society that it cannot be constitutionally encroached upon on the basis of so meagre a countervailing interest of the State as may be argumentatively found in the remote, shadowy threat to the security of New Hampshire allegedly presented in the origins and contributing elements of the Progressive Party and in petitioner's relations to these.

In the political realm, as in the academic, thought and action are presumptively immune from inquisition by political authority. It cannot require argument that inquiry would be barred to ascertain whether a citizen had voted for one or the other of the two major parties either in a state or national election. Until recently, no difference would have been entertained in regard to inquiries about a voter's affiliations with one of the various so-called third parties that have had their day, or longer, in our political history. . . . Whatever, on the basis of massive proof and in the light of history, of which this

Court may well take judicial notice, be the justification for not regarding the Communist Party as a conventional political party, no such justification has been afforded in regard to the Progressive Party. A foundation in fact and reason would have to be established far weightier than the intimations that appear in the record to warrant such a view of the Progressive Party. This precludes the questioning that petitioner resisted in regard to that Party.

To be sure, this is a conclusion based on a judicial judgment in balancing two contending principles—the right of a citizen to political privacy, as protected by the Fourteenth Amendment, and the right of the State to self-protection. And striking the balance implies the exercise of judgment. This is the inescapable judicial task in giving substantive content, legally enforced, to the Due Process Clause, and it is a task ultimately committed to this Court. It must not be an exercise of whim or will. It must be an overriding judgment founded on something much deeper and more justifiable than personal preference. As far as it lies within human limitations, it must be an impersonal judgment. It must rest on fundamental presuppositions rooted in history to which widespread acceptance may fairly be attributed. Such a judgment must be arrived at in a spirit of humility when it counters the judgment of the State's highest court. But, in the end, judgment cannot be escaped—the judgment of this Court. . . .

And so I am compelled to conclude that the judgment of the New Hampshire court must be reversed.

6. *". . . a society so riven that the spirit of moderation is gone, no court can save . . ."*

THE CONTRIBUTION OF AN INDEPENDENT JUDICIARY TO CIVILIZATION
Learned Hand

. . . LOGICALLY, the irresponsibility of an independent judiciary is here an anomaly, like the common law itself; in a pitilessly consistent democracy judges would not be making law at all. Why

Address, reprinted in *The Supreme Judicial Court of Massachusetts* (Boston: Massachusetts Bar Association, 1942), pp. 59–67. Copyright 1942 the Massachusetts Bar Association. Reprinted with permission.

then do we not resent it? In earlier times when the parturition of statutes was slow and painful, judicial license was tolerated partly for that reason and partly because judges fairly represented the governing classes. . . . That is no longer true; both the need and the unison have gone; legislation has become easy, judges no longer speak for the ruling classes. The price of their continued power must therefore be a self-denying ordinance which forbids change in what has not already become acceptable. . . .

. . . A constitution is primarily an instrument to distribute political power; and so far as it is, it is hard to escape the necessity of some tribunal with authority to declare when the prescribed distribution has been disturbed. Otherwise those who hold the purse will be likely in the end to dominate and absorb everything else, except as astute executives may from time to time check them by capturing and holding popular favor. Obviously the independence of such a tribunal must be secure. . . .

But American constitutions always go further. Not only do they distribute the powers of government, but they assume to lay down general principles to insure the just exercise of those powers. . . . It is true that the logic which has treated these like other provisions of a constitution seems on its face unanswerable. Are they not parts of the same document? Did they not originally have a meaning? Why should not that meaning be found in the same way as that of the rest of the instrument? Nevertheless there are vital differences. Here history is only a feeble light, for these rubrics were meant to answer future problems unimagined and unimaginable. Nothing which by the utmost liberality can be called interpretation describes the process by which they must be applied. Indeed if law be a command for a specific conduct, they are not law at all; they are cautionary warnings against the intemperance of faction and the first approaches of despotism. The answers to the questions which they raise demand the appraisal and balancing of human values which there are no scales to weigh. Who can say whether the contributions of one group may not justify allowing it a preference? How far should the capable, the shrewd or the strong be allowed to exploit their powers? When does utterance go beyond persuasion and become only incitement? How far are children wards of the state so as to justify its intervention in their nurture? What limits should be placed upon the right to inherit? Where does religious freedom end and moral obliquity begin?

... Moreover, even were there a hedonistic rod by which to measure loss or gain, how could we know that the judges had it; or—what is more important—would enough people think they had, to be satisfied that they should use it? So long as law remains a profession (and certainly there is no indication that its complexities are decreasing) judges must be drawn from a professional class with the special interests and special hierarchy of values which that implies. . . .

... There are two ways in which the judges may forfeit their independence if they do not abstain [from passing on such basic constitutional issues]. If they are intransigent but honest, they will be curbed; but a worse fate will befall them if they learn to trim their sails to the prevailing winds. A society whose judges have taught it to expect complaisance will exact complaisance; and complaisance under the pretense of interpretation is rottenness. If judges are to kill this thing they love, let them do it, not like cowards with a kiss, but like brave men with a sword.

And so, to sum up, I believe that for by far the greatest part of their work it is a condition upon the success of our system that the judges should be independent; and I do not believe that their independence should be impaired because of their constitutional function. But the price of this immunity, I insist, is that they should not have the last word in these basic conflicts of "right and wrong— between whose endless jar justice resides." You may ask what then will become of the fundamental principles of equity and fair play which our constitutions enshrine; and whether I seriously believe that unsupported they will serve merely as counsels of moderation. I do not think that anyone can say what will be left of those principles; I do not know whether they will serve only as counsels; but this much I think I do know—that a society so riven that the spirit of moderation is gone, no court *can* save; that a society where that spirit flourishes, no court *need* save; that in a society which evades its responsibility by thrusting upon the courts the nurture of that spirit, that spirit in the end will perish. . . .

". . . the judgment of a Court . . . can give a nation the chance to see how its actions look in the long perspective of history . . ."

7.

THE LIMITS ON JUDICIAL SELF-RESTRAINT   *C. Herman Pritchett*

. . . JUSTICE FRANKFURTER . . . has been the keeper of [the Court's] conscience on the self-restraint issue. Of the many discussions of Frankfurter's position on judicial review, certainly that by Wallace Mendelson is one of the best and most authoritative. ["Mr. Justice Frankfurter—Law and Choice," 10 *Vanderbilt Law Review* 333, 349–350 (1957).] He sums up his estimate of Frankfurter's judicial motivation in this eloquent passage:

> In Mr. Justice Frankfurter's view . . . "sovereign prerogative of choice" is not for judges. He would resolve all reasonable doubt in favor of the integrity of sister organs of government and the people to whom they must answer. He would adhere, that is, to the deepest of all our constitutional traditions, the dispersion of power. . . . He is wary of judicial attempts to impose Justice on the community, i.e., to deprive it of the wisdom that comes from self-inflicted wounds and the strength that grows with the burden of responsibility. It is his deepest conviction that no five men, or nine, are wise enough, or good enough to wield such power over the lives of millions. In this view humanitarian ends are served best in that allocation of function through which the people by a balance of power seek their own destiny. True to the faith upon which democracy ultimately rests, the Justice would leave to the political processes the onus of building legal standards in the vacuum of doubt. For in his view only that people is free who chooses for itself when choice must be made.

. . . If the Supreme Court's primary obligation is to avoid taking a position on matters of acute public controversy or where the interests which the Court is protecting are not substantial enough to give the Court a reasonable measure of support if a hue and cry is raised by the decision, then . . . experience suggests that the self-restraint

The Political Offender and the Warren Court (Boston: Boston University Press, 1958), pp. 69–74. Copyright 1958 Boston University. Reprinted with permission.

doctrine needs to be reformulated. Proposals along this line have recently come from several eminent scholars. Carl Swisher, out of a deep and thoughtful concern over the effects of the Court's segregation decisions, has expressed his doubts about the wisdom of judicial intervention in a situation where social consensus is markedly absent. ["Dred Scott, 100 Years After," 19 *Journal of Politics* 175 (1957).] He warns that "when the people are fundamentally divided on basic issues the judiciary will act at its peril if it intervenes unnecessarily to impose a judgment of higher law in support of one political faction and to aid in the defeat of another." Where questions are still in political controversy, where the constitutional language is indefinite, and where public opinion has not yet arrived at the degree of unanimity permitting of settlement in terms of principles of higher law, then it is best for the Court to avoid adjudication of the basic issues, Swisher concludes. . . .

. . . Mendelson's basic position is that "the stream of law cannot habitually rise above its source." This means that the Court cannot for long oppose strong popular movements. It is true, Mendelson concedes, that in the past the Court did for some time withstand public opinion in protecting "moribund" economic claims, but this was an exceptional situation. In sustaining those interests, courts had "the support of influential segments of the community, the very forces indeed to which judges by training and background are apt to be most responsive." But in protecting the rights of Communists, the Court would have no such backing, Mendelson foresaw. . . .

. . . That the Supreme Court should use its great powers of judicial review with self-restraint is a salutary and necessary rule. But that this rule should be carried to the extreme of requiring the Court never to render an opinion on an issue of public policy until substantial consensus has been achieved, and then only in accord with that consensus, is a perversion of the rule which would turn the judicial decision process into a Gallup poll.

It is possible to understand Learned Hand when he says that the law "must be content to lag behind the best inspiration of its time until it feels behind it the weight of such general acceptance as will give sanction to its pretension to unquestioned dictation," and to agree that this may be a valid description of the relation between law and opinion. For example, his statement surely has some relevance to understanding why the Supreme Court declared the rule of "separate but equal" unconstitutional in 1954 rather than in 1950 or in 1938. But Hand's language cannot possibly be accepted as stating a guide for a judge to follow. What respect could be accorded a court whose justices felt obliged in deciding cases consciously to lag behind the best thought of the time because that thought had not yet won general acceptance?

Mendelson fares no better in seeking to implement Hand's thought by suggesting that "the dissenting opinion perhaps is a proper place for recording the 'best inspiration of the time'; for instruction in moral values still struggling for general, i.e., political, acceptance." Again, this is the way it seems to work, but a court could scarcely agree to operate on the principle that the majority decision would confine itself to platitudes, with all bold new thoughts allocated to the dissenters.

The distinction between judicial self-restraint and judicial avoidance of controversy may be a subtle one, but it is the difference between a sound and stultifying principle of judicial review. The Supreme Court *should* reach constitutional questions reluctantly. It *should* be chary of disagreeing with legislatures or executives, whether national or state. But its primary obligation is not to avoid controversy. Its primary obligation is to bring all the judgment its members possess and the best wisdom that the times afford, to the interpretation of the basic rules propounded by our Constitution for the direction of a free society. To be sure, the Court cannot achieve certainty. Its constitutional interpretations are "guesses," and it must be respectful of the guesses of other authoritative participants in the political process. But the Supreme Court is in a most advantageous position for making informed guesses. It has leisure to take thought. Its work is characterized by an absence of pressure; it has sharply defined questions to answer, a continual awareness of its responsibility to the universal constituency of reason and justice. The Supreme Court has an obligation to be humble, but not to the point of denying the nation the guidance on basic democratic problems which its unique situation equips it to provide. . . .

No court can preserve liberty in a country whose people are bent on losing it. But the judgment of a Court, which accepts its responsibility under the Constitution to judge, can give a nation the chance to see how its actions look in the long perspective of history, *sub specie aeternitatis*. It can give a community the opportunity to measure its conduct alongside the yardstick of constitutional liberty. . . .

TABLE OF CASES

(Boldface page numbers refer to opinions printed in this book.)

INDEX